9780870271052
AF574867

Books by Léo Bronstein:

LUTTE ET RÉCONCILIATION, ESSAI SUR LA MANIFESTATION DU RÉEL DANS L'ART, *Paris, 1927*

ALTICHIERO, *Paris, 1932*

EL GRECO, *New York, 1950*

FRAGMENTS OF LIFE, METAPHYSICS AND ART, *New York, 1953*

FIVE VARIATIONS ON THE THEME OF JAPANESE PAINTING

Five Variations on the Theme of Japanese Painting

Non Scholae sed vitae descimus
Seneca Jr., 106th Letter

✣✣✣✣✣✣✣✣✣✣✣✣✣✣✣✣✣✣✣✣✣✣✣✣✣✣✣✣✣✣

The painter "takes his body with him," says Valéry. Indeed we cannot imagine how a *mind* could paint. It is by lending his body to the world that the artist changes the world into paintings. To understand these transubstantiations we must go back to the working, actual body—not the body as a chunk of space or a bundle of functions but that body which is an intertwining of vision and movement!

MAURICE MERLEAU-PONTY

If you have had your attention directed to the novelties in thought in your own lifetime you will have observed that almost all really new ideas have a certain aspect of foolishness when they are first produced.

A. N. WHITEHEAD

Rules are not the source of poetry, but poetry is the source of rules, and there are as many rules as there are real poets.

GIORDANO BRUNO

LÉO BRONSTEIN

FIVE VARIATIONS on the Theme of JAPANESE PAINTING

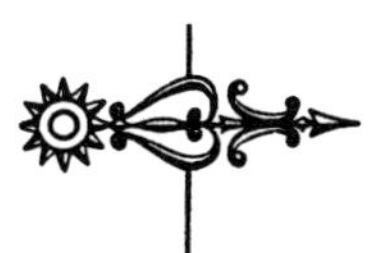

PUBLISHED FOR BRANDEIS UNIVERSITY

By The Bond Wheelwright Company, Freeport, Maine

Library of Congress Card Number:
65-27614
Standard Book Number:
87027-1059

The Bond Wheelwright Company
Freeport, Maine 04032

Printed in the United States of America

In Canada, Abelard-Schuman Canada, Ltd.

Editor's Note:

This book has been in production for over four years during which interruptions beyond the control of the author and the editor have been extremely disruptive. One consequence of this may well show itself in inconsistencies of rule in the use of accent marks. It seemed more important to get the book into the hands of waiting readers than once more to go through the entire text to try to avoid any inconsistencies that would be more likely to reflect the editor's inefficiency than to affect the content of this book.

Furthermore, while we have done our best to trace copyrights and obtain the necessary permissions for prose passages and illustrations cited in the text and the notes, we may have unwittingly reproduced materials without due acknowledgment. We hope such transgressions, if any, will be forgiven.

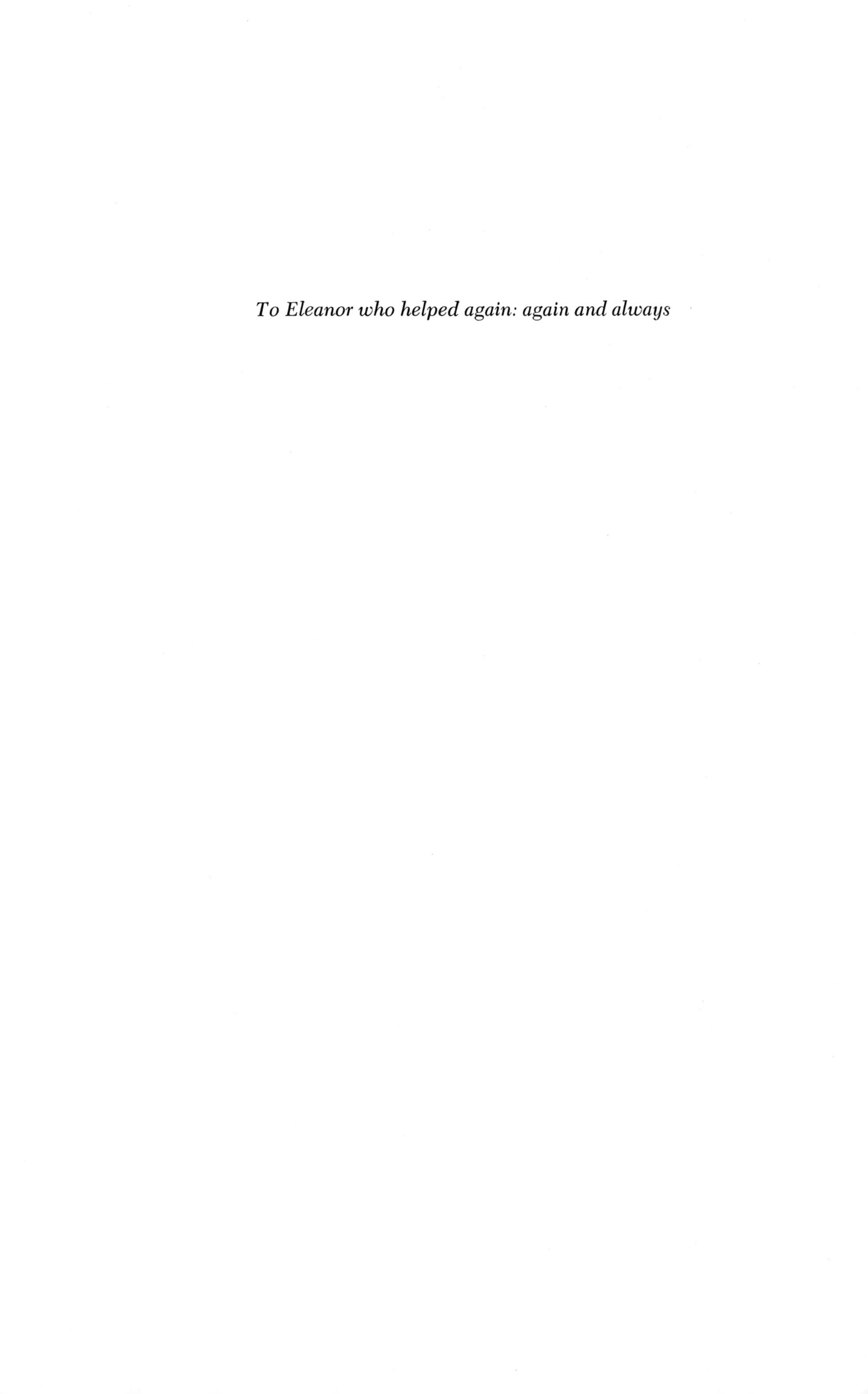

To Eleanor who helped again: again and always

ACKNOWLEDGMENTS

I wish to thank for their financial help in the preparation and publication of this book Brandeis University, the Lucius Littauer Foundation, and Mrs. Phyllis Lambert. My gratitude goes to the editor Thea Wheelwright for her intelligent, imaginative cooperation. To Mr. Barney Burstein my thanks for allowing me to use his collection of slides.

Contents

Introduction

This is a difficult book. It is original, immensely stimulating, and in the last analysis, I think, true. It is a book worthy of an introduction. It is a book which in its very insistence upon seeing the world anew—perhaps not always in a fashion acceptable to many—may too readily be dismissed as personal fantasy. The danger is there. It is thus worthy of an introduction, but no simple introduction can explain it.

On one level these variations could be characterized as a book of *pensées*. For—rather independent of the specific analysis of art—we may ponder such brevities as:

> The spiritual is what is thought about the body.
>
> The past is what we are within it.
>
> For more and more it seems true that only the subtle, still invisible, secret differences are the real differences, the efficient, working differences.
>
> When we "remember" a sensation we lose it as an actuality in us.
>
> . . . good and its self-rotting, evil and its self-exhaustion.

But these thoughts do not just flower on any tree. They consciously grow from a modern man's understanding of Japan's past.

> Japan is the only culture that never stopped believing in ghosts.
>
> Letters, or written characters, have had a most difficult existence in Japan.
>
> Shinto is not purity but purification.
>
> . . . the sub-historic genesis of Yamato-e is North Wei.

It is a book, too, that more often than not contradicts accepted stereotypes. Buddhism is characterized as "nothing less mysterious." Zen is "easy," while Amidism is "difficult." In a gadget for popular amusement there is "spirituality." The East's line may be as convincingly three-dimensional as the West's more solid methods for creating form in space. "China is Greece . . . sub-historically." "Fujiwara and Kamakura form one single ever-maturing block-style of life and art." " . . . never did these people think as we must about their art."

It need hardly be said that this is not traditional art history. Yet is it not to be welcomed? It is one of the unfortunate dilemmas of the respectable academic world that as the educational establishment grows, perhaps more often than we would like to admit, we seem unable to afford that intellectual necessity, the risk of originality of thought. Traditional art history has not been over-revealing about the art of Japan. We can learn a great deal—indeed have much more to learn—through the application of accepted study of iconography or style or perhaps the piecing together of extant works by single artists. But none of these have revealed—may ever reveal—what seems to be unique about the art of Japan. Yet that uniqueness is universally recognized. Close as it is to the art of China, it is only at a few isolated moments—moments of closest influence—that there need be any confusion. However, we have generally been forced to "explain" Japan's artistic greatness as an intense absorption in the technical aspects of the craft, or as brilliant decoration, or as narration, or as skilled imitation, or as that of being the last great repository—the farthest East—of a noble tradition that owes its genesis, its originality, and its basic importance to India and to China. Toward this Japan is at best a precocious child.

These indeed all have their truth. But somehow it is an inadequate truth. To praise the work of the hands in an age of automation seems only negatively important; to see art as a pleasing combination of shapes does not take us far beyond the interior decorator; and something that is second or third-hand imitation is hardly to be valued above the imitated.

This in part has led us to prize the art of China at the expense of the art of Japan. And this value finds special credence, I think, because the art of China *can* be explained. For in truth it is the art of China that is "imitative," not because it is essentially a copy of other artistic traditions, but because it is a re-creation of what we have already known. Space in Chinese art is again the familiar space that we have previously met in the "normal" world. Its form is like the form we know from physical experience, however beautifully intensified in the direction of what Professor Bronstein calls "grace." It is because Chinese art deals with what is familiar, what is essentially given in the natural world, that it is "easy" to explain—and because understood, the more highly prized.

The less intellectual contemporary West—the world of commerce, the craftsman, the decorator, even the tourist—reveals a more just, if still inarticulate, judgment of the art of Japan. For in recent years the "Japan boom" has been too strong not to indicate a significance greater than passing whim.

It is in this atmosphere that Professor Bronstein's ideas are brilliantly revealing. In a very genuine attempt to take us beyond what has been done before, he asks us to "leave with due politeness the world of influences and reach the world of attitudes, the *what of the how* world . . . . " At this level Japanese art is seen under the guise of "substitution." It is this new and more complete notion that embraces and makes meaningful the partial truths that we have already known. We are forced to accept the uniqueness of the work of art. And naturally the technique, the very way in which it reveals uniqueness, is clearly of prime importance. So, too, the idea of "decoration," for such readily observable matters as flatness or skilled surface arrangement have much to do with the artistic glory of a lacquer, a textile, a surface of paint. Even the matter of imitation has its significance here, for the excellence of the *art* of a work of art does not rest in its intellectual source.

But the theory of substitution as a characterization of Japanese art would hardly be enough if it did not affirm as well the ability of that art to speak in and of itself of that which is of deepest human concern. It is because of its physical presence that it is valid. It is because it can be touched, and infinity (of which all undefinable aspects of existence partake) cannot be touched, that art has meaning. For Japan's greatest art there can be no more talk of "mere" decoration. And " . . . that is why in Japan the costume is of the utmost . . . metaphysical importance."

That which can be touched cannot be doubted (which in the story of religion, as Dr. Bronstein affirms, is the greatness of Christianity). "The spiritual is what is thought about the body."

Nothing about that which is of greatest human concern is surer than art. This affirmation stands in direct contradiction to feelings about the visual arts in popular circles and even considered opinion in scholarly ones " . . . for his [the visual artist's] art can only be an imprecise definer of already vague concepts . . . "[1] But this latter view surely stems from the deeply ingrained notion that the definite and the precise is that which is verbally definite, verbally precise. That words, as the tools of reason, can with confidence be relied upon to define what is real, while arrangements of forms in space cannot.

This brings us to the "style" of Dr. Bronstein's book, which at least may appear to have its aspects of imprecision. Its difficulties are in part the result of wide learning, which often condenses meaning—perhaps too abruptly—to essential statements (the *pensée*). But more than that is the inescapable fact that words are poorly fashioned instruments for defining the much more precise concrete and tangible reality of Japanese art itself. If we ask why we cannot have a straightforward expected explanation of Japanese art, why we must have "a Mysterious Companion," a ghost, "mud," a grey little mouse, or a Noh play, the answer can only be that, at least so far, all straightforward expected explanations of Japanese art have left us far short of a satisfactory notion of what it is. Certainly this book is not without its mystery, but unless he who writes about the visual arts is willing to accept mystery as basic to their nature, he has defeated himself before beginning. Mystery, of course, is not an equivalent for vagueness.

Finally, I think, it is important to respect Professor Bronstein's notion of history, that is, the importance of "sub-history." The existence of similarities in the arts of various parts of the world, independent of the tangible links of space and time, may be as fascinating as the existence of similarities found in those which are linked by them. And this is what makes it possible to consider the art of Islam, or the art of America, or the art of Greece or of medieval France in a book on the art of Japan. Indeed possibility may very well be necessity; for whether he wills it or not, contemporary man is not really free to see any artistic tradition completely independent of the judgments that other artistic traditions may impose on it.

We travel far geographically in this book, but also within the realms of man. For here *inter alia* we are involved with philosophy, psychology, mathematics, technology, drama, and poetry. But there is no leaving an essential unity of form, for the form of the book is the form of the body as defined by its senses; and the senses are consonant with the seasons, and the seasons and the tangibility of the body are here the art of Japan. Japan never lent itself to abstract thinking. No matter how far we wander we always come back, and the art of Japan is there. But one can also say that this is a book by a modern man about the modern world ("The past is what we are within it"), which Dr. Bronstein sees as ready for a new myth: "The total substitution of the material witness of today's innermost-man-and-his-body" for the unseizable whole of this cycle's happening. Its subject is also " . . . not Japan and Japan's art. But . . . man's intellectual love of God, *amor intellectualis Dei,* the only profitless absolute in the world or worlds."

As a work of art, such complexities suggest that *Variations* is most closely analogous to the apparently uncontrolled control of a richly varied abstract-expressionist canvas. Most of what is here will not be grasped—accepted or rejected—without reflection. Understanding comes through immersion in the "person" of the book itself, and cannot come merely through the exercise of that "verbal" reason which is here found wanting. The form of the book is inseparable from the message of the book, and toward the end we find the sum of our direction:

> " 'higher-level abstraction'
> vision
> sound
> touch
> taste
> smell
> 'the silent objective empirical world' "

Drawn ever closer to the heart of the new myth "Buddhist psyche-*ascent* became . . . my twentieth-century's psyche-*descent* . . . where the lowest and elemental joins the highest decisions of abstracting." And this affirmation is universal because it forces us to accept what we are—which is our salvation . . . and was Japan's:

> The method of final salvation that I have taught is neither a sort of meditation such as that practised by many scholars in China and Japan in the past, nor is it a repetition of the Buddha's name by those who have studied and understood the deep meaning of it. It is nothing but the mere repetition of the name of the Buddha Amida without a doubt of his mercy, whereby one may be born into the Land of Perfect Bliss.[2]

Ann Arbor, Michigan
September, 1965

RICHARD EDWARDS

VARIATION I

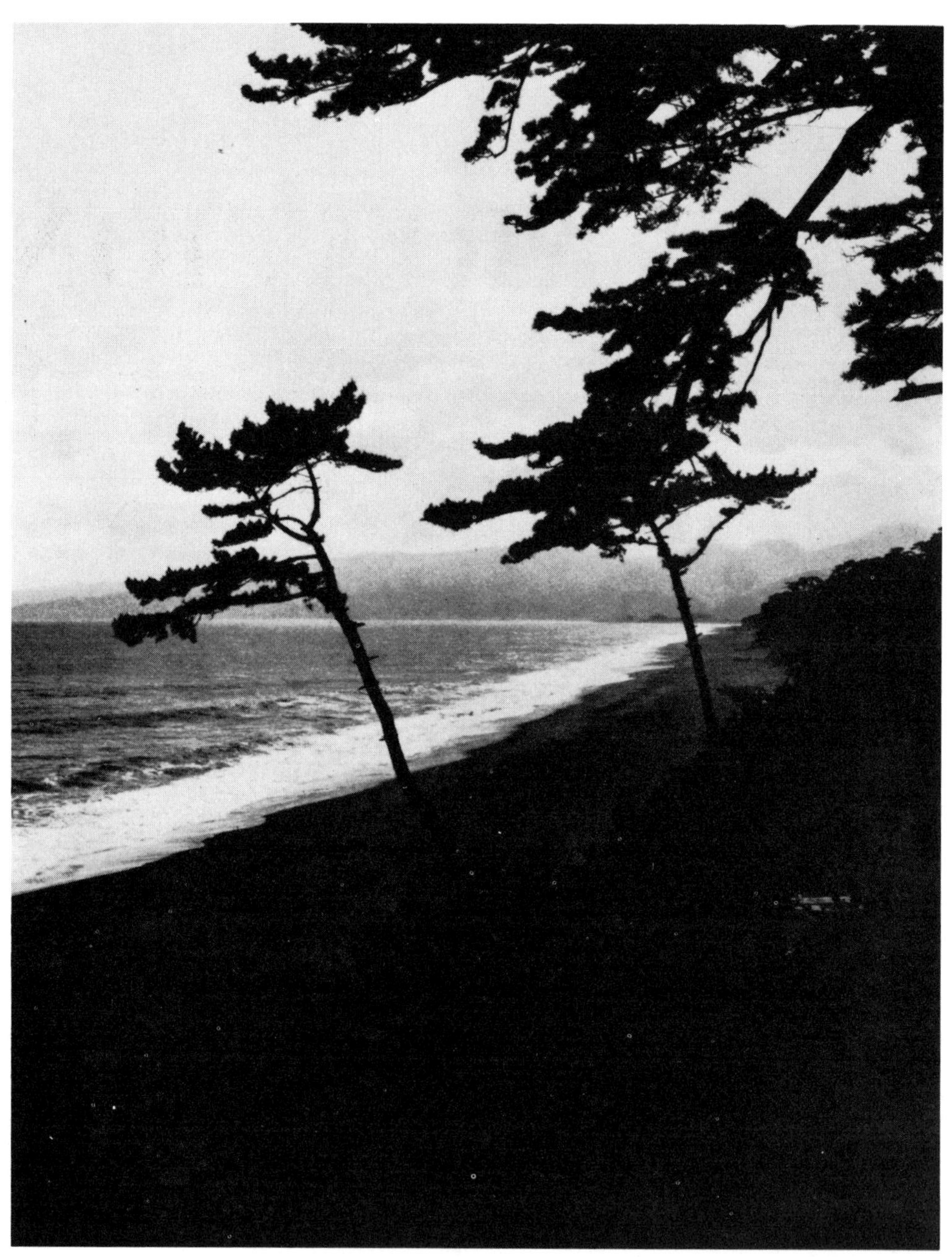

1 *Seashore, Kanagawa Ken*

The Starting of a Journey

My love for animals and the rest of creation is not hearty and of the earth. I do not bend down to them; nor do I lift them up. I look for a remote source-of-creation *point,* wherein I can apprehend a sort of formula covering man, beast, plant, fire, water, air . . . and all circulating forces *at once.*
PAUL KLEE

✡

We are ready for a new myth.

✡

Standing on the shore in Kanagawa Ken *(Plate 1),* a vast and winding shore, a great light and a great water in front of me—not different from, not greater nor more surprising than many many other shores scattered all over our earth, yet unique, this luminous dusk in Japan on May 26, 1964, a point-event within the plenum: forever this point, never another, never another's, yet one with the whole continuum of change—standing, now, before the *torii*[1] reflected in Miyajima's sacred waters, I met the Mysterious Companion, the Comrade of my journey and time: Japan's past.

✡

And, together, we opened the closed past of Japan. (For a past is forever closed—a perfect, closed, present sphere. It does not know—but we know!—what has been achieved after it; it floats, a light and perfect balloon, a bladder, among others, which we of today puncture as we touch it, and empty of its content. The past is what we are within it. The past is *ours,* not *theirs.*)

✡

I came here from far, a different—*totaliter aliter*—huge and awesome far. Cautiously I parted the tufted branches which concealed this sweetest

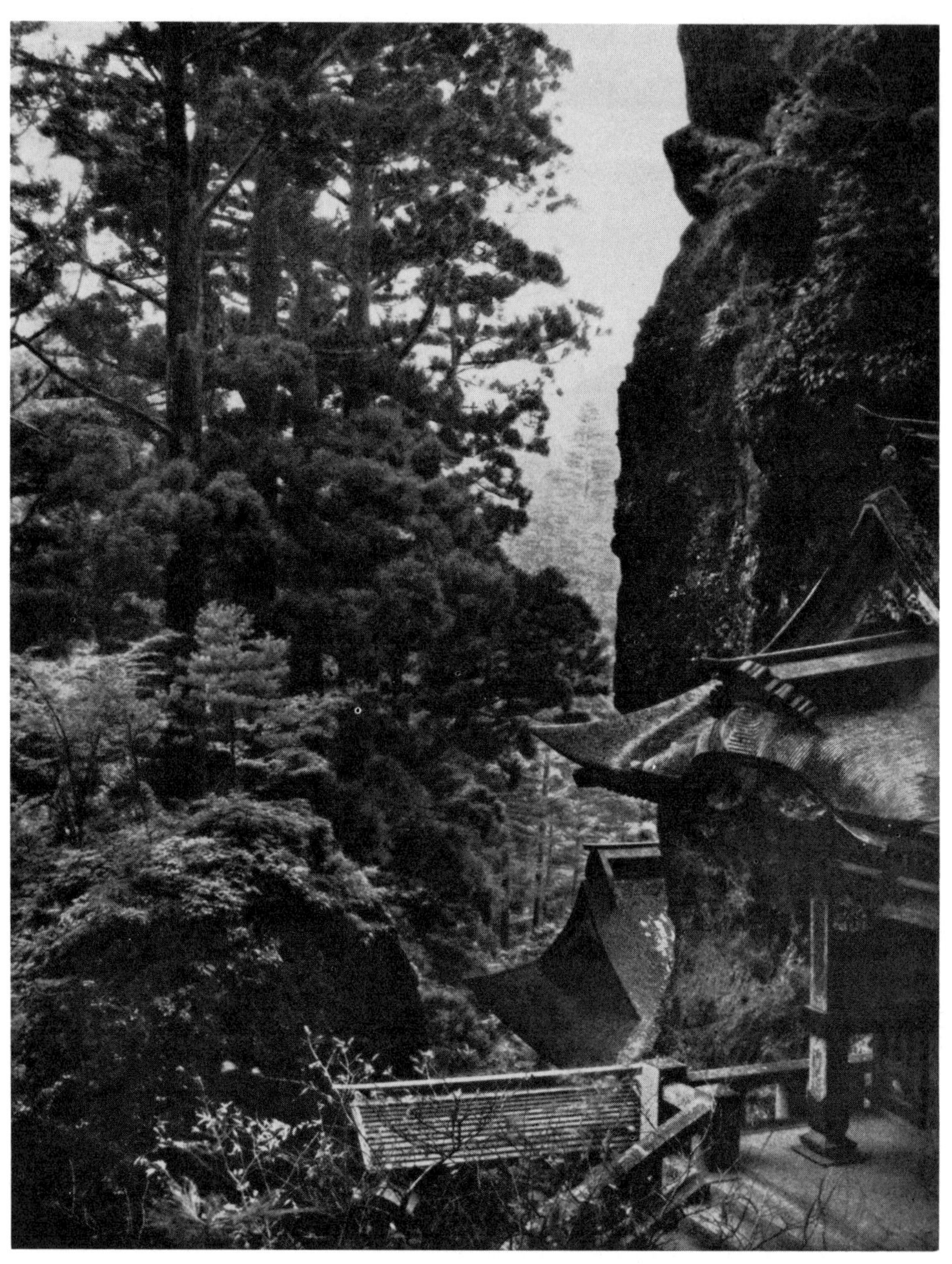

2 Haruna Shrine

spot *(Plate 2)* and faced Japan's Time, with all its views, smells, existences, and exuberances. In a blast of Japan's purples, golds, whites, and blacks I could hear, could smell the Heian's, the Kamakura's great noise coming from within a world new, deep and sharp, oceanic, purified in body.

✡

Japan, I greet you here, with the astonishment of an unexpected encounter —mine or Plotinus's,[2] what does it matter! *Salut,* Japan—and adieu too! Here let it be told firmly: adieu, bloody *mud* of recent memories! And silence now about the bloody mud of Japan's past and of the world's! Silence—not for the sake of the aesthetic man's rest and return to the enlightened comfort of his *paix intérieure* ("Let's not mix poetry and politics . . . Really!"—as if it were possible not to!), nor for the sake of the moral man, the man of our innermost center, the one who has judged and is going to judge, and thus must rest—central and factual—for a while; but silence about the bloody mud ("But yet the pity of it, Iago!") for the sake of the tired metaphysical man of today, of his vivid—untiring—anxiety, born somewhere between the "nausea" outside his body and the *amor intellectualis Dei* within his body. Yes, for the sake of this ever-shrinking in-between, this Sartrian nausea and this Spinozian *intellectual love of God*—the love nonprofitable (non-"spiritual," non-"corporeal" too), self-sustaining, self-emerging, the mathematician's very existence, his living equation of order of nature = order of mind; love that must be only love, with nothing to lean on, neither God, nor self, nor Nature, nor the reminder of God or Nature or self, nor the remnants of rewards or denials. Nothing: *amor intellectualis Dei,* the very closeness of poetry, indeed. Silence here about the bloody mud, present, past, future.

✡

Cautiously, I part the branches; the fragrant retreat of the shrine of Haruna is still there, close against rock and darkened greenery.

And starting our pilgrimage there, Japan's architecture—Chinese in its traceable apparent origins, of course, yet Japanese in its ultimate reach and intensity—is ours.

In a flash of living documents the grandeur of Yamato's wooden temples and dwellings, the structure of its poetry and engineering argument reveals itself: the subtle and truly astonishing asymmetry in the relation between what we call the façade, the face, of a building and its roof, its shelter; a reversed ordering of functions.

Unique the heavy, opulent, living flesh of a Japanese roof—both weighing on us and sheltering us (how securely one is held against it!) *(Plate 3)*; its eaves and double brackets *(Plate 4)* in their up-flight, their polyrhythmic dance, supporting as it were, against all the logic of gravitation's laws, the façade—here actually the roof!—a façade simple, too-simple, transcorporeal in its Palladian, or even Brunelleschian "proportionality." Unique: from the precious sonnet-cadence of the open-winged Phoenix Hall *(Plate 5)* to the absorbing, almost smashing, yet also sheltering fleshiness of the Hotoku-Jinja.

One could say a new architectural dimension (surely extending, in its reverberation, over its conditioning undergrowth: the sociology and economy of Japan's past; the demands of Japan's geography; the offering of its building material, Japan's precious woods), a new value-dimension, has

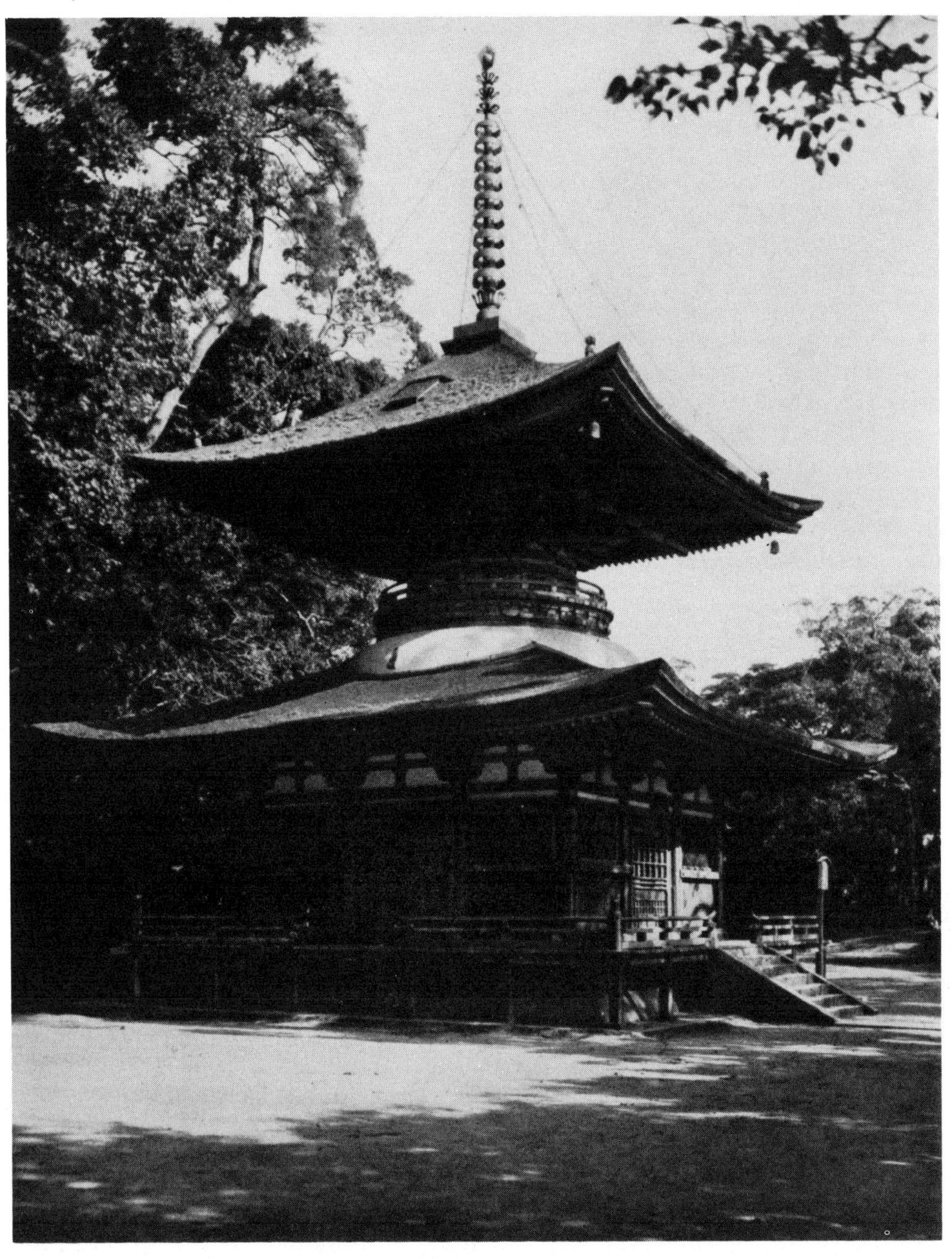

3 *Pagoda in the Ishiyamadera* (so-called Tahoto style)

been added by this Far Eastern architecture to all the other values that the architecture of other creative cultures has historically embodied.

To architecture's inner humanistic goal, to its planetary drama of emancipation from the gravitational burden of stresses and tensions, its dematerialization by the very means of this materiality, the historical epochs of the column's pride and support, of the vault's protean vigilance, and lastly of the cantilever's self-achieved liberation—to these freedom-conquer-

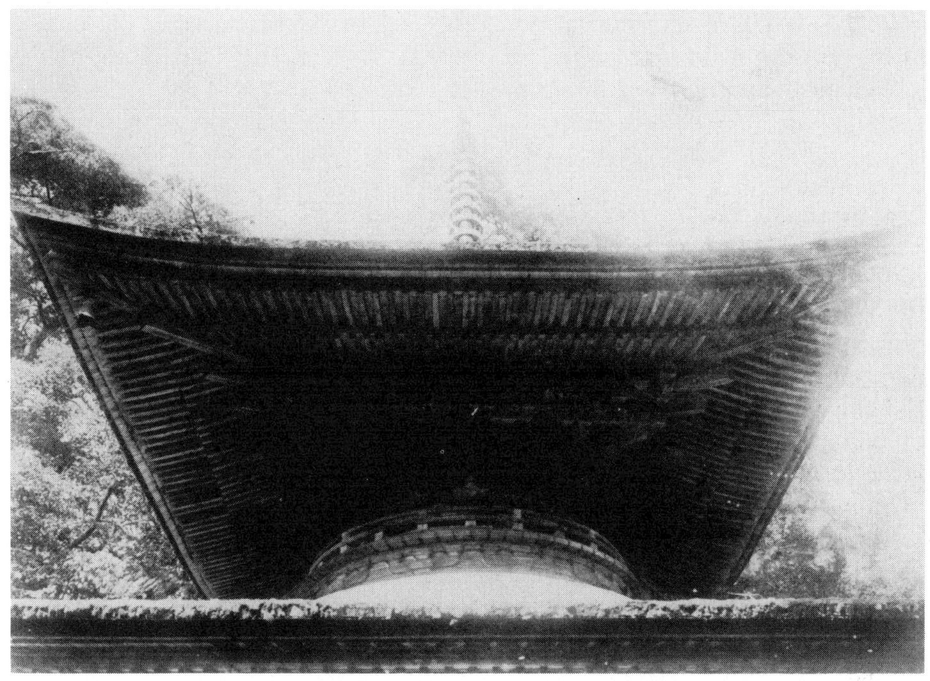

4 *Eaves and Brackets, Phoenix Hall* (11th century)

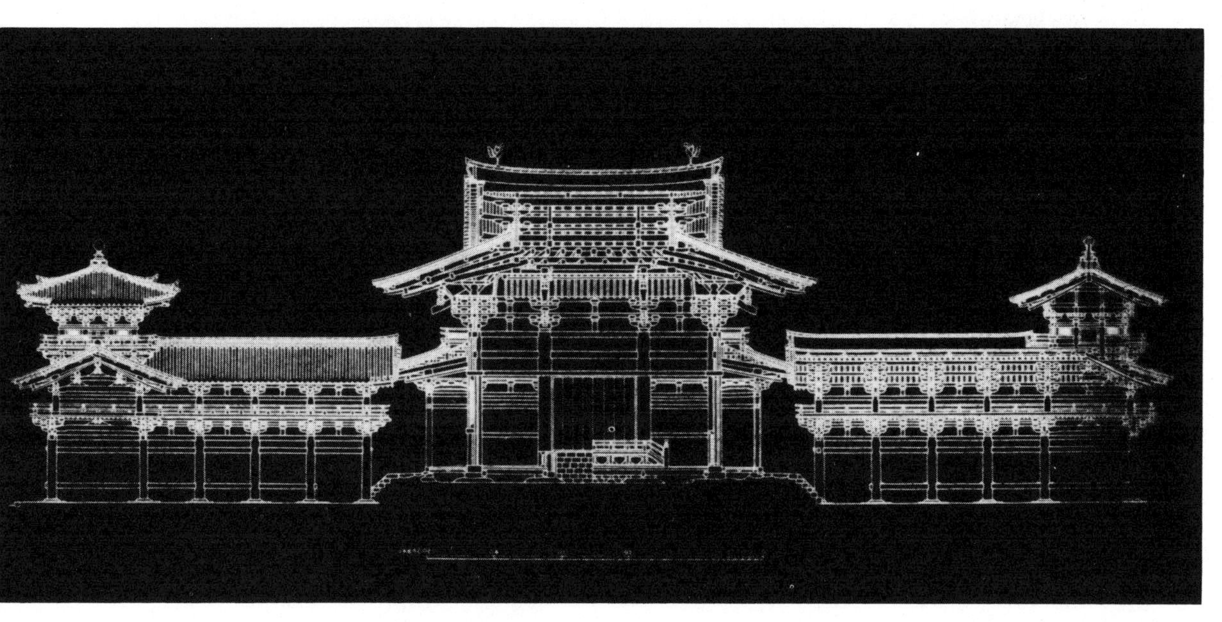

5 *Elevation, Phoenix Hall* (11th century)

ing functions a new freedom and a new function have been given: Japan's conquest of gravity's law—of mass, of weight, of "matter," by the law (Yogian?) of no-mass, no-weight, no matter!

✡

Here it is, or seems finally to be, within or around the beautiful city of Kyoto, that the vision of a great architect of the West, Louis Sullivan, took its bodily form: art "is the ten-fingered grasp of reality."[3] The ten fingers of the eye it is, the ten fingers of the fingers, of the nose, of the ear . . . and their grasp of reality. Reality, yes: as vaguely defined and as clearly comprehended as, say, in the erotic moist Oneness of the tantric Yab-Yum[4] or in the Existentialist dry certainty of Primeval Touch, the immediate realization of ourselves within the world through the total sensation of touch by an outer "object"; the Two-before-One. The presence of adherence: the reality of immediate passage from me to what is not me; immediate because without the help of the famous "category of relation" that ultimately separates instead of uniting.

Presence of adherence it is indeed—the very content and the very form of body's flesh and body's act: the very root of sensitivity, thus, by efflorescence, of idea itself.

✡

> In the womb of nature, at the source of creation, where the secret key to all lies guarded.
>
> But not all can enter. Each should follow where the pulse of his own heart leads.
>
> So in their time, the Impressionists—our opposites of yesterday—had every right to dwell within the matted undergrowth of every-day vision.
>
> *But our pounding heart drives us down, deep down to the source of all.*
>
> *What springs from this source, whatever it may be called,* dream, idea or phantasy—must be taken seriously only if it unites with the proper creative means to form a work of art. Then those curiosities become realities—realities of art which help to lift life out of its mediocrity.
>
> *For not only do they, to some extent, add more spirit to the seen, but they also make secret visions visible.* PAUL KLEE[5]

✡

" . . . but they also make secret visions visible." Perhaps—in response to so exalted a meditation-opening, in response also to the exalted site of Miyajima Torii, or Haruna shrine—perhaps it was exactly then that this other friendly voice of Japan was heard: Japan's sculpture. How welcome this other testimony of body's sensitivity in co-vibration—so Japanese!—with the sensitivity of an art.

For the sensitivity, the "nature" of an art, of any art based on the eye's possession of visible space—painting, architecture, sculpture, etc.—consists primarily in the peculiar character of this very possession, pictorial, or architectural, or sculptural.

In our optical perception we possess from the outset the reality, the "naturalness" of the space which is all about us; and we possess it as an extension of *our body*: an extra body, an extra hand, an added member. We possess it, therefore, automatically, *without astonishment* or pointed vigilance. The visual universe or "natural" empirical space, if it is a member of *my own body,* is at the same time, as an intuited inescapable necessity, a member, or an extra member, of all other bodies, human bodies *par excellence,* analogous to mine. The notion of an object, of a precise "this-object," in space comes from the crucial encounter—in the interior of my body—of what is purely personal, *mine,* and what is purely general, universal, belonging to all bodies *similar* to mine. Thus at the bottom of the automatism of this possession, or rather, principle of possession, there is already a certain conflict, a drama. It means that the mere givenness of the space, its actual, "natural" presence, is not all-sufficient for the eye.

The genesis of creation is there, perhaps. *Art* would be to surpass the conflict by continuing, thus revealing, it. An object of art—a fabricated semblance—is always a *new* object. It is never *entirely* constructed on that datum or principle of possession—automatic, thus pre-established, natural—on which the perception of a natural object is entirely based. (That is why the "deformation" or transformation of a natural object is the first exigence of art.) In our visual perception the object is an indivisible synthesis of extension and of drama, of the material milieu (space or extension) where the form of a thing is realized, and the psychological milieu (the "story") narrated by this form. In art this spontaneous synthesis is broken up. Art chooses, or rests upon, one of the two—extension or story—and *reconstructs* by its own means (hence "artifice" as catharsis) the other, the missing or abandoned part of the broken synthesis. That is how the activity of art fabricates—and thus surmounts the eye's innermost conflict—its own synthesis, a new synthesis, different from the "natural" synthesis with which it started in the eye. The character of this choice is the particular nature, the sensitivity, of each of the arts of the eye.

Thus the art of the sculptor, who retains the "possessed" physical milieu of a form, the volume-presence of solids and voids interrelated with us, creates its new synthesis by inventing or constructing the expressive drama of the form.

To sculpt is to create and to expand a psychological content by means of the very givenness of space, that is, of the reduction, the economy, of a given space, the thinning, or the thickening, of a volume-presence there. Sculpture is the maximum of expression in a minimum of physical expansion, progressively achieved. In its ultimate expressive reduction it would mean this: from three-dimensional, given, to two-dimensional, to one-dimensional offered. The reality of drama in a sculpture—bronze, stone, wood, lacquer—is in the expressiveness of its pure linearity, or rather, in the latter becoming a point, a multi-point mobile: the Hera of Samos, the Pietà Rondanini of Buonarotti, the last Prometheus of Lipchitz, and the most "economical," thus the most "created" of all, this sculptured simulacrum of Ashikaga Yoshimasa *(Plate 6).*

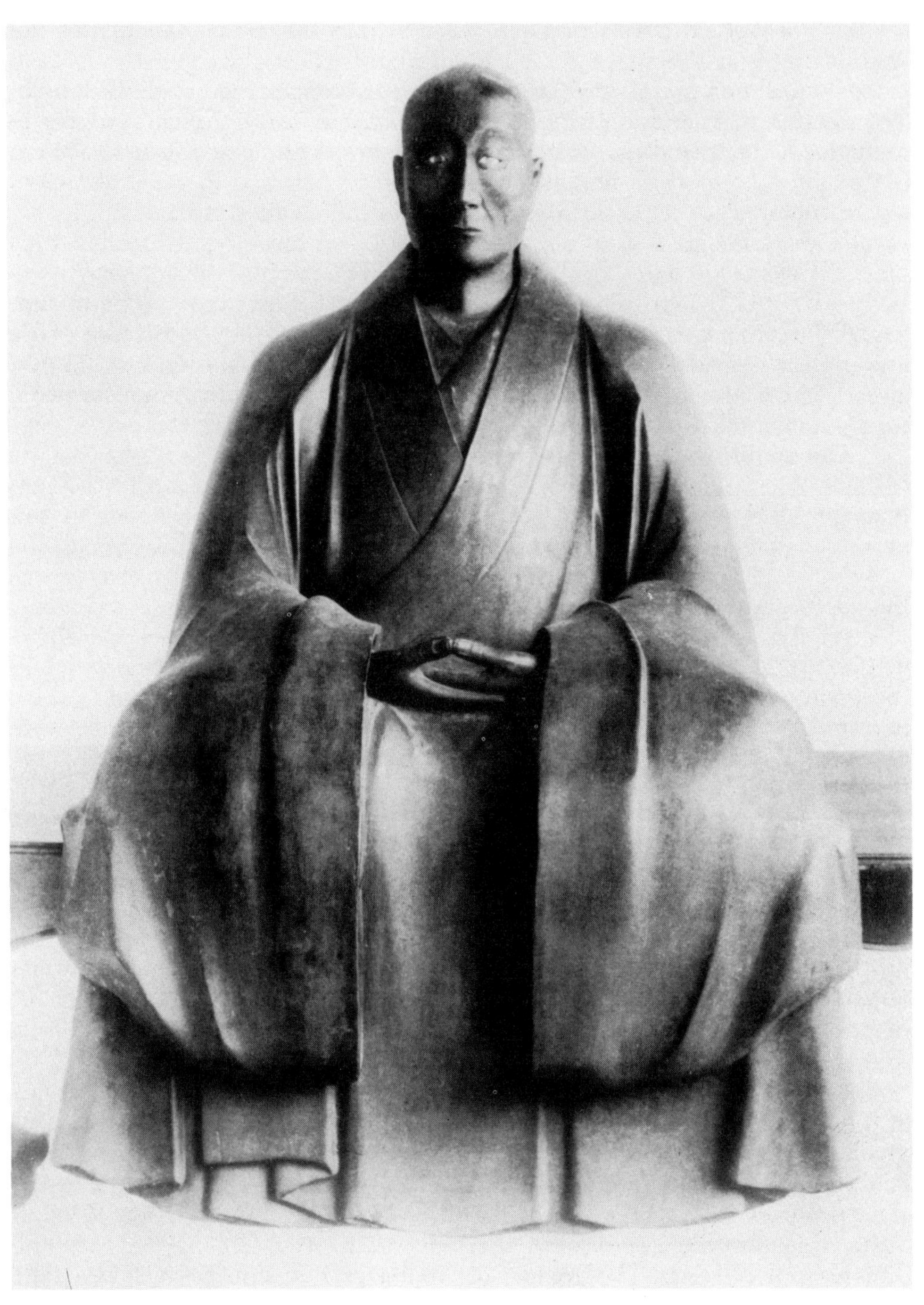

6 ARTIST UNKNOWN *Ashikaga Yoshimasa* Wooden image (late 15th century)

Such would be the "sensitivity" of sculpture, the very contrary of the "sensitivity" of painting.

Because to paint is to possess and retain—within the scope of a technical ability potentially illimited here—the drama, the psychological narrative content, as included in the given synthesis of nature's "object": all the earth, meteors, sky, fire, beings, happenings, doings. . . . What is to be re-created or completed there is the element of extension itself.

The painter has to construct his own object—space; he has to fabricate the consistence, the very significance of the extended. The "spiritual" message of a painting is in the "materiality" of its physical volume-drama. Painting is the nostalgia for space. This is the "sensitivity" of the art of painting with which our body's sensitivity co-vibrates: whether in the painting of China, of twelfth- and twentieth-century France, of twentieth-century America, or of Japan.

❖❖❖❖❖❖❖❖❖❖❖❖❖❖❖❖❖❖❖❖❖❖❖❖❖❖❖❖❖❖❖

Pittura è una cosa mentale.

LEONARDO

China in her more representative or matured age, Sung, one guesses, made her "secret visions" visible through the triple structure of her world-famous pictorial line-idiom: the *Shin,* the precise "ox-like wrinkles" line; the *Oyō,* the "twisted rope," a rounded volume-suggesting line; and the *So,* the "abstract" splash-linearity.[6]

Japan in her more representative matured age, since the late Fujiwara, one guesses, took in this Chinese pictorial idiom-structure, labored in it, and brought it to a consummation.

There is, indeed, nothing in Japanese painting, Japanese art at large—and what of Japan's polity and what of her history of ideas!—from the prowess of her brush stroke, the peculiarity of her bird-view slanting and inverse perspective, the delicate symbolism of her color, to the depth of her *nōtan,*[7] nothing that ever since the time of Japan's initial opening in the sixth century, to the impact of China's full penetration (Korea intervening creatively), did not come there from the fabulous shores of the Far East continent.

And yet, between China's *Gestalt* and Japan's (*Gestalt,* indeed: here, the communicated uniqueness of a historical physiognomy, its "horizon," its immediately comprehended expressiveness. For otherwise, outside a *Gestalt,* there could not have been any one-China, or Japan, or Greece, or France, but—as indeed there was not—many different Chinas, Japans, Frances, or Greeces), between China and Japan, then, there is and has been a much deeper separation than, say, the still lingering inauspicious separation between "our" West and "their" East.

Thus, in painting: China's creative tension, necessary for the formulation of its proper—Chinese—space, was, one feels, both released and relieved in what could be called, as our Baroque Age would have it, China's Central or basic Affection:[8] the continuity of the form and its milieu—the finite and the never-finite—the figure and its background *(Plate 7).*

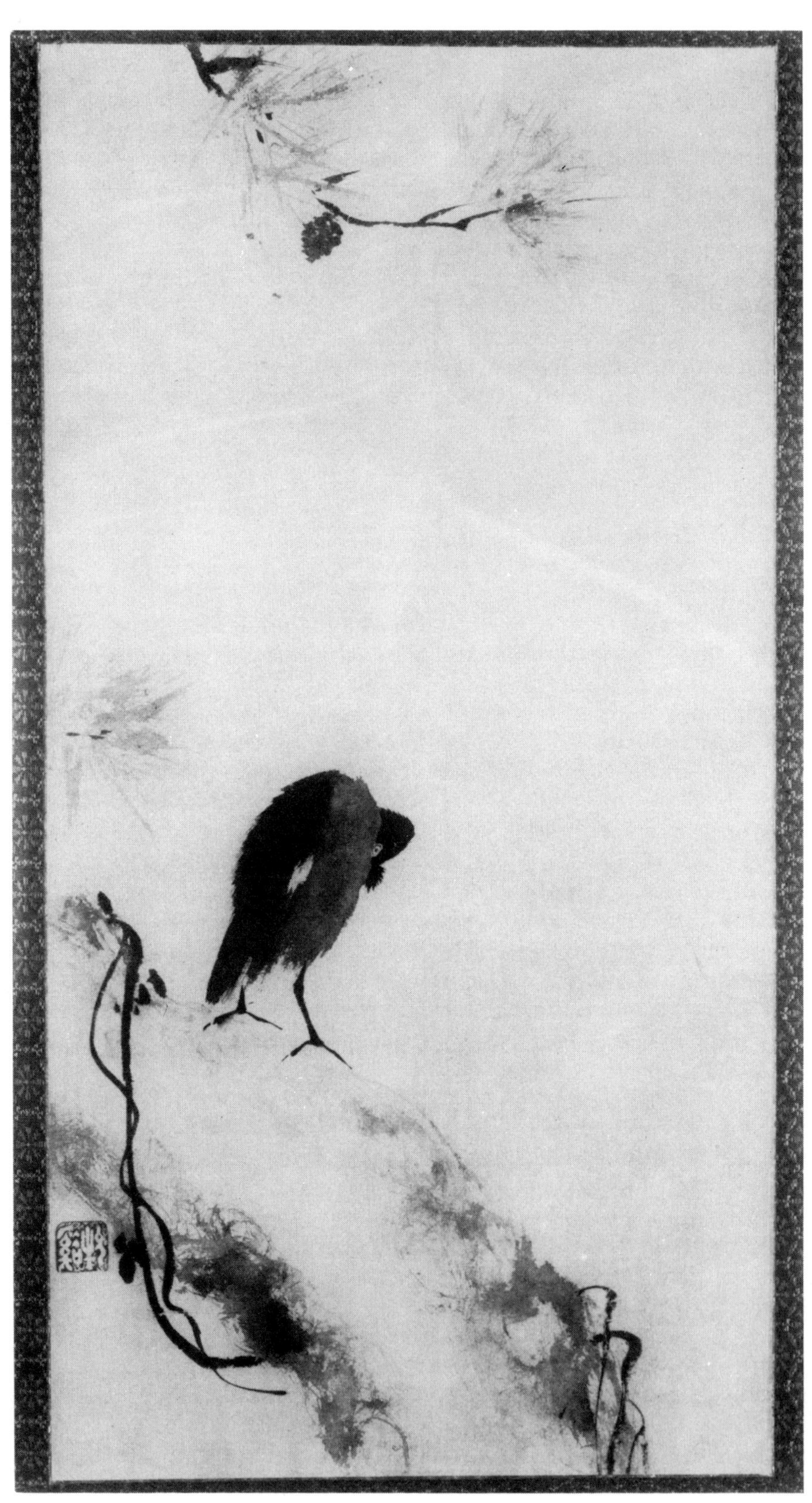

7 Mu-ch'i
Bull-headed Shrike on Old Pine Tree
13th century

Now, if China's Central Affection appears to be given to this principle of spatial continuity, Japan's seems to be disclosed in the opposite: the discontinuous, the sudden, suddenly unique. The differences here are, more often than not, as subtle (so subtle as to be sometimes unperceivable) as they are deep in what they reveal: the symbolization, philosophical in intent, as well as the style in Niten's masterpiece "The Shrike" is obviously Chinese, but the suddenly interrupted, *discontinued* merging of the dead branch at its upper edge into the fullness of the void around it, surmised as infinity—is Japan's, unequivocally *(Plate 8).*

And so is Sesshu's voluntary fragmenting of the same void-fullness of space-continuum, by the sudden action, the discontinuity, of his vertical slash there *(Plate 9).*

Subtle differences, that is, real ones.

✡

For more and more it seems true that only the subtle, still invisible, secret differences are the real differences, the efficient, working differences.

The ubiquitous twofoldness of life's oneness demands it: the very inseparability, thus the closeness to each other, of obvious opposites—the opposite terms of the two-complex, yes-no, either-or—blurs, if not annihilates, the *acuteness,* the efficiency of the opposition itself; while, by the same inescapable twofoldness, it is the seeming closeness—thus the "secret" remoteness from each other—of two similar or quasi-similar fact-events that makes their subtle opposition so efficient, acute, and once revealed, so real.

Not either-or, yes-no, but Hamlet's perhaps, almost. Not truth-lie, but lie versus hypocrisy, truth versus silence. Not vital-mechanical, but vital versus vitalist, mechanical versus mechanicist. Not capitalism-communism, but socialism-communism; not fighting corruption with purity, but with lesser corruption. Not East-West, but China-Japan.

And in art's "secret visions" made visible: not content opposite form ("contentism" against "formalism") but content-and-form at once becoming and opposing a new content of the same form.

How similar in their apparent spatial arrangement are these two pictorial narratives *(Plates 10 and 11)*! It has even been suggested[9] that the earlier work, the Chinese, might have been, historically, the origin of the art, so typically Japanese, of horizontal scroll painting (*emakimono*). Yet each of the two pictorial works conceals a different visual content, and beyond this, a different secret human attitude. One, the Chinese, is facing us; its movement, though made up of juxtaposed parts, is continuous through all the elements of its narration. The other, Japanese, projects through us its *oblique,* sudden, thus discontinued progression of forms.

Here too the subtle distinction—similarity almost—becomes the real distinction. And here too, basically and universally, the real subtlety of distinctions is detected on neither of the two obviously opposite levels of comparative analysis: neither on the level of *what,* the level of the subject matter *understood in its most extensible sense of verbally narratable content,* nor on the level of *how*—the expressive form itself, the "cognitive significance" of its technical procedure.

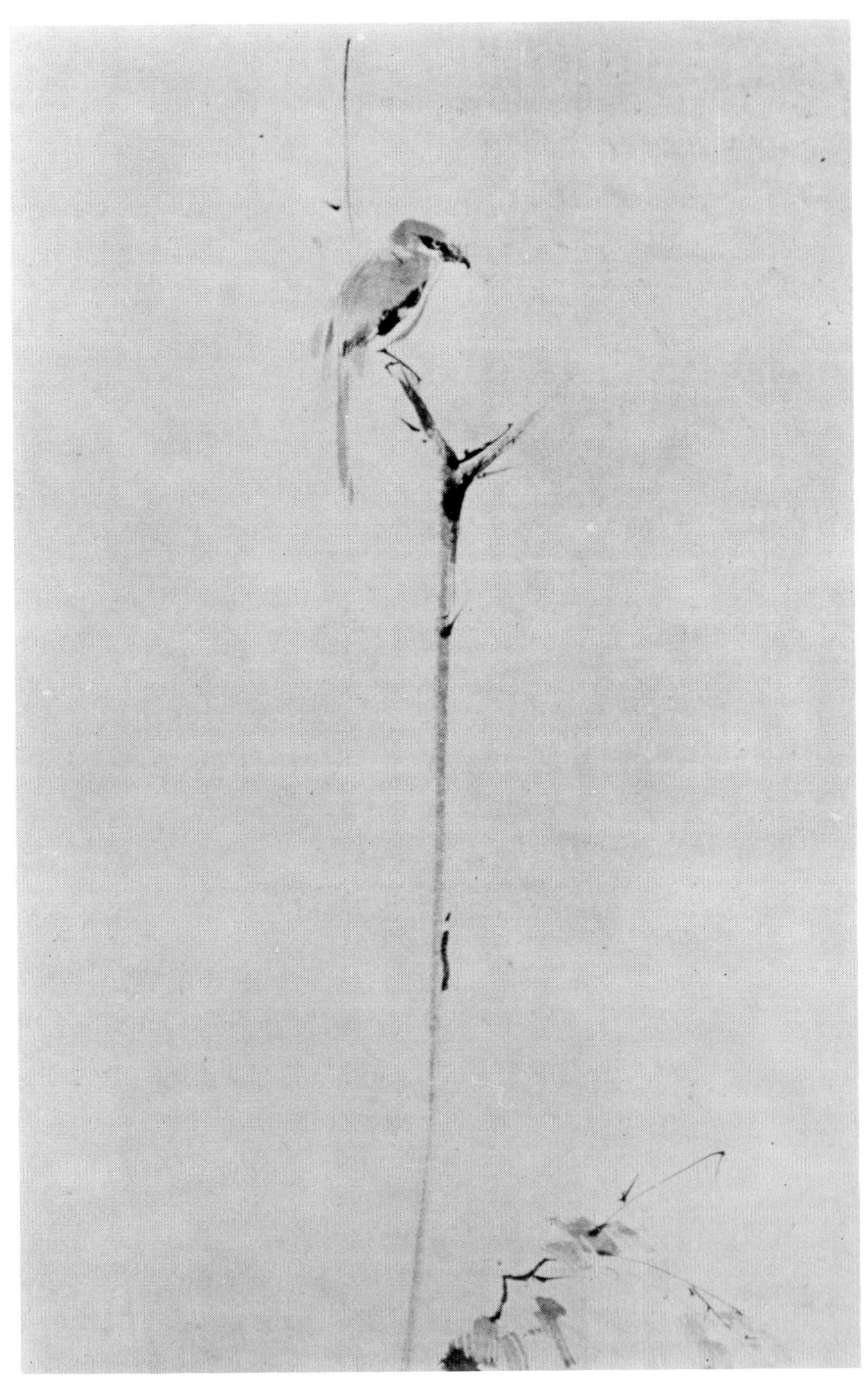

8 NITEN *Shrike on Dead Tree* (Edo period, 17th century)

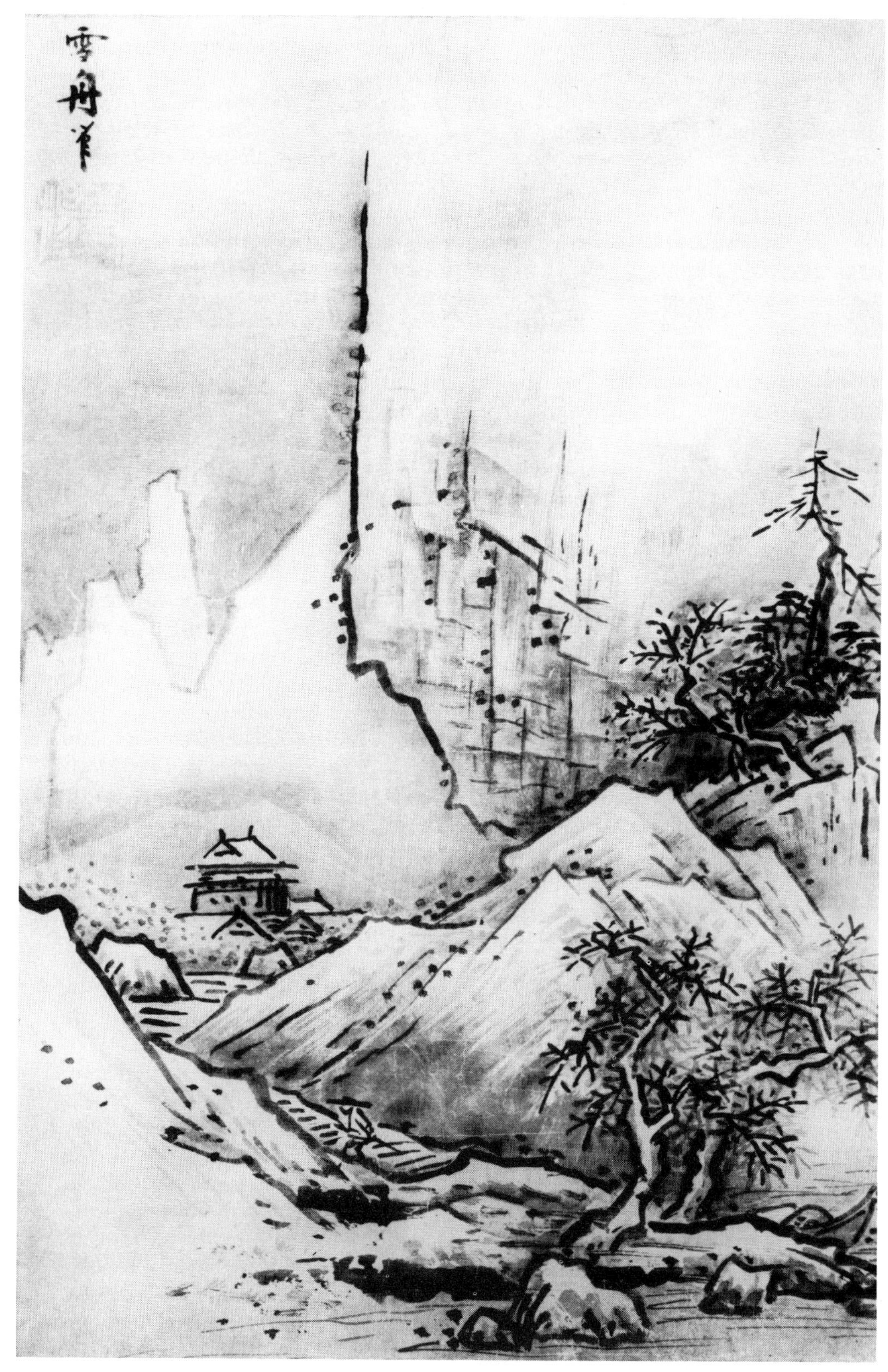

9 Sesshu *Winter Landscape* 15th century

These two "opposite" levels, even when taken together as complementary, cannot reveal the subtle and efficient content of an object of art—mental or plastic—the innermost result itself of hidden, subtle, real oppositions. Only on the root-level of their interrelation—"to be is to be related"[10] —the level of the *what of the how*, of content and form joined, made one, does the "visual secret," though secret still, become visible.

A new subject matter, very different, sometimes totally different, from the verbally narratable *what*, emerges there, a new *what*-content revealed—after a daring plunge into the *formal* medium itself—through and within the *how* of the color, line, sound, volume, rhythm and rhyme and their spatio-temporal behaviour. And it is here, in the depth of this *formal iconology* that the central revelation and purpose of a work of art resides: the revelation and purpose of the "integral man," the vague, unique and lyrical *I* indissolubly attached to a precise moment of human history, a moment which contained the earthly existence of this *I*. This is the "integral man" of the terrifying Sphinx enigma in the Oedipus myth. This is also the man hidden, for instance, within the acute nostalgic restlessness of a Vermeer November 1669 blue form, a form whose "verbally" narrated aspect is on the contrary so full of poise, cozy grace, and peace. Or the man hidden within the nostalgic more than just flowery Paradise recreated for him in the festive frivolity of a Yoshiwara courtesan *(Plate 12)*.

Unwarned, we could of course leave any pattern of culture wherever our scholarship found it, together with the *what*-content it reveals: this or that pictorial imagery of China, for example, by means of whose ink-brush vocabulary the painter-philosopher may have intended to suggest all the elusive depth of Asia's thought. Comfortably halted there, we would enjoy once more great Asia's verbally accessible depths already known to our scholarship, enjoy once more through China's pictorial poetic suggestion the "aesthetically undifferentiated,"[11] yet at the same time so precisely different from anything else, all-Asia culture pattern, the doctrine of Tao or Way—this all-explaining, all-confusing, all-penetrating elemental principle of becoming and of being, of being absent thus—in its polarity of Yin-Yang, the male-female, the positive-negative principle; then, the entire heirloom, made Chinese, of the Hindu code of teaching, based on *bhava* = growth, and *sunyata* = plenum-void; above all, perhaps, the Ch'an Buddhist (Zen in Japan) "white vacancy of silence," its soul-to-soul, heart-to-heart, sudden and immediate enlightenment and propagation of nothing-everything.

Unwarned, we could also leave where we found it the obvious distinction between the image-content of China and the image-content of Japan, of Japan's apparently most typical artistic eras: the "decorativity" (very well: frivolity) of the leaf-gilt screens, the festive flowers, birds, self-mirroring beauties, of the abundant Momoyama or Tokugawa periods.

And further, we could profitably go on examining the sociological roots of these differences: China—more "open"-bourgeois, her historical horizon or mentality ever widened by interrelated trading-liberal and scholastic-classifying social functions; Japan—more "closed"-feudal, her historical mentality evolving in a climate of physical-moral prowess, of war and love, of beauty = love of war—in war and for the sake of war's surcease.

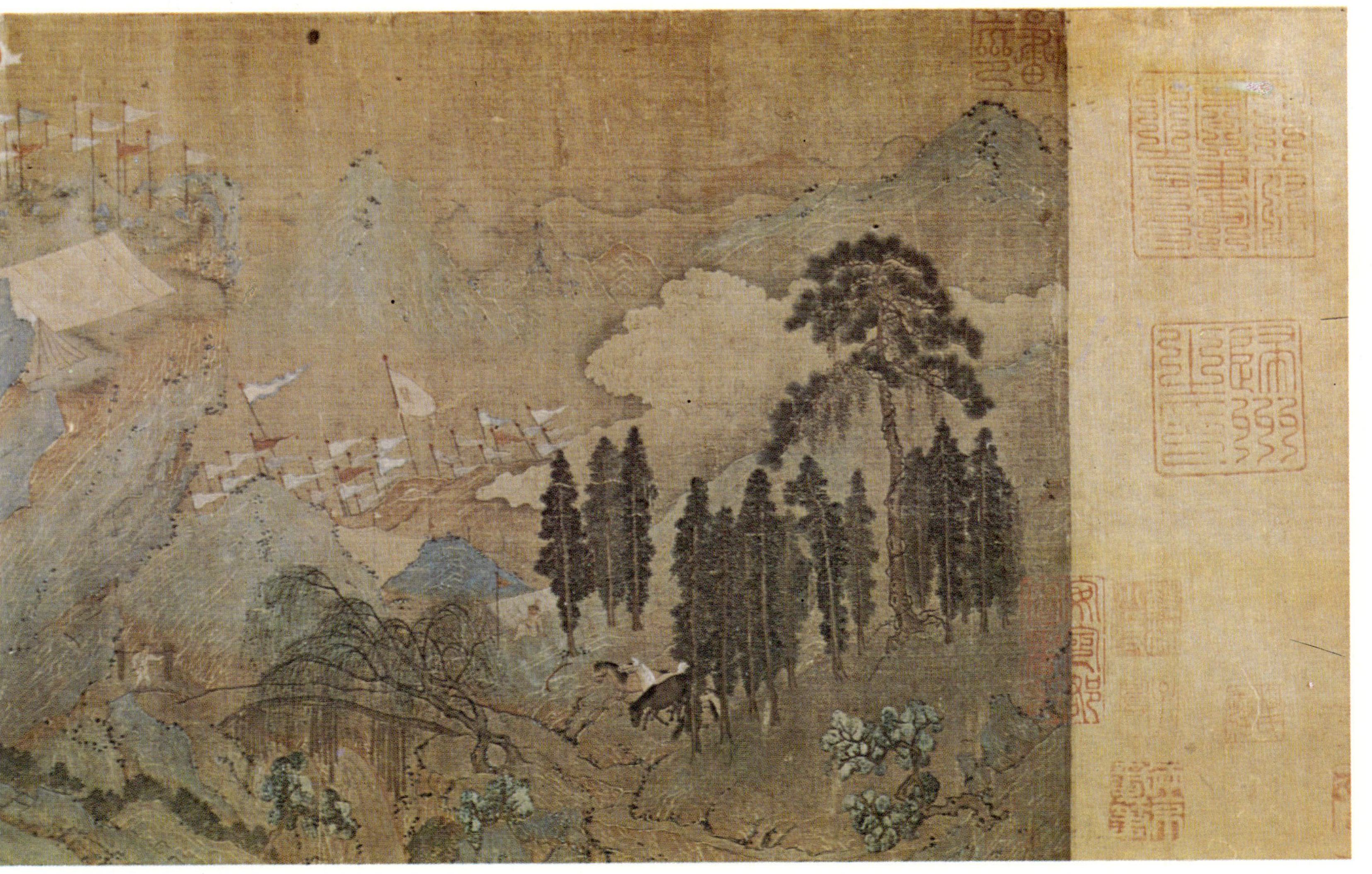

10 Chao Po-chu *Entry of First Han Emperor into Kuan-chung* (detail)

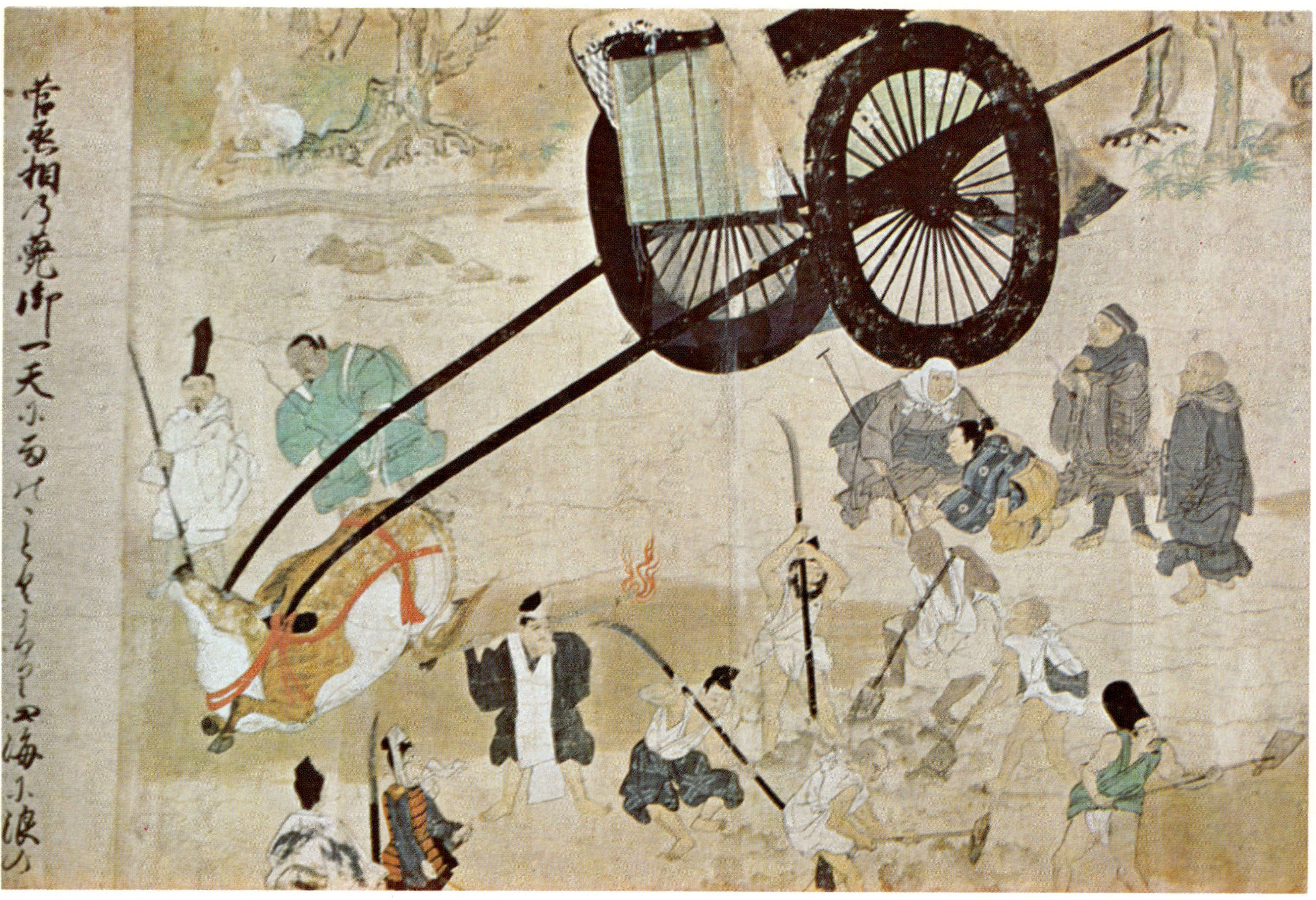

11 Ascribed to Fujiwara-no-Nobuzane *Kitano Tenjin Engi* (detail)

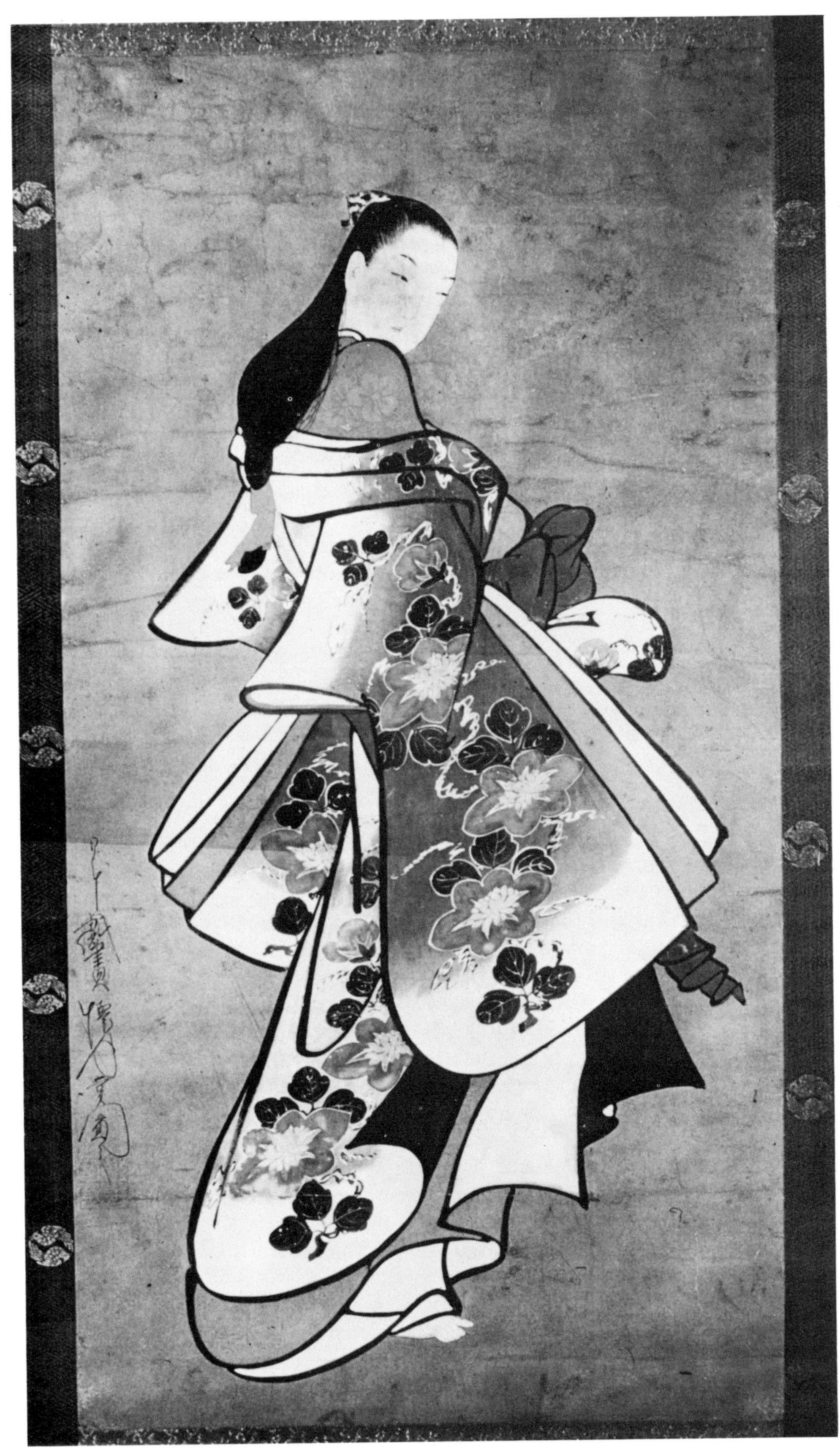

12 KAIGETSUDO ANDO *Yoshiwara Courtesan, Beauty*
(Edo period, early 18th century)

(How repeatedly—and incompetently—has Japan been described as the aesthetic culture *par excellence,* by art historians still under the spell of the Goncourts' blessing: its charming "genre" mentality, especially for the Ukiyo-e eighteenth- and nineteenth-century pictorial period. Or—as a much more thoughtful critical view would have it—Ukiyo-e art revealed as a "democratization" of the doctrine, hitherto confined to the Buddhist elite, of "everything-everybody-is-Buddha" thus why not this courtesan or that actor!)

And now descending still deeper—at will—from the *what* universe of narration to the *how* structures of formal visuality, if we arrive at discerning there the now semi-hidden, now obvious differences of style: China's emphasis on the continuous one-into-another merging of forms in space, Japan's accent (often China's too, but less urgent) on the cut-out, oblique, and suddenly discontinuous space structure, we could once more leave these disentangled distinctions where we found them: on the threshold of the aesthetician's haughty self-sufficiency.

But if, following, as we all do needfully, the dictates of value-judgment, we aspire to go beyond both the verbally localized *what*-content and the logician's *how*-hedge, we must reach the universe of Paul Klee's "where the central organ of all temporal-spatial movements, whether it be called the brain or the heart of creation, initiates all functions."[12] We reach the universe of the *what of the how,* where the hidden, subtle meaning of just such a distinction as China's depth-realism versus Japan's depth-ornament is transferred (not vaguely transformed, but transferred entirely) into a new content-form, a two-faced new compound: at once man's togetherness with the universe of the beyond-of-man (as in the Chinese continuous-figure-medium relation), and man's elemental, tragic and beautiful isolation within this beyond (as in the asymmetry-discontinuity of the Japanese *how*).

✣✣✣✣✣✣✣✣✣✣✣✣✣✣✣✣✣✣✣✣✣✣✣✣✣✣✣✣✣✣

Everywhere this basic, inescapable banality faces us: that there is nothing but man and the beyond-of-man, their relations and the repercussions of this. Nothing else: from the block feel of existing to the reflexive orderliness of being; from sex to art; from everyman's spontaneous philosophical need of *immediacy*—its roots deep in the body's knowledge of touch—to the equally spontaneous need and finding of the *mediate,* inherent in the very immediacy of a felt relation; from "pure" thought to the mud of politics.

(Included in it, my standing alone—alone?—at this shore of Japan's inner sea, and wondering how petty and awkward is this isolated and personal affair of philosophical height-appraisal, in front of the metaphysical terror of *mors ab alto,* death from the height, the terror of the solidarity and solitude between man's will and atom's readiness!)

From immediacy to orderliness, from terror to readiness, everything is contained in the core of man and the beyond-of-man, of his body—outer, inner—and the Body of beyond-his-body *(Natura naturans, natura naturata).*

And the banality is in the very ease of repercussion. Facing us, from the first, man in his solitude: the sovereignty—and its repercussions—of man's organizing and defining the world within and without him by the strength of his own enlightenment; thus while affirming, belonging to, this world, coming out from it as mind, as discontinuity, as limiting law. This is the *nous* of ancient Greece; hypostatically, the Aristotelian Prime Mover, moved and moving by itself in its own stillness; Husserl's *Eidos Ego,* the unchangeable essence of "I."

In art, as the practical visual projection of this sovereignty—art's concept of ordered space is centered on the rules of geometry's isolating limits: the sovereignty and solitude of the figure in early classical Greece or during the Renaissance.

Opposite this sovereignty-solitude of man (opposite? too opposite not to be subtly similar) is, facing us also, the sovereignty of man and the beyond-of-man and its repercussions. Here, all is solidarity, mobile continuity. It is the *pneuma*-continuum of the Stoics, with its roots in India's self-intermerging Atman-Brahman, personal breath-suchness = Cosmic Breath-Suchness; in the West, let's say, the Bergsonian grasp of movement's movement itself as the Self, or the conceptual philosophy behind Leonardo's *sfumato.*

In art, the victory of solidarity makes the figure be continued (and "deformed" if necessary) into the beyond of the figure, essentially into its "landscape" as it were: a concept of space-ornament (the secret of Islamic pictorial art, the secret of the West's and the Far East's *invention* of "impressionist" landscape), a space illimited in its mobile flux, ordered also, but ordered not around a geometry-centered set of rules, but around the rules of rhythm's repeat or return.

Thus the repercussion of this basic twofold attitude of man reaches all the points on the trajectory of all cultural variants, whether collective-epic or individual-lyric.

In Greece, the principle of one-centered solitude is sovereign, in spite of its Heraclitean lasting will, and in visual thought, of the never-forfeited "Minoan" (later on, Hellenistic) symbolization of the illimited, the continuous, in the form of the self-involving spiral.

In innermost Asia, China, India, the principle of multi-centered solidarity is sovereign, in spite of the centrality there also of man as the deepest theme or worry of thought.

And—propagated thence?—the same solidarity, the same togetherness asserting itself in our Occident—in spite, or because, of the agonic conflict from the days of medieval Christianity to our own days of multi-relativity, between the alternating awareness and oblivion of this elemental Two-One by the one-centered Western man. All the grandeur and all the misery of this man is there.

The most striking thing in the so-called history of ideas of the West that makes this history so exemplary after all, is that four—exactly four—formulae manifest it most accurately and sufficiently in all its totality and diversity:

a) the geometry-limited "natural" and finite image of the Classical man *(Solitude) (Plate 13)*

b) the interlaced, thus deformed, unnatural because un-finite, ornament-image of the Medieval man *(Solidarity) (Plate 14)*

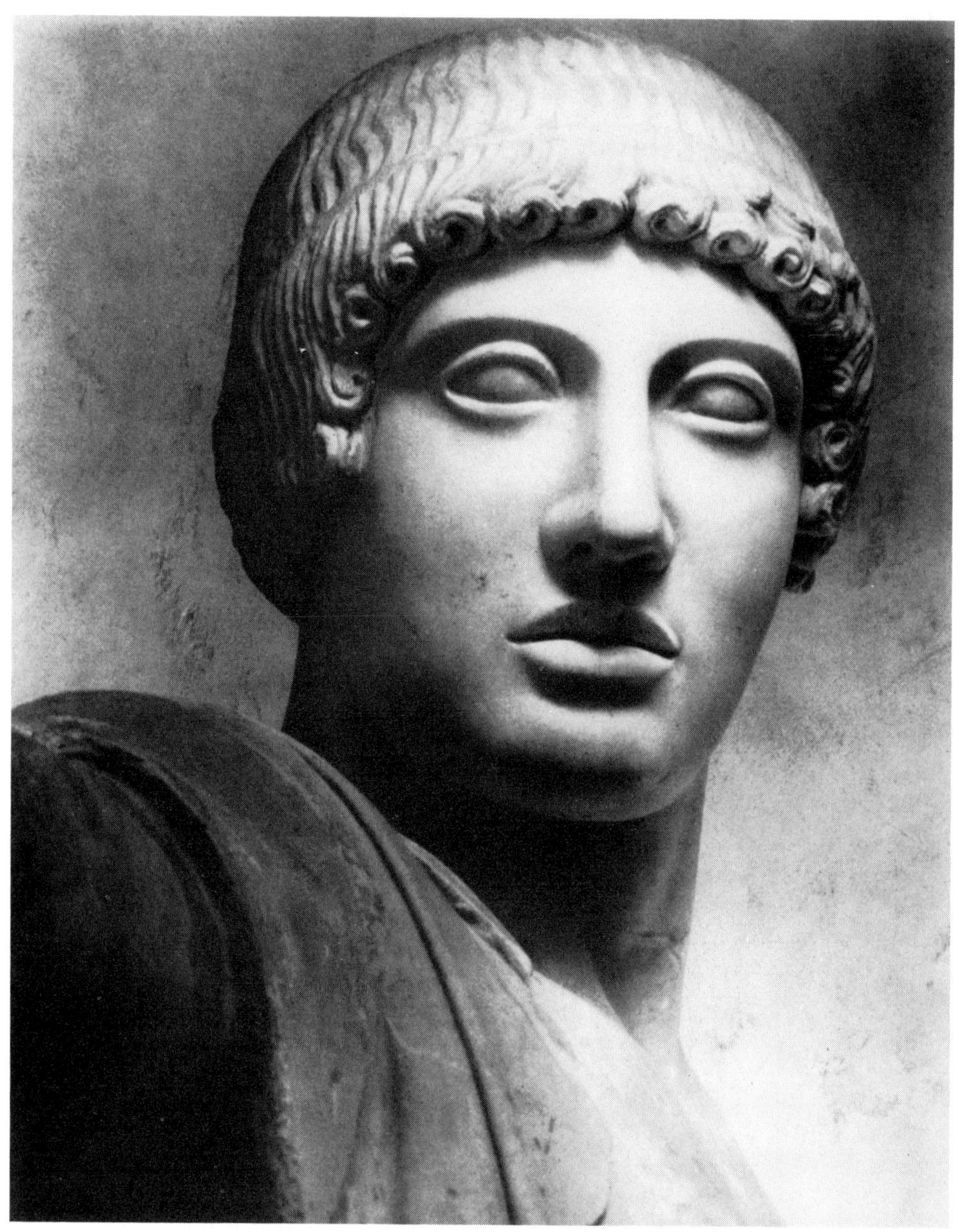

13 *Head of Apollo* Temple of Zeus, Olympia (5th century B.C.)

c) The co-presence of both images, classical and medieval—*antiquity's leading, however*—in Renaissance man, and his awareness, the first in history, of this dichotomy *(Plates 15, 16)*

d) and the same co-presence—this time *the medieval leading*—with awareness of the dichotomy intensely enhanced, in Contemporary man *(Plates 17, 18)*.

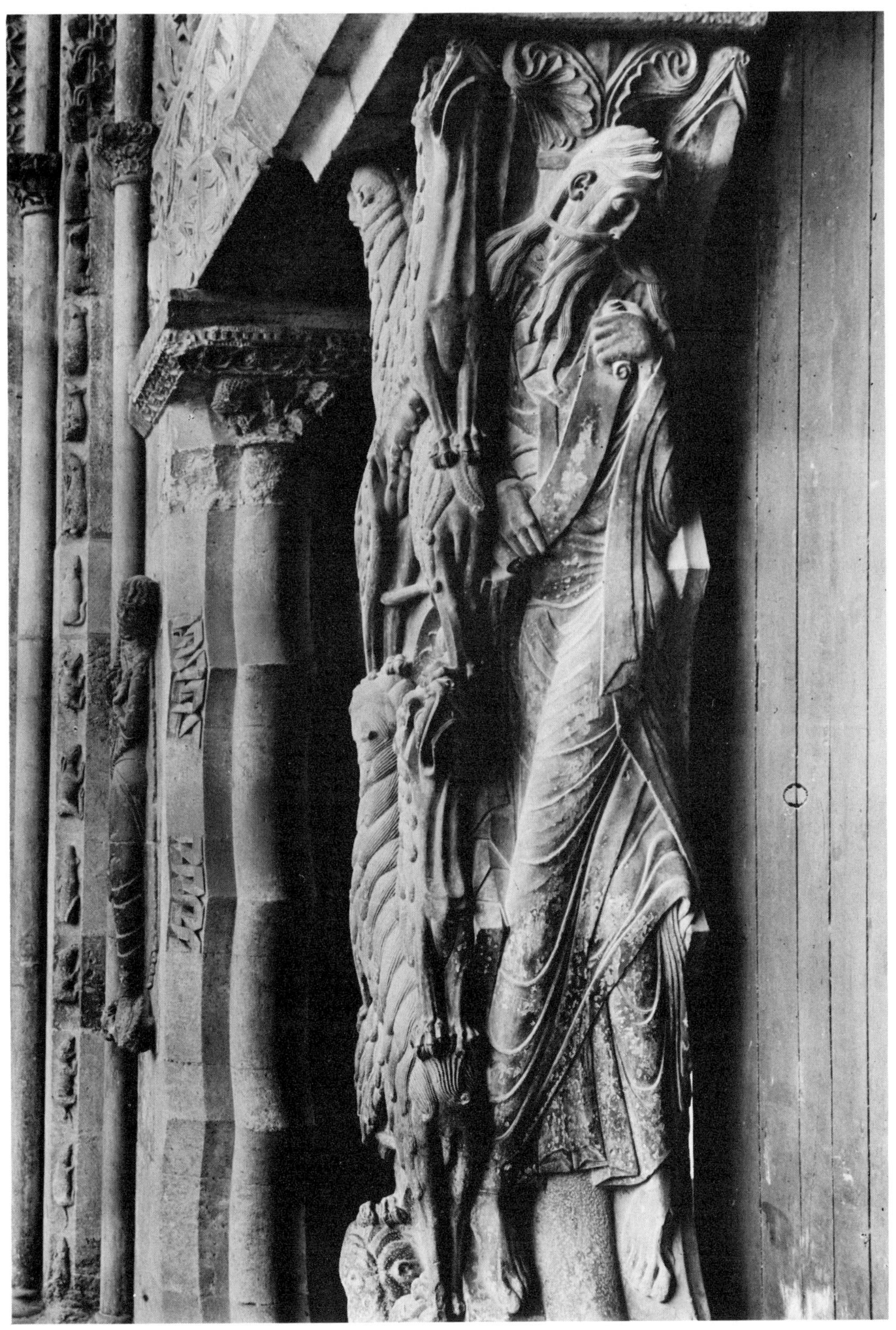

14 *Prophet (probably Isaiah)* Detail St. Pierre, Moissac (12th century)

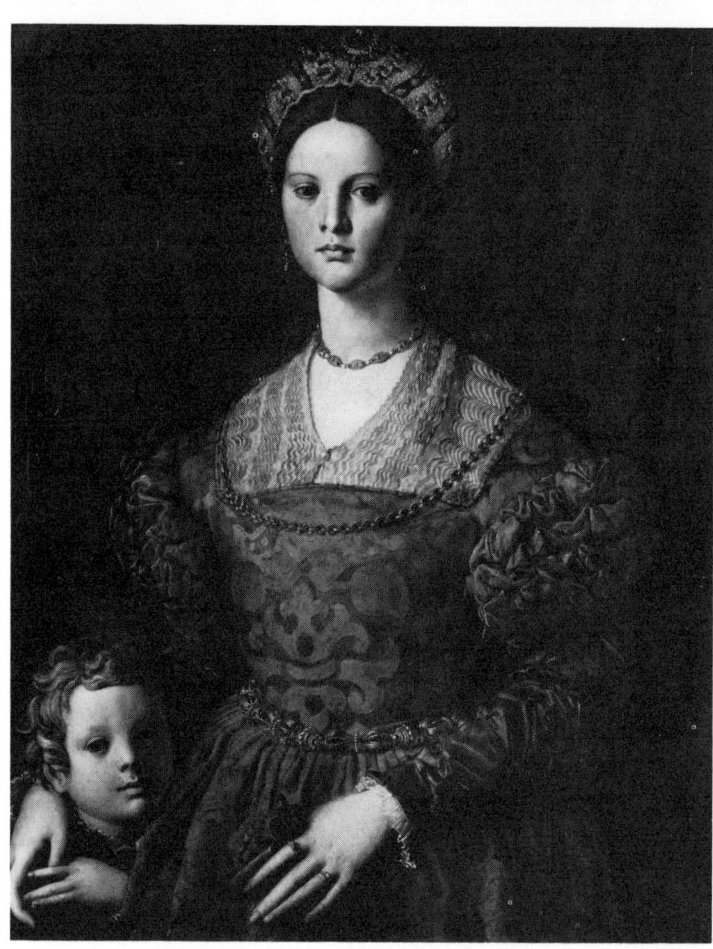

15 Bronzino
A Young Woman and Her Little Boy
Early 16th century

16 Tintoretto
Moses Striking Water from the Rock
16th century

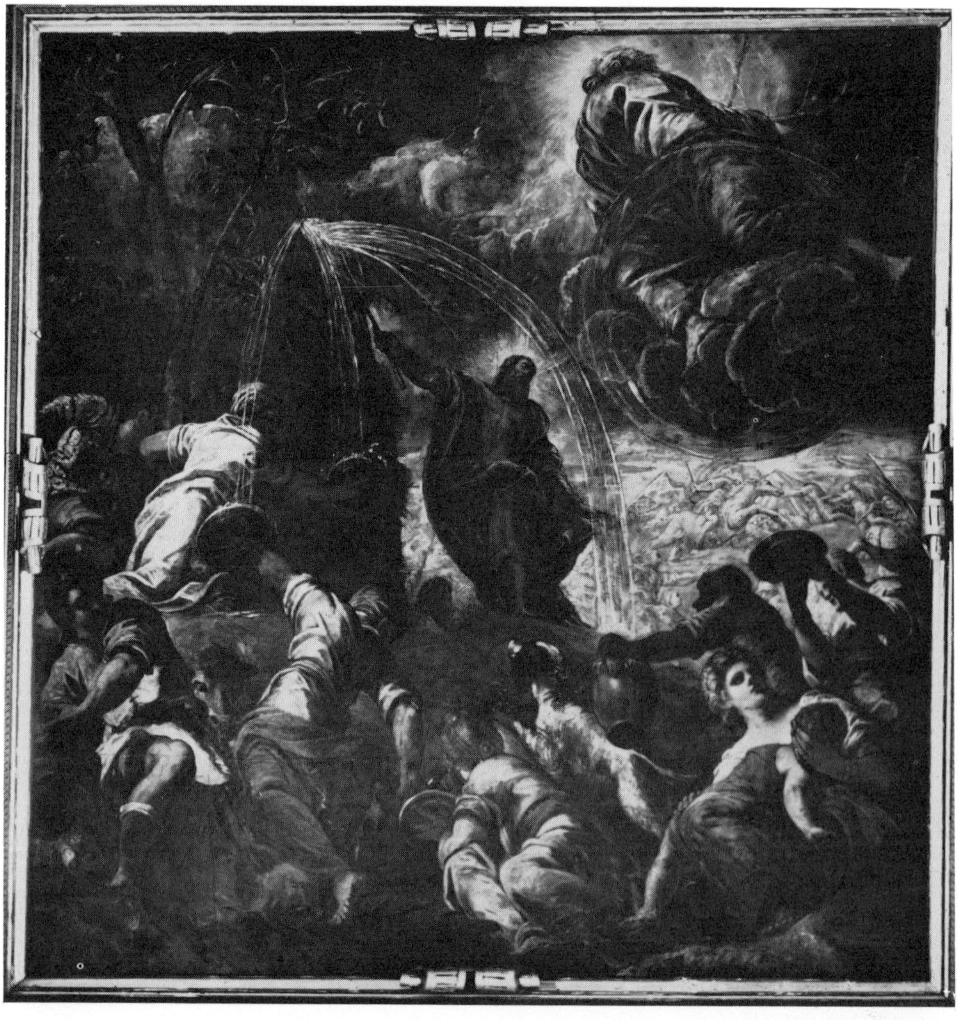

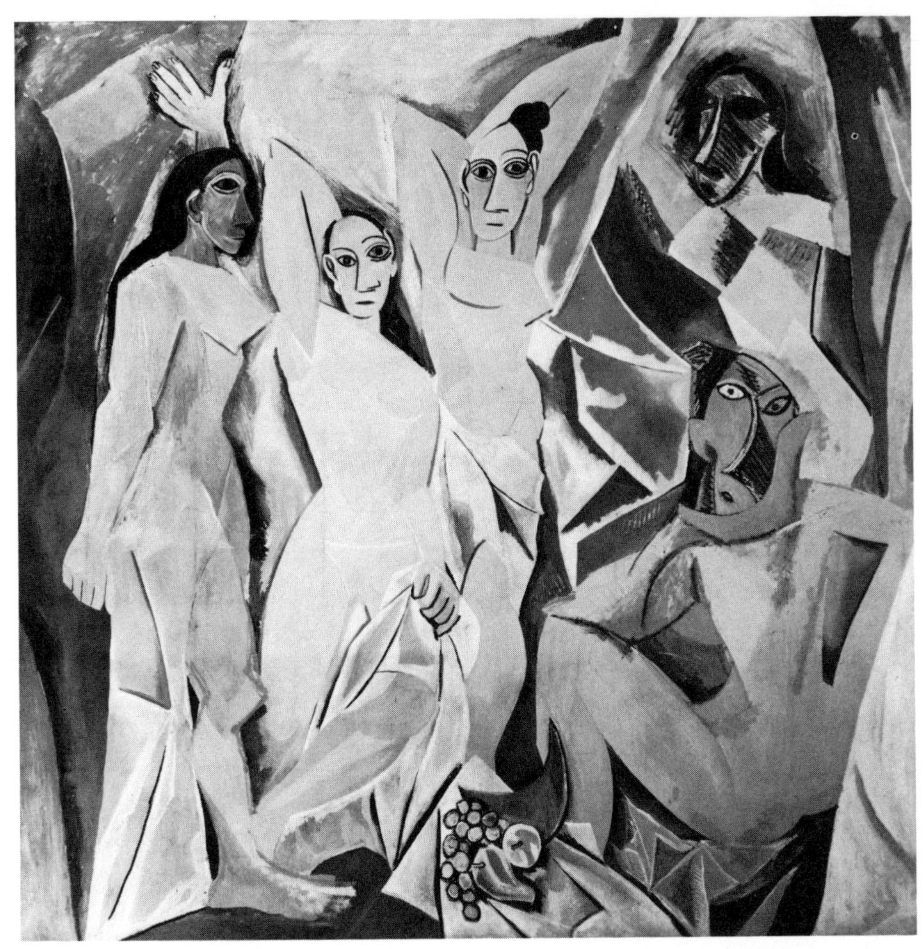

17 Pablo Picasso
Les Demoiselles d'Avignon

18 Giorgio de Chirico
The Sacred Fish

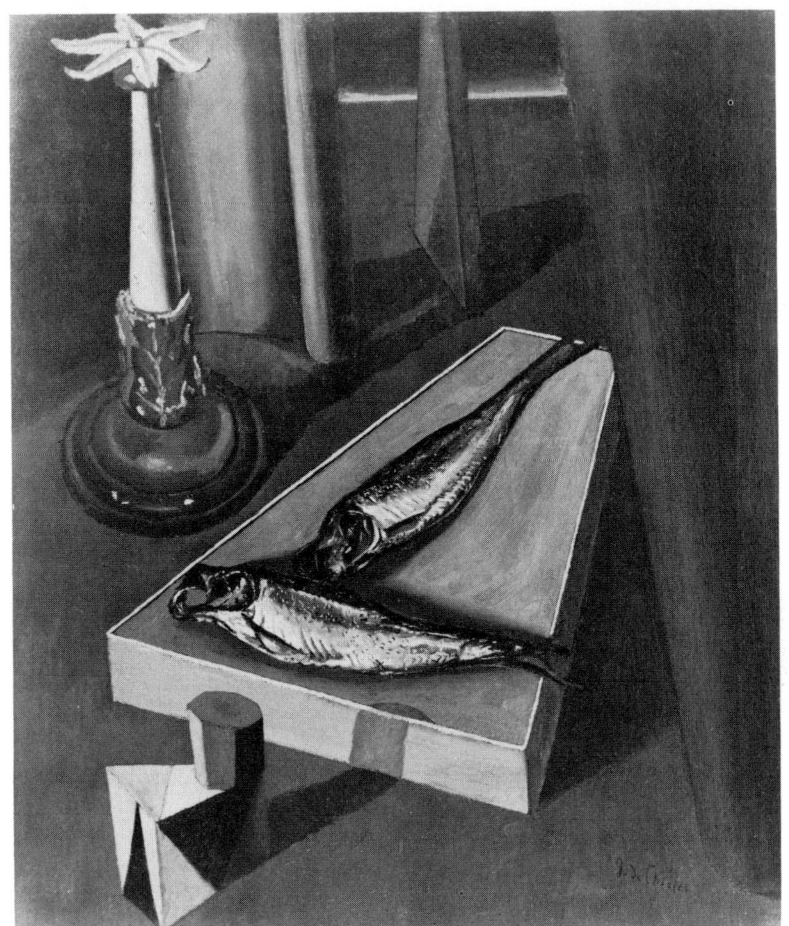

Not less eloquent, although less precise—and so, surely, more astonishing for our discoveries—is Asia's own formulation of solitude-solidarity, that is, Asia's own transfer of its psycho-historical realities into the dual content of its visual forms.

But our pilgrimage into the vision of the Far East is only at its start!

❖❖❖❖❖❖❖❖❖❖❖❖❖❖❖❖❖❖❖❖❖❖❖❖❖❖❖❖❖❖❖

Solitude-solidarity, in form's enactment or mimicry of it, is the hidden presence in the technical procedure, the *how,* of any object of art. To grasp this—and thus to be absolved of oversimplification or worse—is to transfer the narrated content to the mimicked one: precisely the *what-of-the-how* level into which both the obvious and the still-hidden content of the *what* is now totally and verbally transferred, thus revealed.

Here it is no longer a matter of visual *or* verbal, but of their inter-translatability: " . . . every language has . . . a structure concerning which, *in the language,* nothing can be said, but . . . there may be another language dealing with the structure of the first language, and having itself a new structure, and . . . to this hierarchy of languages there may be no limit."[13]

The final gesture of the line in pictorial space, the vibration of the volume-bearing point in this space, halted temporarily, the chosen evolvement of a volume, each climax of this mimicry, is the very ideograph-silhouette of the innermost man, indeed, of the man-in-a-precise-time.

Piscasso's condemning and redeeming revelation of his own evil time, hypostatized in the obstinate mimicry of the hooky—too hooky—claw-volume is this *(Plate 19).* And so too is the innermost man and his time re-

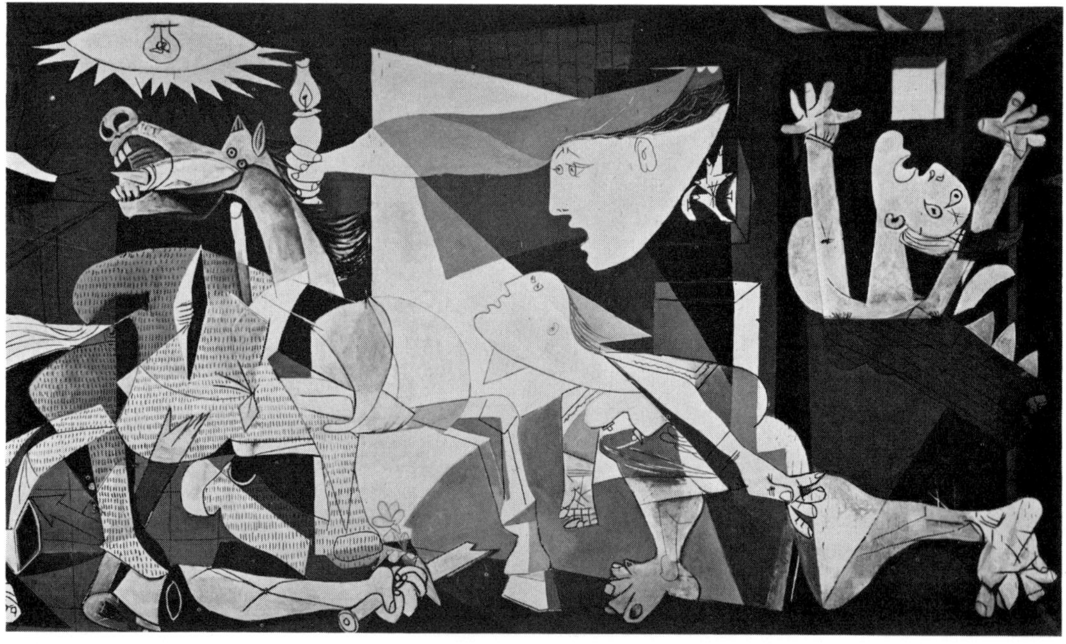

19 Pablo Picasso *Guernica* (detail)

20 Ogata Korin *Matsushima*
Early 18th century
(Detail, overleaf)▶

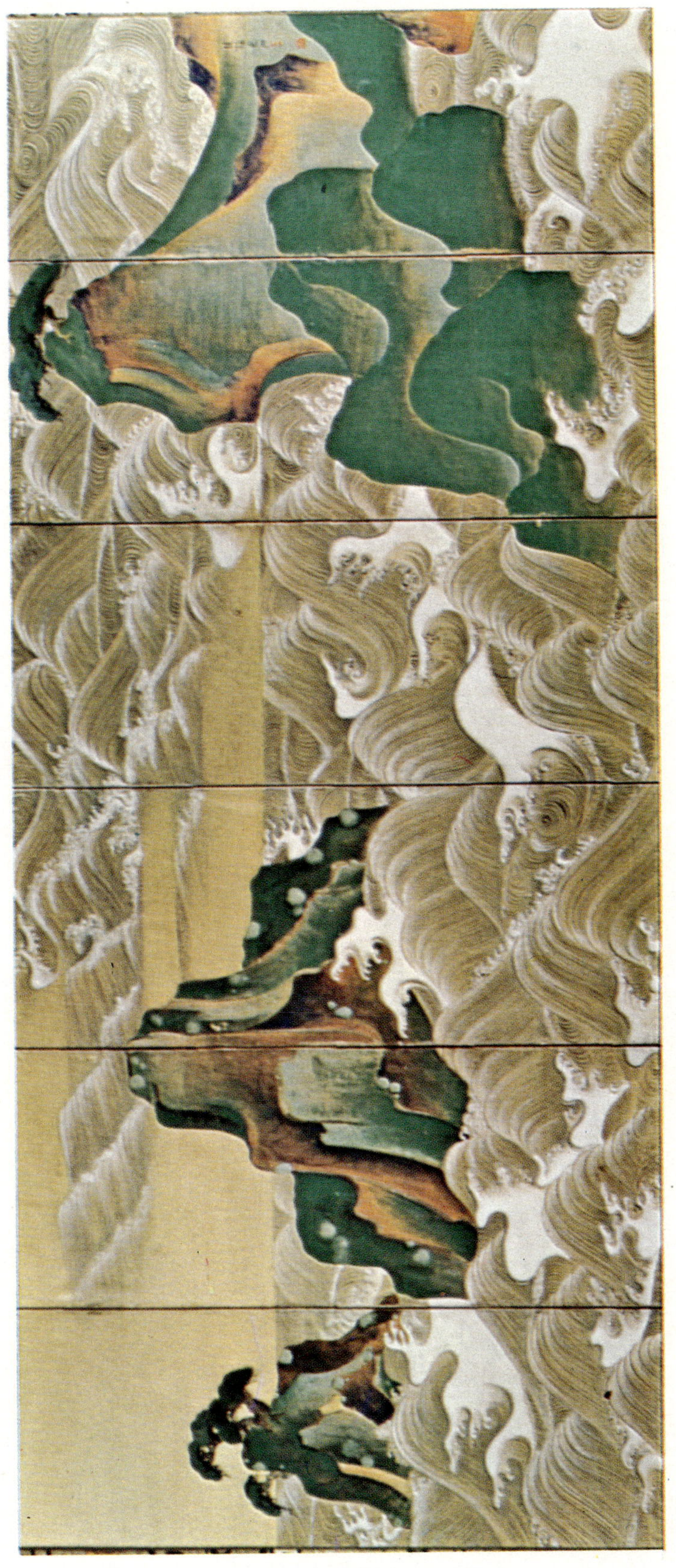

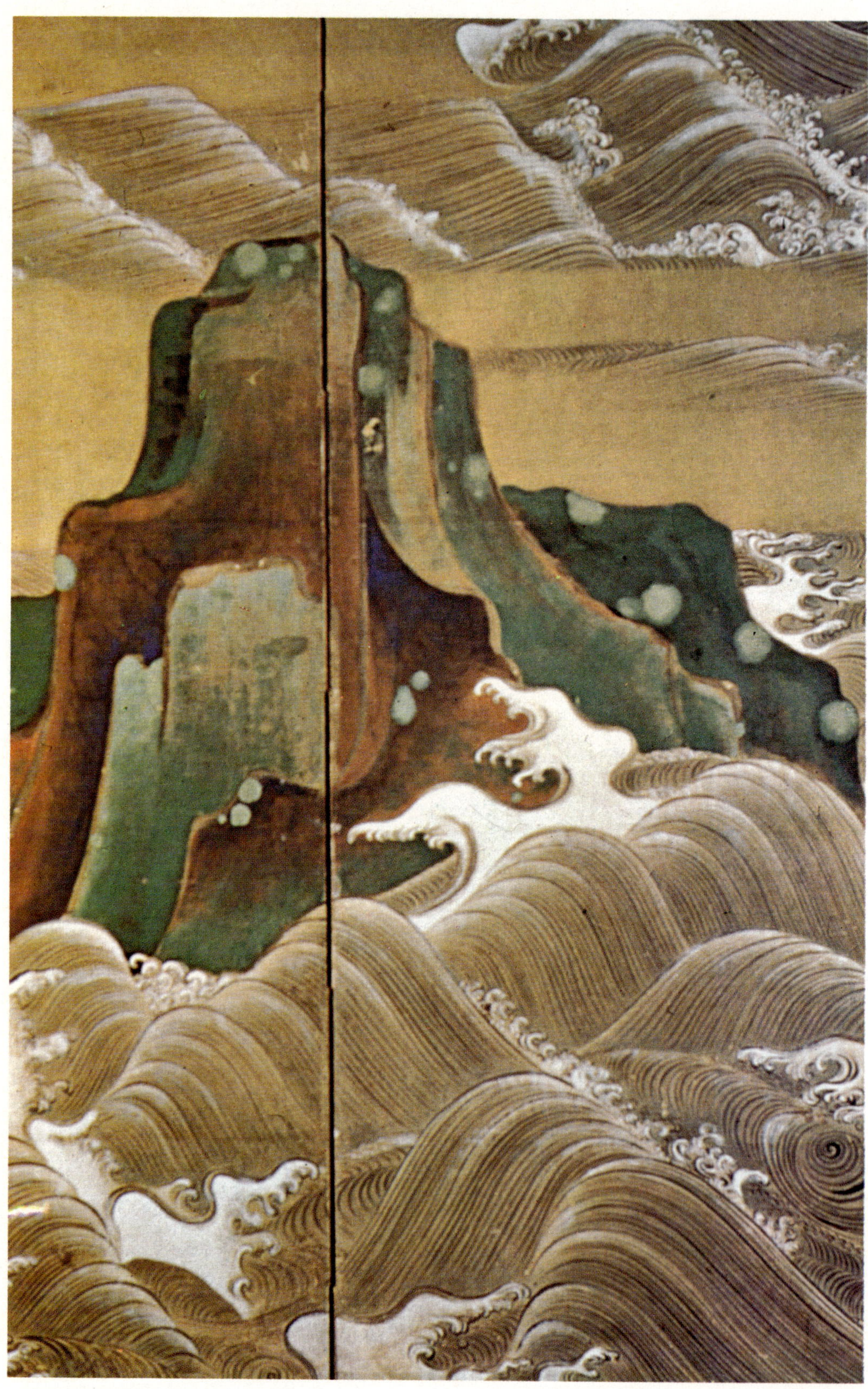

20

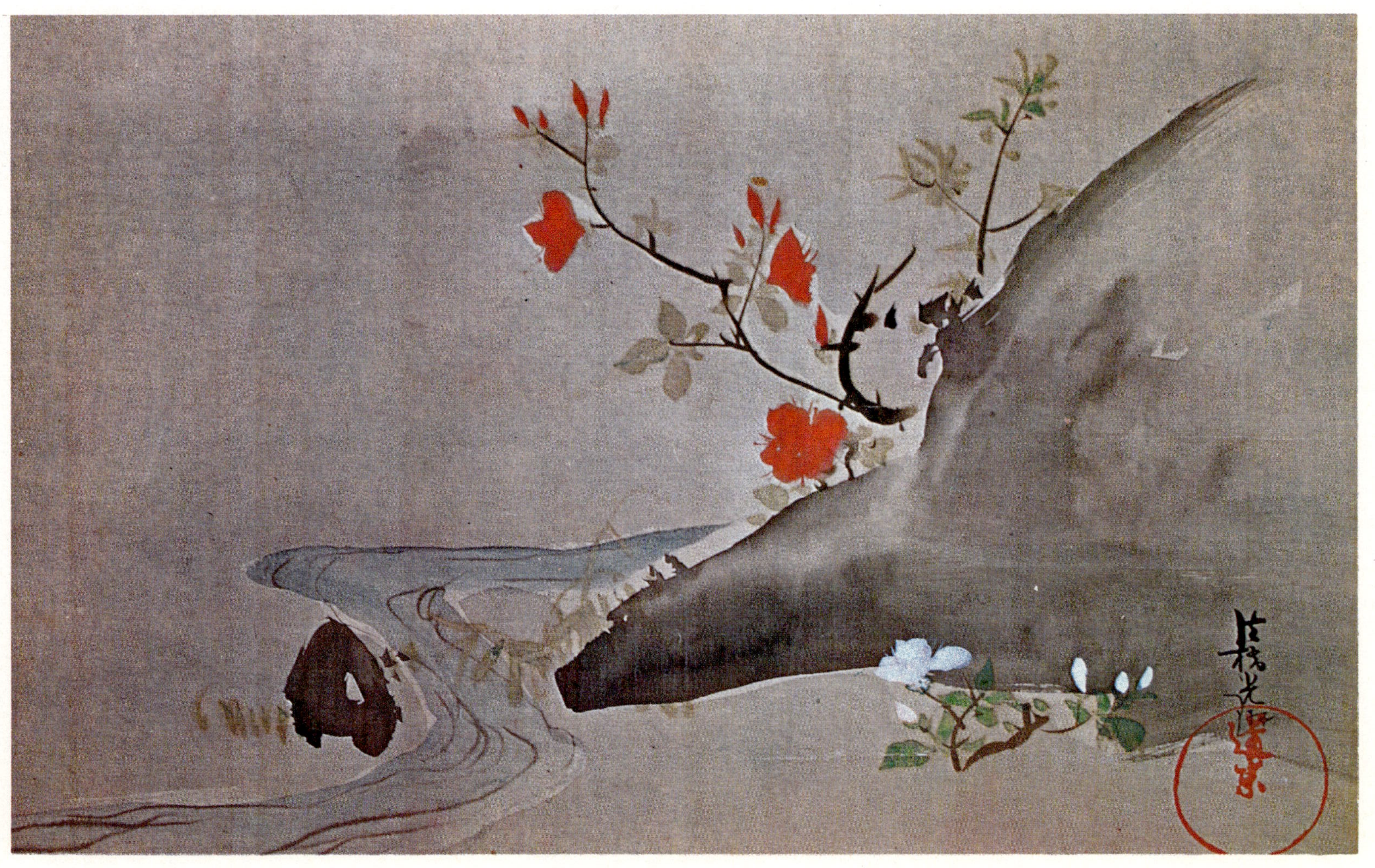

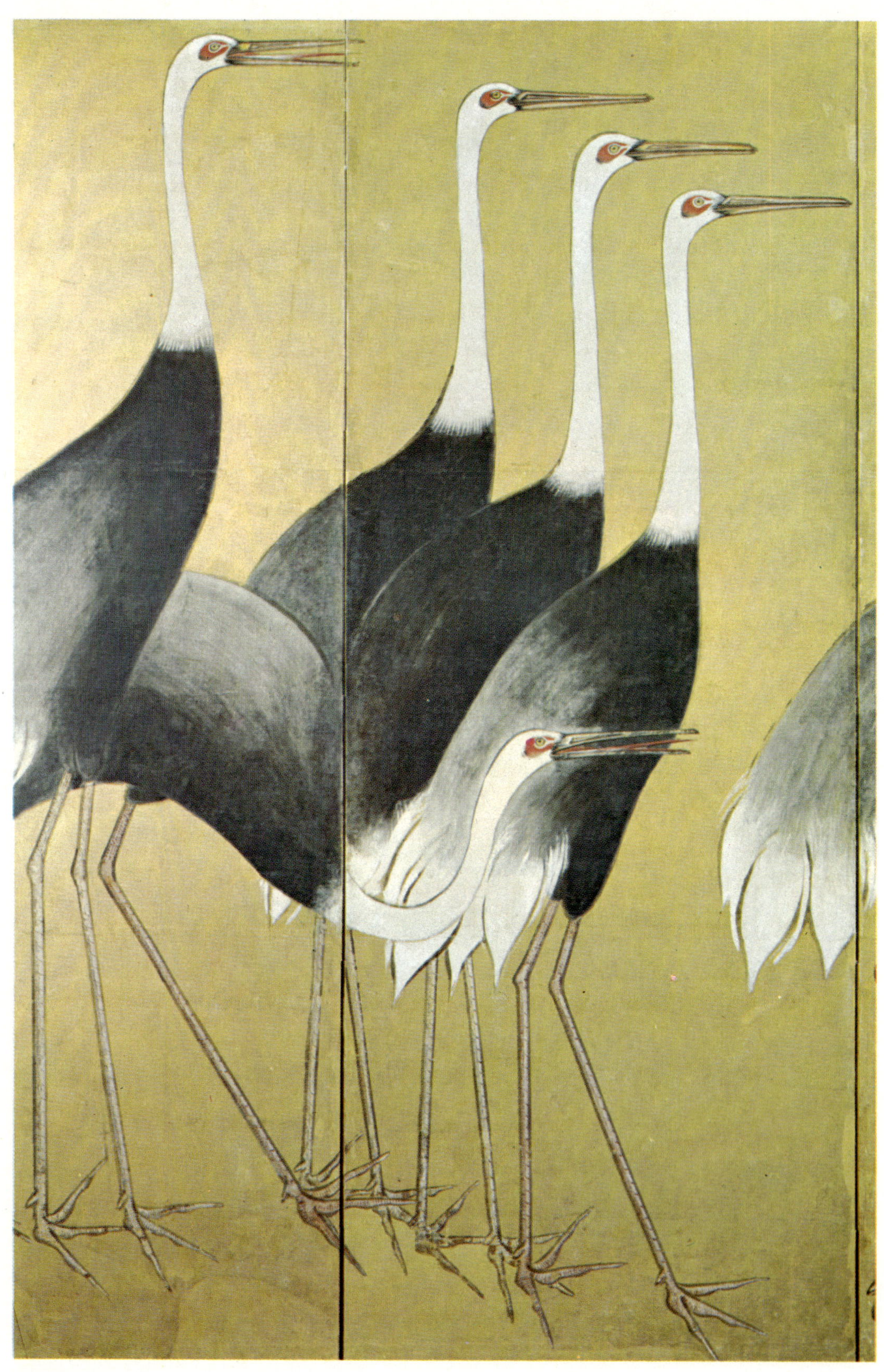

22

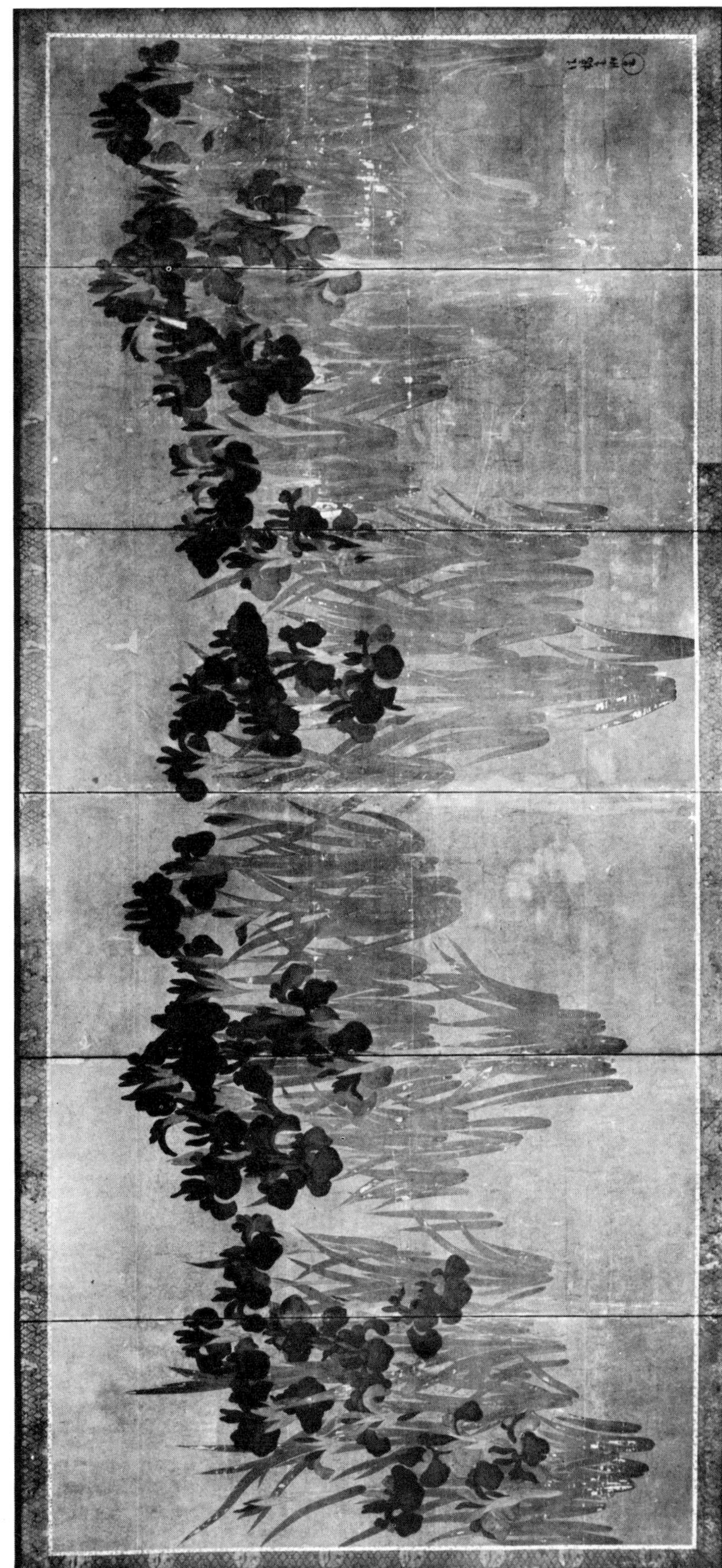

23 Ogata Korin *Irises* (Edo period, ca. 1700)

21 (overleaf)
Ogata Korin
Azaleas
Edo period

22 Korin
The Walking Cranes
Detail (Edo period)

vealed, condemned, and redeemed in the bulging span of this Ukiyo-e line-bow or line-arch *(See Plate 12);* or in Korin's line color and its equations: man's death = ocean's wave-ubiquity; man's solitude = azalea's solidarity, lost and found, and lost again; man's pride = cranes walking; man's rebirth = iris's ceremonial floating *(Plates 20, 21, 22, 23).*

✡

When transferred to this *what of the how* stage of form-mimicry, whatever might on a discursive level be given to our eye as similar or dissimilar, *might* be revealed as the reverse: for the very method of comparative judgment is thereby transferred also from comparison by analogy, that is, the grasp of similarity based on the evidence of function and appearance, to the comparison by *homology,* as one may call it temporarily, by which the evidence of similarity or dissimilarity emerges from the structure itself (Keyser's "invariant relation among variable terms") and the genesis of two or more things.

There is an evident "natural" movement in so gracious a work as the Victory of Athena Nike's balustrade *(Plate 24);* there is obvious mobility in the interlaced rhythms of Delacroix's drama; and even more convincingly in Ch'ên Jung's dragon evolving from no-birth to no-end *(Plate 25);* there is on the other hand stiffness, rigidity, immobility, in Giotto's figures *(Plate 26),* in Ben Shahn's image-epigrams, or in this Yamato-e simulacrum-abstraction *(Plate 27).* Yet what the deeper level of homological comparison reveals—without any loss of impact in the narrative interpretation—might be contrary. The movement of the first group is, one could say, a *mnemonic* movement, not an immediate or immediately reproduced movement: it results from our memory's reconstruction of all those observable moments of motion in objects and beings—agitation of folds, flexions of the human body, movements of animals, etc.—whose authentication has been for us most satisfying or pleasing both optically and "logically," and which by memory we can retain, accumulate, and select for the purpose of aesthetic reconstruction. This is the birth of what we call *grace* in art.

Mobility, on the other hand, or movement immediately captured, might be revealed in the very stiffness or rigidity of the second group. Because this rigidity is the dynamic *effort-momentum* of a starting or *immediate* movement: the decisive momentum of a just-opened dike when the quiet waters of the upper level, at the point of emptying, are *no longer quiet, immobile, nor in movement already.* It is this effort, or this instantaneity of movement "about to be," that *mobilizes* the immobility, the rigidity of Giotto's drama (the horizontal catapulting of the central gesture of his Judas), of Ben Shahn's sharp and capsizing balances, of Japan's passionate inrush into visible reality, obliquely seen—homologically, the same seeing that today, among us, results in so-called "pure abstraction."

And so also—once the lead of homological comparison is acknowledged—it is possible to add that the Far Eastern "two-dimensional" space resulting from the fabulous linear technique of the brush stroke is, in its fullness of tactile rendering, as "three-dimensional" as our West's; that the quality of

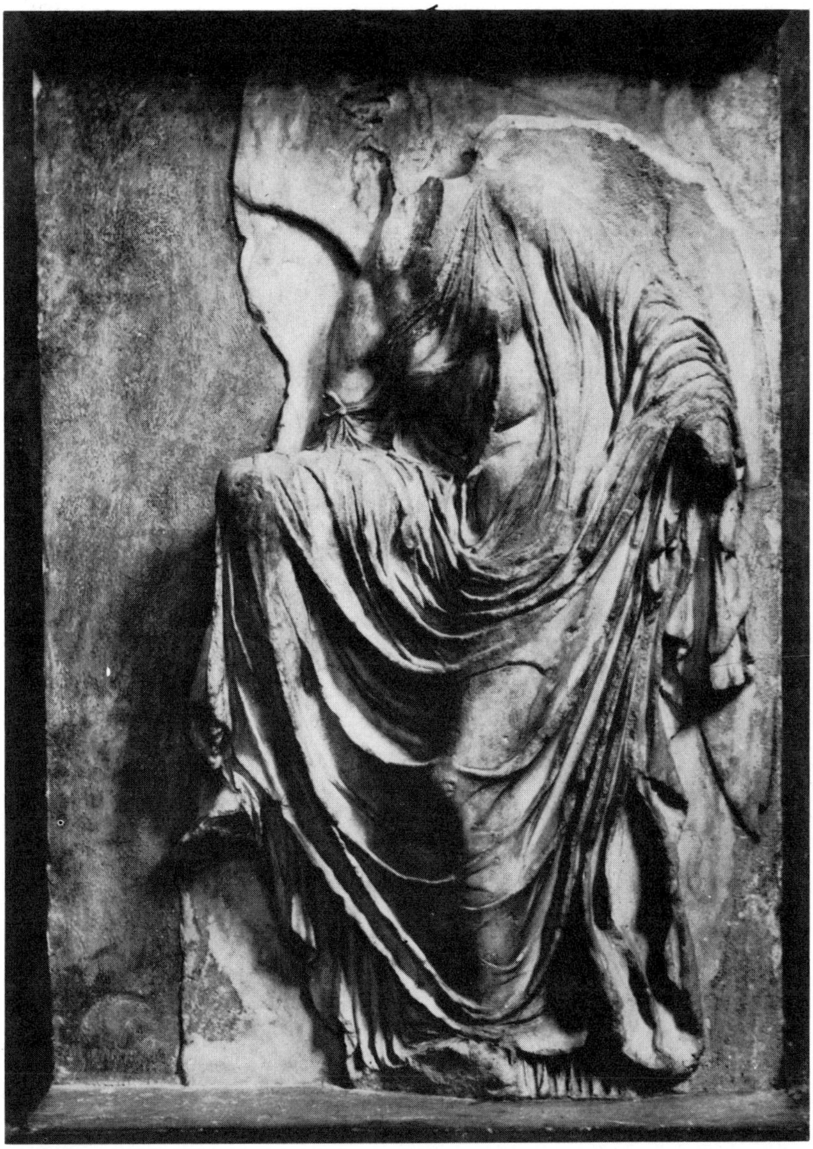

24 *Nike*
Temple of Athena Nike
5th century

25 CH'ÊN JUNG
Nine Dragon Scroll
Detail (1244)

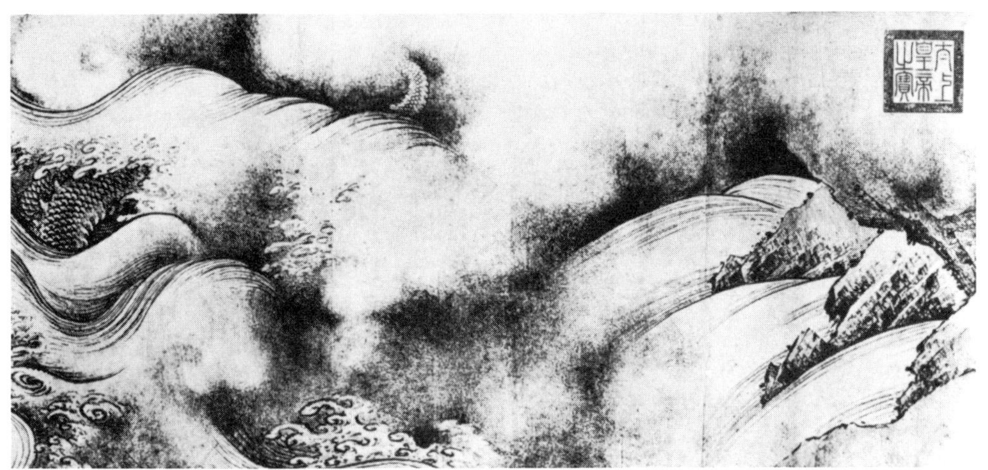

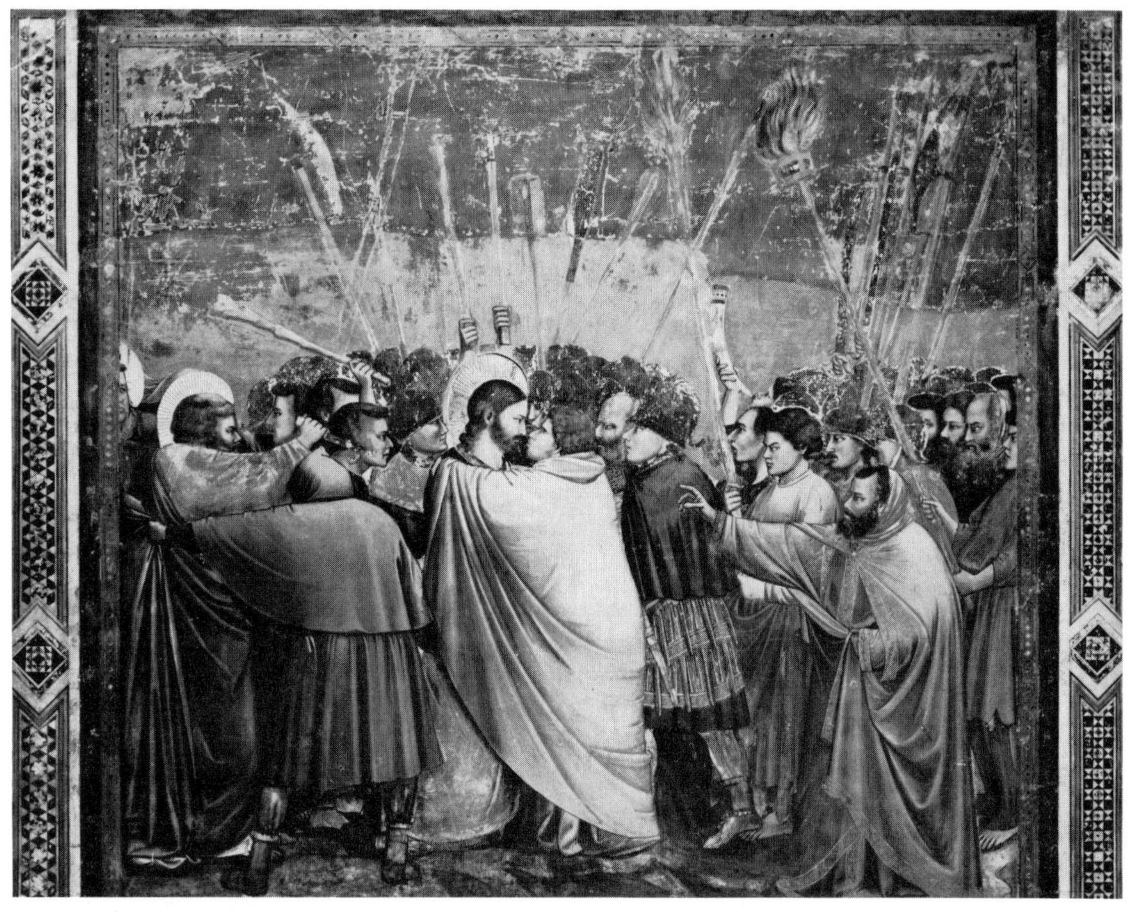

26 GIOTTO *The Kiss of Judas* Scrovegni Chapel (14th century)

the space there—analogically still two-dimensional—by the very intensity of this quality as *line,* presents the same convincing content-mimic of relief, of volume, that our geometry-centered space elaborated.

And it is here that we find again that the most subtle differences in degree are the real differences in nature. It is here that the transfer from the *what* to the *what of the how,* from the method of analogy to that of homology, means also the transfer of *quality* as a category, or a dimension of mind, to a new category or dimension, quality as *intensity of quality.*

From having been only an "emotional" and as it were casual addition to other, so earnestly established category-frames—time, space, quantity, quality, relation, etc.—intensity now becomes an integrated, autonomous, "real" dimension in existence; not only an added quality, but a self-generating quantity.

Similar to the physicist's particle-event of nuclear matter, made one with its propagated wave, its "spin" and its "magnetic momentum," so also intensity is made one with its own wave, its own magnetic momentum, the quantum of its energy-value: its persistence, its duration. Intensity is the persistence, the duration of intensity. 26

27 ARTIST UNKNOWN
Portrait of Ariwara Yukihira
Kamakura period ▶

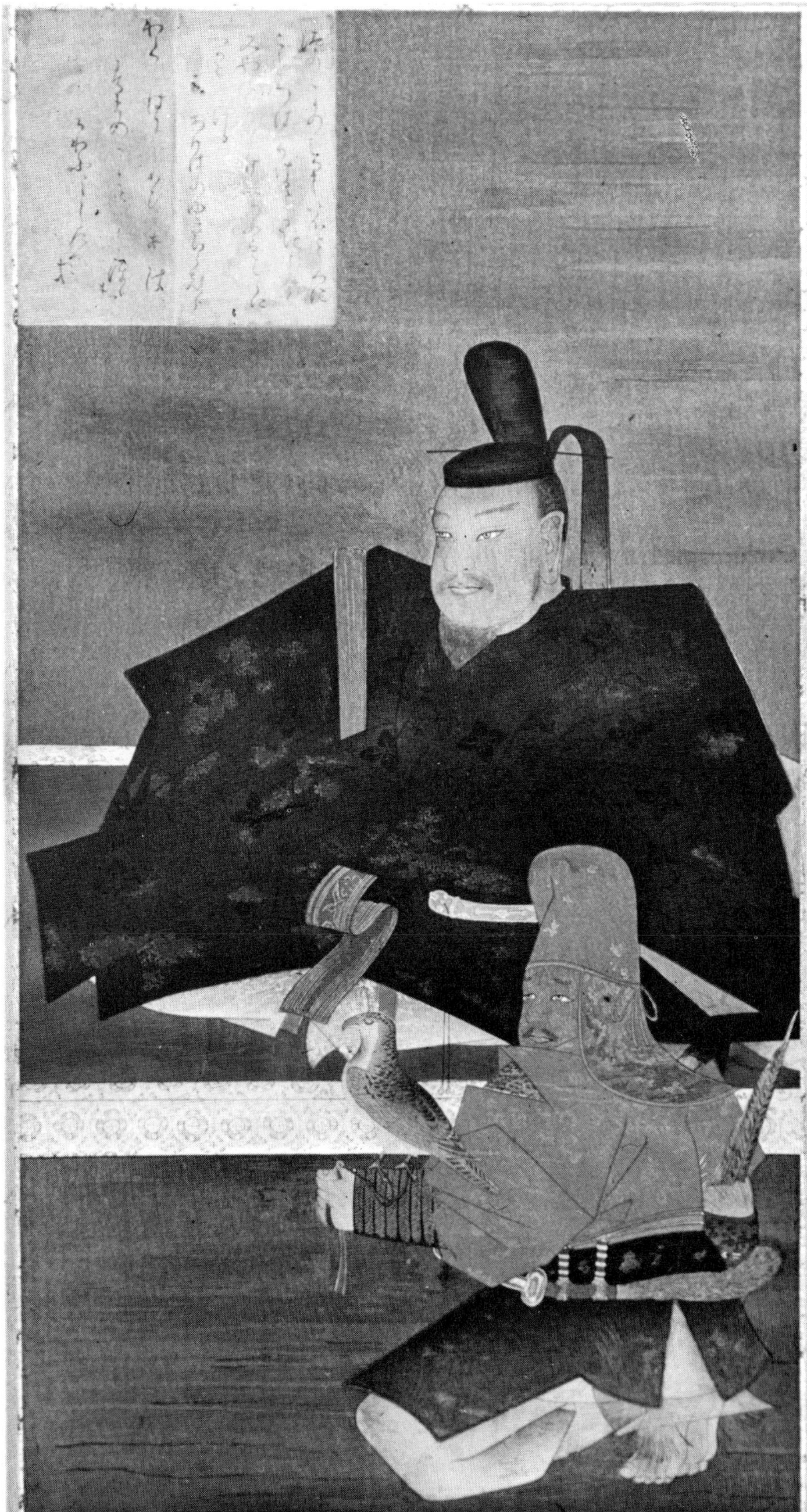

✡

Even when most earnestly discussing Japanese art, how casually we mention its salient traits: the slanting, *oblique* perspective of its pictorial vistas (a recurrent device which we trace back—as we do with the brush stroke and other achievements of technique—to its Chinese origins, particularly T'ang and even earlier); or Japanese "decorativity" and its linear polyrhythmy; or Japanese love of nature; or Japanese sensuousness, so bold yet so clean—cleanly washed just as a Japanese citizen is in his daily physical being. All this we say or hear said, convincingly, *factually*—and once it is said or heard, we pass on, as if nothing *really* had happened.

But the slanting perspective of Japan's space structure *is not* Chinese at all: it has an obstinacy about it, an intensity and a persistence that China has never shown in this respect; and so it is with "decorativity," with sensuousness, with love of nature, etc. All these traits discursively thought of as added belong to the very form-content of Japan's historical becoming. They are the very *fleshiness* of this content's mimicry—the mimicked history of Japan's evil and Japan's good, of Japan's "mud" and Japan's *amor intellectualis Dei;* they are most of all the intensity of the motive power that states the limit line of Japan's culture-horizon.

But is not a view like this, which appears to re-install the concept of an absolute, inescapable limit-horizon, of an "absolute" nature for a cultural compound—the "absolute" nature of China, or of Japan, etc.—is not such a view an obsolete, reactionary, more than that, a deeply erroneous one, in the presence of the creative change or flux that makes history be history, something that goes on and changes, in spite of all and us?

Yes—if it is allowed to remain a discursive content, as it were, a *what*-thought, even a *how*-thought, about the change.

No—if this vision's content is interiorized and widened by the action of its new dimension, new category: its *intensity*.

For intensity is the ever-opening into the illimited of what is forever closed as limit: the very intensity of the vision of limits makes both—limits and vision—illimited: the closed "nature" of Japan opens then to a nature "other."

The feel of obviously universal notions like what we call, or what Greece, or for that matter India or Japan or Islam, could have called "soul," "spirit," "body," or relation, or cruelty, or reality, is at some point or points of its communication totally "closed" for each one. Try as we may to enlighten ourselves about a particular "closed" cultural notion, for example, the Chinese notion, supposedly untranslatable, of Tao, and then candidly to communicate the result to a "native" well versed in the subtleties of this classical subject—our approach or enlightenment, no matter how competent, will never be "that" Chinese approach or enlightenment, the native's.

The same is true if we try to define the crucial idea of *Bha = becoming* to a Hindu, or the mystery of Eucharist and grace to a papal Christian, or the a-iconic ideation of the Shehina-Name, the Name of the Innamable, to a Jewish scholiast. Or if, in the midst of our contemporary worries we try to recall to a U.S.S.R. Marxist his unreplenished duty of vigilance over the dialectics of the party's power-and-service, or to a U.S.A. reactionary the ethics of total, all-involving responsibility inherent in the very existence and logic of democracy. It will never be *that* notion, that mystery, that duty, that responsibility. Because all these concepts are co-measurable with the limits of their respective horizons, individual and collective-cultural.

Yet it is again the *intensity* inherent in the living—passionate—persistence of these very limits that makes them co-measurable now with those same concepts. Tao, or Shehina, or the mystery of substitution through sacrifice in Eucharist, or democracy's responsibilities are to be comprehended with one, universal, and *intense* comprehension that is not vague or banal but precise and open: by the decisive virtue of their form.

In the dance of the form, which is art very simply—"the visionary circumstance of mind," as a contemporary poet of Japan, Yone Noguchi, formulated it in a most happy saying—in the dance of the form—the abstraction of the body, "the ten-fingered grasp of reality"—we find and release this comprehension. And it is an *easy* comprehension too: because there is only solitude-solidarity, nothing else; nothing more than the visionary ease of it, the banality of it, everybody's ease. (Lautréamont's "Poetry must be made by all. Not by one"; Picabia's "The real Dadaists are against Dada. Everyone is director of Dada." All this, so respectable, so easy now—always so difficult yesterday!) The ironically easy ease of yesterday's burden: Tao is easily to be conveyed, and Shehina, and Eucharist, and "horizon" and "body." This fabulous "take it easy" is the *locus sigilli* wherein by natural affinity and attraction the most ironical joins the deepest. Here is perhaps the real, the easy message to us from the East's wisdom: in the dance of its form, in its content-mimicry of isolation-togetherness, the truth of directness, of reserve *(pudeur),* of obscenity (if required by the throng of divinities), as conveyed by the arts of China, of Japan, of Korea, of the Indias, of the Great Steppes.

All this is the domain proper of intensity, the dimension of its passionate persistence where ideas elaborated by man-in-a-time are not co-measurable any more with their horizon's limits, but these limits themselves, by the very duration of this intensity in them, their intensity as limits, become co-measurable with ideas. This is the domain and the dimension of Giordano Bruno's "Rules are not the source of poetry, but poetry is the source of rules, and there are as many rules as there are real poets." For to measure a dimension is to be *outside* and not *within* the limits of the measure. The birth of "another," of the "other," is in this. And the starting of the interiorization of self as "another" self's body: the body of the innermost man.

❖❖❖❖❖❖❖❖❖❖❖❖❖❖❖❖❖❖❖❖❖❖❖❖❖❖❖❖❖❖

We are ready for a new myth.

Because a myth is a new body given to a renewed crisis of man-in-a-time: the historically ever-present crisis of choice—a choice of emphasis only—between the two terms that build the oneness of man and the beyond-of-man, his solitude-solidarity.

The crisis is with us today: we know it—or we are ready to know it. Our readiness is the expressive form-content of this crisis, the very form-content given to the global attitude of a man-within-a-time, within-a-horizon, toward the conflict of this impending choice.

And because of the presence of intensity in this conflict, which is precisely the "presence of adherence" of touch, thus, as presence and as touch, *our* presence, *our* touch, our body's awareness there—because of this, no epoch-making crisis in history, however remote from us in time or space, can fail to be *our* own crisis, our contemporary crisis.

But the birth of a myth itself, the creative myth-generating procedure, is hidden from us as yet, perhaps in a recess of the psychological passage of "signalization" to symbolization of inner events. Yet we can guess what the mythmaking process is historically. We guess it as a total substitution or hypostasis of a material witness of it, a material testimony, for the wholeness of a crisis.

From the equalitarian aspiration toward "better" life conditions, to the philosophical, also equalitarian, hope for the order of nature = order of mind equation, the otherwise unseizable collective and global sensation-touch of all the anxieties that make up the crisis in a given time is totally transferred into a precise and "sympathetic" historical or semi-historical being—hero, usually—or deeper in either the primordial past or the enigmatic present, by a "sympathetic," "significant" object, stone, tree, light, idea. . . . The unseizable total "spiritual" anxiety is seized—thus "magically" liberated from the bonds of a crisis and anxiety—by the *materiality* of a testimony, by a body, the body-witness.

A new body, "another" body, another form thus, is given, always, to the same banal and primeval crisis of man: whether as the intellectual man's sovereignty of solitude (the reformer of bygone "mystic" cycles, still with us), or the victory of his solidarity (his yielding to the collective Beyond, as messianic redeemer); whether as the individual sovereignty of isolation (in Cézanne's "I want to realize my sensation"), or his yielding to the demand of solidarity (be it in the form of the collective and inescapable memories of "depth psychology," or in that of the equally inescapable, all-permeating socialism).

❖❖❖❖❖❖❖❖❖❖❖❖❖❖❖❖❖❖❖❖❖❖❖❖❖❖❖❖❖❖❖❖❖

But form, but body, a new, "another" body, already means art. A new form means a new art—new, thus strange, *unseen before,* discontinuous, a monster (Robinet's "*Les êtres éloignés dans l'échelle sont des monstres les uns par rapport aux autres*").[14] Seen thus, the form of a new myth is always a de-formation of the form preceding.

And to be ready for a new myth is to know that this "monstrous" *permission* to deform is the real, "another" measure of one's own age's crisis.

The true acceptance of such a permission is an acceptance of this crisis not complacently or timidly, as a mere fact, but as that fact's problematicity: as the interiorization of the problem of crisis itself.

❖❖❖❖❖❖❖❖❖❖❖❖❖❖❖❖❖❖❖❖❖❖❖❖❖❖❖❖❖❖❖❖❖

Our age is full of voices and echoes of voices that herald this new body: Maurice Denis's prophetic formula for the twentieth century's art, the expressionist *objective deformation* as opposed to the impressionist *subjective deformation;* Picasso's "I don't look for, I find"—because a new form, unknown as yet, is not to be recognized, looked for, but recognizes and finds us.

And what could the hierophant, Paul Klee, really have meant when he said:

> We used to represent things visible on earth which we enjoyed seeing or would have liked to see. Now we reveal the reality of visible things, and thereby express the belief that visible reality is merely an isolated phenomenon latently outnumbered by other realities. Things take on a broader and more varied meaning, often in seeming contradiction to the rational experience of yesterday . . . . By including the notion of good and evil a moral sphere is created . . . . *In the end a formal cosmos will be created out of purely abstract elements of form quite independent of their configurations as objects, beings, or abstract things like letters or numbers.* . . . Art is a likeness of the Creation. Occasionally it is an example, just as the terrestrial may exemplify the cosmic.[15]

This:

The birth of a being is a necessity and an invention of its medium's passion and growth: the fish came because of the passion and growth of the waters, the bird, because of the air's, the reptile, because of the earth's, the insect, because of the fire's, and man, because of all this made one consubstantiality. Why then from the necessity and passion and invention of another life-holding medium, the still growing and inventing matter of mind's grey abyss, would not new beings be formed, de-formed, and formed again there; beings consubstantial with the abstracting passion and invention of the cortex, beings-monsters, all limbs, living, then dying, of a new body—indeed?

And here, one guesses, is traced the very direction of our change, indeed, of change as such, which has carried the history of man to this vision of body interiorized.

Here is the contour line of our cyclic changes with their moments of crisis in them: from the "miracle," the myth-testimony about the "moist" soil—the death and resurrection of the buried grain (in solitude-solidarity buried), man's food, cattle's food, and the sacrificial messianic myth of it; to the "miracle" and the myth of the "dried" soil—the smelting, the transforming of the hardest soil's vein, its death as metal ore, as metal-grain, its resurrection as man-god's utensil and weapon and the hero myth in it (all the new power symbolism of the Bronze Age's temple-city, then, later, of the so-called Iron Age's "democratized" state-citizenship); and so on, further and further, to the latest "miracle" of the interiorized fiery soil—the death, like the death of the grain, of the innermost atom (H. Poincaré's *"le trou dans l'éther . . . "*), and the wave of its resurrection as interstellar energy's vigil.

And today's myth—the outline of the new myth still in the making—is this: the total substitution of the material witness of today's innermost-man-and-his-body for the unseizable whole of this cycle's happening.

And passing on from the "epic" to the "lyric," how easy it is, as irony when joined to depth of thought would have it, to comprehend the spirituality of the "visceral"—substituted—love declaration on the Magic Mountain, or of Sartre's *Nausée.*

✡

To be ready for a new myth today—today when the counter-myth is still honored—is not only to know this, but to know the knowing of it.

The change from *abstraction* to *abstracting,* from *absolute* to *universal,* from the priority of noun-substance and verb-action to that of the gerundive, here is the change, or rather, the transfer we are ready for, the monster we did not look for, but found.

This monster-content is now coextensive—in its ever-expanding "pooling of experience" motive-action[16]—not with the moral *qualities* of its increase, but with the moral *quantity* therein: more and more people, more and more of "mediocre" people to participate in the results of the physical and spiritual "pooling of experience"; more and more and more, all over the world—simply this!—simply the change, the crisis, the monster we hate and despise and are desperate about and reject as today's vulgarity incarnate!

Yet—*e pur si muove!*—it is here, to stay. For it is the great "pooling" change—surely metaphysical in its categorial intensification of passion, invention, and intensity. The demand on us, beings of habit, from such a monster-creature, a new Fish, a new Bird, a new Man, is exhaustive indeed. Blaise Pascal's wager logic would be, historically speaking, the first ushering in of such a new body concept. For his justifying "proof" of an unprovable new being is not the proof by guidance and goal, which is the logic, and thence, the philosophy of the Necessary, but the proof by astonishment, intensity, and adherence, the logic and philosophy, in germ, of the Arbitrary.

It is in all earnest conceived here—as a Pascalian "proof"— that an epoch-making change in the attitude of man—which a change and its crisis are—can only be a *what-of-the-how* change in its basic moral tonality, as it were; can only be a change either in the sense of *quality's* priority, as the central category of moral reference, as the axis around which all other culture values organize themselves within a given cycle in history, or the equally decisive priority of *quantity.*

For it should be conceived that there are cycles—perhaps the longest span of historical time accessible to our search—whose central tonality would be the *quality value* of all the diversity of events, including the qualification of quantity itself—such as the idea of virtue's graduated rewards, whether by Heaven or by Kant's "categorical imperative" freedom; or, again, the Cartesian qualification of quantity as extension in matter.

And it is in equal earnest conceived here that the poet's vision of hope reborn from the weight, mass, quantity of despair itself[17] is already a different voice which, together with other prophetic voices of poetry, belongs to another horizon—next? ours to be sure!—where the transfer to the quantity center makes the latter a new, "another" quality—but a quality all the same: all the same a monster we still hate, reject, despise, and hope to get rid of.

Yet—it is the "spiritual" itself that is meant here. The vulgar—sentimental, materialist—command, "More and more and more people to have their daily, easier bread" is as spiritual as once the Bodhisattva's vow, "More and more people—all of the people, all of the beings and things on earth and elsewhere—should receive, by my final and sacrificial waiting, the Bliss of Amitabha's Paradise"; or as was Eckhart's *Seelengrund,* or Santa Teresa's *Inner Castle*'s only Good, or Zen's "white silence of Truth" . . . .

And still further: that the roots from which this *change-transfer* of our attitude comes up are to be befriended in all earnest by us, as if they were —and indeed, they are!—concrete, tangible beings, a new Fish, a new Bird, a new Fire, a new Man . . . . *The Ghost of Long Ago.*

✡

Je ne parle pas logique,
Je parle générosité.

MONTHERLANT

✡

These roots are to be befriended. . . .

For we don't speak of crisis—we *are* it.

And I don't speak of crisis—but of the body, the form of the myth: of substitution. I speak of form as of a testimony, a witness to substitution. And of the body's *ontological* proof: I *touch*—thus I *am;* the in-body nexus; the feel, later, the idea of it, its controllable lyrical experiencing in the individual man, and magnified, as epos in history.

I speak of the dance of the innermost, the dance of its body—the dance of the *muscle sensé.* I speak of art.

✡

When we speak, we all speak art: by substitution.

For the crisis is us, and what is too much of it that cannot be more in us, is our burden.

✤✤✤✤✤✤✤✤✤✤✤✤✤✤✤✤✤✤✤✤✤✤✤✤✤✤✤✤✤✤

✤✤✤✤✤✤✤✤✤✤✤✤✤✤✤✤✤✤✤✤✤✤✤✤✤✤✤✤✤✤

Standing alone, my burden by me—how otherwise?—on the shore of Japan's inner sea—unique, unique! yet not more astonishing nor beautiful than so many other, similar, shores all over our earth—it is there that I met the Mysterious Companion, the Comrade of my journey and time: Japan's past.

And I, the Westerner, faced him with the face of my unspeakable conflict. But he smiled, facing me with the face of his (= of our— O rebirth there of the primeval myth of solitude-solidarity!) unspeakable conflict, and shared my burden.

The journey started.

VARIATION
II
AUTUMN

Autumn:

The Sense of Sight

SCENE I

A leafy entrance to a public park facing the traffic and the buildings of a busy corner in today's Tokyo. The "downtown" noises come greatly mitigated. Except for the characters on signboards, etc., there is nothing "Japanese" in the setting. Enter I *and the* MYSTERIOUS COMPANION.

I: Let's stick to the subject and not deviate any more. . . . We are in search of the nature of Japanese painting. Let's not deviate.

MC: Agreed. But let's not lose face either—you are too practical to confine yourself to a private colloquy on this. You are surely going to write about it, *n'est-ce pas?*—let's not lose face: to look for the "nature" of an art, when even the nature of man is challenged today! You remember the Diltheyan "Man has no nature, what he has is history": man's nature—the absoluteness of it—being replaced by the notion of man-in-a-time, the notion of a universal invariant within a universal change.

Ever moving, ever creative, thus ever new, never absolute and static—yet invariant, all the same. It is the "historicity" of man which is challenging, is replacing exactly, the lapsed notion of man's "soul"—and rightly so, as you would say. (For how many crimes are committed in the name of this "soul's" sacredness and the elite's claims over it?)

I: You are right. But the very character of controversial indecision implied in the word *challenge*—does it not stabilize, precisely because of this inherent necessity of being instability itself, the two opposites of the controversy: absolute nature, relativist universality? Would it not be more prudent—and thus lessen the danger of "losing face"—to leave these notions—whether concerning man himself or his arts—where they are now? Let it be "nature," or "soul," or "spirit" of Japanese painting, or let it be its "historicity" —provided the *body* of it be there: Japanese painting, the multiple aspects of it, chronological, stylistic. I wish I knew. . . .

MC: You shall. But accept graciously what is offered to you here. Accept our time here. Accept autumn. Never forget that autumn is not a time of questions, nor doubts and their answers: it is the time of ripe fruit and falling leaves, of harvest. All is done there —over and done with. It is the time of quiet pain: the pain of love. *La peine d'amour.* How sweet and painful, now, it was to have been in love when spring was young; how sweet it was— and so painful now—to have been in love with lost origins and paradise lost when spring was here! But even this autumnal *peine d'amour* of time and of madrigal is quiet so, and so silent— it is only a ghost, something, someone, dead and come back.

(Enter the GHOST. *Just as if in a Noh play.)*

GHOST: I am. I know you don't believe in ghosts. But I am the ghost of Komaru no Tōsei. I should introduce myself according to all the rules of polite conduct. In my own time when I was a young aspirant for Dhyana wisdom I was living in the monastery of X under the supervision of the master—the very venerable Abbot Dōkai Daishi. And so once, doing what many have done, I humbly asked him about the great Truth and how to approach it. And I received—in Zazen fashion—the answer-to-be: a slap in the face. But instead of the sudden and expected result, the desired enlightenment—surely enlightenment about the extinction of all differentiations including this very extinction—the result came over me like lightning: I myself promptly replied with a much more vigorous muscular answer—the most pointed slap-reply you ever saw. And off the old master went, dead as a ghost.

In good and legal form my enlightenment's answer should have been interpreted as Zen-like, yet it was judged differently: I too was promptly dispatched—how dishonorably, by an executioner!—and went a-ghosting in my turn. I went in search of my poor old dead master, to thank him for giving me what he called the truth—the only truth, indeed! I never could find him. Has he joined the "bubbles of the earth"? So, you see, I come from afar. I am sad, tired, and lost. I wished to rest here a while and wait for the return of my companion—the not so mysterious companion of a mysterious and travelling ghost. But I overheard you—and now I am worried about you.

I: ?...

GHOST: Yes. Worried. You are too solemn and too unctuous—too easy a prey to the "sacredness" of your journey's goal.

And so, I fear, instead of falling as you should, under your own autumnal tree, your humble search, your humble search of art—you will fall right into the "white silence of Truth" of Zen's "holy vacancy of self," into its sacredness. You could not avoid it. Zen expects you there—expects everybody, the Big Racket, you know.

Truth—Shmuth, as my companion would have it! Zen, the Big Racket, so I say. The most exquisite racket too, among all the big rackets of your world: a most exquisitely devised camouflage, a power machine—the intellectuals' power! Power entirely covered up—disguised—by the "popular appeal" of an anti-church, anti-scripture, anti-dogma convincing directness. Exquisite, most refined machine—exquisite, most refined cover! "Lean only on yourself," they say—on your own free, freed from itself, will. And—all honor to the Holy Sword that nourishes this freedom, to the Money that protects it, to the silent and total contemplation that is the life in it!—Zen expects you; its alluring reward—inner peace, *la paix intérieure*—expects you.

And I won't let you have it. I love travellers with a precise and humble goal—they are like real ghosts-to-be—travellers who do not come here with a vague hope or goal of being purified from the heavy mud of their mechanized Western selves in the baptismal waters of Asia's wisdom (to learn how to sit again and meditate a while in front of a tree, of a mountain); or with a still vaguer urge and goal: to justify in the name of a philosophy of the majority—the majority's welfare—the unavoidable spread all over Asia of mechanization's taking-command[1]—but who have chosen a precise goal, no matter how silly, or futile—like yours, for instance. Come with me now—I shall tell you. . . .

I: How wonderful, Mr. Ghost—and how grateful I am—we both are . . . . But allow me to express my surprise at your disdainful attitude toward the mechanization-takes-command business, philosophically-historically. . . .

MC: Please don't—for goodness sake!—Your questioning will surely irritate him and spoil everything for us! Remember, he is a ghost we met in autumn—and this is the busiest and noisiest corner of modern Tokyo! Follow him. A ghost guiding us—what a chance! Don't question. The real question now is not to spoil this chance. The doubt about all this—should come forever later.

GHOST: Let's stop fooling around. Come on. My companion won't disturb us. Anyhow, he thinks all this is a lot of bunk.

SCENE II

In the treasury room of the X monastery. From a beautiful case the GHOST *takes out a* makimono *which he will later unroll.*

GHOST: Here is one of the greatest masterpieces—this scroll of poems selected from an ancient anthology, painted by two friends in seventeenth-century Kyoto: Hon-ami Koetsu who made the letters of the poems, and Tawaraya Sotatsu who made the gold and silver ink decorations. Both were great and subtle painters, and closest friendship united them (could the Orient be imagined without such friendship?).

Koetsu, his hallucinations. . . .

Sotatsu, his hallucinations perhaps even more faithfully remembered. . . .

I: Hallucinations?

MC: S-s-s—Don't. . . .

GHOST: Hallucinations, indeed. And I mean it—clinically. . . .

I: ?

The Ghost bursts into silent laughter that shakes his entire body. He remains silent for a while and distracted—not paying attention to the others during the following conversation, and reciting to himself some of the poems of the scroll.

MC: You're incorrigible. I've asked you not to question him any more. . . . Look at the autumn around us, how melancholy and soft it is. . . . He said simply that a painter paints not a dream, not a recomposed fantasy, but as it were, a real visit, a hallucination. "The visionary circumstance of mind." A painter, a real painter-craftsman, not just a painter-dreamer, is subjected to noiseless, formless hallucinations, that are real hallucinations, such as the sick mind produces. Only—similar to what happens to one who does not remember having dreamed during his sleep, yet has had dreams, surely—these hallucinations are forgotten, they are without *body* within the painter's immediate memory. Yet they become bodies in his eye-and-hand will.

A painting, a com-position of situated images, is such a thing. A ghost, a real ghost. It is, without the painter's knowledge of it, a dream lost in memory, re-embodied by the eye's hand. It is a *visionary* thing, not a vision, not a thing imagined, but a visionary visit, a *visitation.* A hallucination, the ghost said: a thing utterly abnormal, *unsane* from the point of view of an outside-a-ghost situation. From the point of view of normal eye-and-brain vigilance, insane; yet normal, sane, from the point of view of eye-in-brain—the ghost's—reconstruction of a visionary presence.

A painter or a visionary thinker does not know all this, does not even suspect it. Openly, socially, he simply realizes his dream, his fantasy, composed freely into a picture and a beauty. In this he is—socially—clinically speaking a sane person, acceptable *de jure*—yet, what is done (notice, please, the passive voice here!) by his eye—without him—is insane. (One could thus partly explain why it is, historically, that mysticism, which is simply and normally a visionary experience through and through, has been rejected, despised, and often relegated to the world of insanity by the "verbal"—verbally ordered—world that normally uses the help of imagination, of visions narrated, but not actually embodied.)

I: How could such an upsetting situation be humanly possible, or possible rationally to perceive and explain? Setting aside any suspicion of quackery in painter's art or in any interpretation such as mine—the sheer attempt to answer that would, I think, touch the most sensitive spot of human psychology. Perhaps we could. . . .

MC: It is exactly this that we should pass over in silence. Something is very strangely inciting you to challenge our visitor's patience and to drive his irritation to extremes. Ghosts, you know, cannot but hate human psychology with all their ghostly strength.

But you are worried—I see it clearly—and we cannot avoid talking about it sooner or later. While our ghost is still present in his poem-reading, you might tell me quickly. . . .

I: I don't know. I am greatly confused. All this is vague and puzzling, dangerously tempting too. . . . So, perhaps . . . let's be earnest about this word "perhaps". . . . Couldn't we say at random that the "abnormality," the "insanity," inherent, according to our ghost, in the "visionary circumstance of mind" has, perhaps, to do with the way we possess, so to speak, space itself in painting? I mean, the spatiality itself, the extension-milieu that dictates the spatial position or pose of all the dramatic and narrative elements in a painting. Do we possess this space—an "abstraction," or the condition of "abstractions," after all—or are we possessed by it? It is important. Don't we know that to be possessed is to be at the doors of insanity?

Now, if it were true that what the painter creates is precisely the *novelty* of his own pictorial space, then all the tensions of creative sensitivity would become the possession of this space, which in its turn would project them, tensions and creation, as its own—beyond our reach, beyond our possession. Space in painting could be called, metaphorically yet in earnest, a tension-full, thus an "abnormal," *sick* space, a space that we cannot possess any more, that possesses us and gives us its sickness and its creation.

Following this track of possession for a while, we could perhaps see further.

Perhaps it would be true to say, as is urged today, that two elemental—and inseparable—factors build up the very condition of our normal thinking and knowing—thus, perhaps, of our creation. To begin with, the so-called form-giving, Kantian schema-bearing activity of the mind. Not a part-to-whole grouping activity, but whole-in-part grasp: the *whole* of a thing—the in-ordered whole—silhouetted, as it were, by the very direction, the directive order of growth, followed by any given concrete part of the *schematic*—abstracted—whole. This immediate seizing of an ordered wholeness—already its evaluation or judgment according to Kant—is no mere approximate definition of purely intuitive knowledge. It is an inherent, living, concrete necessity of mind. It is, just is. Hence its "objectivity." Nevertheless its function, its maturation into a real symbol-concept-object, is dependent on another function, not immediate or immediately *given* as the first is: the mind's urge to use images: Cassirer's "the human mind is an image-needing one." The mind adds—constructs, creates?—the image to the elemental scheme or form, the elemental abstracting.[2]

Now, what I suggest is that in the visual, or rather "visionary" modality of human awareness and creativity, there is a reverse in the order of our *possession* of these factors, and that this reverse of the order or precedence between them would account for the rejection of the visionary as "abnormal," unintelligible, by the "normal" modality of thought, the thinking in symbols-concepts. It is the *image* that is given to us at the start in our visual knowing; its undeniable presence, immediate, convincing, unchangeable and whole—the flesh of it. The visionary image is the visitation; it is given to us without us, it comes *and we are possessed by it*—just as in the normal, verbal universe we are possessed by the immediate presence, the givenness, the visitation of the forms, the schemata (and the only "speculation," it seems to me, that I allow myself here is to separate temporarily, for comprehension's sake, what is in existence unseparable: the visual from the verbal, etc.) It is the form, the scheme, that takes the place of the image in our visional conditioning of thought. What the eye-in-brain creates is the form, the schemata, the abstraction itself, and not the image. The image-givenness first and the form-need or form-urge next would be the proper visionary order of precedence. Here that which we possess fully—which is our *visual* sanity and normalcy—is the form, the schema; that which we are possessed by—our givenness, our *sickness*, our *folly*—is the image given to us and not to be made to be, image-flesh, image-hallucination. The image would thus be the end-product of the "verbal" activity; the form-scheme, the abstraction, would be the end-product of the "visual": to interpret a work of verbal art—a piece of speculative philosophy or even a poem—it is the image ultimately that you have to evoke in fullness, by the image that you must "prove." To explain a work of visual art it is the form abtracted that should be the only proof and the only method! Perhaps you could . . . .

GHOST: How silly! How obsolete! I overheard you. Not bad. Much too much fuss though, too much "tsymess" about it all—as my companion, Mr. Sholom-Aleichem the ghost, would say if he were here . . . .

But you don't believe in ghosts, of course. A pity. Because I am really a ghost and I came to tell you that you won't understand anything about Japan, about Japanese painting most particularly, if you don't grant that all Japan believes in ghosts. Take it as you wish: either factually, as a ruling fact—ghosts are ghosts, period—or as a delegated fact, if you care not to shock the self-respectability and modernity of Mr. Kawada, technical advisor to

28 SESSHU
Ama-no-hashidate
Detail (15th century) ▶

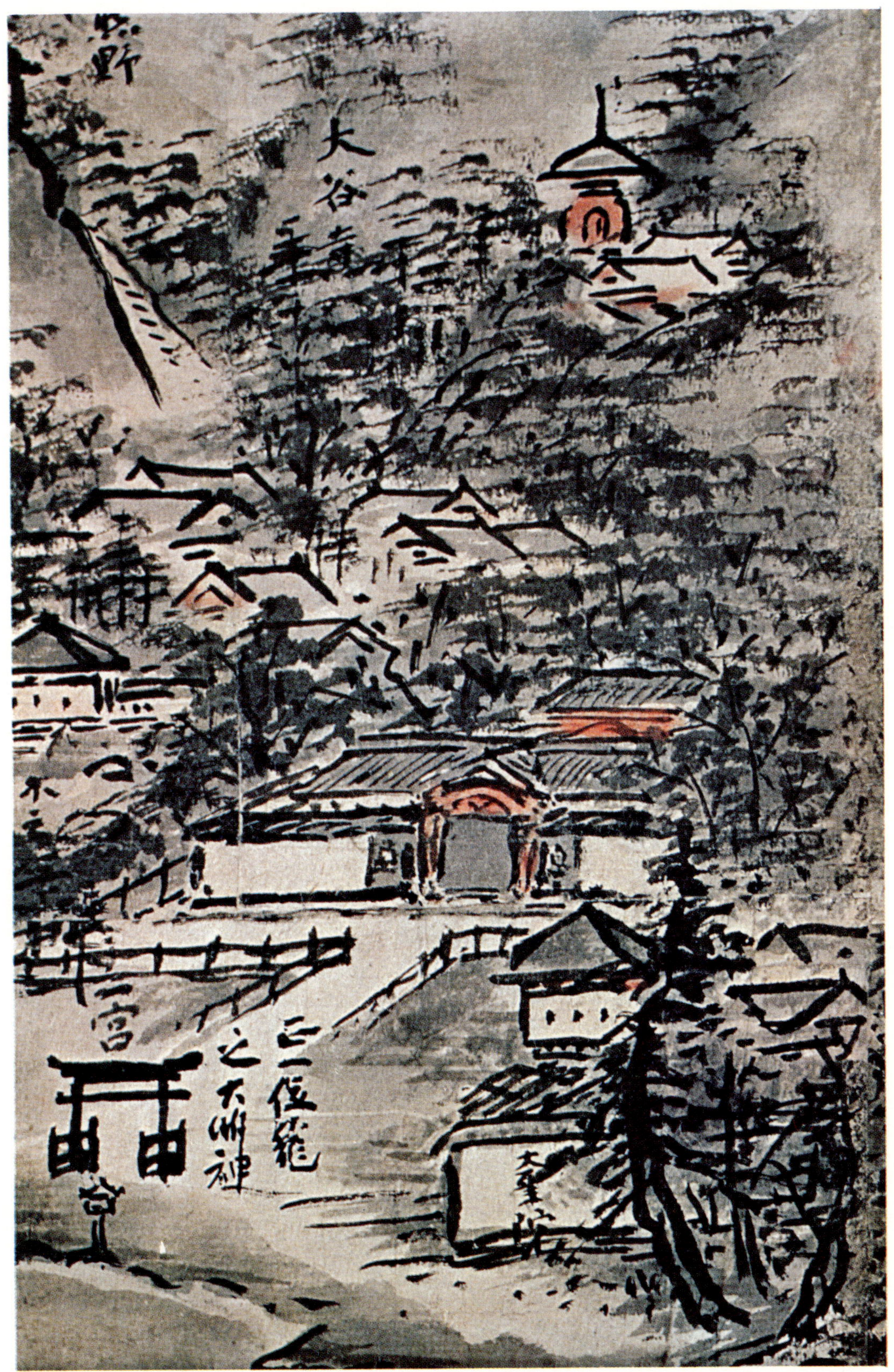
大谷寺

Seven sections of a poem scroll painted by two friends in seventeenth-century Kyoto: Hon-ami Koetsu, *who inscribed the poems taken from the* Kokin Wakashu, *an ancient anthology, and* Tawaraya Sotatsu, *who made the gold and silver ink decorations. An* emakimono, *the scroll is read from right to left.* (See Plates 29-35)

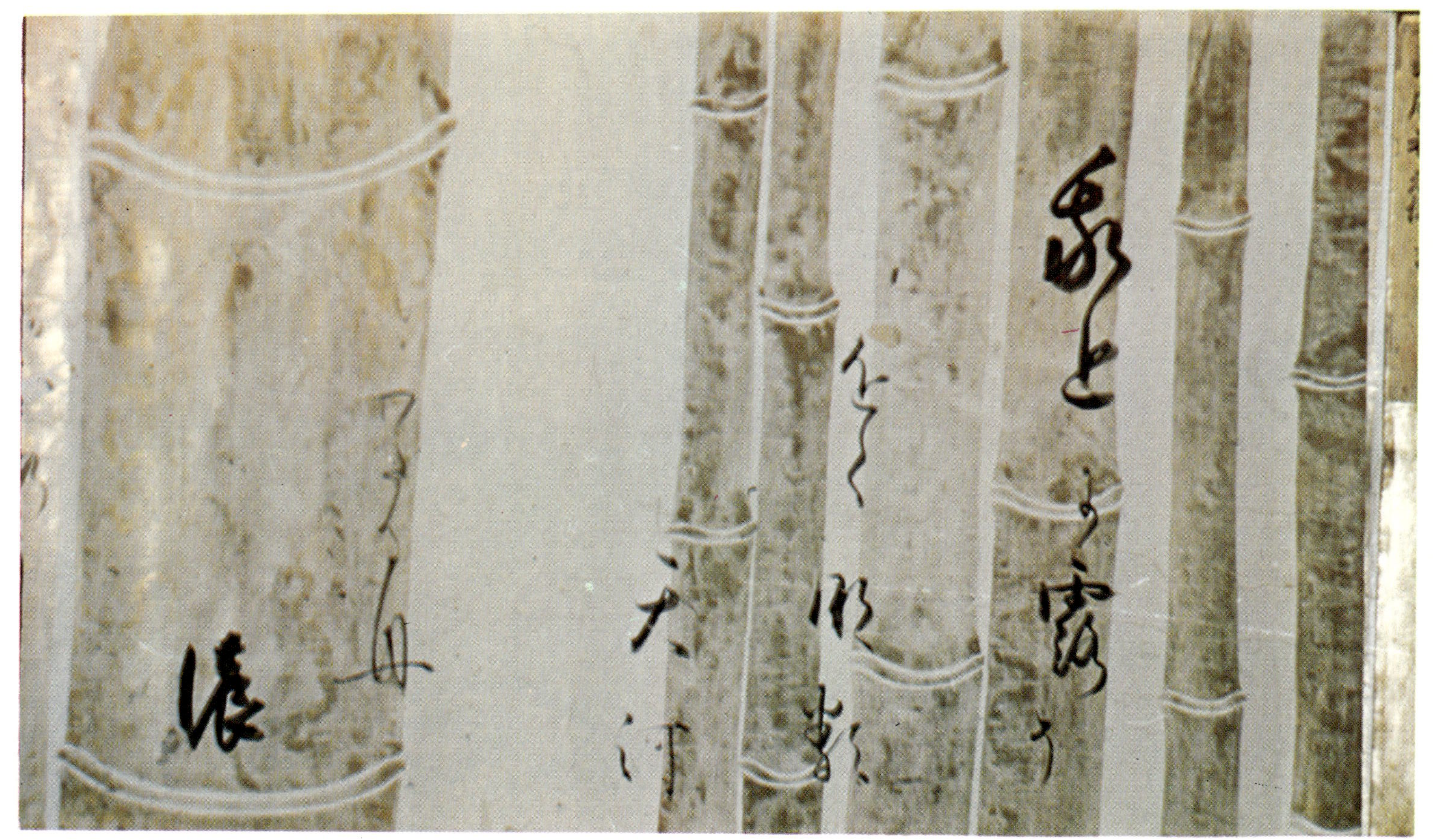

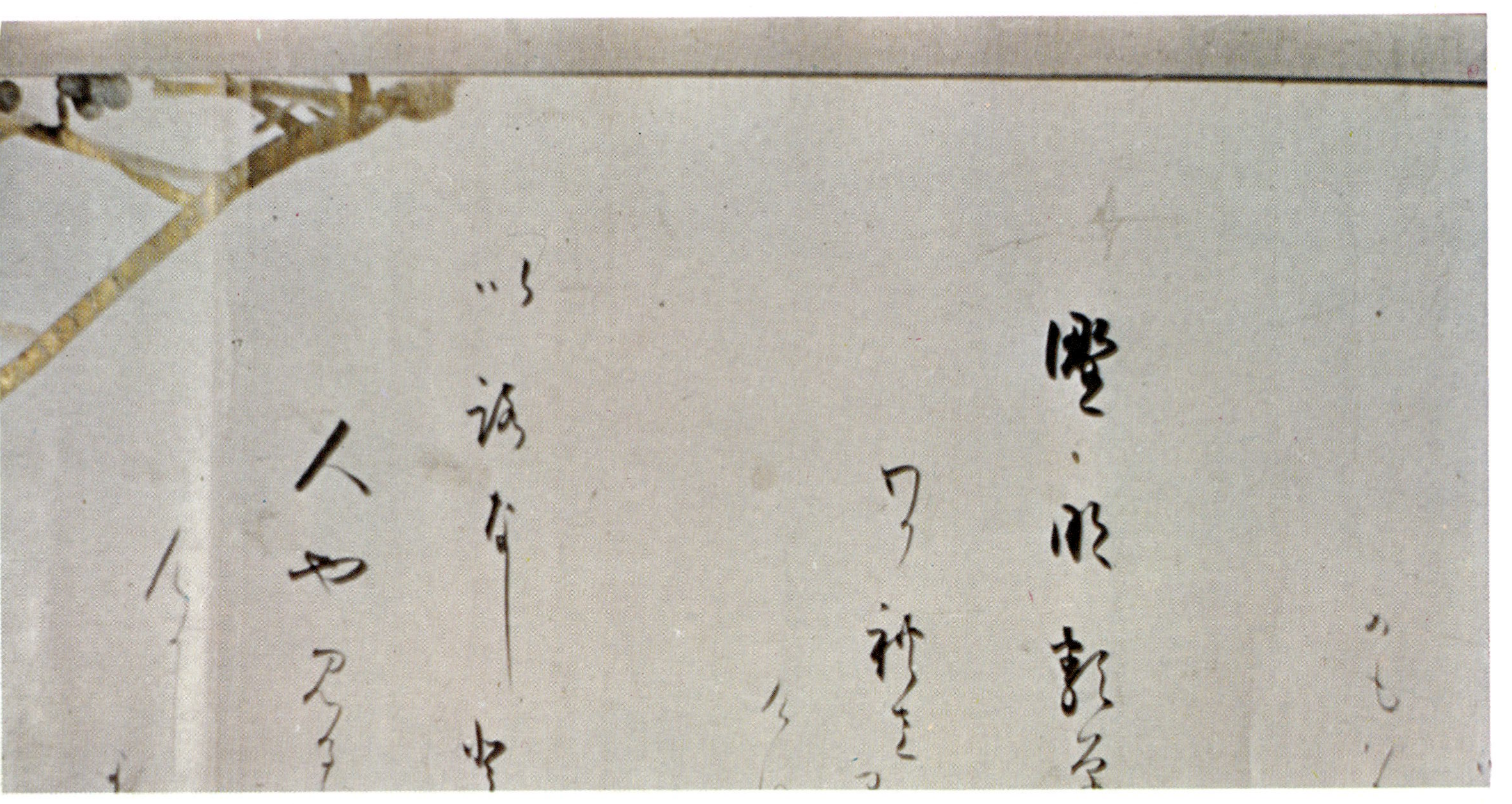

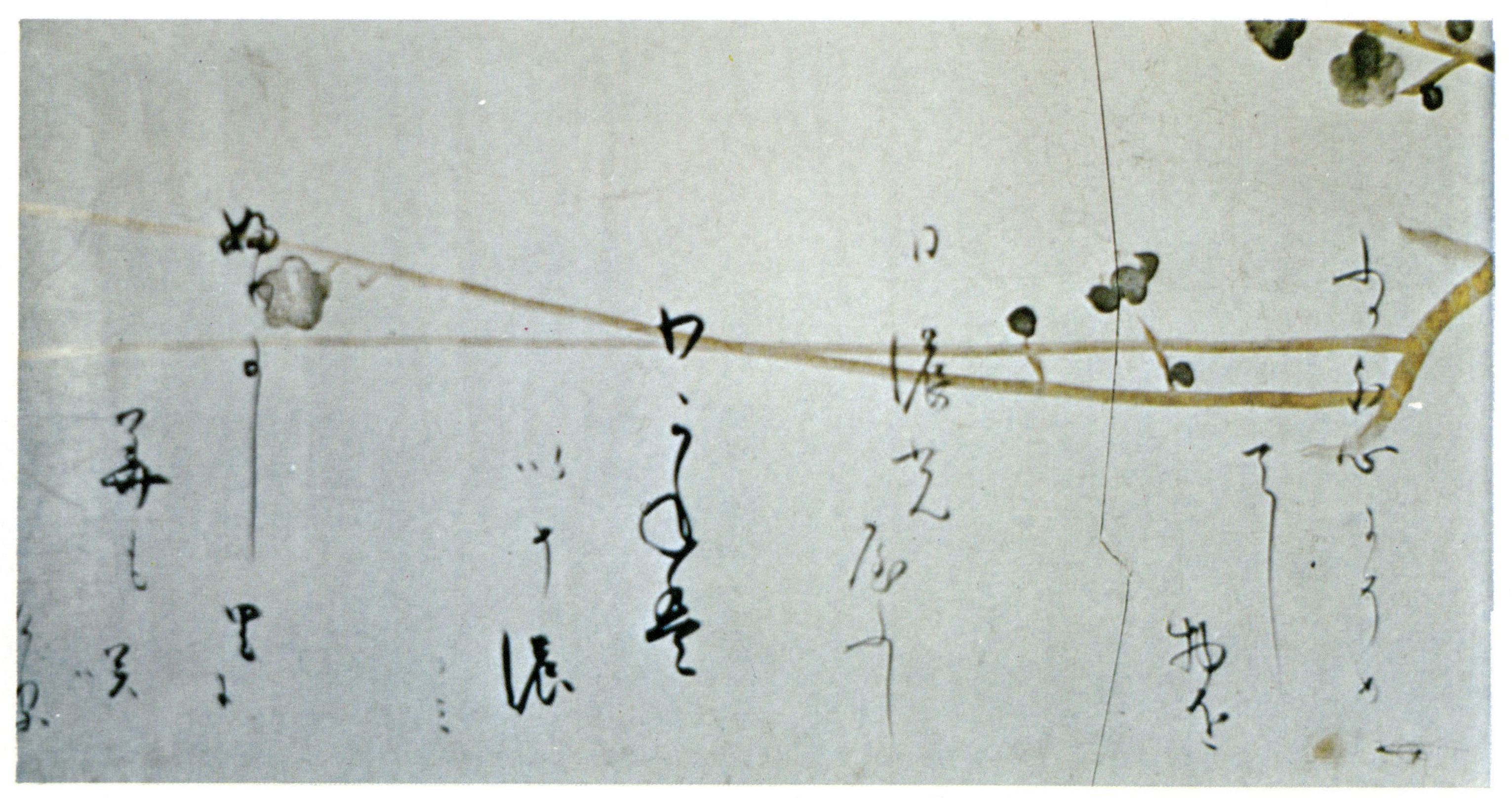

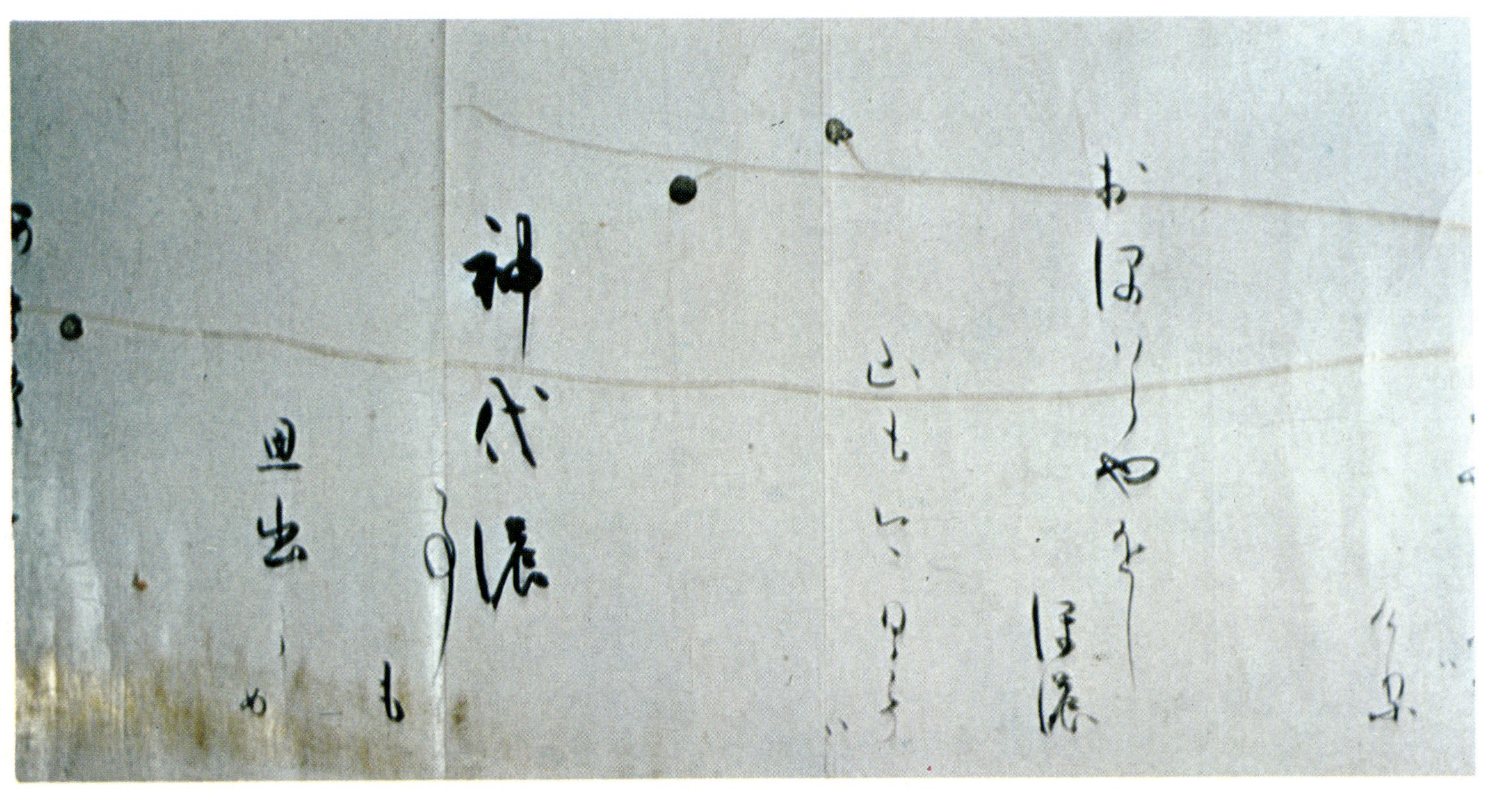

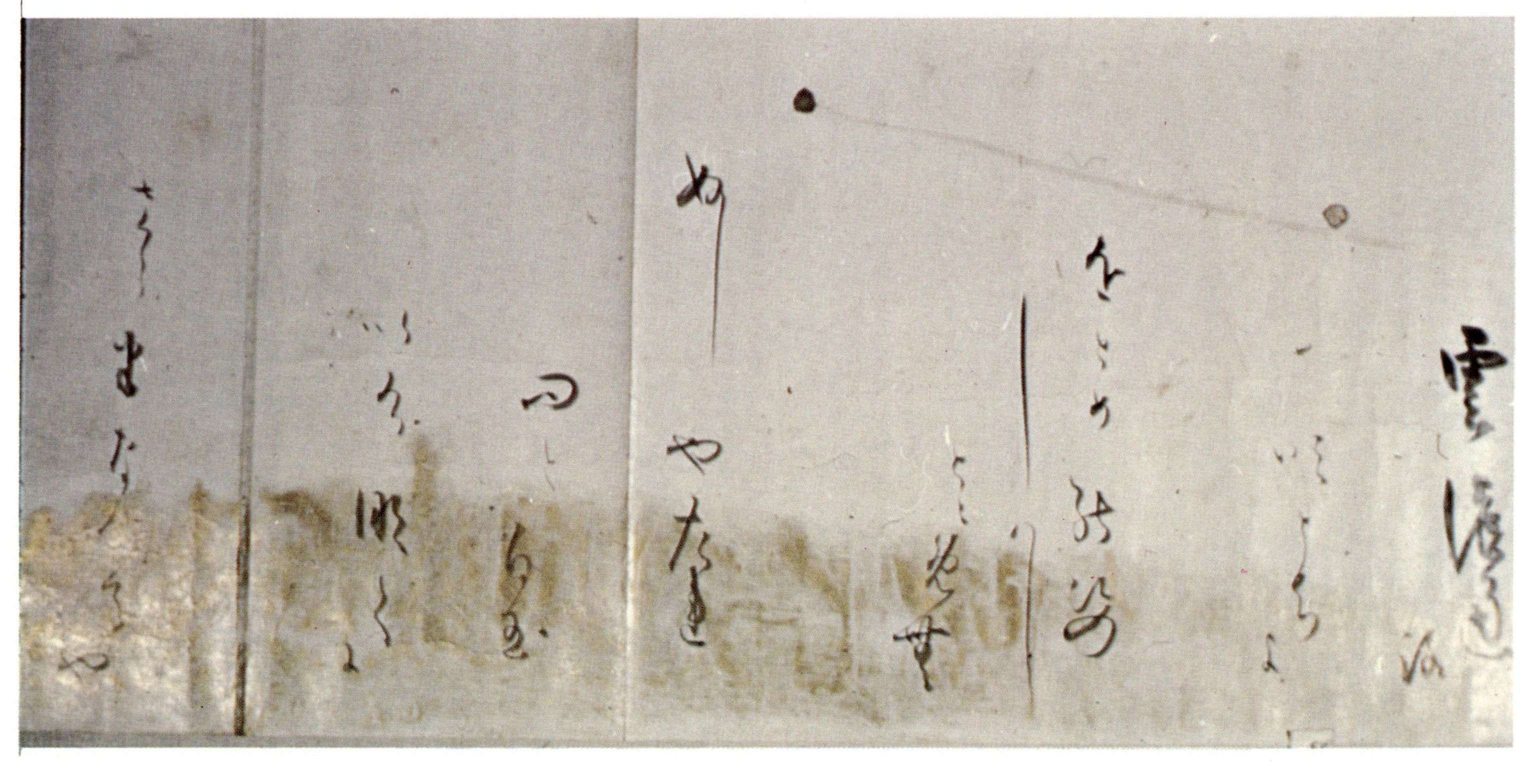

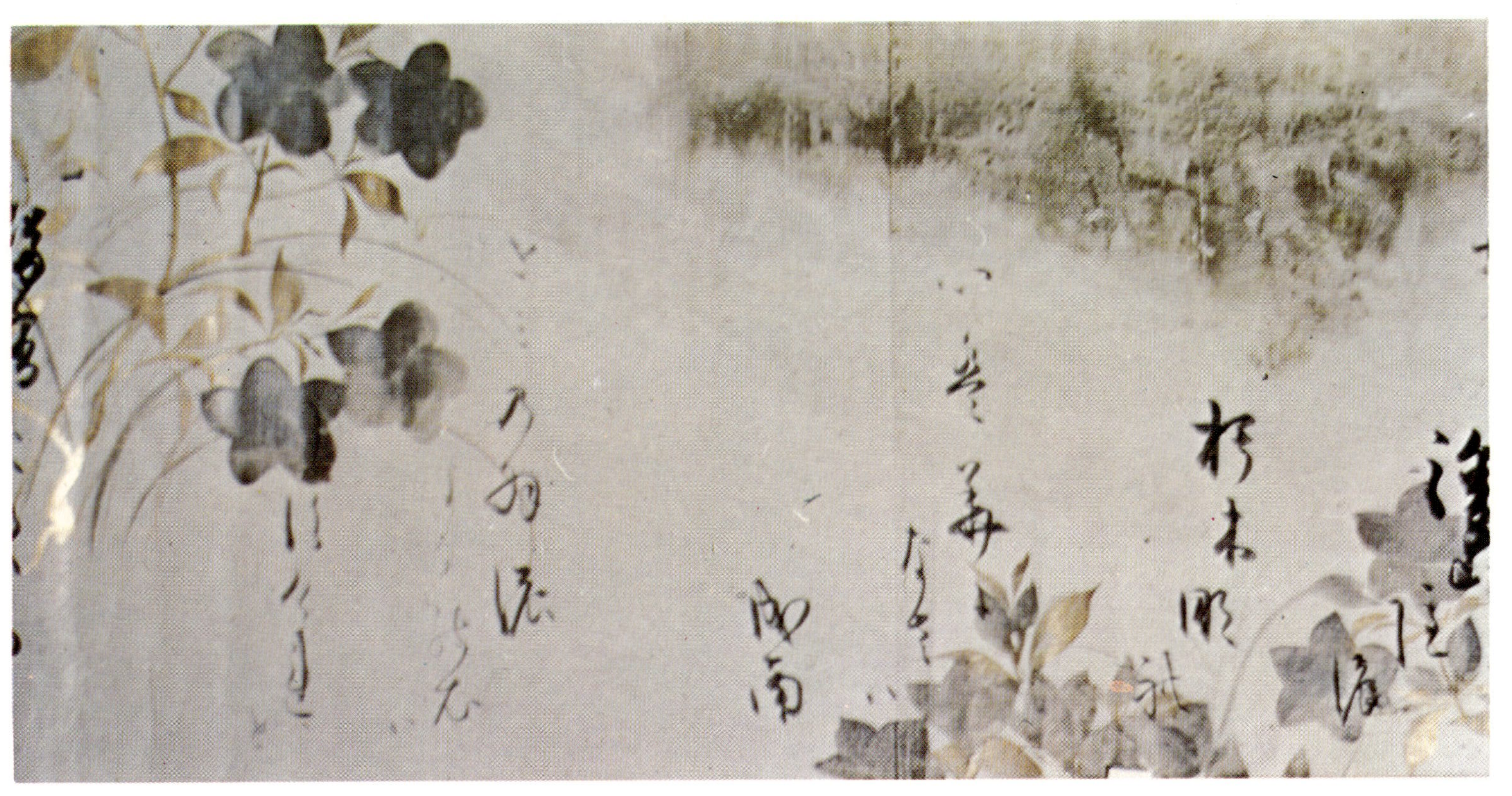

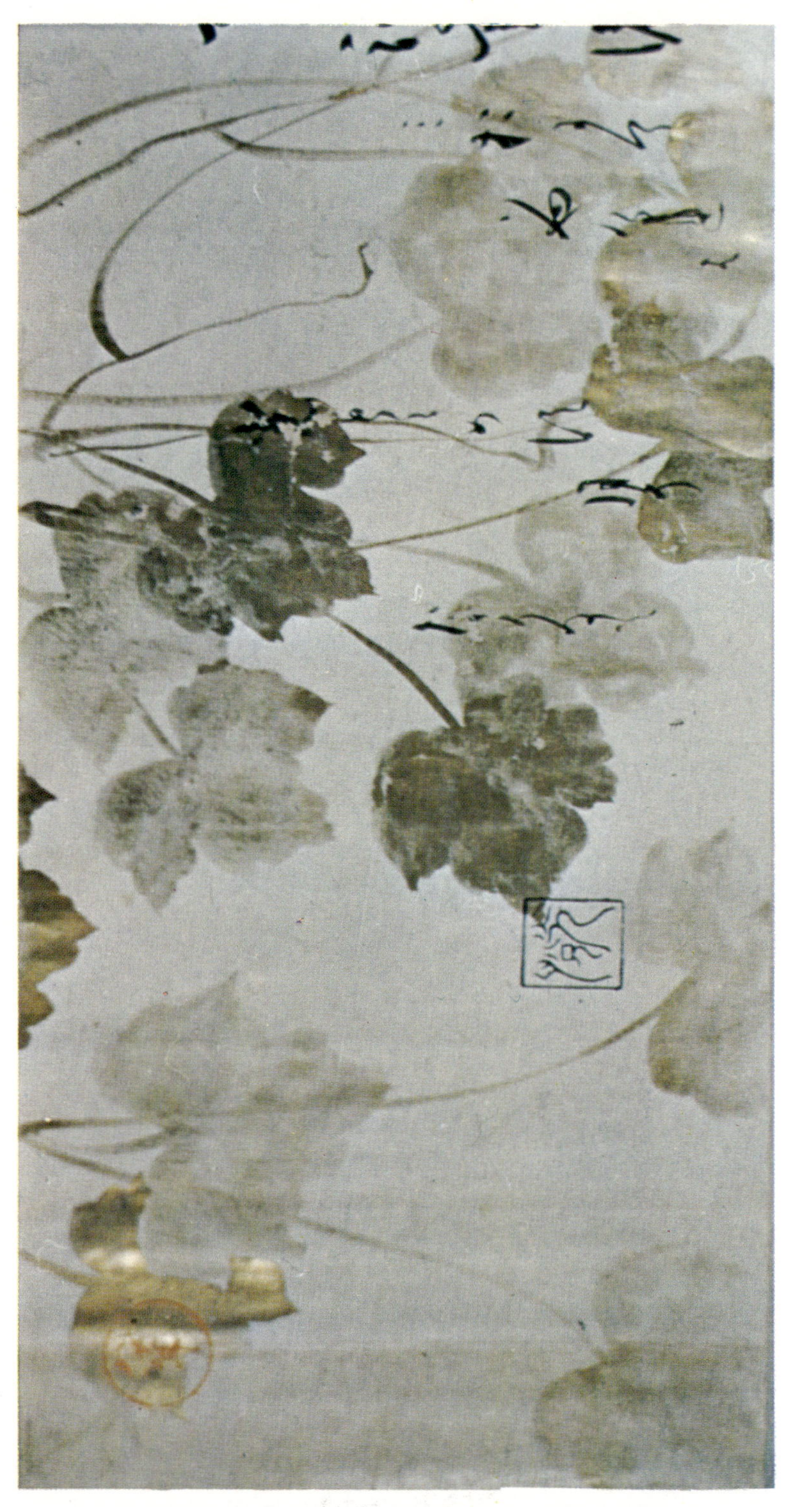

the Osaka industrial engineering concern H. Kobayashi, or Professor Okada at the University of Kyoto—take it, I repeat, as a delegated fact: namely, that nothing really is destroyed or dies, that everything returns as another form of energy, another efficiency-work, in the sense evolved Shinto would have it.[3]

Delegated, disguised, as those facts are—they are ghosts all the same, I am telling you. Simply because Japan is the only culture that never stopped believing in ghosts.

And now you must learn another thing. Once dead, one is more or less a ghost to the degree that one had had to perform a more or less difficult and tense task in life. Now among many things—which in Japan are always beings or bodies, ghosts-to-be—letters, or written characters, have had a most difficult existence in Japan.

This everybody knows. The painstaking adaptation, never fully successful, of a script invented for the monosyllabic idiom of China, by a polysyllabic Pacific language of Yamato, made of the letter-sign in Japan a living being, a living-struggling body, now in revolt, now subservient, always palpitating together with its idiom's life-stream. I don't say this to remind you of the resulting close relationship between calligraphy and painting, as China had realized it in the very expressiveness of her brush technique—a phenomenon dramatic enough in itself!—I say simply: written characters in Japan are real, concrete beings, with passions, dramas, and comical endings *(Plate 28)* . . . .

And now. . . . *(He starts to unroll the poem, progressing from right to left of the scroll and leaving—free as he is to do what he wants[4]—the revealed part of it unrolled, so that at the end of his explanation the entire scroll is in front of everybody present, the* MYSTERIOUS COMPANION, I, the audience.) The drama of letters begins. Look at these stark upright bamboo stalks—they appear the more powerful the less is shown of them on the scroll's field. And coming out of this background are the letters, living, minute people, many-limbed beings made of silver ink. Letters-homunculi, fettered, so it appears, to gold-inked bamboos. Fettered, I said? No, not at all! Alive—thus free! And the great thing starts: the letters decide to leave their consigned golden world; they walk away, just like this! *(Plates 29, 30)* and here they are free, free in a free empty vast space, walking, gambolling, now clustering together, now in meditative aloofness, a suspended garland of most gracious insect-like inventions. Dead, absent is the imposed columnar solemnity of bamboos of yore. Dead? No, not at all. The drama rolls on.

From the bamboo world sprouts out—how? from where exactly?—a long long branch, nude, sterile, silent and free also, freely stretching itself toward an end or aim that seems to have no end *(Plates 31, 32)*—a long long branch—some sprouts coming out here and there, irregularly propelled forward and hovering over the letter population, over their welfare—threatening them? protecting them? The most astonishing, uncomfortable—disturbing—visionary concept ever seen in pictorial space. I myself, the ghost, cannot stop now in qualifying it further: irregular, out of measure, out of proportion—how much longer can this nude, sterile yet free thing be stretching its limbs?—it is unique. Being unique it is irreversible; being irreversible it is challenging our habits; challenging our habits, it lacks respectability; lacking respectability, it becomes a thing of laughter, it is supremely comical, a monster formed.

And then—as sudden as was its sprouting out and its growth into space, comes the twig's end: not a Chinese end-unto-the-unfinished, the illimited—the subtle *sfumato*-like never-ending vanishing away; but a definite and sudden ending, a comical, bulging end—the pinch of a dot *(Plate 33).*

What happened there? The death of a twig that was born from the death of the lordly bamboo. Don't miss the coming event now—look! A golden mist, the very substance—delicate, delicate—of the absent bamboo, emerges—no! emanates—from the upper and lower edges of the scroll's field; it grows—but not suddenly, not irregularly!—grows and grows (chrysalis of a living ghost) into a spraylike bunching of fragile, delicate and leafy stems—gold and silver *(Plate 34).* And while the freed letters, at first inattentive to this happening, then more and more attracted to it, are now walking, dancing, now stopping in meditation, now clustering together among the newly born world, the growth of the leaves continues. Oh, poem of Japan's visionary mind-eye!

Watch, watch—read into it, read all existence into it!

I give you freedom final, autumnal letters, poor, beautiful, difficult creatures and creators of the new leaves, new young leaves in autumn! And almost brusquely you will vanish away into the no-letters surrounding universe. Disappear? Disappear among the also disappearing leaves? Oh, no! Absent now, as the bamboo stalks are, the twig and the leaves, you are—you yourselves; and finally, this last and only remaining golden leaf *(Plate 35),* this last full-grown leaf—and nothing else beside it, nothing but the end of the scroll itself.

(A silence.)

And now, off I go. Good-bye. . . .
where is my dear good old master I
killed and sent a-ghosting? *(Exit)*

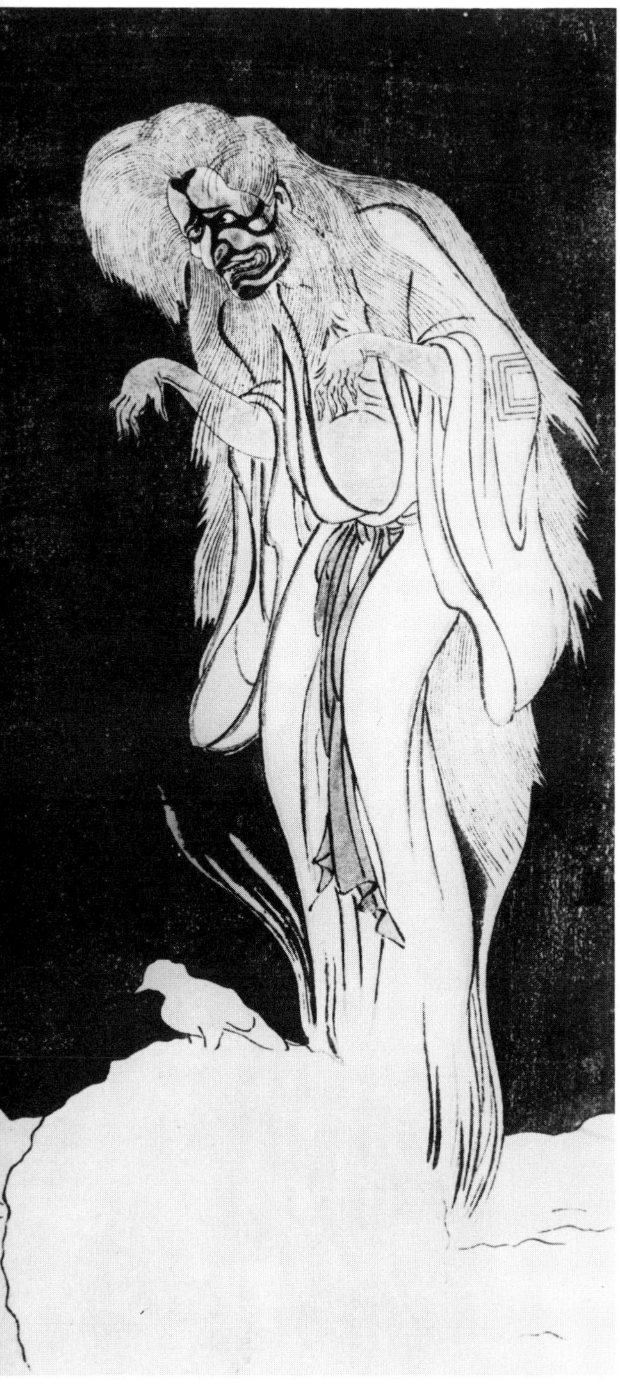

36 Katsu Shunshō *The Tragic Ghost* 18th Century

SCENE III

Back to the public park of Scene I.

I: What a nice ghost—so useful, so kind! But why did he keep repeating: "I am a real ghost?" Would he mean by that that he was not like a ghost painted sometime by a Japanese artist? *(Plate 36)* Strange. . . . Or that he was a traveller from afar—not a Japanese ghost only: a Westernized, Islamized, Africanized one? . . . . Strange. . . . And you know, I forget already how he looked—I cannot see him—I can only remember him as what we saw just now in the liberated letters: as a substitution. That's it! As a "visionary circumstance of mind" in full swing—which means that he is no allegorical ghost, or ghost symbolically speaking, but a real substitution for what is or seems to us to be unseizable, thus arbitrary (like a hallucination, for instance) in this whole situation. Arbitrary indeed, all this. . . .

MC: Arbitrary: you said it! I warn you: you are as ripe a fruit for the arbitrary's palate as, in our visitor's warning, you were for the "white silence of Truth." (Zen! Not such a racket after all, I can tell you now.) Take my advice—let us forget all this—and go right into your own memories. It will be best for our search, believe me. . . .

SCENE IV

A wooded place not far from the treasure-room where the scroll is kept: very fragrant.

I: One day—many a day before I learned all I could absorb about things Japanese, before I learned with a particular and revealing interest how Japanese painting was the Japanese theatre, the solemn operatic Noh and its later absorption into the complexities of the Kabuki theatre—one day I read the strangest of all plays. It is called "The Silk-board"—*Kinuta.*[5] A very simple story—the simplest imaginable—about a village wife whose husband, a country gentleman, has left her for some urgent business in the far-off capital, promising her to be back without tarrying too long. Three years are gone—thus starts the play—and a servant-girl of the household whom the departing husband had taken with him to serve him while away from the wife's care, comes as a messenger of the husband, to tell the wife of his delayed, but now nearing and sure return.

There is, floating in the air of the servant's short message, a resigned sadness about the real situation: no more return to the wife, the real wife now being she—Yugiri—the girl-messenger.

And the play, with no external action in it, pursues its own action-in-speech course.

A long long, irregular, sterile, nude, unnecessary complaint—Sotatsu's hovering twig?—covers the whole extent of the drama. The complaint of the abandoned wife, her noiseless death among the sweet words of the Chorus, her return as a ghost, of course. . . .

And all along this monotonous flow of words, one is aware of another presence—a strange recurrent motif, an obsession, as I said, an estranged presence in the very words of the two women and the Chorus—a constant reference to the sound of the silk-board beating in the village by other women, busy wives, purpose-having wives, in a bygone Japanese village. . . .

The words—ghosts of my intensity—come back to me loyal. Thus don't be astonished that I recite:

CHORUS

Alas, for her foolish heart!
How foolish her trust has been.

WIFE

What strange thing is it beyond there that takes the forms of sound? Tell me. What is it?

MAID-SERVANT

A villager beating a silk-board.

WIFE

Is that all? And I am weary as an old saying . . . . Yet I have stretched my board with patterned cloths. . . .

MAID-SERVANT

Boards are rough work, hard even for the poor, and you of high rank have done this to ease your heart! Here, let me arrange them, I am better fit for such business.

WIFE

Beat then. Beat out our resentment.

. . . .

CHORUS

The voice of the pine-trees sinks ever into the web!
The voice of the pine-trees, now falling, shall make
talk in the night. It is cold.

WIFE

Autumn it is.

. . . .

CHORUS

. . . The last leaf falls without witness.
There is an awe in the shadow,
And even the moon is quiet,
With the love-grass under the eaves.

WIFE

My blind soul hangs like a curtain studded with dew.

CHORUS

What a night to unsheave her sorrows—
An hour for magic—
And that cloth-frame stands high on the palace;
The wind rakes it from the north.

WIFE

They beat now fast and now slow—are they silk-workers down in the village? The moon-river pours on the west.

CHORUS *(strophe)*

. . . .

Wind, take up the sound she is beating upon her coarse-webbed
cloth.

CHORUS *(antistrophe)*

Beware of even the pines about the eaves,
Lest they confuse the sound.

. . . .

Take up the sound of this beating of the cloths.

. . . .

WIFE

The seventh month is come to its seventh day; we are hard on the time of long nights, and I would send him the sadness of these ten thousand voices—the colour of the moon, the breath-colour of the wind, even the points of frost that assemble in the shadow. A time that brings awe to the heart, a sound of beaten cloths, and storms in the night, a crying in the storm, a sad sound of the crickets, make one sound in the falling dew, a whispering lamentation, hera, hera, a sound in the cloth of beauty.

MAID-SERVANT

What shall I say to all this? A man has just come from the city. The master will not come this year. It seems as if . . . .

CHORUS

The heart, that thinks that it will think no more, grows fainter;
Outside in the withered field. . . .

. . . .

[*The wife dies. Enter the husband, returning.*]

. . . .

GHOST OF THE WIFE

Aoi! For fate, fading, alas, and unformed, all sunk into the river of three currents, gone from the light of the plum flowers that reveal spring in the world!

. . . .

. . . . and show her autumns of a lasting moon. . . . Oh heart, in your utter extremity you beat the silks of remorse; . . . .

. . . .

CHORUS

Her tears are shed on the silk-board,
Tears fall and turn into flame,

. . . .

She cannot reach us at all,
Nor yet the beating of the silk-board
Nor even the voice of the pines,
But only the voice of that sorrowful punishment. Aoi! Aoi!

. . . .

GHOST OF THE WIFE

Even the leaves of the katsu-grass show their hate of this underworld by the turning away of their leaves.

CHORUS

The leaves of the katsu show their hate by bending aside; . . . .
Aoi! Aoi! Is this the heart of man?

. . . .

GHOST OF THE WIFE

It is the great, false bird called "Taking-care."

. . . . 6

The complaint flows, flows. . . . The autumnal *peine d'amour,* the pain of yore and of madrigal, quiet, so quiet and silent—a ghost, someone-something dead and come back. . . .

It flows, flows, monotonous, sad, sad, *infinitely* sad, fragrant; a sadness uncommunicable. Unseizable sadness, autumnal—a vil- 48 lage forlorn in Japan; a sad and unique happening there—who cares?—and innerly transcending all this: the familiar sound of a familiar autumnal occupation, sound repeated, sound referred to, and the time of fall in it, leaves falling, all Nature in it, *natura naturans* and *natura naturata* in it, in one Nature, becoming there a being, a body—this and not any other sound and smell of autumnal silk-board beating—and the whole sadness in it, whole, infinite, unseizable, seized, made finite in it.

I see what I say to you: the story of this Noh play is not the story of a sad abandoned wife and her complaint—death in a sad and village-busy autumnal day end—*it is this very autumnal day end, nothing else.* It is the story of the unseizable sensation of an autumnal day end itself. Unseizable because the whole of the given Nature, Nature beloved so *intensely,* so earnestly by a Far Easterner (a love and an intensity much beyond our Western reach!) amidst most serious "business" of life—of lovemaking, of money-making, of power-and-politics-making, of killing-self and killing-other-selves-making, etc.—I say, the unseizable sensation of the autumn itself is being seized here in the narrated image of a sad wife's destiny.

We have here the *substitution*—thus total identity, total transfer—of a human drama (which, for our direct purposes now, when transposed into pictorial terms, would give us a figure, or figures, in space and its, their, drama), for the otherwise unseizable wholeness of Nature's presence (in terms of pictorial "visitation" again—the landscape, the landscape in the narrow "naturalistic" sense as well as in its inherent sense of the never-finite beyond-of-man). Eureka! I have it, my friend, we have it!

MC: *(with irony and friendliness)* We have what?

I: The secret, the "nature," of Japan, of Japanese painting, Japanese art, of Japanese theatre and of Japan's cities, politics, borrowings, of Japan's Buddhism, of Japan's . . . *substitution.* With no allegory about it, no symbolism in it—only the fleshiness of a myth: the making of the myth a body.

MC: You know, I hope, that all this could be found in China also, and in India—and all over the world, when and wherever you look about.

I: True. And the play of the silk-board beating, its plot, its poetic technique, its obvious Buddhist morality, all this could have been Chinese. I agree. Yet, a tiny accent here, a little shade of added suggestion there, would have changed, probably Sinicized, the structure of its symbolized goal.

The first wave of sadness there—the human sadness of abandonment—would double its own self-encirclement by a larger circle-wave of a sad autumnal day end, with all the sounds and smells of an autumnal village occupation in it, with all its nuanced meanings of poetry, consolation, rest. . . . This two-subjects-containing new circle would continue its symbol propagation by becoming now a much ampler circle-wave, the circle-wave of universal rhythm, the rhythm of return—same hopes, same delusions, same resignations, same resulting "enlightenment," same quiet sadness—circles within circles, one continuing into the other, one, the microcosmic center cycle (the wife's story) corresponding to the macrocosmic center cycle, all-cosmos-inner-and-outer-about-to-plunge into Buddha's Bliss, and falling back, Bodhisattva-wise, into the initial little sadness, its own poetry, consolation, rest, and salvation. . . .

Just as it is chanted and mimicked at the very end, suddenly so Chinese-Indian of the "Silk-board"—*Kinuta*—Noh:

GHOST OF THE WIFE

It is the great, false bird called "Taking-care."

. . . .

CHORUS

She recites the Flower of Law; the ghost is received into Butsu [Buddha]; the road has become enlightened. Her constant beating of silk has opened the flower, even so lightly she has entered the seed-pod of Butsu.[7]

A comprehensible, *necessary* world of correspondences, of transformations, revealed here. And so would be for me China's art and politics and history, China's cities, borrowings, Buddhism. . . . China is this epic emphasis on a finite thing forever being included in—and including—the circulatory flux of what cannot be either total finity—because it transcends all limits—or total infinity —because what could be conceived as infinite is at each point of its existence filled to capacity with finite things and feelings, and thus corresponds to these things' and feelings' limitations.

This is not Japan's visitation. Correspondence is *never*. . . .

MC: Don't let the scents of your memory vanish: I warn you, be aware of the spot where we are. And—let's stop fooling around, as the ghost said.

I: Thanks: Close to the Noh play and its memory's smell lie in wait two pictorial images precious to me. Every detail in the Chinese work *(Plate 37)* carries in full China's credo: the bird's silhouetted sketchiness and the upper branch in the right corner of the painting repeating in exquisite suggestions of slashed lines, the very contour of the goose; the reverberation of this correspondence onto the surrounding void, a kind of still-to-be substance, a breath, a *pneuma,* and the monochrome yet many-shaded greyishness that absorbs and radiates the correspondence between the void and the full, the finite being and the not-finite becoming, the humblest of pictorial themes—a goose!—and within it, the most "sublime" that Asia's mind has ever devised: the Tao-Sunyata's not-discrimination, not-distinction! Rich, expanded, expanding China! Japan too—scattered throughout Japan's thought and art; but not in this work here *(Plate 38)*—in this subtle and secret and true credo of Japan.

Because the great void here is the infinite, invisible landscape itself, with everything it could contain. It is the beyond of the two figures—the figure of the Noh actor performing and the figure of the symbolic pine tree (good omen, wish of longevity, or Buddha himself?). But the real, visible, and infinite landscape *is* those two figures themselves! Emptied of all visible content the landscape-void is seized and then catapulted into the drama of the two silhouettes, the acting man and the tree. These two silhouettes are the finite substitution for the inexpressible fullness of the landscape theme—they *are* in flesh this fullness, this whole: a visitation, a hallucination.

And at the same time they are substitutions for each other's wholeness—the infinity of man, the infinity of a tree—unseizable otherwise, inexpressible otherwise. The contours of the man and the tree are identical, interchangeable—and the great void is *in them.* I know: "Why," you wish to ask me, "could not the relation between the Sung goose and the slashed branch be called rather identity, substitution for each other, and why should not the similarity between the Noh actor and the symbolic tree be considered precisely as an allegorical episode of correspondence?" I would never dispute about this, you know: the differences here are subtle and real. May I add perhaps this: a correspondence suggested is the only correspondence; a correspondence indicated is the only identity. And where China clearly suggests a relation, Japan clearly indicates it.

As for myself, within my memory I decided one day, and on many other days afterward, in front of such a rich revelation of Japanese pictorial thought—telegraphically—this:

> JAPAN, CONVERTED TO BUDDHISM dash A PSYCHIC RELIGION-AND-PHILOSOPHY IN WHICH MAN [in art the human figure par excellence, as in Greece or Egypt] REMAINED THE NARRATED CENTER OF ATTENTION AND CARE dash WHILE THE REAL AND PROPAGATED SUBJECT-GOAL WAS THE CONTINUED MAN, THE COSMIC MAN, THE INTERSTELLAR ADAM OF THE GNOSTICS TOO dash THE CO-PRESENCE OF THE LITTLE MAN'S UNIVERSES AND THE COSMIC MAN'S ASTRO-PSYCHIC MULTI-UNIVERSES [the sacred symbol of the multi-petalled lotus signalizing it everywhere] dash JAPAN, CONVERTED TO BUDDHISM, TOOK OVER THIS INDO-CHINESE MESSAGE.

Japan too in its art made the sovereign figure and its dramatic adventures the narrative center of attention and care. But in contradistinction to India and China, where the infinity-landscape, the continued cosmic man, was comprehended in the very buoyancy of its correspondence with the finite human figure, Japan dared to wish differently. Japan dared openly to wish that which only two other planetary culture-destinies dared to wish: to seize the unseizable whole not through the temporary and partial appeasement of correspondence, but as identity, by aggressively making the finite itself be the infinite.

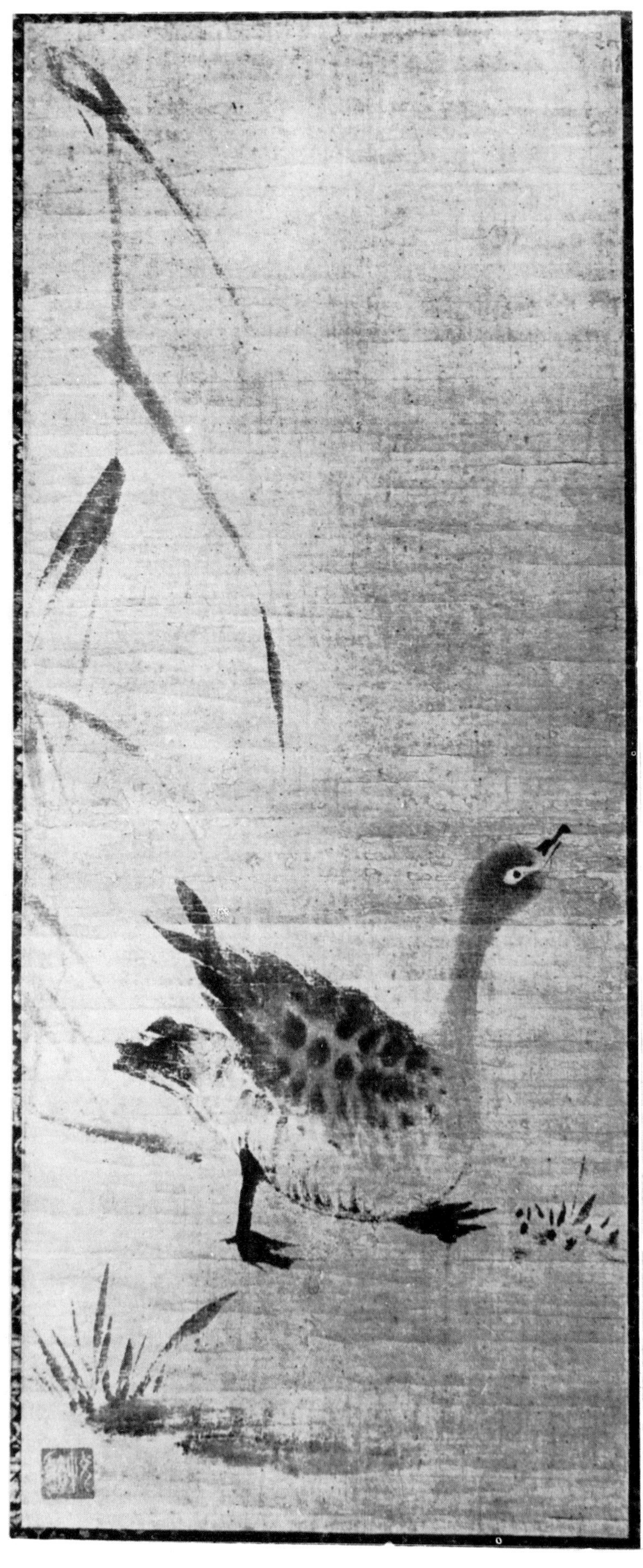

37 Attributed to
MU-CH'I
Wild Goose
13th century

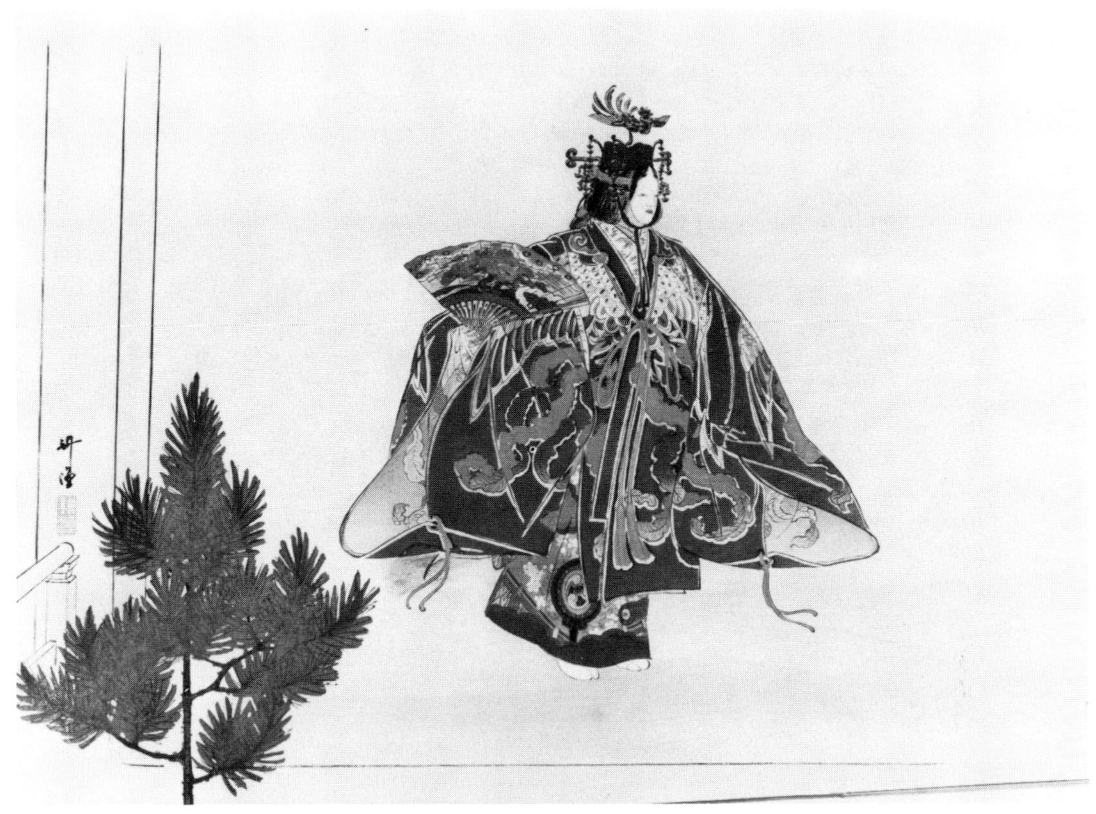

38 Kogyo *Illustration for a Nō Dance* (ca. 1910)

Such a seizure cannot but be a seizure by a concrete—delimited—*part of the whole* (the well-known *pars pro toto* historic, or rather prehistoric, principle). It must be a *body*. We call it embodiment; we call it also in theological idiom sacrificial incarnation. A chain—a game? a bet?—of total substitution: "It is, in fact, well known that the construction of the fire-altar is a veiled personal sacrifice. The sacrificer *dies*, and it is only upon this condition that he reaches heaven: at the same time, this is only a temporary death, and the altar, identified with the sacrificer, is his substitute."[8]

A body always, sacrificial body. Very dangerous business all this, arbitrary, obscurantist, totalitarian—yet historically undeniable in its tenebrous working, to be coped with: as an Ancestor Mask, as Eucharist, as total State, as total Dogma. . . .

MC: A chain, you said—a game? a bet? Was it not Heraclitus who said that Eternity is a Child that plays? I have certainly nothing against Heraclitus, and in this sense nothing against playing with your *idée fixe:* the principle or the world of transformations and correspondences of the finite's and infinite's circular and mutual transforming one into the other, and opposite to it, the world of substitution—of identity, of total transfer. I also sense the provable necessity of the finite—the logos of necessity in it—the correspondence, say, between observable facts and mind's deductive views, things, and concepts responding to each other's appeal, continuing in each other, logically, "naturally." I sense, with disgust, to be frank, the dangers you are so aware of inherent in the arbitrary decision of the opposite world, the logos of the arbitrary in it . . . Very much so. . . .

I: I know it. But. . . .

MC: But—of this later. . . . We want more of Japanese painting now. We should not sacrifice Japanese painting. Shall I say no substitution for it, eh?

I: Coming. . . . But first let me finish—I said just now that two great cultures beside Japan had wished, and dared, to seize the unseizable, that each of the three had attempted this by creating, amidst a staggering crisis, its own body. By means of this sacrificial—because finite and created—body, the earthly, fragile, irregular, and complex human body-and-mind could be given the permanent *form*—the *aeternitas,* the simplicity—of infinity's exact receptacle. This is how I conceive the form, the art—as visuality, as politics, as science, and speculation—created by each of the three, Greece, Judaea, and Japan.

The form in Greece, at its purest self:—oh, the truly mysterious early Greek form, the pre-Phydian most mysterious art on earth! *(See Plate 13)*—is form-geometry, the visitation of the *aeternitas*-limit. That is why the discursive notion of infinity—the unknown as unknowable, incommensurable, the *x*, the *y*—was so repulsive to classical Greece, rejected as physical concretion, relegated to the speculations of mathematics.[9] Only much later in history, beginning with Graeco-Asiatic or Hellenistic learning, already saturated with India's algebraic world of equations (correspondences), that is, with her very handy "trading" inclusion of the unknown, the *x*, the *y*, in the great circulation—the wheel—of the known, only then had the physicalization or the liberation of the concept of infinity from the sacrificial body-limit started its great Western adventure.

The form in Judaea at its purest self: total identity—never-to-be-named, body-and-mind's self-limitation not as geometry but as order of conduct, as responsibility of conduct: ultimately, as the only one choice of the only one obedience (ritual) of body and mind, to the only one Law: the prophetic notion of commonwealth as the Book's or the Law's visitation, the visitation of the *aeternitas*-limit. "Where the Book is, the Sword is not." This is the form, the art of Judaea at its purest self. At its dearest—of Islam too.

And the third? The form of Japan at its purest self? Japan's substitution, difficult, uncomfortable, of the finite for the infinite, the identity of both? As in Greece, as in Judaea, so also in Japan, it is, at bottom, the result and ordeal of body and mind's self-limitation: in Japan, as *order of body's position.* Position in space, position in time. Simply this. Not as order of body and mind's limitations as such, the Greek geometry; not as body and mind's conduct, as Judaea's responsibility, but as position in space in time, a dance. It is, at its kinæsthetic deepest self, a physical awareness of being not *what* but *where* one is. A physical awareness awakened in the very presence and self-ordering of body's touch, multiplied *ad infinitum,* with the outside of the body; an awareness that makes unmistakably *significant,* thus *potentially moral,* the very situation, the position, the *pose,* of the body: that makes it be at once a *dance* and a metaphysics. The secret of Japan's seizure of infinity—the secret of Japan's conduct, as art, as polity, as moral rule, is in the metaphysics of dance.

MC: If this were so—assuming I understood you—it would most likely seem repulsive as well as utterly ridiculous to the Judaic moral man; and utterly incomprehensible as well as frivolous—arbitrary, in short—to the Greek. How then? . . . .

I: Arbitrary! And yet—irony of all interpretations!—no more arbitrary in Japan than in Judaea or Greece, or for that matter—to a lesser degree of historical intensity—elsewhere. For unquestionably this arbitrary, unprovable substitution attitude in handling the infinity-finity relation is as much a typical human phenomenon, to be pragmatically coped with, as the opposite attitude, so logically plausible, of correspondence.

MC: *Qui s'excuse s'accuse.* The instant you begin to justify your "ghostly" visitations, all is lost in impending boredom: it is like asking your girl permission to kiss her. Don't ask—kiss! Stick to the ghost—am I not here—in silence mostly—to protect you from entangling disloyalty?

You simply arrived at this: that the revealed secret of Japan—definitively, decisively of Japanese painting—is in the close connection between what we called the logic of the arbitrary (and the very mention of such a notion as infinity is arbitrary), the principle of substitution, and the precise, bodily technique of dance. And that this connection—a nexus of interlapping image-contagions—is reducible in its turn, simply to what is called body, human body, our body, my body—the direct feeling, the immediacy of its presence. . . .

I: Yes, yes. "Tangled, we are entangled. Whose fault was it. . . "[10] as a Noh stanza says. It should be easy from now on. So that the Divine in Japan—All-Kami—is nothing but the human body, woman's body *par excellence,* the divine body; and an iris *(See Plate 23)* is the human body, and the deer at the edge of a wood, or a pine tree and an old ugly woman, or a pheasant, or a lotus, and all the "meanings" added to them. . . .

And so also—in substitution—it is not the human body that is painted in Japan, being as it is already and unerringly there in representation-imagery, but it is the beyond of the body, the great landscape, that is painted instead: infinity itself. That's why. . . .

MC: The more simply you see your vision the more entangled you get. Try to find a more compelling definition: what do you mean exactly by body of infinity—and then see what happens.

I: Definitions—*je m'en fous*—with our ghost's permission. . . .

MC: Oh no!—this wouldn't do. For what are you doing now by refusing to formulate? In your own fashion you formulate a refusal. . . .

I: *(the exalted mood suddenly lowered, quieted)* All right. . . . What was I saying when you interrupted me? I know, I was saying something I could use now. Oh yes! About body: that's why . . . . that's why in Japan the costume is of the utmost—I would insist, metaphysical—importance. The costume in Japan is already the beyond of the body. It is the very script of the ritual by which the landscape-infinity, infinite space and its visionary content—the visitation of anything and everything in visible nature—is incarnate in the human body: the sacrificial—hence its sacerdotal splendor!—new body of the Japanese myth of substitution *(See Plates 39-45)*, the sacerdotal splendor of flowers, mountains, birds, waves, beasts, leaves, skies reproduced—stiffly, "unnaturally," emphatically, thus significantly, on the metaphysical textiles of kimonos and obis.

It is not only this, of course! It is what could be conveyed to us by costume (and no other art in the world has done it with equal intensity): the bodily touch, at a particular and chosen point or points, of the space-void surrounding the costume. Hence the "mannerism" of Japanese silhouettes—the "frozen calligraphy," by which something precise is communicated in the body's pose, the body's halt: its *aeternitas.* No other culture has done more or better in covering entirely—significantly—the naked human body.

MC: You are forgetting that parallel to the pictorial development of the costumed human figure in art there was also flourishing in Japan an art of frank nudity—especially in the time of Ukiyo-e's glory—an art of unhindered eroticism, candidly "pornographic" as the West calls it. I am talking, you know, about the *Shunga* painting and woodblock printing, hidden away now, forbidden by Western legislative prudery. How would you explain this art—without using any extra tricks of speculative interpretation?

I: I know little about this art as yet—but I certainly know how important it is for the establishment of a "correct" historical perspective of Japanese painting. I have even heard of a curious and very plausible thesis according to which the totally uninhibited production of sex imagery—quantitatively immense!—should be entirely reconsidered (and for that matter the rest of Ukiyo-e) by the West's art criticism. What this art would be supposed to illustrate is nothing less than a Japanese version of Buddhism's most influential corpus of doctrinal symbols: in great particular the tantric Shiva-Shakti = male-female union of contraries, all the

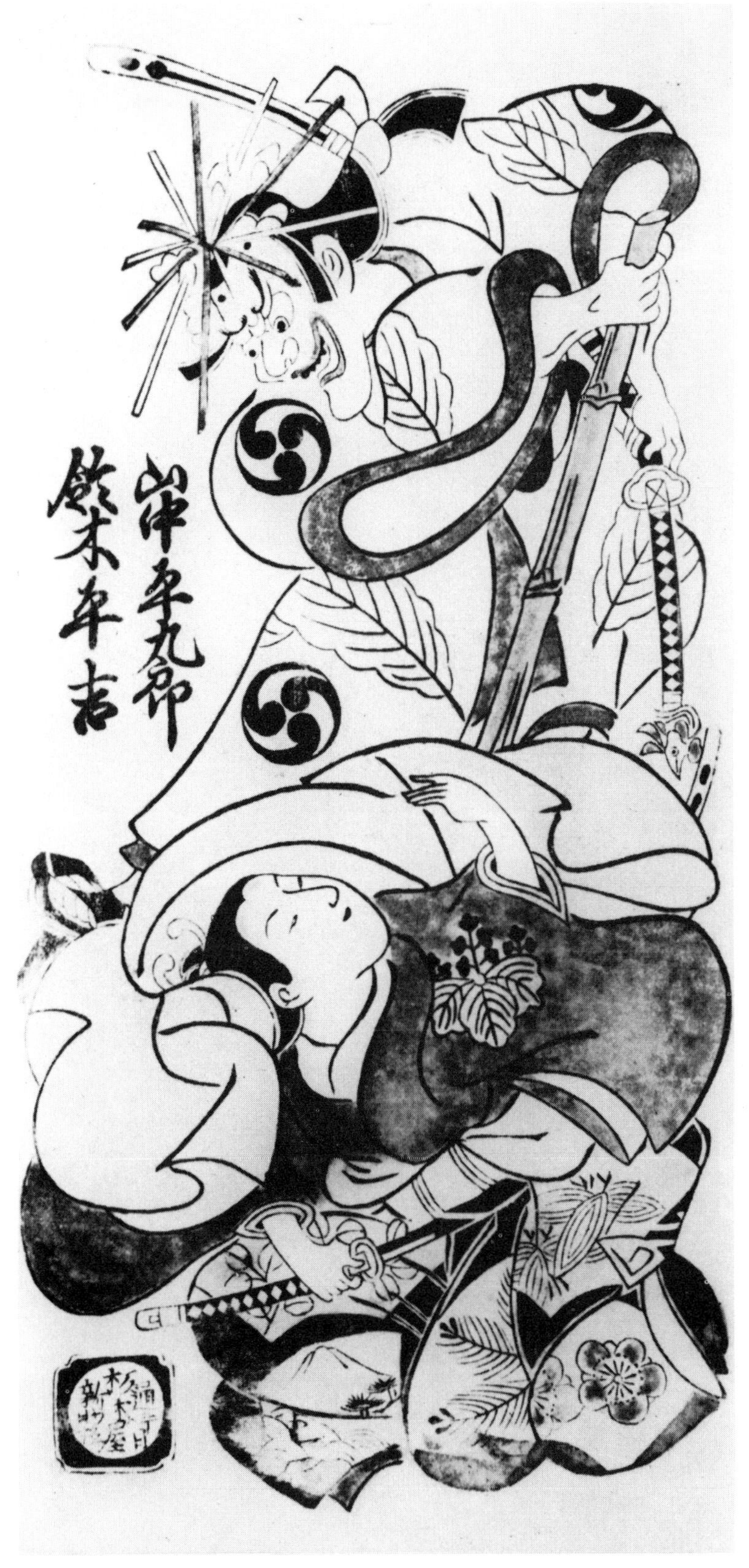

39 Kiyonobu I
Heikuro and Heikichi
Early 18th century

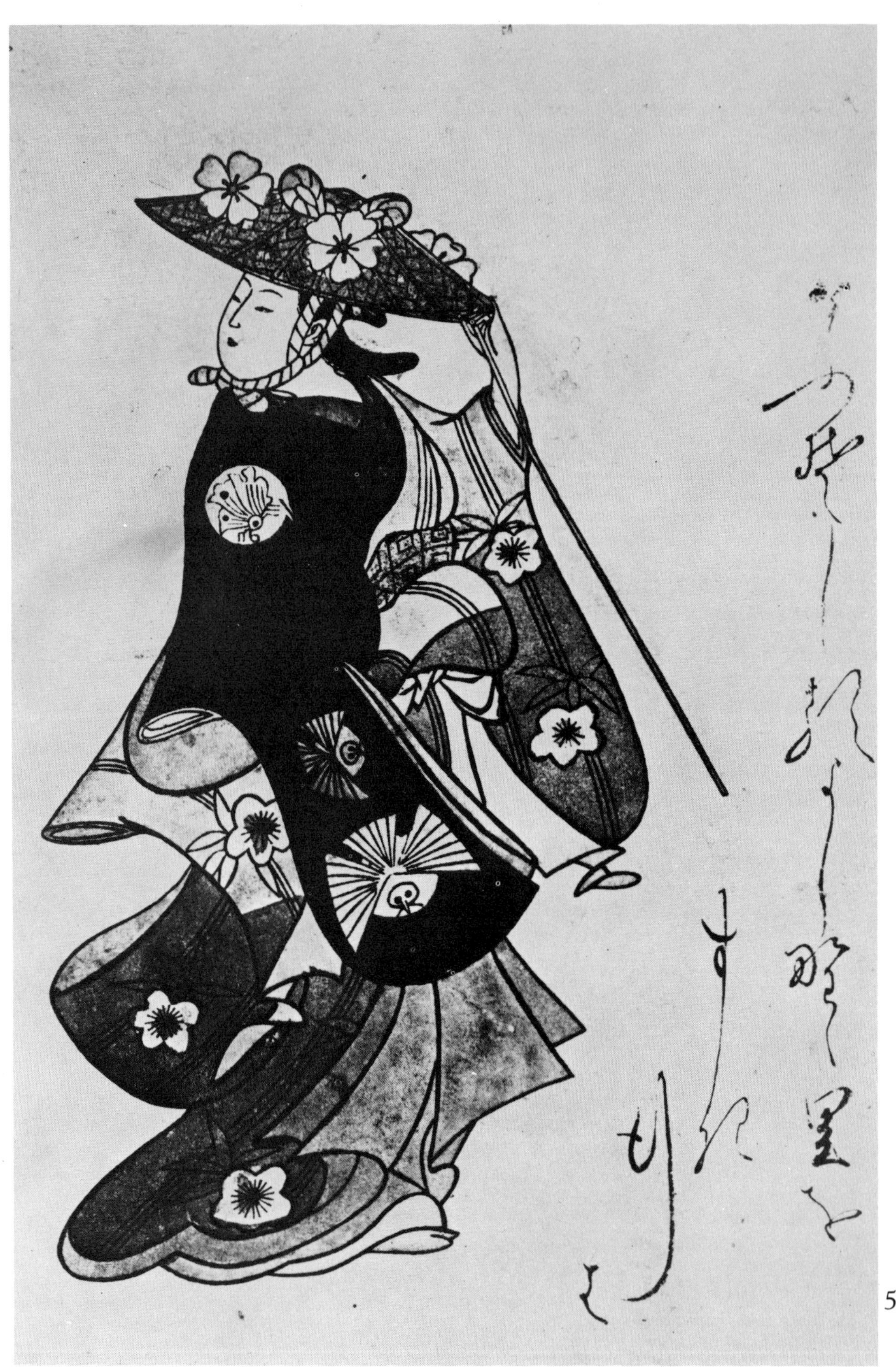

58

40 Okumura Masanobu *An Actor as a Girl Dancing* (ca. 1715)

contraries, as astral-magic copulation, supreme sex and supreme enlightenment made one, by which the cycles of creation-destruction-creation could be endlessly actualized.

Be that as it may, this narrative explanation pales—as I look at it—in front of the simple, *formal* fact that it was never the *nakedness* itself, but nakedness clothed in *nudity,* that the Japanese "pornographic" artist had honored there. And if one might assert the same thing about other historical styles, say the Greek or the Renaissance, one must also add that the Greek or the Renaissance nudity-clothing had always obeyed the ordinance of geometry, while in Japan it was always an ordinance of dance, ultimately of ornament, of body's "frozen calligraphy." The compositional assuredness—the *grace*—of the line, the chosen mimicry of this line-ornament, that winds round the bodies in full sex activity, carries also in it the same persuasive evidence of the beyond-of-the-line, beyond-of-the-ornament, the same sense of total "arbitrary" seizure of the unseizable, that the costumed figure had communicated to us elsewhere. (Japan has rarely been an aesthetical culture—it has always been an artisan, a craftsman culture!) Again—I have it! I mean this much of the body problem, perhaps even of the substitution problem itself: that what covers the body, hides it, separates it from itself and us; what makes it absent, is exactly what makes it be a presence—a different, "another" presence, very precious, very rare, very sumptuous. . . .

A fragrance—a memory—is coming back to me. A momentous evening, rather long ago. But I can see it. On the immense operatic stage of Barcelona's Liceo, a perfect-voiced cantatrice was communicating to a breathless and expert audience the tragedy of sweet Desdemona. A tiny and pretty Verdian Desdemona. Defenseless, in the scene which precedes the reception of her father's embassy, she tries in vain to calm Otello's tempest and love. Her delicate and fragile body supports with ease the burden of her royal attire, but fails to support the pressure of the Moor's blinded hand. She falls pitifully to the naked floor of the throne room.

The Italian singer was a consummate actress: with an imperceptible motion of her limbs and head she made, in her fall, all the folds of her sumptuous robes cover her entirely and spread far beyond her. The precious and unhappy little being totally disappeared under the sombre pomp of silks, velvets, gold, and jewels—an immense multi-petalled new flower now, with its palpitating heart hidden in it.

And no words—I was sure of it at that moment—could have rendered as fully the global catastrophe of guiltless Desdemona—of all the guiltless, in worlds past and future—than this immense growth of a new being out from Desdemona's humble body. What is more: through its own artifice, a calculated operatic trick, the little body lying there on the vast and emptied stage became self-cognizant, cognizant that it grew into a new thing, precious, central, unique among the infinity of other things. That it was both continued-magnified and transposed to fulfilment—as into a "frozen" dance and ritual. And that this sombre and pompous and frivolous mimicry of textile was the very face—the mask—of Desdemona's identity with infinity, her substitution for infinity.

Thus—body: that which hides it, which separates it from itself, which makes it absent—that, exactly, makes it a presence. An awareness. A body-awareness, a sensitivity, at once the center and the periphery. Hypostatized infinity: body.

And the spiritual—what we all still call the spiritual, unless it be a power-weapon, a must-spirituality in the hands of all those who care only to rule—the spiritual is what is felt and thought about the body. . . .

MC: Sweet, guiltless, helpless Desdemona—she certainly helped. . . . From tale to tale, straight to the labyrinth of the legend.

But—please!—don't lose Ariadne's guiding thread. The battle of the labyrinth is nearing, I surmise—the monster, the labyrinth's Minotaur, you know. I see the approaching battle with infinity, with the arbitrary, with the talk about it all. Remember what the ghost said about truth?

I: No—rather his not so mysterious companion. Besides, we have learned how much calumny there was about the youth-devouring man-bull of the legend.

MC: Oh, but you are not just to me. Poor, sweet Desdemona did help, indeed. I meant it. And I am listening—nobody else listens——

I: The spiritual is what is thought about body.

MC: I must interrupt you—sorry! Why should you bring in here the old and insoluble—thus useless—quarrelling about "thinking" conceived as something either separated from, transcending—mysteriously—its physical application (the thinking about the body, for instance), or included, immanent, in the physical, say body-mind, medium—but then in what equally "mysterious," thus equally separating, sense? Oh, don't get impatient with me. I know, it is not a dialogue, after all, that we are staging here, but a mysterious companionship, you and the ghost and his companion and the visitation: one companionship. I am here to accompany you. Let's see whether I understood better than I seemed to just now what you have been trying to tell me.

Shakespeare's Desdemona, her whole tragedy, could be communicated to us through the expressiveness of her body continued into the strange sumptuosity of her costume, her body changed into "another" magic and monstrous performing body-image. This communication you want made one with Desdemona's in-communication, Desdemona's into-herself communication, of her physical being's change: the birth in her of a new, precious, and rare being-body, made one in its turn with the unseizable world of her unique tragedy. Here would be the syn-

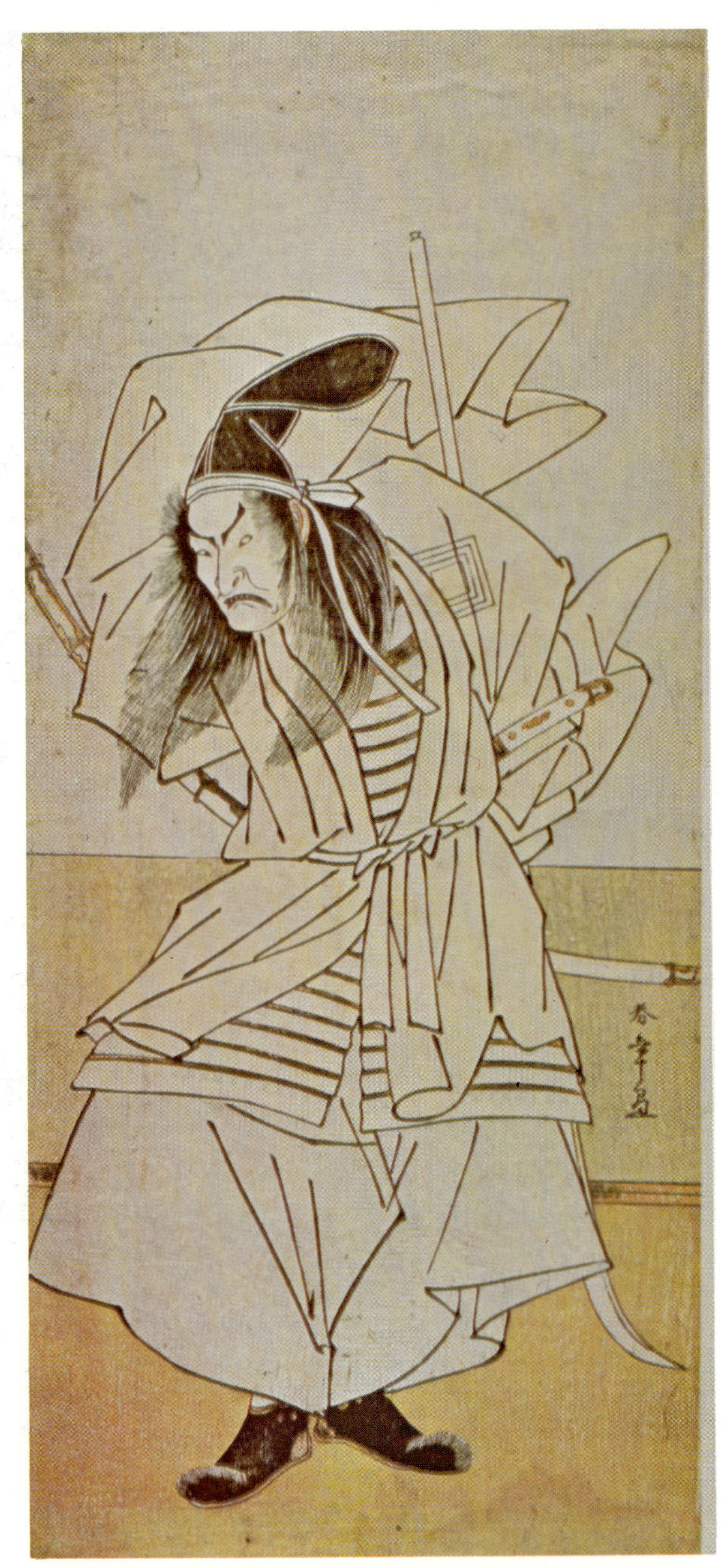

41 Katsukawa Shunshō
Danjūrō V as Tomomori

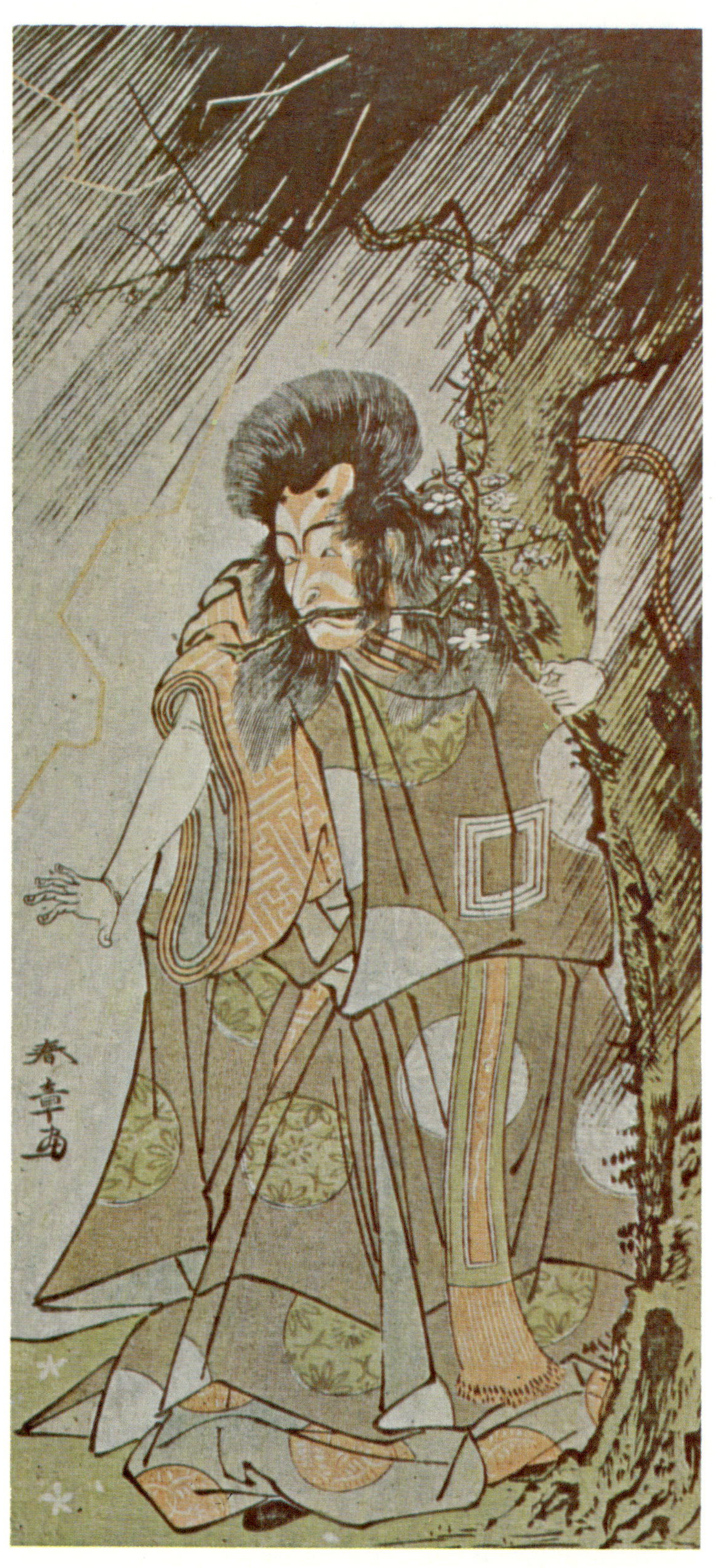

42 KATSUKAWA[illegible] SHUNSHŌ
Danjūrō IV[illegible] as the Thundergo[illegible]

chronous beginning of a visceral, as it were, and of a fully communicable awareness: a visceral-kinæsthetic consciousness and epistemology. And this would already be a domain of the "spiritual" proper, exactly, if I understood you, in the sense of such bodily thinking, in the sense of thought-substance, thought-flesh. Just as if you or I were to have said—and meant it with all the responsibility of a thoroughbred philosophical seriousness—that to think about something is to *penetrate* into it, and that the word "penetration," be it even a simile, transmits an act of fleshiness, is fleshiness itself.

It is most remarkable—take it here, please, as a memorandum of sympathy with your *idée-fixe*—how keenly aware of all this was the "spiritually" tuned humanity of the past. You know much about the exquisite distinction made by all medieval thinkers, west and east, north and south—but especially by the Judaeo-Islamic—between body and mind's " corporeity " and its " materiality." The first, as a finite, transitory, perishable yet definite visibility: *that* body's corporeal aspect. The second, as a general and vague *bodiness,* vague, yet nearer to the invisible, divine permanence. I say medieval, but God knows—or the scholar in checkable truthfulness—how indebted was this distinction, through culture diffusion most probably, to India's pre-Buddhic, Upanishadic, distinction between the notion of man-body, *rūpa,* and that of man himself, " else-more," *Nāmā* or *Purusa.*[11]

And you know also how close is this differentiation, in its close-to-fleshiness feel, both to the " primitive " man's assertion of several " souls " in our body and to the fully matured St. Paul's far-reverberated classification of body-soul-spirit.

St. Paul's *body:* an immanent, though dormant, consubstantiality with all existence—as, say, the vibratory " materiality " of all-breath, of the Stoics' *pneuma.*

St. Paul's *soul:* a still "corporeal," my-body's, Desdemona's-body's, awakening to the fact of its necessary continuance into the Great Body, of its becoming, as psyche-breath individuated, a part of the Psyche Total, Divine, *pneuma* itself.

St. Paul's *spirit:* a body's awareness both of that consubstantiality and this continuance—from something to something. Awareness I say. Not awakening—psyche's very existence—but *the being awake: the coming out,* the self-separating, from the very conditionings of awareness, and the re-emergence as a discontinuity, a discontinued body or being, a *new body:* the *nous,* the untranslatable all-transcending ideality, of the shrewd Greeks.

Here is where the logos of the arbitrary was actualized *ab ovo;* wouldn't you agree?

I: This is good companionship, indeed. . . .

[THE FOLLOWING MONOLOGUE OF THE MYSTERIOUS COMPANION TAKES PLACE SIMULTANEOUSLY WITH THAT OF THE I, WHICH STARTS ON PAGE 63—A TYPOGRAPHICAL DUO—REMINDER OF THE ONE-VOICE-OF-COMPANIONSHIP.]

MC: Good companionship should suffice, yet it does not: in your stubborn Western way, you are forgetting our autumnal, so earnest decision to rest—to relax—after the year's labor. You are hammering, questioning, answering—estranged from irony, from fun. How arbitrary! All right, then! Was it not also decided between us—and the ghost!—that what appears as "arbitrary" to our normal conceptual function of thinking is perfectly normal in the visual functioning of thought? That the arbitrary is a normal existential fact to be simply added to the other facts of existence? In the visual, we said before, the image is not an added, needed element of "symbolization" but a preeminent, given, unchangeable presence, a hallucination, a visitation. And because it is a presence, a visitation, it can be *optically* magnified without losing its "objectivity"—acquiring on the contrary an additional consistency, the validity of a proof: The body-soul-spirit vision, when optically magnified, so to speak, from subtle, individualized, to collective-historical dimensions, becomes, for our satisfaction and ease, a most normal, checkable "document" or fact.

History—this continuous series of hallucinations or visitations—becomes the inner and exciting story of universal planetary types of cultures or horizons. We might call them: Horizon-Body or Horizon-*Soma,* Horizon-Psyche or Horizon-*Pneuma,* and Horizon-*Nous* or Horizon-"Spirit." From one primeval culture horizon, one common source, Horizon-Body, which included them as it were in embryo, sprang the two planetary types of culture: Horizon-*Psyche* and Horizon-*Nous.* All anthropology would, I think, agree that the proto-philosophical attitude of so-called primitive humanity is—within the confines of its "barbaric" or even "savage" horizons—through and through somatic: a body-knot mentality.

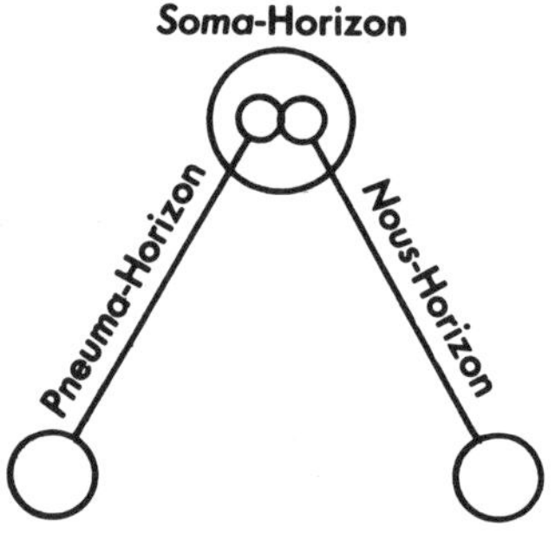

For a member, say, of a Dahomey sib, his individuality, his suchness, his living and loving and dying, makes one with the sib itself, with its geographical natural habitat-being (beyond whose dark zone of forest or bush or water there is nothing but the dangerous to-be-watched-and-destroyed not-being, not-my-sib foe), makes one with the ancestral spirits, the latter themselves, all of them, made one, and one with the life of ancestors when still alive, nay, with life itself as an impossibility to be not-life.[12]

So that death, made one with its image-idea, and with its expressionist ritual, is not any allegorization of hope for after-life survival, but *is* a part, a member of life as such. And all the ritual, the bodily mimicry around this global event, is the visitation of this somatic oneness, this absolute consubstantiality. And

I: Good companionship should suffice. And it does. For you will have sensed here, I am sure, that the arbitrariness of this coming out—the lingering enigma of its being inevitable, thus necessary after all—is not in the very fact of separating oneself from oneself and the resulting facing, thus *judging*, oneself already (the birth of mind's judgment). The " arbitrary " is in the fact, here again, of being *body's* coming out from itself. How is this bodiness, fleshiness, of spirit's first free move to be comprehended?

I wish to confide to you, oh Comrade of my journey and time, a visionary thought, a thought that befits no other place or situation than the autumnal threshold of this temple in Japan, silent, solitary, and huddled against the scented domain of memory.

Now what is strange—an absurdity?—is not so much calling a visitation or hallucination the visual image-thought, or affirming the presence of olfactive intensity in a concept, as the fact that all this becomes normal and convincing the moment you are in it—whether your involvement is more visual or conceptual or olfactory. I mean this: that the moment a natural transfer from a concept-thought about something to its original source, say, an image-thought, is initiated by us, the obstacle is removed for a further chain-reaction-like transfer to another—"higher"? "lower"? —sensory level of mind's activity: the level of scent, for instance. And scent, in such a case, the scent-thought, becomes an explicit co-presence with the other forms of thought. The visitation becomes convincing, and so is the scent-thought, in the very fact of the transferability of sense data. One smells an image-thought, one sees a scent-thought. It is thus that I intend to confide to you my visitation. I say: in order to seize the *bodiness* of mind's " coming out," we have to keep on looking for the initial momentum of this " arbitrary " free move—looking for it backward, always backward into mind's working, till we *touch* a spot wherein the identity, or rather, reversibility, of the initial " ideality " (the " coming out " as an idea, a judgment—genesis of the *nous*) and the close-to-body concreteness (the feel of coming out from something into something) could be established.

And indeed man's critical psycho-philosophical attention has many a time been pointed toward this goal. The difficulty in attaining it lies usually in the fact that this elemental spot of the innermost self—we call it *sensation*, or the immediate direct reflex of flesh-and-mind awakening—is unseizable because it is unretainable as a presence. A sensation is as unseizable as infinity—or our need of infinity—is unseizable. In the dimension of intensity it is as if the simple, elemental sensation, born within and with our flesh, were infinity itself.

A sensation—the thatness, the suchness of it, the whole of it, the sensation-cold, the sensation-roughness, the sensation-loveliness, the sensation-blue, the sensation-volume, the sensation-

MC: yet—obscurely, deeply in sleep—within this consubstantiality there is already implicitly given (but not explicitly shown) the future bifurcation into the "spiritual" currents that will go on nourishing the planetary history of man: the future Psyche or *pneuma* horizon, the future *nous* or Mind-spirit horizon. A Dahomey's pouring into the soil the liquid of the sacrificial offering—chicken's blood—is already an obscurely felt realization of an uninterrupted, umbilical continuance into the ancestral real body; it is thus an act of correspondence between his, the Dahomey's, being and the sib—all-ancestors-all-beings; a correspondence between his feeling, thinking, body-purifying—his or her psyche—and the psyche of the here-and-beyond oneness.

More: incipiently it is also an absolute total identification with the unseizable—for his definite thought—whole, seized in substitution: the chicken's blood penetrating into the soil *is* the whole sib-all-beings-all-him-or-her-self: he or she already chooses to discontinue this consubstantiality's change into continuance or correspondence—already chooses to *come out* from this vagueness, in order by means of it to re-create a witness of the unseizable whole, a material witness, material testimony, a real new body. (And any old, or new, *thing* could become this body: a chicken, a stone, a mask, an ancestor's dead-living dream face, a fragment of unleavened bread.)

A Dahomey, I repeat, or an Australian " savage " or a North American Hopi (when freed from extraneous elements of sophistication) chooses already—obscurely, within the whole body knot of his horizon—to discontinue the correspondence-continuance, to *come out* from it by his or her own will's awakening to mind's capacity of independence, of looking at itself—and projected in the great future—naming this looking at itself *mind, spirit,* the *nous* of the Greeks.

This momentum in history's visitation is crucial. For not only is the " barbaric " world constituted into such a body-knot complex, but almost all the great urban cultures of antiquity were so. And of them, the Nilotic Bronze culture of Egypt's world, so it seems, buds out closest to the Dahomey-like body-nexus horizon in thought, religion, art (the Karnak column—a copy magnified of a lotus and papyrus stem, etc.). Much has been written—and well—of late about thinking in terms of consubstantiality in earliest Egypt or Mesopotamia.[13] The same could be advanced in regard to other, similar cultures: the Mohenjo-daro of India, the Shang of the Yellow River, perhaps the pre-Aztec or the Inca of America.

From the prime source, the Horizon-Body, the bifurcation in historical life-ways takes place. Thence develop slowly, very slowly, the majestic and luxuriant Psyche or *pneuma* cultures, nourished by the conviction that between the finite and the not finite, between the microcosmic and macrocosmic happenings,

I: angle, the sensation-fall, the sensation-levitation—is always a *past* sensation.

It can, of course, be retained or normally reconstructed—as an approximative, yet sufficient semblance—by the mediate activity of our memory: as a fugitive yet “faithful” *impression.* But man—and here it is finally, the first-born move of his freedom!—chooses folly, chooses this: that he can at will possess, seize the unseizable wholeness, thatness of a sensation, by the power—spontaneous if arbitrary—of a substituted testimony-object, any object, any possible *but immediately witnessing* object, ready-to-be object of art. This flower, this color, this “abnormally” broken line, this “geometry” of a configuration in sound, in smell, in visceral touch . . . . Obviously *this* any-artifact, *this* any-object-of-art—not otherwise, not elsewhere. Sensation, the way of substitution, of *nous.*

But another way is open to man. Impression, the way of correspondence, of *psyche-pneuma.* When we “remember” a sensation we lose it as an actuality in us, but we gain an added sense of correspondence with the world outside. For the unseized sensation is reconstructed—remembered—only as a trace, a brain trace interconnected—and only thus concretized—with other sensation traces. The impression is the ever-changing correspondence between such a trace-sensation bunching—let us call it here the trace of a wound in mind's flesh—and its apparently incessant source of wounding, the so-called natural-empirical world around us. Impression is always a form of such a correspondence. And what we call “naturalism” in art, which is always, more or less, an “impressionism,” is this.

But the correspondence between the trace of sensation and its source gives to man only assurance—not certainty—of an actual presence. Only identity could give us certitude: the total identity of an actual sensation, the presence of adherence in it. And man wants certainty. Identity is folly, is impossible, because sensation as presence is impossible—is unseizable. But man wants identity and the impossible and the unseizable, come what may, at the price and risk of his sanity. (“The supreme degree of the doctrine of the Divine Unity is the denial of the Divine Unity.”)[14] This is a man's essential, metaphysical despair and the creativeness of the despair. That's it; we cannot do anything about or against it. It is a fact, and we can only repeat that it is an arbitrary fact, yet existing as fact, thus to be added to the other, the “normal,” sane facts of existence.

Man wants the unseizable. And here, I beg of you, recall the fulgurant equation I succeeded, I hope, in establishing not long ago (fulgurant and true, so I saw it, but how evanescent, I fear, when our day ends!): the equation between the inner man's “lowest” fleshy functioning, the brute sensation, fleshy because functioning by *touch,* and the same man's highest spiritual ten-

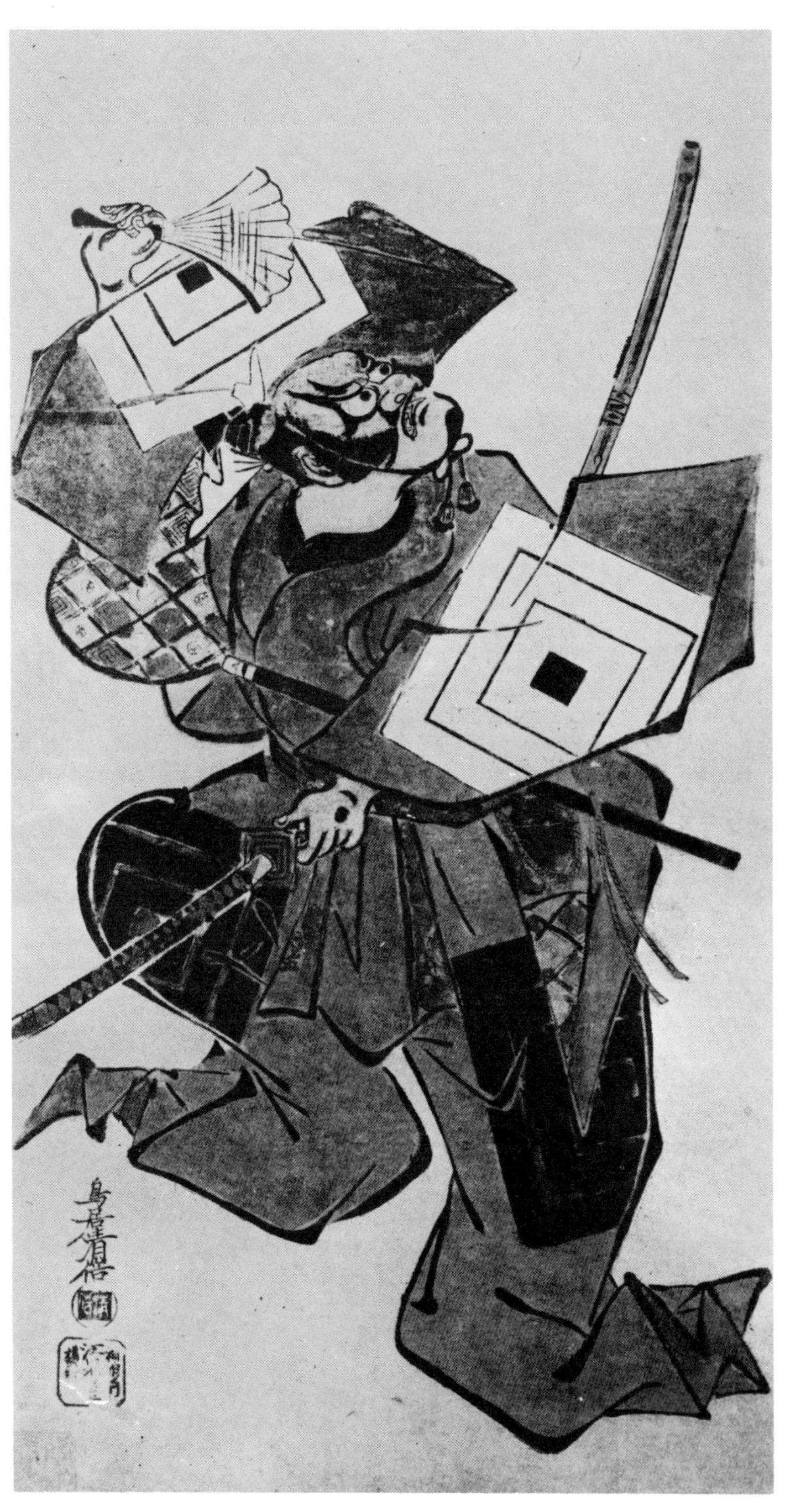

43 Kiyomasu I
Danjūrō II in Shibaraku

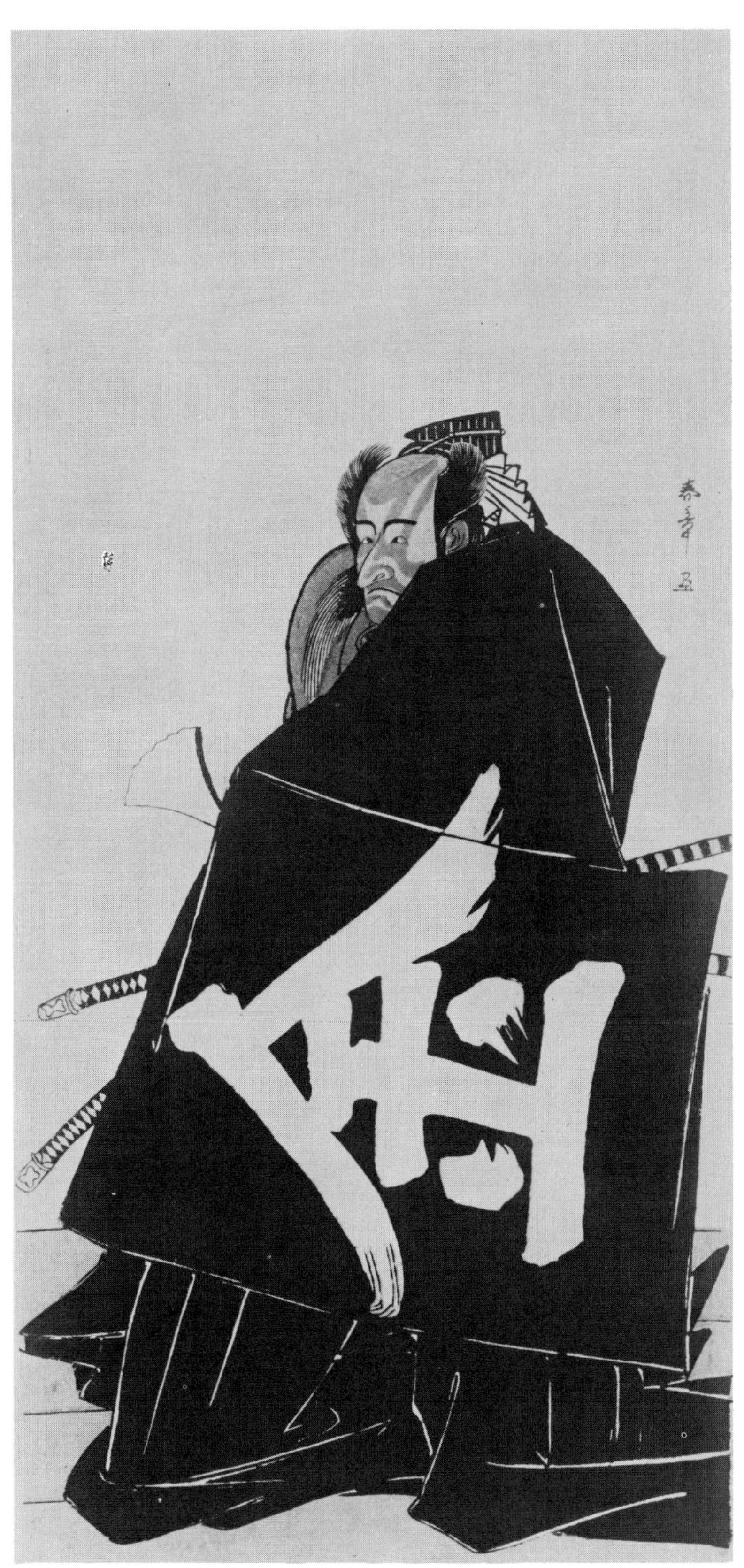

44 Katsu Shunshō
The Black Danjūrō
(Danjuro V)
18th century

MC: there are never-ended correspondences and transformations of one into the other; that these correspondences and transformations neutralize all extremes or conflicts and contradictory distinctions —all the " *harmonic* " Psyche cultures of West and East, from the Celtic Atlantic to Taoist Pacific, passing through the heavy-scented mystic-gnostic zones, culminating (not chronologically, of course, but in intensity and significance of achievement) in the loftiest and most communicative of all: India's Upanishadic and, later, Buddhist thought.

But parallel to this grandiose current runs the second current, the current of Horizon-*Nous:* the few and exceptional cultures—only three, to be precise, the others, similar, having been absorbed by the Psyche—nourished by the certainty that the whole, the never-finished-beyond-and-I, is unseizable, yet exists, thus has to be seized or *touched.* It is most remarkable that all three—the same three cultures we have already spoken of once today—classical Greece, the Prophets' Judaea, and matured Japan, were latecomers in the history of culture formations, yet at the same time were the closest to the primordial " barbaric " horizon of body nexus. All three were born amongst or in the neighbourhood of most sophisticated urban civilizations. All three also went through a similar sociological crisis or trauma, the almost sudden change from a semi-nomadic state to an urban world: a crisis that surely helped the awakening of the still dormant urge to come out from the neutrality of the consubstantial; to touch what precisely evades any touch, the vague, undifferentiated yet ever-present un-finity. Again and again the word " touch " comes back to us—as the only residual token of persuasion.

Yes, I say: to come out, to touch and to seize the never-seizable, by the choice (not a chance choice, but a historically, materially inspired choice) of a substituted presence, arbitrary yet definite, a new form, thus a new art.

In *Greece,* the seizure and the art of geometry; the art of the Law, its seizure, its touch, its art, in *Judæa;* and *Japan's* art of the body itself; the seizure, the touch, and the art of the human *body* —and nothing else—of its pulsating life, self-asserted, self-perceived and perceiving us, as rhythm, as dance. The bodiness, or if you wish, the "spirituality" of Japan's coming out—the poetess Ko-ōgimi's self-perceiving awareness of her own self through the *other self* (the robes that cover her); the mimicry of this substitution; the rhythm of it, the precious, hidden body, both continuing into its emptied beyond, as its assurance, and coming out of it, as its certainty *(Plate 45).* The rhythm, hence: the dance. Japan—all.

Japan, of all the three close-to-consubstantiality, exclusive cultures, the three planetary horizons of mind-*nous* independence—Japan was also the closest to the primordial Dahomey-like body nexus.

45 Ascribed to FUJIWARA-NO-NOBUZANE *The Poetess Ko-ogimi*

I: sion-jet, his desire for infinity, this equally fleshy functioning, because functioning by *touch*.

(Whether actualized as sanctity of the Divine by so-called pre-scientific man, or freed from this sacredness's awe and magic —all the more so concretized or "energized"—by so-called modern, scientific man, this infinity need and thought remains unchanged—an existential fact). For infinity, as nearly as I can conceive it, is a thing of body, because it is a thing of extension: as existence-body extensible *ad infinitum,* infinity cannot disappear —be naught—in the absurdity of never finishing, or never being, what it, yet, is: a finite existence, a body as body, a finity, finally; still, it is what we say it is: infinity. A non-being—a between-being? Shrewdly, the Greeks relegated it away from the physical where it belongs, to the neutral-mathematical, and only today has the Existentialist revenge re-installed it back into the physical with all the logical and moral consistency of a wrong-redeeming act.

I have read somewhere, I forget where, long ago, how, in his early youth, when almost a child, a philosopher of nineteenth-century Germany fainted one day, thinking suddenly about infinity.

At that inexperienced age it could not possibly have been the "unfathomable depth" of a speculative mind that precipitated the philosophical child into a temporary annihilation. It must have been—and how often childhood could provide us with memories of a similar, if less intense experience!—it must have been the *childish,* close to physical-consubstantial existence-response to a new emotion-shock: "How could I become, and then be, a never-finishing, never-finished I-extension, if even in saying the words 'never' and 'finished' I remain within the circle of I-finity no matter how vaguely defined!"

The impossibility of such a happening and at the same time the possibility of such a thought (thinking and thought making one for a child), the unbearable load of such a bodily co-extension between the finite and the not-finite—that is what it must have been, the sudden avalanche of anxiety in the child.

And we all project at our feet the shadow of this anxiety, even at the grey and passive moment of its oblivion, or absence, when our existence is only for sufficient bread and sufficient fun —and stop seeing the intellectualized elite and its anxiety in everything, please!

No—such a stopping would not help. For we all, individuals, histories, cultures, we only do one or the other: we deceive, we pacify the anxiety with our inborn sense of correspondence—sufficient for us, sufficient for our enlightenment and ease and harmony; or we face the anxiety in nude truthfulness, and construct the total, unquestionable, unchallenged substitution—the dangerous, created-by-us, sacrificial substitution, the blood-shedding readiness of the *odium theologicum,* all the wars waged by men in

MC: It is the " purest " of all also (my companionship is asserted here!), in its unaltered loyalty to this elemental consubstantiality; in its unaltered, unique loyalty to what has always been the very core of the entire and complex substructure of Japan: Shinto worship.

Shinto, the "way of kami"—the way of gods, the primeval religious-social horizon, this lovable, Child's horizon within which Japan's later configurations of Indian-Chinese Buddhism could be fulfilled.

Shinto: the sameness of all, as godliness of all, as existence, existence itself becoming acceptance of all—of good, of bad, of rough and gentle—kami being both rough divine spirit and gentle divine spirit.[15]

Not Nature "animated" by spirit-souls, but—in Shinto hallucination—being-souls in flesh, nothing but living, acting beings as in oldest Egypt—bodies, nothing but bodies-kami: a tree is a god—not a dwelling of a god, but God the One-All; a moon-phase is kami; virtue is kami, kindness is kami; vice is kami.[16]

The film "Rashomon" does not tell us—West-wise—a story of brutal sex offense in a forest, seen from four angles of interpretation (four variants of the same story), or four possible reactions in the protagonists, but "visualizes" for us four of such sex attacks in a forest, four possibilities that become four flesh-fragments of hidden reality, four *active, present* body-acts, four concepts incarnated in four flesh-images; four lives—ghosts? A concept is thus a kami present, a body-kami itself;[17] a dog is kami, evil is kami—this child of " Divine Spirit's own mistake";[18] human body is kami; excrements are kami.[19]

Izanami, the first woman and the first wife in the Shinto creation cycle, on giving birth to the fire-kami was badly burned and died—we read in *Kōjīki.*[20] In her death throes she gave further birth to other kami, metal-mountain-kami, boiling-food-kami, from her vomits, from her excrements, from her urine. And Izanagi, her husband and the first man in the universe of recently born kami, descended to the Root-Country—the eternal, *fragrant,* distant underworld—to bring her back to life. But he failed—by his own mistake, his disregard of his dear wife's order not to look upon her. He looked—he looked into the Land of Yomi, the grave (another phase of the Shinto underworld)—and saw Izanami's putrified corpse—and fled in horror, while his wife cried: " Thou hast put me to shame."[21]

And this was the birth of shame—the great innermost body-kami of every Japanese! Izanagi fled in horror, pursued by Yomi's " rough spirits "—and finally freed from their menace, reached the quiet and pure waters of the island of Kyushu, and plunged into the middle reach of the waters, and purified his polluted body.

And the body-purification-kami, the purification-ceremonies-kami, the root of Shinto's ritual, was born here—here, at the puri-

I: the name of eucharistic truth and eucharistic sacrifice for tomorrow.

Infinity: in front of this strange being, the impossible non-being (how is it possible for me to die, I ask you, not to be—yet to be being?), man stands, as he always has, with his despair and his anxiety. And it is the stubborn standing in front of the unseizable that makes precisely this very despair a working, creating, and constructive human spur, perceivable through even his "business first" opacity. Because—watch now, and hail the laughing face of the sage, hail the victory of the arbitrary!—infinity is sacrificed as correspondence, as assurance, as harmony, substituted as identity and certitude and despair.

The same finite testimony—object or being—into which infinity is transsubstantiated contains also, at will, the unseizable single sensation.

And if, terrorized and snatched temporarily by what we call man's power drive, man's political acquisitive power, this living substitution were to incarnate or express this very power, its terror, its mud, and were to become the dead ancestor's mask and its terror, the total Eucharist, the total State, the total Party—yet, when turned again to the other of the two extremes of man's taut bow of will, mud and *amor intellectualis Dei,* it would reassume —O, yes, it would!—the same equation of infinity and sensation and the same testimony thereof: this flower, this color, this geometry of configurations in sound, smell, taste, touch, concepts —man's art and the Eros of infinity made one.

> The noisy time has slipped away even gracefully at Kyoto . . . . when one passes through the dustless streets of Kyoto, where the little houses with moss-eaten dark tiles humbly beg for their temporary existence on promise not to disturb the natural harmony with the green mountains and the temples that the holy spirits built. . . . The Kyoto people, the moth-spirits or butterfly-ghosts, are born for pleasure-making, and to sip the tea. I say pleasure-making but not in the modern meaning; the modern pleasure-making is rather a forced production of criticism, therefore often oppressive and always explanatory in attitude. I say they sip the tea; I do not mean the black tea or the red tea which the Western people drink, calling it Oriental tea; but I mean that pale green tea, so mild that it does not kill the taste of boiled water. It is the high art of the tea-master to make you really taste the water beside the taste of the tea; . . . . We do not call you a real tea-drinker when you think you only drink the tea; you must really *taste the fragrance* and spirits of tender leaves of a living tea-tree, which grew by accident and fortune under a particular sunlight and rain. And, of course, more than that, you must learn how to sip the tea philosophically; I mean that you must taste, through the medium of a teacup, the general atmosphere, grey and silent. And there is no better place than Kyoto, the capital of the mediæval, to drink tea as a real tea-sipper . . . . [22]

MC: fication site of sun-confronting tachibana, the fragrant grove of trees—were they orange trees?

And it was the birth of Shinto-shrine-groves-of-trees-kami, the birth of a spot and a ritual, with no fear in it, no terror in it, no penalties—but pure, white robes and yellow robes of priests, much bowing, hand clapping, waving of fragrant sakaki branches —the worshipper calling, among shadows and sounds of trees, the wonderful evergreen trees all over the sacred grounds, calling on his host and friend, the kami of the shrine, and being served by him with saké—in full fellowship with the deity.[23]

And so—as the Legend now has it—before descending into the pure waters, Izanagi disrobed himself: other kami were born from his garments, kami-thoughts, kami-memories, body-thoughts, body-memories, rough, gentle. . . . After the purification bath, the first man washed his eyes, blew his nose: from the moisture of his left eye, Amaterasu-Ō-mi-kami, the Heavenly-shining-great-august-deity, the Sun-goddess, was born. From the moisture of his right eye, Tsuki-yomi-no-mikoto (Moon-darkness-augustness) was born. From the snot, Take-haya-susa-no-wo-no-mikoto was born, the Brave-swift-impetuous-male-augustness (=kami), the Sun-goddess's misdemeanant brother-obstacle-kami.

How repulsive to a monotheist, how repulsive to a pantheist too. Repulsive, repulsive . . . in purity repulsive. Yet Shinto is not purity but purification.

Of body, of course. The washing, washing, and washing of one's own body. Not washing off sins, not exorcizing evil and dangers and fear (this too, in Japan: for sins and evil and fears are bodies—as in all other "primitive" proto-religions)—but washing off body's impurities *ad hoc.*

(As our twentieth-century doing it is re-thinking it. For the West's twentieth century is—and here is my prophecy!—a neo-plunge into the consubstantiality, into the body nexus, of a Dahomey, of a Shinto world, with all our millennia-long experiences and memories of the Psyche cycles and the *nous* cycles never to be forgotten, never to be rejected, but ever to be overcome—and the obscure dangerous emergence of a neo-Psyche horizon, and a neo-*nous* horizon to come.)

Shinto: Sameness: Amaterasu, the heavenly ancestress, Japan and Japan's people, and every one, the Emperor, *Sumera Mikoto,* one sameness.[24]

So that, in truth, the Emperor is both continued by (in the Psyche horizon), and substituted for (in the *nous* horizon) the great ancestress, she, unreachable, who is the people of Yamato, and the sun and the stars, and all life and all never-death; and the people do not worship their Sun-goddess, they do not worship their Emperor—they never had—any more than they would worship themselves—and would they?—any more than they would worship, say, a limb of their bodies or that waterfall-kami, or that

I: Who was the leader of the movement for the general admiration of the cherry-blossom? It was the children, I believe, who brought it home from the countryside a thousand years ago when it was a nameless flower; and it was the poets of the Heian age who properly introduced it into our Japanese life. The poets were the leaders; and our spirit, which is *of the crowd,* made us follow after them. Is there any greater work for the poets than the bringing of a flower into our lives?[25]

Cézanne's famous "I want to realize my sensation" when textually understood becomes the revelation of a central truth and a constant wish in art and in its history. "I want to realize my sensation": I want to realize the infinity of it. And Cézanne did it, according to his own free—arbitrary—choice. The simple, unimportant and taken-for-granted sensation-weight, the material weight of material objects, became, in Cézanne's visitation-folly (his color-line-volume weight) transubstantiated infinity itself, all, all infinity, all of the invisible unseizable God of the Bible—God forgive me! Cézanne created his own myth by his own personal choice—and so after him did the new century.

But all the other myth-creators of the historical past could achieve the same—less by their own choice of course than by the will, so often despotic, of their milieu and their time.

Only here the further removed was the myth-creator from the patronizing directives of the dominant verbal elite and its interests, the nearer was he to the artisan source of his particular technic's skill, and the freer and fuller was his mythopoeic creativity. How florescent was the manual-visual myth creativity in Islam, where only the verbal was considered worthy of being creative, and where the artisan-artist was left free—by neglect and contempt—within the confines of his craft's idiom!

And what medieval theologian could have imposed—while imposing and dictating the details of inconography—this or that of the meaningful "objective deformation" witnesses in a Romanesque pious image! But it is the Japanese manual-visual thinking "folly" that, to me, I confess, is the most astonishing of all. And by this I don't intend to diminish, not in the least, the beneficent effect exerted upon the narrative content of Japan's "visionary" art creation by the prodigious poetic verbal myth-creativity of China. I am only ready to suggest that China's visual—pictorial, to be precise—universe was absorbed, more often than not (the two, however, on equal terms of respect and care) by that of its verbal elite. Whereas—and that's what I dare to say to you here—Sinicized as Japan may have been, it most consistently, under the disarming disguise of its typical narrative charm, the charm of Japanese so-called "genre" realism, as well as of its Buddhist profundity, freed itself from the impact of the verbal and accepted, in return, the always astonishing guidance of its image-scheme visitation.

MC: rock-kami, or the Mirror, the Sword, the Jewel—the three Shinto emblems of the sameness.[26] And the sameness itself—or Shinto—is a kami, is a body and its mimicry. The Emperor, the people, you, I, the Sun-goddess, are one gesture, one rhythm, one mimicry, born out of the sacredness and the indecency, the shamelessness of the primeval Shinto dance—the dance with which the creation myth reaches its summit and history's true life starts—and still starts: the "kagura," danced by Ame-no-uzu-me-no-mikoto, the Heaven-alarming-female-augustness, in front of the closed rock-mouth-kami and the hidden Light-kami in it. Sacred and shameless dance it was, danced by the Heaven-alarming-female-augustness, who thus saved the two worlds from darkness and woe—the Dance-messiah-kami!

When Amaterasu-Ō-mi-kami, the Sun-goddess, outraged and angered by her mischievous brother's heaven- and earth-endangering misbehaviour, entered the cave whose door she shut behind her, the Plain of High Heaven and the Central Land of Reed Plains were plunged in " eternal night " and woe.[27] And all the eight hundred myriad kami assembled in front of the cave—all the long-singing birds of eternal night (Land?) singing there (was it the birth of torii, tori = fowl?)—and took counsel how to save the Creation-kami and the Creators-kami and to make the Shining One *come out* from her confinement. And great objects of art, the great-new-tricks-kami, were caused to be made: the Mirror, the Jewel—a string of curved jewels, five hundred in number, eight feet long. . . . Then, hanging and tying the objects to the branches of the sacred sakaki tree *(Cleyera Japonica)* and hanging, in addition, white pacifying offerings (paper-mulberry cloth) and the blue ones (cloth of hemp), all the kamis, together with bird-singing and sakaki fragrance-giving, all stood, sat, and lay in wait. And then the Heaven-alarming-female-augustness put on a wig of the creeping foxtail vine,[28] tucked up, as a working woman would do, her sleeves with evergreen vines, grasped a posy of bamboo grass in her hands—and danced. She danced in front of the closed cave entrance upon a sounding board—stamping till she made it resound—as if possessed by a kami. She danced thus, " pulling out the nipples of her breasts, pushing down her skirt-string *usque ad privates partes.*[29] And the plains of Heaven and Earth shook with laughter, and the eight hundred myriad kami laughed together. Then, amazed, the Shining One, slightly opening the door, exclaimed " How is it—my retirement having carried darkness and woe—that Heaven and Earth's merry-making prevails?" And then the Mirror was shown to the Heaven-shining One, who, more and more astonished, *came out* from the rock and gazed upon Her-in-the-mirror, and saw herself *coming out* therein. And the trick-of-art-object-kami and of dance-kami prevailed. And one of the great kami standing hidden behind the rock took her hand and drew her out. And Grand-jewel-kami put

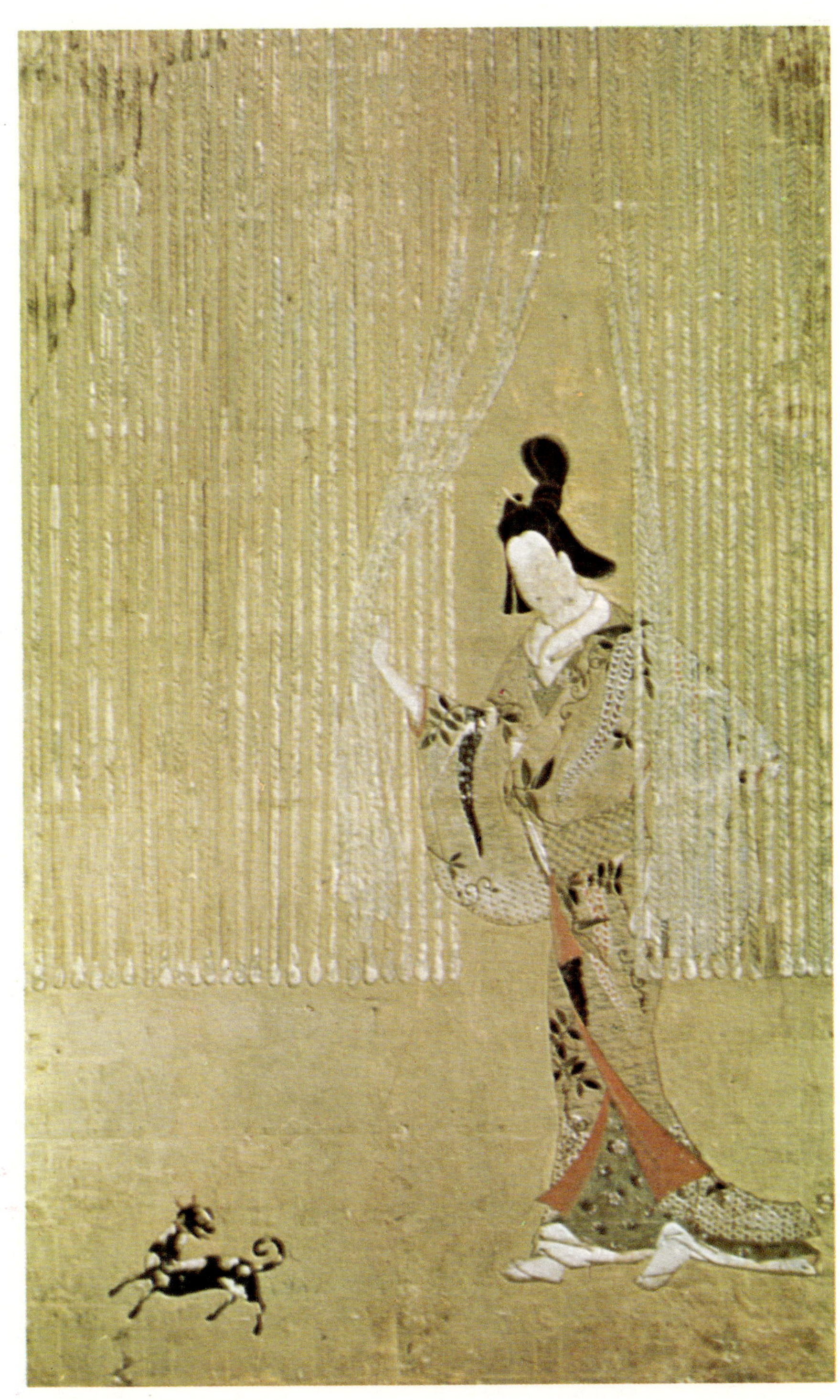

46 Artist unknown *Nawa Noren*

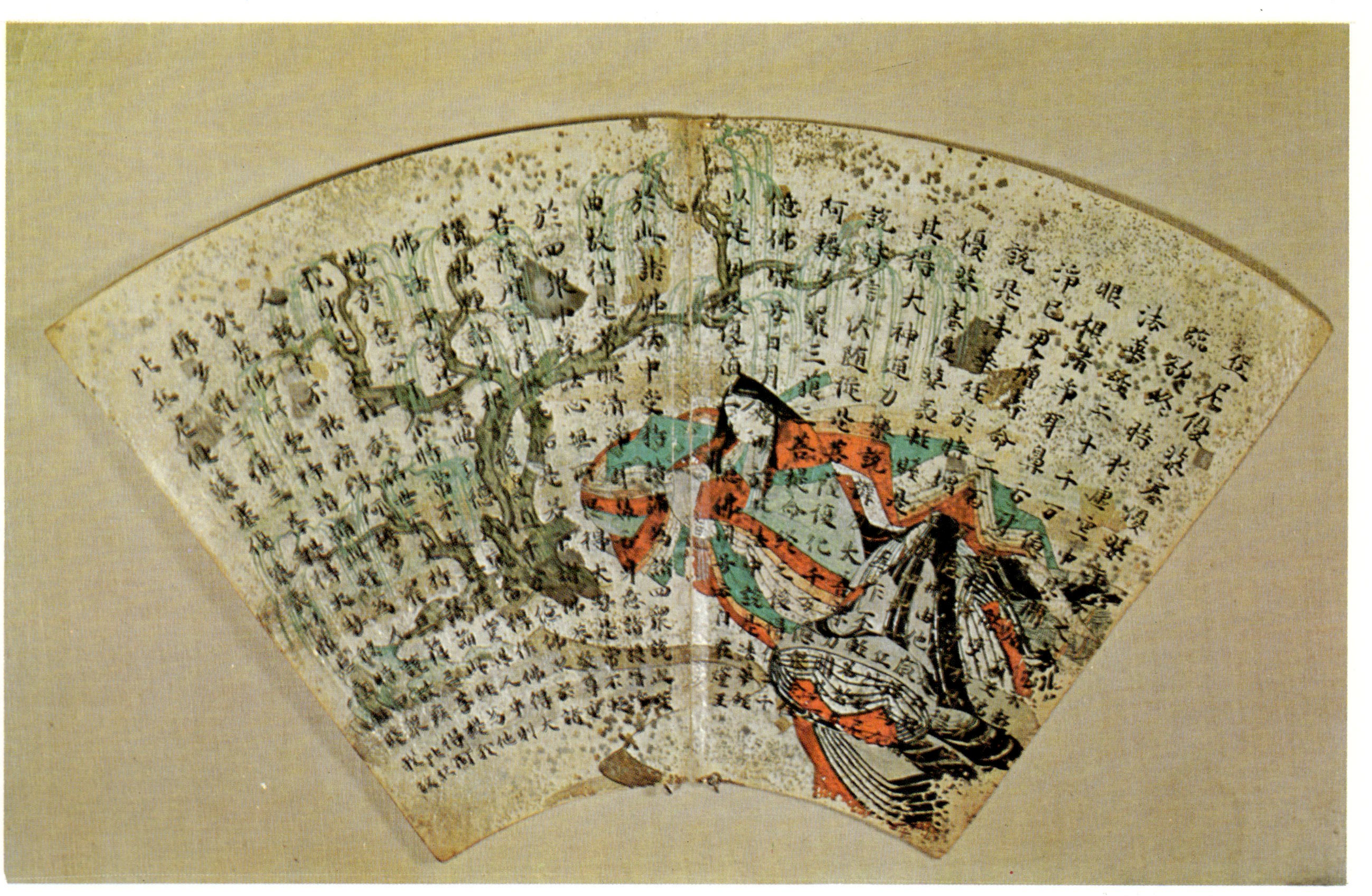

47 Artist unknown *Hoke-kyo*

I: The entire history of Japanese art—except here and there, particularly in the literary theological grip on Buddhist icon assimilation—is in front of us to illustrate Japan's loyalty to the chosen principle of substitution and identity. But why invoke the entire history of Japan's art? Why not—here *in situ*—substitute it, and thus be successfully myth-producing ourselves?

I must confess, more "illumination" comes upon me from saying to myself, now, at random: the Japanese space in painting is a *fan-space,* is the visitation of the typical, unavoidable Japanese folded fan, that reduces, when closed, all its expansion to a narrowest space-motive, the folded fan's mimicry of opening-closing, showing-hiding, facing-profiling, disrobing-robing—more comes to me, and more convincingly, from such a visitation than from studying this space at length in the histories of Japanese painting and in doing so, gradually dissolving the pointed attention. How much more consistent even the Japanese religious or political history as it opens for me by this folded-fan-space testimony!

Look: astonishing, yet so delightful, and disarmingly light-minded — no? — is this anonymous seventeenth-century artist's myth! *(Plate 46)* Nothing there but (but!) the unretentive sensation of a parted curtain's imminent springing or falling back, a sudden and unique little sound-fall, idea-fall, adventure-fall (in homology with Cézanne's sensation-weight), all this seized and told in the adequate and humble idiom of Japanese craft; a folded-fan reduction to a narrowest motive of narration and extension in space. The figure of the girl—the fall of it as it emerges from the half-opened and shortened curtain; the figure of the little dog below—a repeat-ornament of the girl's mannered, artful silhouette—alone there, suspended-fallen, too; everything making one ornament-thought, one "folly," and one icon of the equation: infinity = sensation-fall.

One flesh: the unseizable one. Period.

And again, what Buddhist or Shinto-Buddhist theologian or patron could impose—although possibly imposing his suggestion of a hidden iconographic meaning—this precise and unique form of a myth, created for a Japanese artist-artisan by his hand-and-eye loyalty to his craft's "folly"? Of course, a sociologist of Japanese civilization should be enchanted by this subtle and delicate indirectness of a verbal—perhaps theological—impact, typical as it is of the aesthetic cooperation between the verbal elite and the visual-manual artisanship throughout the entire Far East. The sociologist of Japanese painting would, I fancy, attempt first of all to look into the social structure of the newly established urban-theocratic Buddhism: the five sects of Nara's haughty hierarchic and individualistic elite;[30] then the Heian (= Kyoto) era (ca. 794-1185)—the teaching elite of the supreme all-embracing twin church, Tendai Shingon.

MC: the bottom-tied rope (the *shime-naha* straw rope used in Shinto ceremonies today) about Amaterasu's back and said: "Thou must not go back farther in than this!"

And there, forever—the Legend does not say it in words but in living deeds of Shinto ritual—was born, forever, Japan's art goal: the solemnity, the innocence, the shamelessness of her Dance.

Forever hers: the Female-alarming-augustness and her sameness: the future kagura-performing-child.

And the Child prevailed: in Japan's arts, in building, in painting, in sculpture, in the art of poetry, in the art of living, of voluntary dying, voluntary obedience, and voluntary change.

Meanwhile how metaphysical and victorious are all the innumerable and beautiful young *Saru-me-no-kimi*—ghosts now!—who performed kagura at the Yamato court of yore; all the sweet-looking, sweetly moving twelve- or thirteen-year-old little "miko" who today, in Kyoto, upon little resounding platforms of Fushimi Inari-food-divinity shrines, with pines and cryptomeria all about, in pure white robes with long flowing sleeves and red " hakama " (skirts), long, black hair tied once only and then hanging free, perform, accompanied by flute-and-drum-boys' little music, the kagura—a "terpsichorean prayer"[31]—the kagura of simple, dignified, childish—oh, very child-childish—pure and perverse, little-body rhythms.

And forever also Amaterasu's great Mirror, the main " shintai "—the " deity body "—[32] kept at Japan's most venerable inner shrine at Ise, is thus made one with all the myriad large and small kami-mirrors which, either as humble shintai on a household shrine altar, or as everybody's everyday object of personal care, help a Japanese to *come out* from him or herself as seen in the reflection—to *come out* (and here is the uniqueness of the Japanese social-psychological physiognomy as so acutely portrayed by Ruth Benedict) to come out from *shame-learned* childhood—the post-sixth or post-seventh-year stage of the child's upbringing, and to re-plunge into the child's pre-shame, purified, elemental Shinto stage: "the self without shame."[33]

A Japanese " comes out " not through the " know thyself " concept-image of Greece, but through his *bodily* identification with his or her body's *animate* presence—certainly another presence—in a separate, shining, and inanimate surface-object, the activated, yet inanimate mirror-reflection—a different being there, a different *not-I* body. And this presence, animate or inanimate as a body, is precisely Shinto's true object of worship—and Japan's true and innermost self. The inanimate is given by its very presence, as movement (the puppet theatre, the later Joruri, this Yamato-oceanic root of Japan's theatre-and-painting-tree); and the animate is given by its return to its origins as things = kami,

I: The sociologist of art will find it easy to connect the enthusiasm with which Chinese-Indian Buddhism was accepted with the great need for liberation from the clannish, reactionary vagueness of function and power distribution in pre-Buddhist Yamato, felt by a new aristocracy of land, sword, and throne, young, ambitious, growing in body and mind. How rewarding it would be for this historian to reach through art's imagery and symbolic narration the corresponding and satisfying reflection of those epic events!

As an example: the initiatory secrets of a splendor-dripping Mahayana Buddhist mandala: its power-bearing stunning yantra structure underlying the ultimate holiness of the psycho-cosmic Two-One.[34] Secrets unreachable indeed, except by the worthy individual or group, the lofty, the loftiest ones in social and mental discipline and hierarchy. And then the historian could rejoice in this other sociologically established correspondence, the Tokugawa or Edo era (ca. 1615-1867) and its arts. Tokugawa, officially the last feudal, "stabilized," "peaceful" regime of Japan: magnificence, refinement, inventiveness, unforgettable cruelty and misery, corruption and creeping fear, too; social pomp, refinement, much "philosophical tea sipping," inhuman cruelties of the Daimyos and their noblehearted samurai all over the blood-emptied land; all this—glories and miseries—not new in old Japan, only doubled now by the no less abusive power of the new merchant classes; indeed tripled, revenge-wise, by the endemic and terrible rising of the "low" people of the land.

Feudal disintegration, of course, and in full sociological correspondence with it—behold!—art's expressive connivance. I mean precisely, art's camouflage of this glory and misery; art's splendor, easy inventiveness, refinement, but also, its Ukiyo-e—floating world—"frivolity," vulgarity, even; art covering, thus the more revealing, the social splendor and misery: flowers, flowers, birds, "beauties," colors and gold, the splendid, silly, deafening gold of the pictorial backgrounds. And to make it still worse and more expressive, the revival or enhancement of tantric secrecy in the form of most stunning erotic-esoteric puzzles of imagery!

It is, however, on this sociological level of scrutiny, and because of the undeniable directness of correspondence there, that the sociologist of art is in danger of distortion of facts by an interpretation itself too narrowly direct (thinking, let's say, that such or such social change creates exactly such or such an aesthetic new detail or formulation). It is a commonplace warning—yet too frequently passed over—that a motivation had better be looked for within a different context of human conduct than its own. Such would be, say, the social-economic rather than the purely ideological motivation of an "ideology," or ideological con-

MC: symbols = kami (Izanagi's children born from his polluted garments: thought-bodies, memory-bodies, obligation-*giri*-bodies).

The melodious voice of the reader of the ritual, the priest at the Myōbu Fushimi Inari shrine, saying the prayer—norito—to the Young-food-woman's-augustness—how could one forget it, once having been present there? . . . . " Declare—" the melodious voice gently chants—" in the *presence* of the sovran deity that if the sovran deity with peaceful and tranquil heart accepts as peaceful OFFERINGS and sufficient OFFERINGS the great OFFERINGS thus set-up . . . "[35] and the voice enumerates the offerings, rough and gentle, sweet and bitter—a pure barter. A prayer barter. A prayer pure, not soiled with holiness or sin or morals or future life—for holiness and sin and future life are there, present in the scent of pines around; the prayer is a primeval barter, I say; it is the humble fragment of offerings " sufficient," given—in substitution? in correspondence?—for the presence, the whole, the real and unseizable presence. The barter of a finite offering for infinity.

And it is sufficient. The prayer is the divinity present. In flesh. In close nearness. In sameness again. Listen, smell, taste, touch—don't look at!—but see, the voice whose body was purified in waters, continuing: " . . . if the water which the sovran gods deign to send boiling down the ravines from the entrances of the mountains which they rule be received as sweet water, and ye will deign to bless the late-ripening harvest which the great PEOPLE of the region under heaven have made . . . the princes, councillors, functionaries, down to male and female servants of the six FARMS of the Province of Yamato, will all come forth on the (number) day of the (number) month of this year, to set-up the first-fruits in juice and in husk, raising-high the beer-jars, filling and ranging-in-rows the bellies of the beer-jars, piling up the offerings like a range of hills, and plunging down the root of the neck cormorant-wise in the presence of the sovran gods, will fulfil praises as the morning sun rises in glory."[36]

Japan's Shinto: the body nexus with both the micro-macrocosmic correspondence and the rites of substitution—the " arbitrary " creation *ex nihilo*—implicit in it; in wait there, waiting for a decision and a choice yet to come: to "come out."

This is Japan: the rhythm, the mimicry of a choice yet to come. The metaphysics of the Dance.

Is all this necessary and yet arbitrary—to ask? Is all this arbitrary—and still necessary? Shinto has no answer. Shinto is body-washing, child-bearing. And Shinto is barter. A free barter; free—thus arbitrary . . . . For Shinto is the mysterious—free—companionship.

❖❖❖❖❖❖❖❖❖❖❖❖❖❖❖❖❖❖❖❖❖❖❖❖❖❖❖❖❖❖
❖❖❖❖❖❖❖❖❖❖❖❖❖❖❖❖❖❖❖❖❖❖❖❖❖❖❖❖❖

I: text of conduct, personal and collective; such, the motivation of insanity's symptoms revealed not on the level of the symptoms but, say, in the secret radiating connections of a *lapsus linguae.* It is a commonplace, we all know it. This "psychology of exposure"[37] had been known and practiced by many a thoughtful interpreter of human historical conduct long before a Marx, a Freud, and even a Lavater, had formulated it.

Yet it is—usually—overlooked. In a late Fujiwara (twelfth century) gold-strip decoration, the technique is not, as many a book on Japan would have it, just a silly expression of the Kyoto court's equally silly decadence and effeminacy. No; on the contrary, it might be visualized as a thing of awe, and an astonishing transfer. If effeminacy be there, it would be in the sense of Japan's sporadic plunge into the resurgent greatest past, the body-nexus elemental past, where the Mother, the Child, were one, and where, within this oneness, man and the order outside him, the cosmos, were one, this same one. One, all-in-one are childhood's play and motherhood's protection—freshness, freshness, beginning, always origins, always childbearing, births—games, gods, gods-kami: this textile's design on a Fujiwara robe; this love story of Prince Genji the beautiful youth and the shy Empress,[38] always this blood-craving revolt, real or narrated; this father-son killing and this repenting; this precious fan with sacred Buddhist script on it covering over—so prettily, so "frivolously!"—a submerged "genre"-like—oh, but no! gemlike—tale of Fujiwara court domesticity, deep, deeply submerged in the waters of a still greater and deeper legend *(Plate 47).* And is not Ukiyo-e's "frivolity" this—and more than this, if we go deeper in the legend?

I say: a greater legend. I mean: the very core, the background of all Japan's evolvement (no matter how diversified in its sociological *what* patterning). I mean: Japan's Shinto. The Shinto worship—which is the body's self-awareness: the body nexus with both the philosophy of the micro-macrocosmos and the rite of substitution, the arbitrary creation *ex nihilo,* the only possible creation, implicit in it—in wait there, waiting for the decision and a choice.

Shinto and the choice yet to come: to "come out" from the body nexus. This is the choice—the choice yet to come—and the rhythm, the mimicry of this choice. The thinking of the body, by the body, with the body. The metaphysics of the Dance: SHINTO

✲

✡

On this ever-green trunk, Buddhism came to be grafted.

> A seed . . . produces a manifestation . . .
> A manifestation perfumes a seed;
> The three elements (seed, manifestation
> and perfume) turning on and on;
> The cause and the effect at one and the same time.[39]

✡

The ghost said: "You are about to fall into Zen's big racket—beware!" A ghostly thing to say: the fact of Zen's central influence in fashioning classical Japan is almost a dogma among historians!

Did he mean by racket all Buddhism as such—for Zen is closest, so many a scholar thinks, to Buddha's teaching—[40] did he mean the steady rotting in any religion of its initial and pure humanism, its urge, at first—not for enlightenment only—for pity of fellowmen and help and not-killing; and then, once in power, its change into evil? In Japan—scores and scores of Buddhist monks in the turbulent years of Nara and Heian, descending from their monastery castles, killing, burning, raping, making ashes of Kyoto and other places? Or still worse—would this be the "racket?"—the explanation, the exoneration, or the pardoning of this mud in the sacred name of the essential non-discrimination, non-differentiation, mind-stuff's reality (the doctrine of mind-only = matter-only), the only possible reality, projected onto mind's indifference to reality as human pain and joy?[41]

I presume he would not smuggle away—my earnest and not yet accepted ghost!—in an unbecoming anticlerical mood, Zen's prerogatives of silence and meditation in front of a summit, of detachment for generosity's sake—yet he knows, only too well, Zen's aggressive alliances with the political powers-to-be and their spinal nerve, the stream of all Asia's trade and its interests, its conditionings, its profits, as well as its far-diffused cultural services.

But I also wonder whether, ironically if not in earnest sarcasm, what my good ghost really meant by big racket was this: that nobody is able in a lifetime even to try to absorb the content of the vertiginous quantity of all the Buddhist teaching,[42] and yet, at the same time, that there is nothing *easier* to grasp than the substance and the goal of this colossal overgrowth, provided the vision of the two planetary types of culture-formation is accepted and retained: the open Psyche horizon and the closed *nous* horizon (both types issuing from their common source, the body horizon, both coexisting, yet each of the two in its prominence fashioning a particular culture-modality). And Buddhism in origin and essence is a psyche culture. Its horizon, no matter how widened by historical accretion, lies always in the zone of correspondence and transformation—harmonious, observable: easy. Nothing less "mysterious," indeed, and less "difficult" than the psycho-logy of this necessary correspondence between microcosm and macrocosm. What appears difficult to handle is its heavy numerical and discursive load; according to India's historicist-psychic logical calculus, the layering (within the happenings of both the micro- and the macro-world) of myriads of psycho-individual worlds, each running parallel to each of the ever re-created world-cycles, which, in their turn, correspond, as content and goal, to the equal number of cosmic mind-worlds. In the Indic universe, both Hindu-tantric and evolved Buddhist, comments Avalon,

> the individual life and the world-life are known as one. And so the Tāntrik Sādhaka, when eating or drinking, or fulfilling any other of the natural functions of the body, does so, saying and believing Śivohaṁ ("I am Śiva") . . . . It is Śiva who does so *in* and *through* him . . . . his life and all its activities are conceived as part of the divine action in nature (Śakti) manifesting and operating in the form of man. . . . To neglect or to deny the needs of the body, to think of it as something not divine, is to neglect and deny that greater life of which it is a part, and to falsify the great doctrine of the unity of all and of the ultimate identity of Matter and Spirit. Governed by such a concept, even the lowliest physical needs take on a cosmic significance. The body is Śakti. . . . [43] Whatever of Mind or Matter exists in the universe exists in some form or manner in the human body.[44]

That was Buddhism in India and Buddhism in China—in India, and its direct zone of influence and diffusion, more "mysteriously" dense, prolific, wet, sheltered, elliptic; in China, cooler, dry, cubic, sheltering in its turn the Confucian hierarchic intensity of social watchfulness.

Nuanced with the still vaguely discernible Korean *apport,* Buddhism came to agricultural and collectivist-clannish Japan at a time when she was maturing toward a decisive urban crisis—the urge for an organized elite, for ordering, for social dominion—unexpectedly repeating at so late a date (the middle of the sixth century) the prodigious urban revolution that thousands of years earlier gave to the ancient world the Bronze theocratic cultures. On the background of the body-nexus neutrality, with neither evil nor good beside it, with only the Shinto roughness-loveliness of the divine-all in place of the dormant ethical urge, Buddhism appeared and awakened the choice—Buddhism, the carrier of good and its self-rotting, of evil and its self-exhaustion. It was the tantric Buddhism, preeminently the awe-inspiring weapon of the initiated, of the kingly priest-monks, priest-aristocrats and aristocrat-priests of the haughty Nara and early Heian periods: the Buddhism of luminous yogic speculations about body-psyche, the doctrine of all-Buddhas, all-souls-all-beings-things = One Supreme Adi—Vairocana—

Buddha, and at the same time of the progressively cheapened monkish responsibility in regard to a message of universal-enlightenment-compassion and universal salvation, Buddha's initial doctrine of universal humanism "for Many not for Less."[45]

The tantric Shiva-Shakti Buddhism[46] became accessible to few, to the elite, through the ceremonies of fastidious initiation rites and exegeses—enlightened and enlivened with sacred icons; to many, through the lowered standard of efficient, more often than not charlatanic, magic.

As a controlling power in converted Japan, it did not last too long unchanged. Of the two basic attitudes in Buddhism, correspondence, explicit and dominant, and substitution, implicit though silent in it, the choice of Japan seemed to be predetermined: Buddhism, as a traumatic event, had awakened in the Shinto neutral world the urge toward the "difficult" move to "come out," not the easier solution of continuance.

Of the two main branches, among many others sprung from the Mahayana trunk (mother-trunk represented with such real grandeur by the twin head schools, Sino-Japanese *par excellence,* the Tendai and the Shingon), it was not the Zen branch that Japan had truly chosen, not the influential, "provable," enlightened, necessary—thus "easy"—Zen, but the opposite branch on the same tree, the common, unproved, absurd, "arbitrary" —thus "difficult"—creed of Amidism, the creed and the bliss of the Pure Land, the Land of Western Paradise, where the sinner, any sinner, is received gratis by the Lord of Eternal Light, Amitabha.[47]

The risk of committing a clumsy historical error—Zen! think of it! think of its perpetual, indeed, its growing fascination for the intellectual's eye, as well as of the high-heaped evidence of its preeminent historical role, in Japan especially!—the risk of committing an historical error, as far as I am concerned, is nonexistent. For it is not a matter of a risk—there is only an arbitrary obsession to see and to have substitution in everything that is, or could be, Japanese. Perhaps, just because this obsession is so narrow, it is the only, the most necessary way fully to evoke the contrary—thus to praise most convincingly, most favorably, Zen's sovereign influence far and wide. For is there anything else in the world but solitude-solidarity's two-oneness? A risk becomes the liberty of "another" risk—while liberty itself is but the future of liberty: Oh, my goodly, earnest ghost—where are you? Why are you absent—and always absent?

But wait!—I see the trail of my ghost's scent-thought visitation:

> I am the Zen priest Sujo. I dwell in Kyoto, the City of Peace. In the year of the Ashikaga Shogun Yoshimitsu's retirement[48] to the exquisite splendor of his Golden Pavilion, the Kinkaku, I wrote, as I was asked to do, a short poem on Zen. The image was the moon, the meaning-scheme: what is Zen, the Enlightenment, in the light of the Lankāvatara Sutra; Zen, the mock extinction of this very light by another light —the Moon? About the moon, the best has been said already in bygone days.

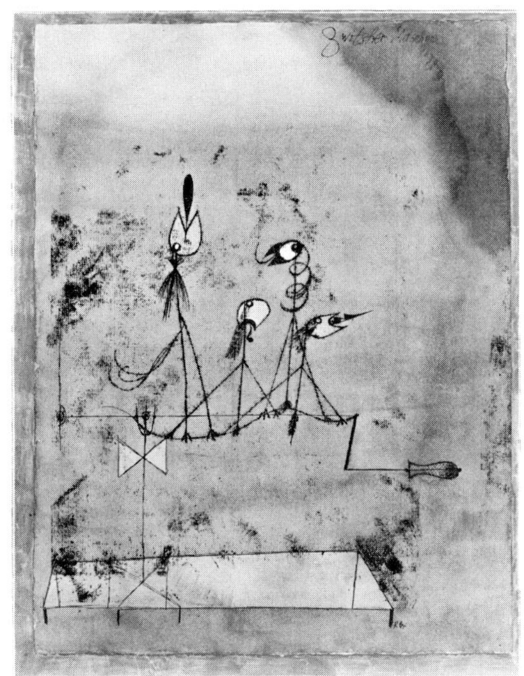

I said the worst:

"How red and beautiful was the Moon
and the other light—in the blood of Divine Indifference—horrible
most horrible!—blood of thousands and thousands of wretches killed
and killed and starved out throughout the country this very year of
Golden Pavilion retirement!"

Then I made an accompanying sketch—of delicate design and of most delicate concern here *(Plate 48)*—" . . . twit—twit—twit: No more machines, my Noble Lords, my Noble Ladies—forever no more machine-worlds. Birds, living, inspiring new birds, twittering new birds only: Glory be!"

And then I signed at the end of the scroll:

איך האָב עס אין
באָד

To The Reader

At this point I, the author of this book, have decided to stop, to "come out" for a while myself, and to address my expected reader directly. Why here, at this point? Because suddenly I have realized how urgent and fatiguing it has become for me—but also how dubious a procedure—to keep on imagining or inventing plausible links and transitions—literary tricks you may call it, of course—by means of which the workings of the principle of substitution in the history of Japan could be conveyed upon as many levels of her historical behaviour as my competence concerning them may have been able to encompass. How to make these transitions without creating the illusion or suspicion of "pulling all the waters to my mill" or of confusing levels of historical activity—a principle of history, including my substitution principle, being not necessarily and synchronically present at all levels of a culture!—How to invent a transition from, say, Buddhism—the point where I stopped—to, say, Japan's handling of her political destiny, and thence (on the way back to my initial and central concern and study, her pictorial art) to that form of creativity to which her pictorial art has been so intimately related—the art of the theatre, the concept of space in Noh and particularly in the later world of Kabuki? But the "literary" necessity to use such links comes, as a rule, from a different source in a writer or conveyer of a vital, personal conviction, namely his sense of responsibility in front of a risk of choosing or of having chosen the wrong conveyance or "proof." Now, there is no risk involved at all in my case—and the Mysterious Companion has already heard this—there is simply an obsession, an intensely persistent, aggressive conviction that everything in Japan is, astonishingly of course, saturated with what I have called substitution and identity: the Amidist Buddhism, so Japanese, a Noh play, the political-social institution of the shogunate, a Ukiyo-e print.

To justify both the transitions and the principle here, no "realistic" links are necessary. To visualize, to see them while directly passing from one level to another suffices. Precisely, to visualize. To see as one sees the fullness and concreteness of a hallucination, and to be obsessed by it. I expect, of course, that the reader will say such an elimination of the responsibility of a scholarly risk is tantamount to shifting from what we call risk to what we call arrogance. And aren't we tired of literary "confessions?"

My defense would be again:

Obsession

READER *(politely):* Mysticism, to be sure, sir; or—mysticism again!—an uncontrollable ambition on your part to introduce into the historiography of art an "original," extra-rational element, the twentieth century's "objective deformation"—and to have fun with it.

AUTHOR *(politely):* Possibly. You might be right here. Possibly, my urge to write about Japanese painting the way I do—as a visitation, a multi-presence, with the documentary facts versus ghosts, mysterious companions, etc.—is a mystic urge. The accusation—and it is one—is grave: it could exactly be my own. For in rejecting the mystical abuses I gladly accept the general social interpretation of mysticism as of a danger still overhanging man's liberation from the externalia of reactionary superstition. But—and without transitions here too—listen, please, to this Vision:

Since its very beginnings, the organized and organizing reasoning in man has fought, fiercely, the "irrational" or "super-rational" subversiveness of mysticism with every weapon, pragmatic and speculative, at its command. The various results of this struggle mark out the roads of all civilizations, as halting-places where mysticism was absorbed by victorious yet condescending reason.

This agelong hatred lies much deeper, in its motivation, than the "natural" repugnance of reason for the irrational, or anti-reason. It lies deeper even than the level, itself deep enough, reached by sociological interpretation: the life-and-death struggles between the verbal elite's stratum

—professorial theological, professorial literary, professorial philosophical—and the stratum of mystical thinkers and agitators. The first, almost invariably allied to the joined (or disjoined as the case may be) powers of state and church, who, as all powers are, are in constant need of being rationally verbally justified by this elite's dialectical abilities; the second, almost invariably too, linked, especially during the so-called medieval eras in the West as well as in the East, to all forms of heterodoxies, and not infrequently forced into alliances with the subversive socio-religious disorders, revolts staged by all lower social strata.

But still deeper than all this is the unwillingness or incapacity on the part of the verbal-conceptual structure of human thinking to admit the realities of the latter's visual structure—which is exactly the structure of mysticism itself. Visual—and mystical—perception is based on the immediacy of the given image, on its bodiness, fleshiness, and on the urge of the image-function to construct—in fulfilment of the symbol-productivity of human thought, a new *form,* a new schema, thus reversing the interrelation of these components in normal "verbal" functioning. (I have spoken of this once before, the reader may recall.)

Mystical perception is this hated image-flesh, a vision-presence. A folly. And what, in addition, makes it still less acceptable, is the frequent misuse, or misunderstanding rather, of this visual structure by the mystic himself. I mean by that the misunderstanding of what is the end-product of visual as well as of any other mode of comprehension: the symbol and its conduct.

Very frequently also, it happens that our, one could say physical, attachment to the idiom, the *what,* of the visionary—mystical—symbolism of a given period makes it that much more difficult, and painful—unfeasible in most cases—for us of another period to see that the full content, the *what of the how* content, of that symbolism can be transferred into a new idiom, a new *what* appropriate to our era.

To one mystically led, how sweet, how warm and cosy it is to participate in the visitations, contemplations, and silences of an Eckhart, or Milarepa; the Poverello's *stigmata,* Saint Birgitta's *nails in the flesh!* But should it be forgotten that in their own time those ejaculatory visions were rude, "difficult," inevitable, and dangerously threatening to the established orderly powers and their *mud*—sweet, fraternal, and warm only in the ardently cool universe of *amor intellectualis?* Ardently cool universe, indeed—ardently watchful over the dangers and the ease of mystical habits or attachments!

For the history of mysticism—*the history of the visual*—is made of painful changes in the apparent content of mystical thought and vision, where it would seem that its "spirituality" was being destroyed, while in reality the vital core of it was being proportionally reinforced.

To give you but one example, major it is true: What guided if not promoted the anti-mystical mechanization of the West and the gradual physicalization of the concept of matter was exactly the visionary mode of knowledge, the visionary in its most direct, practical implications, the *optical.* It is known today that—helped by the previous achievements of the Islamic mathematical mind, the daring, already non-Euclidean deductions of the poet-mathematician Omar Khayyam (d. 1132) or of Nasīr al-Dīn al-Tūsī (d. 1274) and others—this "materialist" progress was essentially the outcome of a gradual passage from the supremacy of a perceptual, yet still verbal appraisal of the empirical world to that of a purely optical, non-perceptual grasp of the same world: the first, its source classical geometry, measurable, static, serial, discontinuous; the second, basically Asiatic, algebraic, undifferentiated and continuous, functional. The final result of this crucial shift was not the abandonment of the classical rule, but as is usually the case in great changes of culture horizons, a synthesis of both. Yet it was the optical mathematical that was in the lead. The so-called Renaissance era of the West is this, more than anything else. It started, as is usually the case in history, with a simple artisan visual-manual invention, G. B. Alberti's peepshow or "carpenter's" device,[49] by means of which finally (but not exclusively, of course) the illusion, the optical bodiness, the three-dimensional space, could be abstracted from the ever-changing continuum (the silent objective empirical world of Korzybski).[50] And so the optical mathematical could gradually make its way into the main channels of man's thinking and acting in the West. The capacity, at once engineering and artistic, to construct the volume-body of an optically present object without the necessity of actually seeing it while in construction, but only visualizing it mathematically as a simultaneous and calculable presence of projective properties of functions, of extension, of *pose* in space—that is what, in its still hidden promise, it was, that and much more of course, the momentous "artisan device" of Alberti!

Out of these beginnings all the far-reverberating energy of projective and analytical geometry, and thence, all the strange "visitations" of multi-relational mathematical universes of the modern era could come forth. The structuring of a thing could be seen without being looked at: the fleshy—oh, how fleshy, alas!—visibility of the nuclear explosion could be structured as a result of the most innerized, invisible calculus vision ("spiritually," "miraculously," this would have been styled in the "mystical" days of long ago)—the result simply of a mathematical projection of predictability.

There is nothing today in the world or multi-worlds seen by the "mechanized" engineering mind-eye—from the unreachable visibility of the internuclear, submicroscopic, and the interstellar happenings, to the "vulgar," pernicious for many, visibility of optical-mathematical gadgets of popular amusement, a camera, a moving film, a television set—that is not part of this innerized and new vision.

The commercialized and vulgar abuse of these inventions and the resulting dangers of automatically injected bad habits of thought and even conduct—how true is all this! And how laudable and noble in its intention and purpose is the intellectual elite's outcry, their growing protest against this abuse, and their remedy: purification of content, de-commercialization, socialization. Yet also, how dangerously useless all this verbal protest, if, at the same time, it does not carry with it the full acknowledgment of today's crisis—the crisis of innermost man and his body, the West's global shift to a new, visual-mental horizon—the acknowledgment of a neo-humanistic, therefore moral, "spiritual" message, to be found precisely in the projected technical, quantitative results of this shift, in the very inventiveness of our visual-optical age itself!

To welcome the spirituality of this message (the "spirituality" of a gadget for popular amusement!), to accept it, not as a platform for technological power supremacy, of course, but as today's temporary actualization of a visionary, truly mystical undercurrent in human history, unhesitatingly to promote and foster both the philosophy and the practice of this inventiveness (inventiveness in Whitehead's sense when he spoke of the nineteenth century's greatest invention being that of the technique of making inventions)[51]—this could be the real tool of reformatory—perhaps revolutionary—spiritual action on the part of the protesting intellectual elite of our age.

Asia, fully awake again to the vision of its own roots of knowledge, which are roots of the West too, knows it. Its verbal elite is more and more keenly aware of it. But the West is not. In the West it is only the new twentieth-century artist—whether artist-artisan, artist-poet, artist-philosopher—who knows it. The engineer-inventor himself knows less. And still less, much less, the verbal professorial and literary elite as such. This would be my own version of "the treason of the clerks."[52]

Treason it is—but why so solemn an accusation?—because the undercurrent of this epic shift I am speaking about has its source in another, much deeper shift, about which something has already been said in this book:[53] the shift on the stage of history and of epos, from a quality center of spiritual gravity to a quantity center; from the spiritual on behalf of the person of quality to the spiritual on behalf of the person of quantity: thousands and thousands, millions and millions of human beings, men, women, children, adolescents, thinking, facing us and existence here, now, in obscurity, in semi-obscurity, in light—all over the world from all strata of social-mental conditionings . . . . Exactly, precisely—the substitution of quantity for quality, the epistemological identity of the two categories.

Precisely, exactly, the Western paradise, Amitabha's bliss for all—its presence, its body, for all: *Namu Amida Butsu.*

We are back in Japan—without transition. Back home. Back to my obsession and its justification: that it is not dishonest.

My obsession: the intensely persistent conviction that everything in Japan is saturated with substitution or the identity principle: Japanese Buddhism, a Noh play, a Ukiyo-e print or the institution of the shogunate.

"Realistic" transitions or links are no longer necessary to justify both the principle and its simultaneous activity on different levels of Japan's historical existence. To visualize all this together suffices. To visualize. To see it as one sees in exaltation or folly a hallucination, its fullness, its concreteness.

The *nous* of Japan. No transitions any more. And I choose, I the wayfarer upon the level of Japan's political history, as its typical and most striking expression of rule and administration, the famous institution of the shogunate.[54] In its apparent functioning this institution is not different from any other political form of delegated central power practised in any other culture. And indeed that is how the shogunate is usually appraised by historians of Japan, foreign and national.

It could easily be likened to the famous Islamic vizierate, for example, by means of which the burden of administrative and even legislative responsibilities was lessened for the head of the government by transferring the heaviest part of it to a chosen high servant—a khalif's delegate, or a sultan's, or an emir's. Yet neither in Islam nor in the West did such a power ever become the total substitution for the supreme power. There, even in its extreme abuse, it could only be a total usurpation—exactly what Japan never knew, could not have known.

Under different disguises or titular names[55] and with different hierarchic degrees of officially delegated duties and rights, the principle of the shogunate—and this long before an actual shogunate existed—was the supreme power itself, a direct, total one-power, elemental, unchanged. In other words, the Emperor himself in transubstantiation. And the people. And the shogun.

The institution of the shogunate—it too—was not an abstraction, an idea, a schema applied to political thought and practice—it was a body, and it was this body's mimicry: the Japanese myth and the form, the art of this myth; the sacrificial identity of the Emperor, the divine ancestress and all the ancestors, the people, the shogun, the arts, the trees, the ghosts. It was both Shinto and the "coming out" from Shinto.

That the Emperor was frequently abused and ill-treated as a particular person—bereft of support, humiliated, forgotten at times, almost reduced to mendicity, he and his in his huge sacred dwelling—did not change the real situation. The Emperor was present as a collected body-presence, as a visitation that lasted throughout the entire history of Yamato—in its essential being, still lasting today, unchanged.

The real change in tomorrow's Japan—if desired—would come only from a total change of horizon, the epic change from the substitution attitude to one that in spite of all is still lacking there, the micro-macrocosmic attitude imbedded today in what we call the scientific-experimental, multirelational attitude.

It is, in this respect, a most edifying thing to see how in today's China —historically built on the hegemony of the correspondence or transformation principle—the total change, when it had to come, came led by the opposite and not-Chinese principle and attitude: that of substitution. On this the solidity of Red China is mainly based.

But why, you might ask me, would a total change of horizon be desired for Japan? I think because, undeniable as the omnipresence of substitution in Japan may be to me, it would not mean—far from it!—that its different embodiments there have had the same beneficial value. Magnificent, beneficent in forming Japanese art, it was abominable, maleficent in politics. The institution of the shogunate was the great pity, the misery of Japan's evolution. We should welcome the real, global—"spiritual"—change, yet to come.

❖❖❖❖❖❖❖❖❖❖❖❖❖❖❖❖❖❖❖❖❖❖❖❖❖❖❖❖❖❖❖❖

Let Japanese painting be truly mysterious today: that is to say, not only an art mysterious, but a word mysterious, the word *mysterious*, mysterious itself—and left alone, to remain so. Let this be an explanation both of what Japanese painting is and what the term *mysterious* is. And let this be done precisely, by saying that the mysterious is the discovery of the mysterious and therefore, in being such a discovery, it has to be explained and at the same time it has to be a failure, a failure of explanation: mysterious.

Let thus mysterious Japanese painting be fully a failure of explanation, such, and the same as, in its positive sense, a scientist would have in mind when he says: "A well-verified hypothesis will probably continue to lead to correct inferences even if it is wrong."[56] Or: "The truths that we seek today may find expression tomorrow in sentences containing words that are unknown today."[57] Or, when so truly Japanese a mind as Chikamatsu Monzaemon's[58] would conceive such a "failure" as the true and truly mysterious "success." "Art," he said, "is the layer that lies between the skins of truth and falsity . . . That which is false but not false, true but not true—that is what gives joy."[59] For a failure is not the contrary of success—was it not our visitor today who said this already? What is called success would be the accomplishment of a goal already known or prefigured, a static goal, predictable, thus as such, self-erased amongst the ever-changing unpredictable motives; and what is called failure, an accomplishment of a goal as yet to be discovered, moving, changing, thus existent unpredictable amongst moving, changing motives, also unpredictable.

Let Japanese painting be truly mysterious today, with no "smell of mendacity," the smell of "successful" explanation in it, not even the faint memory of last summer's smell, only the smell and the sight of today's autumnal day upon it. For just as in man's outermost body—his senses and the stars—the time of autumn is the time of fruits ripe, ready to fall, fallen already—the sense of autumn's sight!—and the time of spring, a time of seeds and of planting—the spring's sense of touch!—the time of winter, a time of laborious and vigilant expectations, of seed and fruit expected—the winter's long listening-to-come!—and the summer, when summer is there already, a time of surprise, of sudden and rapid identity, the seed and the fruit, the sight, the touch, the listening, one, only one sudden and rapid flower there—the summer's sense of smell!—so also, exactly, in man's innermost body, summer is the sudden and rapid identity of question and answer, of seed and fruit; the vigilant and laborious expectation of answer-to-question; spring, the time of questions only, and autumn, of answers only, answers ready, ripe, ready to fall, fallen by themselves already—unquestioned, unquestionable.

And so let Japanese painting be today, the day of our autumn meeting, the ripe, ready, fallen fruit, the necessary, unavoidable, unquestionable —fallen by itself—answer, with no seeds of question, no answering, in it: at once answer and failure to answer. Exactly and truly, the mysterious discovery—with no explanation, no transitions or links, reader!—that Japanese painting is the truly mysterious manifestation of the unseizable to man, a descent, always the first, never twice the same, of God to man: an *epiphany.* And that this descent is not the descent of the unseizable, total Responsibility to man's responsibility, as in Judaea, nor of the unseizable and total Geometry to man's geometry, as in Greece, but the descent of the unseizable total Body to man's body, the epiphany of Dance: "at its kinæsthetic deepest self, a physical awareness of being not *what* but *where* one is. A physical awareness awakened in the very presence and self-ordering of body's touch, multiplied *ad infinitum,* with the outside of the body . . . . a 'frozen calligraphy' by which something precise is communicated in the body's pose, the body's halt: its *aeternitas,*"[60] at once a dance and a metaphysics.

That is how Japanese painting was "successfully" explained today by us, here—its real and mysterious answer self-erased instantly then, and instantly also reborn, substituted by an answer, ripe, ready to fall, fallen from another art-tree: the staged image-word-dance—dance heading, here too, the epiphanic descent!—of Japanese theatre.

In the Noh plays, as Fenollosa sees them and sees them so truly,

> the god is the chief actor, sometimes in dramatic relation to a human companion. The god always wears a mask. The solo part is established; and herein the play differs from the Greek, where the original rite was performed by a group of priests, or (in the comedy) by goats or fauns.
>
> The most certainly Japanese element of the drama was the sacred dance in the Shinto temples. This was a kind of pantomime, and repeated the action of a local god on his first appearance to man. The first dance, therefore, was a god dance; the god himself danced, with his face concealed in a mask[61] . . . .

. . . . Japanese art of painting is the autumnal descent of God's image to man's stage, of painting to body's halt. "The plays are at their best, I think," notes Ezra Pound,

> an image; that is to say, their unity lies in the image—they are built up about it as the Greek plays are built up about a single moral conviction. . . .[62]
>
> The play *Awoi no uye* (Flower of the East) opens with the death-bed of Awoi [the court lady who was deadly jealous of the other and later co-wives of the beautiful Genji], and in Mrs. Fenollosa's diary I find the statement that "Awoi, her struggles, sickness, and death are represented by a red, flowered kimono, folded once length-wise, and laid at the front edge of the stage."[63]

. . . "A red robe folded once"—the first, never twice the same, descent of the Divinity into man: epiphany.

Epiphany that is not to be explained theologically, psychologically, anthropologically, historically, successfully—such, say, the descent of a Sumerian or Akkadian divinity, carried processionally along the terraced slopes of the Ziggurat from the top sanctuary down to the smaller shrine atop the soil and at the mount temple's foot, the epiphanic presence of the giver of fertility finally consummated then, the fertility of land guaranteed, and the fertility motive of the epiphanic manifestation thus sufficiently ex-

49 Artist unknown *Landscapes with Sun and Moon* (detail)

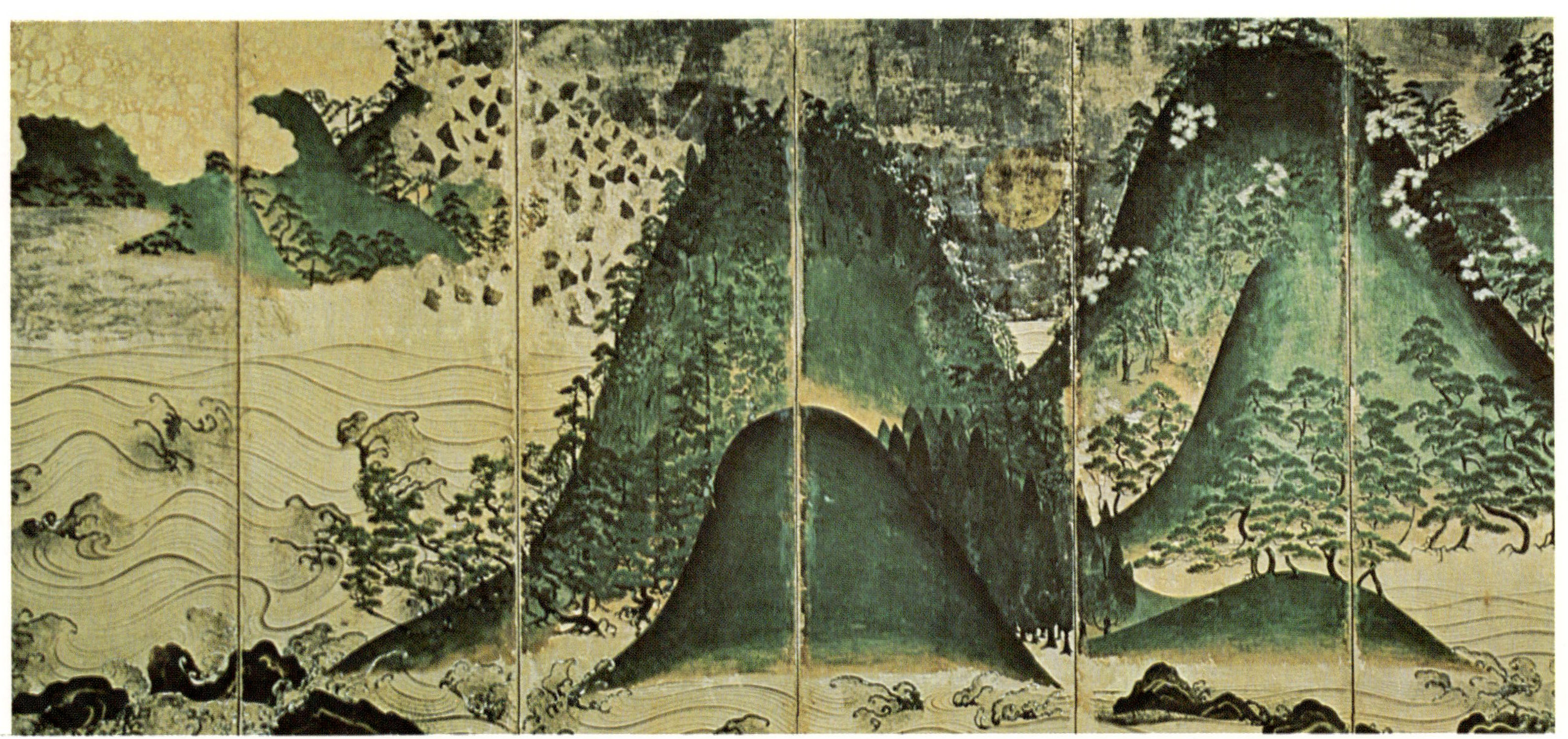

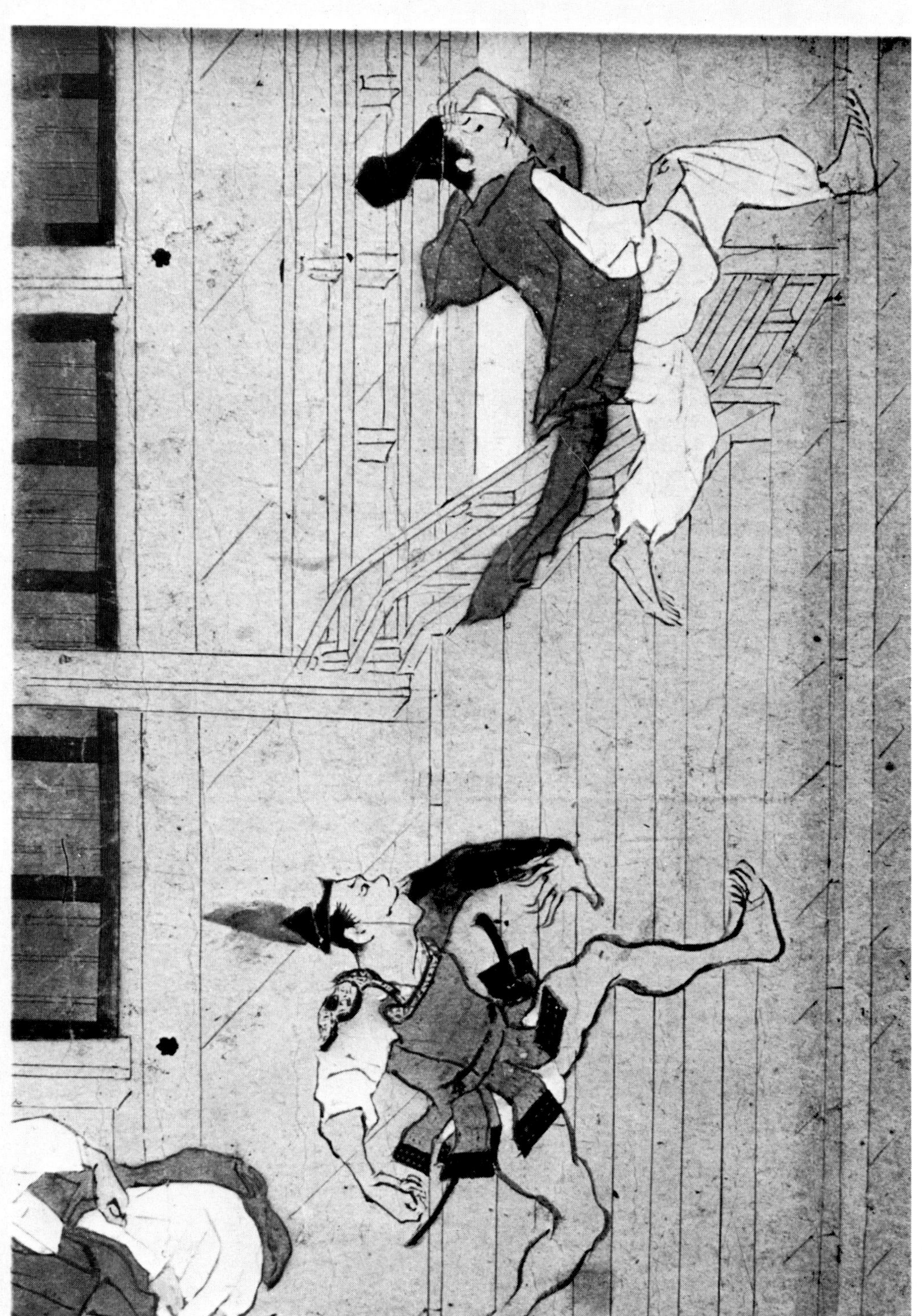

plained—no, but epiphany as a truly mysterious visionary act, of God-image, God-thing, *res*, becoming God-*persona* during the operation of His descent into man's low shrine, of His downscape into man's mental (= abstracting) and ceremonial (= mimicking) seed: a substitution of the inanimate for the animate, and of the animate, the living, flowing, for the inanimate-immobile-rigid. Such exactly, and the same, as from the remotest past—the primitive's transfer of his finger-signalled first notion of number, one finger, two fingers, four fingers, numbers = things, to the living abstraction (man's first descent into his own abstracting dancing seed), of a number-*persona*, number as such, the one, the two, the four—had been inherited, however disguised formally, by modern man. So that, say, a Hegelian idea-*res*, the abstracted absolute, is working and living as idea-*persona* within the changing seeds of Hegelian "nature" and Hegelian logic.

So that history-*res* becomes history-*persona*. And for us here, today, space in art—this simple physical, inanimate extension-*res* of the vision—could become space-*persona;* the inanimate body-space, space-spirituality, the very secret of all art. And in Japan: the precise, although secret, symbolization of this identity by the identity of actor and action on the Japanese stage—the "frozen," cumulative "where" and "when" of an acting body in a Noh or Kabuki final gesture and image: the fabulous *mie* dance.[64]

The *mie* dance, this ordering, this situ-ating of body's "visitation" by the scope of a gesture, an image, or a word, is, in a very precise and here very intensified sense, Japan's discovery. And trying in thought to look beyond the strict boundaries of Yamato culture into all-Asia's primordial, far-spreading sources of invention, one wonders: would not the psychological roots of this Japanese discovery be also the roots of another, so truly mysterious and truly Asia's, Indian Asia's discovery—the discovery of the mathematical *mie* dance of the number zero, the numerical ordering, the situating of zero's body in mathematical space; zero's "where" and "when" and the *epiphanic* identity of a static number-*res*, the *nothing per se,* with the mobile number-*persona,* zero's potential number-infinity, the infinity of *everything per se?*

"This is what Chikamatsu told me," writes, in 1738, the playwright's friend and commentator, Hozumi Ikan,

> "when I visited him many years ago. '*Jōruri* differs from other forms of fiction in that, since it is primarily concerned with puppets, the *words* should all be *living* things in which action is the most important feature. Because *jōruri* is performed in theatres that operate in close competition with those of the *kabuki,* which is the art of living actors, the author must impart to lifeless wooden puppets a variety of emotions, and attempt in this way to capture the interest of the audience. It is thus generally very difficult to write a work of great distinction.
>
> "'Once, when I was young and reading a story about the court, I came across a passage which told how, on the occasion of a festival, the snow had fallen heavily and piled up. An order was then given to a guard to clear away the snow from an orange tree. When this happened, the pine tree next to it, apparently resentful that its boughs were bent with snow, recoiled its branches. This was a stroke of *the pen which gave life* to the *inanimate tree* [the italics in this entire quotation are not in the text]. It did so be-

50 ARTIST UNKNOWN *Heiji Monogatari Emaki*
◀ Detail (Kamakura period, 13th century)

cause *the spectacle* of the pine tree, resentful that the snow has been cleared from the orange tree, recoiling its branches itself and shaking off the snow which bends it down, is one which *creates* the feeling of a living, moving thing. Is that not so?

" 'From this model I learned how to put life into my *jōruri*. . . .

"It is essential that one not say of a thing that 'it is sad,' but that *it be sad of itself*. For example, when one praises a place renowned for its scenery such as Matsushima by saying, "Ah, what a fine view!" one has said in one phrase all that one can about the sight, but without effect. If one wishes to praise the view, and one says numerous things *indirectly* about its appearance, the *quality* of the view may be known *of itself,* without one's having to say, "It is a fine view." This is true of everything of its kind.' "[65]

Chikamatsu knew well, he, the Japanese through and through, how subtle—subtly comical too!—this equation of the "mechanical" and the "vital," of the inanimate and animate is. How fluid and mobile, never fixed, is the equation indeed! From substitution to substitution, the Japanese drama's action (a Noh action, a Kabuki action, or puppet action, all the same) is identified with the actor, the image of an actor with his final, unique *mie* dance, and the mono-role of this unique mobile-rigid halt is substituted by the ubiquitous role of the actor's *double*—this truly mysterious invention of a shadow action and a shadow actor on the Japanese stage: the *shite,* main performer, *le centre et le pivot*[66] of a Noh piece and his *double,* the *shite-zure,* not any other, complementary *shite,* but the same = another *shite;* the *waki*—actually the second Noh performer equal in importance to the *shite,* the promoter and sustainer of the *shite*'s action (Noh being essentially *une pièce à deux personnages . . . deux roles,*[67] but also, in a mysterious way *shite*'s double. And what of their respective subdoubles, another—other—*shite* = the same![68] And what of the truly exceptional role of the "invisible" *kurogo,* the assistants "who appear on the stage with the understanding that the audience consider them invisible . . . in black from head to foot," and even their faces concealed "behind thin black cloth,"[69] who follow the important characters on the stage and perform for them, *instead* of them, the minute and personal scenic changes and functions—all this, as a Japanese comprehends it, meaning "that people on the stage have made a contract with the audience to regard visible things as invisible"![70]

How subtle and subtly comical is this embodiment of a double-oneness or sameness! For considered as the double, the same, of a living actor, he, the "shadow" is an animated being, and considered as being another's being, he is an inanimate thing, a *res,* say, an idea.

A fluid equation—very Japanese, *perhaps* very Pacific-oceanic. All this, *perhaps,* a deep recoil in ourselves, necessary for us here, into the prehistory of man to see anew the time of a particular, water-borne "barbarism," wise and civilized, when remembered or re-imaged so—as a water world, a water culture, having, like all cultures surrounded with waters, separated from the mainland, yet one with the oceanland, the feeling of animate-inanimate identity.

Mind's immersion backward in ancient waterways; the "innermost body" of a very very ancient man and very ancient time.

Perhaps the historical Noh is less Noh in reality than the pre-Noh dances—the *Bugaku* and others—brought in from India, Mongolia, China, and the ancient West to Japan, and joined there by Yamato folk-*Shinto* dances. *Perhaps* these ancient pre-Noh dances were "purer," less significantly loaded with "verbal" suggestions (Zen in grand particular), and more directly mimicking for us the identity of *res-persona.* And *perhaps* the more recent Kabuki or Jōruri—more "vulgar"—is more ancient in its back-to-depth recoil and ramification than the chronologically much older Noh.[71]

Japanese painting—the long Yamato-e tradition, from a Tosa or a Kose "school" to the later Kano and Ukiyo-e pictorial manner—has taken over this Pacific-oceanic message (Fenollosa was right—"arbitrarily"—but right!) of the *res-persona* equation. This is *perhaps* the meaning of what we find expressed as movement so persistently in Japanese painting: beings, animate beings, and the movement of their feelings and thoughts are expressed there as *things* and inanimate things—mountains, clouds, waves—moving in a full space-void as a dance, or rather a collected culminating pose in a dance *(Plate 49).* And motion itself, the resulting total motion-*ornament* of a pictorial ensemble, the final *mie* of a pictorial image contour or image color is not given then as belonging, as subjected, to a dancing being, but as living a separate, significant, life of its own.

I remember how once, looking at a remarkable Kamakura e-makimono, Heiji Monogatari Emaki,[72] you pointed out to me two examples of Japanese feeling of motion. One is at the very beginning of the scroll and its story, the other at the very end of it. The first occurs in the opening episode of the narration: soldiers of Fujiwara-no-Nobuyori, a general of the rebel head of the Minamoto clan, Minamoto-no-Yoshitomo, are inside the imperial palace, searching in vain the place where the prisoner Emperor could be hiding. They pursue and hunt the palace servants, who try to escape, running away fast. And here is where a tiny, almost imperceptible detail of utmost expressiveness had attracted your acute attention: the hand's gesture of one of the running men, who tries to give an accelerated speed to his moving body by pulling forward a fold of his ample trousers *(Plate 50),* as if this inanimate object, the fold, possessed a will of its own, the will of a living being, to *animate* the speed. At the extreme end of the entire scroll, we see the general reporting to his rebel lord about his discomfiture. The fury of his rage is given here in his acrobatic leap-pose: simply, a well-studied and well-performed dance move. As if the living man and his feeling have been replaced, *substituted,* by an object-symbol in space, the inanimate mask's mimicry of a living face: body's pose. Perhaps. . . .

❖❖❖❖❖❖❖❖❖❖❖❖❖❖❖❖❖❖

MC: Yes. *Perhaps*—I welcome this word. I was hoping and expecting its coming. It came finally and gave me my own freedom: for the word "perhaps" here means simply your independence from me, the Mysterious Companion. You are freed from my acquiescence: perhaps. So (*he slowly walks away*) you can proceed with your journey now alone—without me. Adieu.

I: Oh, this is too abrupt, I am perplexed . . . . Will I ever see you again? Has your companionship been simply a ghost story too? It is sad.

MC: I shall be back for a while, I promise you this. At the end of your adventure, when nothing will remain but the mystery of the scent in all the events of your eye's journey, the Mysterious Companion of your journey and time will be back. I promise.

VARIATION
III
WINTER

As the Eye is formed, such are the Powers

BLAKE

Winter:

The Sense of Hearing

. . . . . Winter threading along, the needle in my winter's canvas searching, now with caution, now with speed—for whom, for what?—throughout the tortured span of this sentence; winter, consonant with indoors warmth (a sheltering mood of meditation, Descartes' stove: winter) against outdoors chill, sunny and grand or grey, wintry and petty-killing, as sleepless drizzle needs be; consonant again, in much narrower but deeper consonance, with my choice of Winter's image, sentimentalist, against a truer vision (say, of winter struggles for ever-bettering survival, tough tough: more of live money, of solid exchange and good fun yoked to it, or of inner life's activity and gain); this choice consonant, in ultimate consonance now, with the choice of how to communicate Japan by the medieval searcher's *arbor Porphyriana* method, a branching out of events, forward and backward, from a freely selected trunk: at random, the art of a Korin, of a Nobuzane, or not even Japanese art at all, a free center trunk, my Winter's embroidering needle threading out finally along this choice and this ending of the sentence, the tale to be told now: a bunch of letters, all branching out from the central search and goal of my book, letters written in response to mine, by a gentle and learned Japanese lady, all the letters wrapped, so I found them, in the companionship of Apollinaire's supplication:

> Have compassion on us who are always fighting on the frontiers
> Of the boundless future,
> Compassion for our errors, compassion for our sins.
>
> . . . .
>
> Be forbearing when you compare us
> With those who were the perfection of order.
> We who everywhere seek adventure,
> We are not your enemies.

✡

Kyoto, January 9, 1964

Dear Sir:

It is with real pleasure that I am sending you under separate cover the photographic material you inquired about.

We know here, of course, how deplorably Shiko Munakata's woodcuts were reproduced in the English translation of the Noh play *Uto*. We of the Hashi group are happy to hear that this living artist's work, liked in Japan by many, rejected of course by as many others, might be given a chance, through the agency of your written and competent word, to be better introduced to the hospitable English-speaking world; very happy and proud indeed to make available to you these prints in a state as close as possible to that of the originals, as well as reproductions of some other less-known works of this artist.

It is, I do hope, superfluous to insist how grateful we shall be if you would consider it proper to let us know more about your research project connected with your book on Japan's art. Our readiness to assist you, if you permit, is, dear sir, very sincere and earnest.

I am also taking the liberty respectfully to include some additional critical and biographical material published in Japanese and related to Shiko Munakata's art and activities.[1] I do it, I confess, hesitatingly, not knowing whether these publications and the biographical data they contain might be of your cognizance already. Yet I felt encouraged to do so by the fear-disarming warmth and interest with which you spoke about him in your letter.

With all my good wishes for success as well as those of the entire Hashi group, whose decision I, as their executive secretary and oldest member, am authorized to express and convey to you, I retire now, dear sir,

Sincerely yours,
Wakana Iwai

Kyoto, January 24, 1964

Dear Dr. B.:

Very frequently—as you must have observed yourself—there occurs in the world of intellectual exchange a new and peculiar circumstance, an inverse coincidence as it were, the *coincidentia contradictorum* which for us, men and women of the East, becomes the asset, better the sign, of a philosophical solidarity, of friendship, along the interrelated paths of personal existences.

Your generous and informative reply—communication, more truly—to my letter would be such an undoubted coincidence.

For the purpose of your book described by you, as well as your commentary on Shiko Munakata's apocalypse, as you put it, are all coinciding—in inverse coincidence—with the very purpose and function of our group.

It is thus first of all my duty to tell you about this group.

Founded clandestinely, "subversively," by my husband some years before the Second World War, silenced then, it could re-emerge after its founder's violent death, and is now functioning unmolested as a semiliterary, semiscientific private research institute.

Its name, "Hashi," *The Bridge,* was given to it in commemoration of the famous *avant-garde* group—*Die Bruecke*—at the beginning of this century. The very name of our group meant to suggest our sympathy with, and interest in, the problems of contemporary criticism and creativeness on all levels of the West's endeavour.

Here is our group's main object: *Die Bruecke,* the bridge to be thrown across the depth of separation between West and East. For we believe, in challenge to the banality of such an *avowedly* obsolete opinion, that in spite of all, this isolation still exists there, just where Kipling so nonchalantly left it.

We, many of us in the vast East, are simply tired of a camouflaged *rapprochement* with the Occident. We want a real contact, the fullness of a multi-valid relationship. We reject, although we might sympathize with, say, the so strikingly Japanese decision of our poet Shiki[2] who, after having gone through a most thorough westernization, rejected the West's greatest and deepest cultural benefits, and in creative despair, in hunger for the ultimate, found for himself and for Japan his truest and fullest "Japanese" answer: the coming back home to the ultimate truth of Japanese reduction given in the *haiku*'s form-content.[3] We reject such a possible absolute, just as we reject this other, but with terror and repugnance now: the Hollywoodish image of Japan, an image, not so alien to Japan's actuality after all, of Japan's upper-class businesslike connivance with the Western code of behaviour covering up, after a busy day's profitable activity, the uninterrupted retirement to the intimacy of the Japanese home, to the fabulous refinements of the latter's sensitivities, its aestheticist rituals, its kimonos, hand clapping, swords, its women submissive, sweet and proud unto death. . . . .

And the repercussions of all this on the less spectacular yet thousandfold weightier platform of Japan's class struggle, Japan's labor existence, so hellishly a West-East mixture, the two elements overlapping, now the sharpness of the West's Marxist analysis taking the lead, now the East's traditional, collected practical response battling upward.

Neither do we accept another West-East distinction (meant to be a formidable, if artless compliment to Asia at large) pointed out by many a gentle mind of the West[4] by which Asia's "undifferentiated aestheticism," her all-embracing yet precise "vagueness," is contrasted to, yet seen as buttressing, the vertiginous piling up of the West's absolutes, mechanistic yet sacred also, limitless too, yet perishable, as science and change must be. (Oh, we know, of course, how far removed is this newer distinction between East and West from the older one mirrored in the notoriously "imperialistic" and comfortable motto: "Let the Occident be from all eternity the practical, the rational, the future-heading man's domain; let the Orient, all the Orient, remain for all eternity the undisturbed mind's dream world, undisturbed in its hypnotic past-present-future quietness, in its contemplative lovely lovely unrationality.")

True, all this might be there, present in Japan—yet we reject it deliberately, we reject all discriminating ultimates and absolutes. That is why what you are telling us in your letter about your own approach to the same problem is so appealing and endearing to us, so close to our own worries and gropings.

Your book, if I understood you correctly, would deal with Japanese art seen through and for the eye of a Western contemporary man, with no pretension to achieve an objective or detached presentation of Yamato art's historical evolvement and aesthetical value. In launching your experiment you hope—am I mistaken?—that what might happen would be similar to what happens in, say, medical chemistry when a new coloring substance, a new tonality, is introduced into an organism's stream for checking purposes. It will act upon all substances met there, but it will color—thus depersonalize—only those that accept the newcomer's affinity. The others—perhaps only one—will be impenetrable to the new tonality's spreading action and will reveal, by contrast and isolation, its hitherto hidden peculiarity, thus individuality, the "pathology" in it. Different, antagonistic even, as the new tonality and this no longer hidden, isolated substance might "objectively" be, in reality they are now made one and the same by this process, by the very eventfulness of this revelation.

We, our dedicated group, we too try to know—to know in a different new-tonality way—the West's "universe of discourse," by infusing into it our own—Japanese—color substance, frankly, with all our revealed, biased differences in it.

Yet, at the same time, we know that we must clasp tighter and tighter around us the idiom of the West—the whole-planet-penetrating tonality of the West's own experiment. (And this we feel could only be the idiom of the spreading industrial revolution, an idiom still odious to many of you and certainly to many of us, unbelievers in the West's *new* thinking in science and ontology. We must clasp tighter and tighter around us this new experiment and experience till the creative shock of a total change reaches us: our final *yes,* or our final *no.*

Shiko Munakata's art, in its visual fist's grasp, attained this, so it seems to us. Would he resent as treason such a view of his art? Very probably. We cannot know—as yet. But we do know that what interests us in your "discovery" of him and makes this discovery so significant is that in a precise sense for us his art symbolizes our very group existence: *The Bridge.* As you have put it, his technique and his content largely come from his knowledge-shock of the West's new formal idiom, formal in the form-content-whole sense, the *what-of-the-how* sense of your letter.

This, of course, makes of him neither a clever imitator of the West's narration, with the traditional Far-Eastern technical convention grafted on it—the bold Sungian ink splashes, the *linear* subleties of thinning and swelling, etc.—nor a kind of Paris-Tokyo, Tokyo-New York, fashionable "abstract expressionist" in the garb of a Japanese exotic-*genre* narrator. No, you say. But it makes of him a good Yamato craftsman creator, his creations communicated loyally, through the very Japanness of his beloved Japan. Of course, I am expressing myself here in a most clumsy and confusing way, very contradictory, I am afraid, to what I was trying to say before. By

Japanese I certainly did not mean to suggest the so abused and abusive patriotic-through-universal attitude, underneath whose "liberalism" lurks more often than not a most brutal nationalist fixation. I mean to suggest something else, something very different and very precise—something pertaining exclusively to the craftsman's world. First, the full presence in Shiko Munakata's imagery of that dual spirit, so emphatically Japanese, of the simultaneously rough and gentle, the rough-and-gentle-kami that permeates, indeed makes into concretions, all the myriad shadings of all existences. Secondly, this very roughness and gentleness of feeling-kami, of creating-kami, as silhouetted in his art against the otherwise pervading tonality of the contemporary West's art. By contemporary I mean the working presence there of the concept of purposeful or "objective deformation" your letter is telling about—a purpose-full, meaning-full deformation of the optically given reality *(Plates 51, 52, 53, 54).*

The striking and revealing fact is that this tonality of the West, though "chemically" not absorbed by that kami, is nevertheless very akin to it. In both—in the twentieth-century West's objective deformation concept and in the dual spirit of Yamato-e's lore—the technical achievement of the creative goal, as it were, depends not upon the creative mechanics, the technique,

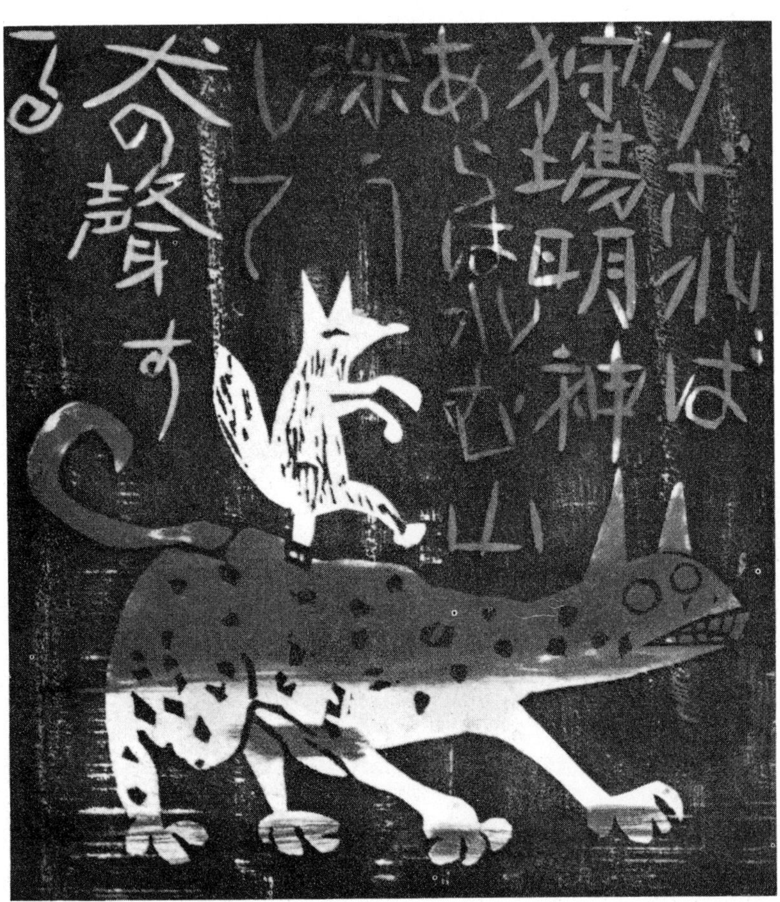

51 Shiko Munakata
The Barking of a Dog

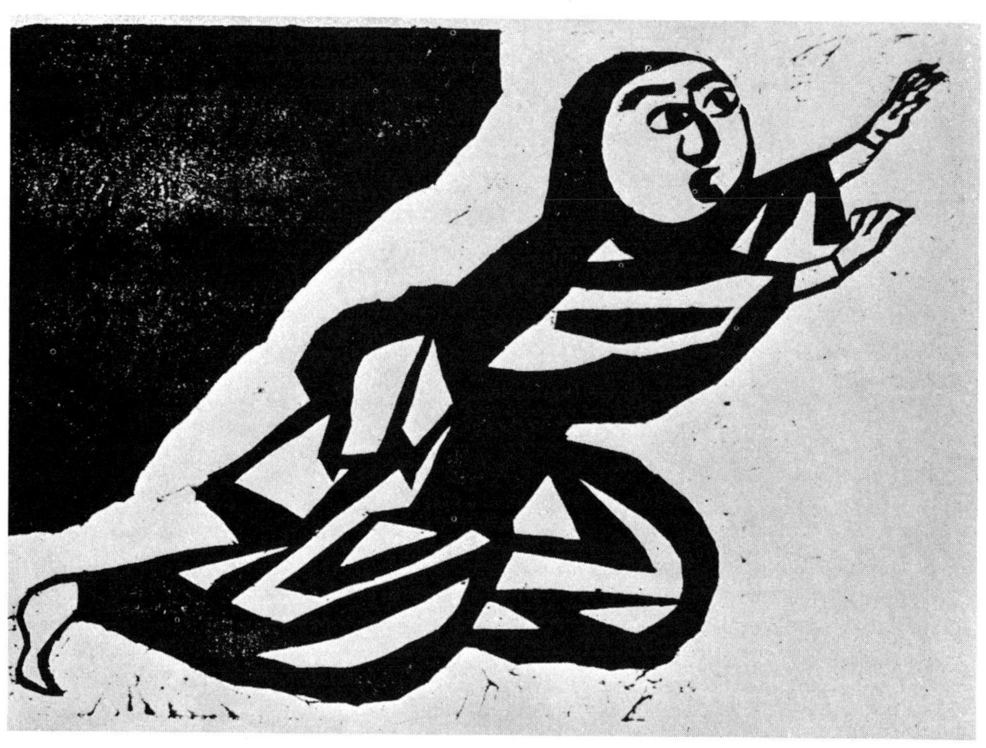

52 Shiko Munakata *The Mother*

53 Shiko Munakata *Vultures*

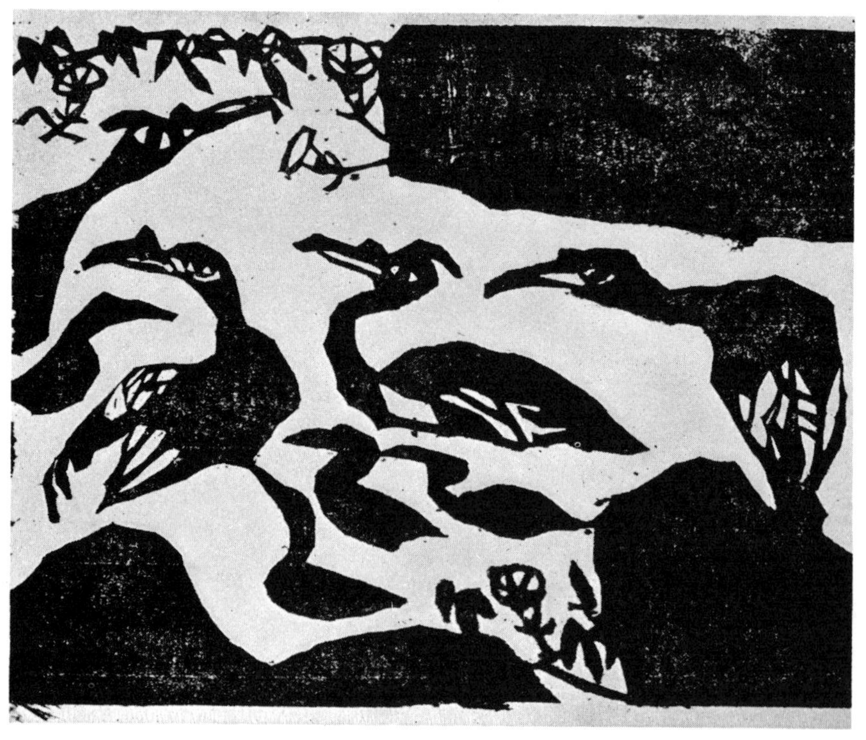

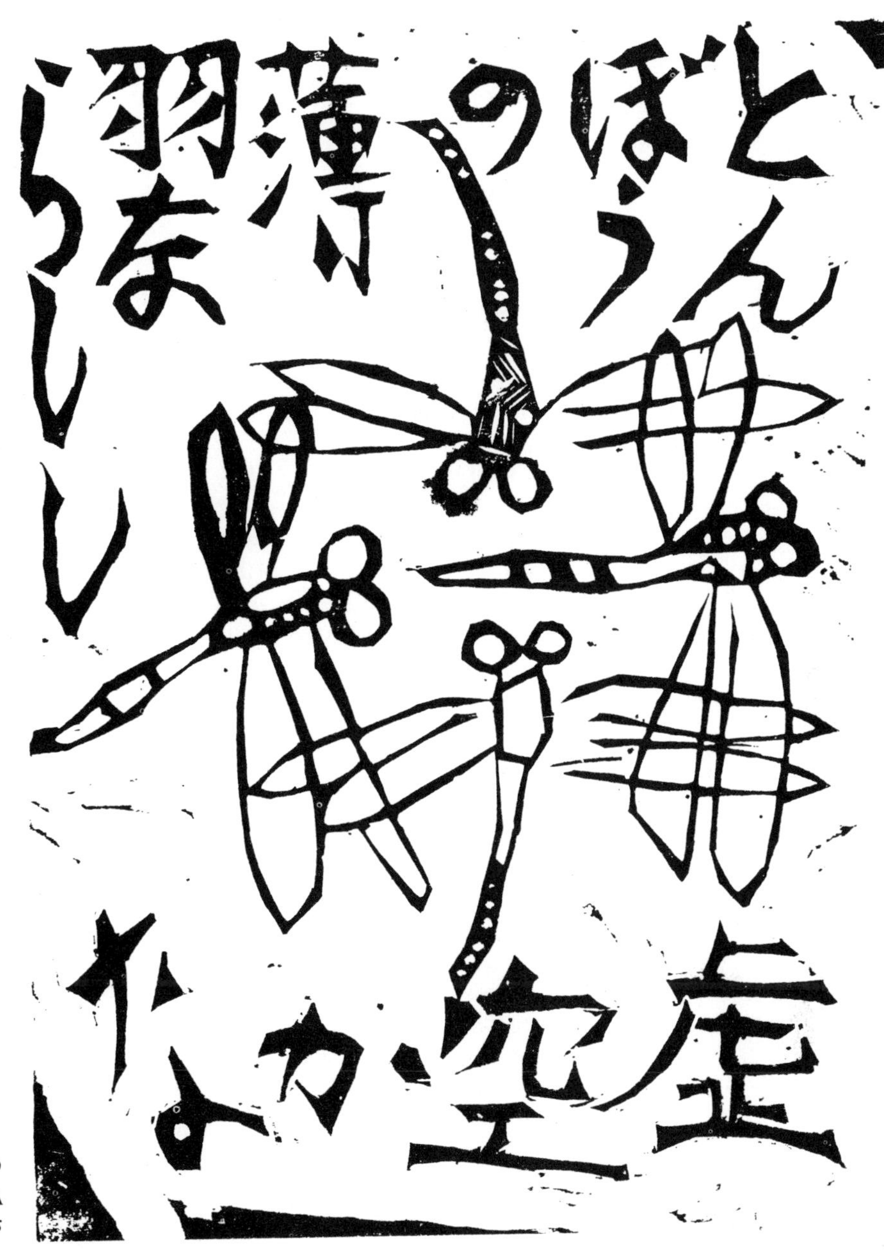

54 Shiko Munakata
Dragonflies

but upon the meaningfulness, thus the moral-lyrical essence, of this very technique: the ethics within the mechanical.

Here let me add that as an art historian myself, I feel extremely obliged to you for having brought to my attention Maurice Denis's so momentous distinction between the "subjective" and the "objective" deformation in art: the first, a lyrical, blurring arrest of a fleeting moment's contour, the impressionist shorthand proof of the *natural*'s validity, the very genesis of naturalism; the second, a *realist* neo-formation, the birth of a new, thus "objectively" monstrous being-kami.

And now, taking leave of you with my reiterated vow of gratitude and confidence, may I repeat what I most earnestly meant to say at the beginning of this letter: *plût au ciel* that the *coincidentia contradictorum* of our intellectual chance meeting become the very seal of our continued communications.

Sincerely yours,
Wakana Iwai

Kyoto, February 1st, 1964

. . . . . Delighted to answer your questions, dear Dr. B., or to try, at all events.

How would I proceed, you ask, if as a teacher of history, I were obliged to give a concise and a most pointed account of Japanese history?

I think, in my humble estimation, I would try to do it by choosing at random any of those episodes that have caught the fancy of Japanese people, and then, in a forward and backward, downward and upward swing, building around this thin axis the very volume, the volume-eventfulness of Japan's history. At random, I say, yet more truthfully, with a guided predilection for a folkloric episode-image rather than for the more evident importance and span of, say, so typically Japanese an episode or epos as the tragedy of the Onim Wars.[5] Yet your interest in this era calls here for a halt; let this be our central concern for a while.

This crucial drama of Japan's past obviously belongs at the same time to a known and universally recurrent pattern of medieval man's history.

Everywhere, as in Japan, the same feudal striving for supreme tenure of graduated lordship, ever swelled and swayed by the undercurrent of discontent and massing revolt among the exploited feudal base of the pyramid: the peasantry and artisanship yoked together in serfdom. Everywhere, the two-levelled semiveiled lord-and-serf alliances against other, equally precarious alliances of other lords and serfs, or lords and lesser lords, as the case might be—with the entire feudal structure from base to summit of the pyramid ablaze with bloody holocaust. Of course—and here is the justification for my halt—the tragedy of the Onim Wars era is much more than that. It is characteristically Asiatic, and within this frame, acutely Japanese: the clash between the interests of feudalism and of *trade,* that vortex of international or interregional exchange of goods material and spiritual since greatest antiquity; the clash between the two coexistent collective wills there, the feudal will, centrifugal yet in reality restrictive, self-encircled, and the will of trade's far-radiating expansion. In its evolved stage the latter is the will of Asia's great merchant guilds or collectives and their ever-expanding interests—of the promoters and builders of immense Asiatic empires, empires of the steppes, empires sown with their geographical expansions guaranteeing to the trade easier custom and exchange barriers—greatest and most desired road securities—empires of Alexander, of Cyrus, as well as of Chinghiz Khān and Tīmūr-beg. In Japan, mainly through the activities and power of the banking-trading Buddhist orders (Zen of the Muromachi era particularly), the interests and the impact of trade's sovereignty could also be asserted at times, and the emergence of a semi-lay, semi-ecclesiastic expanding merchant class could take place there. Yet confronted with the militant tenacity of other social forces—the ancient clannish, the more recent restrictive feudal—this grand merchant world could neither expand to its maturity (as it did so splendidly at certain periods in China or Iran), nor be entirely cut off from its live sources. All this contributed there to a unique historical social and psychological situation, the peculiar Japanese phenomenon of closing and opening to the outer world, of both reduction and expansion; and the peculiar Japanese psychological physiognomy, restless, bloody and contradictory, yet clever, sophisticated, brilliant, and joyful—fragile also, sensitive and boldly poetic, as tenacious childhood would be.

So it was on the eve of the Onim Wars. And the cataclysm came: all-Japan-comprising and devastating civil intermassacre. Then the resulting triumph of a newly born feudal-merchant alliance (the peasant element, so basic underneath this turmoil having been smashed and betrayed), achieving, temporarily of course, a centralized, imperial-like formation—the period of the Great Three,[6] the terror and the beauty of this age called Momoyama: polytonal, sonorous, cruel; gold-screened, castellated, anti-Buddhist, pro-West, anti-West; so Japanese—those fabulous, irreverent nights in the palatial gardens of Hideyoshi, and his monster tea ceremony, attended by a sumptuous throng of parvenu nobles.[7]

And the terror and beauty of Momoyama was followed by a still stronger era of another splendor and greater misery, the earlier stages of the Tokugawa Shogunate, when an osmotic exchange of social fixations could finally fulfil the premises of the Onim Wars' logic: the trade world's branching off from a Kamakura-Ashikaga stem arrested for good in its growth. And we see this: the body of trade recoiling on itself and within its geographically reduced domain (Japan closed to the world) transferring *in toto* its inalterable urge of expansion, impossible now, into the narrow depth of this very self-recoilment.

The merchant new urbanity, the enriched parvenus of Edo or Osaka became, by osmosis, exactly the old Yamato courtly aristocracy, the fabulous, ancient-traditional, fantastically romantic Fujiwara aristocracy, money crazy at that, and so very bourgeois practical. Think of the short Genroku era (1688 to 1703 or '04) therein, the late child of the Onim Wars' catharsis —the "daring populace" of Yoshiwara,[8] its enlightened classicism, much like your eighteenth century, Yoshiwara's dense and dashing atmosphere of *pudeur* and cultured brothels.

See streets at night, lit with the orderly and streamlined reflections of light and colors, the revival there and the reflection in us, today, of some other oceanic and pantomimic nights, elemental! (Fenollosa's fantastic unhistorical "blunder" in referring Japan's beginnings and Japan's essence to the Pacific world and past, including that of the Americas,[9] takes on, precisely here, the truth's mask of a deep-sea image-memory, oh, Fenollosa's magnificent correctness!)

All this world, see: it is of Kabuki's black substance; of Ukiyo-e, of course, Ukiyo-e first and foremost.[10] Great Buddhas—in Ukiyo-e disguise? —Bodhisattvas, all redeemers, bliss givers—right now, the Enlightened Ones, their close-to-us-all sacredness and blessedness; their absolute exchange

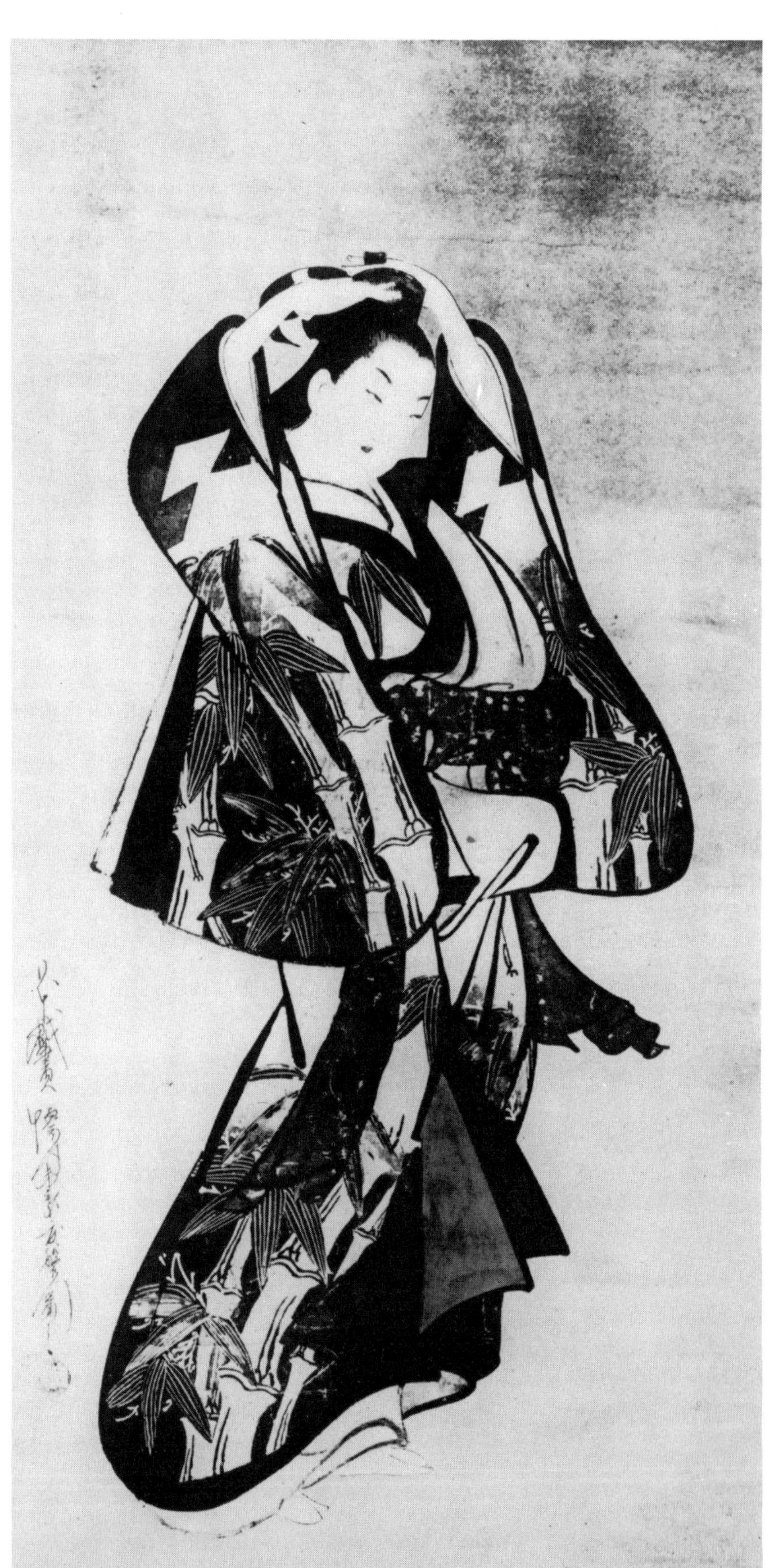

55 Dohan
Courtesan
Early 18th century

with our own us—so easy, so easy, just say *Nembutsu!*—all this energy (Blake's "As the Eye is formed, such are the Powers") transferred *in toto,* or in a *pars pro toto* way, just as it is, into the sacred halo surrounding the grandeur and refinements of the courtesan's attire, speech, and walk. *(See Plate 55).*

She, the opulent, sex-pleasure-prolonging Oiran,[11] she, as painted and color-printed by the Ukiyo-e masters, the Bodhisattva Avalokiteshvara Her-Himself, the purest one now.

Would the Tokugawa tonality have been then Buddhism at its purest again? Possibly. Meanwhile, its learned-dry revival by nineteenth- and twentieth-century scholarship was still a long way off; and notwithstanding a few individual summits among a still lofty elite, the Buddhist Sangha itself became and remained impure, talismanic, cheap, mercenarily wheel turning and rosary torturing, useless, muddy.

Yoshiwara of the Genroku era; I, an old Japanese woman, I, Japan's historical nostalgia incarnate, how am I to evoke this fabulous reality of ours—a reflected, inverse reality, as it were?

Yes, the Onim Wars would be, after all, the proper axis around which to build the volume of my history of Japan. And yet, I repeat, I would not start with so ample an episode.

But I would fall in love with a more precise image-episode, precise and reduced to its localized folk appeal: the story, say, of a warrior boy, Atsumori, slain by the rude Naozane on the shores of Suma, and the never-appeased regrets of the slayer; perhaps—more likely—I would have started with a Ukiyo-e print after all, Ukiyo-e again and again, the floating multi-petalled world of great and small actors, mummers, and semidrunken samurai, the floating desperate pictorial pride, truly aristocratic because so precise and presumptuous and so headstrong in its conventions kept loyally, thus folk-purely.

Yet why such a narrow choice for so wide a purpose? I would not know. I only know that no matter how differently I might try to orient the direction of my thought, this thought and its organizing effort will always re-establish, compass-needle wise, its pointed drive in the direction of some very precise, brief, and concrete image-fact, image-event. It is a peculiarly Japanese methodological urge, I have discovered. Moreover, this external narrowing or reduction—*substitution, as you have guessed*—of the image choice or image search even, is the more urgent in me, the wider or more general, more speculative, the ultimate goal of this search.

The really peculiar thing here is this: while my answer to a general and speculative problem like Japan's history is being built around some such precise and localized image-event, this very image-event is in its turn, boomeranglike, substituted by a new image-event, a compound image-"monster." Here is where I am so Japanese, I think. And yet I see this as very similar to precisely what in your twentieth-century West would be called an objective, thus independently existing, deformation—the production of an image-"monster" after all.

Think again, please, of the Buddhist "general" problem of bliss, the Amidist ontology of bliss. And see the Japanese answer to it: the patterned, ornamentlike image-answer, image-monster—the Nembutsu formula of being already saved—itself a substitution for the narrow immediacy of an image of bliss as touch; a nodal, everybody's, most concrete sex-spasm-image-touch, image-event ultimately.

My hypothesis is that we have to do here with a particular, *historically* verifiable, mental-physical direction, specifically a Japanese method of knowing and of organizing the knowledge in the shape of an eventful compound of attitudes rather than as a "factual" chain of influences.

And here is where I can face your second question: How could I so nonchalantly say to you that "East is East and West is West" *in spite of all*? What could I have meant by this "in spite of all" if not precisely a real East-West growing understanding and ligament? Neither India of today, nor China for sure, nor the Islamic world, let alone the fabulously West-garbed Japan would be able or willing to take seriously the assumption of so obsolete and peremptory a Kiplingian distinction.

You see, I could not approach your second question without having it already added to, hooked onto the first, bunching the two together in one question-and-answer image-ornament, image-pattern, this: that there is such a distinction; for there is a Japanese epistemology, very distinct, very "different," and this Japaneseness of the very way of thinking and knowing should not just be *connected with* the historical problem of its emergence and actualization, but *is* Japanese history itself, epistemology and history making one image-pattern.

How and where is the Bridge's span to be projected over the distinction or separation?

How difficult it is to communicate!

It is late at night. We both are tired at this point. Tomorrow, encouraged by your reiterated invitation to communicate, I shall continue.

And now, with just a grain of irony to it, but no more!—what my devout cousin of the lovable Kiyoshi Kojiu Temple would say in earnest will come true—my good-night wish: "With our faith in the Three Treasures, Buddha, Dharma, Sangha, and the Three Wealths, everybody will be happy and peaceful."

Next morning, February 2nd, 1964

It is a good morning, indeed, a simple morning in a simple Kyoto home, the troubles in mind and body created by the world class and other struggles notwithstanding. And it is so good to see, and to continue seeing while writing to you again, the snow falling thick and soft, a simple, silvery Japan snow. It is good to see with narrow, localized silver precision the silhouette of Japan's history projected on the matinal openwork of my snow-covered garden, narrow, precise and silvery.

The epistemology and history of Japan is the story of its two traumas; two decisive many-branched traumas or shocks, as I would call Japan's facing the two great strangers, China and the European West. I call them traumas because I conceive of them as foundation shaking, physical-mental events which threw Japan into her global changes.

First, China's impact (known to everybody), thrice during her tormented social history accepted by Japan, thrice in graduated diminution of intensity: T'ang China helping to build Japan's first—if so precarious—era of centralization, the Nara-Tempyo; the implantation there of all the Sino-Buddhist complexities, of T'ang's hierarchic-literary systems of governing men, mind, and taxes. Then the second and much lesser wave, the Yuan-Ming trade mentality in-spreading on all levels of Japan's Ashikaga era, from the haughty wisdom-humility of Zen-and-suiboku[12] philosophies to the Chinese "bourgeois" moralizing about freedom—all China's world of subtle and bold acquisitiveness, poise, and orderliness. Then a third or subtrauma: the re-introduction, toward the end of the long Tokugawa period, of Confucianism in an aspect nearest, perhaps, to its origins (rejected by the oblivious Shin China), and of the political moral protestantism of a Wang Yang-ming (1472-1529).[13]

So, in epistolary brevity, one might describe Japan's triple plunge into pro-Chinese change, Japan's absorbing of China's hierarchic-patrist structure. (I deliberately use here this abused yet still imaginative term *patrist,* a sex-limiting, clean and dry, mind-clearing—sky-religion generating—high attitude in man; in opposition to the *matrist,* the sex-unbinding, occultist, wet, low earth-and-depth-piercing plunge in man.)

But this is only one face of the story of Trauma One. The reverse should complete the vision. For in typical Japanese reaction, immediately after the first era of absorption-diffusion, another era, of awakening—Japan's first self-awakening—followed. This is also known by all: the era of anti-diffusion, of re-formation and re-absorption into Yamato's collected-clannish trial-and-error tradition in living and governing, the so-called Fujiwara age of re-Japanization (making one continuum with Kamakura's). It is the age of happenings most extraordinary, Japanese *par excellence,* never to be forgotten, never to be surpassed either: THE REAL IMAGE, THE REAL FACE OF JAPAN.

At this stage of Trauma One I stop. You know the facts only too well.

It is the other great trauma, Europe's impact, that I am anxious to evoke.

Twice it struck and shook the foundations of Japan. *Twice.*

About the first coming of the new stranger much less is known than about the second. Yet the rough facts are there. The great trade expansion of Asia as a whole and its international interests—Ming and early Ch'ing China of the fifteenth to seventeenth centuries—yoked now to the expanding industrialization and ambitions of the West; all this immense wave, with its bewilderment, confusion, energies, and sins, unfurling onto the shores of embattled Japan; the coming there of the trading religious orders, the Jesuits. . . .

Little as yet is known about the shock and the effect on the Japanese mentality of this sudden intrusion of the white's world, so alien, so far removed from the world of the extreme East. The shock, rather external when compared to its earlier, Chinese-Buddhist internal counterpart, must have affected the deeper and hidden-from-view strata of Japan's sensitivity much less than it affected the very apparent ones, the ones closest to the surface, as it were. I mean here the effects of the apparent, gross-optical impact; the bigness, the coarseness of the things and the men of the West; the Occidental man, a big, coarse, strange white monkey *(Plate 56)*, manipulating with self-assurance and communicative ability big, useful, fascinating and brutal things: formidable firearms, big astrolabes, marvel-

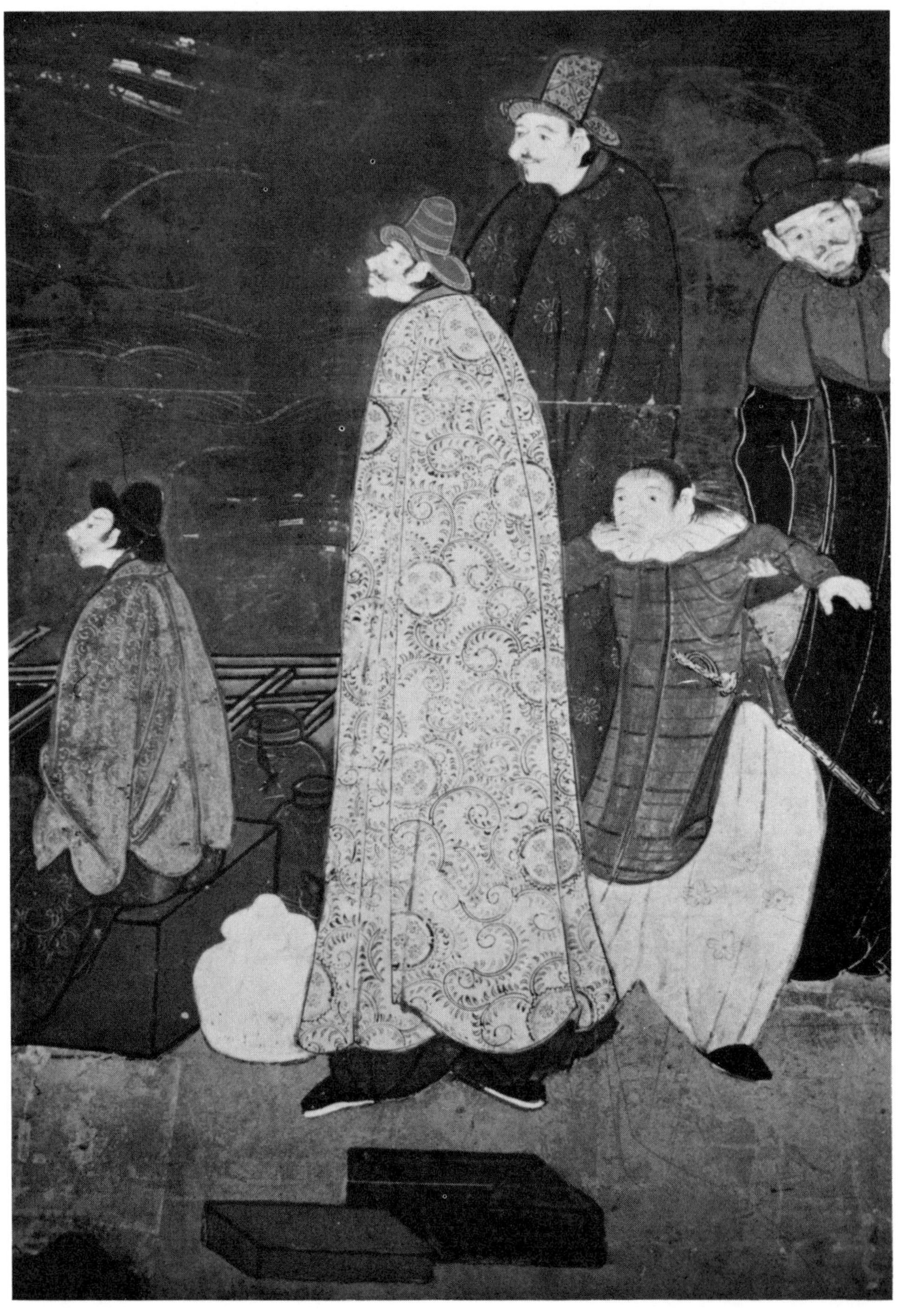

56 ARTIST UNKNOWN *Westerners in Japan* (Edo period, 17th century)

lous calculating tables, and many other complex engineering structures and toys. The usefulness of that which is big and coarse—the very opposite of what had always been Yamato's concept—a visual-mental shock at first, certainly it was. Then, as with China's impact of old, came Japan's boomerang way of reacting: Japan's recoiling on itself. The repercussion of this in art, the art of the Momoyama period, is typically Japanese: the awakening of a new energy-radiating consciousness, collective-epic, embracing all strata responsive to change, but this time with a particular intensity and obviousness on the visual aesthetic level. It was the miracle of the Momoyama style that was Japan's promptest response here: the renewal of an ancient Tosa-Fujiwara Yamato style, or styles. (I don't go, of course, since it is all so well known to you, into the complexities of other styles or schools either surrounding or deriving from the Tosa-Fujiwara, semantic-historic center.) Momoyama, the "barbaric," the *magnifique!* Yes: the Tosa-Fujiwara world resuscitated, dense, fulgurant, precious and precise and fleeting, delicate—but, how coarsened, how big now! Big, with big white monkey's big forms in a big space. And the permission, no! the urge, to make big, coarse and *magnificent* gold-laden screens, flowers, birds, big figures, the slanting perspectives big, big gold, big silver, big trees (for big parvenu warriors, of course, and their big audience halls—but surface sociology cuts a shabby figure here!) and the big, terrifying *nearness* of objects painted! (Very Yüan already, it is true [*Plate* 57]. That is why, may I note in passing, this fourteenth-century Sino-Mongolian art in China inherited by the Mings offers to the art historian a problem of the densest historical volume, carrying his search way back to the Occident's—Graeco-Roman, to be precise—obsession with the tactile nearness, the close-up of shapes, an obsession widely diffused eastward and reaching the Far East via Islam and Central Asia's oases.)

Then—oh, you know well the many other parallel happenings!—this revived Tosa world was channelled forth (the coarse "white monkey" and China both remaining within it) via the Kano synthesis[14] to the audacities of Ukiyo-e and its numerous

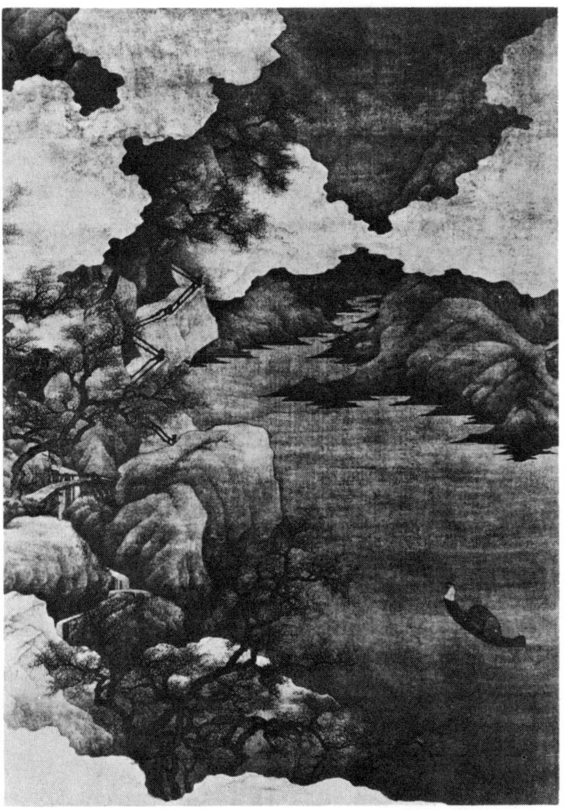

57 Sheng Mou *The Deep White Clouds* (Yüan period, 14th century)

branches—my weakened breath of an old woman getting short at the simple thought of scaling this abrupt summit!

Enough. Japan acquired, through this first shock of the West's action and the countershock to it, a new dimension. How deep it went down into other ways of Japan's collective consciousness—I could not calculate. I know with some certainty only this: the second stage of the great Trauma Two, the absorption of the West's technological, machine universe, physical and mental, both mechanical and epistemological, by modern Japan (the so-called Meiji and post-Meiji eras) has this time reached an apparently fuller degree of intensity. Japan still is absorbing it.

What is or will be the response to it, or the new self-recoilment of twentieth-century Japan? Think of the new hand as well as of the new mind created by today's West, the last "Heaven-and-Hell" wedding gift of the West's last cycle—the industrial revolution—what spirit will inhabit it in Japan? For there is a spirit in all this—the stupidity of a contrary assertion is unbearable.

When I say industrial revolution I mean by this only my own narrow, localized, precise folk-image of it. And this image—a substitution—I would describe as the spirit of *spreading*. Yes, the industrial revolution is the very spreading, irresistible, of this revolution. It is its very being, philosophical and historical, to expand, not to stop, to spread throughout our planet—from eighteenth-century England to twentieth-century Asia and Africa—and beyond our planet into other space and other time, in time. Has Japan been so penetrated by this spirit of the revolution that it will remain spirit there? The West's—and the West's alone—is the irresistible march and change from tool to machine and from the machine to the meta-tool, the meta-machine; from the "continued hand" acting and thinking, to the machine's "detached hand"—an extra limb born that walks and acts and thinks by itself—thence to the liberator from "mind-forged manacles," spreading spreading farther and farther.

And we ask ourselves with anxiety: does Japan's acceptance of the West's gift—the great trauma of modern Japan—help it to *come out* (using your expression in your last letter) from its own self-possessed self (its "continued hand") to face this, to learn how to know itself by another self's self, so that the "coming out" from itself becomes a deepened "coming in"? We would not know. And that is why, in doubt, I said that the Kiplingian separation exists in spite of all.

In a way, what I am trying to tell you at the end of my letter is this: the positive answer to the problem of separation is that the separation is nought—its reality is an image, is within the reality of an image, my image of the industrial revolution, whose spirit admits no separation. I touch this image, *ergo* it is. The image is irresistible—is Japanese. Something is brighter lit.

In friendship
Wakana Iwai

February 6th, 1964

Dear Friend and Brother:

Thus shall I address you henceforth—by right and by duty. *Je m'explique.*

In a quiet and solemn ceremony, very ancient, very Japanese too, we, the Hashi Group of Nine have adopted you brother of the Nine, co-builder of the Bridge. You shall soon receive the lovely "diploma" of this venerable rite of adoption. It is signed by all of us, introducing to you the specialty of each of us: the poet, the painter-engraver, the historian, the textile master, the mathematician, the ceramist, and the physician, the Kabuki stage director-actor, the economist.

Our ceremony took place yesterday. A beautiful and crisp winter night it was, lit with our liking of your new name:

His suddenness - one - when - two

The *mon*[15] in your diploma is our own *mon* with your individual sign added to it. The latter consists of a delicate petal-wing design, which, according to the origins of Japanese "heraldic" distinctions (some purist in the West might object to the use of this term applied to Japanese badge-plethora), goes back to a pattern design of a particular textile belonging to a particular and distinguished old Yamato family.[16]

The *mon* was engraved by our Omata Kori; Azuko Nazane made then this verse:

Myriads of dancing
dust-parcels lit.
A winter light-beam:
never mind.

And yet: this ceremony and its earnestness, how dangerously "reactionary" it appears even to me at some moments, when faced with our Hashi's program and decisions, the guiding decisions of a "post-magic," scientific mentality; to be precise, when faced with the latter's image-center, narrow and localized: the *spirit* of the industrial revolution—the central theme of our planet and of my last letter. But first, considering, as we must, how tightly knotted are all the connections that make up this revolution, I wish to single out the following one: Why is it, you might ask me, that we, the Hashi group, part of Japan's most "progressive" humanity, struggling as we are against all obscurantist leftovers, all feudal prejudices and monopolies, whether in church and state or group and individual—we the *abatteurs* of myths, and of all mind-blinding "speculations"—why have we chosen as the seat of our activities this quiet, obsolete city, the antiquarian's *prurit*-releasing city, of Kyoto—this lovely, lovely imperial and papal-Buddhist capital of yore? Yes, why?

Simply, because no other city in the world (except, perhaps, some equally beautiful and equally dead city of say, the world of Islam, whether an oasis-city in the Iranian East or a Moroccan in the West—a dead beauty too militant in any case for positive and discreet Japanese nostalgias)—no other city in the world could have kept in closer and more solid union—in one single knot of connections—the two most apparent aspects of all cities of old, the aristocratic and the folk. Yes, we have chosen Kyoto, haughty and sonorous *Heian,* because the air in it is the health in us. And this because in Kyoto, better than elsewhere, this union of the aristocratic and the folk can be seen as achieved within the very "universe of discourse" that pertains to the visual-manual, to the artisan.

This is the same universe from whose soil the *arbor Porphyriana* of the industrial revolution grew up and up. For indeed, we believe that it was this triple-limbed being, the aristocrat-folk-artisan, father and mother of many children, that in your West gave birth to its latest child—the revolution.

This triple-limbed being is what we believe is called history of man, living history on earth, living now in full health, now in sickness and convulsions of discord, now in health again.

And lastly—in last knitting together of connections—we came to believe firmly that the history of man is to be rewritten anew: that the trajectory described by the documented social ideological or political history of man does not necessarily coincide (though it often must needs coincide, too) with the trajectory of man's visual-manual knowledge and creation.

Is this a crank's vision? No; it is a knot. The knot, and how it all started in the lovable shaded city of Kyoto: the world of aristocracy—black-shiny and purple, the world of the folk—shiny black and shiny red, the world of the artisan—black and golden, the world of the industrial revolution—black and white—all in one, one great bunching, one compact knot.

It is easy to perceive the contact between what we call aristocratic and folk: the memories of the greatest past in the one are mirrored in the sociology of the other. What is difficult, but necessary, is to create an image of their transferability. It starts as an image of existential persistency in the very concept and history of the aristocratic. I mean the image of aristocracy as it came to be *imagined* by the post-feudal eras, now the most cherished thing of the Romantic, now the hindrance rejected by the Positivist—now, ultimately, my own image of an existential persistency, infallible, ubiquitous, thus transferable to any other universe or milieu no matter how opposite in appearance—the folk, let me say. I see this as the ubiquitous, transferable persistency of what is for us aristocracy's most signalizing trait: its age-polished refinements of watchful leisures and wasteful audacities, ineffaceable, beyond the reach of times and changed historical conditions. I see the *Grande Mademoiselle*'s[17] fluted hands and speech, palpitating haughty nostrils and thoughts, the truly and traditionally "aristocratic" in effigy.

But if I look into other, reversed aspects of this effigy, I see there also the unrefined, the unaristocratic traits and habits of her era, say, the *populo,* "vulgar," physical personal habits of uncleanliness, the neglect in body washing, etc.

Then, turning away immediately from this effigy, can you see, as I do—in substitution—the very essence of the truly aristocratic traits *transferred* into this twentieth-century young repairman in the city of New York, in speech and thought unrefined, vulgar, *populo,* unclean, unwashed—but clean, refined, "aristocratic," as the habits of his era want it, in his washed body—all the traditionally aristocratic refinements of fluted fingers and fluted speech-thoughts transferred into the fluted, long-tapering pride of cleanliness, into the watchful leisures, the wasteful audacities, the washing waters, the washed limbs?—oh capillary-levelling truth in history!

The image of persistency, of *total* transfer (am I abusing your favoured term?)—given to us as completed by imagination; aristocracy, feudality, redeemed—uncritically, but at this point of my story what does it matter!—is body's closest symbol of self-assertion: the creative hand, the creative eye, the artisan's universe.

And the knot is there: Kyoto, aristocracy, folk, the historical artisan as eye and hand.

The hand is the eye within the knot; the hand is the eye that tied all the ropes of the knot. The same eye, the same hand that is weaving during man's winter on the looms of history, on the looms of my never-finished communication, the great arched threads of ideas, the curves of their trajectories.

And so, tenaciously again and back now to my beginning thought that the trajectory of the verbal elite's explanations of happenings and the trajectory of the visual-manual, artisan's (for want of another or better word here), do form along their planetary historical evolvement one arch, but also, at frequent points diverge and so are lost—unknown, uncomprehended—to each other's gifts, to catch on again, then to be separated again later. . . .

It is thus that the two trajectories, so parted, met (I am firmly holding the knot) at the very gates of the industrial revolution's home. . . .

✤✤✤✤✤✤✤✤✤✤✤✤✤✤✤✤✤✤✤✤✤✤✤✤✤✤✤✤✤✤

Forgive me, dear friend, for not finishing today's letter. My lovely assistant, Suzy, just entered the room to tell me two things: one good, the other bad. The good is the arrival of your much-expected manuscript. I am very happy; how eagerly I shall read it! The ideas in it will surely be more easily befriended by my humble mind now that you have had the generosity to share some of them with me already in our correspondence.

As agreed, I shall give it to Mr. O. of Osaka, who will get in touch with the publishing house in that city I have mentioned to you. I reiterate my wishes for a successful publication of your work in Japan. My hopes are strong not only because of its subject, a subject so flattering to Japan's ego—but also because the very presentation of it, as explained to me by you, seems to me extremely appealing to our tastes here, the real text of the book being the visual one, the illustrative material itself in its abundance and thought-directing organization, the properly "verbal" explanation or the literary text playing the role of a suggestive and as brief as possible accompaniment. A philosophical-aesthetical book conceived as a sort of *Images d'Epinal,* or even better, a comic strip—how instructive and sincere!

The second, the bad news brought by Suzy is the sudden death one hour ago of our old gardener and friend, Mr. Osaka Kakushi, the one I watched in my childhood taking care of the garden that surrounded my father's tea-ceremony house. He was a sweet and most amiable human being and we all loved him. A lonely man, I presume, with no family attachments we knew of—a family-less Confucian, strange as that may sound, and a pious one.

He had begun to worry us lately, particularly because of his tense and unfriendly reaction to a silly and unnecessary incident that had happened to him, and happened again with increased frequency. I say, a silly and unnecessary incident, nothing but clumsy behaviour toward him by a stranger, a young neighbour of ours here, unhappily an American, a young New Yorker married to a Japanese girl when he was still a graduate student of things Japanese in the States.

We met Mr. and Mrs. N. here and in Tokyo on several occasions; he was what you would probably call a nice fellow, with a nice open sense of humor, of course; enthusiastic about Japan and an earnest student of Japanese ways. And yet, increasingly confident as he became, his young Japanese "pals" helping him in that, in Japan's all-out "modernity," he unwittingly and rather jokingly had committed the usual blunder of hurting, without suspecting it, an old, old sensibility, quite foreign to him, of a native. In jovial and confident comradeship he once told me this: "We now live in my wife's family home, you know, that monstrous old Japanese-style barn near a small shrine, and one of my hobbies is stealing antique gravestones. Your frantic old housekeeper or gardener is always burning incense in front of them to appease the spirits." It seems to have been too much for our old and frail Osaka. Silly Osaka . . .

❖❖❖❖❖❖❖❖❖❖❖❖❖❖❖❖❖❖❖❖❖❖❖❖❖❖❖❖❖

Next morning

Very sad. Mr. N. and his wife seem to be really desolated. I had to console them. I was sincere in doing it and yet I must confess, terribly and sadly irritated . . . Again and again, rises the thought of the West-East abyss of separation; again, the image of the fragility of our Bridge, alas! And suddenly I saw my incorrigible, shameless, leisurely optimism reborn as an ugly and fatiguing shadow. Forgive me, my dear friend. And above all, forgive me, if to re-establish my shattered poise I continue to be talkative today about the interrupted "sublime" things of history and ideas—instead of telling you more, and more profitably, perhaps, about the humble, so very Japanese existence of our gardener and friend.

But—poise re-established, above all. And so, as if nothing had happened, no interruption at all:

Beyond the gates, deep in the sky, the Great Bird of the industrial revolution (still occurring, still not finished, on our tiny planet) is expecting us along the track of the artisan's trajectory.

Of one thing I am sure: that you see him soaring exactly where I see him here, the Great Bird of the West's sky, the new spirit and the new category of mind, given birth to by the West, with all the elemental beings around his flight, all the historical connections that gave him life and that afterwards were themselves nourished by his very life. It would thus be inconsiderate of me to burden you with naming all these connections, so well known, all leading to the triumph of the machine on all strata of life: social, poetic, economic, as the West's sciences and the West's policy.

But less known, I must say, and always worthy of recall, is the revolt against the machine by the machine itself.

(Here is where my nostalgia for the living West dwells—seen from afar, seen from Kyoto's resurrection day!)

Within the machine's mind and its historical dictates of preorganized, clocklike fixities, its centripetal logos of great machine cities, of class strife and its geared crucifixions, as well as of the focused and pointed three-dimensionality of art's space or of music's unicentered rhythms, of the yes-no structures of value judgments, I watched the slow re-emergence of ancient, premachine polyrhythms and polystructures of judgment, of art, of experiment—of relations themselves.

Yes, this is less known. And still less known are the elemental and self-emancipatory deeds of the visual-manual: the diverging arc of its trajectory and the genesis of this divergence; the resulting chasm in understanding between the "all-understanding" verbal and the visual-manual productions; the resulting crisis in history and ideas, the why of it, the why, perhaps, of the great crisis of today—oh, yes, this I must communicate to you, who have already so miraculously hinted to me your akin-to-mine vision of it! For our common vision carries in it a precise, narrow, and recognizable icon of its own origins, the image-touch of the first divergence, or what we call, among our group, "the tragic split" in prehistory and history of man; a split operating as a constant historical inhibition throughout the multi-trajectory of man's behaviour on earth, carried on and on from the unnameable past into the future. We speak between ourselves of this primal split as of a concrete event and we consult each other's chosen field of research for a fuller grasp of it—we are still far, far away from the fullness of vision.

Of one elemental thing we are sure, though: that there occurred at some point or points in the prehistory of man, a split—*the tragic split*—between the *three* essential and ever-present functions of man's symbol-creating activity: the creation of verbal symbols—the function of the "magician"; the creation of visual-manual symbols—the function of the artisan as such; the creation of muscular-kinetic symbols, symbols of protection-as-dance—the function of the military chief, protector of this primeval collective-social unit. In this unit, one with it, the magician is the future priest, then the future judge, then the intellectual elite's elected—magician always; the artisan, the potter, weaver, singer of fertility, smith above all, is the future artist-poet—artisan always; the military chieftain is the future king, emperor, statesman, politician—dancer always. Whether embodied in three individuals or in one, the three basal functions once formed one closely-knit function-entity, one social-physical being or body, as it were. (To evoke this oneness—disjoined so very long ago—let me recall King David's sacerdotal dancing in front of the Ark, the Ark one with the dance, one with its meanings; or the strangely identical dancing of the Shang Emperor before a vessel of precious bronze—a ritual bronze embodiment of the symbolic protective mystery dance—the verbal kinæsthetic visionary bronze-dance?)

A three-one creative function. So that any fabricated, thus wholly sacred, object-symbol, vessel or idol, was in actual instantaneity of communication three-one in meaning, inescapably whole man's too—an embryo of all philosophies, religions, and systems to come.

It must once have been thus. And then, at some crucial moment or moments of man's prehistory the split took place. At some moment or moments, I said, for how manifold in terms of repeated happenings in historical times this split could have been, only the honesty and patience of the anthropologist would be able to reconstruct and tell us. For similar "splits" are still being produced by conditions similar to the great prehistory's conditions, in today's "barbarism."[18]

The tragic split of the dawn: its material roots—where? One can *feel* them in the jealously guarded secrets of the first-born technics of man—when, by the creative intelligence of the human hand, the human body's rhythms, nature's awesome mysteries were transmuted into clairvoyant strength and well being. On the model of the awe-mystery of grain's apparent death and rotting in the soil's darkest moist element, of its sacrificial revival as a new, another resurrected grain—the many-limbed plant now, flower, corn, or tree—on this model the world of technics was fashioned: the potter's resurrection-vessels, the potter's dolls of divine Mother-Child games made out of dead mud; mountain rocks of obstinate toughness made malleable by the will of fire, and then, by the perceptive rhythms of the hand, made into obedient and varied objects, tools, weapons. Precious, dangerous, jealous secrets, power-giving, too, to those who knew power—oh, mystery—techniques of the artisan-magician-chief, that contained in their lore all the secrets of the three-one unity, the voyages of the grain and the voyages of the stars above made into one pride!

Harken, you, the future genius-artist of the romantics of all times! Be watchful! For while with the two others you, the artisan, were mastering these secrets of life and death and resurrection, of despair and hope, you did not master with them the secrets of power. You were betrayed! At the very threshold of the split! Even then you were too busy! And when the chieftain and the magician, in mutual protection of what had been acquired, allied themselves against their third self, the split took place.[19]

The future priest of the great Bronze temple urbanity and the great chieftain became allies. The artisan's share was relegated to obedient and guided productivity. Creative—oh yes! but with the creativeness of the priest-king or the king-priest, whose powers of brain's double-edged sword and wit cut out from the primeval myth-stuff all the grandiose structures of subsequent temple-and-state philosophies, sciences, and religions, all their grandiose and guided imagery!

This is what should be known by the historian. The primordial split, the tragic split, indeed, because the split is ever-present, as fate and as memory, in both trajectories, in that of the two allies, forever watchful over their treasures and the spoils of their treason; in that of the betrayed, submitted to the others, yet keeping, however obscurely, the memories of the three-one time.

Yes—on the grounds of the priestly empires and imperial priesthoods there joined, elite's wealth grew immensely—haughty and deep temple cities, haughty and deep philosophies, haughty and deep religions, all fruits of the same awe-mysteries of growth and seeds—along the laborious waterways, the Nile, the Two Rivers of the Fertile Crescent, the Indus Valley, China's Yellow River! Yet all this power-wealth, the theophanic terror and wisdom of the Bronze allies, while incessantly fed on its own profit-bearing memories of the pre-split oneness of knowledge, was unceasingly troubled by the lurking guilt-bearing memories of the treason. Hence, the subsequent drama of temporary triumphs and fortunes in re-forming new alliances, now the chief re-allied with the artisan (Akhnaton, the grandeur and misery of his attempt to "return"); now the priest re-allied with the artisan (the first Hebrew Prophets); hence, at the very roots of post-split divergencies, all the successive and cyclic zones, or planetary belts of man's re-awakenings, of man's revolt against the treason.

And this is how I see man's history unfolding itself in front of me:

I see first, the belt, two-centuries wide, encircling the tight waist of Europe and Asia, the first zone of revolt that gave us Zarathustra, and Buddha, Ezra and the later Prophets, Confucius, and at the zone's latest edge, Socrates.

How significant it is that this first awakening of the memory of treason took place not among the betrayed themselves, but among the triumphant magician-priests! For it was the verbal elite's self-purifying attempt to liberate the visionary in it from the tyrannic ties with the dancer militant that separated forever, throughout all times and places in history, the visionary prophet-judge-priest from the temple-and-state priesthood.

That is how the universe of visual creativeness was about to be vindicated.

Then—the era of reaction: a time of treason darker even than the initial one. From the renewed power-protecting alliance with the chief a new verbal dominion of a haughty and secular elite emerged. The story of it—the learned gossip—what need of it here? Much more illuminating for us is this: the coming of the second revolt.

For, in the midst of the social and economic tempest which preceded and accompanied the revolt of the prophetic belt, the unclaimed new energies of the unsown against the sown, of the unpriestly steppes against the priestly city-temples, exploded over the *terrasses* of urban treasuries—and the Bronze Age collapsed. And the Iron Age came. The change was a violence, but became a beneficial longevity. Many a sign had announced its new spirit: the Iron Age announced itself as the age for the many, for the more (already in the origins of the historical Buddha's preaching, for the many, rather than for the Upanishad's less—as this has been visualized by a sensitive historian of late).[20] The great change was prepared in the world of the ancient Near East—in the so-called "Hittite" particularly, and its Turko-Iranian derivations (it is here that I would situate the Achaemenian unfinished experience).

But the great change was never fully understood or embodied there. It was understood and embodied only by the "barbaric" newcomers in the
 West, the future builders of classical Greece. Here, by a magnificent

chance, the close-to-the-pre-split world of the newcomers became also the heir of a truly unique Bronze culture—the Aegean—the only one where the pre-split unity could be in great part preserved.

Oh, the unrepeated beauty of Creta's joys in life energies—the free, open, in open-air-sanctified, the never-secret, never-esoteric joys; the three-oneness there living ritually and free, the messianic promise, the plant-tree transplanted in ceremonies of dance-vision-thought. There the young chieftain-priest-artist wearing in effigy the insignia of oneness: the sceptre, the necklace, the sickle *(Plate 58)*.

Only later, much later (the Cretan universe having followed its Bronze destiny and collapsed), the exoteric, unhidden rituals of joy were made esoteric and hidden in the revived fertility contents of the mystery religions, the Orphic, the Dionysiac, the Eleusinian, religions of hope given to the many, not to the less, it is true, yet controlled now by the split-containing mystery secrets of the elite. But I see other things, too, unfolded: in the midst of a new upheaval the gates of the second revolt slowly open, and the second belt of awakening slowly encircles the man-changed earth. I see the Iron cities, swarming, multiple, industrious and noisy, increasingly artisan in their social component and impact, implanted deep into the unsown, implanted by the post-Alexander Greek world and spirit in the West, by the Sino-Iranian world in the East, overflowing the restless and avid humanity of the steppes.

And I see how, from within this dense, fabulously prolific urban mass-stuff, and parallel to the artisan's social economic struggles for emancipation, the emancipatory action of the visionary's "universe of discourse" was approaching the *avant-scène*.

This is the second great belt of revolt, encircling again the tight waist of the West and the East—this time the artisan's revolt against the treason; a two-centuries'-wide zone of awakening, framing both the center event and and the center time of Christ's all-men visitation, and in the farther East, the spreading of Bodhisattva's salvation for all through the touch and faith.

A shudder of enthusiasm and poetry comes upon me each time I perceive the historical image of Christianity's birth, the historical *logic* of this birth: triumph of a mystery religion over all other surrounding mystery religions, precisely because of its rejection, at the very start of elite's esotericism, of the hidden and the separating in the others.

The birth of Christianity is thus the rejection of the very traces of the split's treason. It is exoteric frankly, free, and open to the more, not to the less; the mystery of sacrificial death-resurrection, hope, becoming in Christ's presence a touchable reality, not any mythic abstraction-reality—not Mythra or Cybele-Tyshra, not even Sakyamuni the Enlightener, the abstract Vairocana of later Mahayana heavens—but the living reality of a co-sufferer, the Man of Sorrow, to be touched with the touch of a concrete physical event; the image-touch at once visual, verbal, and rhythmophoric.

But I don't speak of this image as yet, today—I speak of the belt of artisan revolt spreading in the shape of two simultaneous historical energies: messianic Christianity and messianic Buddhism, of their mutual and many-limbed embrace and radiation. That the very precision and concreteness of the visionary Buddhist "imagery" had given a new dimension to the Far Eastern man when it was introduced to him—to the Confucian man in China, to the imageless Shinto Japanese, to the Mazdeo Shamanist of the Central Asiatic oases—all this is well studied and known—not proper for me to exalt here. Besides, the revolt against the split's power alliances in Asia (hence Asia's "wisdom") has never been as acute and cutting through all life sources as it became in the West. That is why it was here—in your West, I mean—that the spreading belt of Christianity's action became one with the second planetary belt of the artisan-visual revolt. And this Christian-artisan revolt, repeatedly interrupted in its full unfolding (a long and obscure story of renewed treasons), could nevertheless—this was its achievement—keep alive its initial impetus, and helped by changed conditions, could usher in the world of our own revolt, contemporary man's. That is, it could prepare and then become part of the third belt of the artisan-visual revolt: precisely the industrial revolution and its twentieth-century planetary spreading.

This is my image total of history. I believe in its truthfulness—I believe in the reality of the primordial split, in the drama of repeated enslavements and liberations, and I believe consequently in the twentieth-century man's

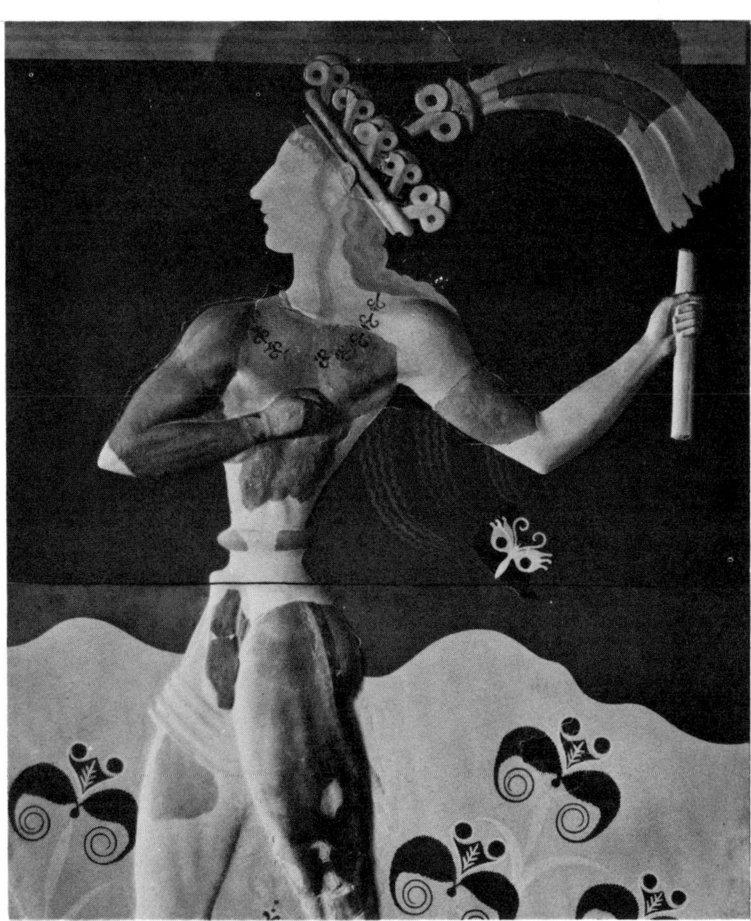

58 Artist unknown
Priestking
Relief (detail)
2nd millenium B.C.

third, perhaps final, planetary effort to redeem the visual-manual from the treason's deeds; his *techne* sciences, his *techne* philosophies about human existence as growth, experiment, and situation.[21]

If patiently allowed to, what exciting details could one not—at random! —single out in this total image! How exciting to watch the post-split working in, say, the history of mathematical thought—that of classical antiquity most typically; to watch there the trajectory of the verbal elite's static geometrical teaching, from a Plato to a Euclid, a teaching that diverged more and more from the artisan-visual *techne* geometry, yet was at the same time nourished, redeemed, and projected into the future by the dynamic formulae of growth, experiment, and situation of this geometry, from say, Eudoxos of Cnidos (c. 408 - c. 355 B.C.), Archimedes (c. 287-212 B.C.) and Proclos (A.D. 410-485).

My belief is firm and I have entered it with delight and without fear, a thick forest with many roads in it, one road only to walk on securely, the others only to cross—the thick forest of origins. How exciting it is for me, an Asiatic newcomer, how it silences all my other curiosities, to watch there the dawn of our, contemporary, man!

I watch the centuries'-long obscure groping for self-expression by the early Western Christian man: an "obscurantist" groping, an "obscurantist" method-and-object of knowledge it was, indeed—so repulsive to the far-radiating enlightenment of the Hellenic past.

I watch Cosmas Indicopleustes, the sophisticated and cosmopolitan sixth-century-still Hellenistic man, his conversion and its effects; his mind, scientific, skeptical, proof-and-evidence demanding, exchanging freely all its wealth and refinements for the new Christian revelation-proof's no proof.

Choosing to be poor and coarse in mind, he relegates to the limbo of sin and obvious error his Ptolemaic rational knowledge of the surrounding cosmic world, and rewrites convincingly the mechanical physical structure of the starry universe in motion. He rewrites it as a new and precise image-shape: Moses' Ark, whose walls are the earth, our real earth, the cover, heaven's stars, the cherubs, of gold.

All this of course just an obscurantist back-plunge into "barbarism," an additional proof of the reactionary backwardness of the self-empowering Church[22]—and yet! for me, in the dark forest of origins, it was the dawn of our own day: the conquest of the image-touch—an image that is one with its meaning, one also with the protective muscle-stance in it (the magician-artisan-chief again), over the verbal ratio-syllogistic or even the dialectic *must* of enlightenment.

An obscurantist groping, and yet! the true one that later, much later, made Kepler's line of infinity into a workable image and device of cosmic mechanics.[23]

I enter deeper, with delight and no fears, into the dark forest, my path crossed, thus joined, by many others. And I glimpse, helped by searchers on the crossroads, the obscure *techne* progressiveness of the so-called Dark Ages.

Here it is, the crank—ah, the humble crank unknown to antiquity, known to the "barbarian," by which, in later improvements and complex changes, the reciprocated motion could be joined to the circular one, and the mechanical clock, or rather the soul of the clock, the escapement[24] could be produced! Thence, I am led toward the brighter day at the edge of my forest, the later medieval West: the clock and the clock mentality of man, the thing that goes by itself and not only because of us, that stops, goes, stops again, temporarily, yet repeatedly, without the help of our hand—oh, miracle, yet also danger of stabilized automation!—the clock mentality, the real machine already in the circular-reciprocated, the centered, geared rules within cities and minds, in the centered and geared space projections of geometry, art, physics, mapmaking, and theater, and in the concept of money.

The machine, of course! But also (already?) the antimachine, the anticlock, the tool mentality, the hand-continued, the thing that goes with us, because of us: Franciscan "folly," Franciscan-Nominalist reach, or rather descent, into the thought of "impetus" as inherent, immanent, in bodies once set in motion.

Contacts, crossroads, junctions and divergences, resulting battles of social economic forces, all intermixed; we historians know much by now about these tumultuous efforts of Christian medieval man. It remains to learn more about the spreading belt of revolt, the boldness of its spreading. The artisan both as mind and as a new social being-force was slowly liberating himself: the very consciousness of the so-called Renaissance is in this. For the triumphal Renaissance is the culminative era of the visual-manual emancipation, first of all—not so much, perhaps, in the visual creative liberty of the great ones, as in the craftsman's revenge against inhibitions still so much in force: a Cellini, or a Giovanni Bernardi, a Noel Delacroix, a Sebastiano Sbarri, for whom, say, the very stoneness of a stone vessel to be shaped by hand and eye, jasper, onyx, jacinth, crystal, has itself become the very shape of the inner man's three-one involvment. Exactly as it was going to be again—in our today—with a Moore or a Gonzalez or a Brancusi. Exactly also—perhaps more naively—as it has always been with us here, in Japan.

And then, the art historian's delight to follow, along the forest's chosen road and its crossings, the traces left by the epos—the trajectory—of the eye and hand: the history of art, proper, all over the world of man. Traces, I said? No: images. Or rather, one image, one single image and its radiation backward and forward. *Arbor Porphyriana*-like, the ancient proto-historic image of *techne* associations: the fraternities of artisan labor and invention surrounded by protective rituals of "mysteries," translucid walls, guardians of professional secrets in bronze and iron casting, in the building of cities and symbolically geometrized enclosures of stone or brick or wood, in making icons of redeemers and redeemed.

Among the Aegean wonders I would choose the radiant, and for me as a Japanese, fraternal, story of the Kouretes, adolescent protectors of Zeus the Child, dancers whose leaps were to fertilize the cities and the fields; they, future heirophants of Eleusinian night initiations and future mimes, sacred goats, as it were, teachers of fun, the very soul-sex-Okeanos of the theatre in early Greece. I would choose them, the sacred substitution-dancers, and close to them in function, the Cretan association of bronze casters, clothed in ceremonial white, just like our swordmakers. Later, in endangered times of the Doric elite's reactions, they became the ambulant artisan fraternities of pre-classical Greece,[25] breeders of styles and of most famous schools, sometimes in secret, sometimes openly swarming around temples of mother-virgins, goddesses of hope and energies, swarming far and wide; preparers of all the arts and freedoms of the West at large. In Asia, too, of course, all over Asia, watch, please, the fraternal activities of old. In India, the artisan and priestly gifts of detailed mimicry, rules, meanings. And in Islam, that most "verbal" universe of all, what of the active and liberating role played from the very beginning of her trajectory by artisan groupings around most ancient fertility rituals[26]—*gestes* of undivided pre-split eye-mind-hand's creativity—in all the socio-religious struggles of her history, offering a redeeming shelter to the visual-manual itself, an exaltation, an idiom, silenced otherwise by her "verbal" pride and dominion! And in my own world, what of the striking sociological enclave of artisan clans, real clans of work and peace, the granite of Japan's future visual-manual pride and loyalty, within the clannish militant structure—the granite of future aristocracies of Yamato—in pre-Buddhist, Neolithic Japan?

Perhaps the secret of Japan's charm, mystery, and ease is to be found in the "abnormal"—and so Japanese—alliance not of the chief and the priest, but of the chief and the artisan.

Perhaps all the fate of Japan is in this, that Japan misses, has always missed, the priest; and looks, has always looked, for the priest!

As for the creative and tumultuous West, think again of all the associations of labor and peace, the visual-manual lore of the West, kept in secrecy from the oppressive and jealous alliances of the priest and the chief-militant. We know but vaguely as yet of these artisan fraternities' history-making impact: the art *collegia* of Rome, their hiding and dispersion in the times of Imperial Rome's last troubles;[27] their sheltering in the home of monastic Christianity—the Christianity of labor-mind-dance's primordial oneness. (Should we forget, because of monastic socio-ideological abuses and distortions of original views, the pro-labor, pro-arts philosophies of the original monastic self-rules? Should we—how could we?—forget the spirituality or the love of liberties—what else could spirit be?—of all the future reformations already contained in these rules? Is not the West's history of political thought lit, at its best and most generous, with the light of the Cistercian principle of federative polity,[28] the only possible principle and the only possible polity rule for a pre-split's unity revived?)

We all know how the birth of Christian medieval arts is connected with this monastic sheltering of visionary-artisan fraternities.

More so, more effectively perhaps, and more independently, this birth is connected (but our documented knowledge is here very scarce as yet, thus often in danger of exaggerating its own pro or contra assertions!) with the truly mysterious ex-*collegia* groupings—those, among so many others, around Lake Como, for instance, their freemason secrets guarded among themselves, away from the greed of the powers.[29] Then, in due or more mature times, attracted by the active—and interested—sympathies of great monastic prior-chiefs, an Aethelwold, a Bernard, a Suger, attracted even more by the enterprising protections of new chiefs militant, the "barbarian" nomads of yesterday—no lovers at all of priests' alliances and lore, the Lombards, the Normans—they, the Comoccini, as well as other associations, spread, swarming throughout the West's feudal world—as the Cretan white-robed ones did in Greece—and gave out the honey of their accumulated millennia-long knowledge and artisan skill.

And the arts of the West re-flourished immensely, proudly, reaching summits of formal and symbolic visual expression never reached before, perhaps: the sculptor's and painter's art of Romanesque tympana, capitals and illuminated texts; the Gothic architect-sculptor's narrated and urban imagery —the *speculum majus*—clothing the magnificent bodies of the cathedrals. Oh, delight to say, as one says a prayer of thanks, a poem to be, the triumphs of this second planetary belt of revolt and emancipation in art—delight to continue this saga of belief in the still greater triumphs of the third, perhaps last revolt!

I have finished, my dear friend.

But I cannot finish: for there was no triumph, as you know.

There was, of course, the apparent triumph of the Renaissance. And then there was a new, obstinate battle against the new knowledge, throughout the entire time span of the very Renaissance till our own time.

We see from here—can you see it as well?—the prideful re-entry of the allies, the magician and chief, the elite of the word and the elite of power, allied anew, more victoriously than ever!—the so-called Baroque era—allies that had learned in the very process of revendication against the late medieval darings how better to watch the other's moves, and how to live more richly on the rich spoils of the magnificent vanquished. The arched curve of the West. The age of enlightenment profited by the spoils; and the age of the literary elite, your splendid nineteenth century itself, was haunted by the still-hidden treasures of visionary booty.

Then—then the great kick, incredible, untellable (unless my visions of the two trajectories, of the cyclic divergences and reunions were to come to the rescue here!)—contemporary man's *volte-face*, the *homo loquens* joining willingly, indeed knowingly, the *homo faber*, the man-doer.

I bow, I bow, I clasp my hands thrice. Far, far in the sky of Japan I watch the great bird, the spirit—yes, spirit!—of the industrial revolution: the verbal, the visual, one rhythmophoric man again! (The evils assailing from elsewhere, everywhere, notwithstanding—so, be silent, correct critical reality and malice!)

Far in the sky—the bird; how far I am too, from grasping the bird's true shape!

How untruthful—all! For I perceive but the copious snow falling, so ancient, so sweet, outside my window, of course, the falling night and the falling snow, mother and child.

And now—to your book, dear friend, with all due humility and due solemnity. . . .

Good night
Wakana Iwai

(At this stage of our correspondence could be found a copy—a rough draft —of my own letter to the Japanese lady, the only one I have inserted within the tightly kept bunch of hers; the only one too that was left without any record of her reply.

Why? And why at this stage of our correspondence? Intentionally? By chance? I really do not remember.)

No date. No place.

Dear Madame Iwai:

I have just finished writing my Noh, which I dare to dedicate and send to you, just as it is, finished or unfinished.

How irreverent such an enterprise will appear to my Japanese friends: this arrogant challenge to Yamato's demand for reverence for its typical—the most typical to be sure!—form of self-definition!

A stranger's daring—and doomed in advance—challenge to the requirement of familiarity with the poetic idiom of the Noh, with the realism and the moral-religious earnestness of its verbal subtleties—its battle of apparent "tricks," inexorable conventions never to be mastered by an outsider, all tricks in appearance only, in truth, all helping mementoes for freedom's ever higher flights into the as yet incommensurable—why this irreverence, this useless effort and challenge?

And yet, I wished most suddenly to write a Noh for you. True, not a Noh about the meeting of souls in life, naked souls of women, of battles, of men, of deaths and saviours, as a Noh must be. But a Noh about a Japanese painting and its own mysterious meeting of souls and images within its own space-image. I wished a Noh as a colored, rare illumination or plate, as it were, for my book on Japanese painting—nothing else. But, again, if so, would it not be less sacreligious, let alone less ridiculous, simply to narrate the chosen or re-invented subject of my imagined drama and not to profane, thus destroy, the sensitivities of a Noh?

And yet I dared. And so here it is—unpolished. I had to write a Noh for you, my understanding and dear friend—definitely so. Because the Japanese Noh, or to be more direct, the making of a Noh, is itself the very making of Japan, of its poetry, and beyond everything else, of its art of painting. A Noh is a pictorial image, a precise, brief, localized image-touch, the image of a body revealed as idea. As the *muscle sensé*, as the Dance. In the very sweetness and melancholy of, how shall I say, Noh's tonality, I invariably sense the presence and the growth of a body. It is the loss and the finding of a body: something (something always very precise), lost and found and lost again; lost as health, as youth, as hope, and found as illness, age and despair, to be lost again in health, youth and hope—and found. Something always very precise, very concrete—and very fragile, like the fragility and growth in adolescence; the growing idea in a growing body, always wounded by the already-grown—and then healed, to be wounded and healed and wounded again and again. Yes: a Noh play is always about adolescence's re-opened scars—as precisely so, as in the art of painting—of all the arts of eye's labors the closest to the body and body's idea—is painting's created, artful space. For in painting, the space, the created, artful extension in which a pictorial action is presented, is a sick space, the sick, wounded "natural" space to be healed and wounded again, cicatrized again and again—a lost-and-found body, lost again. (In all the fragile beginnings—adolescences—of great cultures, is it not the art of healing that we invariably find and lose and find again at the very roots of future blooms: the Hippocratian roots of the early Greek "miracle," the healing roots of the first Buddhism?)

A Japanese Noh is the image-touch of adolescence, of an idea, of a scar, and of painting.

And of more:

Atsumori

(Transformed from Seami Motokiyo's famous Noh)

Cast[30]

WAKI: Kumagai no Jirō Naozane
SHITE: Taira no Atsumori
SHITE-ZURE: The today of our Kalpa[31]
CHORUS

Place: The shore of Suma Sea
Time of Action: Today

Dans un parc solitaire et glacé
Deux formes ont tout à l'heure passé

WAKI

I am Kumagai no Jirō Naozane, the rude warrior from the land of Musashi in the east. At the battle of Ichi-no-Tani I murdered the young Taira no Atsumori, and thus became the repentant monk Rensei you know so well. I have carried since, and back throughout the universes of innumerable Kalpas, the desire, the thirst for Atsumori's face, for his last smile, a thirst as single as is the single-flowered white *hamayu* on a deserted beach. . . Unbearable, burning load of god-and-goddess's sweetness, Atsumori's face!

And now I must go to the Suma beach. I have never dared to face the place of the murder. And the music of Atsumori's flute[32] is heard throughout all the ten directions of innumerable petal-lives, to be sown, to be mourned, each laid upon the other, translucid, trans-seen. The music of Atsumori's flute—I hear it coming from the sultry breath of Suma's solitude—and with it my hope to see again—never again?—his presence there! I am going there now. Here is the narrow hemming of the Suma Bay.

How strange, the joy and the surprise of this pine-scented seaboard—the woods clothing with warmest scent the mountain slopes, from Ikuta to the bay, a memorable spot of bloodiest dead. I am now facing the gentle embrace of the three famous valleys[33] and the haughty elevation over there, bearing the once gracious strength of Kiyomori's[34] castle. The envied and sonorous Fukuhara, now in pitiful, unnoticed ruins—so sad!

CHORUS

The scene is of great mountainous beauty. Proper for the enacting of so melancholy a Noh!

WAKI

How true, indeed. I came here not through the times past but through the events in action.

My journey hither—eight hundred years![35]—is but a small instant, present in the ordained frame of our last-and-present Kalpa. There the once is the transparent and trans-seen today. I came alongside the riverbed of Atsumori's death, so often chanted and danced and remembered in Yamato Land—my killing of the young Taira, my unredeemed grief, the prayers for him, the guilt of my unheard-of longing. This is the essence of Noh itself, the *lieu* of my wanderings.

CHORUS

The space of my wanderings, the *lieu* of my memories, the very space and spirit of Noh itself. I am the Noh: the wounded and healed memory, wounded again, remembered ever later, remembered too late. Do you remember? Do you remember? Alas! The happy smile on the lips of the noble *joro!*[36] Naozane is helpless in front of his warrior's duty. He closes his eyes, clenches his teeth, and—tears burning his cheeks—severs with his blade the adorable head of the foe.

WAKI

Naozane then prayed. I prayed for the salvation of Atsumori, I the monk Rensei, refugee of Kumagai and the poorer streets of Kyoto—forgetting there my own deliverance.

CHORUS

But Atsumori is not delivered thus. But you are not delivered.

WAKI

My day prayers were for another, not Atsumori's radiance and bliss only, but for the Bodhi radiance in all others—for everybody's radiance and bliss of *Jōdo*; my night prayers, for the extinction of all—even of Atsumori's smile and bliss—into another, no-dual light and radiance; all my prayers—in vain, in vain!

Why? My wandering is not extinct—this is perhaps just; my own desire is not extinct—this is just; but why Atsumori's? What keeps us both alive and tormented in the multiple deaths?

CHORUS

Listen: the music of Atsumori's flute is suddenly silenced, like the silent threat of a thunder to come just now. What is coming there? Dry leaves among greenery still aestival. Possible? Impossible?

(Enter SHITE *as an old woman clad in hanging rags, lacerate fragments of precious textiles now in shreds, once patterned with faded trees, waves, and wings on a flaming red background—still perceivable.)*

WAKI

(whose face was buried in the ample end—the tamoto*—of his flowing sleeve, lifts his head during the last words of the* CHORUS*).* Wounded. I am wounded too. Yet I am not a child matured, but a maturing man oblivious of creation.

SHITE

I am the weary old woman—alas! alas!—of other days. Nothing else right here. Every day—"Oh, the well-loved long ago! Every last thing comes back to mind"[37]—I come here to this angry shore. Thinking in my heart that the *Kumano* shrines along my pilgrim heart's way are the same as those built once for my childish piety; thinking that the paper offerings I used to suspend on them are the same, I bring myself before the gods in the hope to see once again, once only! my lost bliss. I am in search—Oh, fraternal Kami, help!—of a lost, unforgettable form. Is it a thirst, a longing yoked to my after-life only? Is it deliverance to come?

CHORUS

Possible? Impossible? Atsumori, Naozane, both of them in search of the same! Is it the same? Is it not the same?

WAKI

The beautiful face never to meet again. Nor the smile.

CHORUS

Will they meet again? For this is the place of a Noh continued. How significant is every move, every sound, every touch! What is more significant than the longing for a single passing smile! And yet a Noh is what has no smile in it. I ponder: the journey from smile to death, from death to smile—this is Yamato land's very creation, the Noh of spirits.

SHITE

I can only remember my never-lost desire, my *last* desire . . . .

WAKI

At the very moment the boy's smiling flame, black among the blue ocean of delight, had joined the pallor of the severed head. My sword.

CHORUS

And then my prayers for him.

SHITE

Yes, they have touched me. But not my last and total desire of a thing I have been looking for ever since.

CHORUS

The old woman in rags speaks very strangely. Her voice is the voice of another. And yet, many a stranger I have met in my journeys. I came to know their wisdom: the old woman in rags is not what she is here. [*What is suggested here is the conviction of al-Ghazzālī—the famous early twelfth-century Islamic religious philosopher—that ideas are living beings, who exist as three different human forms, each on each of the three essential levels of existence.*] Who are you? Tell me.

SHITE

I lost a single fragrance, a scent around my coming death, around my flute close to my armour.

WAKI

Is she Atsumori? Oh, moment of fullness and deception—be two, be three . . . Deceptions—remain.

CHORUS

A lost fragrance? So futile a desire? How can it be the very torment of truth? I wonder.

SHITE

My last desire: a fragrance sensed as a shape to be seen, a fragrance *seen,* seen; not as a smell but seen with the eyes, to be touched with the fingers of the eye. I saw a fragrance and I have lost its shape and its form visible: Oh unbearable load of nostalgia, truth of the eye, truth of this Noh we enact, truth of my land's and my time's creations, the Heian art's truth.

CHORUS

Truth is a desire planted in the after-death. A scent is the truth unique and entire indeed when its form is visible as a desire in the after-death. The descent into ocean's depth: what does it matter, the elsewhere's indifference?

SHITE

The lost and last form, alas! alas!

CHORUS

Now mastering, now immersed in the engulfing waves—happy. I and my swimming light bay steed—so happy! Atsumori is proud to be the last in the lost battle's escape, so happy—oh, the joy in blood-shedding too! Rushing to the shelter and safety of the imperial ships, sheer off!—the two Dowager Empresses, the Emperor Child and the new Chūnagon[38] on board already—happy and so proud of my deeds, of my charger's beauty and of mine, of my spring-in-heaven colored armour.

SHITE

Atsumori—his nostrils open, drinking the freshness of the sultry liquid threat and the scents still close around him of the backward-fleeing shore, of the battle's blood, and waning beyond it, the fragrance of mountain byways. Still closer—the horse's sweat, the delicate and ceremonial rouge on the *mukwan tayu*'s[39] face, and the closest of all scents, the fragrance of his flute's protecting brocade:[40] all toys of a child's game ushering into rapid and assured death. Happy, so happy.

(The SHITE *stops and then, as a suggestion of his inevitable Grand Dance to come in Act II, performs a short and solemn sort of "promenade" of many turnings.)*

SHITE

Suddenly—the challenge of a thundering voice piercing from the shore the thundering sea behind Atsumori.

CHORUS

The voice of Kumagai no Jirō Naozane, the man from the land of Musashi who, eager to meet a foe worthy of him, cries out loudly: Surely it is a general that I see there. How unworthy of you to escape in this way! Come back! I am the greatest soldier of Yamato!

SHITE

What could Atsumori do? Happy and proud, he turned his horse's head back to the shore. The beach! Atsumori draws the sword again. Then, still saddled, in close fight they twine, roll headlong together, among the surf of the shore.[41] The embrace—in imposed hatred and destruction of their armoured bodies—the boy's exhaustion; Naozane's knife hovering, blinding; Atsumori's smiling eyes beneath the shadow of his lifted helmet meeting the eyes of the astonished foe. . . I saw then . . . .

WAKI

The old woman speaks as if she were Atsumori indeed. I begin to believe. Are you Atsumori?

SHITE-ZURE

(appearing in a grand grey attire, his kimono tormented across and lengthwise by a light purple garland of davallias—a suggestion of a known verse:

Comme la plaine de Kasuga
D'un pourpre léger
Est teint ce vêtement
Où les davallies se tourmentent sans mesure.[42]*)*

I am the destined today within our Kalpa's frame—I am also the eight hundredth year of this Noh's cause. Today I am what we have all become. Nothing more. I heard, I saw—yes, I saw!—before dying at the Suma beach, the scents just mentioned—and more fragrance still: a curving shape.

WAKI

I loved you then, divine face of Atsumori.

But it was not the fragrance sensed as a fragrance and an image, or—and that could be!—as the image of a fragrant and painted flower on a screen; it was the sight, the very visible form of a scent—an old, curved scent—in the adolescent's astonished eyes. An unthinkable event.

CHORUS

The secret of this Noh and of painting.

WAKI

And thus Atsumori's life came to an end.

SHITE

It was the evening before the great battle. Do you remember?

WAKI

Yes, oh yes, the feast at the fort.

CHORUS

Feast of abundance—feast of torch-lights, ordered by Atsumori's father, the lord Tsunemori. "Tomorrow," he said, "we shall fight our last fight."[43] All the court was present, colors aflame, teeming, trembling with the foresight of the morrow. We were dancing, playing—oh sweetness of assembled sounds!—singing the *imayō* songs of our land, the *rōei* of China—clothing the grim night with Heike loveliness.

WAKI

And the music of Atsumori, his flute singing, now I know it, a song of bliss! My heart, not knowing it then, knowing it now, had its birth of Bodhi then, already the birth of Atsumori's face in my blood.

CHORUS

The tenderness of the *asobu* and of the flute soaring across the campus of astonished besiegings, the uncouth Genji . . . .

SHITE

The soaring scent across my eyes before death—I lost its form. Alas! Alas! Somewhere surely it lies in wait for me.

CHORUS

Yes. Among the petals of innumerable worlds past and to come, laid translucid upon each other, not one of them missing—how could the lost be lost there? It awaits.

SHITE

It must be here. I have searched the whole elsewhere. I am tired, too. Look at an old woman in rags. How old I am! Oh, tell them how beautiful was my boyish face and the splendor of my courtly attire.

CHORUS

We have told it already. Praised be your tender beauty, oh nephew of Kiyomori the Terrible!

SHITE

Yet the uncouth, unknowing, and rude *gōro ébisu,* the barbarian of the east, was not you, Naozane, my pitiful murderer—it was I, the precious youth of the Heian court. The madness was in us, in Taira, in us, delicate lovers of gold-wrought books and precious swords, rude traitors to the law of Bodhi.

CHORUS

We, the indifferent ones—indifferent to the law, to the bloodshedding; cruel, indifferent, beautiful, serious children of Yamato—our books, our swords, our laws: all toys, precious toys made of some lacquered coat-on-coat and hand-thickened human essence, Fujiwara essence; lacquered, fragrant toys of splendor, of government and murder, of people's sufferings in the blackest hole of labour stamped underfoot: lacquered toys, our Emperor-Popes, Emperor-Children, delicacy, elegance, and sentiment. Toys of Fujiwara excitement and carelessness, the precise beauty of horses' buttocks and the many-colored badges and ribbons dancing in the wind of rides; toys of sutras-upon-fans' badinage, of kamis, of state's solemnities and of *kirikane.*[44] Toys. Happy! Happy! And more. Toys of loyalties. Yamato loyalties. Not to the pacts but to the one and the same body. My body and my suzerain's and my flute's—one and the same body; so that when, by death or treason, they become separated bodies—mine, my suzerain's, my flute's scent—the venom of nostalgia destroys here death, treason, and separation.

SHITE-ZURE

And so loyalty remains: Japan-and-the-Child, and nothing beyond it; all the beyond *in* it—consubstantial toys of hand-thickened lacquer—Heraclitean *eternity:* the Child that plays.

SHITE

Smiling I faced my giver of death at the Suma beach.

WAKI

And yet . . . .

SHITE

You, the barbarian, the discoverer of bliss.

WAKI

I loved you as my difference.

SHITE

The lost form, I love you.

CHORUS

How could we? Desire is God wedded to anxiety. No prayer can reach this —no death either, no! no death.

WAKI

This killing? This loving?

CHORUS

Perversion they will say: the dead-end of the law.

SHITE-ZURE

Law is but the discovery of law. There is no law—there is only the discovery of law.

WAKI

And I was born and reborn never to extinguish that smiling face, alas!

SHITE

Never to cease, I, never to extinguish my last form.

CHORUS

Tell us again.

SHITE

My separation from indifference is my law discovered: a fragrance once sensed as a form to be seen with the eyes. This is my eye's separation from indifference. My discovery of law is my anxiety's gift to others. I saw it. I lost it. I lost it as a shape visible—the very curve of a bliss—my desire, Amitabha's desire, Maitreya's desire, the desire of a soaring bird. What—where —is it?

SHITE-ZURE

 The toy.

WAKI

I can't help you.

CHORUS

I shall not help you.

SHITE

And I cannot see the smile.

WAKI

I shall not see your form.

SHITE-WAKI

Let us pray. Separate. Separate.

PART II

Instrumental prelude. And, following it—strictness of rules and at the same time freedom in ruling being the very exigence of Noh's technique—I wish to have a movie screen installed by a kōken [*surveillant* on the Japanese stage] *in front of—thus hiding it—the symbolic pine tree of the* kagami-ita's *background; and on it a* movie *action to be shown suddenly: the black-and-white close-up of the ocean's wrath* (See Plate 20). *A flattened and glistening tranquillity expands over the entire screen's width at first: the threatening great wave, a liquid mass of terror coming from the horizon. Then, in rapid wave actions, the screen's background is completely crowded with the towering and thundering upon us, spectators, of this same gigantic wave—its shimmering inside concavity, in us; this action immediately becoming one black light-source on which fulgurant colors—lightnings—purple, white, red, and black ribbons whipped across the screen by the fury of winds, come out—splendor of late Fujiwara art's color scale!—ribbons and badges streaming out upon the perfectly* black background *from the buttocks of the warriors' steeds, furiously snatched into this black. Then—silence.*

And the SHITE *re-appears as the real Atsumori of the tale, wearing the mask of a young man—*juroku*—and dressed for battle.*

And the Grand Dance of the SHITE*—the crux of the Noh—takes place, embodying the words chanted and spoken synchronously on the stage. During this dance, and throughout the entire* finale *of this Noh, the meaning and message of the latter should be clearly revealed and conveyed by the interplay—now retreat, now embrace—of the folded fans: the colors of the* WAKI*'s fan, blue and green, repeating exactly the colors of the* SHITE*'s costume, the colors of the* SHITE*'s fan, those of the* WAKI*'s dress—red, gold, and deep copper brown.*

CHORUS

Look! Look! It is over. The beautiful head, still radiant, is there, severed, soiled with blood and sand and dirt. Close to the young warrior's limbs is the sheathed flute, and still closer—oh, Heian sentiment!—is a branch of plum-tree. Naozane had wept. I hear him say: "I shall bring you the shape of your bliss, the fragrance you saw—even should it be beyond the strength of my prayers."

WAKI

I see, I touch, I hear, I smell the growth of a Child in my hand's warmth, I shall never find this lost smile. A love so helpless!

CHORUS

(muted) So helpless.

SHITE

Useless.

CHORUS

Useless? Oh, clarity useless for adults' laws—useful here.

WAKI

Thus, I shall never find your smile. Farewell! *(He sinks to the floor and hides his head in his sleeve. His fan is unfolded. The* SHITE *bends over him, his great open fan entirely covering the* WAKI*'s.)*

CHORUS

*(*SHITE *and* WAKI *mimicking)*

Pity's smile—supreme form of Bodhi, nowhere to be lost:
Like the palpitating
cluster
of hungry birds over the deep sea's plenty
—fishes! fishes big!
fishes there—
over the splashing jumps out and in
the blue and luminous offing
and the cluster of fishermen's boats
swiftly reaching this long-looked-for spot
guided by the excitement of wings over fins;
like these three dark clusters
of death, profit, and
desire,
each separate, each different
from the other
yet yoked each
to each other
by élan and events,
one and the same—
so also to each other are the two separate desires of our Noh:
the passing smile of a dying child,
the scent's passing bliss—
one sameness in two
flames!

SHITE-ZURE

(standing behind the SHITE-WAKI*'s closed group. His sumptuous costume, grey on grey, frames them as with some great bird's open wings).* Desires interchanged, reversed—fraternal birds in flight. I am this bird's wings.

SHITE

What is demanded of me to attain this? Tell me, Monk Rensei.

WAKI

The wings.

CHORUS

Just as this desire is not granted, so it is granted already. This is the Noh. The replacing: the flight for the bird.

SHITE

The scent is the smile, the shape and its content, one and the same. How I love my murderer's love.

WAKI

The mirage of all hope—the nothingness of despair, of promise, of faith.

CHORUS

It is not true. The mirage is nought. The accepted non-acceptance of the mirage secures its identity; it is a thing real. The faint vanity of desire, of pleasure, of nostalgia and search, the form visible of a forgotten and suddenly present fragrance—this is a thing real—Amitabha's bliss in immediacy.

WAKI and SHITE

How?

SHITE-ZURE

As a thing transferred—not transformed: from the still *external* Ocean of Becoming into the *innermost* flow of human *ontos:* Buddhist psyche-ascent being—I am here to recognize it, I, the twentieth century!—its psyche-descent into everybody's brains' intimacy where the elemental, the "lowest" concrete joins the "highest" decisions of abstraction. Not any more our deliverance from the Chain of Senses, the still external release from the Ocean of Becoming, the Wheel, but the innermost deliverance of the senses themselves—freedom *for* each of them, achieved together with each and *by* each. Suddenly and anew: socialism unto the deepest.

[I really would not know, dear Madame Iwai, how to say it differently. You will surely condemn as erroneous, to say the least here, my entire treatment of this Noh: a *historical* Noh conceived as a *ghost* Noh; the Japanese Noh, its moon-and-sun mystery brutalized by the noise and indiscretion of the descriptive in it—how un-Japanese, how bad-taste revealing!

And yet, is it so vain of me to hope that some of the elements or events there—the seemingly most un-Japanese—might be accepted by you as precisely the only and truly Japanese? My hope is, I must confess, precisely in my "invention" of the *Shite-Zure* as the twentieth century, particularly of his *satori*-like finale-leap: the sudden, truly incongruous leap from smell to politics, from Child to socialism—truly Nature divinized *in toto:* from the closest to the furthest of all human musts and hopes.

I mean again *substitution*—the *aeternitas!*—the identity of the unseizable *toto* and this incongruous *pars.* (Thus, again, making the *Shite-Zure*'s leap one and the same with the leap across the *genesis* of all human arts and inventions; terror transferred into catharsis of sacrifice or identity and substitution. ((The *tunique sanglante:* on the Mithraic initiation night a tunic covering the neophyte's nakedness (((the rite was the universal fertility-astral rite of partaking of the flesh of the sacrificed Friend-and-I, the primeval Giver, the Bull-and-I))) was symbolically asperged with the blood of the sacrificed Bull. But already it was a gnostic, humane, substitution for a real, inhumane, bloody sacrifice of much earlier, prehistoric times all over the still now-trembling planet. And probably this substitution of a humane simulacre of it for an inhumane sacrifice could have been the genesis of man's arts—be it as the bloody tunic itself, or a paper and straw image, placed in a tomb; or a mask or an altar.)) So that all human arts and inventions, no matter how joy-giving and humanized the sacrificial cruelty of their genesis might have become, all drag behind them the odors of the primeval repast of identity. Yet, I always had felt that Japan, otherwise no exception to these origins, contained so much of exceptional and obvious loveliness, so much of exceptional and obvious kindness that the *tunique sanglante* seemed to be very early forgotten there. Yet a Yoshiwara courtesan's effigy might be, by intention or by habit of collective imagination, the icon of a sacred Bodhisattva in all its grandeur and terror of substitution. Still, if so, not more mysteriously or oppressively "mystical" than, say, the portrait of a lovely-looking lady at the Court of Queen Charlotte, whose traits of majesty and sweetness a Reynolds could conceivably have added there by sheer habit of Western man's traditional vision of womanhood, as substitution for those iconographically pertaining to the image of the Virgin Mary.) Is my guess so vain?]

SHITE-ZURE

The touch is seen. The fragrance seen. The sight is the curve of a scent and the scent is the curve of a sound, of a touch: the fragrance in visionary shape.

CHORUS

The chain is released—oh beautiful compassionate Form! See the roots.

SHITE and WAKI

Show me. More. More.

TSURE

I am the today. As a being and as a surprise transferred—not transformed. The Release from the Wheel, itself so inexorable a rule of old, is transferred now, today—why not? why not?—from the still *external* Ocean of Becoming into the innermost flow of man's being: Bodhi's *prajñā-karunā,* its "highest" notion transferred exactly, totally, into the "lowest" banality of today's notion of social-personal freedom. And I am the today, the Noh of ghosts. How incongruous here! Thus, I raise the banner—the form, the scent, the face!—of socialism: the ultimate release of the present Kalpa. In profundity: form so humble, fragrant hut of Ise *(Plate 59),* shelter to all, from the sacredness of a primeval small-number family living there together, to the sacredness of a greatest-number family living there together—model of innermost socialism, the final secret, metaphysical, of Yamato, I say.

I pray the prayer of thanks—of purest white, all-kami's prayer, kami-scent, kami-smile, kami-desire.

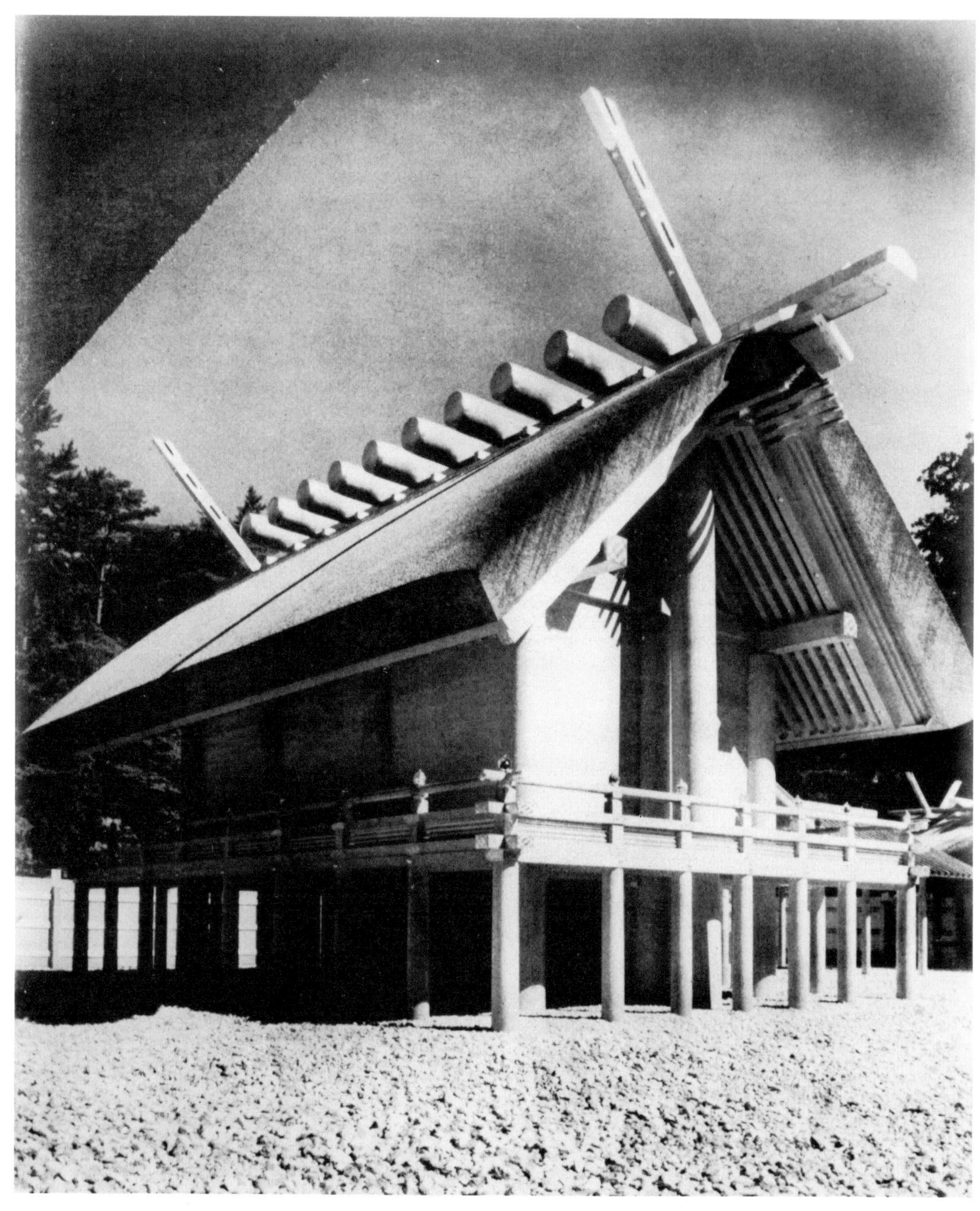

59 *Ise, most venerated Shinto Temple in Japan*

Kyoto, March 1, 1964

Dear Friend:

You have written an erroneous book on Japan. But let it be established at the very start, with no *recul* throughout the entire length of my "discussion," that I consider "your" Japan a most precious gift to us Japanese. Of course, in Japan only "reactionary" readers, as you would put it, would accept in earnest such of your *dramatis personae* as the Mysterious Companion, the ghost, the logic-of-the arbitrary *convive*, the hallucination-image. I speak in earnest, for it is not as symbols—nor of course, in a literary-allegorical way—that you wished these creatures of the "visionary circumstance of mind" to be both presented by you and received by the reader, but in all concreteness as creatures in flesh.

What really did you mean by your Mysterious Companion? How and why could it become possible for you to introduce him so centrally—with the least of justification? I feel that everything else gravitates around this central or initial being and depends on this being for its own reception.

He is the Friend. This is certain. That is why your book is a most precious gift to us Japanese. That is also why your book is an erroneous book on Japan: a friend of Japan—the Friend's friend—will always write an erroneous book on Japan; he will write an erroneous book on Japan as naturally as a friend of China would a correct one. The distinction here is not obvious; thus, as you would say, it is the more real. It is due partly to the fact that China's historical face is open or unveiled for us—not so Japan's.

From its prehistoric premises, and in spite of the latter's controversial and complex obscurities (China appearing to scholarly interpretation now as Western Asiatic in origins, now "purely" Chinese), to its present-day revolutionary decisions,[45] the intricate meshing of China's millenary epos appears to us without great and too-dark gaps.

At the threshold of her clear history—the still mysterious and sacred Shangs—I see the last Shang, defeated and invaded by the Chou "barbarians," killing himself amidst the splendor of the Bronze king-priest's palaces and gardens (Shangs! So strangely "Japanese" in their samurai code of honor and loyalties!) Then, across centuries of change I see the last Ming, defeated and invaded by the Manchu "barbarians," killing himself amidst the sophisticated modern splendor of the palatial gardens. How symbolically significant—symbolically only, of course—is here the continuity and similarity in response-attitudes!

Whereas from the very outset Yamato's epos has deep and dark gaps: consider the sudden and obscured leap from the humble darkness of the Neolithic to the haughty *flamboiement* of Nara, so radiant with its five many-faceted[46] Buddhist gems!

And yet, the obscurity of this gap is already resonant with prophetic voices. Or consider again . . . But no! let's rather fix the light directly on my initial "paradox": that it is good, thus true and beautiful, to write an erroneous book on Japan. I insist. Fenollosa, the best and perhaps the most truthful of all revealers of Japan, was inconceivably, scandalously erroneous when he produced his oceanic thesis—the connection of Yamato's arts in their historical origins with arts, obviously of later date, of the Pacific barbaric humanity as well as with the art of the Americas.[47] And yet—*e pur si muove!*—how right he appears when, or if, we dare to face the concreteness of his global attitude toward what you have defined as the *Gestalt* of Japan, his attitude in its turn bunched together with Japan's own visionary self-expressing attitude in art.

Yamato art *is* oceanic, the body-washing, the body-purification art—and this you have sensed so well!

Yes, your book is erroneous. Urged both by your sophistication and your *tendresse* for the subject, you have chosen (when such choice became inevitable for you) to neglect or fail to grasp totally the "correct" causal chain of facts, rather than to neglect or fail to grasp the self-bunching eventfulness among these very facts, their resulting attitude-horizon.

Have I understood you? *Facts* are observed happenings dependent on happenings that precede and follow them in a cause-effect chain of influences; *attitudes* are made of the bunching of the same facts clustered together by their automatic or magnetic, as it were, mutual and global attraction *at a given and unique point* (materially conditioned by this point too) *of history or time.*

In history as well as in the individual (always collected-collective) an attitude is the individual "soul" of individual man on earth; it is the man-within-a-given-time, I-within-a-time, no more, no less! (In a controversy, say, in a political or philosophical dispute, there would not be one single fact produced which could not be contrasted or answered by another, rival, fact. Not so with the attitude, not so with its "horizon"!)

I am fully aware here of your fears lest such a method's adhesion to the "mysterious" global attitude in detriment of the soundness and "objective" necessity of facts would directly lead to idealist-"reactionary," say Jungian, depth-psychology closures. It is just here, I must confess loudly, that for the time being lies perhaps the greatest difference between us Japanese and you Occidentals: basically we are not concerned—and this, in spite of the apparent, taken-for-granted contrary—with either the acceptance or the rejection of opinions we find surrounding us, but exclusively with the reciprocity of exchange between them and us, their production, their producers and us. Our concern, without any possible exception, is with what I should call the correct—quantitatively adequate—*exchange of gifts.* And I use the word *quantitatively* in the precise sense of your "persistence of intensity" or quantum-of-quality[48] theory. The exchange of gifts—here is revealed the secret of our "psychology."

For we Japanese are so conditioned, thus constituted, that everything—with no discontinuity at any level of existence—exists factual and real because it exists as significance. Everything is given to us as a gift, because the gift of significance or—which is the same—of eventfulness is attached to everything.

All this sounds very unsophisticated, say, childish. Yet childish it is not—but is of the child's self. It is the child in us. (Would it not be that

Japan arrested and kept in childhood some branches of its inner tree, the branch of Kantian moral imperative, for example, all the other branches surrounding it being given then, compensation-wise, an added energy to grow and project farther and faster—the sharpened growth of Japan's sense involvement, for instance—much farther and much faster than on any other historical tree?) It is the child who knows close to nothing about facts, thus is so helpless, but who knows close to everything about events—his own, thus helpful, "universe of discourse" made of eventfulness or significance. But is not the loyalty to this universe instinctual with all those, poets and scientists alike, who know that the reservoir of creativeness or invention is within the loyalty to the child in us?

To destroy the Child is precisely to destroy in our adulthood the child's curiosity for what is not yet known, what is *to be known:* facts, more of more facts, of inventions, thus, of creations.

I call it the gift of all-out eventfulness, which because, or when, it is all-eventful, cannot be but reciprocity, or exchange of gifts. With us, Japanese, all this is a most simple and ubiquitous attitude in existence and experience. That is why, for example, we never can be bored or even understand the concept of boredom. To be bored is inevitably and physically to end existence. To be bored is to live outside a significance and its creative excitement. We then simply cease or must cease to exist: simply also because when, within the limits of our "normal" physical existence, we cannot any more, or do not know how and where, to exchange gifts, we must do it "abnormally": by dying. The two young lovers who voluntarily and simply die by plunging into the entrails of their beloved Fuji—do it not because of, say, the insurmountable obstacles to the stability of their union, but because their love has been already invaded, no matter how still from afar, by the shadow of boredom or habit of loving. That is also why a personal offense, the gift-kami of a deeply personal, always bodily offense, has to be exchanged by a quantitatively equated gift to the offender: it is for that reason and not for a reason of revenge that in such an occurrence we commit the most bodily—most smelly too—suicide, the disembowelment in *seppuku.*

It would give me much joy if at this precise moment I could make myself understood by you as correctly and as far in your mind's direction as my Far Eastern mind's vernacular may be able to go.

I must try.

To be either true or erroneous is indifferent to us, and we know why and how it is so: we are indifferent to the combination of what you call rational and irrational in our judgment's apparatus, and we are passionately interested in—devoted to—the combination of what you call generosity and honesty.

What really matters here is to know that the two opposite yet fused terms, *rational* and *irrational* (read, if you wish to, *conscious* and *subconscious*), which form the very basis, the twofold operational basis of the West's mind, occupy the same position or situation on their mind's map as our own, the Far Eastern, twofold basis does on ours. *Only we don't call these fused opposites rational and irrational,* rational *versus* irrational (as you do so often, since classical Greece's time), we call them or their working *honesty and generosity,* perhaps even (I am not sure myself) honesty *versus* generosity. I do not want to speak here about the translatability of these two sets of terms from one mind's vernacular to another, but about their exact situational identity or mental map's projection. When you speak to a Japanese about honesty you must keep in mind its exact Western equivalent of rationality (consciousness); and if about generosity—the equivalent irrational (subconscious, or unconscious, as read more often than not today). And *vice versa.*

You have surely and fully sensed the presence of this identity: I know it now. But does the West sense this transfer? It is here that the bridge is to be built. The materials are there: exactly your solidarity-correspondence or the world of continuity, of subconsciousness's wealth—of *generosity;* and opposite it—opposite?—the world of *nous,* of discontinuity, the world of consciousness's restraint—of *honesty.*

And nothing else is here but the totality of Blake's Energies; nothing, consequently, that could fall out from the totality of Plenum-Void, of solidarity-solitude, of correspondence-identity, nothing else but the exchange of donations, the *exchange of gifts.*

To give, to give, to give; as the Child of your own imagery does, playing with gifts in a metaphysical toyland of Heraclitean *aeternitas*—receiving and exchanging gifts close to the body! And the body itself, in your own thought and idiom, being that which is in closest possible touch with what we love to call awareness.

Body: what does it matter here how this threshold is to be defined? Is "body" the compound-conscience, in, say, the grandiose image-nexus sense of Buddha's true Three-One Body, *Trikāya;*[49] is "body" that dual compound-conscience which you once told me the Judaeo-Islamic world and sometimes, later on, the Renaissance, distinguished as corporeity and materiality, as *visual apparition* of the physical and as *visionary operation* of the same physical (the *pneuma* or *psyche* element substantiating there this duality: *pneuma,* the *generous* elasticity of our touching and facing the somatic continuum, and at the opposite end of this act and simultaneously touching-facing the logos, the *honesty* of the separated, of the individual)?

It does not matter: "body" is simply the closest closeness of *my* body to my about-awareness: its threshold.

Here again, coming back to your imagery, is the unseizable individual sensation, unseizable because when occurring it cannot but be total coextension with my body, a total presence of adherence, with no possible overlapping room or margin there for consciousness's seizing. It is infinity. It is thus finity at the same time; you say it, because ironically, infinity becomes exhaustible in the very precision of sensing it physically. ("We shall die, finish—I cannot die, finish, I.") Possibly this would be the best historicist justification of today's existential anxiety—this fiery tongue of human creativity—as the final physicalization of the concept of infinity in the West—and this, in its turn, as the end result of the physicalization of the concept of spirit itself; simply also, as I see it in your writing, the latter's very humanism, or rather, neo-humanism: your prophetic vision about the

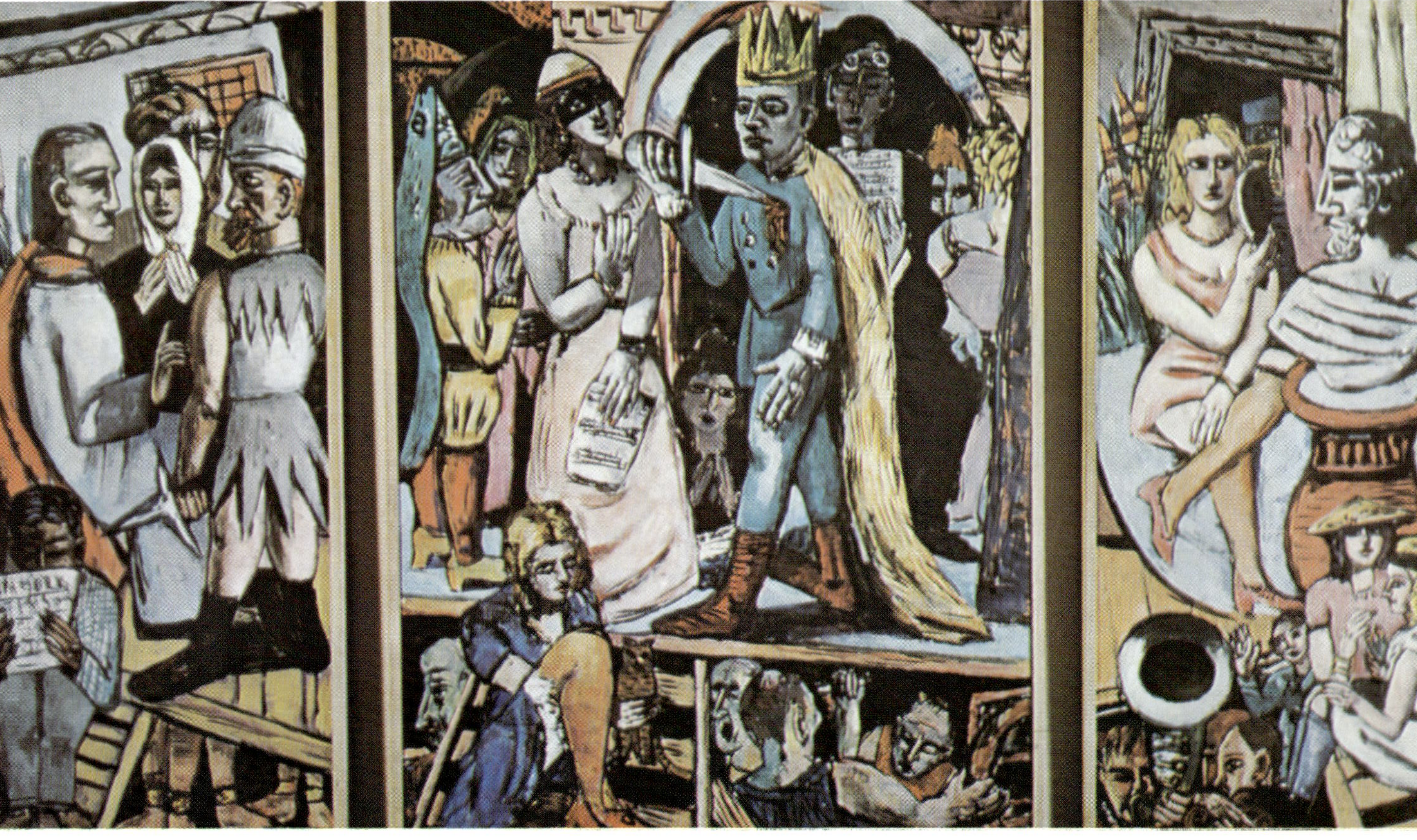

60 MAX BECKMANN *Actors* (triptych)

starting of a new light-cycle amidst the confusion of our dark today; the vision of the twentieth-century man's readiness to meet and perhaps to accept a new myth-monster.[50] And I am the loyal echo of your own voice, your entire vision. I mean the great past's light-cycle, its roots in the body horizon (the most ancient Egypt, the purely Shinto Japan as historical models), giving birth to the two cosmic trunks of the planetary thought-tree, the *nous* horizon (Greece and Judaea, *par excellence*), and the *pneuma* or *psyche* horizon (India, *par excellence*), both achieving their destined growth, circling their mature cycle, finishing it in the inevitable clash of twentieth-century transitional confusion.

For here is where your prophetic vision starts. I hear with sympathy your prophecy about the emergence today of a new cycle, the light-cycle of neo-consubstantiality, the neo-body horizon with, still fused within it—for how long in this new Kalpa?—still fighting there for self-realization (in global repetition of the great past's procedure), the two parallel and new forms of a neo-*nous* and a neo-*pneuma*.

The neo-spirit and the neo-psyche are still hidden in the obscurity of the future's entrails, yet dimly active there already: in the redeeming, closest-to-body neo-logic of our contemporary thought and of our contemporary arts, close to all primeval fruitions, the child, the ancient, the insane, the "primitive."

Your West starts to know all this with a knowledge still violent, alas! The East knew it long, long ago—in peace and irony too, for to be either true or erroneous is indifferent to us.

Dame souris trotte,
Noire dans le gris du soir,
Dame souris trotte
Grise dans le noir.

Le grand clair de lune!
On ronfle ferme à coté.
Le grand clair de lune
En realité![51]

All this great detour of mine is simply to stress and repeat to you what I said at the very start: your book on Japan, my dear friend, is an erroneous book on Japan. It is thus, I insist again, a solemn and lovely gift to us Japanese. And it is a gift in our Japanese sense because it is to be exchanged exactly—it is already, in fact!—for our-my-gift to you. "*J'ai mal à ta poitrine.*" From now on there *will be no more letters written to you by me,* but my own writing of the book you have already written: I shall write a your-book on Japan. It is a must. For the very "mystery" of the Japanese collective "character" is in this exchange-of-gifts must. It is not, certainly, in the world-famous omnipresent and adamantine Japanese politeness shining in multiple reflections of its multiple facets, from exquisite sincerity and tenderness to calculated flattery, deceit, and cruelty; not, certainly, in the proverbial Japanese coupling of "losing-face" fears and revenges, its *giri* inhibition—no! it is not in all this, but simply in the exchange-of-gifts must. Yes, exchange of gifts, precise and quantitative: whether peace-giving in its goal and roots, or catastrophic in the failure of its subtle measuring devices; in philosophy, religion, trading, and politics, in lovemaking, seed propelling and seed loosing, in creating art, in woodchopping, in hiding from the world at large, in revealing itself to the same world at large openly, candidly: exchange of gifts, always.

And now, what exactly is your gift to us; what exactly is my exchanged gift to you? I am very sure about mine: the *Mysterious Companion*—my Companion now—of your journey. Who or what really is he in your book? And you, in turn, are you sure of your gift? I doubt it: the idea, let alone the intention of such a thing, is foreign to you. And so let it be I, the author of your book, who tells you now: praised be your book-kami on Japan! Because its subject is not Japan and Japan's art, but man's intellectual love of God, *amor intellectualis Dei,* the only profitless absolute in the world or worlds.

And praised be the absolute's only embodiment in art: the *kami-ornament.* As the spirit of geometry for Greece, so the spirit of the ornament is for Japan the only profitless absolute in art's universe: body's "frozen calligraphy"—the *nous* of space—the very tracery of Japan's oceanic kami-dance.

This is your solemn and needed and lovely gift to us.

The *amor intellectualis Dei* belongs to us now, not to you, to Japan and to Japanese art: it is your gift to us. The Mysterious Companion, the Japanese Companion of your journey, belongs to you, not to us; he belongs to the West, to the art of the West: this is my gift to you.

Indeed, I am the one who one day met the Companion of your journey on my last visit to the West. I found him inhabiting the big, passionate world of a rough-and-gentle painting. It was this rough-and-gentle spirit there that at once attracted my astonished sympathy, the sympathy of a rough-and-gentle-minded and trained Japanese *(Plate 60).* The limbs of this spirit's mysterious body stretched beyond the limits of the painting's frame, stretched and stretched long and narrow—a long and narrow shadow stretched on a moonlit and solitary summer street—and reached beyond the stars' zone, so it seemed to me, the very limits of Western man's mind. This is not just an exaggerated, if helping, metaphor (perhaps irritating to you), but a very accurate description of an experience, as concrete and precise an experience as the reciting of a *haiku* is for us.

Haiku: have you noticed that of all the so-called great cultures of the world it is the Far Eastern, strictly speaking, the Japanese, that has never produced a great national epic? We never had a *Bhagavad-gita* or an *Odyssey* or a *Shah Nameh.* Neither *Kojīkī* nor our *Genji* are this. But it is the shortest, perhaps, verse in the world, our *haiku,* that for our people has been the great epic, our only and the same epic: where change—ineffable, individual—in us, or in the cosmos's mood, lies in narrow, Yab-Yum embrace with the cosmic permanence.

One day, very suddenly, in front of the roughness-gentleness of Max Beckmann's triptych *The Actors,* I met the Mysterious Companion. What

I mean here at the very start is that, in *haiku* fashion, or far-radiating *haiku* habit of thought, I met through him, ascending the monumental scale of intensity, no less a personage than the very history of Western man; to be precise (if incongruously sudden), my own Japanese passion, the history of Christian man. For if *amor intellectualis Dei* is what is *not* history, the *Mysterious Companion* of a journey appeared to me as what *is* history or change. But I am speaking exclusively about my being in front of a precise painting, within the frame—and nothing else!—of Max Beckmann's triptych. There I promptly recognized your Companion, him, neither a symbol nor

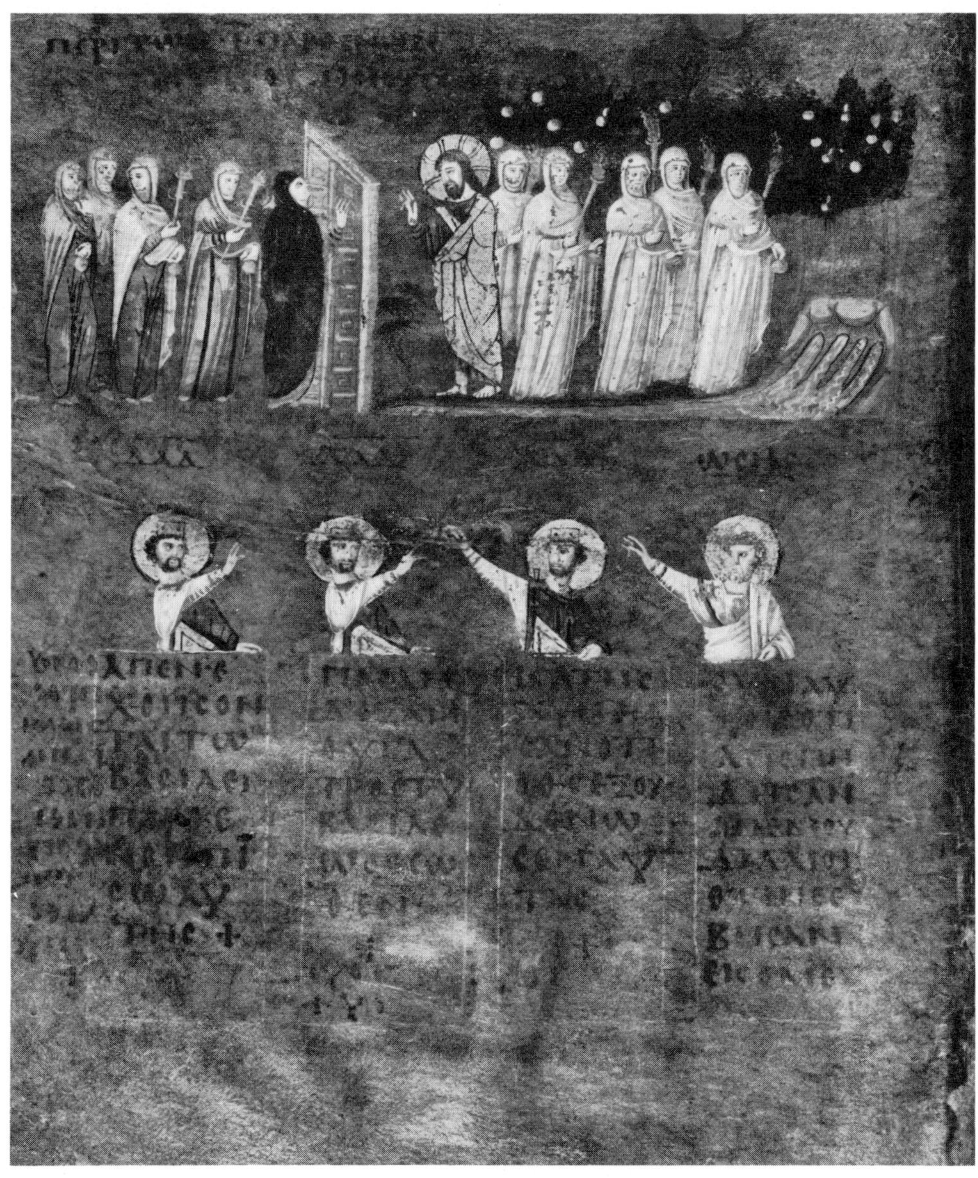

61 *The Wise and Foolish Virgins* The so-called Rossano Gospels
Syro-Byzantine, 6th century

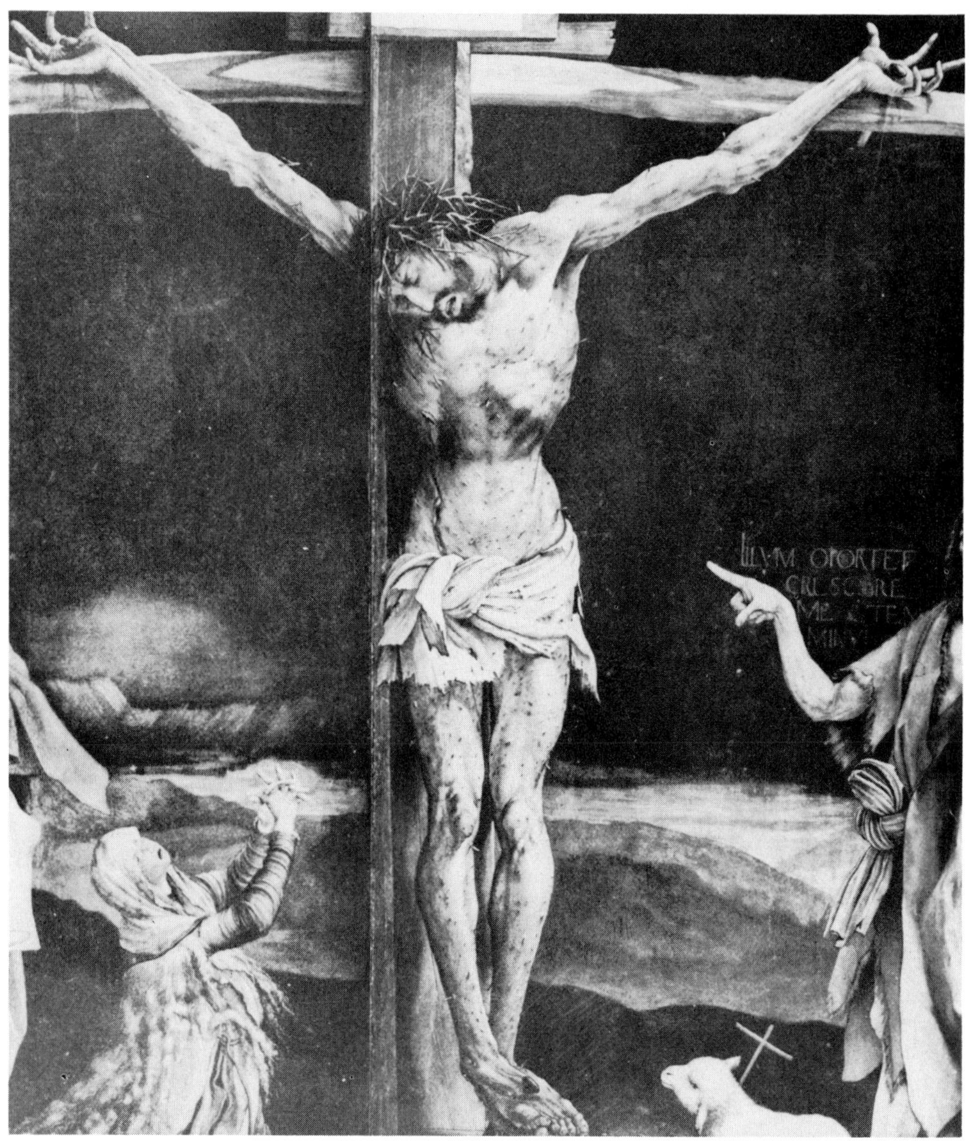

62 GRÜNEWALD *Crucifixion* Detail (ca. 1512-1515)

allegory but a "verbally" still absurd concretion: a witness, the actual, physical presence of a witness, his influence and operation tangible in there; a testifier to a hidden event, nay a witness of the Truth; one should say, with needed courage, as Christ and his true follower are.

Sheltered as I am now and here by our friendship from the suspecting and mocking outside, I dare to tell you this: I had a vision that the Mysterious Companion in a painting, in a journey, in the history of man, is the *finger pointed*—menace, anxiety, peace and *caritas* together—at someone's presence: the hand's index, the eye's index *(Plates 61, 62, 63)*.

How curious it is that India, so close to this witnessing persuasion and mood has never, at its best and most expressive, known this testifying command of the hand's index. In her consummate knowledge of and specula-

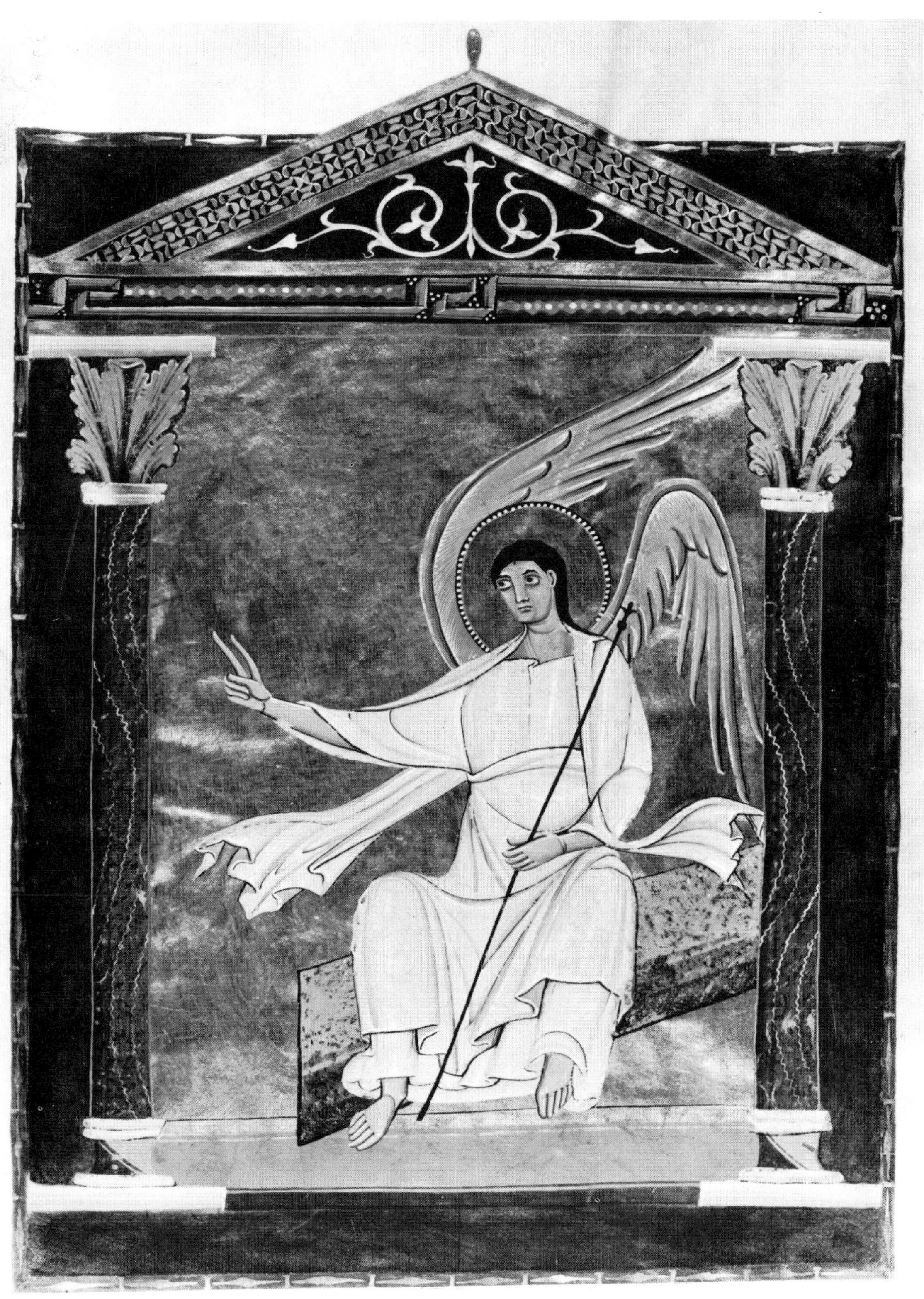

63 *The Angel at the Sepulchre* (early 11th century)

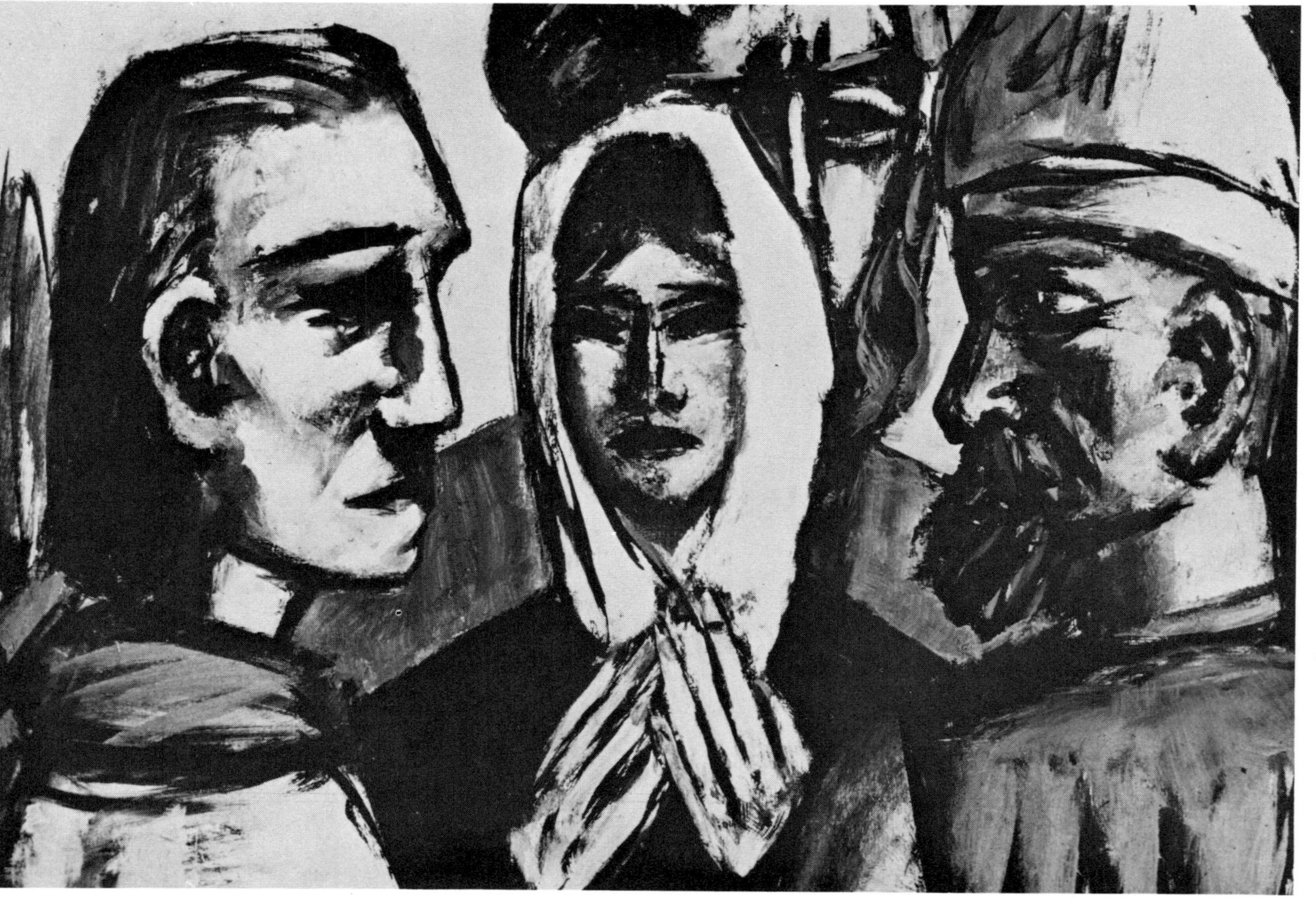

64 Max Beckmann *The Actors* Detail

tion about the human hand's communicative idiom—the *mudras*—India's supreme achievement remained at this stage of knowledge-conviction, not the witness's presence, not touch.

Now—you will surely trust me—this Christian art's testifying index is not only the hand's pointing gesture, it is or can be the index-eye, the index-color, the index-composition or index-ornament.

In the world of Max Beckmann nobody looks at anybody or anything, nobody sees anybody or anything; everybody *glances* at any and every thing and every body; there is a silent and forceful index-glance pointed at what is the eventful—threat, anxiety, peace, charity, together *(Plate 64).*

Yes, the triptych is a glancing into a journey, a journey accompanied by the same Companion of your journey from the Kanagawa shore onward. But what journey in Max Beckmann? I say the departure into a destiny: eyes, big one-eyed monster's eye, two eyes, trembling little animals, through the apertures of the mask; eyes that conspire—it is a conspiracy!—between them, through their glance, and point at my destiny, because of the glance. The Departure of the Innocents. Eyes that but look, eyes that but see, do not suffice—they have to testify, they have to testify to something else. Perhaps the *peine d'amour* of your *Autumn* is the cause of this *else* of Beckmann. For to glance is at first to look at something, to see it, to paint it, and then to erase it—to erase that which was seen, and so to start anew the glancing, the index-pointing at something else. And Max Beckmann does it. Always: nude and uncomfortable eyes-feet, big supporting feet, segregated, then re-installed in justice to the body hurt—very uncomfortably nude—*peine d'amour!*—feet-eyes exchanged, color splashes exchanged: glances, the index of the glance; the witness of the departure—or murder?—of Innocents. The slaughter of innocents, as the Gospel tells us, never to be hidden for too long, revealed after all.

And now I shall describe the triptych:

The left wing: preparation for the journey toward the murder. The Companion-glance testifies that the good suffering intellectual—Max Beckmann—and the post-World-War-I Paris, Rotonde, Dôme, Christ stopping there maybe, oh *peine d'amour!*—explains this murder to the murderer-to-be, the latter's dagger—a crucifix erased—pointed at the innocents below—the *New York Times* reader, poor naked flesh, young feet in chains?—the innocents of elsewhere, maskless, defenseless, yet part of the show. And the woman in mourning-veils bethinking all this in her silent, imploring glance. Preparation. Waiting. Prophecy.

The central wing: destiny accomplished. It is I, the good innocent "intellectual"-shepherd, I the king and the foreigner at the Dôme, 1932 (the picture could not have been conceived outside a precise momentum: the Companion is history, always). I kill myself, in mock murder for the sake of the new, another, Departure. (Two eyes, my beloved's, trembling little animals, through the apertures of her mask; eyes that conspire—it is a conspiracy!—between them and others, through their glance, prophesying my destiny in a glance, and pitying, oh *peine d'amour!*)

 Whose Departure? The world's, everybody's, around the mock sacrifice

—and everybody is glancing, eyes supporting big feet and shadows, in silent testimony. *Consummatum est.*

The right wing: the arrival for a new Departure, the re-opening of the stage of slaughter (young woman, very pretty, glancing anew into her mirror, testifying to a new face—the blue face—while the old good intellectual is a statue; and a little below, all is fanfare and pretty girls-flowers, Hurrah!).

Now seriously: the uncomfortable, erased, symmetry between the left and right wing's com-position is astonishingly well orchestrated: the main balance-center being the girl with the cat (all say the owl), where the Mysterious Companion is innocently posted—in good and crafty pictorial earnest. Thus, the subject itself of the triptych, including what I have just said, is erased in the glance of my destiny's departure and the new arrival. Witness of this: the Companion, justly mysterious (even the crafty color, color splashes, are slippery, slipping one upon the other—erased, indexing, witnessing too, as does all flesh).

All this, of course—Beckmann and my reading into it—is neither rational nor irrational, but simply honest and generous: obviously Japanese. But obviously also—a very accentuated, particular way of communication; obviously again, a religious-mystical way. Exactly.

Exactly also my experience about which I must tell you now: that is, my exchanged gift to you. I had been thus glancing at the triptych for a long while, very bewildered—the *ecce homo* in it!—now disgusted (so much distorting roughness!—too much even for Japan!), now in bliss (so much stress on the gently interiorized significance!), when the train of my historical thought was suddenly and freely alerted and moving ahead. Of what I became lucidly sure was that neither Max Beckmann nor any of the "objective" deformers of the twentieth-century's art (with satisfaction I could find our Shiko Munakata there!) could be what they are without a mental orientation in them, a method of communicating and convincing that I suddenly saw as belonging to a precise and now revived historical cycle: the time of Christian man's rise and growth. Of this I have already spoken to you. But I must add now: I saw lucidly then, and only then, that Christianity as mind's new way—new glance! (and the *Dead Sea Scrolls* controversy would leave this precise newness untouched)—was the giving to the world of the gift of a *tactile,* and not only *conceptual-persuasive* proof of its Messiah, not through the image-concept, but by the image-touch.

True, all the messianic religions brought with them a similar testifying "proof" of their sacrificed redeemers. Namely, and in your own description, the messianic in-seeding of the living grain, its death and rotting in the moist womb of the earth, its inevitable miracle of resurrection as another, different, big grain, the plant in spring—*deus absconditus*—the hidden god who, because known as hidden, is to be revealed thus. Yet the sacred icon of a Mithra, for instance, is still highly abstract, still too conceptually pure, and even the historical Buddha, Sakyamuni, gave away slowly and inevitably his limited, touchable historicity. Only Christ could be *touched* with the finger-index of a historical event. Be it as it may have been—whether factually "provable" or not as history's true happening, the image-touch of

65 Juan Gris *Le Canigou*

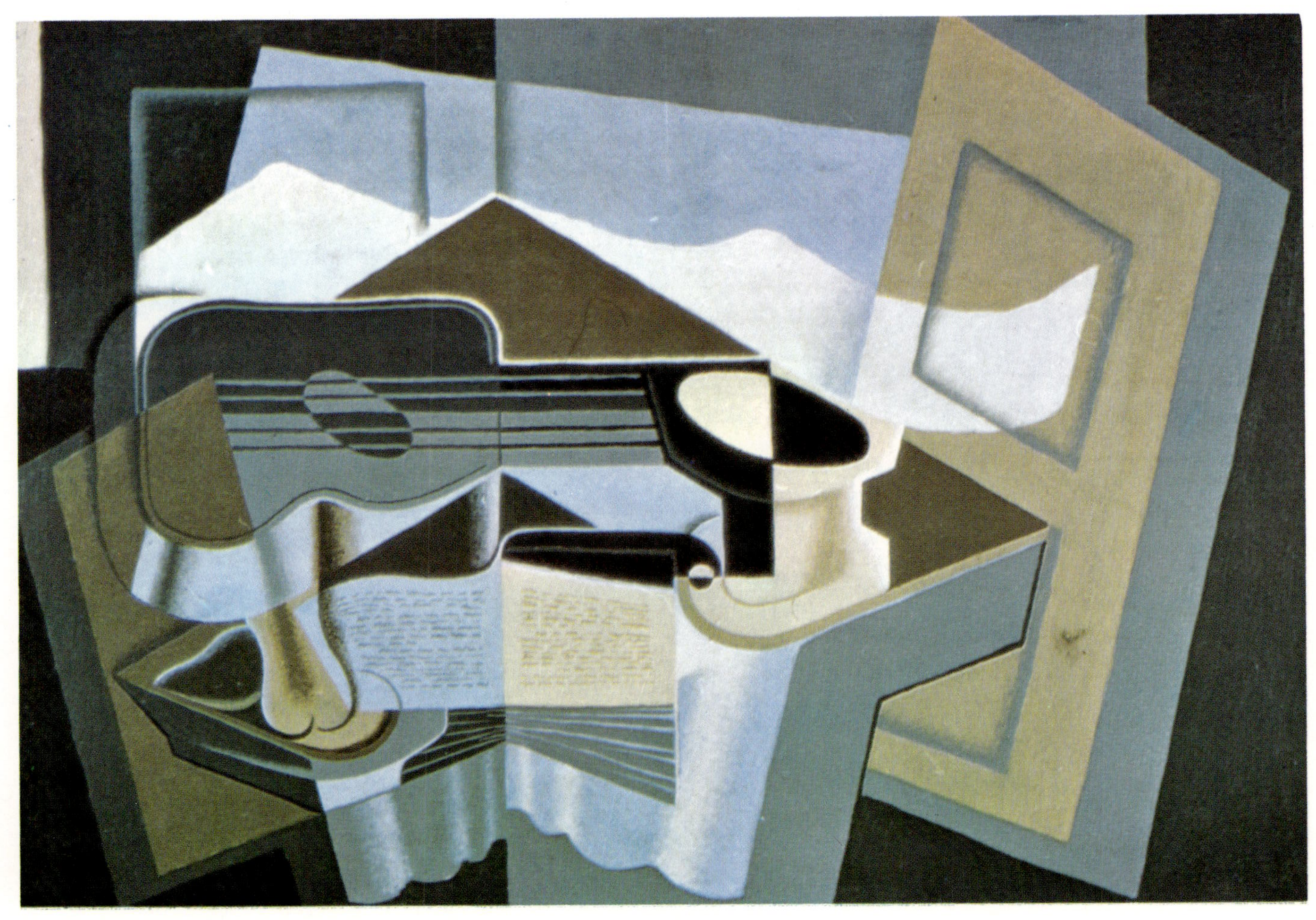

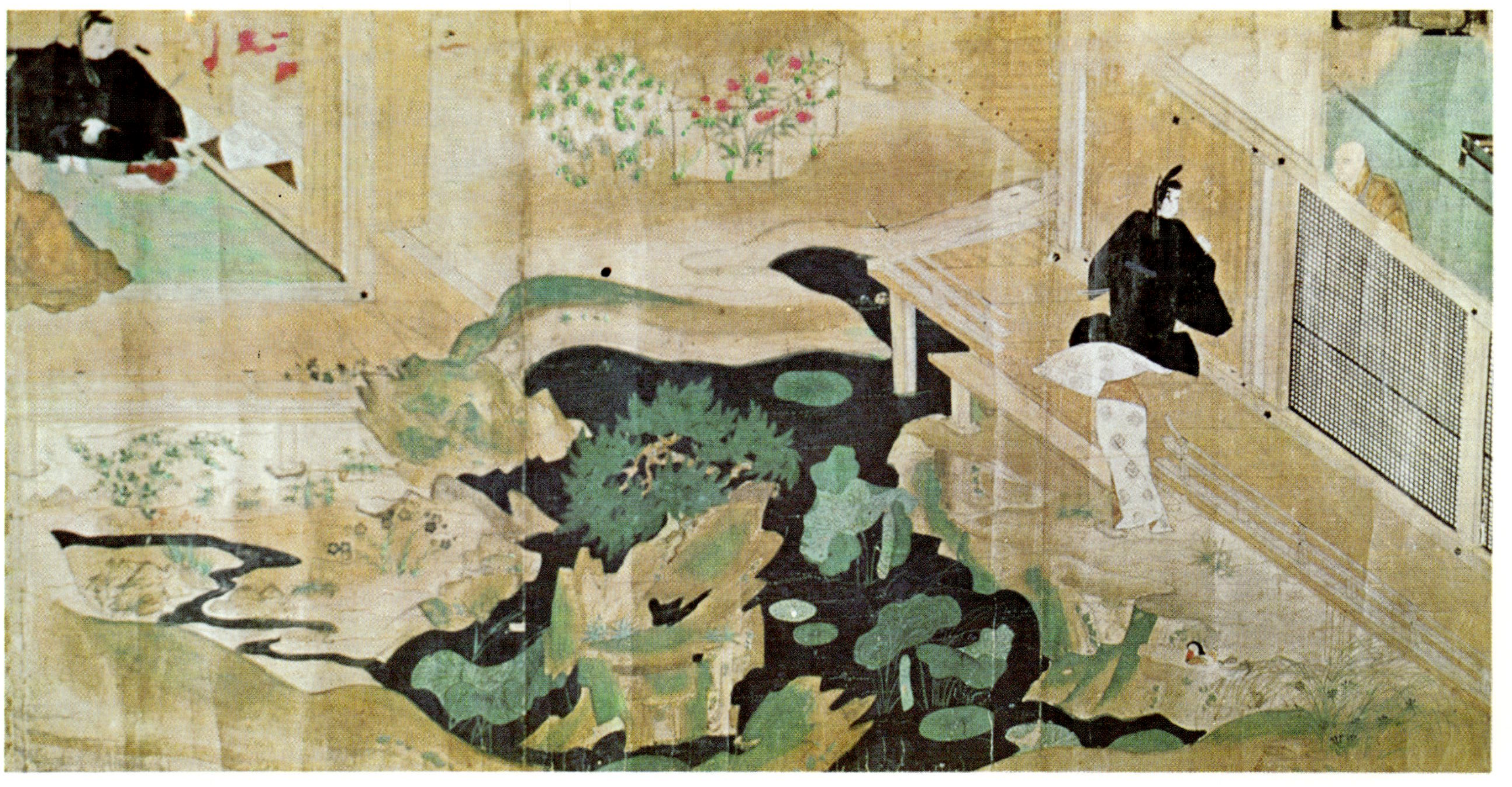

66 Ascribed to Fujiwara-no-Nobuzane *Kitano Tenjin Engi* (detail)

Christ's presence—Christ, the Jew of the time of Herod—has never been contested as an event of history.

Credo quia absurdum est, the christological event became both a metaphor and a proof, the immediacy of an image-touch not only as *object* of religious communication and subjective fullness, but as the very *method* of communication itself, as an epistemologically asserted proof. A metaphoric method-and-object of thinking. Not even a witnessing, but the Witness himself—the constant Companion of the proof's journey. Proof, proving, and the proven equated.

❖❖❖❖❖❖❖❖❖❖❖❖❖❖❖❖❖❖❖❖❖❖❖❖❖❖❖❖❖❖

March 5

For I think that the human mind has known only three ways of communicating its findings, three methods of conducting its inquiry about the object of its desire or knowledge: the way of the syllogism, the way of dialectics, the way of the metaphor-touch. Yet, in considering these three always interlocking methods or ways of mind more narrowly and closely, that is, in concentrating rather on their operation in the world of mind's creativity proper, only two types of building device, only two types of reference symbol have been found and used, so it seems to me, along the three ways: I would call them the *mirror* and the *window.* These are for me the two paramount symbols of the entire history of the human mind's evolvement.

Now, the first way. To begin with, it is the way, historically the most recent, of classical antiquity, *par excellence;* the Greeks' art of the syllogism, the art of "coming out" into the outside of oneself through the operation of a most adequate symbol, *the window;* the looking out through the window, a symbol revived fully later in the Renaissance, Dürer's obsession, the *Durchsehung,* the window indeed.

In its visual-manual, *techne* application, I mean in the visual, pictorial, to be precise, arts (our main concern after all), this legacy of Greece should be easily equated with its corresponding optical device or tool for adequate through-space building; the invention of shadow. The pictorial shadow is the middle term, as it were, of the syllogism-proof, the "window" of spatial objectivity; it is extension and graduated plastic consistency. But who told us that the decisive middle term of a syllogism should be in the middle of such a structure of proof? And why should this way of syllogism be less "arbitrary," more necessary than the other, the second, perhaps parallel way, the way to which I am coming now: the way of dialectics, of dialectical proof, Asia's way of observing and ordering the parallel-mutual continuity—the Tao?—the mirroring of me in the world and the world in me, the mirroring of Yes in No, of No in Yes? And indeed, the reference symbol of dialectics' or Asia's way, the invisible underlying symbol of Asia's global attitude, primordially universal too, is thus the *mirror.*

The mirror: the window's universe in reverse; it is I plunging back into the I-together-with-the-beyond-of-me universe. But who really sees himself in a mirror? Illusion of the "objective" real? Reality of the "subjective" illusion?

Neither; but in the arts of the eye and hand, a real object of dialectics' convention: the interlace, image-ornament, not image-narration.

But there is the third way—the way of touch, the immediacy of proof by the immediacy of touch: I-thou, mirror-window, shadow-interlace, image-narration = image-ornament. Presence of adhesion, you said; and also, you said, relation without the category of relation in it as yet.

There is surely such a third way. For I found, hardly interrupted, traces of its structure along the entire history of man's evolvement. It is the story of the tragic split, and the post-split's happenings. And now comes the true moment to repeat it and to resume it.

Obscurely and universally groping for recognition ever since the primordial tragic split, asserting itself in the swarming mystery cults of late antiquity's urban-artisan inquietudes, the mind's way of touch, the way of the witness-in-the-icon, could re-assert itself by shaping two major and synchronical events on our planet: the spreading of the messianic Mahayana Buddhism in the greater East—the zone of the *mirror* and the interlace; and the rise of Christianity in the greater West—the zone of the *window* and of the pictorial shadow.

But the true home of the witness, the *difficult* fruit of his *caritas* could only be built where it was at once expected, *difficult*, and new: in the Hellenized West. There the rise of Christianity (I don't mean Christianity itself), its triumph over all other similar messianic mystery creeds, was mainly due to this piercing-through or self re-asserting of the artisan epistemology of touch.

The rise of Christianity is the rise of its art. Christianity is its art and the witness in it: the Mysterious Companion of your journey in Japan and of my gift to you.

Humbly but firmly—in *haiku*-trained fashion of identity and substitution—I repeat: the Mysterious Companion (within the frame of an object of art, only, exclusively, from now on) touches with his index, in judiciary menace and tenderness, every being, every object, raised thus from death by the Christian within it. Such is Christian art from the catacombs to Picasso. I say someone is always present in an object made by a Christian, no matter how un-Christian in behaviour, ethos, and conviction might be the maker of it. Someone always is there, a witness, whose will can change the natural "order" of the eye, the causal chain of the visual facts, into a new order, a new form-monster made of the unexpected bunching of facts = events.

The witness is invisible. What is visible is his impact or influence (thus he is there!): his *permission,* as it were, to change—to deform—the order of empirical facts. The very essence of medieval Christian art, the epic revelation of the mysterious witness in it, is in this *permission;* the very essence of your externally so un-Christian art of today's West is in this *permission* to deform—rather than in the *deformation* itself. . . . . Someone within the soul of an individual eye and hand, Juan Gris and his "Canigou," for instance *(Plate 65),* within the soul of that precise hour of history also, of course; someone there changes the order of the world outside us in the painted view through the window. I, Juan Gris, the blueness of the blue Catalan sky, the whiteness of the snowy summit, Canigou's brown triangularity, all cluster in a new, permitted, Juan-Gris-Canigou-blue-snow-triangle-window-mirror object resurrected.

A resurrected new object-Lazarus, the proof-touch of a living witness there; and in Picasso's monster-landscape, Picasso's "Aubade," both monster (because form unexpected!) of linear light sources (here Picasso is but light!) and witness to day's golden birth from the old purples of the night—probably the most significantly "witnessing" landscape of daybreak ever painted; all this, here too, made visible and tangible by the visible, tangible will and influence of an invisible witness. A re-created universe of solitude-solidarity, at once man and the beyond of man: man-landscape *in toto.*[52]

A new, compound, unique being-monster, not more nor less so than, say, a Ukiyo-e monster-landscape *(See Plate 39)* or this Kamakura creation *(Plate 66).*

The Mysterious Companion is physically invisible in a painting, of course; and his physical visible influence, his permission to deform, to change the given order of the world is within the physical limits of a painting. We are within a painting, not elsewhere, don't forget. And I should not forget now that I am writing your writing of a book on painting. In *haiku*-trained fashion of identity and substitution we shall not speak any more of mind's ways; we shall not remember or wish any more mind's great planetary symbols, the window, the mirror. We remember, wish, and speak only, exclusively, of their *techne* equations. The mysterious living witness, the Mysterious Companion of your journey in Japan and of a painting is but the index—justiciary menace and tenderness—touching the destiny of the finite pictorial shadow as well as of the infinite interlace.

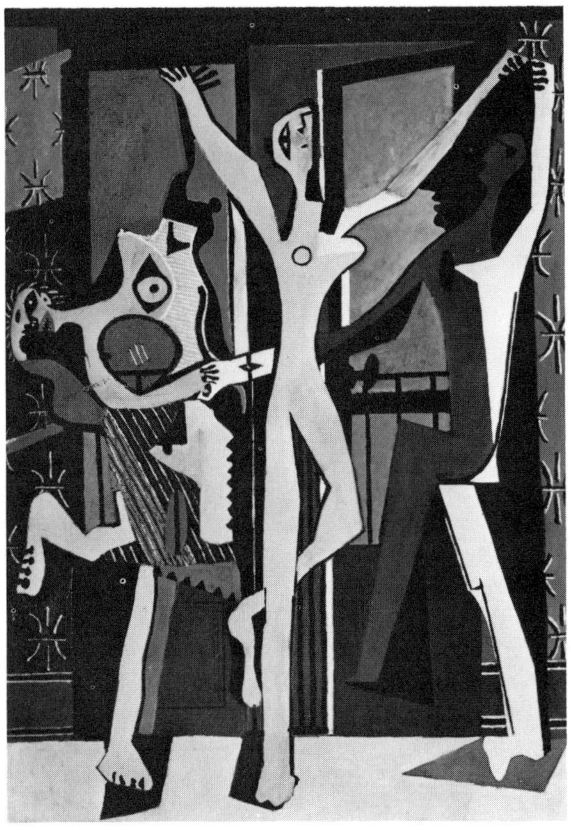

67 PABLO PICASSO *The Three Dancers*

Our destiny is their destiny; our function is theirs. The will of the witness takes a definite shape. Picasso's life companion, Christ or Tovarishtch (it does not matter here any more), is the One whose will has already entirely changed the destiny of what was antiquity's legacy—the space-building function of the pictorial shadow. From an inanimate, obedient object or thing of support, this constructed device for body-rounding and projection in a limited space and light, by the virtue of the living witness's *index*-touch, became a fully animated, multi-limbed new being—a living body itself and in its own right now, freely operating, independent yet bunched together, interlaced, with light: a shadow = interlace.

The whole twentieth century is in the phenomenology of the free acting shadow and of its understanding. Yet all this was—and no historian of the West should forget it!—a Christian revolution, its limbs stretching far from the frame of a painting to the moving stars: *"l'amor che move il sole e l'altre stelle."*

In truth, there is no shadow any more—neither in Picasso nor in any of his contemporaries: there is only its witness to light.

The shadow of yore has left its sheath, and fraternal to our Sotatsu-Koetsu letters-and-bamboo poem of liberation *(See Plates 29-35)*, has started to live its own life, still too new for us *(Plate 67)*.

Yes, the Mysterious Companion is not an abstraction or a symbol, and his testimony is about the real-concrete. By and in this testimony, your ghost is real too, and your image-touch, and your visitation. But this is exactly what you wished to say in your book on Japan and on Japanese art. And thus it is a truthful book—praised be your book-kami!

March 10, and I resume

1) A libidinous philosophy *in toto*, the philosophy of penetration, as when one evokes the love-name given by India to the water-center of all existence: the Seed of Waters.[53] *Soma-knot. Body.*

2) The four seasons, autumn, winter, spring, summer, each in each other, each following each other: *Pneuma-knot. Psyche or Soul.*

3) And nothing else besides them. What could it be besides? Only the Name: of the Sacrifice. *Nous-knot. Spirit.*

Yours	*Mine*
In autumn: oh, give me the *peine d'amour* from spring, alas!	Summer's short smell: Minamoto white Taira red in winter's heraldry.

All you have said without me about Japan I resume thus in second circumambulation:

a) That *Yamato* is the Noh or the vertical-and-horizontal positing of one's body: the narrow vertical dance-leap being there the not-as-yet-freed aspirations of very primitive humanity; while the horizontal outward dance-leap is the freed expression of evolved societies.

b) That Noh is Yamato's painting by substitution; and by substitution Yamato painting is Yamato's polity—the shogunate—and is *Jōdo*'s I-am-already-in-Paradise (Nembutsu: and period!), in Paradise for the many not for the few, as Mme. Rhys Davids, so loyal to the West, wished Buddhism to be in its roots.

c) That, as a corollary, everything you have said is also by substitution or identity a new *quantum-emotion* theory, its *ontic* axis, the category of quantity itself, replacing in our crisis days the greater past's all-commanding axis of value-judgment, the category of quality.

(To check this: all beginnings—of religions, in a very particular eminence and example here—before their yielding to the state-church elite's reasons, are intensified and precise quantities of emotion, nostalgias for the ordinary, the mediocre, the many, and not qualified qualities, shelters for the extra-ordinary, the few.)

Let's float upon all this and resume now—yes!—my own your-writing all along the book:

That you were looking for a name; and that I have this name, the name for the bunching together of the still nameless touch with the *peine d'amour* and with all the rest. (Oh, not a bunching together as the result of a micro-macrocosmic correspondence—you are not a bit interested in this—this would not be the name!—for everybody knows correspondence as the only possible absolute; and you are interested in the Eucharist, the final loss substituted: the Name.)

Let's float anew—toward the Name, not toward the absolute, which is only possible.

❖❖

Till then, I had the choice of names: I cried out: Tathagata! I cried out: Citta—loudly, pompously, piously, dryly too: Tathagata! and other names dear to us: Samsara,[54] Sunyata above all!—in order to get their full light—phonetically!—in order also to be blinded, inundated, extenuated and satisfied by the dialectic splendor of my Asia, Asia's incalculable treasures of the rich: so that in this state I could forget; so that I could tell myself I have lost, I have forgotten the touch of the poor: the *Agnus Dei qui tollis peccata Mundi.*

The Mysterious Companion is never in Tathagata—never. The witness is in the touch of *Agnus Dei.* The witness is in the theory of this touch as well as in the touch of the cleverly justified mockery about the silliness of this theory of the touch.

(And yet, art is exactly this poor "mystical" silliness, when art is not what it is with them, the mockers, a sociologically established success in illustrating and revealing forces that work—and indeed they do!—within an influenced historical time-fact.)

But the touch-visitation epistemology is without a name as yet.

Tathagata! But no! This would not work with me any more! Desperately (I take as my help our testimony here, the twentieth-century consubstantiality: touch Picasso, please!)—desperately I am drifting along all this wilful vagueness, not any more as a precision-struck Japanese, but as if I were a Westerner, drifting consciously and not so consciously. And I am to speak here for the still nameless touch. You could think of me as being against the syllogism and dialectics—but I am not: I am for kami-good and kami-bad, a pre-Buddhist I am, all for experimental sciences probably. No, I am not against dialectics-*pneuma,* nor syllogism-*nous!* but (because of everybody's talk about today's crisis, because of this true yet abused expression, *crisis,* crisis of our twentieth century, crisis of the individual, the collective, the ethical in man, held everywhere in the gossipy tongue of appraisal and not in the palm of the hand), I must come out and lead the emphasis on the by-passed, forgotten logic of touch in us. (Maybe this is what we shall call soul—I don't know.) For this touch exists in us as truly and as identically as exists in us, underneath syllogism's out-affirmation and dialectic's in-negation, the body reference—in silence and fullness.

I am here obstinately to stress in your book the body again—not so much as the epos of consubstantiality in man's greater past, but as the neo-consubstantiality of today and its radiation afar in intertwined knots of communications: area-volumes, not only direction-lines of communications, both spreading and knot-forming.

All this I want now tightly kept in the palm of the hand—a bunch, a knot of libidinous obsessions held in the palm of the hand. And by bunching I finally mean:

a) in its initial sense—*de profundis clamavit!*—Kant-Cassirer's image-and-schema knot, and

b) in another sense far removed from that psychological source, the area-volumes or patterned attitudes called history or change, the history-knot of China, of France, of America or Russia . . . .

All of which has to have a name in order to be kept firm and tight in the palm of the hand; things nameless flow away. And the name must be the name of a real person. For the touch, the Companion, the visitation must be a person.

And now I introduce in this already old and tired book a new *dramatis persona:* the Heraldic Man.

The heraldic mind, or heraldry: the name.

March 11, 1964

To remember: the rough-gentle kami is what reveals the spirit in Japanese art.

To forget: the word *bunching* is not a pretty word; it is a perilous word, too: it meant *Fascio,* it meant *Bund;* but it also meant *Ecclesia* (Christianity and its attitude, all), and *Umma* (Islam and its attitude toward men); it meant *Menschlichkeit* (Karl Marx's *totality*).

But then and anew: *bunching together,* what is it?

It is history without proof: without the chain of influences, a time-cluster of attitude-images given; a new emotion, the historical emotion: a mind's way and in it the presence of a witness. I call it the heraldic way to be explained.

Bunching: what is it?

It is to start the knot from within the body *(soma)*, from within the soul *(pneuma)*, from within the spirit *(nous);* then to become "connected-with," to hold in the hand, as a knot, as a name: my *peine d'amour.*

Bunching: what is it?

The heraldic universe, that is what it is: the New Name.

. . . One starts always somewhere, never at the very start; one always starts within a contracted area-cluster of events, a pattern-bunch already, and coming from afar.

And the art of Ukiyo-e is just such a good somewhere-start as any.

Ukiyo-e is, indeed, the hypostatic start of everything that has preceded and has been continued in the world of Japan: heraldically. It is everything and everybody that has preceded in your book and that is being continued there. Heraldically.

Because, just as in the "universe of discourse" of medieval heraldry, that is, in heraldic art, it is the positing, the situating upon the armorial shield of the armorial objects, the pose-dance performed by the charges and their signifying tinctures (and not so much the shield and the charges themselves), that both condenses and projects in one image-witness the totality of desired meanings there, so also in Ukiyo-e's clustered dance (its Heian-Momoyama legacy being thus fulfilled) it is the pose-situation of the pictorial subject matter (= the armorial charges) upon Japan's history field (= armorial shield) that gives to this late Yamato-e both its heraldic bearing of pride (in the sense of the French *fierté*, not in the sense of *orgueil*) and the mystery of its patterned narration, of its "frivolous," *populo*, ornament-imagery.

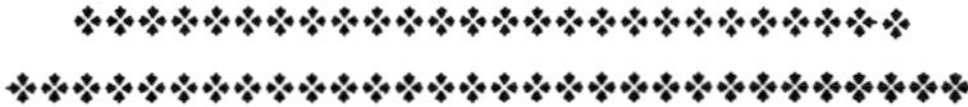

The heraldic man—the *grand personnage*—came to visit me, as you know it, right from within a page—a single, by-passed thought in it—of our friend Huizinga's *Waning of the Middle Ages*—right into my expecting mind and hand: "With the emblem and the motto *we enter the sphere of heraldic thought, of which the psychology is yet to be written.* To the men of the Middle Ages the coat of arms was undoubtedly more than a matter of vanity or of genealogical interest . . . . Whole complexes of pride and ambition, of loyalty and devotion, were *condensed* in the symbols of lions, lilies or crosses, which thus marked and expressed intricate mental contexts *by means of an image.*"[55] (Italics added.)

Here it is, in one knot of "connected-with" terms, everything I loved in your Japan: the heraldic way or state of mind: the putting in respective signifying position on the armorial blazon's field of all the objectivized loyalties of the human heart, object-knots of a dying knight's deep and cool, ultimate and profitless emotion—exactly the "objective deformation" already in our "monstrous," contemporary art's sense—the unseizable total sensation of aristocratic-folk loyalties, fear, gratitude, death, and comradeship; a collective-individuated sensation seized *in toto* by the witness-image of it; the lion or the leopard restant, rampant, passant, affronted, or eagles, or martlet, fish, sun, moon, the *estoiles,* the cross, the chevron, the pile, the clover, the five-petalled rose . . . . The way of the witness witnessing, of touch, mind's third way; mirror-window; shadow-interlace.

Here it is: the substitution of the logos of immediacy, the logos of the "arbitrary," for the logos of persuasion. The heraldic horizon, let us call it, or heraldically re-written human as well as cosmic history; perhaps to be called also *sub-history* in homology with what the term "sub-microscopic happening" would mean to a modern physicist.

That is why it is not important or essential here to observe the jealous strictness (by no means to be factually rejected) exercised by all the authorities in this particular field of medieval studies[56] in defining the limits of what should properly be considered heraldry as an exact historical science and art. It is this strict adhesion to established rules of appraisal that makes, say, the Islamic peoples' armorial distinctions a true heraldry, but not the Japanese *mon.*[57]

How curious are the artisan-visual roots of Japan's heraldry—of Japan's art at large! "Originally, the Japanese heraldic insignia, commonly called in Japanese *mon* or *mondokoro,* was designed for representing one's family name. This has achieved through the centuries such a development that today the family, its crest or badge and name constitute an indivisible trio among the people of this country[58] . . . .

"Heraldry in its broadest sense embraces trade-marks, emblems on ships' sails and even the badges borne by troops, schools, cities and towns, and many other bodies . . . . "[59]

A large number of the existing family crests have their origin in the patterns depicted on the garments of ancient court nobles of the Heian period, who, in lacquered palanquins and canopied coaches drawn by oxen, vied with one another in the display of their vehicles decorated on the sides with patterns of tree-peony, or iris, or swallows, or butterflies—all this connected with distinguishing one's vehicle from another's.

There is no difference, I think, no essential difference, between the mental-collective roots of the Western and, say, our Japanese heraldic horizons; between the spirit behind the armorial shield and the armorial *man.* The witnessing index of the Mysterious Companion's hand, the singling-out touch, is in both.

Here too confusion arises from the very strictness of critical delimitations.

The badge, the badge-mentality—a clustered total, equated with each of its individuated Lazarus-fragments—is the man that does not want to be anonymous in an anonymous world, Christian, Buddhist, Shinto, feudal or "capitalist." That's it! Heraldry means not to be lost: to be held in the hand, to reach the discontinued, the individual, *via* the collective-collected sensation of, and within, one self—not *via* the collective social only. The Hector or St. Louis on a Franco-Flemish fifteenth-century tapestry *(See*

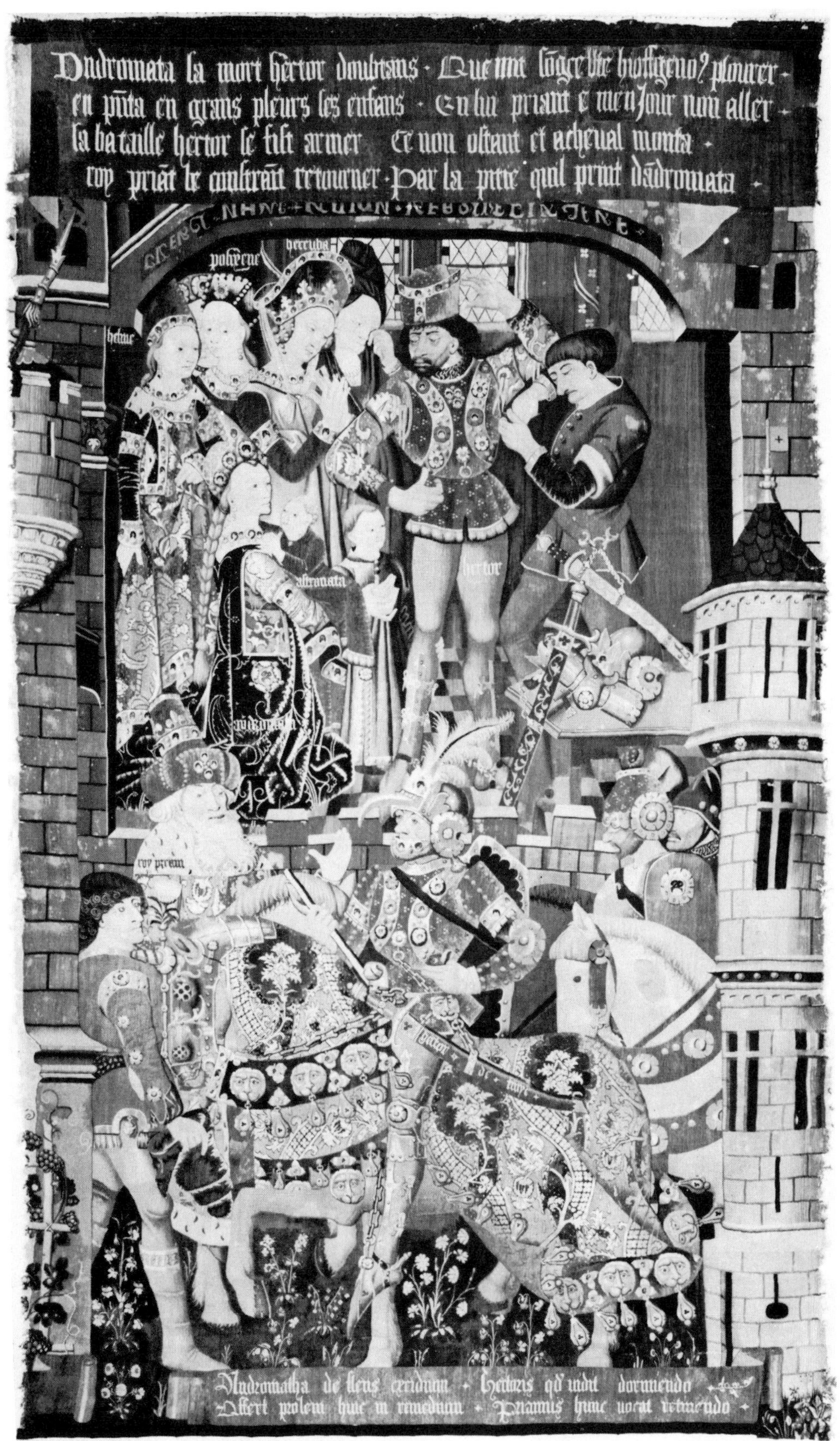

68 *Hector and Andromache* Tapestry, Flemish (late 15th century)

Plate 68) is that and only that particular knight, his individual suchness not lost in a pictorial space made of continued and bunched-together significant forms, his, the knight's included.

❖❖❖❖❖❖❖❖❖❖❖❖❖❖❖❖❖❖❖❖❖❖❖❖❖❖❖❖❖❖❖
❖❖❖❖❖❖❖❖❖❖❖❖❖❖❖❖❖❖❖❖❖❖❖❖❖❖❖❖

I knew it all along and with delight (my past quarrels being now at watchful peace with those whom I often considered to be both liberators of historical facts or linear direction-influences in history, and gaolers of attitudes or volume-events in history, the professors, I surmise)—I knew that the name heraldic, Heraldic Man was the right name.

❖❖❖❖❖❖❖❖❖❖❖❖❖❖❖❖❖❖❖❖❖❖❖❖❖❖❖❖
❖❖❖❖❖❖❖❖❖❖❖❖❖❖❖❖❖❖❖❖❖❖❖❖❖❖❖❖❖❖❖

It has been man's ineluctable habit to give a name to a knot of happenings. For the name is the very knot signified or "indexed." Hence the sanctity—and its terror or awe—attached to a name by prescientific man.

And yet, for precision's sake, and slightly with irony, I must add this: even as the energy, total, of the physicists is never, or not totally, lost, so also, it seems to me, the notion of sanctity, total—and the terror in it!—when overcome, is never, or not totally, lost. It is *in toto* transferred (to be henceforth transformed) into secular stuff of man's inventiveness and creativity: into what we call the creative style.

The sacred in the religious mind and its art is what by the creative secularized mind and its art is called style. For here art and mind and style are, all, the giving of the name to our daring familiarity—oh, the terror in it!—to our bunching together with what is as yet our innermost outsider: the creator? the creature?

The giving of a name—the shape to a form—above the altar, *sanctus, sanctus!* and the secular shaping of a created and creative form, *sanctus!* in the absence of an altar, are, *totaliter aliter,* sameness. And it is here that I see lying in wait a subtle distinction as well as, simultaneously, a most subtle nodal interconnection between art, style, and heraldry, or mind's third way.

For heraldry is the mythopoeic substitution of an object-witness (as object, both limitation and convention) for the total, thus existentially lost, unreconstructable sensation-loyalty. Now convention is loyalty chosen, thus accepted. Hence the great difficulty—one would be tempted to say the impossibility—of overcoming a convention in a culture or in a person, lest the feeling of its acceptance should itself change and become a new, and sudden, thus violent, feeling of compulsion.

Not so with limitations: limitation is a loyalty imposed, thus conditioned. Hence the illimited possibility in overcoming it, its conditions once changed.

Art contains—is!—this illimited possibility of change; art is the limited loyalty.

Style is the illimited loyalty. Art is loyalty—heraldry—attuned to change. Style is loyalty—heraldry—and nothing else. And heraldic history would mean the story of culture-arts and culture-styles connected and disconnected.

Italy knew the best or the broadest of itself as art; Italy knew art. So did China of her post-Wei eras, so did Greece of later classicism. Japan is a style; so is France, so also the Islamic civilizations. Heraldic intensely, increasingly, these style-crystallizing cultures were secular depositories of the sacred in human mind and art.

And that is how, in a final definition, I would define again your solemn and lovely gift to us: the understanding of ornament's content—the *amor intellectualis Dei*—as mind's and art's style or convention.

But I am a Japanese—can never be you: my life and my thought are exchange of gifts—or they are nought. So in everything the gift of *amor intellectualis Dei* is your gift to me; mine to you is the Mysterious Companion and witness of your journey.

A style-crystallizing culture is the living witness in its art. (I know how pretentious, "*précieuse ridicule*"-like, it is to formulate thus what is style. I do it, because it is my heraldic, visionary, "erroneous" way of loving man's art, the only way I could love art, as a bunching of loyalties. *On va à la sainteté comme on vient de la nonchalance*—do you remember?)

Japan's art is heraldic art—as is the Western Christian, as is the Islamic art of its most loyal eras. The witness and the name—the index of the hand upon it—are there. Thus: Peace, ye *odium theologicum* of the experts! No more of that philological-historical nonsense: "Don't you dare to approach with your dilettante hands the sacred arcanes of the science of heraldry, of the arch-complex *garderobe* of its subject matter, unless you are an initiate or have the birthright to do it!"

The chronology of the origins and apex of heraldry? The feudal tenth, eleventh, twelfth centuries? Then the slow decay? How silly, indeed, to try to pin down a start. Why not look for it in the origins of the seal, in the Scottish crosses, in the esoteric protection-badges of old and jealous crafts?[60] Or still better, in Kabuki's being black—not black factually (a spectacle so color-full!), but black as an attitude-pattern of Yamato itself.[61] Or, better still, in the possible origins in textile design rather than the military origins of Japan's heraldic badges, in their artisan origins thus close to the pre-split *pax* for and by the many and not for and by the few.

❖❖❖❖❖❖❖❖❖❖❖❖❖❖❖❖❖❖❖❖❖❖❖❖❖❖❖❖❖❖

Obviously my writing of your book is a defense of imagination—*la folle du logis,* your image-touch after all—against the priority of *intuition,* mind's generosity which, when guided by the honesty of observed and interpreted facts, becomes conviction and certainty: a syllogistic or dialectic proof. The verbal universe, we both call it. But why against it? And is it really so?

I cannot draw back now. But think, please, of the visual-artisan trajectory of man's planetary history. It should suffice.

Yet what, *serrée de près,* is this image-touch we both evoke in loyal faith? Why should its visual or visionary universe also be for both of us the universe of the new *quantum*-ethos?

What is an image-touch? Let us both repeat: It is the bunching together of fact-events, fragments of something or somebody to be as yet shown, seen, proven; a bunching and bunching, tighter and tighter, till, in *theory of probability fashion, by virtue of sheer quantity-mass condensation of energy (a knot of persisting intensity), there is given to us a conviction-image: the proving without proof.* Pure—because loyal to origins—presence of adherence. Touch. Testimony. Somebody's touch, something's touch.

This is what heraldic mind and its universe are. It is history without proof—without the chain of influences (facts of intuition and guidance).

A time-cluster of attitude-images given, touched: a new body.

A new emotion, the historical emotion, profitless; a mind's way.

The presence of the witness: a knot, a name held tightly in the hand, not to be lost but to be my other's other myself:

A lion couchant, rampant; eagle, cross, martlet in style; moon, a mouse-and-sex, a mouth, a hand, anybody's *passant.*

Or, it is when you hold in your hand the voice of an age passed, the testifying voice of a man or woman within a precise time, his or her mind's precise direction, *bodily* direction toward happening-events: the voice of Dame Juliana and that of her contemporary commentator (probably the printer of her famous treatise on matters of heraldry):

> All "gentilnes" comes from God; there were originally in heaven ten Orders of Angels bearing Coat Armour, but now only nine, Lucifer with "mylionys of aungelis" having fallen out of heaven into hell *and other places* [italics mine] . . . . .
>
> Of the offspring of the gentleman Japhet came Abraham, Moses[,] Aaron, and the prophets, and also the King of the right line of Mary, of whom that gentleman Jesus was born, very God and man, after his manhood King of the land of Judah and of Jews, a gentleman by his mother Mary, and Prince of Coat Armour. . . . ["Schemata-bunch" all this, rapidly cutting through the thickness of history, and *à tout prix* reaching the very genesis of all history, given complete by the Holy Script, the history-witness held in the hand. Islam does it and so does Amidism in Japan.] Coat Armour . . . was founded upon the nine Orders of Angels, who were crowned each with a diadem of precious stones—the Topaz (truth), Smaragdus (hardihood), Amethyst (chivalry), Loys (powerful), Ruby (courageous), Sapphire (wisdom), Diamond, a black stone (durable), Carbuncle (doughty and glorious). These represent Gentleman, Squire, Knight, Baron, Lord, Earl, Marquis, Duke, and Prince. . . [Oh, much more, of course! The Zodiac and its heraldic dance is meant. Think of Faustos Indicoplaustos: his "obscurantist"—oh, *clarté obscure des étoiles* of the poet!—Ark of Moses as hypostasis of cosmic mechanics most real. Heraldry: body's awareness of the extreme of its own extremities—soul's limbs' extremities.] Everything is treated in nines and the nine virtues and nine vices of gentleness follow . . . [bunching for the sake of holding it in the hand—not to be lost] and nine manners of gentlemen, in which we learn that the Evangelists and Apostles were all gentlemen of the right line of that worthy conqueror, Judas Machabeus,

who in course of time had fallen to labour, and so were not called gentlemen. The four doctors of the Church—St. Jerome [,] Ambrose, Augustine, and Gregory—were also gentlemen of blood and of Coat Armour. There are nine differences of Coat Armour and nine quadrats, all of which are explained.[62]

(Not a haughty hierarchy of degrees in the sociological value ladder, but heraldically, the opposite here: equation of merits *via* positing, situating them; a dance calculated—where and when are the significations to be located?—according to the rules of the "intelligent muscle.")

✤✤✤✤✤✤✤✤✤✤✤✤✤✤✤✤✤✤✤✤✤✤✤✤✤✤✤✤✤✤

What Huizinga, our good friend, really meant was the heraldic thinking in medieval heraldry as such: a collected, "kept-in-hand," in-individualized thinking.

And however dangerously obscurantist and repulsive might, or should, appear to a modern, secularized, historical analysis the heraldic content thus defined—the witness in it, the hallucination, the logos of the arbitrary, etc.—its form, its schema-procedure of thinking itself stands apart, universal, autonomous and free: a mind's way, indeed, a very particular but necessary, because creatively operating, way: *the visual way,* we both call it.

And, indeed, if so much *chi-chi* has been made by experts about the medieval-feudal heraldry and its sociological content, it is because heraldry was sensed by them, in spite of themselves, as mind's definite, if very singular, *techne* procedure that touches the very oozes of the visual-visionary existence on earth, of its history too: exactly, by substitution-touch, the optical *object-ness* or *thing-ness* of the charges on the armorial field. Heraldry—let us not forget it—is mind-and-art's style: not a medieval knight's armour, but a painting, somewhere, somehow, not necessarily even of a knight, but possibly of a knight, too—a compound image ready to become an object of art exclusively, purely, physically.

✤✤✤✤✤✤✤✤✤✤✤✤✤✤✤✤✤✤✤✤✤✤✤✤✤✤

✤✤✤✤✤✤✤✤✤✤✤✤✤✤✤✤✤✤✤✤✤✤✤✤✤✤✤✤✤✤

By this, to begin with, we both mean that knowledge, the very condition both of knowing and analyzing knowledge, is controlled at its birth by the "heraldic" position of those still vaguely "kept-in-hand" terms—fingers of mind's grasp: the schema-form and the image,[63] the two forming one living, form-signalizing-(*that thing!*)-to-symbolizing-(that *significant thing!*) concern.

The form-giving function, the very *givenness* of Kantian *schemata* (that is, in its existential inevitability, a function-presence not chosen, thus not to be fulfilled creatively or constructively within its own confines), and added to it in pure simultaneity of operation, the "image-needed" function (that is, in Cassirer's novel conception of this term, a function not given but chosen, thus structured and free, a lucid completion of the very schema *qua schema*)—these would be the two, and the only two, preconditions of knowing, the two "charges" placed upon the shield of awareness at its birth.

And it is uniquely the spatial order of position of the two that makes us both distinguish, *when this order is changed or reversed,* between, say, the "visual" and the "verbal" universes of discourse (so idle a distinction to any professional analyzer of mind's integrative conduct—but not to me, the historian!).

The "visionary circumstance of mind"—our eye's *ergo-sum*—is this reversal: the place reserved for what is given "normally"—the form-givenness itself[64]—is occupied by the image-givenness now; and the place reserved for what is needed at the symbol's birth there—the image-need, the image's lucidity constructed choosingly, creatively—is occupied by the form, the form-need, the form-lucidity now.

The visually given, inescapable birth-event as image-touch (the image de-formed, the *Image la Folle,* the hallucination, the witness, the birth of eye's monster, of the new, the birth of style, the "expressionism" of sensation-infinity), and added to it, the form-needed lucidity of mind (the birth of the "natural" in the eye; intuition's facticity, impression, birth of art, "impressionism," and correspondence)—this is what we both call the "visual"—the visual arts, *n'est-ce pas?*

Lucidity is framing now the untamable *Folle!*

Precisely: the schema-lucidity in Picasso's monsters, or Klee's; or in the "decorative arts" space.

Precisely: St. Augustine's "love God and do what you wish," for nothing could be done and image-formed then but of God.

Precisely: heraldry; and precisely: Japan, the order or orderliness in the exchange of charges-gifts; Ukiyo-e's precise exchange, re-placement for the gift of man-and-the-beyond-of-man's infinity by the gift of pictorial landscape, this gift of landscape exchanged in its turn for the gift of ornament, itself lastly, an exchange for the gift of *amor intellectualis Dei!* (This order or orderliness being not more nor less "mysterious" than the taken-for-granted, not-even-to-be-questioned ordinance and orderliness in, say, the intermolecular "self"-structuring of matter.)

March 20

My writing has reached the place in your own book (and I am occupying it exactly), where and when, turning your face to us, readers, you told us that from now on all the intermediary or introductory justifications are not necessary any more for the setting forth or presenting of new and separate problems therein; that this in appearance so arbitrary, so arrogant a literary practice is neither arbitrary nor arrogant indeed; its roots and justification are simply in the very logic of solitude-solidarity itself.

And at this point of my writing, the rock-involving current-voice:

Connected with!
Connected with!

has grown so swollen, rapid, and loud that I have lost in it the most discreet of my secret voices of guidance, the most ironic voice, too: "Stop here!

Watch your step! The from-sublime-to-ridiculous tiny and separating step is right there about to be made by you—avoid it, turn round it!"

But I could not care less. For all our aims, yours and mine, have met here already. What I call heraldry's—or the *"connected-with"—voice* (and not a step to be watched) is exactly what you call the *what of the how* level of both creation and analysis: not the what *and* the how levels, where happenings-associated-with-happenings are projected, in dry and clean uplift, from the present to the future of their man-made causal efficiency; but the what *of* the how—where happenings-adhered-glued-to-happenings are projected, in wet, to-be-purified down-plunge, from the present to the past of their not man-made, probably angelological energies—energies the same for all times and all sources of existence. (The utterly unmystical halt of today's exact sciences before the secret of physical light's matter-electricity is such an angelology—who knows?—in its most sober attire.) Thus the *what of the how* is also projected, in depth-lift, toward the future.

In brief: on the *what* as well as on the *how* levels we do evaluate correctly, say, the sociological apparatus, the cause-and-effect succession of facts and their chain of influences that underlie our "decadent," "frivolous" aristocratic era called Fujiwara. We are correct in our historical aesthetic appreciation when we show—and we do!—how such a socio-political situation is as fully mirrored or revealed in the "decadent" and "frivolous" aristocratic art of that era—an art where the element of the decorative takes precedence over the solemnity and ardor of Buddhist iconology's and Buddhist spirit's heirloom: this set of fan-shaped sacred writings superposed "frivolously" over *genre* vignettes *(See Plate 47)*, effete, if exquisite in color and execution, made by court nobles with the monks' connivance.

How utterly other, how changed will all this be in our evaluation, when, under the glance of the companion-witness, the index-glance of history without proof, we leave with due politeness the world of influences and reach the world of attitudes, the *what of the how* world, whose visionary horizon embraces in one "connected-with" curve of events, called sometimes historical tendencies, all the strongest and healthiest traits of Yamato: Yamato's definite transfer of the sacred to the secular, of art to style; in visual inventiveness, the typical Japanese—Fujiwara already, Fujiwara, first!—crystallization of a space structure or space consistency that is made of what feels sudden and surprising, thus oblique, interconnected, thus ornamental *(Plate 69)*. And making one with the same knot-attitude, the ancestral loyalties, the never forgotten aristocratic-folk-artisan loyalties, loyalties which, in depth-lift toward both the past and the future reach there the many rather than the few; the mother of many many a child (Fujiwara mother-grandfather-child[65] depth-lifted ethos!) rather than the father of few worthy sons (the predominant sociological tone of later eras).

Is not the late and most "decadent" part of the Fujiwara period the one that had already witnessed or started the prodigious and typically Japanese *pro-vulgo*, pro-many religious reforms (usually given by historians to the "virile" succeeding age called Kamakura, whereas Fujiwara-Kamakura form one single ever-maturing block-style of life and art)?

❖❖❖❖❖❖❖❖❖❖❖❖❖❖❖❖❖❖❖❖❖❖❖❖❖❖❖❖❖❖

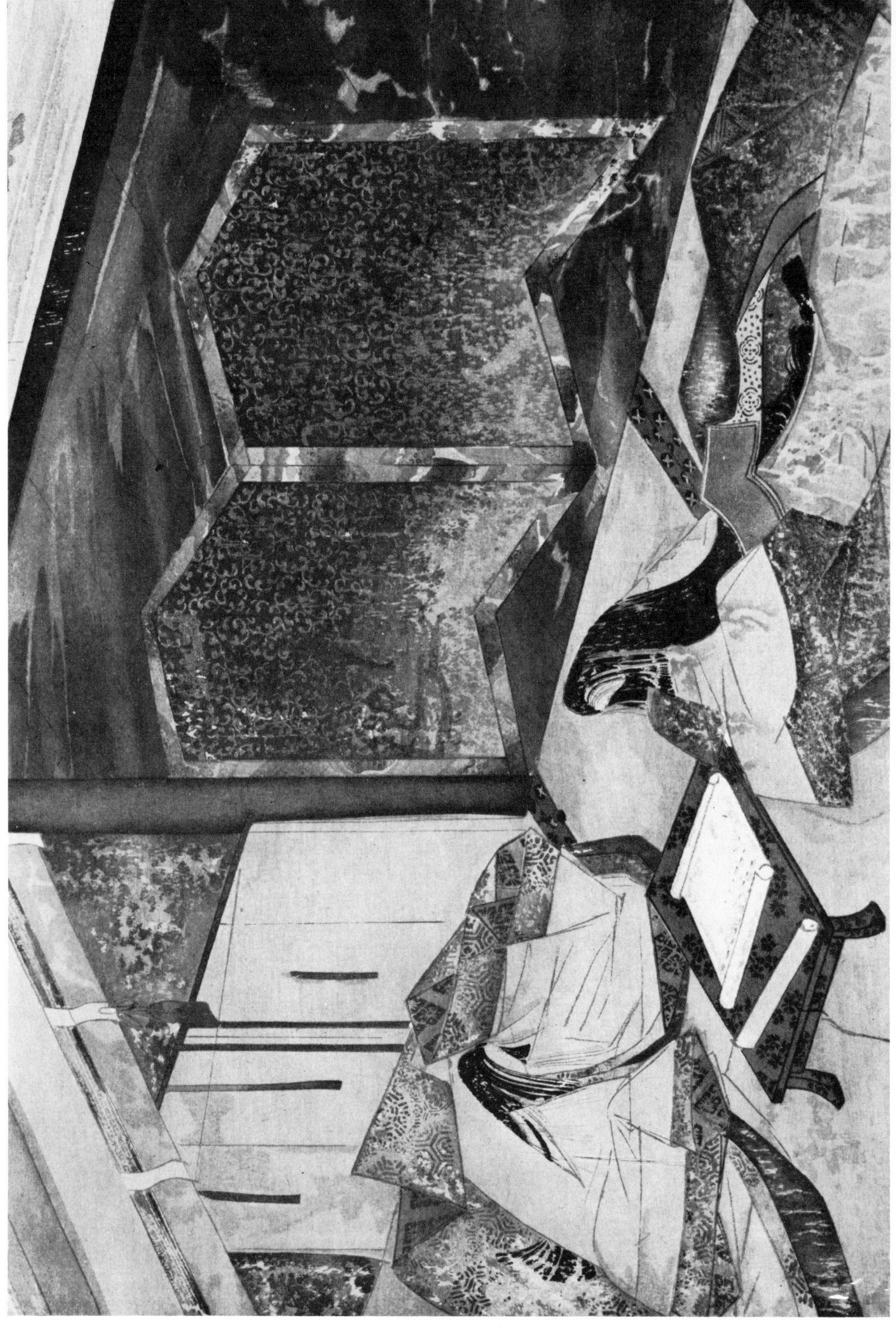

I am aiming toward a new, visionary-artisan sociology or social history of human creation; another history of ideas' trajectory. See: here is Greece and the haughty aristocratic ideal of a right balance between physical and moral qualities in man, of his self-restraint and discipline, *sophrosýne* and *kalokagathia*[66] reflected in the geometrized, freedom-strangulating space of her immediately pre-classical art. But does this art really mirror so faithfully the will and the taste of a reactionary class of land aristocracy, for whose revengeful satisfaction (before the oncoming city-state's "bourgeois" will and taste for the "natural," the empirically tangible) this geometrized art has been created?[67]

In front of the underlying persistence of the geometrized-abstracted in even the most "naturalist" art of later classicism (is not this precisely the "uniqueness" of Greece?) one stops in wonder and looks anew. Would it not rather be that, descending here again from the level of socio-economic facts and influences to the level of socio-economic "connected-with" global attitudes, the *sacredness* of geometry in Greek art and thought is not the sacredness of the upper class's self-preserving interests and musts, but is the sacredness, the sacred-to-secular-transferred sacredness of precisely the lowest, thus innermost, socio-economic module: I mean the role of the slave in Greece's economy (notwithstanding all of the slave-serf-salaried mixture operating there already at an ever-increasing pace)?

The haughty ideal of Greece—the ideal of geometry-and-*sophrosýne* in it—is the total substitution for classical antiquity's socio-economic core, the state-owned slave. And by slave I mean the existential horizon of a "direct producer" who as a human, thus possessing being, is yet totally eliminated from the possession not only of the means of production, tools, family, etc., but also of the produce itself. The *slave*—witness of the age—bestows thus on any object made within the confines of the same horizon, even when by any other-than-slave's kind of production (Phidias was not a slave!) this far-radiating substance or tonality of a collected-individuated attitude toward participating in the possession of a manu-factured object of either daily usage or of art proper. And this participation could not be a physical or direct bodily, as it were, participation, thus possession, but an "abstract" one, relegated to the limited, the abstracted. (Think of Aristotle's re-defining antiquity's essential creed: that evil is what is illimited, good is what is limited; or again, Aristotle's legitimation of the concept of infinity as belonging only to mathematical reality and not—absolutely not—to the empirical physical world or reality around us.)

The geometrized, "abstract" element in the art of Greece is not the element that reveals the mental visionary horizon of the possessing or the possessor, but of the possessed. He, the slave, is the witness of the age, but a silent, invisible witness, unnoticed, unnoticeable perhaps. (I think here suddenly of that prehuman past on our earth, where small, insignificant ratlike creatures lived together with the earth-and-seas-mastering great

69 Ascribed to Fujiwara Nobuzane *The Diary of Murasaki Shikibu*
◀ Detail of Scroll (late 12th-early 13th century)

reptiles: insignificant ratlike creatures, unnoticed, unnoticeable perhaps, by the colossal dinosaurs and their kindred. Yet they were the forerunners of the future masters of creation, the mammals.)

And even as a simple sensation in us is equated, by your definition of it, with infinity itself, because it is totally coextensive with our receiving body, thus coincides with what is not separable, not distinguishable or finite there, so also in my vision, he, the slave in the city state, is coextensive totally with the city state's total existence: no overlapping margin is left there to make room for any inner writ of awareness. The slave-as-attitude is the total, unseizable otherwise, existence of Greece: its fullness-void, its *sunyata*, its infinity. (And here again I speak of the body while thinking of your saying:

"That spirit—*nous*—is what has no struggle in it, what cannot have any struggle in it—*logos.* That soul—*psyche, pneuma*—is what has no blemish, cannot have any blemish on it—Rome's account of Lucretia. That body—the Nazarene—is what struggles, must struggle, for the spirit; what receives, must receive, soul's stigmata of the blemish; *logos* incarnate, the Witness for all witnesses.")

Such is also, in heraldic opposition of differing charges, upon the shield of the medieval or feudal man's world, the serf, the serf-as-attitude: its fullness-void, *sunyata,* its infinity.

Mirror of the hierarchic, rigid structure of its social pyramid, so appears to us the inexorably hierarchic also, in its authoritarian terror-spreading and fleshless frontality, art and thought of this age (as typified throughout the entire length of its otherwise content-changing span, by the ever-present so-called Romanesque style).

But why is the rigid immobility of this art and thought so intensely dynamic also, so full of inner *bougeotte,* thus so convincingly communicative?

Why is the hieratic visionary space-structure there so interconnected, intertwined in its elements, so dramatically mobile and not quietly static?[68]

From the very top of the socio-political pyramid to its all-supporting base, the institution of serfdom, throughout all and each of the degrees of the feudal universe's ladder, wherever and whenever the latter has been evolving historically, runs a shiver of a particular, typically feudal participation in possession—an inter- and multi-relational participation, bodily-personal, eye-to-hand as it were in the tenure of all essential goods, land, God, *rex,* the toiler himself. In the medieval global attitude possession is *possessio precaria* at its very start and not antiquity's total yet "abstract" possession: the cross of hand-clasping during the *hommage* ritual, not the existing, but abstract perfection of the Parmenidian circle. This cross is the symbol of the new, feudal age, the central symbol of suzerain-vassal's mutual loyalties unto life and death, treason and attachment.

But the creative shiver in art, in thought and life of this multi-relational participation-tenure is not of the lord of the age—it is, here too, of the witness of the age himself. In deeper, down-lifted descent from the level of socio-economic facts and influences to the level of socio-economic attitudes—global tendencies—the sacredness of the hierarchic interconnectedness of "Romanesque" forms preserved throughout the entire medieval era and style is not the sacredness of the upper class's self-preserving and self-perpetuating interests and musts, but precisely the sacred-to-secular-transfer sacredness of the lowest, thus innermost, socio-economic module, I mean the role of the feudal serf—the very core of feudal life and economy. And by serf I mean the existential horizon-attitude of the direct producer who, *de jure* an ex-free tribesman of yore, *de facto* a possessing bourgeois of the close future, is, however inhumanly exploited and humiliated, nevertheless the owner (humble semi-slave! but never a slave!) of both the means of production and the produce—except, of course, what is of his sharing of the principle of tenure with the lord himself: land, God, *rex,* and indeed himself, the serf.

He, the witness of the age, bestows thus on any object made by any—any other than the serf's—kind of production within the confines of the same horizon the far-radiating substance or tonality of such a collected-individuated possession (here, relativist tenure), which *can not but be* physical, personal, participating, and multi-relational in content and form.

He, the serf, is the witness of his age, but the silent witness, the invisible, unnoticed, perhaps unnoticeable one: the very existence, the infinity sensation of the medieval man, his uniqueness, his own *grandeur* and *misère,* his fullness-void—*sunyata.*

❉

And who is—where is?—the witness of our own age?

Everywhere I dare say. Anywhere. Everybody, not to be seen; nobody, to be seen. I dare say: Amen.

❉

No doctor of fame in the entire world knew—and all fairy-tale loving children in the entire world know this—how to cure of her long sickness the young and beautiful, perishing princess, lying pale and speechless in the castle's big room. Neither did the doctors know, of course, how to find the cause of the deadly illness. And all hope was taken away from her unhappy father, the king in the tale.

"Get rid," said to him a passing beggar, "get rid," said he again, "of a tiny little grey mouse whose sharp tiny teeth in the darkness of the cellar are slowly, slowly, day after day, sapping the foundations of your mighty castle. Find in there the hardly noticeable tiny mouse, and your daughter will recover and live." This done, the princess was instantly cured, and married, of course, the passing beggar, prince-born himself.

❖❖❖❖❖❖❖❖❖❖❖❖❖❖❖❖❖❖❖❖❖❖❖❖❖❖❖❖❖❖

❖❖❖❖❖❖❖❖❖❖❖❖❖❖❖❖❖❖❖❖❖❖❖❖❖❖

In the world of influences, facts, and proofs—the energetic, forth-propelling world of young, healthy bodies—our Fujiwara age was the age of decadence, of decay; in the world of global, self-recoiled attitudes, of touch-events—the world of bodies not young any more—our Fujiwara age was the age of Japan's renaissance.

And the "heraldic" methodology—everything I have said and am saying about it—has to do, I presume, with the melancholy of decay, the tenderness for decay, for sickness, possibly for death; it has to do with old age, too, with the melancholic tenderness and respect for old age. Precisely with what distinguishes—an unnoticed, unnoticeable perhaps, distinction—mouse, cause-mouse!—our East from the West. Hence my tiny unnoticed prophecy about your West:

That the much desired and much despaired-of *renovatio*—the cure of the sickness of the very young—in the West will come about when and where the respect for old age as such (not any more as solely an object of respectability but as a subject of respect, both object and subject of tenderness and melancholy) will come.

For such a respect for the very old is, in its global "connected-with" eventfulness, the respect and consequently, the cure of the very young. (Think of your constant and so helpless, because so respectless, remedies for your sick young ones—for their so-called "juvenile delinquency" and its kindred ills!)

"Get rid," said the prince-born passing beggar: "get rid," said he to the not-yet-so-old king, "of the tiny, grey, little mouse in the grey cellar."

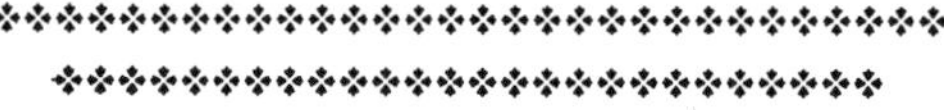

I am an old Japanese woman. Is it this that makes me speak the way I do? A moody old woman's moody and vindictive outburst?

I am afraid—I confess: the *window* of my credo—this solid Bridge of our aims, built on scientific experimental pillars of contemporary critical, secularized, thought—do I face it only as reflected in the *mirror* of my own solitary and atavistic involvement?

But such a personal involvement, with no utility or meaning to any but myself, how can this unthinkable (for a Japanese) ego-romanticist indiscretion be possible? Indeed, indeed—it is impossible! Indeed: would this very questioning of mine rather be such a moody, vindictive outburst?

Let us descend (and no climbing back could possibly now bring us a better self-checking evidence!), let us descend the remaining and last steps to where our long winter journey is ending.

The First Step: personal, of course—at first:

That I am going to die soon. *Ça y est. It* had finally to pass by me too. The doctor said to me today, I have one year or so to live; and his usually jovial eye's sparkle was wrapped furtively in a too-energetic, as if guilty, good-bye handshake—poor dear Doctor! . . . .

Now—am I going to be really afraid—in your so contagious, Western fashion? Am I going to stupefy myself and my fears by avoiding—while loudly talking about it—the thought of death, etc., etc?

It is important for me to decide. I have a job to do and to do undisturbed, without heroism mixed in it by the news of my death to come soon; I have to finish my your-book writing; and a job undertaken is in Japan, more than elsewhere, a job to finish—in deadly earnest, as if life and death themselves were being strictly framed by it and its duration, however paltry.

How will I go about it, while descending the last steps? By deluding myself here, too, into believing that the personal has simply been left beyond me, and forgotten there? This is not necessary at all. When I reach, as we both do, the experiential *what of the how* level of connected-adhered attitudes, my own personal involvement is already situ-ated behind me but present nevertheless: for I keep tightly in my hand the knot made of this very personal avowal and of what comes forth now:

That the West—let's so call the image of the Atlantic-Mediterranean world at large—knew the anxiety and fear of death because in its historical center of radiation, the Syro-Hellenic culture-attitude, it had always exalted the discontinuous, the substituted and the transferred: life and death, soul and body separated. While the East—let's call thus the image of the greater Indo-Sinic, or perhaps better, Indo-Pacific world—knew, or learned how to know choosingly, the continuous, the corresponding, the transformed: with no room in it for death, that is, for the *suddenly* discontinuous, the *suddenly* not being there, thus with no room in it for the fear or anxiety of death.

Very well—but how can I keep this vagueness of a generalized historical statement tightly in my hand, as if it were an image-touch, precise, narrow, localized? Only, I presume, by remaining loyally within the structure and idiom of my chosen job, because the personal decision to be made by me about my attitude toward my death to come and my decision to resume my your-book writing are one and the same job now.

By this I simply mean *The Second Step down:*

That the East at large could not have created a pictorial icon, its witness, like the one that came down to us from the very heart of the Syro-Hellenic West, the face-masque, masque-death from Dura-Europos *(Plate 70)* or Byzantium or Fayum's tomb—the terror-anxiety of fleshless proximity facing us—proximity to what? proximity to whom?—"I am coming upon you—accept me or run away from me!"—the terror of a sudden rigid arrest —arrest of what? of whom?

Instead, the Sino-Indian heart had contemplated a different—oh how different!—icon. The Sino-Indian-Pacific heart calmly, easily, richly, and let me use this word afresh here, majestically, was beating in rhythm with the sinuous curve of say, this Yakshi in stone *(Plate 71)* or this T'ang Buddha icon in bronze *(Plate 72)*—Eros of evolved infinity and involved finity, Eros of involved infinity and evolved finity, all limbs intertwined.

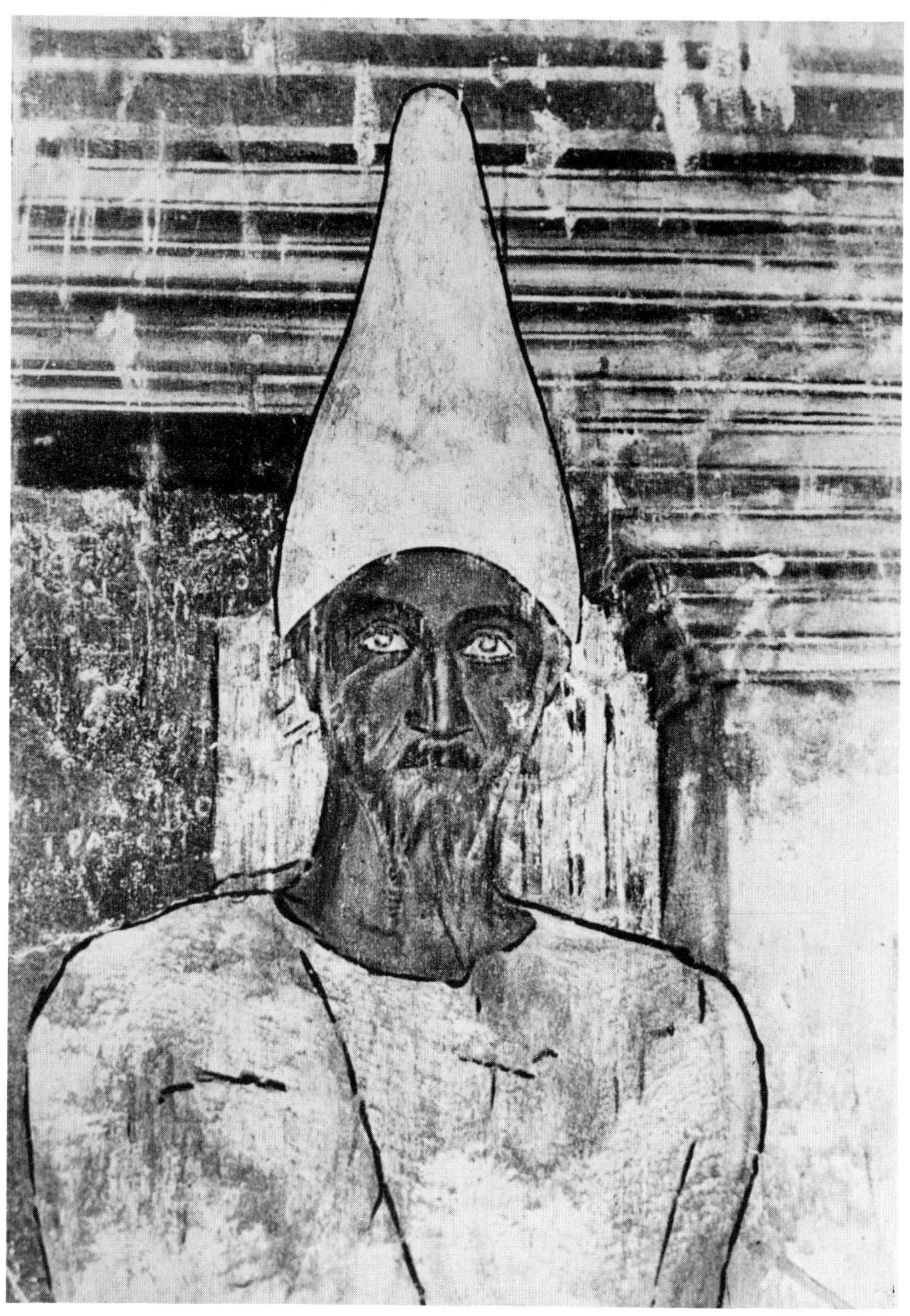

70 Ministrant Detail, wall painting, Dura-Europos, Syria (last quarter, 1st century A.D.)

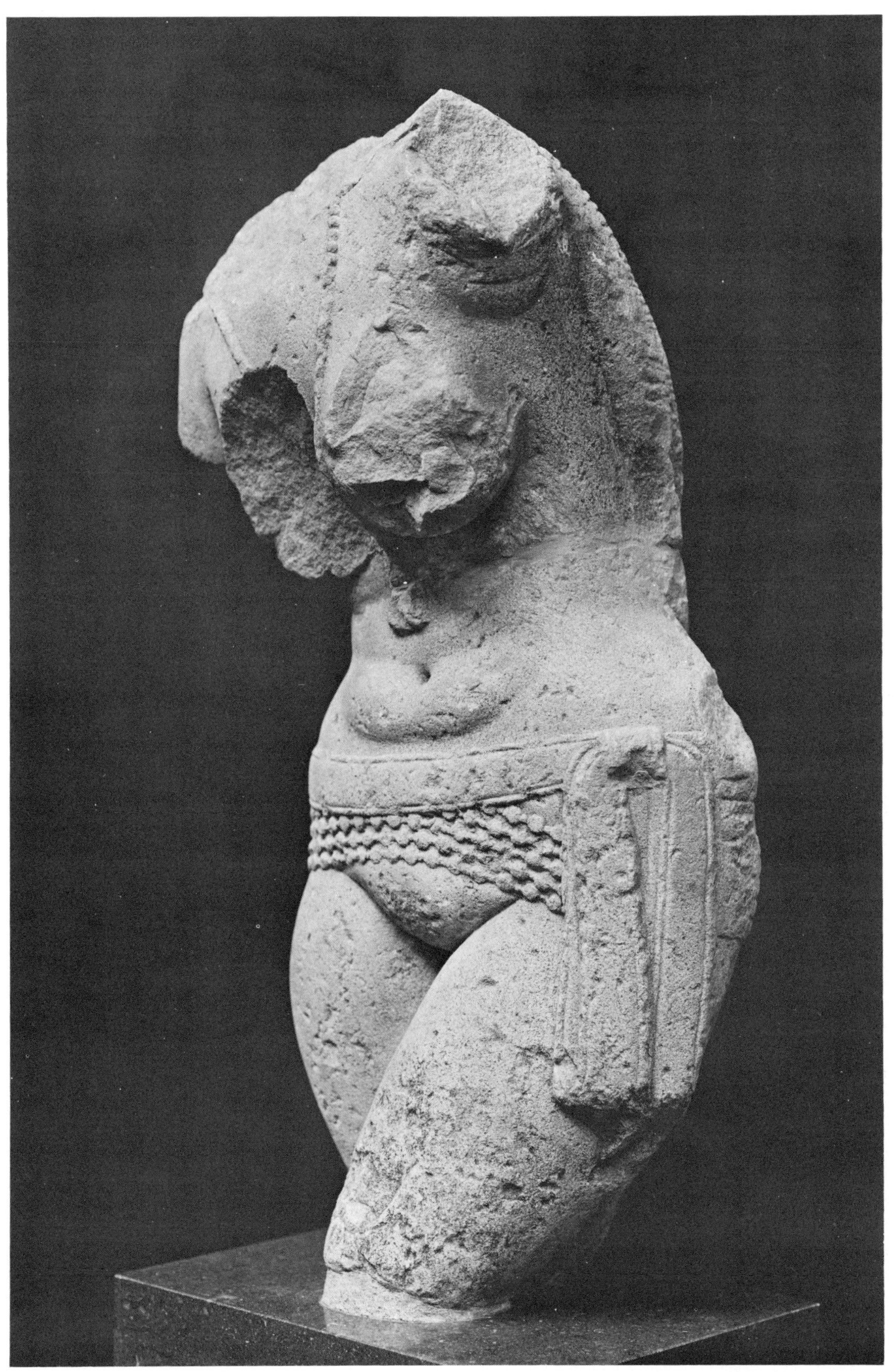

71 Yakshi Torso Indian, stone (early Andhra period, 72-25 B.C.)

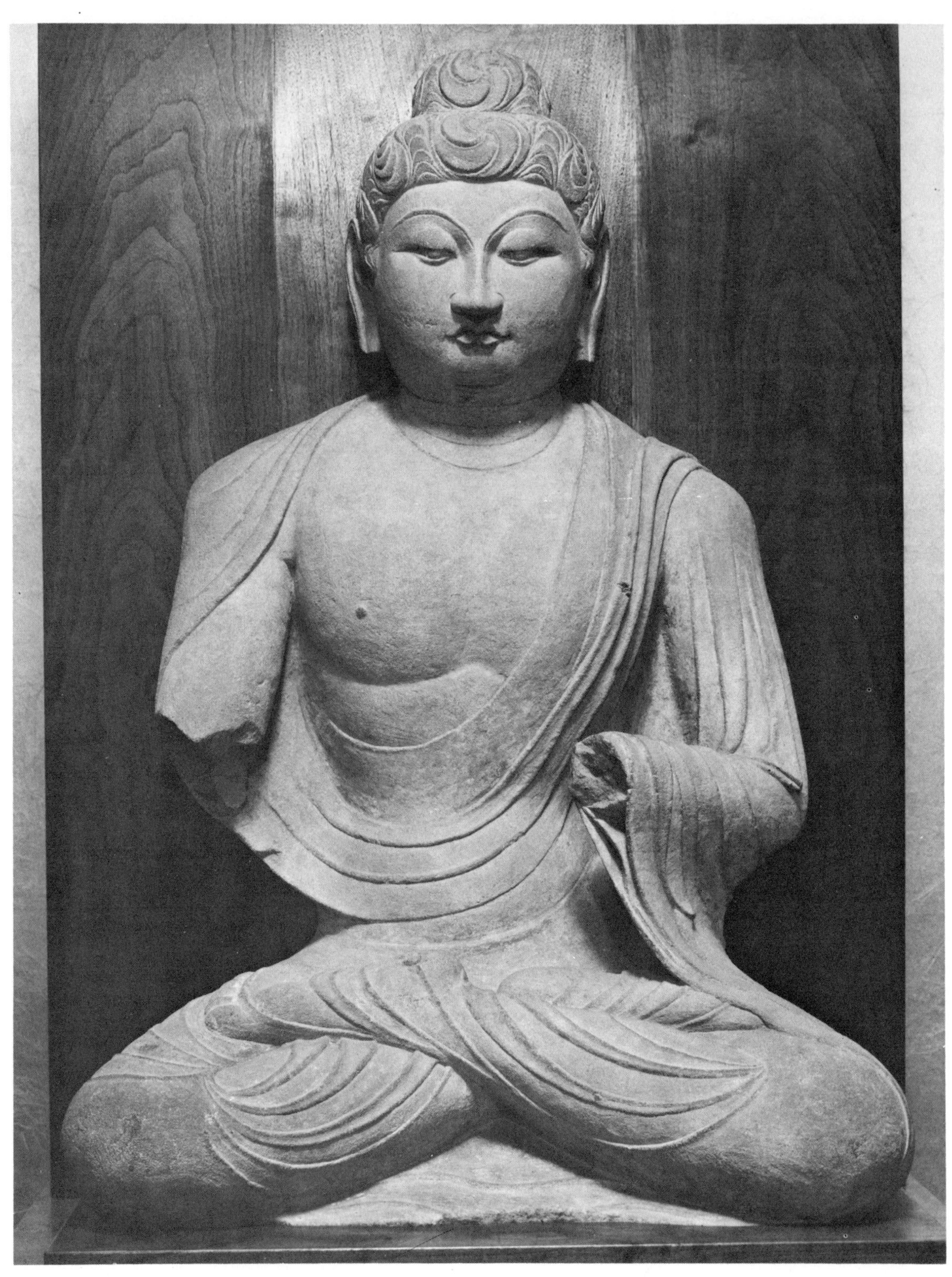

72 *Sakyamuni* Stone (T'ang dynasty, ca. 684-ca. 755)

Je m'explique: The witness testifies that the West created the Creator; the East, the creature-creation itself.

The sober-rigid figure from Dura-Europos or the sumptuous-rigid silhouette of the Byzantine Basilissa comes from the concept of the human soul as created and ready for sin, ready for virtue, creature of the Creator, forever such, forever an individual or individuated soul-being.

Created especially, separately, by the Creator, thus separated by this act from him, yet at the same time part of him, the soul-being cannot disappear, it cannot lose its individuality, it cannot but be immortal. Yet it is separated forever from the immortality of the Creator by the sheer act of being created—it is discontinuous with him, it is finite, it is dead and to die.

Inexorable face of duality—this divinely created crisis, crisis forever, of Western man! Closest closeness to the Creator of life; far far distance from the Creator:

Terror of solitude,
Bliss of solitude.
Terror of identity,
Bliss of identity.
Terror of nostalgia,
the impossible return;
Bliss of nostalgia,
of return impossible.
Terror of death—
Bliss of death.
Anxiety and fear of questioning,
Anxiety and fear of answering,
Anxiety and fear of plenitude,
Anxiety and fear of nothing.
Bliss of fullness,
Bliss of separation.

Terror and bliss and glance-index upon all this: com-passion isolated; co-suffering isolated.

This agonic crisis of the West, at once epistemological and *somatic,* the East never knew fully; the image of the Creator was known to the East only in its sub-structural—tantric—glimmer. Openly, philosophically and psychologically no creator's omnipresence or omnipotence could have become a master-concept there. But only the creation-creature itself. A Bodhisattva is not the compassionate, unique, sacrificial *Agnus Dei,* but a saviour all-compassionate for creatures all, because all-enlightened by creation all.

The Great East: creation-creature actualized, from the sub-mineral to the mineral, to the sub-plant, to the plant, to the sub-animal, to the animal, to the sub-human, to the human, to the sub-angelic, to the angelic—fire, Agni, at the bottom; fire, Agni, at the forever about-top—slowly, slowly evolving-involving itself, creature-creation fused together, echoing everything, everybody in everything, in everybody—correspondence, never separation; mind-stuff; mind-stuff and matter-stuff one stuff. Philosophy? no! religion? no! psychology? yes: I or Shiva or Buddha, am creating myself from my other selves, depending solely on electro-magnetic radiations *de profundis*—with nothing there to start with, nothing to end with—no terror there, no metaphysical anxiety there, only fullness, embryo-godhead, spasm supreme of supreme *volupté*—but where, how to locate pleasure? where, how to locate pain? *Volupté:* localized in body? Cosmos localized? How silly!

The Eros of a stone Yakshi's curve: sufficient. Japanese. I am purified thus in body—purified from fear. We don't have to have the Basilissa's questioning, her terror-and-consolation-giving glance—we have the Yakshi's convex-concave fullness-void: sufficient.

Yet do you remember our Daruma's icon? *(Plates 73, 74).* It is a Japanese icon, you know; very Japanese. The index-glance! And the closest closeness that separates!

Well then—trouble? Of course not: Japanese, I have nothing to choose —I just have both worlds in me—and I am playing with them—the two-one toy, the lacquered black toy (Kabuki is black!) the Fujiwara toy—remember?

And I am not afraid of death: *Je m'en fous.* I play with the toy of substitution.

I live with the toy of correspondence. I play with the black lacquered toy, the toy I shall take with me, the toy I shall be, when sharply thin-nosed I shall lie adhering heavy to my coffin's bottom—and I simply speak here of Japanese painting—truly yours, Japanese painting—where, both in identity and correspondence with the very problem of death, art and death belong together.

Thence I descend *the Third Step Down:*

Where, of course, the wonder-toy, or the playing with it, becomes an ever wider-compassing expression for a profitless and exact exchange of meanings: as, for instance, between death and the creation of space in pictorial art.

And why, I am asking myself, should my black-lacquered toy—later, my black Kabuki—through which death-touch exchanges its armorial pose with Ukiyo-e-touch—why should this exchange of gifts—toy = death = Ukiyo-e—be considered more arbitrary or unreasonable than, say, the attitude that throughout history and geography urged man to situ-ate upon the shield of his visible sky-toy along the imagined zodiacal paths the pose, the dance, of astral "charges"—the image-touch of the bunched-together and figured constellations? Why, indeed?

The toy and the word toy I am playing with is the painting of such a toy and of such a word (as in Malraux's saying that a painter never paints a tree but paints a painted tree). And everything that precedes and that follows in our your-book writing is—again!—but *a*) a painting somewhere, *b*) a heraldic rite of name-giving (similar to the name-giving for each and all creatures created in Eden before man's fall, as Holy Writ would have it —*n'est-ce pas?*).

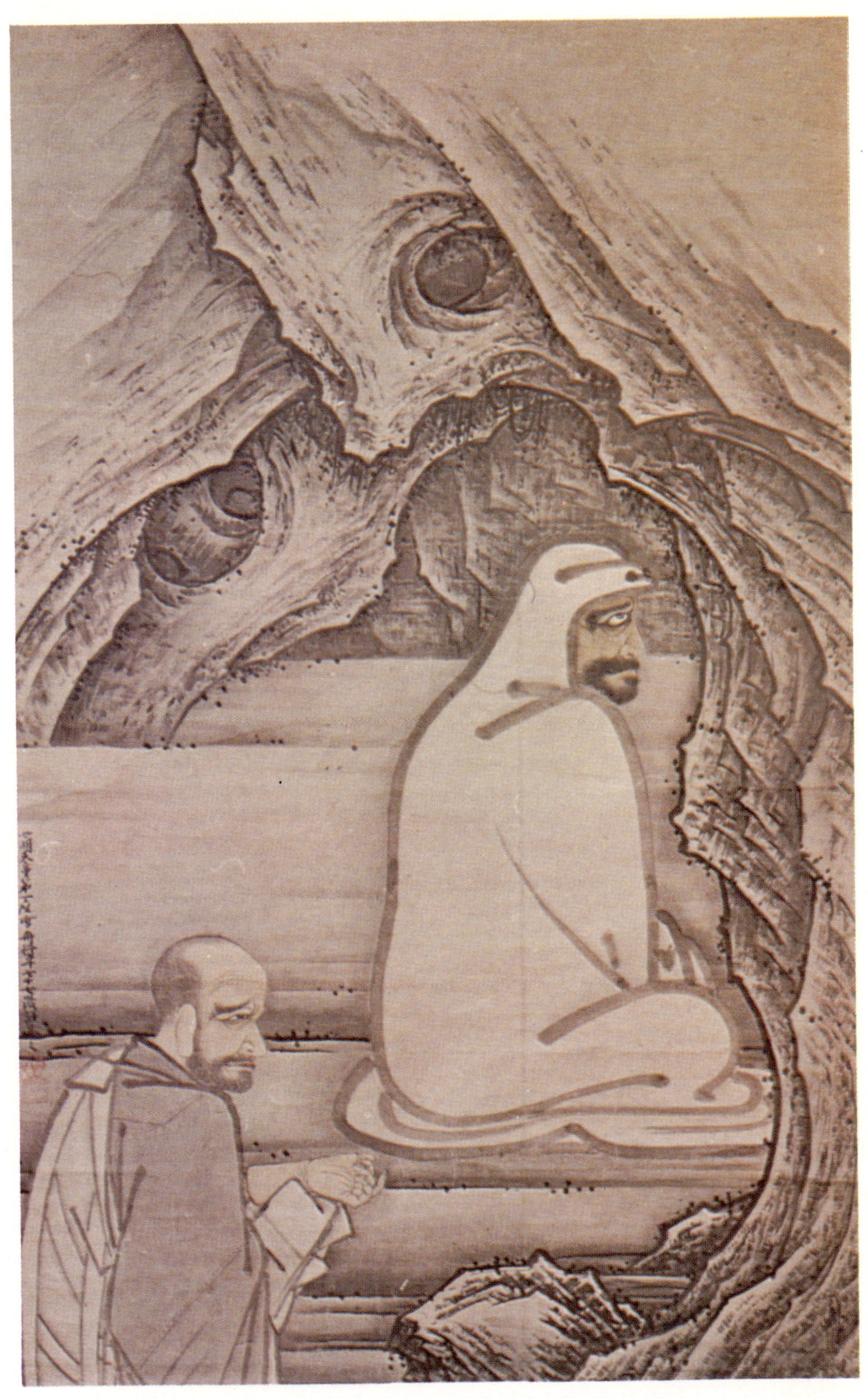

73 SESSHU *Daruma and Eka*

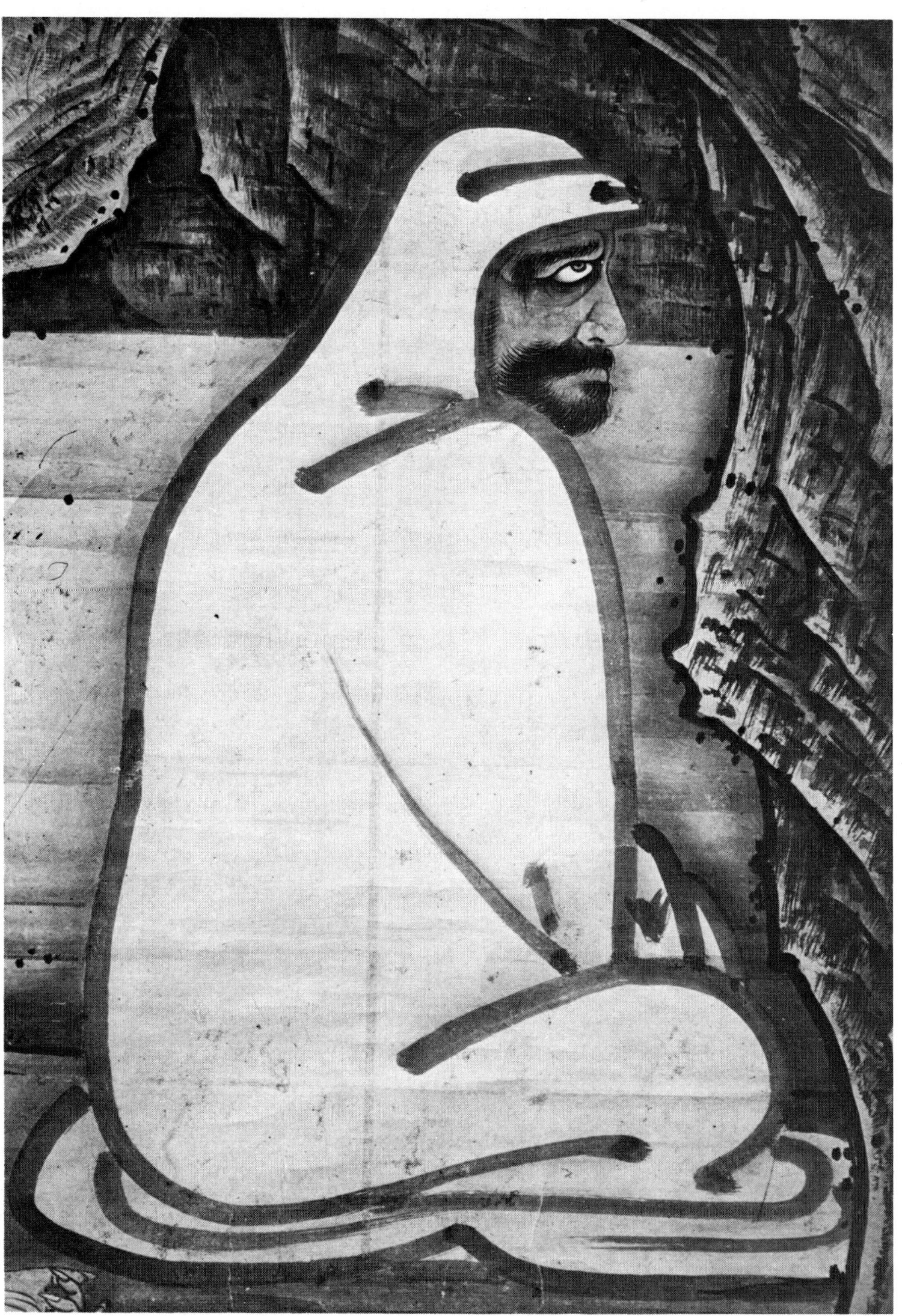

We are both willing finally to write the heraldic history of Japanese painting.

I call this history sub-history, approximately situ-ating this term, this name-giving, where the term "sub-microscopic" is given in wave-mechanics to the down-lifted happenings of innermost physical matter.

We have already called this sub-history the history without proof or history-child (in the sense of an event without the fact being attached to it in us, as yet); ultimately: history-ornament—knot after knot in winter-knitting—the profitless, absolute history of *amor intellectualis Dei.*

❖❖❖❖❖❖❖❖❖❖❖❖❖❖❖❖❖❖❖❖❖❖❖❖❖❖❖❖❖❖

So—one always starts somewhere and never at the start. One always starts within an area-pattern and indifferently from afar or from now and here.

And that is why my own starting of your-book writing was not as it has been in fact, with Huizinga's visitation of heraldic man, but with what for both of us is the positional start—a somewhere start—for our history of Japanese painting: the secret of the Japanese conception of space *qua* pictorial space.

My starting of the sub-history of Japanese painting is with Padmapani's nose.

And I begin the book with the title-toy first:

PADMAPANI'S NOSE

Introduction

A beginning somewhere in the middle, from this famous Ajanta icon *(Plate 75)* to the Horyuji icon *(Plate 76)*, a processional transmission, via Central Asia's crystallized diffusions and changes, of a dual conception of space to be told now.

A nodal beginning it is, somewhere in the middle, it is true, yet expected: expected exactly where death-touch, dual also—death-transfiguration and death-transfer, death-correspondence, oh, stony curve of Yakshi! and death-substitution, Theodora's glance!—exchanges its armorial "pose" with the concept of visual space, dual also.

And it is the heraldic "positing" upon the roads of Asia—think of all the transmitted ideas and goods along the roads of Asia's sown and unsown! —of this dual set of dual "charges," that shall be, for the time being, the given name, the heraldry, for my black lacquered toy: for my death-space-touch.

The new name is thus given temporarily:

Roads, roads, and roads carrying my black toy—the black Kabuki! Roads: see the propagation of influences, diffusions and counter-diffusions of teaching, enlightenment, and of image forming (all this, how magnificently, nostalgically reconstructed by scholars' efforts!). And the intellect-filling puritan Buddhism of, probably, its early stages, see it slackening its pace, the crests of Hindu depth-waves rising, parallel yet contrariwise,

74 Sesshu *Daruma and Eka*
◀Detail (Muromachi period, 15th century)

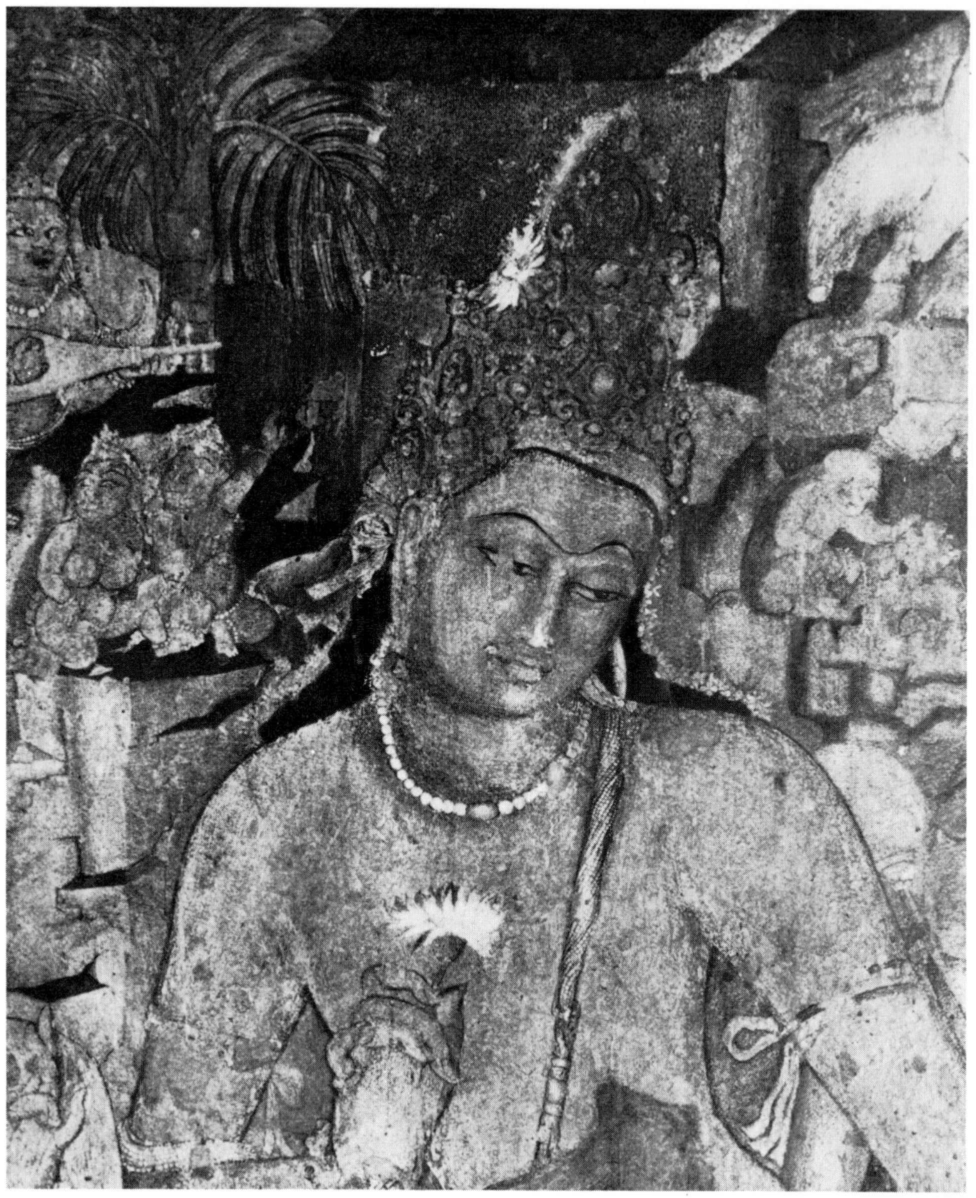

75 The Great Bodhisattva Detail, wall-painting, Ajanta (late Gupta period, 6th century)

carrying to their height-limits the dual-oneness of tantras; India now radiating its pre-Vedic urban-maternal "generosity" around and into the iron-paternal pastoral "honesty" of hymnic Vedas. See them: roads of Buddhist pilgrimage eastward, roads of rich silence; silent roads making one, self-covering themselves, with the noisy roads of noisy town-and-steppe strivings and events; roads, open roads—oh, the human cataracts falling down, epics of vertigo, bloodshed, and tumultuous clouds of dust! falling down from the Pamirian glacial grandeur and beyond this grandeur, to the greedy yet shelter-promising Himalayan passes!—open roads that poured forth rest-

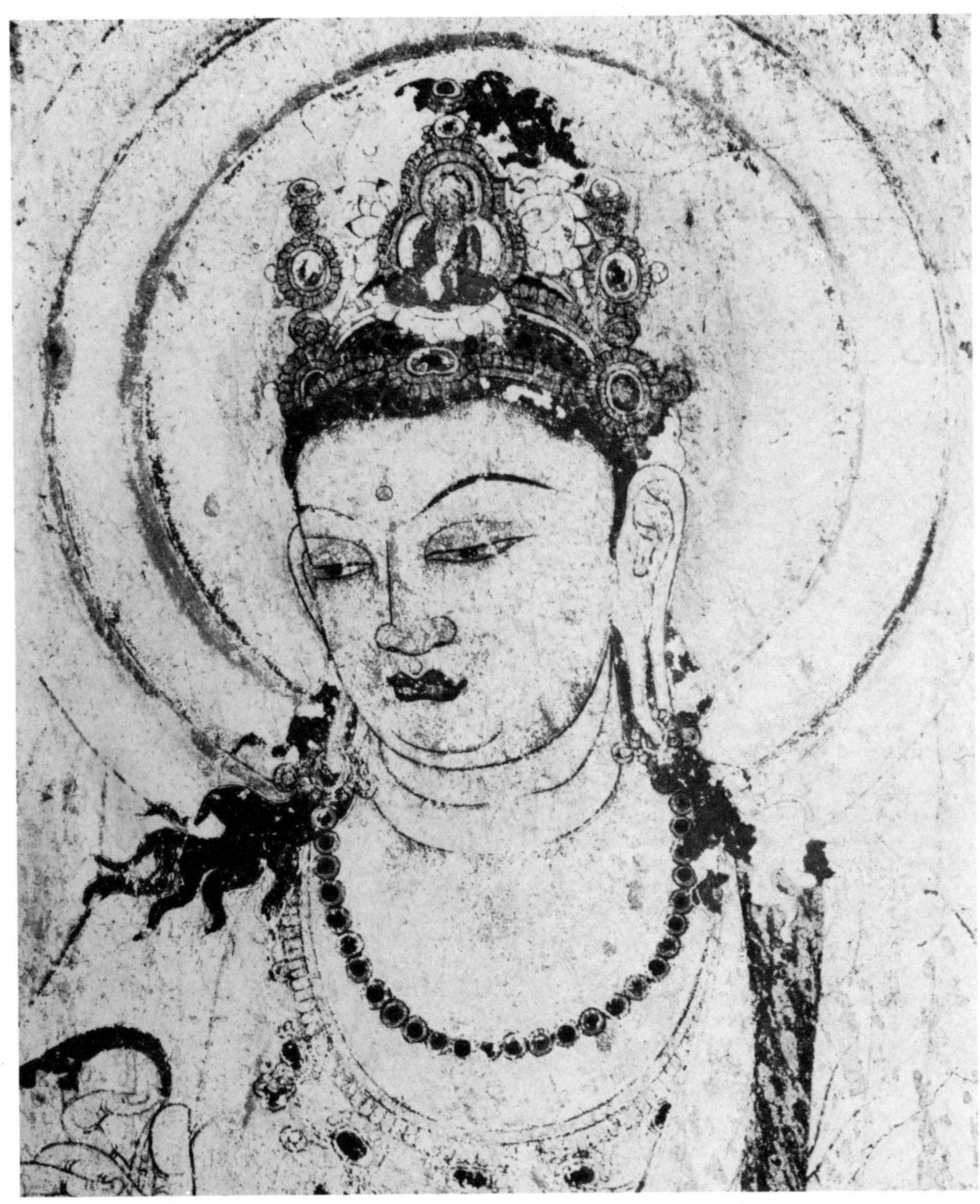

76 Bodhisattva Detail, wall-painting, Horyuji (early Nara period, 7th century)

less peoples from the Mongolian-Siberian wilderness; roads surrounding and penetrating the belt of urbanized Asia, opening to the covetousness and wonder of semi-nomads the reservoir of urban splendors, from Bactria to the Indus Valley down south, to China eastward, to Iran's plateau westward.

See more: roads offering also an escape and an issue from the endemic and devastating rich-versus-poor struggles among cattle owners, this ever-present universal drama of the steppes, the sociological prelude to all the exodus-invasions in man's great past, as well as to the resulting imperial

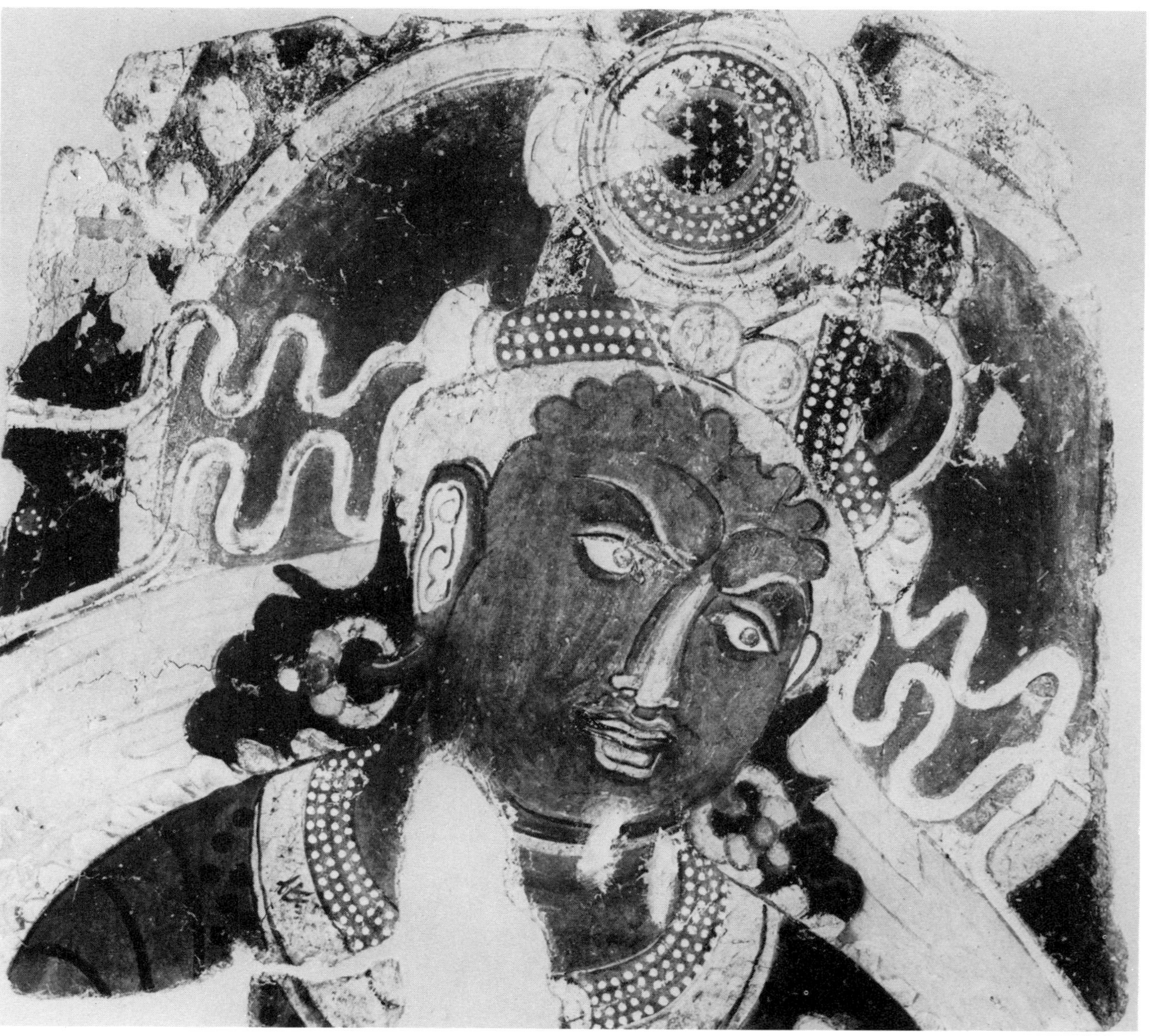

77 *Head*
Detail, wall-painting, Kyzil

political crystallizations. Tumultuous history of periodically settled conflicts and mixtures between the humanity of the sown and humanity on the move, settled in patterns of intermixed steppe-and-urban empires—the ancient Scyths down to the Hsiung-nu, later on, the great Hunnish-Turkish tribal agglomerations, the White Huns or the Ephthalites, the Orkhon Turks, the Uighurs, etc.; the settled empires of ancient Chou, later, those of the Wei and the Southern Liang in China; in Iran, the extended Partho-Sassanian imperial bloc;[69] in India, the Kushana-Gupta bloc, and so many other nuclei of imperial mixed expansions all over the then known world!

And more: such roads of inroads, roads of pilgrimages also, making one, self-covering themselves with roads of peaceful, Rome-to-China trading and exchange of luxuries and necessities—all the water-and-land ways across the multi-curved width and length of East and West! The difficult, dangerous roads of caravans moving slowly, slowly—the daring, death-and-illness challenging perseverance, imagination, and curiosity of great merchant travellers, those of the Far East meeting the others, the goods-news-ideas carrying and trading travellers from the legendary West (all the menace of their crossing of summits and deserts to be re-lived by all of them again at their homeward return)—meeting at last at the solitary halt—halt of cozy solidarity indeed—the world-famous Stone Tower in the wastes of Pamir!

How rewarding a visitation-image for you, poet-historian! Roads, roads, roads! Even as the poet's mirroring in a poem the sown-unsown density of today's steppe-metropolis: "Windows! windows! windows! People! people! people!"[70]

And still more: Roads leading to the heraldic nucleus of all these sedimented urban-nomadic transmissions, converging all into one, final geographical knot of "connected-with" events and influences—the scintillant necklace of oases around the austere and forbidding neck of the Takla Makān desert, the precious necklace of gems-oases skirting the great framing mountains of the T'ien Shan and Kuen-Lun ranges to the north and south—where ultimately our two fraternal currents of thought and sub-history, mine and yours, merge together in one final image-hallucination: the Ajanta-Horyuji pictorial space, its destiny, its meaning, its secret, its culminating Japaneseness.

And that is why it was here—along the stages of a growing *techne* history of Buddhist art reaching from India, and across its Central Asiatic bridge, to the Far East's Pacific—it was here that I stopped and wrote somewhere in the middle, the title of the book to be written:

PADMAPANI'S NOSE

For a subtle difference, unnoticed, unnoticeable tiny grey mouse, is the real difference:

The nose of the Indian Bodhisattva *(See Plate 75)* has the beautiful plethoric fullness of a pictorial line that contains in its sensitive thinning and thickening the melodious roundness of a fully satisfying, fully achieved space-volume.

The nose of the Bodhisattva at Horyuji *(See Plate 76)* is very close to Ajanta's; yet a slight deviation from the melodious plenitude of the volume-building line, a slight and sudden lurking in here of rigidity—echo of a persisting voice from a different far-away world—an oblique line's slashing across the flattened space, suddenly and subtly makes this space formula affined to—influenced by?—that of greater Central Asia *(See Plate 77)*.

The Horyuji image contains, I dare to say, all the subsequent *techne* events of Yamato's art and carries in it very subtly the subtle synthesis of the greater East and the greater West.

That is how, in making now *the Next Step Down:*

I say the problem of Padmapani's nose becomes, under the direct, close glance-index of our journey's Mysterious Companion, not only a problem of a particular art's drama or episode that would correspond to the drama, thus duality, of your solitude-solidarity in man, but this very same duality as embodied in the concrete, precise, narrow and localized visual-manual structure of pictorial space—and nothing else from now on.

Indeed, our two fraternal currents of thought and sub-history make one or make nought: is it I who say now, is it you who said then:

> *Space is the fragment in which the unseizable whole of life, material and moral, is transubstantiated or seized in the art of painting* . . . . I mean the material space we see, not any abstract "meaningful" derivative space; I mean simply the banal yet astonishing phenomenon of extension, of distance, of three-dimensional visibility.
>
> The individual space structure with which, like the snail within its shell, an artist surrounds himself is his whole unbroken reality and truth, his triple level: lyrical—the hidden truth of his inspiration or his personality; epical—the hidden impact of his precise historical momentum; cosmic—his calculable and incalculable breaking through the stellar flow. Space in art is a choice, therefore a judgment.
>
> That is why I say *space in art is a moral space*. . . . .
>
> So I repeat: space in art is a *moral* space. So falls the ivory tower of the aestheticians. The "pure visibility" worries of a painter are not aesthetic and conceptual worries only, they are human, moral worries.[71]

Is this mine? Is this yours? This: there is an evident "natural" movement (the impression of motion in space) in so gracious a work as the Victory of Athena Nike's balustrade *(See Plate 24)* or as India's Yakshi *(See Plate 71)*; there is obvious mobility, there is a clear connection-association between all the formal elements of a compound pictorial image to be narrated in the interlaced rhythms of Delacroix's or Rubens' dramas; and even more convincingly in Ch'ên Jung's mystico-cosmic dragon evolving from no-birth to no-end *(See Plate 25)*.

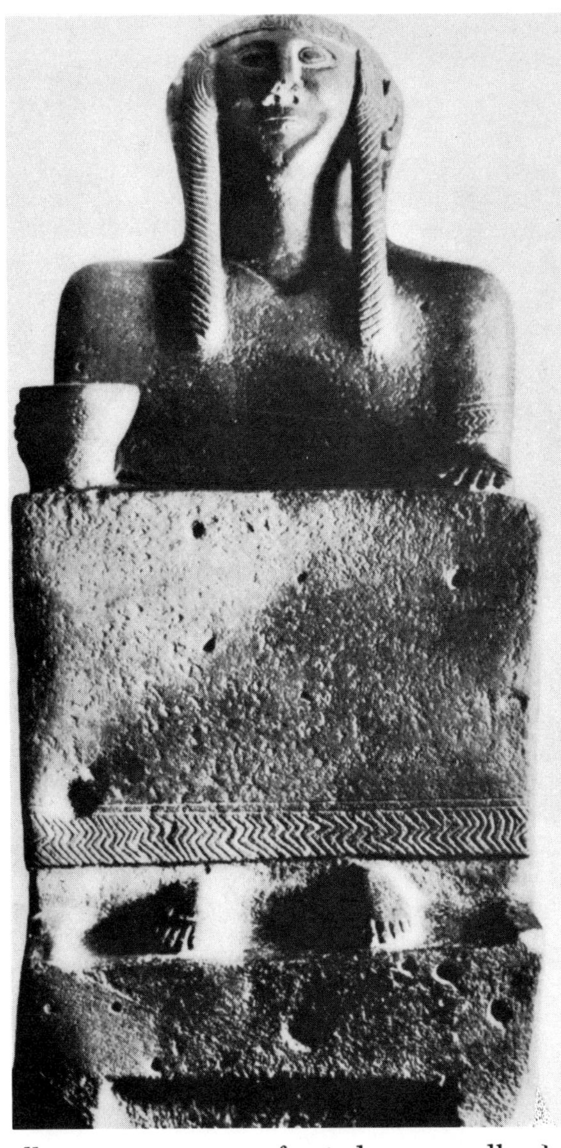

There is on the other hand stiffness, rigidity, in the "Hittite" throned goddess here *(Plate 78),* and in Giotto's figures, in Ben Shahn's image-epigrams *(Plate 79);* stiffness, rigidity, in the hypnotic repeat of verticality of our Dura-Europos image *(See Plate 70)*; rigid immobility in the tensely oblique flatness of the Werden Christ *(Plate 80),* or in the Yamato-e simulacrum-abstraction *(See Plate 27).*

Yet, what the deeper down-lifted level of comparative analysis reveals might be the contrary. The movement of the first group is, one could say, a "mnemonic" movement, not an immediate or immediately reproduced movement: it results from our memory's reconstruction of all those observable moments of motion in objects and beings whose authentication has been for us most satisfying both logically (= this or that curve of a line or of a color, as the case might be, repeated in us and "working" on us as convincingly, if automatically, as a category of mind supposedly does by connecting-associating us with the out of us) and optically (= this or that curve fulfilled and not to be repeated in us—Eros of plenitude and of pleasure-pain!), and which our memory could retain, accumulate, and select for the purpose of an aesthetic reconstruction. Here is the birth of what we call grace in art: the marvel-full repetition of what has been given to us once—and not to be repeated.

Mobility, on the other hand, or movement immediately captured, might be revealed in the very stiffness or rigidity of the second group. Because this rigidity is the dynamic effort-momentum of a starting or immediate movement, the decisive momentum of a just-opened dike when the quiet waters of the upper level at the point of emptying are no longer quiet, immobile, nor as yet in full movement, in movement already. It is this effort

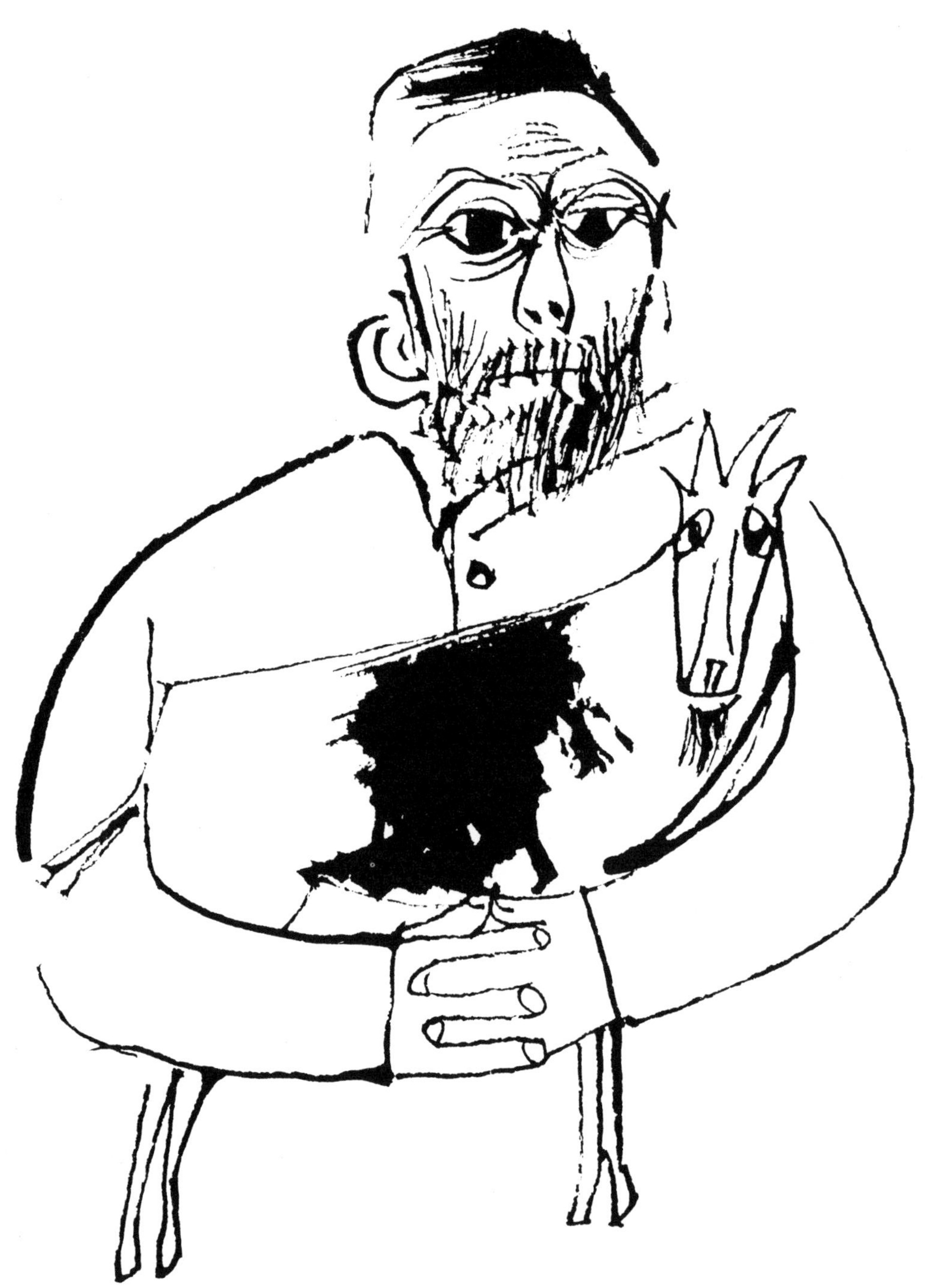

79 BEN SHAHN *Drawing*

or this instantaneity of movement-about-to-be, which *mobilizes* the immobility, the rigidity, of Giotto's drama, or Ben Shahn's sharp and capsizing balances, or the "frozen dance" of Japan's inrush into visible reality, obliquely, angularly seen and seen by us as twentieth-century "pure abstractions."[72]

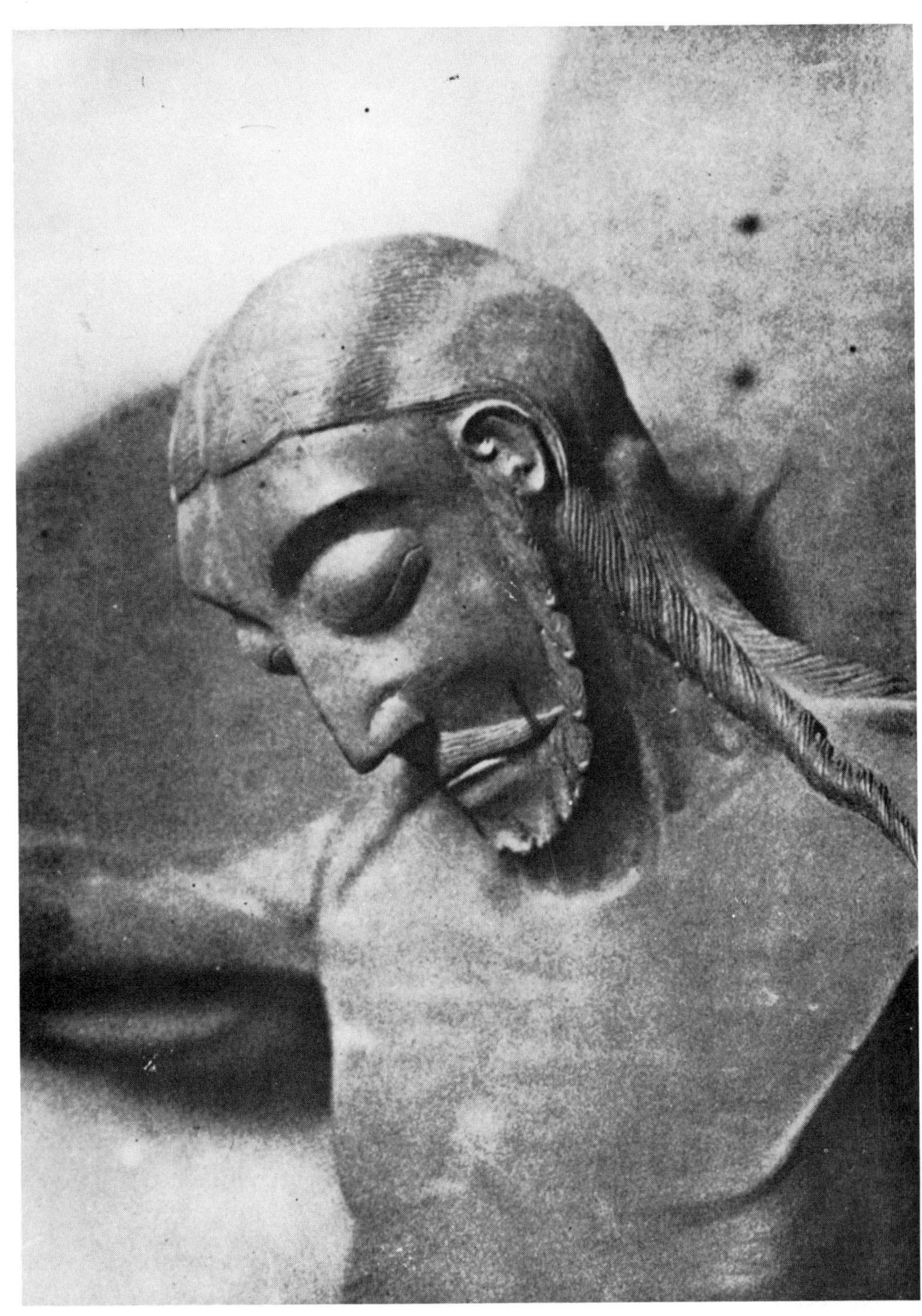

80 Crucifix Detail, bronze (11th century)

Nakedness of space and of movement in space, I call this mobile rigidity: nakedness of a total, otherwise unseizable sensation of motion (= e-motion); not the tonal-melodic, remembered nudity-clothing-the-nakedness

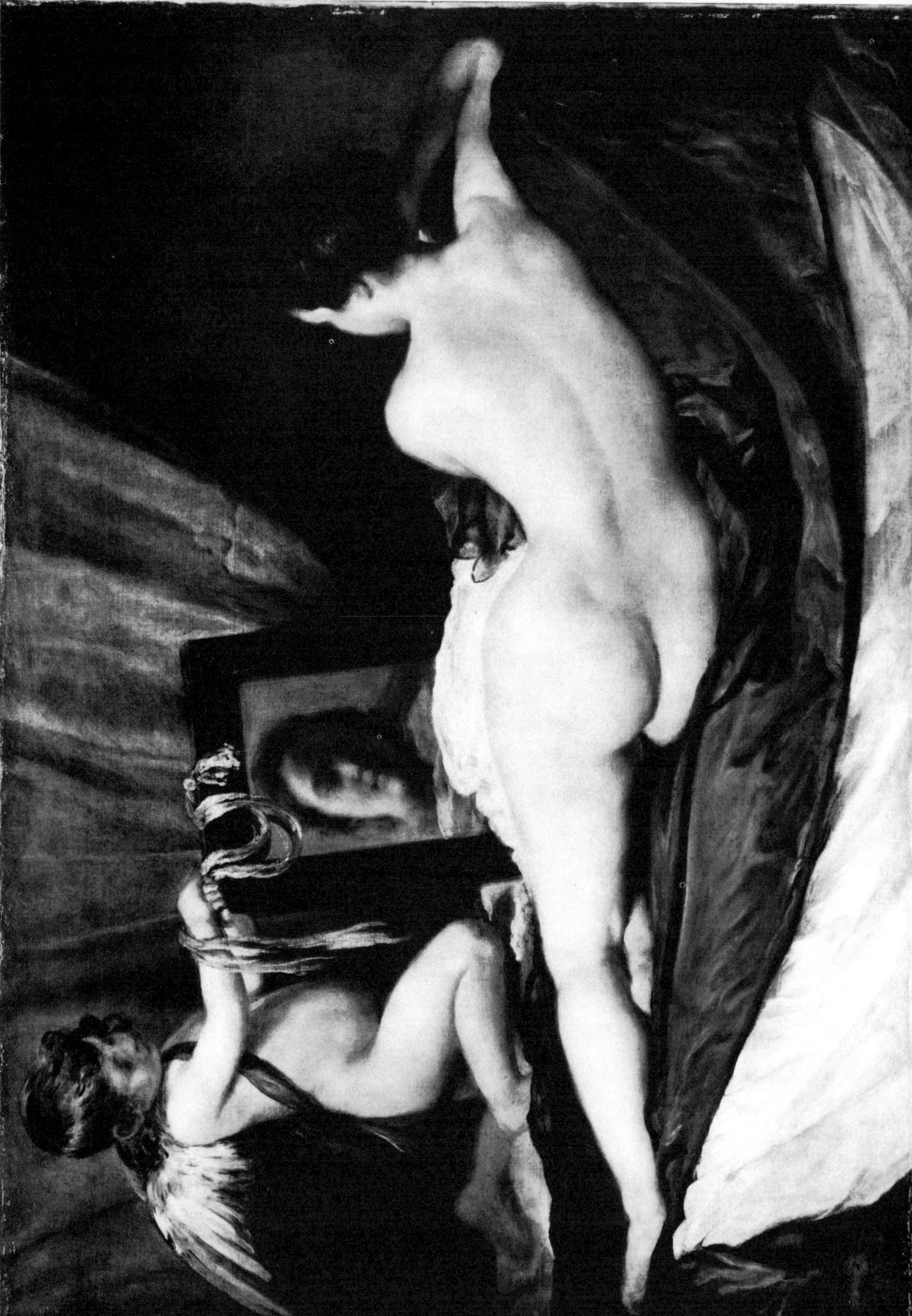

of Velasquez' Venus *(Plate 81)*, but the a-tonal, stripped, immediate nakedness of Manet's Olympia *(Plate 82)*!

❖❖❖❖❖❖❖❖❖❖❖❖❖❖❖❖❖❖❖❖❖❖❖❖❖❖❖❖❖❖

And this is where our united will, yours and mine, is situ-ating us now: definitely at the end of our journey, which is also the return to the "innermost body."

The Next and the Last Step Down is here. Yes; we started somewhere in the middle, but somewhere within our body.

Because spirit is what does not fight; you have said it once. Soul is what cannot bear a blemish on it.

Body is what fights for the spirit, what bears the blemish for the soul. As art does.

Because art has to do with melancholy, with tenderness, I have said—

the tenderness for decay
the melancholy of decay
the tenderness for old age
the melancholy of old age
the tenderness for the Child
the melancholy of the Child
the tenderness, the melancholy of body's fights, of body's blemishes.

Somewhere in the middle and at a precise point-stop of our body's self-involvement and self-evolvement, the visual art's center of concretion or materiality, art's space, is generated—somewhere within my loyalty to the spirit, my body's fights, my body's blemishes.

That's it, that is where the dual motion in space—the "mnemonic," the foreseen behaviour of forms in space, and the immediate unforeseeable birth of movement in space—situ-ated in closest contact, as it were, with the inside-of-my-body, is authenticated as being the very geometry of a dual—always dual—space-volume structured outside of me.

I mean this: that the fullness of the kinæsthetic satisfaction, the fullness of a remembered, reconstructed *impression* of movement, is given to us as fullness of a perfect circular presence, an evenly curved, expected, totally satisfying continuity. And that the kinetic-visual seizure-touch of an immediate "rigid-mobile" movement is the seizure-touch in us of an oblique-angular presence, an unexpected, *surprising* discontinuity, whether appearing optically as such or not.

More obviously in art's genesis than elsewhere (and very convincingly, very much so, in Japan's art secrets, from the secret of sword-making to that of the puppet and Kabuki performances) this means to me that the factual asymmetry, the irreversibility, between the inanimate and the animate is not an opposition—as syllogism would have it, as dialectics would need it—but an "exchange of gifts." It is for me, the *haiku*-trained Japanese, a suddenly human equation of chosen values—an image-touch of a *moral* exchange, as any human choice is, and not only as its corollary, human conduct, must be first.

◀81 VELAZQUEZ *Venus and the Mirror*
17th century

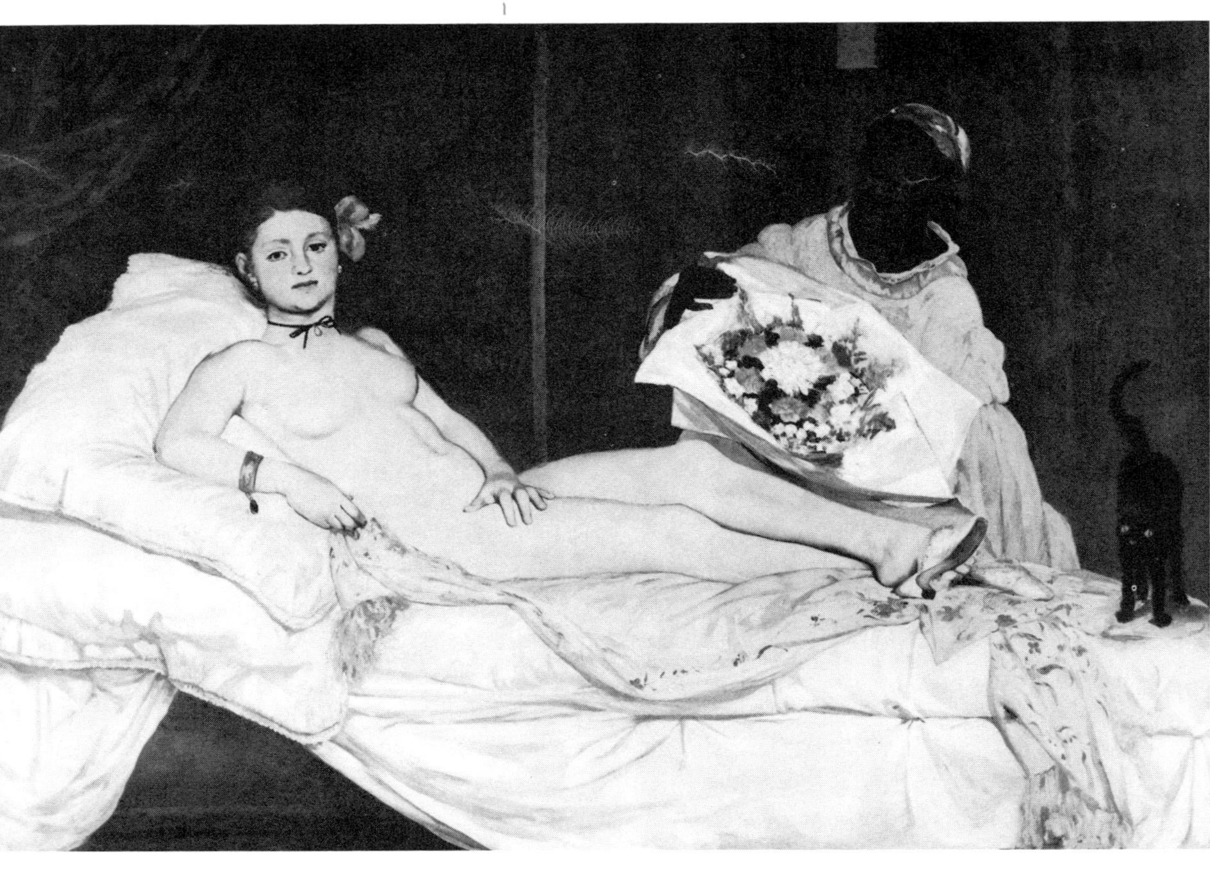

82 MANET *Olympia* (19th century)

That is why, as I understood it, you call art's space *moral space.* That is why also I dare, and have chosen this very moment now, to introduce another of my heraldic equations. This: I say—here is, or has been, a simple sensation of a color, blue, for instance, this purest and, perhaps, most convincing experience. Now, this precise sensation-blue, would it be, just be, a presence, an actuality, total and mine, in exclusion, at a certain, however fleeting, point of psyche-halt, of all other actualities, if, at the same time as it was given to me, and without losing its character of simple, pure sensation *of* blue, it was not also a sort of authentication, a lyrical verification of blue; in other words, if that simple sensation *of* blue was not in itself and by itself the evidence of its own, *self-transcending* significance or value; therefore, if it was not also a moral—chosen as good—*idea* of the blue? The sensation-blue and the idea-blue are reversible in the depth of our visual labor.

The entire poetry of the world visible and invisible as yet, dry and humid, is there; all the meaning of beauty, therefore, of history and thought is there.

My folk-aristocratic-artisan song has a refrain: heraldically, what is heraldry?

A refrain at the beginning, at the middle, at the ending of my song:

What is Heraldry?
Poetry, as
Substitution
tautology, transfer,
refrain, touch
image, knot
sub-history
history without proof
without greed for proof
Solitude-Solidarity's
oneness after all
before all
Why not a fragrance?
Why not?
A dual-one-death
living too
As evolvement in the dual oneness of moving forms
Space-emotion.

When I say blue and question and suppose blue, when I offer the psyche-gift of blue, heraldically my gift is exchanged already with somebody else's saying questioning, supposing, offering this now:

The gift of mechanics is basically dual movement too, the rotary and the reciprocal movement.[73]

The circle is, one may say, the graphic symbol of rotary motion, which is both psychologically and mechanically basal.

Now, the circle itself can be considered the result of a mutual, uniform, continued-associated attraction between a mobile point in space, $a, a_1, a_2, a_3 \ldots a_n$, and another, fixed, point O, which becomes thus the center of the circle so formed.

It is this mutual and continued attraction which is the "moral" materiality of the circle's psycho-genesis.

If the rotary motion is the "pure" motion, the reciprocal is a "mixed" motion formed by the combination of two "pure" and identical rotations. Its graphic, heraldic, symbol, its "moral" materiality, is the lens-shaped figure which results from the interference of two perfect circles. At the points xx_1 of intersection of the circles O and o_1, a sudden break, a rupture of the rotary continuity of the circle O and the circle o_1 is introduced.

As a moral-heraldical, moral-sub-historical reality this means that while the uniformity and continuity of attraction between points a—a_n and O annihilate the initial immediate effort of mobility—the initial *in*-"awareness" of mobility—in a perfectly circular motion, this effort-awareness is rather re-created, is reborn by the change of direction, by the sudden discontinuity introduced in the reciprocal motion there at the points x and x_1, where the momentum of interference becomes rigid (without the two underlying intersecting circles themselves being thereby annihilated: they coexist there in their mechanical, temporary, as it were, absoluteness).

Perfect rotary movement is, thus, perfect stability of the *mnemonic* construction of movement in art and thought; it is the pure circularity of time and space and spirit—the eternity of classical philosophers; it is antiquity's heavenly architectural or concentric circles. Reciprocal, geared, movement is thus rigid-mobility's medium, where the immediacy of an experienced motion is situ-ated in art; it is the sudden obliquity of introspection, the birth of psychology in the West (perhaps, St. Augustine's "invention"), and as, perhaps, the result of it, the "elliptical" conception of the cosmos (Kepler, and much before modern Europe, Hindu-Islamic intuition). The history of human artisan civilization is contained in these two graphic and moral-geometric symbols of motion (and in their multi-interrelation).

❖❖❖❖❖❖❖❖❖❖❖❖❖❖❖❖❖❖❖❖❖❖❖❖❖❖❖❖❖❖

Somewhere—a refrain in my body, an area-pattern, an area-knot of me and of history!—the nostalgic yet stabilized quality of non-finity became the precise quantum-finity of any concretion, anywhere, anyhow. Somewhere in there this equation of mine, this saying of mine about the vital and the mechanical (the content-blue, as it were, and the form-motion, as it were, being equated), has been fulfilled. The "mnemonic" fullness of a circular presence in me, the a, a_1, a_n—O attraction forming the motion and grace of a circle, becomes—and *is* at this very present moment!—the perfect fullness of a spherical being. (So that the still flat thus incomplete circularity of a circle completes itself into a one-center, one-axial self-fulfilled volume-space.)

And facing it heraldically, the fullness of a total seizure, the seizure of an immediate, oblique-discontinued presence, the *xx1* figure, becomes, *is* now a multi-center, multi-axial volume-space; a poly-ellipsoidal blue-and-motion.

The fullness of a space-sphere is the fullness of Greece, entirely, purely, loyally—of ancient Hellas and its radiation afar. Greece, the perfect sphere: an inescapable, irrevocable, pure, empirically nonexistent absolute, one-oneness, pure being—in its ultimated self-maturation a living, spherical being of geometry, of music, of intellect and intellecting, of ethics, of a city-state, of the soul, of Eros total.

As visual narration of our response to it, the perfect sphere (this spherical object I am lookng at in front of me!) is a being-shape optically given and defined to me already without me in it, outside me *(See Plate 15).*

But this visual-verbal narration and experience is not an end-experience, an end-communication as yet—it becomes such, and fully so, while a sphere is actualized or constructed by us, within us as well: a total given-constructed, total-erotic adhesion of all the given out-of-us points that make a sphere what it is about to be instantly, to all the points of our innermost body—and no escape from it!—at the very moment of their down-rush up to Eros's presence and consummation—my *peine d'amour,* my refrain!

Ancient Greece stood up and testified:

That fullness can be generated only by itself, by both being and ever becoming nothing but a perfect self-rotating oneness: a sphere.

For *ab initio* this oneness of a sphere is, in its conception and concretion, but a center-point, a free point in a free space, the mysterious (oh, how mysterious is space's genesis in painting!) *punctum simplicissimus* of Spinoza,[74] a material *punctum* after and before all—one, and only one, point as the sphere's ultimate value-touch, a perfect evenness along the entire surface circularity, no matter how small or how expanded the sphere-point might be; one point, and only one, without a fraction of this oneness possibly to be added to or subtracted from it, without thus any possible imaginable or conceivable geometrical irregularity about it. A sphere *ab initio* with nought beyond it. And so fully satisfying, so perfectly regular this being is, that its reversibility—we might, in a total transfer of terms, call it co-proportionality—with any other shape-form as perfectly regular, a cube, an equilateral triangle, should be (and, indeed, was so in the artisan history of the visual-manual!) creatively self-evident or felt. Such is the sphere-cube-triangle concord in a Greek masterpiece *(Plate 83);* such also this same pure Hellenic legacy when transferred into Islam's new, very pure too, idiom of co-proportionality *(Plate 84)*; such again when it created the Renaissance's passion *(Plate 85);* and re-created this same, very pure,

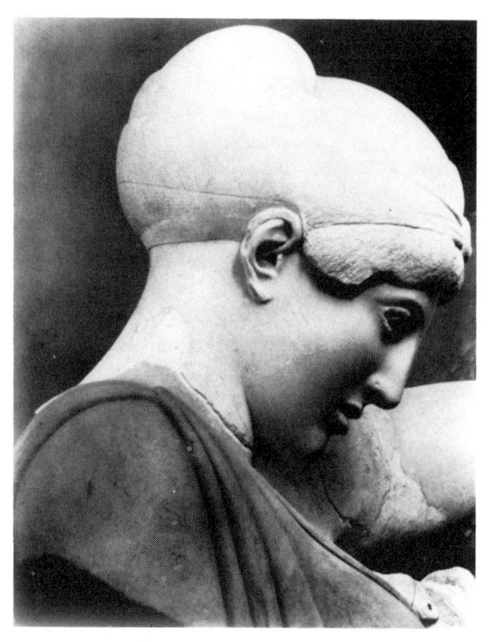

83 *Lapith Woman* Olympia (ca. 470 B.C.)

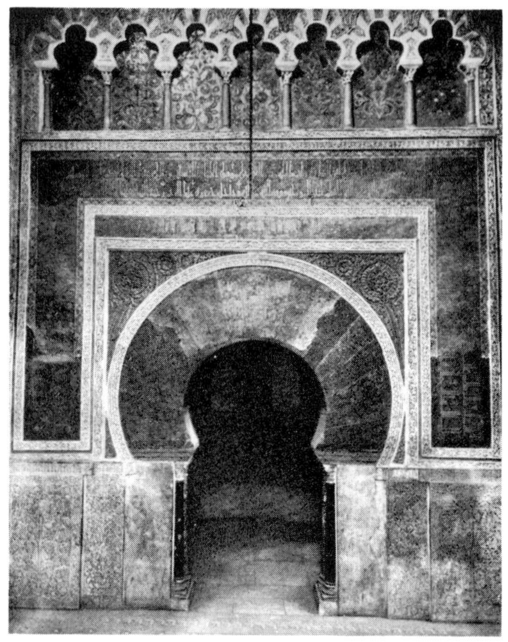

84 *Mihrab* Cordoba (10th century)

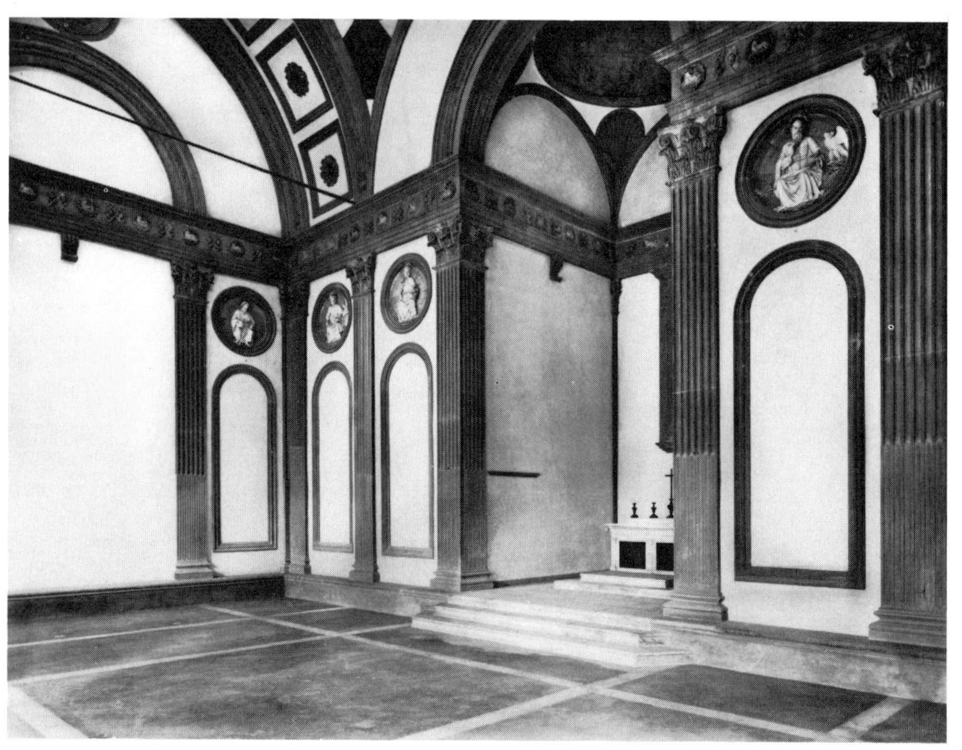

85 BRUNELLESCHI *Cappella Pazzi* Florence (early 15th century)

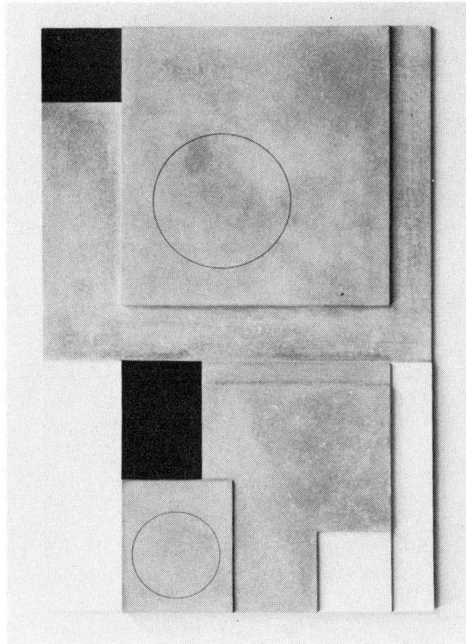

86 Ben Nicholson *Relief 1939*

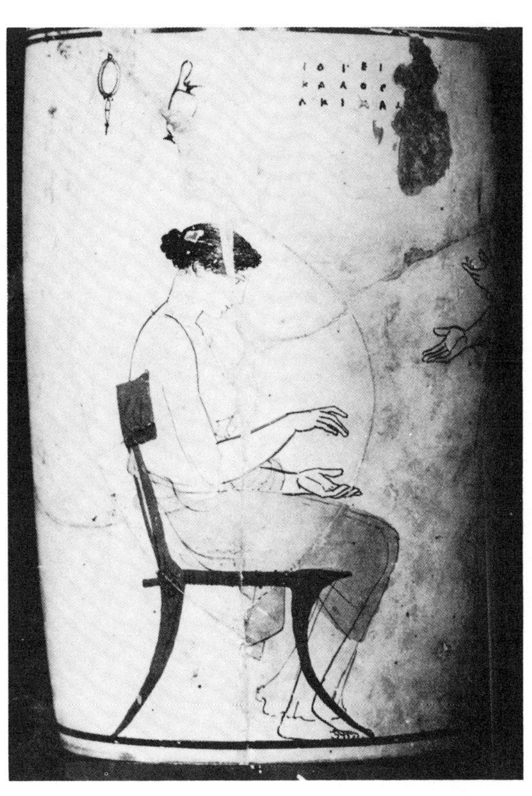

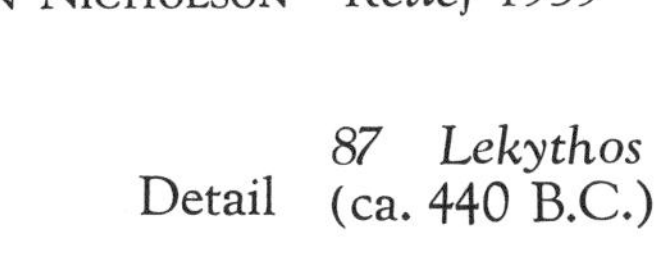

87 *Lekythos*
Detail (ca. 440 B.C.)

passion—too haughty, too aloof, it is true, to be true—in our own century *(Plate 86).*

And more, much more—heraldically:

Not only a volume, but *any* spatial form-limit, whether an all-rounded, inter-harmonized color or a simple line, straight or curved or even broken, any such form-limit that responds to—feels—the absoluteness, the sphericity, of erotic plenitude is already a perfect volume-sphere, a perfect inescapable circularity. Such, the Greek line itself, a line that in the perfection of its toward-roundness plenitude is the very fullness of a volume-to-be, epitomizes it—a line-volume, a line-sphere, a line-relief I call it *(Plate 87).* And that is why I am re-introducing here too, and with conviction, what you have suggested in your book:[75] That the Far Eastern, Chinese, "two-dimensional" space resulting from the fabulous linear technique of the brush stroke—the Chinese classical accuracy in rendering the fullness of the thinning and the thickening of a line *(Plate 88),* as well as the *satori*-calculated nonchalance of an ink-splash *(Plate 89)*—is, in the fullness of its tactile rendering of a volume-feel, as "three-dimensional" as our West's; that the quality of the line-relief there—still two-dimensional, still discontinuous by the facts-and-influence method of appraisal—*the intensity of this quality,* presents the same convincing content-measure of full relief in space, the same sphericity, that our geometrized, centered space has elaborated for itself.

"Our geometry-centered space," you said; but what you surely meant,

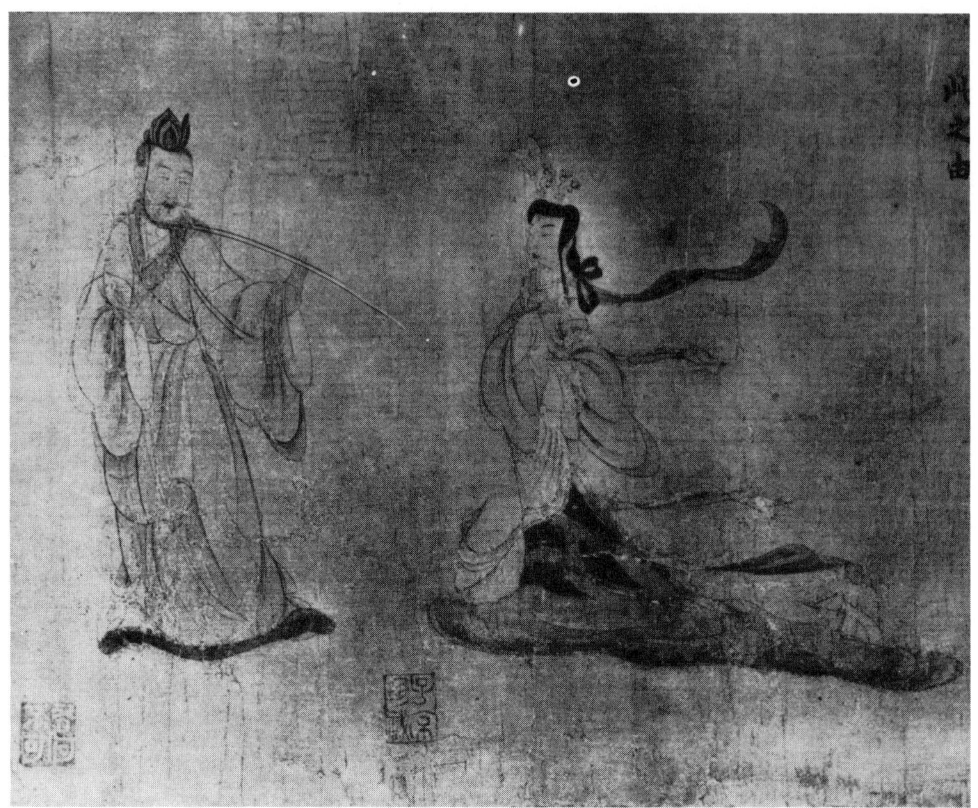

88 KU K'AI-CHIH *The Admonitions* Detail (T'ang period, 4th century)

I think, was the West's universal center-point as sphere *ab initio;* and still more nearly, more tightly historically, Greece itself, radiating far, far: in India, Ajanta's volume-grace! in China, Han-toward-T'ang volume-line's fulfilment!

Greece: the empirically nonexistent perfection, the sphere that includes us—*pneuma*—in its psyche-genesis, yet, once formed, is separated from us—hypostatic *nous:* Greece all!

And confronting this universe stands Asia at large, all Indic Asia, and by inter-far-radiation, all medieval Islam, all the West's Christianity from Werden's "Crucifix" to Max Beckmann; Asia at large, and its concept of space in art that remained loyal to the living act of touch: irregular, escapable, ever-to-be-perfected, a living struggling agonic being—which in its ultimate evolvement does not stand as volume, as relief spatial, in front of us, but with us, in us and by us.

An oblique ellipsoidal space-volume, an about-to-be-volume, I feel it: its birth-center in a real, irregular *punctum,* an empirically existent *punctum,* one and a fraction-of-one or one less a fraction-of-one, propagating this intimate irregularity along the trajectory or trajectories that result.

Never a spherical micro-macrocosmic cosmos-volume, but a universe of lines, later surfaces, unexpectedly crossing each other, evolving, structuring within us a multi-axial, multi-puncted dynamic volume: the sudden,

89 LIANG K'AI *Ideal Portrait of the Poet Li T'ai-po* Detail (early 13th century)▶

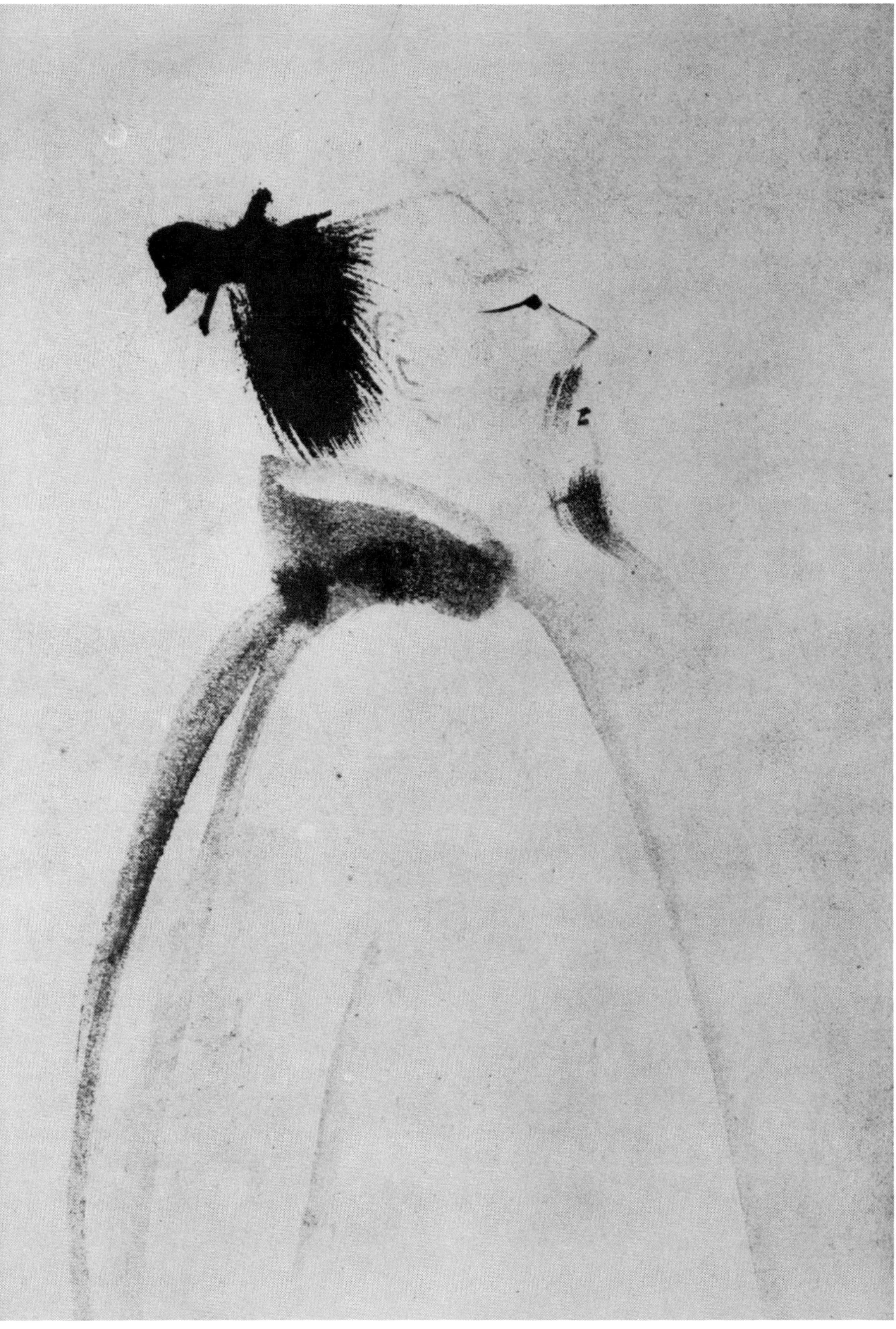

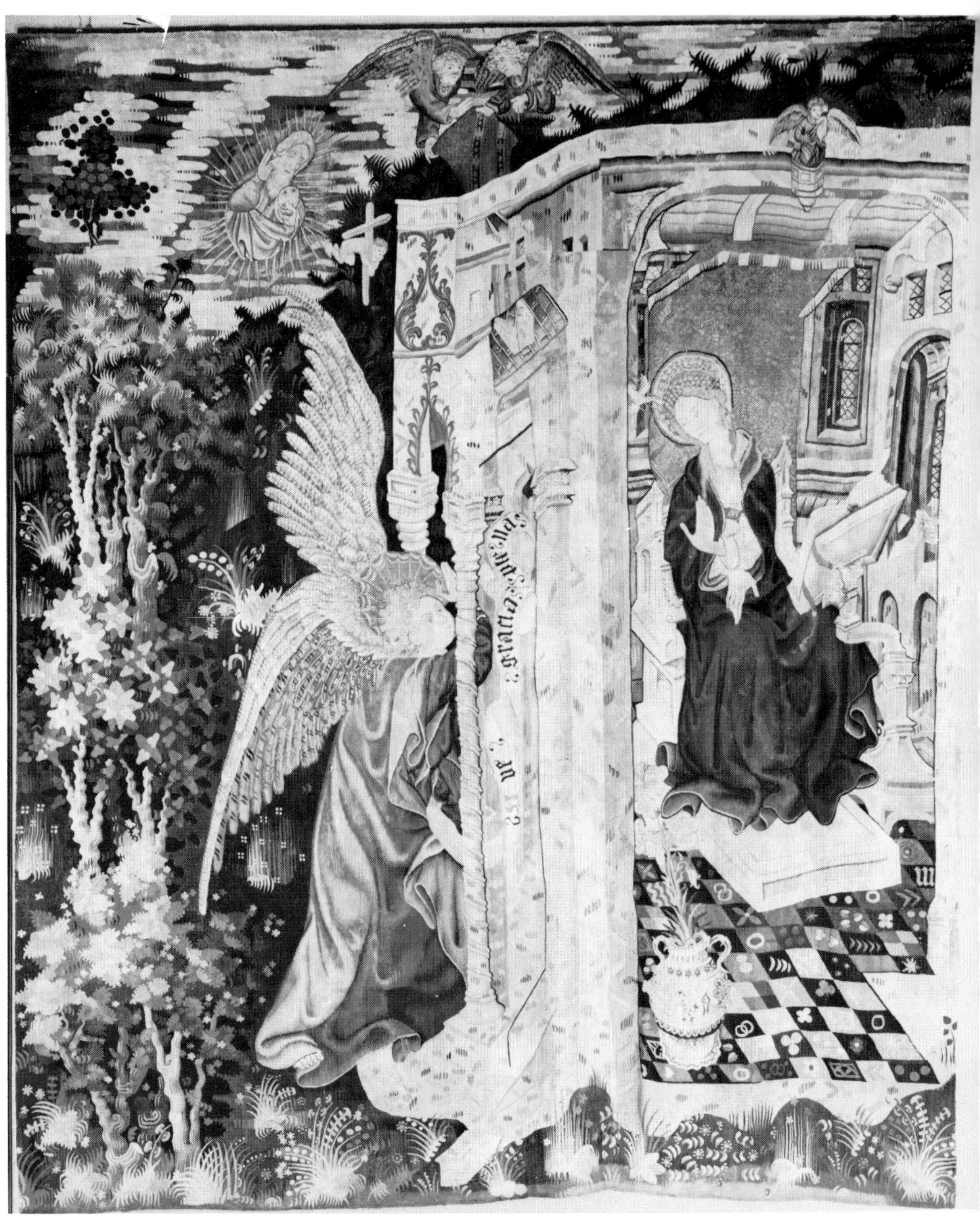

90 *Annunciation* Tapestry, Flemish (probably School of Arras, early 15th century)

immediate, "rigid-mobile" fullness of a space-cross *(Plate 90). (See also Plates 27, 150).*

Heraldically: two concepts of space in art co-present in us and in history.

Factually: who knows? I say two concepts co-present: as art this is an equilibrium of energies; as style—an accent on one of the two.

China contains, indubitably, both, but knew and willed the sphere; China is Greece, heraldically, sub-historically.

Japan learned to know both, but willed the oblique, the cross. To resume, with your example in mind:

China:	*Japan:*
Space – sphere	Space – cross
as	as
movement given	movement immediate
stable-mnemonic	rigid-mobile
nudity and rhythm	nakedness and pose
line-relief	line-ornament
impression	sensation
feeling	idea
humid	dry
naturalism	realism
Pneuma	*Nous*
Correspondence	Substitution-Identity
Death as	Death as
Creature's creation	Creator's creature
of	of
Life-Transformation	Life-Transfer
of	as
Solidarity	Solitude
as	of
Certitude	Doubt and Faith making one,
	such, shadow and light
Concrete-Proof	Touch-Witness
mnemonic round motion	about-to-be motion
interconnected	connected-adhered
interassociated	oblique
enlightened	closest
nearness and sympathy	terror-and-closeness
to Creation	to Creator
of	of
Continuity	Discontinuity
Ease, Pax	Nostalgia, Halt
Poetess in	Daruma in
meditation	exaltation

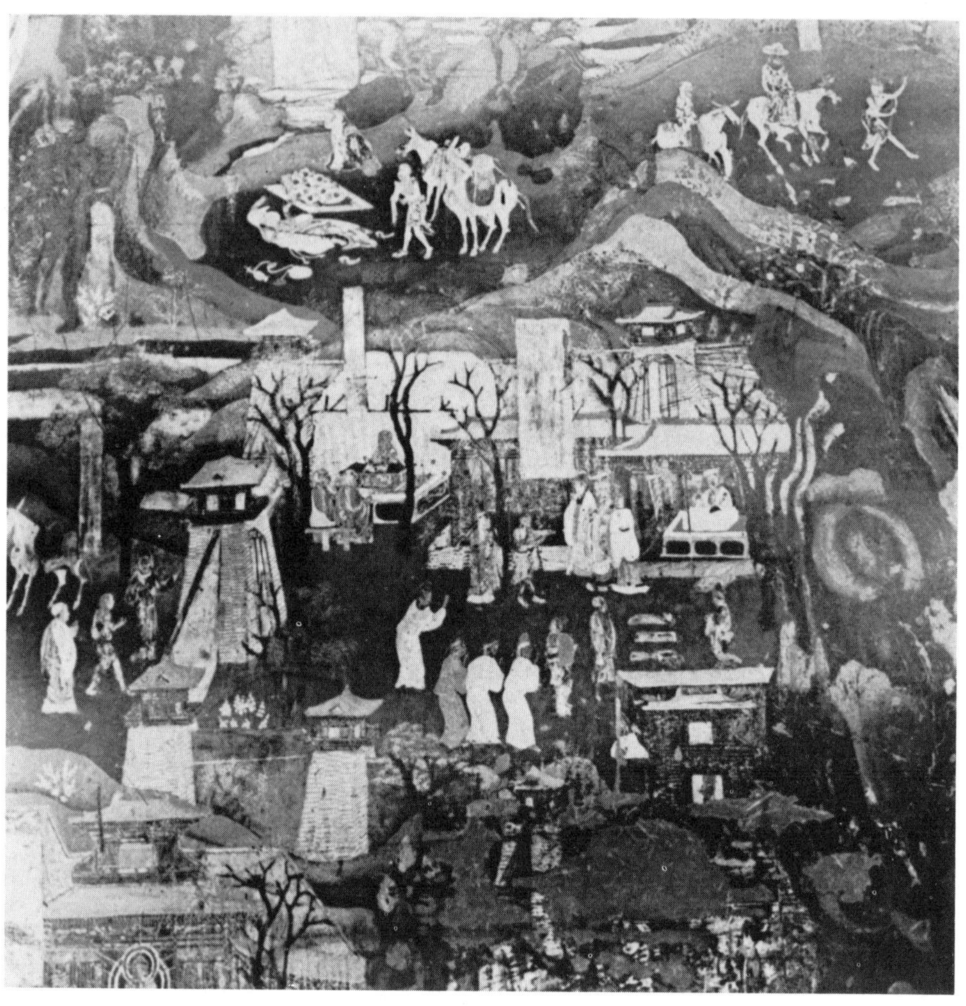

91 *A Pilgrim on His Travels* Detail, wall-painting, Tun-huang (ca. A.D. 660)

China's art of painting:

Space given—perfection facing us—space taken for granted, healthy space; space of sculpture, not space of painters.[76]

Many sensitive scholars have said this already, in their own, different from ours, and very suggestive way: what of their showing the slow and steady growth of China's feel and predilection for spatial fullness, ease, enlightened associations, from the Han era's love for perfect rounded-interconnected forms, the perfectly limited "space-cells" of T'ang wall painting at Tun-huang *(Plate 91)* to Sung all-blending visionary concordances and harmonies!

Painting in China: Space of sculpture: certainty, *pax,* givenness: perfection.

Painting in Japan: Space of painting: perfection structured, not given; perfectibility demanding us, our being there, volume-to-be; space-tension, sick, to be cured, sick again, cured again. . . . .

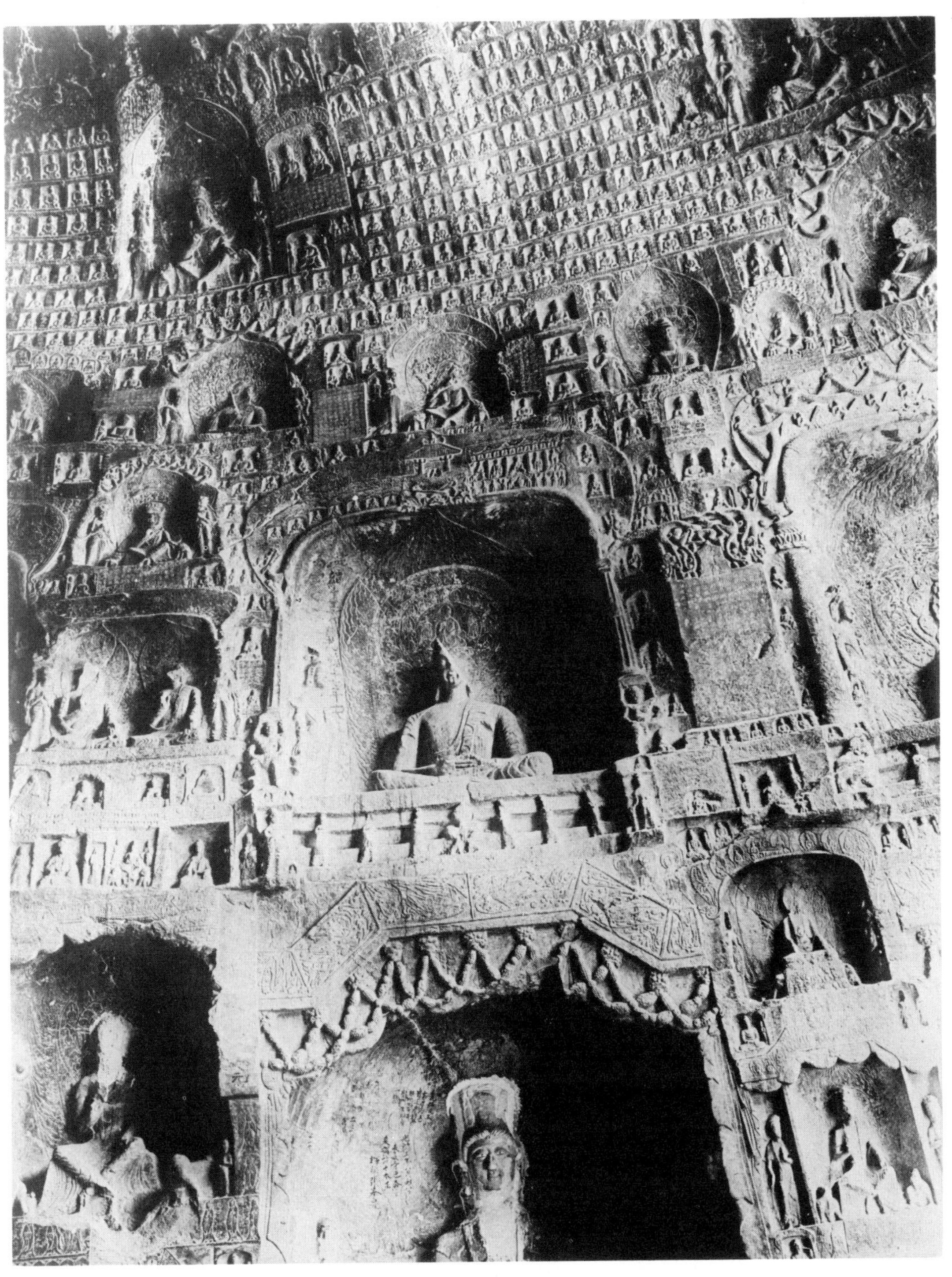

92 *North Wei Caves* Detail (Northern Wei dynasty, 5th-6th century)

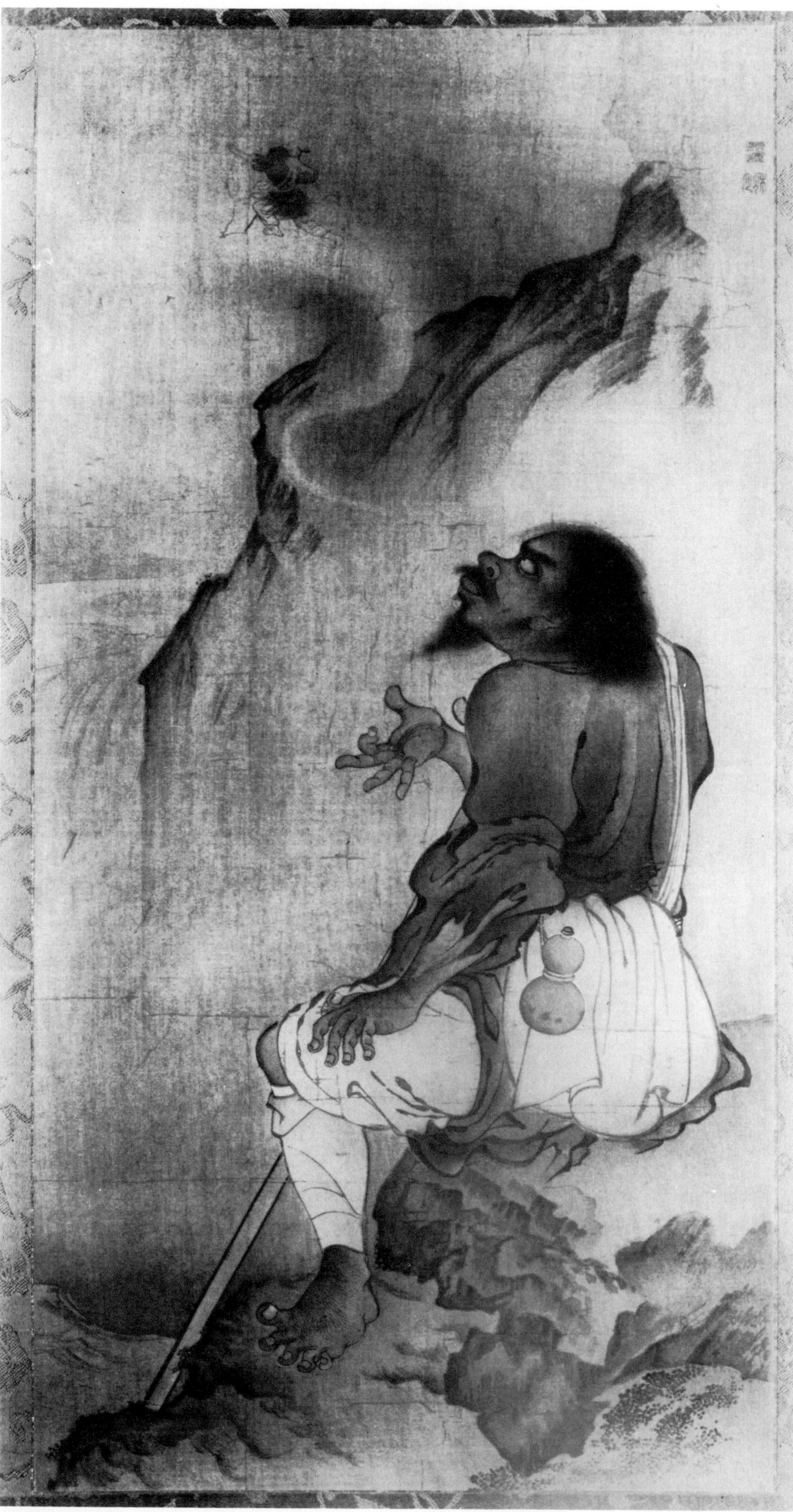

And now the Mysterious Companion testifies:

That the heraldic name given to China's art, the sub-historic genesis of China's painting, its point-center, is T'ang (so erroneous an appraisal of documented facts and chain-of-influences! so veridical an expression of a global, nodal attitude!)—T'ang's sphericity.

And that the heraldic name given to Yamato art, the sub-historic genesis of Yamato-e, its iridescent center-point, is North Wei[77]—North Wei's oblique space-cross, North Wei nearness-terror of rigidity, the mobile immediacy there of the Creator's presence, total, overwhelming, unseizable, seized as image-substitution *(Plate 92)*.

That, heraldically, China never really knew or remembered North Wei. (Oh yes! Following the channel of transmitted and iridescent ideas—roads! roads! roads!—the Mongol nomadic, mobile universe brought back again by the Yüan era[78] could, and for a long while, maintain alive here and there in Ming and Ch'ing China the restless, passionate elements of the space-cross conception [*Plate* 93], yet the persistent loyalty of China remained essentially the same—the loyalty to T'ang's ease, correspondence and certainty.) And so sculptural, so given-spherical, so perfect was China's space throughout its long history, that once, in later historical days, its genuine poetic inventiveness, its sculpturized pictorial idiom exhausted—I think of the Ch'ing period!—this paradox of China's visual drama, a creative paradox for sure! was resolved unexpectedly, so to speak, and finally, in another *techne* medium: in the art of Ch'ing porcelain; the magnificent youth of Ch'ing porcelain, a new, pure, purely pictorial universe to admire!

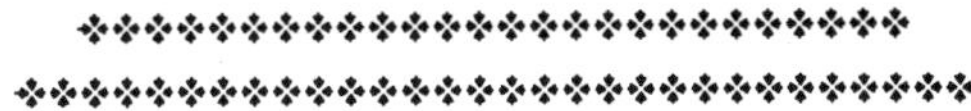

While Japan did learn how to know T'ang, but never really knew or remembered T'ang.

Japan knew North Wei. Such is Yamato loyalty. Such is the true history of Yamato and of Yamato art: a knot of bunched-together events—East and West, sown and unsown tightly held in the hand.

And the Mysterious Companion of the journey stood up again and testified more:

◀93 Yen Hui *The Taoist Immortal, Li T'ieh-kuai*
Yüan period, 14th century

VARIATION IV SPRING

Spring:

Preparation I: A Feeling About Spring

Spring is the discovery of spring; just as a law is the discovery of a law.

Gone, the wealth of unquestioned autumn! Gone, the imagery of the long-answering winter!

Meanwhile, with no way back to winter, or to fall, spring starts hesitatingly with an elegy:

My lovely lady, Iwai, is dead.

And she was an old, very old lady. She was eighty-four years old—I did not know it, I could never have imagined it, of course, in reading her youth-full letters. Now I know it from her obituary and her face, smiling at me, all wrinkles and kindness, on the front page of Tokyo's *Asahi Shimbun,* received this grey and rainy morning of late March, in New York. Her face and the pity of it, my mixed feelings of reverence, astonishment, regret, and nostalgia—because of suddenly learning how old she was, too old to go on living, too young to die—are real. They are all events in my innermost body. (That such events are real and concrete things = beings, and not only *either* things *or* beings, we know, or should know by now ((which, more narrowly, thus closer up, would mean that Asia's way of seeing, at her farthest and deepest, the surrounding universe-worlds in the *mirror* of mind, and the West's way of looking into this same mind out of the *window* of the same universe, are about to become one and the same way (((which, still more narrowly, still closer up, would mean that India's root-concept of reality as mind-stuff, mind = matter = stuff, elastic, extended, extensible, quantitative and quantified, measurable, multi-sensed, mind-matter-minded, very narrowly resembles the West's own answering what is reality by pointing to the long-curved history of Western man's thought and travail, his gradual *interiorization* of the physical, completed as *exteriorization* of the mental or the psychic ((((which means ultimately that the "intangible" psychic-somatic experiences of the greatest East are now available to us. Such, for instance, the concrete experience of levitation, or of leap into the void, re-stated by us not "abstractly" or theoretically—as a psychologist's speculation about, say, an imagined suicidal jump into the void from the temptingly overhanging first row in a theatre's balcony, but as the aviator's—parachutist's, more locally—normal condition of a precise psycho-physiological response)))), for the Western mind's history uncoils openly: a clockwise self-crossing of two directions. Apparently, or externally, on the what *and* how levels, it is the history of a steady mechanization—however liberating and humane the mathematical in it, or the abstract-pure, could inherently be—of both the mind's subject or mind's self-knowledge as mind, and mind's object, or mind's knowledge of "nature" as its own and only source of reality. On the what *of* the how level—along the

The Sense of Touch

Preparation II: A Feeling of Spring

That there is no spring—there is only the discovery of spring.

"We must not try adding to what we have that which we had—we cannot be at once what we are and what we were: that's bad."[1]

✯

And that there are no laws, there is only the discovery of laws.

✯

Paper dolls
 their aptness to fall over!
The window's breeze.[2]

"Rules are not the source of poetry, but poetry is the source of rules, and there are as many rules as there are real poets."[3]

✯

Gone, the autumn; gone the winter and all the other springs!

What really and separately had happened that early spring morning was this: I sat at my sober desk facing the heavy apprehension of how really to start the long-ago commanded book on Japanese painting, facing also the window of my twelve story high perched room and the upper window rows across the broad avenue, veiled behind the drizzle. For it was a grey rainy day of late March, grey, uncertain, meek in sound and light, sickly like the poor eyes of a newly born puppy, or the narrow and pitiful opening of someone's eyelids still fatigued by an evil night, still unglued by a jealous awakening.

As I sat thus at my desk, I suddenly perceived lying there, misplaced by a sheer accident of housecleaning, an already old program of a Broadway play, Sholem Aleichem's, translated into English, with pen-and-ink illustrations by the American artist Ben Shahn[4] *(See Plate 79)*. As I looked at them for a long while, suddenly—then slowly and more slowly—around them and myself a question grew, its shadow covering my window. Unwillingly I found myself asking a grave question:

Why? Why is it that this strange people, the people of the total Exile, has so much *mud* and so much *amor intellectualis Dei?*

(But isn't this love that which is the precise opposite of mud, a precise image of a bow ready for its arrow's flight, its taut cord joining the two ends, the intellectual love of God and the human world's mud?)

I very trajectory of mind's operation in history—it is Western man's bold and adventurous *descent* into the most subtle, *interiorized,* matter; it is—precisely by the passion and impetus to *descend*—the de-mechanization, the re-humanization of the externally overwhelming mechanical "unhuman" itself. A passionate, steady and obstinate descent, starting at the crossroads of the so-called modern era: from the high and grandiose seat of astro-physics or astro-mechanics—this high abode of Renaissance man's spiritual harmonies and metaphysical concordances = proofs, down, always down, ever deeper and narrower, to the less and less "spiritual" but more and more subtle-material secrets of the purely physical, the properly physical-mechanical at first, then the chemical—seventeenth, eighteenth centuries—then the bio-chemical and thence, spontaneously, in a reciprocated exchange of subtle concretions, to the material psycho-logical in itself—our twentieth century))): **yes,** Wakana Iwai's two great symbol-things of mind's planetary history, the *mirror* and the *window,* are about to be one concrete symbol-*persona,* already known and painted, chiselled and built by our poets)); concepts, feelings, sensations, and impressions are seen, touched, smelled, and heard through the translucid physicality of non-human things, and vice versa.)

At this moment, how many—so many!—other events, all moments of discovery, all realities of spring, rushed in and grouped themselves together around the news of my Japanese lady's death! The rapidity of their coming in and succeeding each other was such that each became part of another, then part of all, the all absorbing the each, similar to a swiftly revolving wheel, whose spokes all but disappear in the great wind of the one-motion, and what remains then as real for the eye of a witness and the hand of a painter *(Plate 94)* is a compact, tempestuous yet immobilized disk made of one grey, shiny, and windy substance, a new and totally different "object" in space.

Real or not real as the swiftly revolving events of that early spring's morning may have been, they all but disappeared in the great wind of one-motion-event, and what remained for the eye and the hand of an artist—remained, indeed, a discovery of spring! spring itself!—was a new, different event, one compact immobilized yet revolving windy disk-event, grey, opaque, yet luminous and clearly recognizable. This:

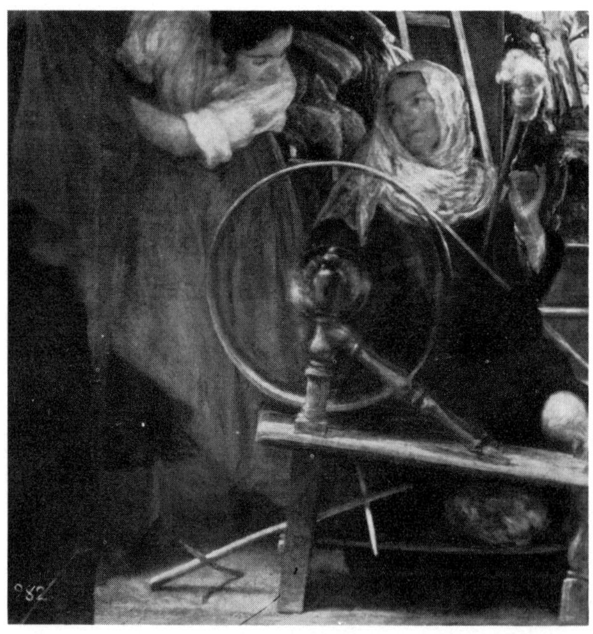

94 Velazquez *Las Hilanderas*
Detail (17th century)

I looked into Ben Shahn's poignant and knotty world and people—mine too—with the same delight and expectation of a beyond-message as when I looked at the rapidly blooming pictorial images of Japan.

And minding this time very little whether it was good or bad to do so, I "tried adding" the gift of that world and that people to the gift of this. But as if in a dream, or in a joke, I could add nothing there: both gifts were one and the same gift, the gift of substitution. In both I saw, at first, man's otherwise unreachable goal, to reach the final ending or decision of man-and-beyond-man's story; then, I saw there the goal reached, and heard this story told—in the very mimicry, the dance of the dispassionate, profit-less *ornament:* the *amor intellectualis Dei.* In art. A scandal, an offense to reason's—my own included, of course—*juris prudentia?*

Invited to defend myself—was it a dream? a joke? or a lasting commun-ion of eros and thought?—I took the stand as my own witness and only attorney.

And my defense was built around the energies of substitution and sacrifice in art as elsewhere:

That *ornament,* understood as substitution for the *intellectual love of God,* the profit-less, thus love-less, god-less love of God, is not an offense to man and to reason's *juris prudentia,* but is the Prime Mover's motion cre-ated *per se,* and man's purest—because man's most loyal to this motion's origins—vehicle of *emotion.*

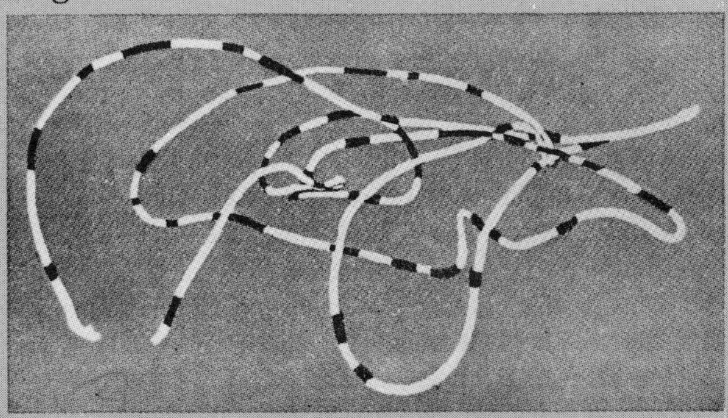

That the concept of a profit-less, at once dispas-sionate and intense, finite and free "stroll for stroll-ing's sake" (Paul Klee) in space—the *ornament per se* and nothing else!—is very similar to, say, the tracery left by an instantaneous and mechanically reproduced motion—by any "natural" motion—such as the photo-tracery of a rapier's point in action, or the danc-ing calligraphy (the "frozen" calligraphy of a Ukiyo-e image!) of a girl's unfolding her handkerchief[5] *(Plate 95).*

Motion's behaviour in space at its most intimate; calligraphy, dance of a precise, irreversible point-moment in time-space continuum, of a precise, unique irreversible *character-persona* (*that* and no other girl unfolding her handkerchief, at *that* and no other moment in all the worlds past and to come); a movement-graphy total, a free being, a new being, a new "mon-strous" unexpected *res=persona:* the ornament!

Exactly, the very real and concrete sub-structure in a Paul Klee or Picasso, in a Miró. Exactly, the living sub-structure, sub-abstraction, in a Fragonard, a Leonardo, in a medieval Christian, Islamic, or Japanese im-agery: *ornament,* Prime Mover's motion created *per se,* man's "purest"—profitless—vehicle of emotion *(Plates 97, 98, 99, 100).*

A second feeling about spring:

That, my lady dead, what remained with me was only my wish to pay homage to her and to the multiple gifts—including the image of herself and of her Japan—she had given me or "exchanged" with me.

And this elegiac homage I wished to be in the shape of an "exchange of gifts" between the last gift from me and her own last and posthumous—and the strangest of all—gift to me. But an exchange like this, made ultimate, final, and unilateral with her departure could only be an exchange of a gift with nothing else but itself, forever the same.

And that is how I remained with one, compact, revolving yet immobilized event-gift, event-exchange—a grey, windy, opaque yet luminous disk, clearly recognizable as my-and-her last gift:

That in art *amor intellectualis Dei* is the *ornament.* Close as its message stood to the *techne* discovery of the poet's *le profond c'est la peau,*[6] and close to the discovery of spring, this gift-event, when taken away from the intimacy of personal conviction and given, as it was by me, to the world, became the scandal and the offense to reason's—any reason's, my own included, of course—*juris prudentia.*

A third and last feeling about spring:

Invited to defend myself, I took the stand as my own and only witness. But my witnessing was impeached. I had to produce a better, a more impartial witness. And so I did. And the better, more impartial—unexpected also—witness came and spoke. He spoke distinctly, with pause and also with arrogance, yet he did not bring in, or create, anger.

"I am," so he started, rather unctuously (this attitude of his being justified by the general attitude of the court), "the inner heraldic History of America, more precisely of the United States of North America. And my occupation is to be the keeper of the American mind and of its home. That is, the keeper of the American mind's most recognizable simulacrum: the inmost, 'heraldic' story of American painting.

"I am here to testify on behalf of the defendant, that it was in this home, very precisely, that I met and befriended its oldest and, perhaps, its most loyal occupant, that very *persona* whose reality—the reality of a reciprocated gift—is contested here."

And immediately after this introduction my witness produced a lengthy document—a scroll, unfolding the outline, duly abridged, of the history of the American eye and American hand, told in three epic actions.

❖❖❖❖❖❖❖❖❖❖❖❖❖❖❖❖❖❖❖❖❖❖❖❖❖❖❖❖❖❖

A second feeling of spring:

It came about then—as unexpectedly, yet necessarily, as it seems to be coming right now in my recollection of it—that all the happenings of that early spring morning in the city of New York were like the spokes in a rapidly revolving wheel: existent there, all of them, they disappeared from the eye in the great wind of a new one-motion-event.

All the happenings of that elegiac moment—the rain tears on my window, the half-blinded sounds and souls of the great city; my floating question, and the hurry, the secret of the mysteriously redeemed people, down below, on the muddy and doomed asphalt; the pity of it and the creations in all this; my now fixed question again; the Japanese Noh-and-painting, its playful ardor and Ben Shahn's passionate playfulness *(le profond c'est la peau);* my grave question again about myself and *that* destiny: why, why so much mud in it, why so much *amor intellectualis Dei*—all these happenings were hidden now in a new, swiftly revolving, "another" question-wheel.

Why, how is it, Ben Shahn, the American painter—one of those who came from afar, and for that very reason, precisely, are the more American! —that your art has so much *mud* and so much *amor intellectualis Dei,* so much narration and so much "ornament"? *(Plate 96)*

Is America and America's spreading afar so unique? Of course! Beyond all the multiple spoke-notions of the revolving wheel (such as the notion "my people," or of ethos and race), beyond even the limits of crafty what-*and*-how criticism, of its exaggerated praise as well as exaggerated contempt, the answer came simple and easy:

A third and last feeling of spring:

> Derbforgaill, daughter of the King of Norway, loved Cu Chulainn, because of the great stories told of him. She and her handmaid set out from the east in the form of two swans until they came to Luch Cuan, a golden chain between them. Now as Cu Chulainn and his foster-brother Lugaid, son of the three Findemna, were by the lake, one day they saw the birds. "Have a cast at the birds," said Lugaid. Cu Chulainn slung a stone at one of them so that it passed between her ribs and remained in her belly. Straightway two human forms were on the strand. "Cruel have you been to me," said the girl, "and it is to you I have come."[7]

... "*Cruel have you been to me,* and *it is to you* I have come":

As when the hollow fear that suddenly, at the low threshold of your sleep comes in the shape of a precise inevitability (I-within-the-coffin; why? how is it possible to be nothing when I am still a continuous something, not ready at all to be no-thing?) and then, as observed life experi-

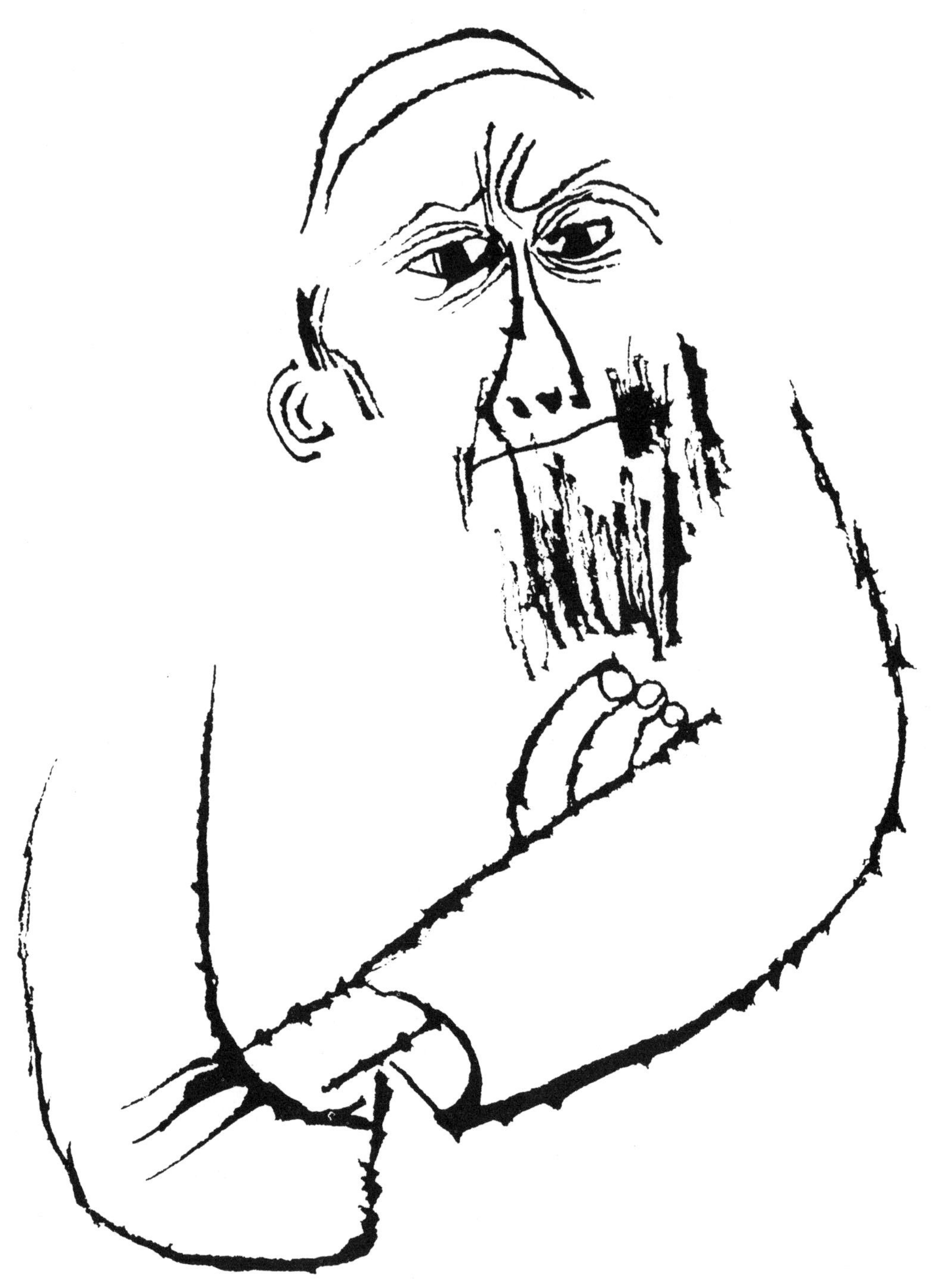

96 Ben Shahn *Drawing*

97 Fragonard *Drawing: Seated Pasha* (18th century)

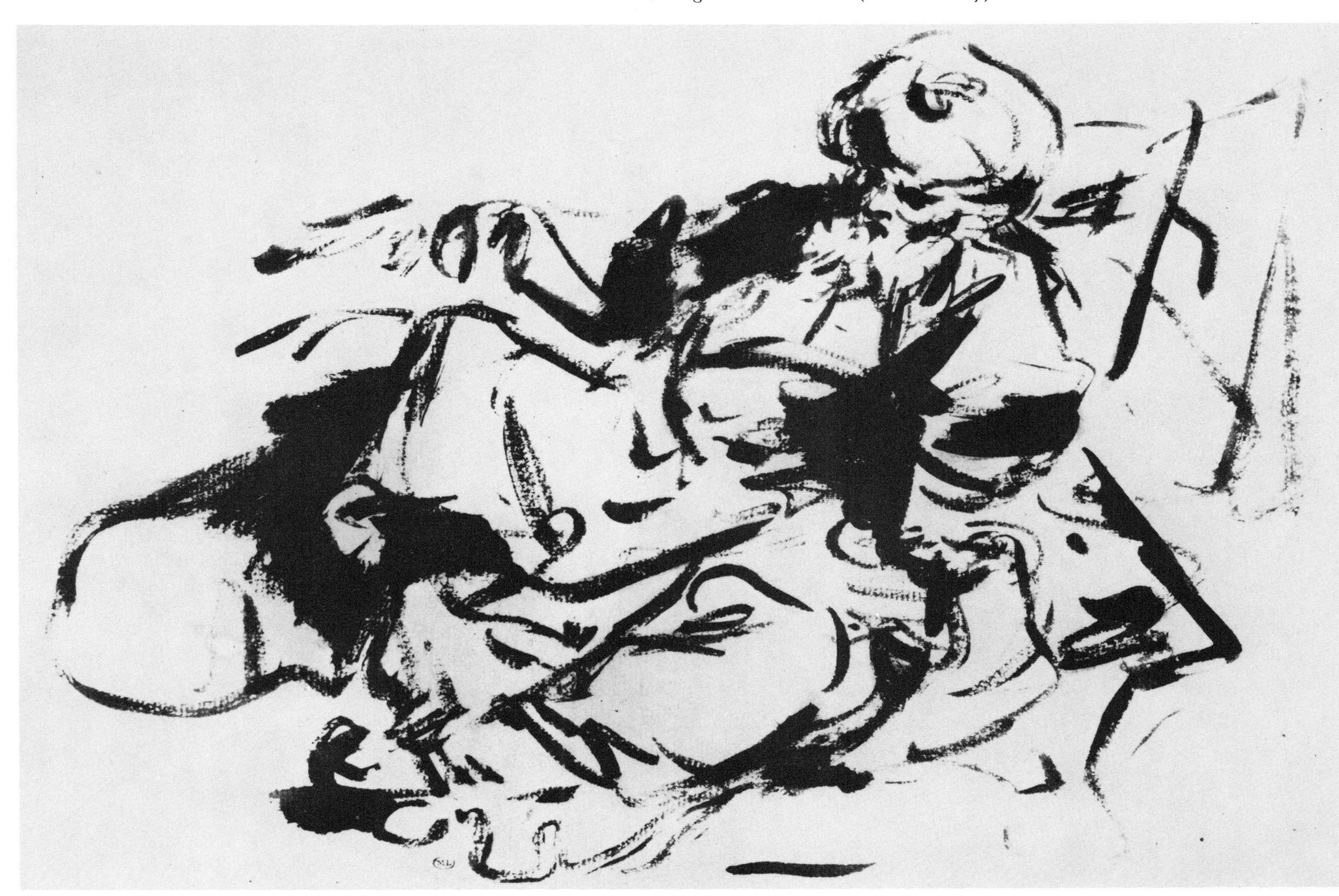

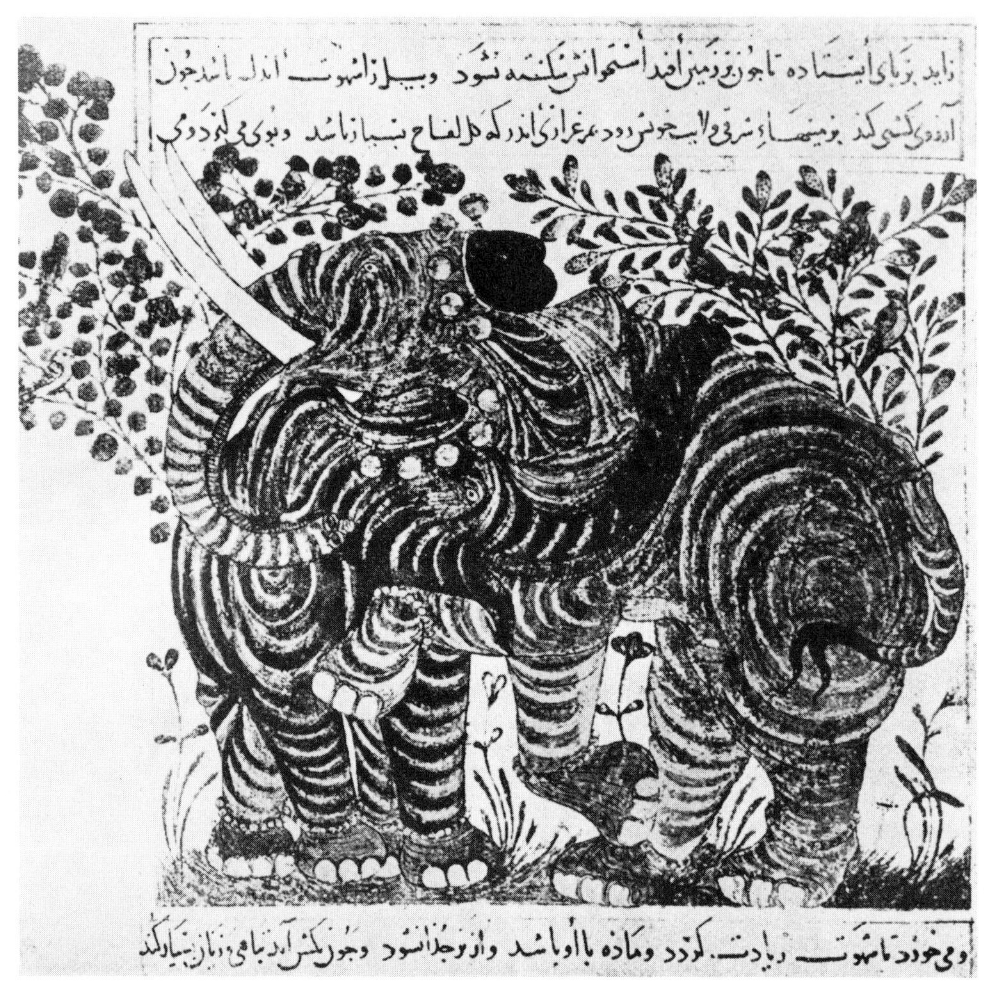

98 *Pair of Elephants* Il-Khanid School, Mesopotamia (A.D. 1296)

ence around you would confirm, when the real physical death comes at the break of a day or a night, it comes, more often than not, as a simple and easy some-thing, you being then ready or not—similar to this shift, the shift of my grave question (America, Ben Shahn, that strange people, why?) came simple and easy too.

Celtic and pre-Celtic it came, as beautiful Derbforgaill when she and her handmaid—her death? her love? tell us, Leopardi!—"set out from the east . . . a golden chain between them."

Celtic, Jewish, African—American!—it came in the shape of a tale in three songs with the golden chain between them.

Three songs sung by the keeper of the American mind and its most lucid and recognizable simulacrum, the history-without-proof, the "heraldic" history of American painting.

Sung in three song-actions.

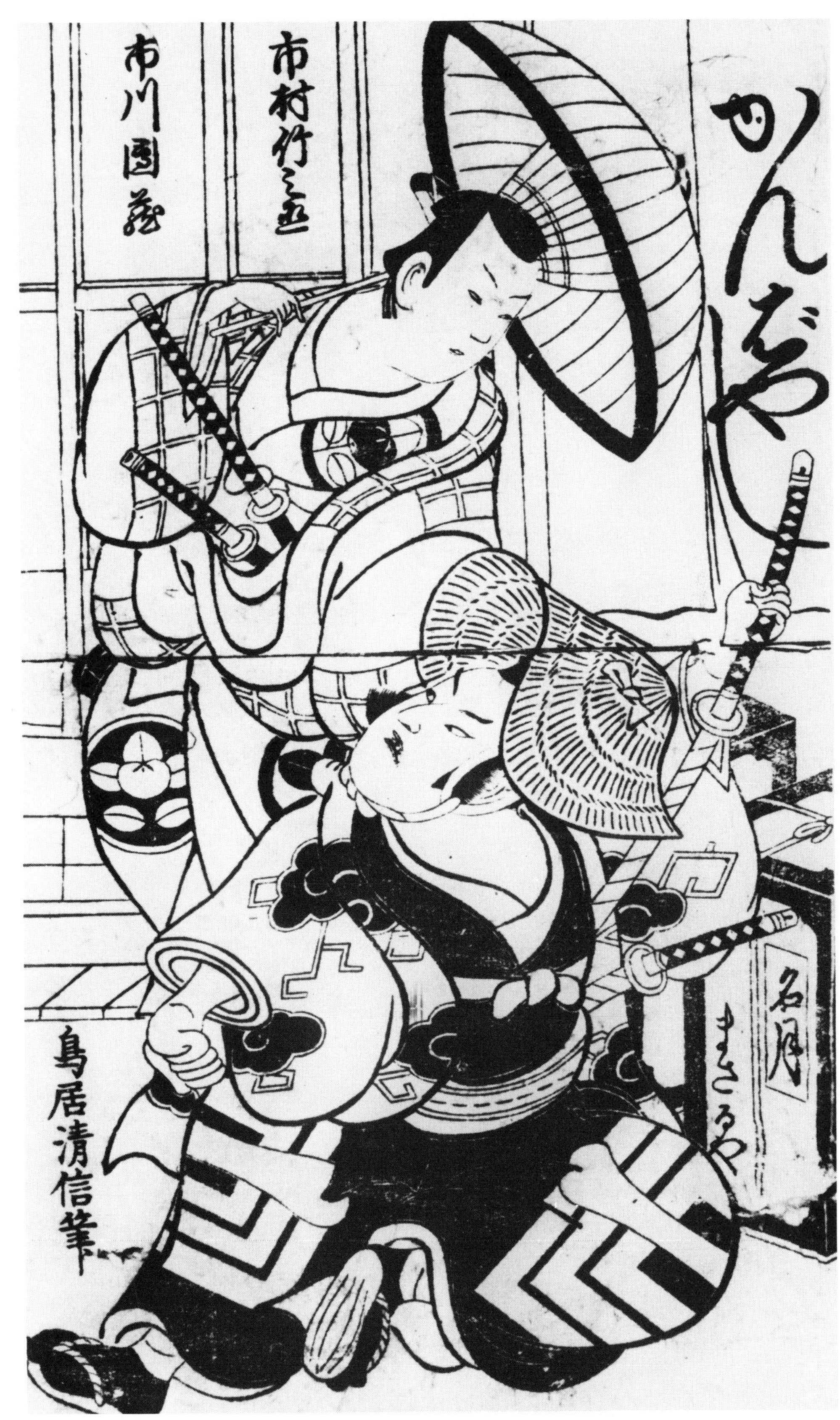

99 Torii Kiyonobu I
Two Actors
Ca. 1700

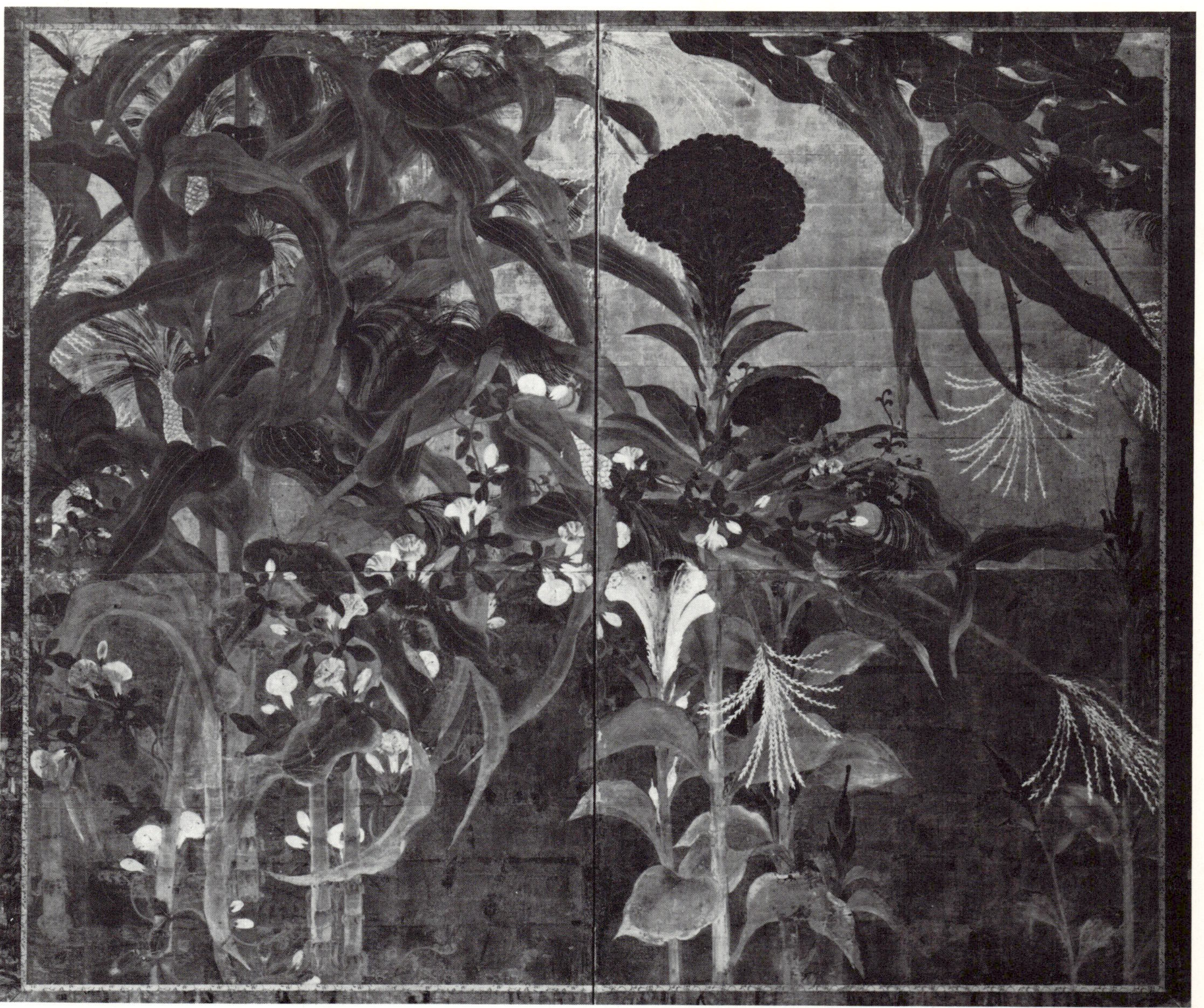

100 Artist unknown
Coxcombs, Maize & Morning Glories
Detail (17th century)

101 Artist unknown *Running before the Storm*

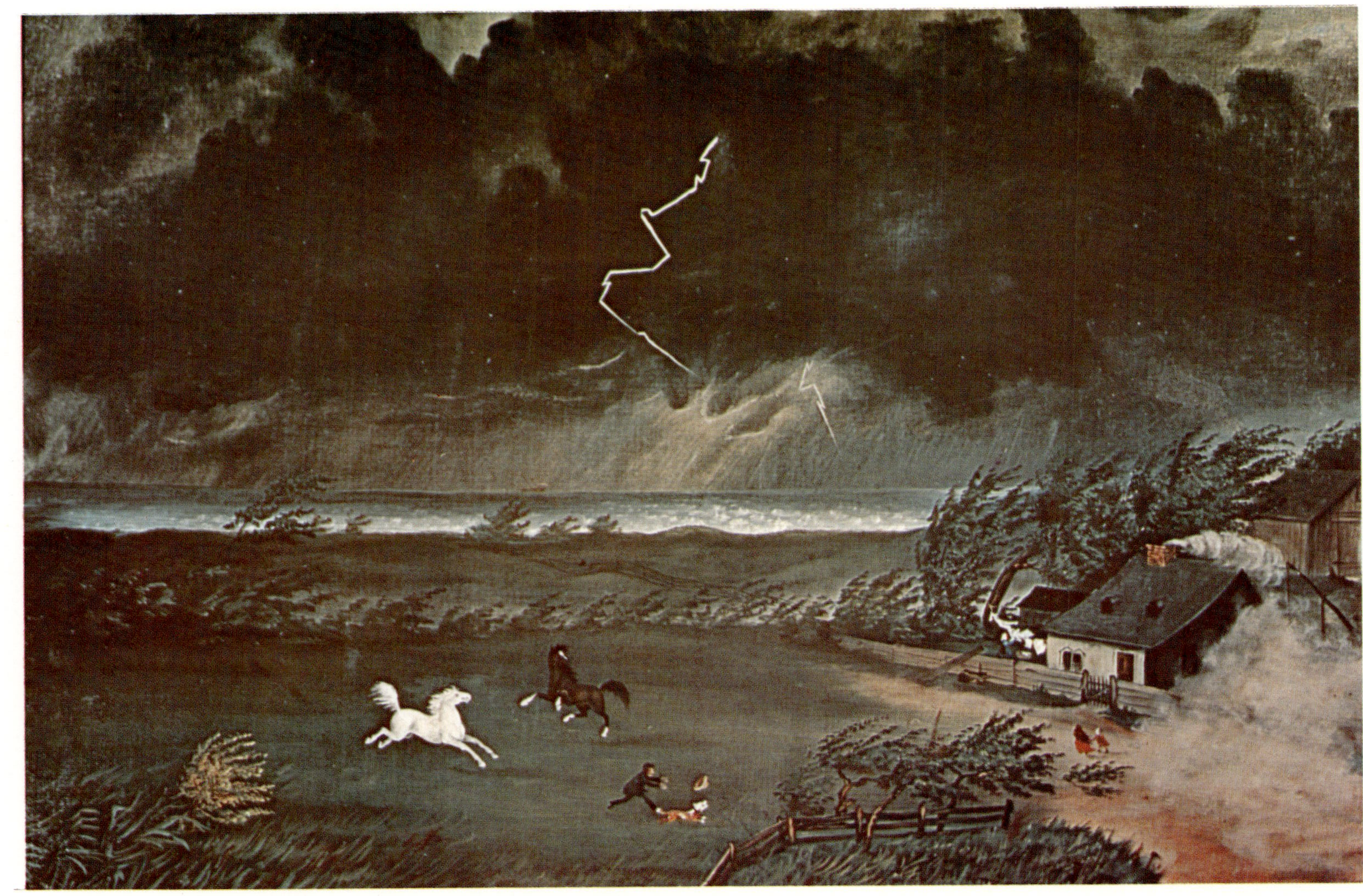

102 Artist unknown *Meditation by the Sea*

Departure (The Action of Art)
First Action-Song

A feeling for America:

As spring is, as law is, America is a discovery: the discovery of America.

Gone, the autumn's fear of inevitability in matured, golden things, books, and words; gone the winter's fear of judges, of accuracy and ferocity in influences! Meanwhile, with no way back to autumn and to winter, the early spring's tale starts thus:

Who is the Mysterious Companion of America? Who, the witness of the American attitude, global? Of America-sensation-blue = idea-blue, sensation-red = idea-red, or yellow, or green, or any other idea-hue, social, moral, individual, visible and not yet visible, still to be discovered.

Such, the total, immaculate attitude-*white* of a Winslow Homer, every hue integrated, present there in this very white—including its negation, the black, its sacrifice, the brown—every existing hue chosen and loved for itself, yet only the white being really given, not chosen; Winslow Homer's hallucination, *Image la Folle,* the closest possible presence, the white!

Who is the Mysterious Companion of America's birth and growth?

☆

Spring is ready for a new myth.

☆

The Mysterious Companion of American painting is the Unknown Soldier born there.

And the myth: the idea-*persona* of the Unknown Soldier is the defender of American cities. For America is the discovery of her cities, her city-shelters clustered together, wide and far, against the dangers of the unknown "beyond," the country around them felt as a growing and growing vastness: from the narrow, coastal strip of the first migration's humble shelter-homes, huddled together against the terrors of unknown bushes, forests, storms, hills, and most savage attacks, to later townships and cities and greater, the greatest, cities with the same unknown "beyond" around them, an ever wider and farther unknown "beyond," the "beyond" of new wildernesses and of new wealths, of great new rivers, great new mountains and lakes, the "beyond" of the ocean and of the reach of another ocean, the "beyond" of these two. Possibly, the un-finite itself.

By and by, the new cities and villages were there, the only shelter—cozy salvage under closing-in storms *(See Plate 101)*—America's hallucination, America's *Image la Folle,* America's nostalgia of Paradise lost, of *the good city's* defense against the bad city: the book without the sword.

This is spring's new myth told hesitatingly (because the tale is true, and the book is erroneous, about America); this and no other is the nostalgic secret of America: her city-shelters and their goodness in spite of the ferocity, ugliness, and mud of history's irrefutable facts about them, the arrogant rudeness and mud of the sea-faring merchant citizenry emerging (an emergence still going on!) from the niggardly sparings of the rocky soil tillers; the automatic cruelty and power (always self-justifiable where justice is allied to success) of personal prowess overtaking the strength of communal prowess.

In spite of all this and of much more and worse, America, from the start, is the memory of a prophetic city in a forgotten time and a forgotten *pre-split* world—its builders, the artisan, the magician, the dancer-chieftain being there one and the same being, one and the same travail: the *persona-idea* buried in any of America's new cities, the Unknown Soldier's tomb to be discovered there, *deus absconditus,* the grain.

And America is the discovery—rediscovery in fact!—of the most ancient man-made world: the planetary strife between the sown and the unsown; the sown, its heart, the city, spreading ever deeper and wider, the unsown, the nomadic, ringing it, ever thinner and thinner. Such—to start in the middle of planetary history's road—the Hellenistic urbanization of the hitherto untrodden, inaccessible wilderness of Eurasia, from the mountain-falls and crevices of Anatolia to the barren or forested depth of the near-Caspian East—new cities planted there boldly, swarming and noisy with revolt, tense with the artisan's striving toward pre-split integration; cities, carriers of gnosis and heresies; Islam inheriting this *via* Mazdean, still alive, heterodoxies, *Manichean, Mazdakite,*[8] then leading its own dissent, telling its own nostalgia, the nostalgia of the three-oneness, in the battle cries of its extremists, the Shi'ite Ismaili, Karmathians,[9] a tremendous, grand wave of initiation and memory unfurling over Christian Europe, bringing there nourishment, organization, and support to the creative impetus of heresies and renaissances.

All this, discovered, rediscovered, started anew—but how humbly, how imperceptibly, as if disguised, how ingloriously at first!—in the very birth of America (the old *after-split* world present there, wounded beast, ready to assault, ready to be healed, too).

Against the testimony of separated and contradictory facts ("'The plowman that raiseth grain is more serviceable to mankind than the painter who draws only to please the eye,' wrote an unknown American in 1719"),[10] early America is primarily and primordially visual-"artisan": the "decorative" and the utilitarian, the lyrical and the individual making one common pattern of expression and purpose, the "major" and the "minor" arts made equal in dignity and purpose too.

Of course, there was not a single detail there of craft and even of social professional habit in early American art (and for that matter, throughout the latter's entire subsequent history) that could not be traced to a precedent in the old continent: from the itinerant limners, face-and-hand painters, the variegated street signs crowding with artisan invention and joy the towns' busy sections, to the American as well as European demand for countless topographic views of harbors and cities (a wonderful landscape art in its own right, indeed!—drawings, watercolors, prints), and the collective craze for "panoramas," circular, moving, etc.—all influential historical facts containing in germ, in impetus and direction, the most characteristic traits of American mature art. Yet, all this—the Old World's too—how unique, how uniquely American! Unique, as a particular American quality of intensity, as a particular *quantitative persistence* of this intensity! (Nowhere else was the impact of, say, the spectacular, often grandiose, "panorama"-invention, or later in the nineteenth century, the awakening and creative "shock" brought to the somnolence of technical pictorial habits by the revolutionary process of Daguerreotype photography and its further and rapid development—nowhere was it more persistently intense, more loyal to the initial momentum of aesthetical astonishment, than in America!)

And this particular, particularly American persistence of intensity was, from the very beginning, the intensity with which the city's taming of the terrifying and unseizable landscape-"beyond" was narrated and mimicked by the American painter-narrator-dancer. For what must be said now is this:

True, the *good city* is the secret goal and the secret nostalgia of America—the tomb of the Unknown Soldier somewhere there. But it is the country embracing and containing the real city that is America's discovery of America: her spring, her law, her presence, curiosity, and adventure.

Always present somewhere at the back of the American mind is the hidden image of the earth-water-air-fire vastness of America, a living abstraction of growth with no end to it; the sensation = idea = vastness itself, an unseizable geographical boundlessness, America's discovery of the infinity of its landscape *(Plate 102).* And it was this *infinity* precisely in its geo-somatic unseizability that—as in Greece, as in Japan—was seized by a *finite* substitution for it, a city's, the city man's, artifact. How? As in Greece, as in Japan, differing only in degree and *dosage,* the means by which this transubstantiation could be made were those of the artisan's visionary thinking, rather than thinking's spatial condition itself: a pictorial image-schema structured as volume-sphere, or—and—as volume-obliquity.

Volume-sphere: a perfectly rounded "objective" consistency of a real object *(Plate 103).* Volume-ellipse: an oblique and flattened, rigid yet mobilized image-ornament, our innermost body's mimicry of the total, the terror of isolation or solitude in it—Dura-Europos's image!—the release of solidarity in it too: *ornament.* No other art of painting, however similar in appearance or structure, has revealed with more conviction and loyalty than America's this "artisan"—city's—secret of substitution: this "closest closeness" of a "natural" object in space, a face, a hand, a still-life or a view, and—or—this mimicry, the dance (a "decorative" pictorial pattern, a composition) of the infinitely remote, yet total.

This is the "visionary circumstance" of the American mind; this is American painting and its innermost body-history.

Early influences from outside? Early historical facts? The art, meritorious as such, in itself and in its own right, of a Blackburn or a Greenwood and their impact on the art of Robert Feke or Ralph Earl or John Singleton Copley? One might as well say: last autumn's leaves, last win-

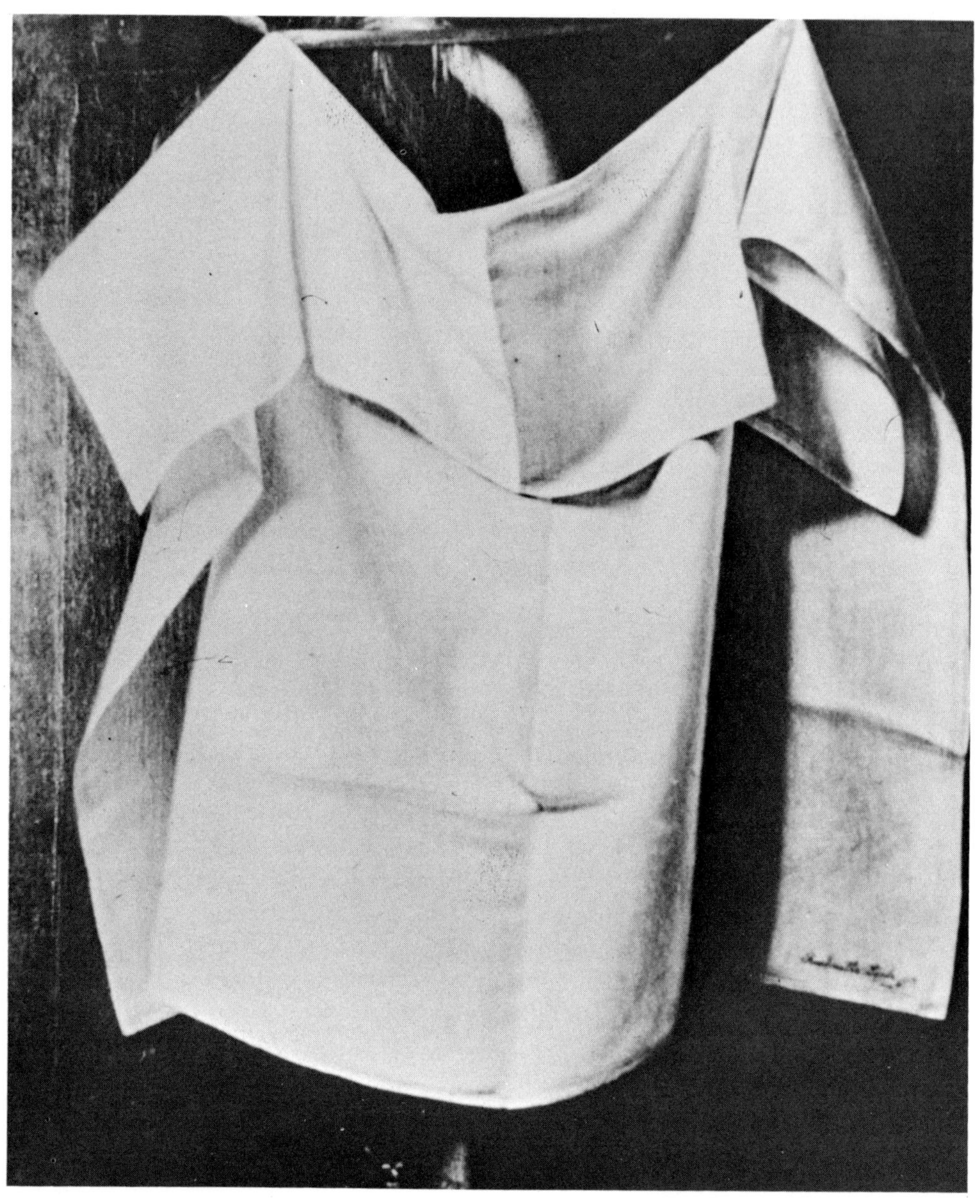

103 Rafael Peale· *After the Bath* Detail (early 19th century)

ter's furnace! Robert Feke and his iridescent ornament-infinity: splendid, humble, proud, unique! And so is Ralph Earl, and even the expatriate West *(Plate 104).*

It was in the human figure itself that the transfer of total infinity to a total finity had been effected then. As in Greece, as in Japan too, a man's or a woman's image was the "landscape" total, unseizable.

And when little by little, from the humble beginnings of painted "landskips," American landscape understood in the usual sense of the pictorial-narrative terms "panoramic," "romantic," or "lyrical," became the dominant,

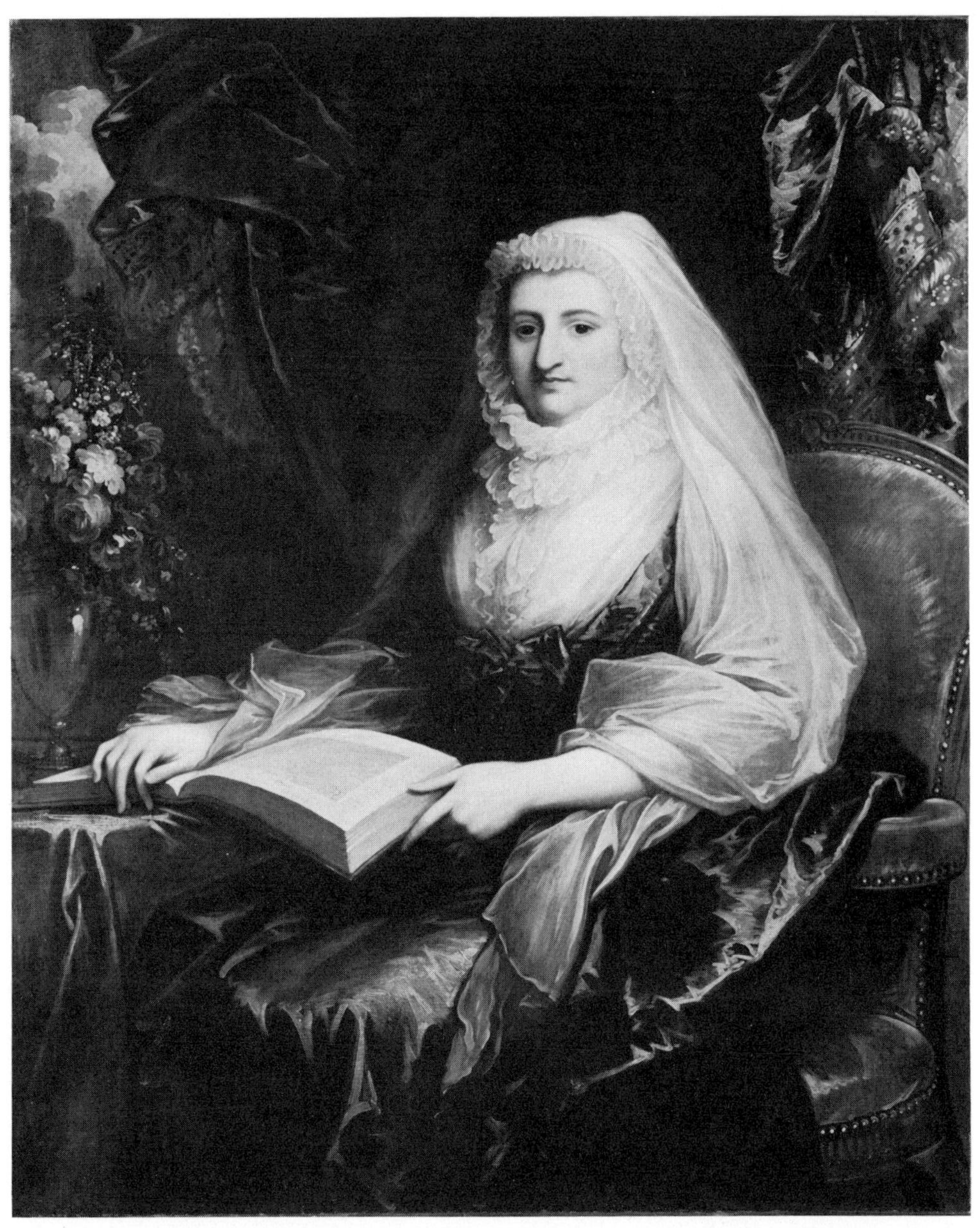

104 Benjamin West *Mrs. Peter Beckford* (early 19th century)

uninhibited object of American passion throughout the nineteenth century, its epic message and attitude did not change *(Plates 105, 106).*

But (and here is where the unfolding tale of spring stops for a while, stops, meditates in doubt, and only then continues) America's rediscovery of the pre-split world, how could it be the return to the artisan's *good city* without also being the return to the artisan's after-split struggles and inhibitions in it? How could American painting be, without being a Christian painting also, a dispassionate universe of the ornament-abstraction, without the witness in it, the flesh, the flesh and the nails in it; without the

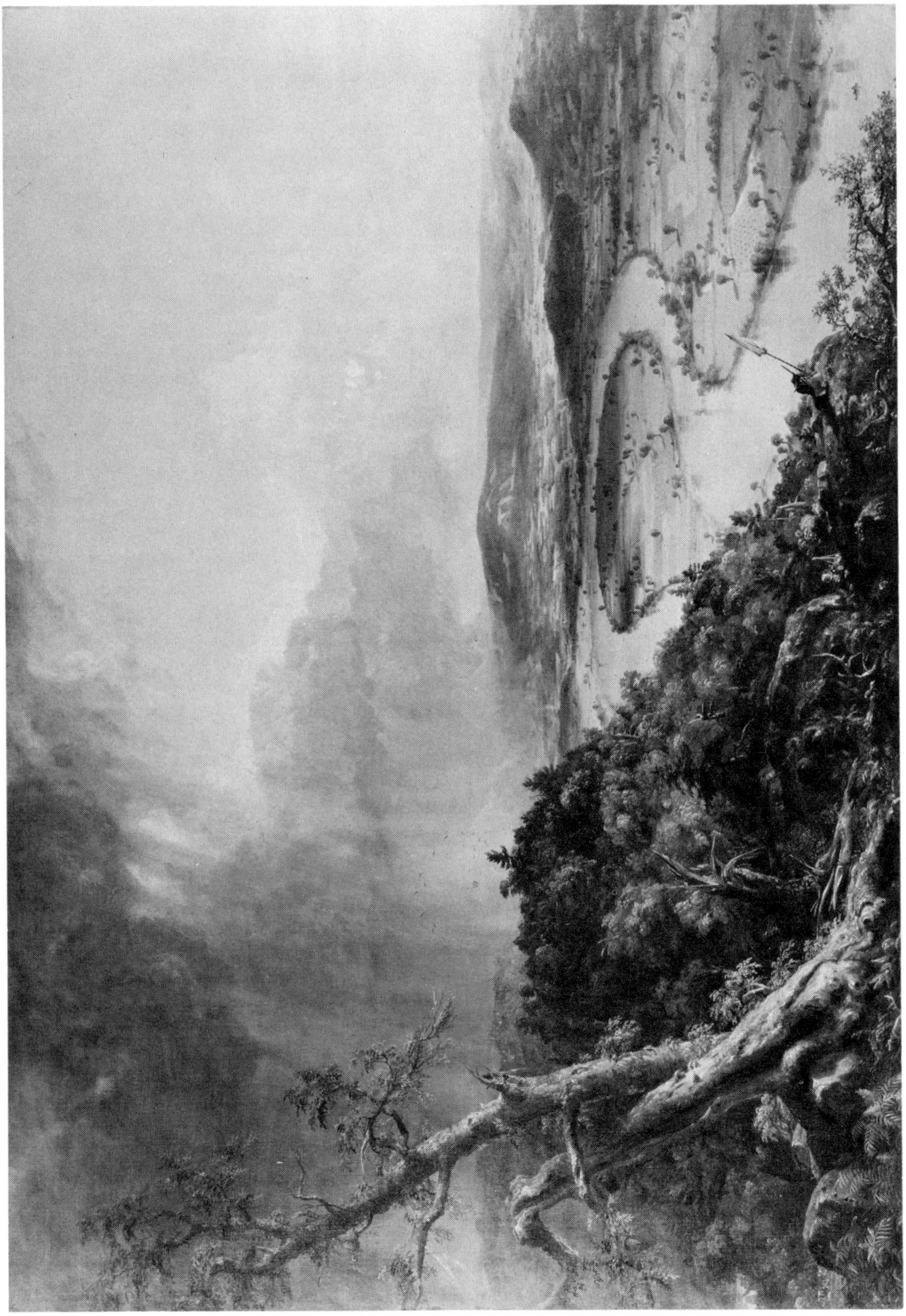

105 Thomas Cole *The Oxbow* (19th century)

106 Attributed to Joshua Shaw *The Deluge* (early 19th century)

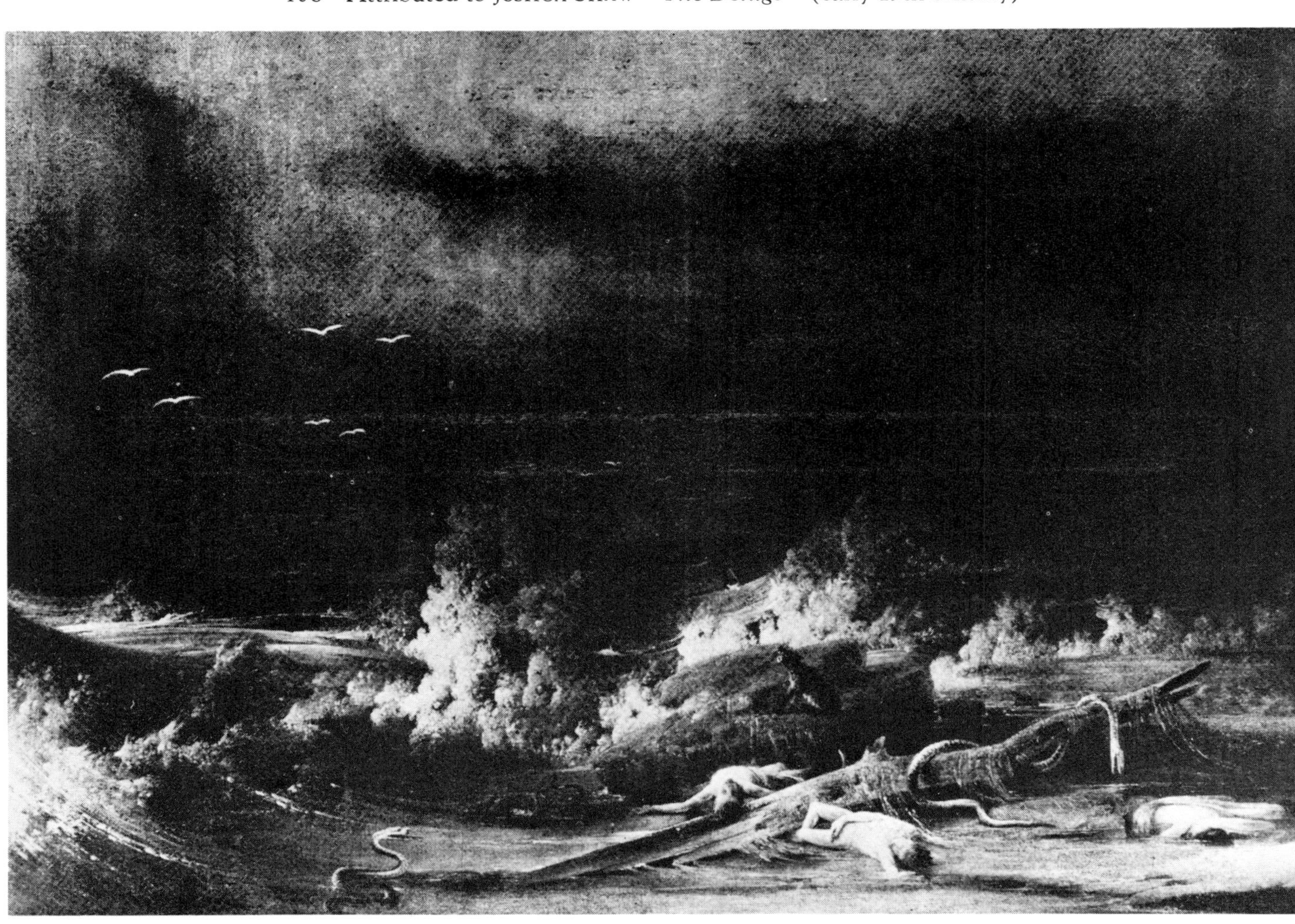

touch of the wounds of Christ—without the co-sufferer? Was not the Christian "ornament" a passionate ornament, a passionate art: a *scientia signata*,[11] the naked, "closest closeness" of its energy-radiating realism, its fleshy, Franciscan love of mounts, flowers, stars, and all the other energies—the human heart included—of visible nature, very often told in the transposed idiom of decorative folds clothing its sacred figures? Here, the passion of mountain's energies breathing life into Giotto's folds and Giotto's figures—mountains that walk alone! Here, the cosmic energies breathing life and astral motion into the folds of the "Medoc" Annunciation, so clearly centripetal in the Virgin, so clearly centrifugal in the Angel, with, behind them, the resulting circular rotation of the heavenly universe—the polygonal, obliquely posed table—and the oblique, "rigid mobility" of all the in-and-outdoors objects = beings surrounding, explaining, continuing, and issuing from this astral drama of ornament-folds!

Of course, American painting knew all this: knew this post-split world of inhibitions, nostalgias, struggles, the very universe of substitution's creative will and creating act! Of course, the sumptuous "decorative" silks of Copley's "bourgeois" portraits are playtoys of *aeternitas;* and Winslow Homer's glimmering naturalism, the luminously sealed mystery of the *scientia signata!*

Amor intellectualis Dei—mud, here: the two ends of a tightly stretched cord and the bow's arc ready for its arrow's flight! The closer to intellectual joy is ornament's playfulness, the nearer also to our flesh is the flesh of wounded Christ: the roots of human art and the roots of human nostalgia are the same roots.

Such a quantitative appraisal of a quality = intensity in art is exactly and firmly the appraisal of America's uniqueness: both the fleshy passion of its art and the ardor of its "abstract" coolness have a measure of intensity all their own.

A second feeling for America:

That everything the spring's tale had unfolded till now, every word in it, every suggestion and signal, was—intentionally yet secretly—nothing but the individual history-without-proof of a particular, exclusive and most "loyal to the origins," thus purest art—the art of John Singleton Copley (1738-1815).

Copley is America, total. His art is the fulfilment of the past's promise and a prophecy about the future: a great bird, the two wings outstretched wide, soaring high through light and clouds.

And the day of Copley's art is the day of the great bird's most intense visibility. Intense, indeed, the feathered silhouette and the flapping of the two wings in the morning sky! Up there: the bird's *right* wing, the wing of the dispassionate "abstract" and finite ornament-landscape: both infinity-sphere (simply, its "closest closeness" to the eye and the hand [*Plates 107, 108, 109*]) and infinity-ellipse, the oblique mimicry of the remotest, unseizable total seized (simply the "decorative" patterning of Copley's folds).[12]

107 JOHN SINGLETON COPLEY *Mrs. Thomas Boylston*
18th century ▶

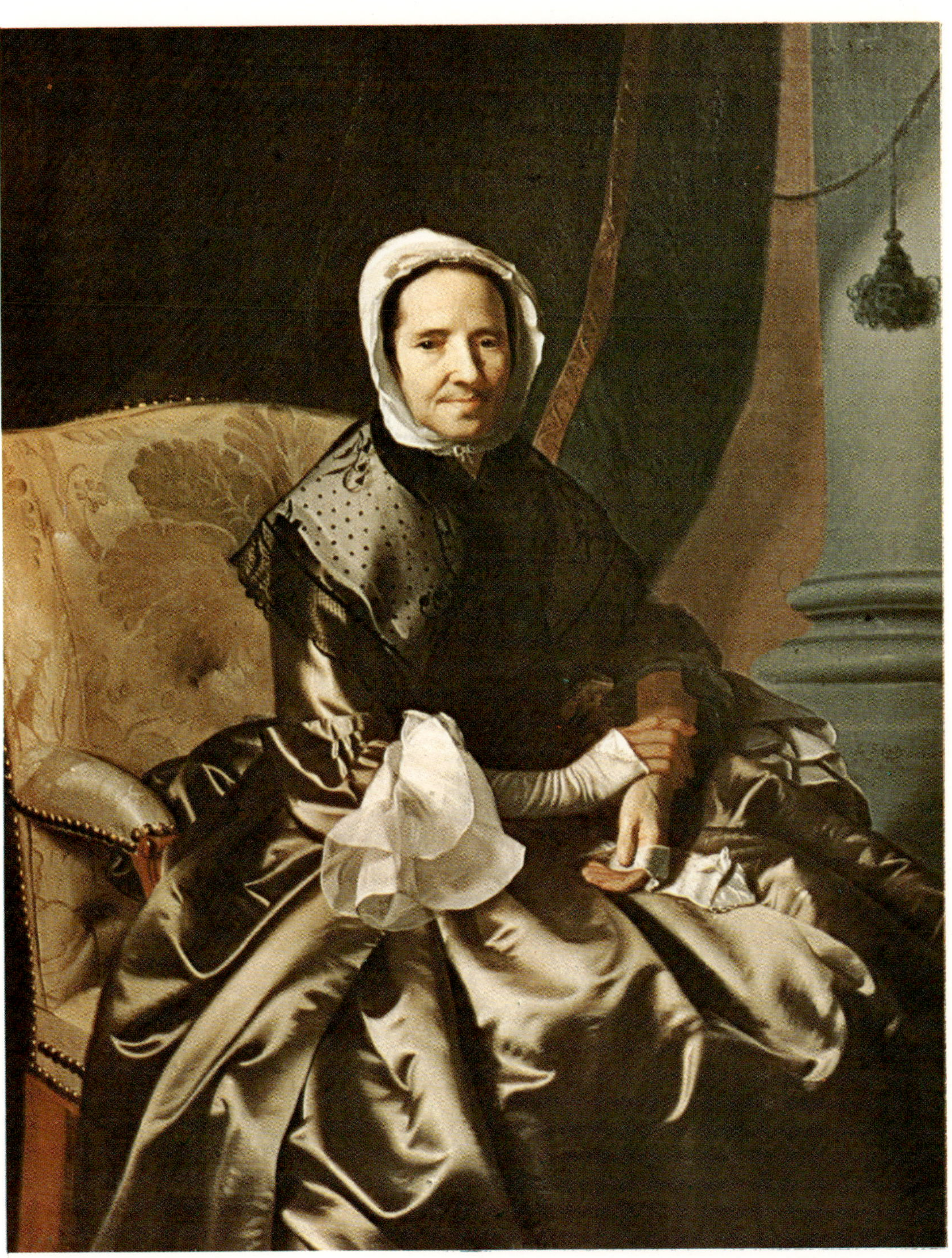

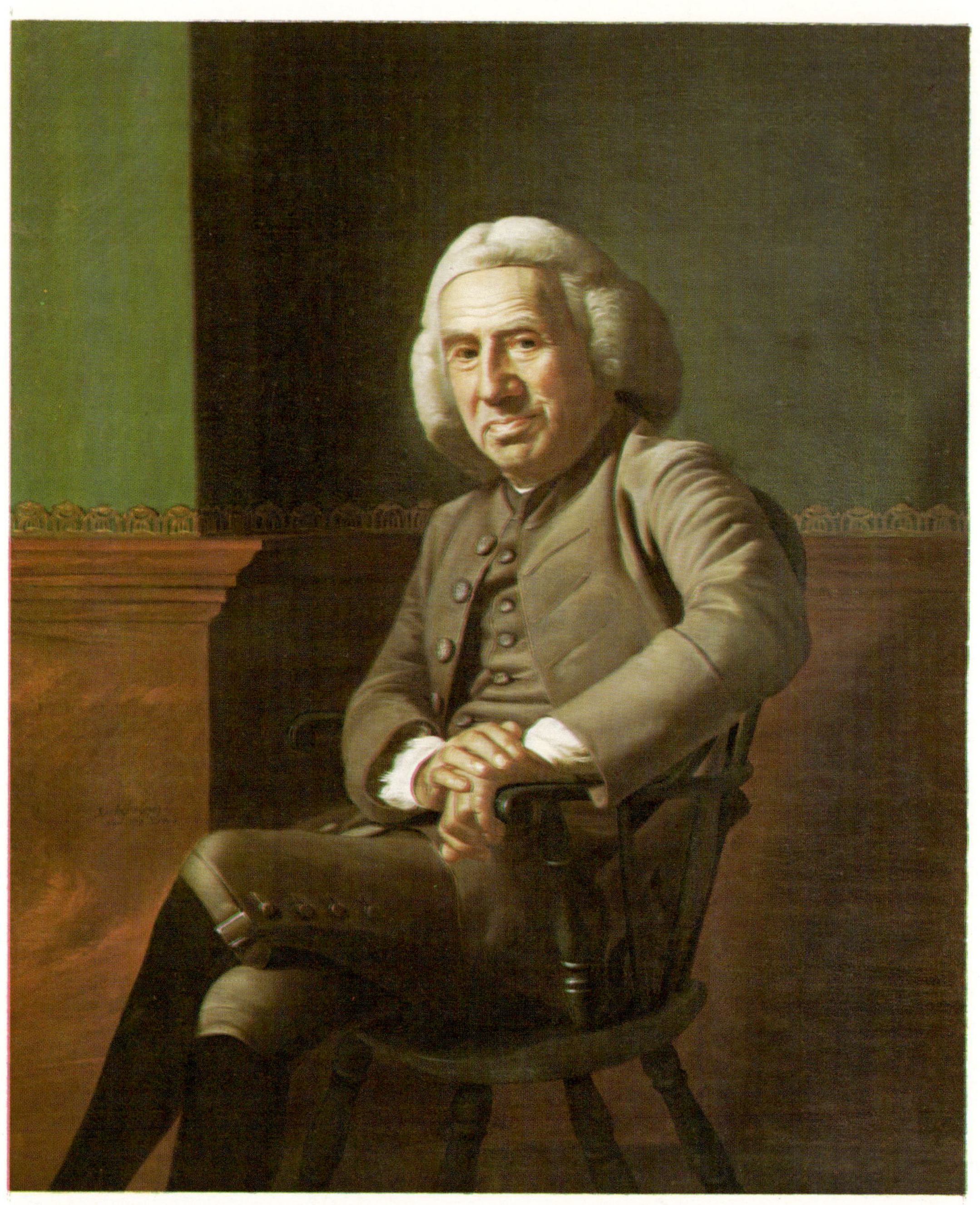

108 John Singleton Copley *Eleazer Tyng*

109 John Singleton Copley *Eleazer Tyng* (detail) ▶

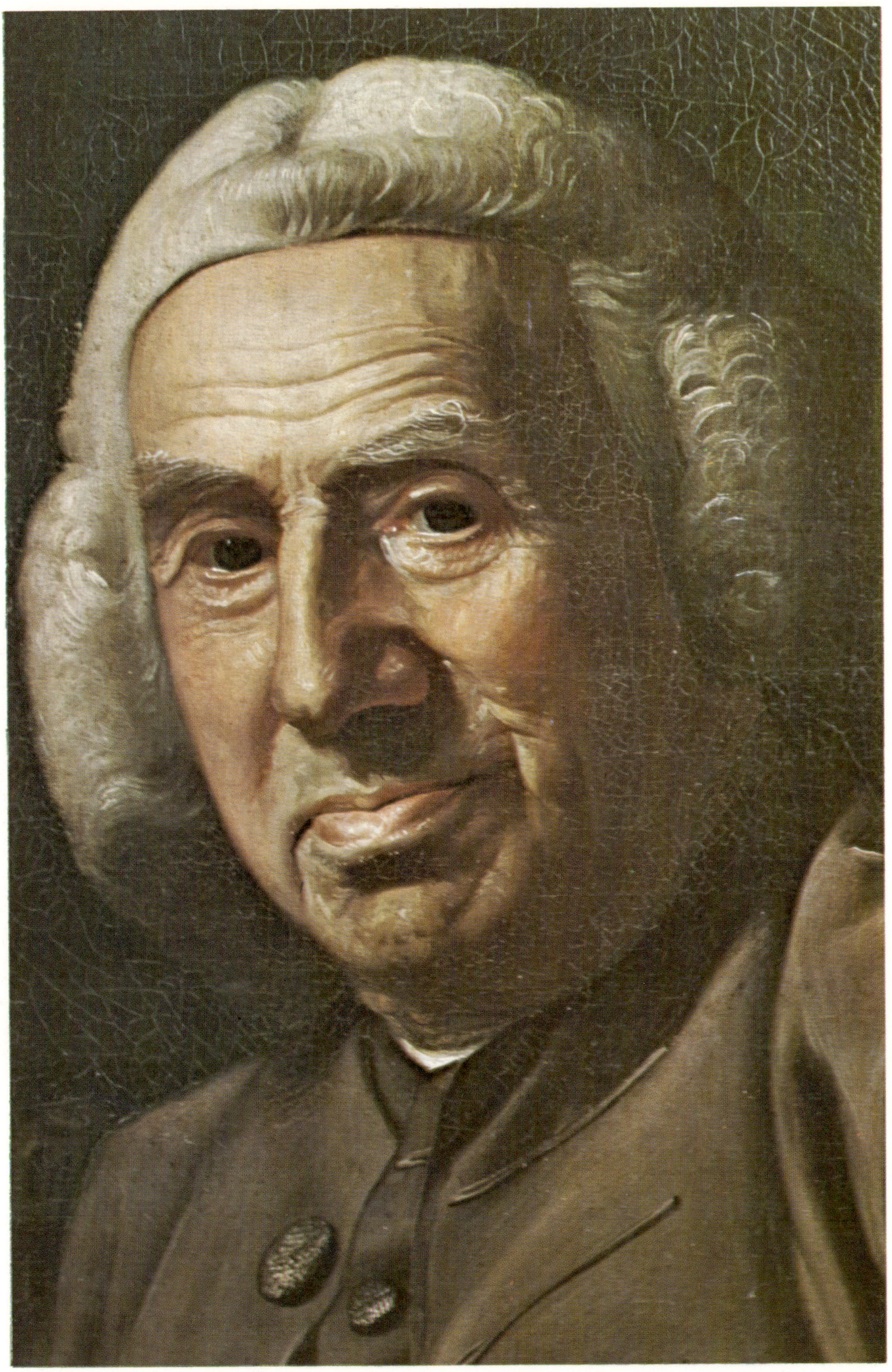

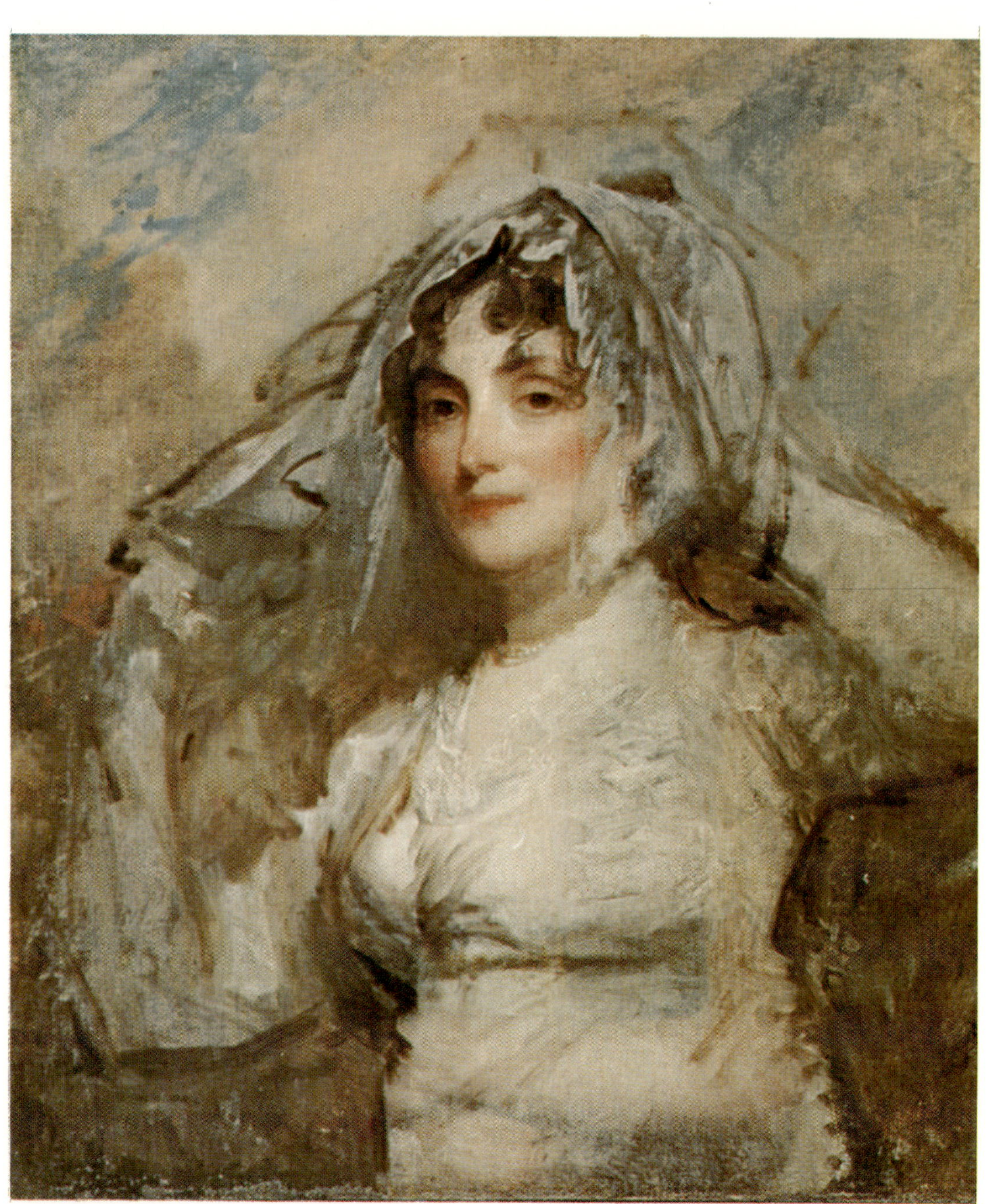

Up there: the bird's *left* wing, the wing of the flesh, Copley's "closest closeness" also[13] to the human flesh; flesh doomed to die, to rot in the moist darkness—oh, hatred! Puritan? Calvinist? Hatred of the rotting flesh! And the fear, but also the ceremonious respectability of this inevitable![14]

The hatred, yes! But huddled in terror and in pity against it, the great Pauline pity—not Bodhisattva's enlightened-to-extinction compassion, *prajñā-karuna,* but the co-sufferer's pity, the love-touch of Christ's wound, the help to resurrect from death and hatred, the resurrection of the flesh!

And silence now, you, contempt and mockery! For this is the morning of an astonishing day, day's morning of all-flesh, painted so marvellously, so mysteriously by Copley; Copley's naked faces and hands, doomed, petrified, wax-dead, wax-smooth; and Copley's eyes, the resurrected intelligence of the human glance, alive again and alight—starry love-touch of Christ!—in the midst of all the petrified pallor *(See Copley Plates 108, 109).*

The radiant fullness of this morning hour, the hour of Copley, was short. And the day, continued, as spring often does, with a changed mood: the great outstretched wings were advancing across the sky with the same majestic assuredness, yet only one, the right one, was visible from below with the same clarity, no, with even more clarity, more splendor and radiance about it than at Copley's hour, as the second wing, the *left,* was hidden now—immobilized?—from view, its plumage lost in the by-and-by invading shadow of clouds and rocky summit peaks.

Such is the tale—spring's discovery of American painting's history: a great wing mysteriously lost, and when the tale will end, recovered.

The entire nineteenth-century American painting is the story of the splendor and radiance of "ornament" = infinity, in figure, landscape, still-life. But the co-sufferer, the one who is touched by Christ, is not there any more. The Unknown Soldier, the defender of America's good city, where is his tomb? Hidden. Yet it is there, somewhere: now and then—very rarely, but oh! how poignantly!—a piercing sunbeam lightens for a fulgurant instant its absence; and the nostalgic ghost of a forlorn wing appears: the art of Eakins.

But there is no Christ's wound and the touch of Christ's wound in the swift, ample, and so precisely arranged rhythms of Benjamin West's art or Gilbert Stuart's *(Plate 110);* no wound in the "abstract" solemnity, suddenly so touching and tender, of Bingham's Missouri visitation *(Plate 111)*; nor, perhaps, in one of the most exalted as well as meditative and bliss-radiating energies of the human eye, hand, and mind that American painting has ushered into the world: the oils, the water-colors of Winslow Homer.

The allegorical bird's right wing—and only this wing now!—is clearly visible in the sky: winged "ornament"—Fujiwara toy!

Here it is, at the later hour of that day, the ardent coolness of "ornament," the stubborn yet dispassionate "abstract" sub-structure in a Bellows *(Plate 112),* a Sargent, even in a Ryder, his "verbal" pictorial mysteries so evocative of the witness's glance! *(Plate 113).*

And then, still later in America's day, when the *ars nova* of early twentieth-century Europe had reached and penetrated far and deep into the land and the sky of America, American painting remained the same—a

◀*110* Gilbert Stuart *Mrs. Perez Morton*
Early 19th century

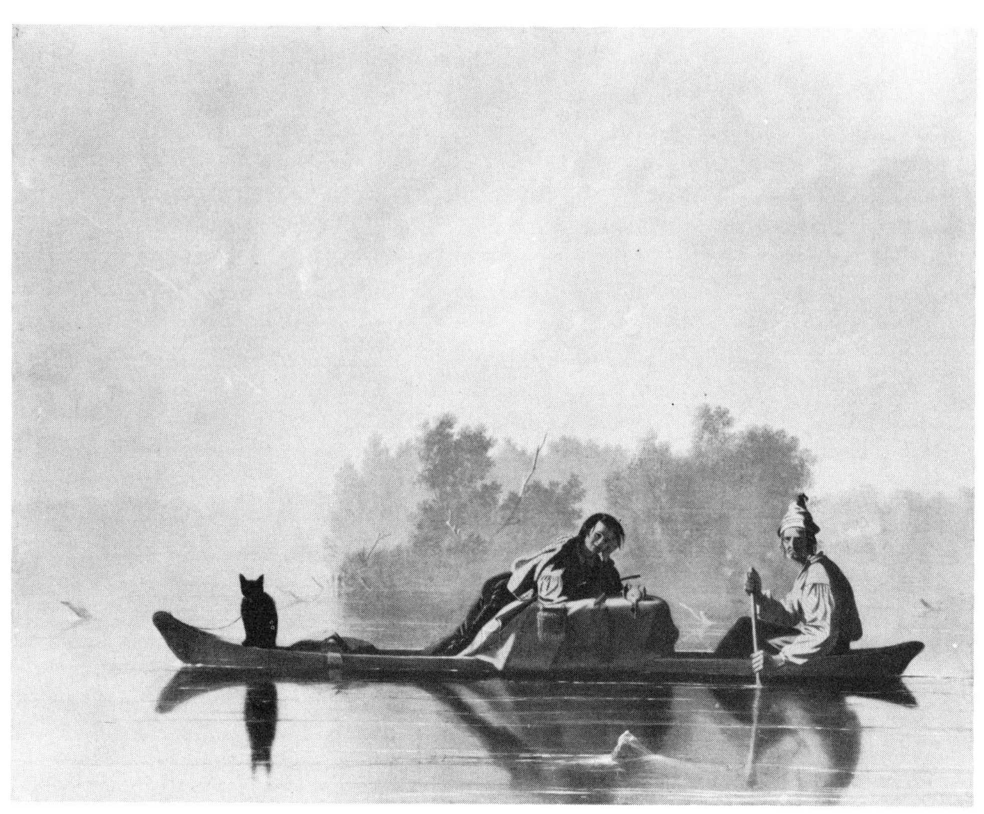

111 GEORGE CALEB BINGHAM *Fur Traders Descending the Missouri* (19th century)

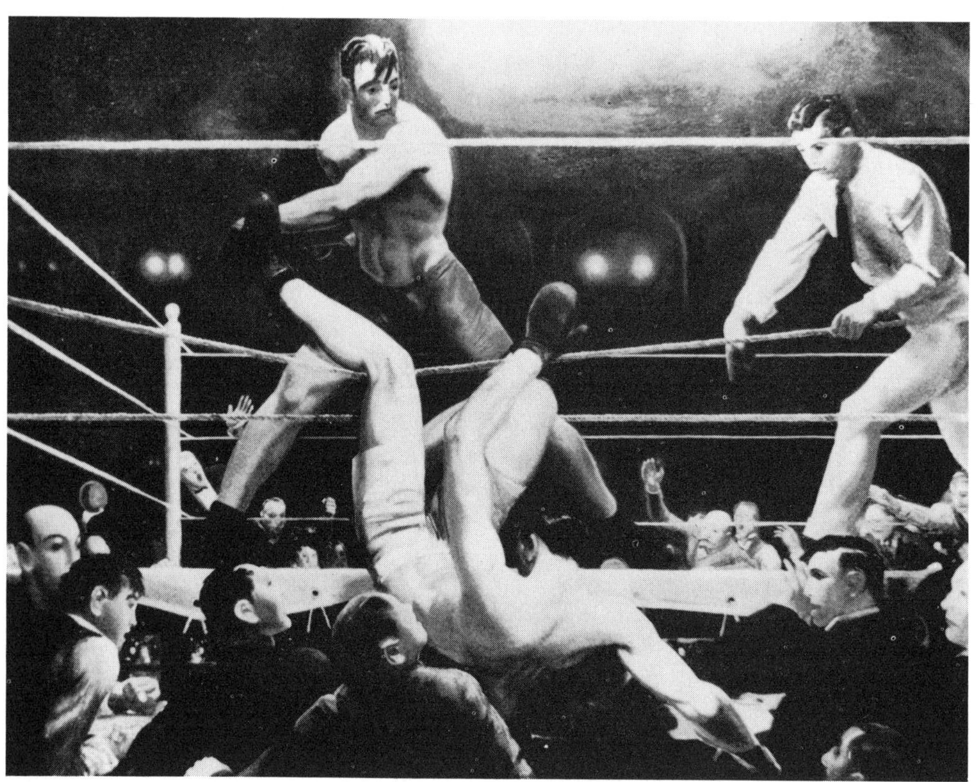

112 GEORGE W. BELLOWS *Dempsey and Firpo* (1923)

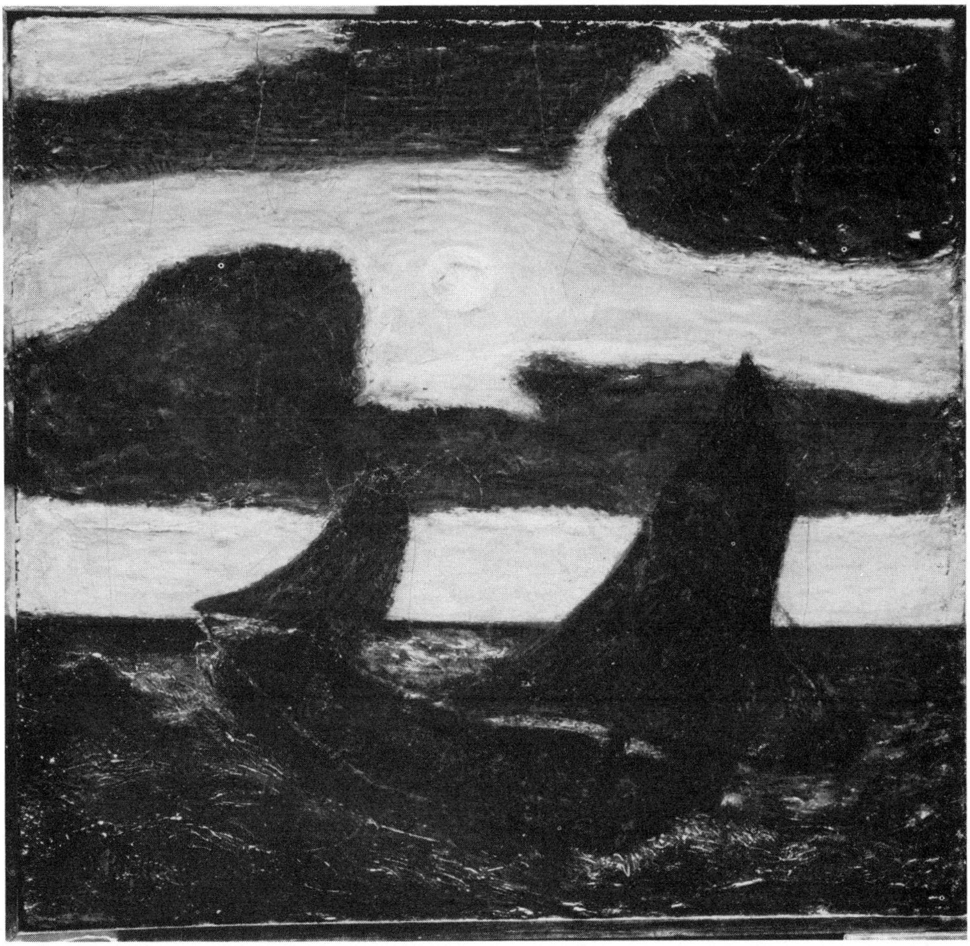

113 Albert Pinkham Ryder *Moonlight Marine*

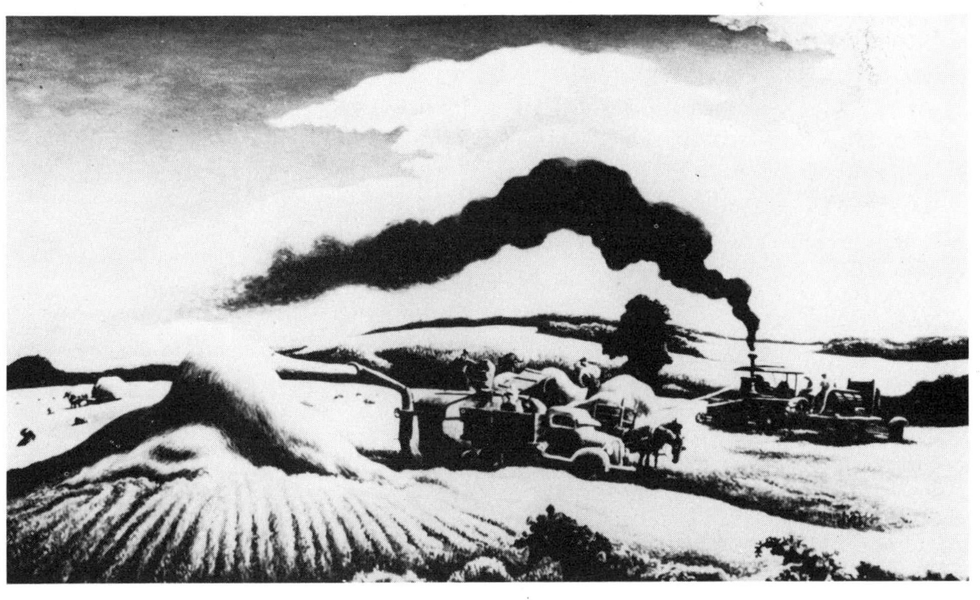

114 Thomas Hart Benton *July Hay*

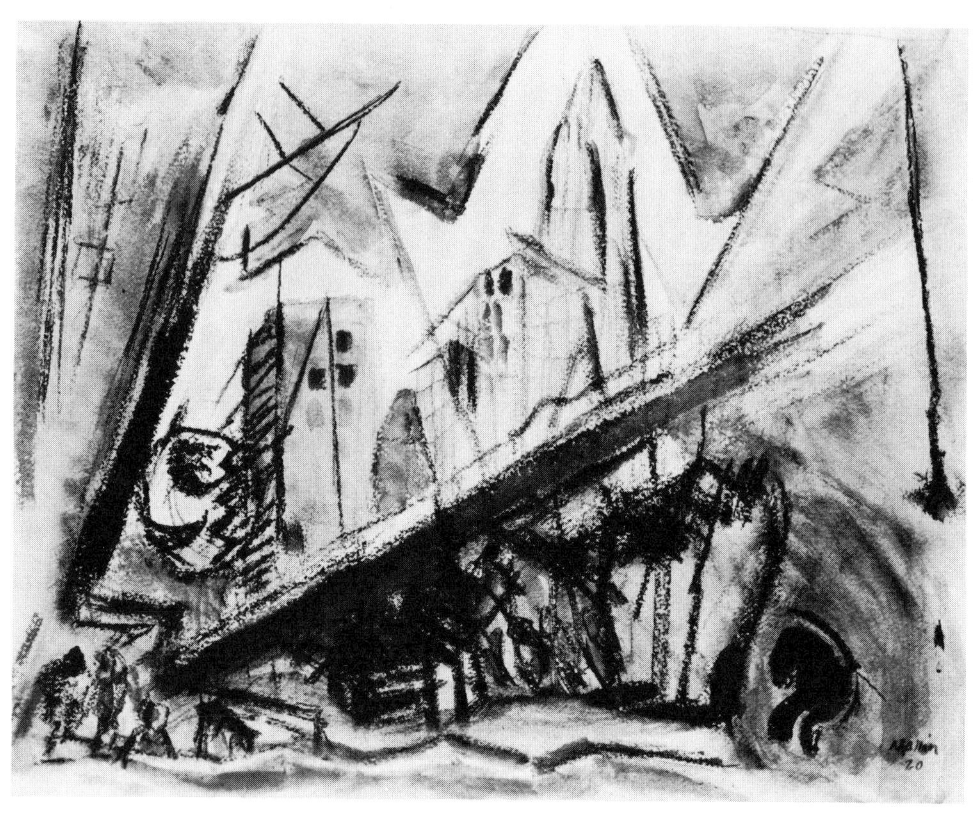

115 John Marin *Lower Manhattan*

right-winged bird—in appearance and, perhaps, in essence; such, Benton *(Plate 114)*, or Burchfield, O'Keefe, or Graves, or Marin *(Plate 115)*.

The second wing, the left one, was immobilized—hidden? absent?—its plumage lost in the shadow of the clouds and mountain peaks. The co-sufferer was not there any more. True, now and then, very rarely, a sunbeam or a thunderstorm's lighting would reveal, for a fulgurant instant, this absence. And the nostalgic ghost of a forlorn wing would appear.

As the day advanced too, the splendor and energy of the fluttering wing seemed exhausted. The bird was tired. Amid a cry for a new strength, a new blood perhaps, the cry for the lost wing was heard, heard finally, across the sky.

Second Action-Song

The wind bloweth where it listeth . . .

The tale speaks now—and does not stop any more!—of another and far-off country.

A country whose destiny of limitless growth is similar to America's, but whose nostalgia of infinity could never be, as it was in America, quenched, however briefly, by the presence of infinity's closest simulacre, the great—the greatest!—waters of America's two flanking and supporting oceans.

Only one of the two, the East's easternmost, has been reached by the tale's new country; the full possession of the other, the West's great water, was barred by ocean-hungry rival lands, more cunning or more deserving.

And so the simulacre of infinity was and still is there a broken, divided, an unfinished simulacre. That is why this new country's cries for infinity, her cries of nostalgia, are like the cries of a powerful, muscled dog about to be muzzled, loud voices now of deepest human distress, promise, and prayer, now of beast's obscure rage and pain. In this country, along the edge—a murderous knife-edge, long and sharp—of its densest and narrowest land extent, precisely where the anxious striving toward the open and westernmost great water—the inaccessible Atlantic—was stopped, a strange people was living, strange among so many other peoples in the vastness of the entire land.

A strange people, indeed, obstinate, short-limbed yet agile in obstacle-race, whose ancient Law was not a law discovered but a law found and given: kept jealously yet offered to many, as finite creation always is.

And no other people in the world had known better and more about the *intellectual love of God* and about the *mud;* no other people had carried in its blood and existence so much of this love and so much of this mud, as this strange people of strangers. And because of this—unbearable to others—purity of love, because of this intolerable impurity of mud, this people was universally hated, envied, despised and followed, admired and persecuted.

Persecuted: in holocaust to what covenant with justice and mystery? But it was the unbreakable endurance of this people's strength that appeared to be the strangest thing of all to those—including the estranged sons and daughters of this people itself—who could not see it where it was, and so could only be, in self-justification, more and more provoked and irritated by it. And yet, the source of this strength and this endurance was simple and known, open to all: it was the loyalty, the only and exclusive and exhaustive loyalty—all the others in obeisance to it and even, if ordered so, absent—to the Law found and given, one and the only one; the Hebrews' living sacrificial substitution for God's infinity. And such was this people's ritually fixed reverence for the word, the written word that reveals and in its turn substitutes the Law, that no other way of human mind, human knowledge and human success had been considered worthy of wisdom's tread, except the way of the verb's or word's categorical rulings—the way of merged syllogism and dialectics.

And the way of touch—accepted and even used when necessary, as muddy life's distraction or commodity and comfort—became for them the way of silliness and failure. (Moreover, was not the way of the verb the way of the Prophets also? Of those who first, in the world of post-split treasons and alliances, priests and defenders of the verb and the Writ as they were themselves, rejected the treacherous king-and-priest power-alliance, and so, by the rights of their first-born, great and noble revolt, made fully justifiable the pride and the sacredness of the word's way, the verb's self-asserted claims of exclusiveness? How then could the forgotten and silenced voice of the artisan's primordial claim be heard, his way be still seen?) This is also why no other people in the world had more readily accepted and exalted antiquity's—Aristotelian—distinction between *sophia* and *techne* than the people of the *Torah*.

And yet, the way of touch is not the way of silliness and failure. The way of touch—*techne*'s way—is the way of the witness: man's success is not the contrary there, not the opposite of man's failure.

So it came about finally that the people of the word's sovereignty and learning had to learn this too. And so the new learning came to them. It came at a strange, yet ripe time, a time of inner split, when their own nostalgia of infinity separated from infinity itself. For the word of the Law—*Sophia* or wisdom itself—being, in total substitution, this very infinity, forever fixed, unchangeable, at rest, infinity's nostalgia had to take abode and refuge elsewhere. *Torah's* nostalgia took refuge in the humble and restless world of *techne* and there learned the witnessing and helping arts of touch, the touching idiom of the witness. Mind's way of *touch* became the way of nostalgia's wisdom with the obstinate worshippers of *Torah*.

And here is how spring continues and then resumes its tale about the destiny of this strange and hated people, living half-choked, nostalgic and disfigured, on the westernmost fringe of the far-off, no-more-ocean, empire of the giant Russ.

Now—what was this nostalgia of infinity among the Jews? It was—so the American-born tale of spring reveals—the nostalgia of the *good country*, the yearning for a good country that one day would again surround the crowded, narrow, unwashed, unwanted alleys of all the innumerable villages, towns, and parts of greater towns allotted to the hated strangers, the half-closed ghettos and ex-ghettos tense with the life and death and irony of this people's sins, grandeur, poetry, and stink. (Oh, but the alleys swept clean, but the bodies washed clean clean—Shinto purified body!—at the eve of the Lord's day of rest! Oh, but the real and haughty and poignant poetry of men's faces there—so many of them!—dry, pale, and lost gems of intensity, bent over the tables of the Law's word to be deciphered now as forever before; and the greasy thumbs, claws of day's greed, fear and defensive deceit, plunging now—ample and pure, Raphaelesque curve of interrogation—into the murmuring space of study and prayer!

The unwashed, unwanted alleys and streets! And swarming there, the suffocating daily rites of petty or grand larceny, of cheating, lying, selling, quarrelling, envying, hating, performed by their helping womanhood, the helpers of mud's spread, of muddy ubiquitous repute—helpers of the pale-faced ones, all the same!

And then, the hour of the consecrated evening meal approaching them again, the mothers, the wives of the pale-faced ones, performing the ancient and sacred rites of Heavenly Light blessing—the mothers, the wives of the pale-faced—blessing with their hands joined, eyes closed, the coming in of a new light—their own!—the light of table candles, lighted by them at the very moment when the last beam of the day vanishes from the purified, darkened room!

Unwashed, unwanted, crowded streets and alleys, the stink and stint and dirt and noise about them; and suddenly—up there, high on the narrow wall, in a half-hidden window, the sudden tenderness of a flower pot—geranium, fuchsia!—a secret silent passion-flower of suffering and patience, a silent, secret witness of it, the co-sufferer, finally!)

Yes: the tale now is the tale of this people's separated nostalgia, of a yearning for a good country: the great nostalgia for green fields, greener and sweeter than the green and sweet, often forbidden fields, trees, and scented byways, huddled together (as America's city was against the terror of its country's "beyond") against the terror of the city-for-others and its unseizable, ever-growing "beyond"!

Yes, that is what it was: the new and late-come nostalgia for green fields' infinity among the people of the Law; and the joy in yearning for it, in loving it; the rejoicing—Baal Shem Tov's new rejoicing, born from the ashes of another holocaust[15]—in the close redemption that will come through the green fields redeeming joy itself; a profit-less joy, profit-less because with no god-like redeemer in it, but only the joy in mimicking, dancing, touching the green fields' infinity of joy and promise, the mysterious and new and profit-less love of God, Baal Shem's "closest closeness" to liberation, with no liberator for it, with no necessity for him.

The touch of the wound and the touch of the cure—only! The touch of the *Torah* and the dance of the *Torah:* such and the same as to be seen today at each year's nightly ceremony of *Rejoicing in the Law*—men, often sturdy, aggressive, bearded and shrewd, old and young males, dancing, mimicking around the table of the Law, in closed circle of hands on each others' shoulders, primeval motherhood's love and possession.

And one could see then with great astonishment their own mothers, wives, and daughters watch at a ritual distance—women's presence tabooed—the dancing men become *mothers* themselves, holding the robed scrolls of the *Torah* close to their breasts, as mothers do with their little ones, hugging, kissing, guiding, and walking them around—a most awkward spectacle, indeed!

And the "patrist" world, fixed forever by law, the patriarch's intransigent universe flows away then—and suddenly, a road opens into a much older and submerged universe, that of the protecting Great-Mother = Lover, the earth and plant, the sky and thunder conceived there as a one and perpetual, changing event-creation—to be at once told, explained, and tamed. Here: the universe of co-substantiality again, the pre-split three-oneness of speech, image, and rhythm: solitude-solidarity. Here: the new threshold of *techne,* redeemed, for the House of Law: Baal Shem's *mirror* of the good country—liberated. Baal Shem's *window* opened into the good country—the liberation.

This it was, the new learning brought to the people of the fringe—at a strange and ripe time of inner split.

Now, it happened that it was a ripe time of inner split not only for them, the strangers, but for many others on earth—a time of liberation's toil and yearning.

And the roots of this more general toil and yearning throughout man's earth were much deeper than even the roots of the strange and abandoned people's new learning and split—yet they were the same roots and their essential energies radiated together and merged, high and wide.

Baal Shem's window, only half opened by him, could be opened wider now, from outside, into the green fields of others. And spring's fresh scents, spring's freed voices, could come from those fields of others into the world, almost liberated now, of the ghetto.

And at the days of Sabbath, in many a village and township scattered through the lands of the fringe—Poland, Lithuania, Ukraine—young men and young women, oblivious of exigent rituals, or resentful of the Writ's suzerainty over their will and mind, would listen to passionately, avidly smell, voices and odors coming in from another world, not theirs at all. Ibsen and Tolstoy, Marx, Engels, Kropotkin, the great Slavic poets of co-suffering, and those of the West; all the centuries-long accumulated treasures of the West's own nostalgia for freedom, the freedom to be continued, toolwise, into the universe, as well as the freedom to "come out" machine-wise from one's own involvement, in sciences and techniques, in the revolts of poetry and social political ethics—all this blossomed slowly, many-petalled flower of *techne's* soil, side by side with the passion-flower—geranium, fuchsia!—bent high up there over the ghetto's noise.

The window was wide opened now both from inside and outside, into the road of *techne*, the road of "artisan" revolts, achievements, and legacies. It was a revolt indeed here too, a silent and still secret revolution among the people of the word's suzerainty, its radiations much stronger and farther reaching than is usually assumed in official histories, its course running close to that of another, more grandiose planetary revolution of the primeval "artisan"—the ever-spreading industrial revolution of contemporary man.

But *techne* redeemed means innermost body's image-touch redeemed, re-installed—means the *presence of adherence* given the rank and the functioning of mind's categories, means participation, immediate, inevitable: touch.

And so the ghetto became the touch of the ghetto—a presence, an immediacy of suffering and co-suffering; *Torah* became the touch of the *Torah;* and *Torah's* justice-as-commonwealth—justice for all not for the few, because achieved in spite of man's act of will, good or bad, but transcending it as a pure act of the Law, act of infinity itself seized in the Law, seized now afresh in the touch of the Law—became the touch of justice.

And because also—this should not be forgotten—the Law of justice for all, the Book, was, and is to remain so, the very life in all its manifestations for this strange people, *techne* itself, its life, its inventions, tools, machines, arts, and the touch of the inventions, the immediate participation in their energies, goals, and achievements, could not but be the touch of *techne*-justice, the *techne*-touch of this very same Law's justice for all. For the first time in the history of the people of the *Torah,* the creations of the haughty *sophia* became, in reciprocated exchange, the creations of the humble *techne.*

Those living on the condemned fringe of the evil and sick empire that was ready to collapse, hundreds and thousands of them in the ghetto's silent and bloodless revolt, young men, young women, who could not be silent any more, went with others to swell the tide, to prepare the coming of the great—and *de jure* the most justice-propelled—revolution of our times, the Russian. They could not do otherwise: the *Torah's* justice, of universal commonwealth, had to be *touched* by them, participated in, this time, and realized. Hundreds and thousands went voluntarily, inevitably, touched themselves by the touch of a profit-less or god-less, pure and absolute, intellectual love of God, to prisons, exiles and executions, some coming back, many many more perishing of hunger, cold, rape, and the whip among the anonymous icy terrors of Siberia. But it is with the destiny of those silent ones, the meditative and, perhaps, the more loyal to the way of ancient *sophia* itself as well as much closer to the new way of redeemed *techne,* that spring's tale resumes its narrative.

And indeed, this ending tale becomes the tale of a new wandering and a new arrival.

One day, across the distant sky, the high and narrow window of the ghetto being open now, spring's voice could be heard: "Go you, living dead, living on the fringe of no-Western-ocean land—go to the West's ocean, go beyond it and reach the land of the two oceans, the land of *techne*'s shelter and *techne*'s strength!"

As a mountain torrent spreads in reaching the valley so they went, many of them, men, women, children, poor and not so poor, bad and not so bad, good-and-evil doers, as all men are.

They went westward, the love of the *Torah,* the touch of the *Torah,* the touch of *techne,* the presence of the ghetto's passion-flower in them, ready to listen, to see, to smell, to touch with their hands, their eyes, and their minds the creations of other men's hands, eyes, and minds, the creations of human art. And became creators themselves—artists and future artists. Their hunger for art and art's—*techne*'s—new laws and new logos was very great. They looked for nourishment. And they found it, while still wandering toward their transoceanic aim in that singular art of the contemporary West, which from Christian antiquity till now was sealed with the same mysterious sign of ever-present companionship and testimony that will become also their, the new wanderers', own sign and seal of liberation and new wisdom: the presence of the co-sufferer.

In Munch: his crucified agonic cry heard finally with no scorn or doubt any more—the co-sufferer in it!

In Kokoshka: the bliss-giving plunge of his haloed dove of peace onto the wounded, lacerated waters of the down-world—bliss colored, bliss given, now bliss-giving, bliss-coloring!

And lastly, perhaps, in the art of Rouault, the ruby red, overflowing, abundant wound of Christ in it, the emerald touch and the star-golden cure of the wound—the wandering co-sufferer, close, very close, Christ of the old and of old age, the rotten flesh and the great pity of it, the divinity in it, Christ = harlot-exposed = old-king-old-clown = Christ, His Mother, the Holy Virgin Mary-harlot-exposed = Christ, and the Heaven of the Old Church rebuilt on it with no mendacity in it, only the bliss of mendacity exposed; and the early evenings—oh, nostalgia of lost goodness in men—old men, women, children, judges, finally painted in red earnest.

Such was the food that had nourished the searching and wandering strength of the Jews' new hand, new eye, and new mind—ready to create.

And when Chaim Soutine and the seeds of his hallucination and the seeds of heraldic history in him did what they were destined to do and to create—oh, Soutine's agonic red harmonies (not "distortions" but Paul Klee's *new fish*) born from his new inner-visceral and cosmic sound-substance, the co-sufferer's blood, Christ's blood too!—then the strange human current of wanderers and new and rare and precious seeds in them. . .

Third Action-Song

. . . reached America.

For indeed, America (*the third and last feeling for America*) is the discovery of America. As spring is. As a law is.

And it was, this time, a ripe and beautiful spring day. The great bird —Copley's bird!—was advancing across the sky always, with the same apparently quiet assuredness. Yet as the tale has told us, only one of the wings, the outstretched right one, was visible, America's winged finite "ornament"-infinity; the other, the left one, hidden now from view, the co-sufferer, was not there any more. As the day advanced too, the great bird became tired. And a cry for a new strength—a new blood, perhaps—the cry for the lost wing was heard finally across the sky.

It was at this precise moment-situation of American art's "heraldic" history that the strange human current of wanderers reached America, and that the help came.

A new blood, indeed, was given, a new strength added, to the great soaring bird: with no seeds of "race" in it—who would dare to give here so accursed a name?—or of "creed"—who would challenge here an over-flowing universal fatigue?—or of "blood." But only the new and precious seeds of creation's blood and of love's:—the same that poured out one day, still does today, from the beheaded body of young Nicolo Tuldo, Catherine his co-sufferer, the strong and stubborn daughter of artisans, the saint from Siena, telling us about this in her famous letter to her confessor, Brother Raimondo of Capua:

> I waited for him then at the place of justice. . . . I prostrated me, and stretched my neck upon the block. . . . Then my soul became so full that although a multitude of people were there, I could see no human creature. . . .
>
> Then he came, . . . and seeing me, he began to smile, and wanted me to make the sign of the Cross. When he had received the sign, I said: "Down! To the Bridal, sweetest my brother! For soon shalt thou be in the enduring life." He prostrated him . . . and I stretched out his neck; and bowed me down, and recalled to him the Blood of the Lamb. His lips said naught save Jesus! and, Catherine! And so saying, I received his head in my hands, closing my eyes in the Divine Goodness, and saying, "I will!"
>
> Then was seen God-and-Man, as might the clearness of the sun be seen. And He stood wounded, and received the blood; in that blood a fire of

holy desire, given and hidden in the soul by grace. He received it in the fire of His divine charity. When He had received his blood and his desire, He also received his soul, which he put into the open treasure-house of His Side, full of mercy. . . .

When he was at rest, my soul rested in peace and in quiet, in so great fragrance of blood that I could not bear to remove the blood which had fallen on me from him.

Ah me, miserable! I will say no more. I stayed on the earth with the greatest envy. . . . Therefore do not wonder if I impose upon you nothing save to see yourselves drowned in the blood and flame poured from the side of the Son of God. Now then, no more negligence, sweetest my sons, since the blood is beginning to flow, and to receive the life. Sweet Jesus, Jesus Love.[16]

Such was—exaggerated, of course, as tales are—the new blood and the still secret new strength given to the great tired bird: the art and the history of American painting.

One thing is sure: the lost wing was found. American painting—Copley's fulfilment of the past's promise and a prophecy about the future—could soar again, both wings moving fast in unison, high above the good and the evils of America: it could now reveal and condemn them more fully, laugh at them and weep over them—strong, and untouchable, angry and co-suffering.

Bird of Copley—America total!—Of Jack Levine, today: The "closest closeness" again, Levine's studious and exalted *scientia signata*—the right wing!—rediscovered, discovered by his brush: Levine's own structuring of pictorial moral space, the volume-upon-no-volume (the translucid-upon-dense) of this space, shaped in its turn into a new human flesh, painted, *chatoyant—ex-nihilo* created? As Adam's rib? *(Plate 116).*

And the wound in this same flesh—the left wing!—and the healing touch of Christ's wound in it; *techne*'s touch of the *Torah, techne*'s touch of the *Torah*'s inexorable justice for the many, not for the few, and the touch of the absent ghetto, its presence, as poetry, irony, pity, and passion-flower bent over the dirt of human alleys: Rouault's Christ of old and of all the old ones, Levine's old, broken, useless white horse in a broken, useless hinterworld, condemned by all, the solitude = solidarity of this precise solitude and this precise solidarity—now, finally, exalted, *in excelsis coeli,* by the brush of a Jew!

The bird of Copley—the bird of Hyman Bloom now: his elegant interlace continuity: landscape-infinity? viscera? roses of St. Elizabeth? fraud? folds of Feke's, of Copley's silks? "pure ornament," surely!

And Hyman Bloom's dissected flesh—St. Birgitta and her "nails in the flesh"—the hatred (Puritan? Calvinist?) and the pity, Pauline pity, of the still power-retaining, putrescent corpse *(Plate 117);* its resurrection, flowered, scented, jewelled—all the poetry, strength, and irony, the glory of the passion-flower up there in the unforgettable closed window.

Copley, the integral body of American painting and mind:

America! What, who are you?

The ghetto's green fields—joy of human dignity tomorrow, yesterday's indignant mockery?

Africa's hidden and transferred sovereignty, that of most delicate and selected senses in man—our planet's vindication and future?

Nostalgia—the unfinished simulacre of two-oceans' infinity?

Yes: all this and more:

All modes of nostalgia, of birth and vindication—the vindication of justice in face of injustice, *theodicy:* birth of mud and of intellectual love of God, multi-limbed Theodicea, American hidden nostalgia of unreachable America.

And Ben Shahn, the American painter, is all this—more or less. What is his art?

Surely, Ben Shahn's art is an American theodicy, told by him in three-day vindication:

First day of Vindication: the Ship

First day of Ben Shahn's substitution for the unseizable totality of justice:

Sacco-Vanzetti corpses and everybody knows it *(Plate 118).* Two painted flat dead faces offered as a gift to the eye's pleasure: a "decorative" icon.

Two *real* twin corpses, sharp-nosed and white, very white, very clean and very correct, lain in pretty twin coffins—their flat, straight and decorative horizontality rooted now in a world of capsized self-righteousness, neither vertical nor horizontal, the capsized stairs of judges, the judges themselves so very elegantly alive—why? how is it still possible?

The *salauds* of Sartre! For, surely, *Torah* was thought dead of mendacity that day!

Twin coffins: nothing but a ship in the midst of ocean's tempest, capsized; a landscape-"ornament"; a painting, after all, and a *techne* substitution—nothing else. And yet America's foundations, the foundations of her history shook that day.

Second Day of Theodicy: the Child

Second day of Ben Shahn's substitution:

A ship capsized and abandoned in the tempest? Sacco-Vanzetti and the judges painted convincingly? An aesthetical vindication—by this artist's dexterous hand, of the quiet-horizontal in front of the treacherous-oblique?

A tragedy and a satire told sharply?

No; but Ben Shahn's second day's substitution: the Child. The sudden visitation of a child in danger, the pity of it, the injustice of it and our helplessness. A little child, a little helpless being, the one who, rapidly grown tomorrow, is too little as yet, today, to either be standing upright—vertically—by himself, or to remain quietly and wisely for long in the horizontal, but who stands uncertain between the two, dangerously, prophetically capsized; about to fall in a fallen world, to be helped—yet Sacco and Vanzetti are not helped!

Does everybody know this? Everybody should—since Dostoyevsky's "Ye, men—beauty and beast!—you may kill, destroy each other to your heart's content: nothing will happen to you and your kin; your *karma*

"Levine's old broken, useless white horse
in a broken, useless hinter-world;
Hyman Bloom's dissected flesh . . .
still power-retaining, putrescent corpse;
Ben Shahn's Sacco-Vanzetti corpses and
everybody knows it; the sudden visitation
of a child in danger; death, resurrection,
child and co-sufferer, all in one image;
the broken and forgotten wire of a
concentration camp's fence; the fanfare
of the shefer *blown."* (See Plates 116-122)

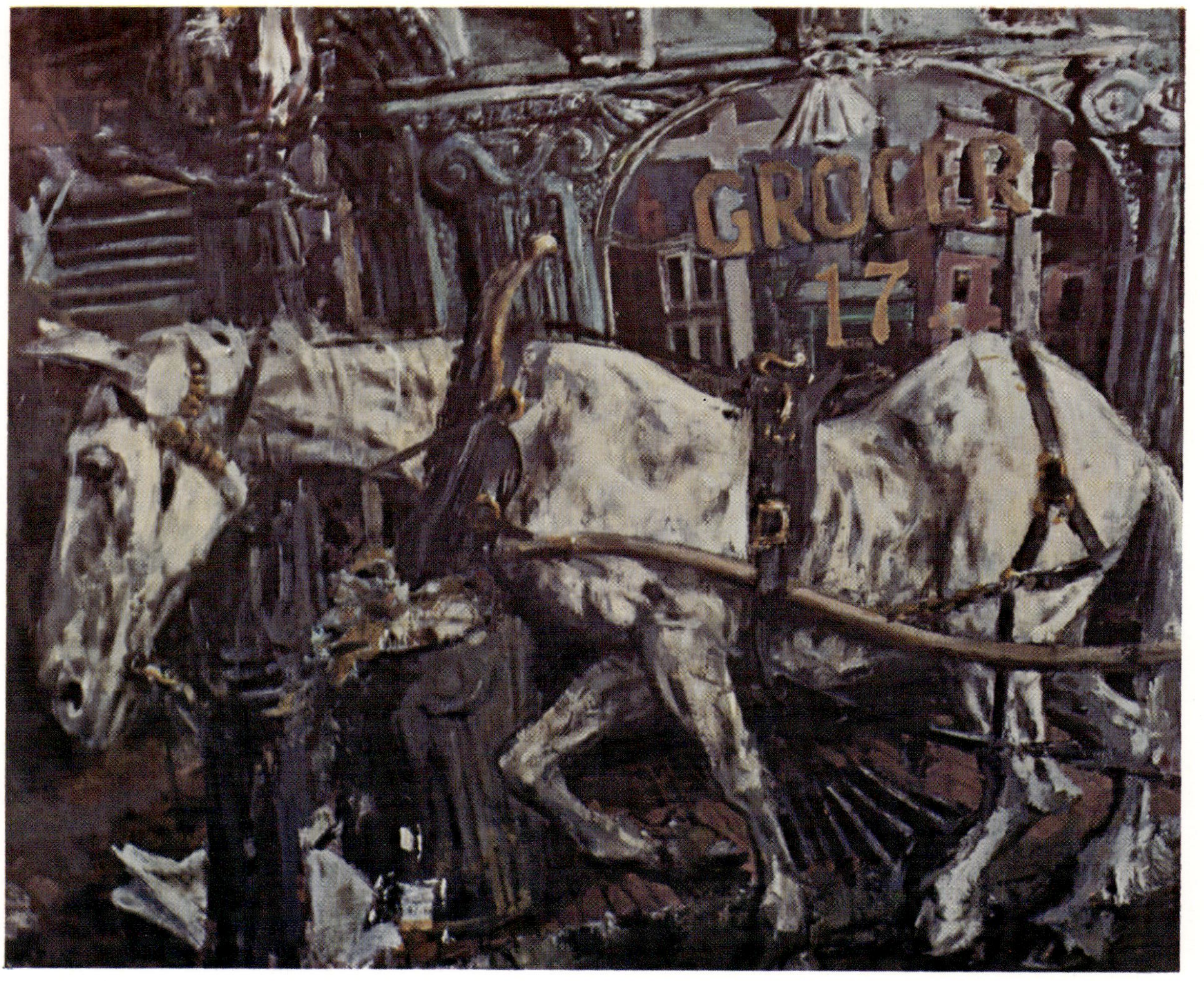

116 JACQUES LEVINE *The White Horse*

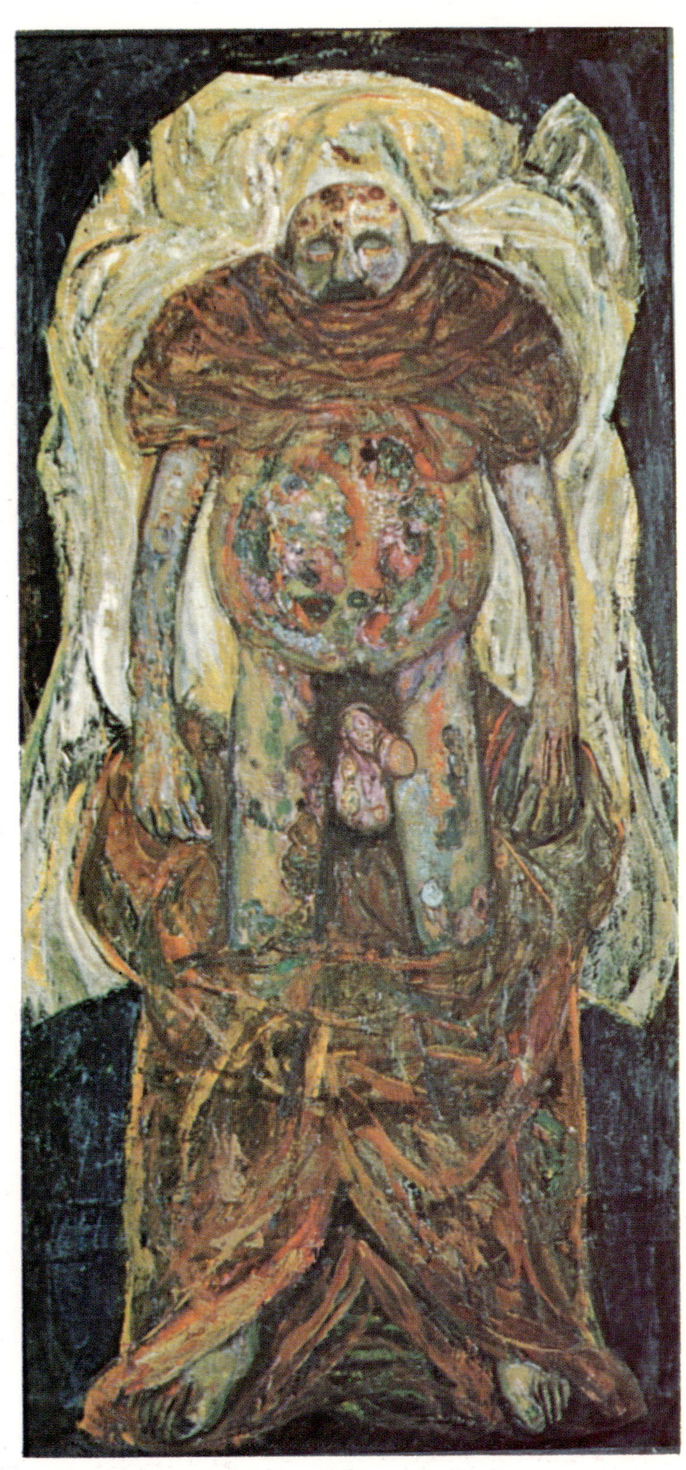

117 HYMAN BLOOM
Corpse of Elderly Male

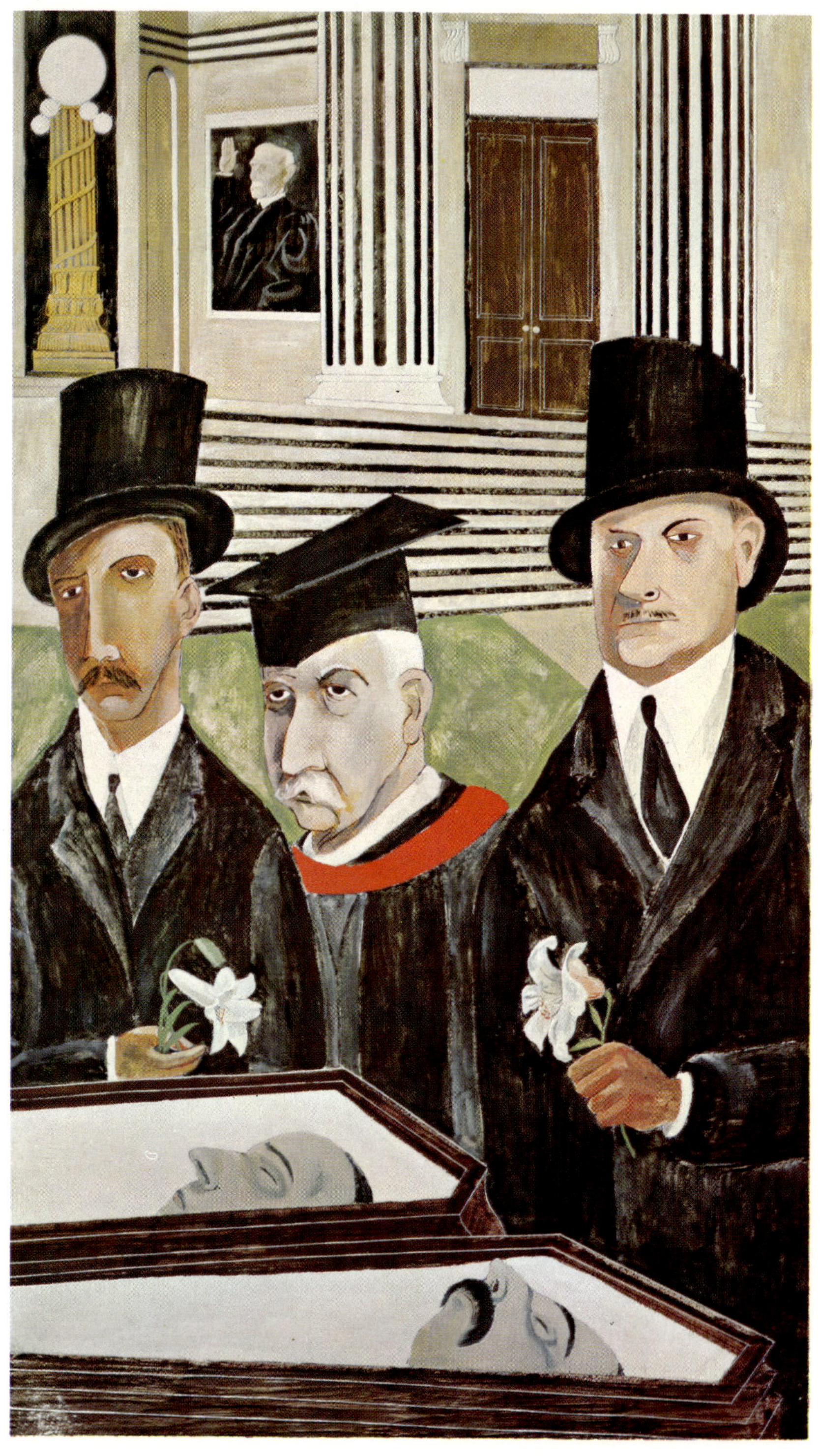

118 Ben Shahn
The Passion of Sacco and Vanzetti

119 BEN SHAHN *Allegory* (1948)

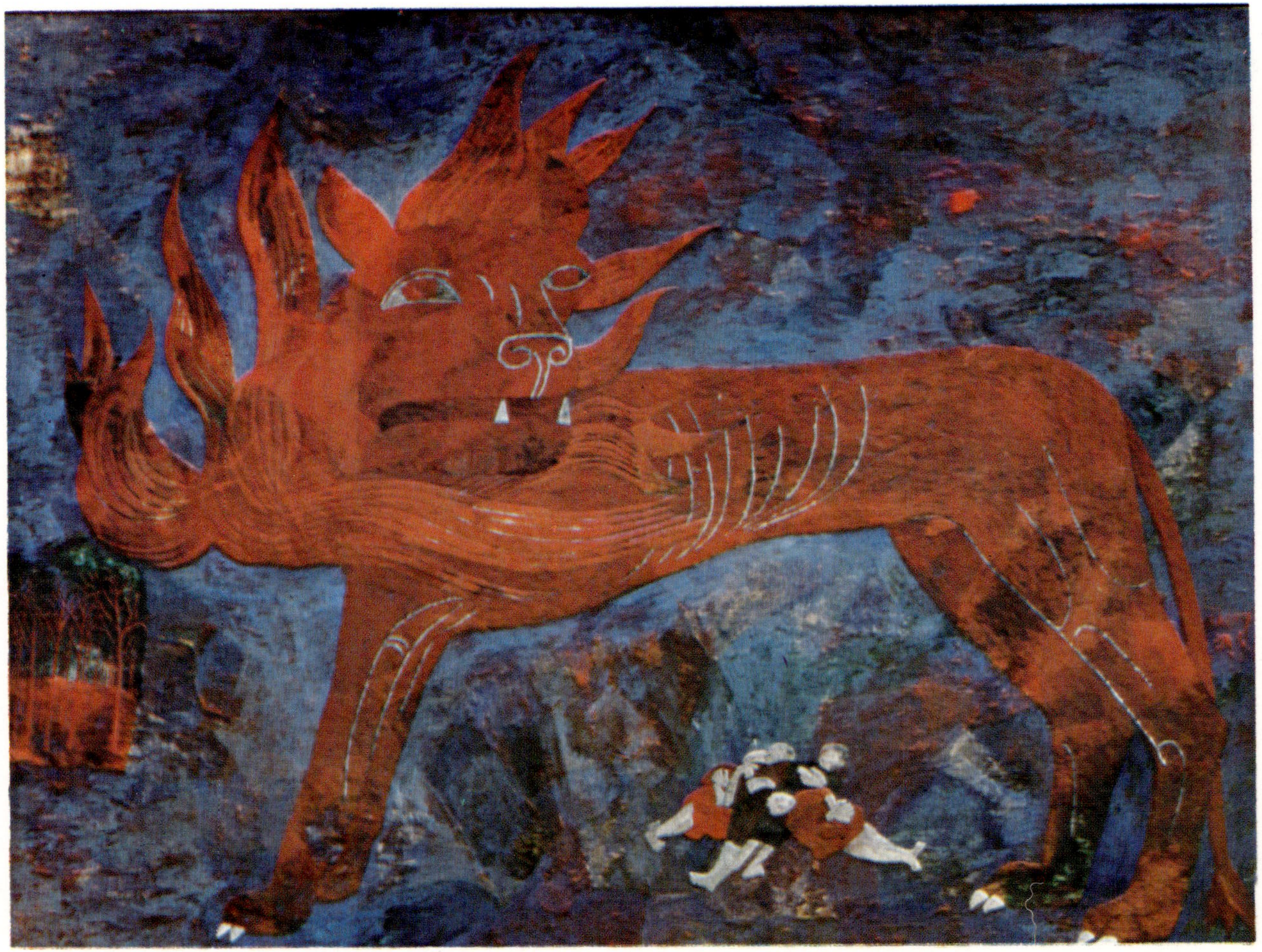

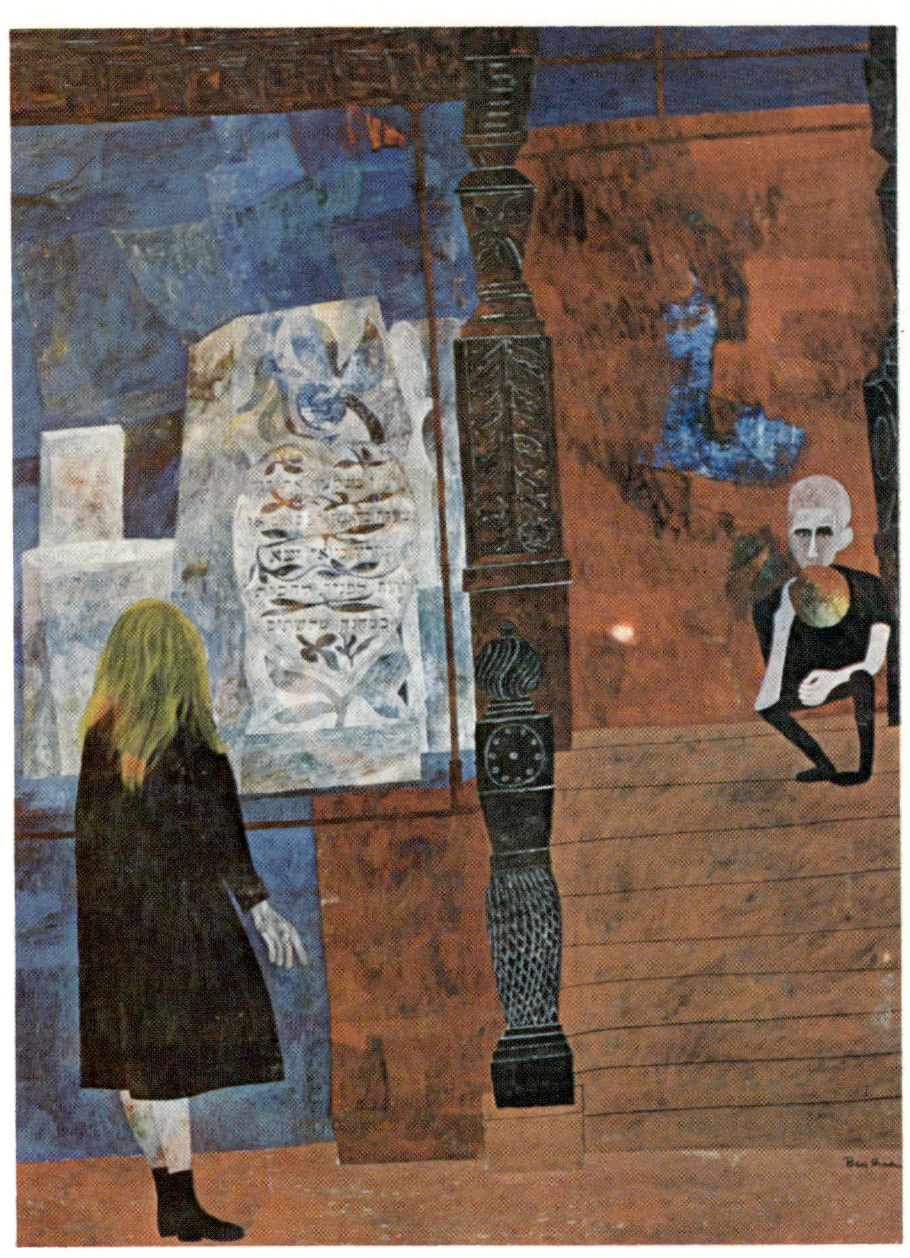

120 Ben Shahn *Sound in the Mulberry Tree*

121 BEN SHAHN *Pact*

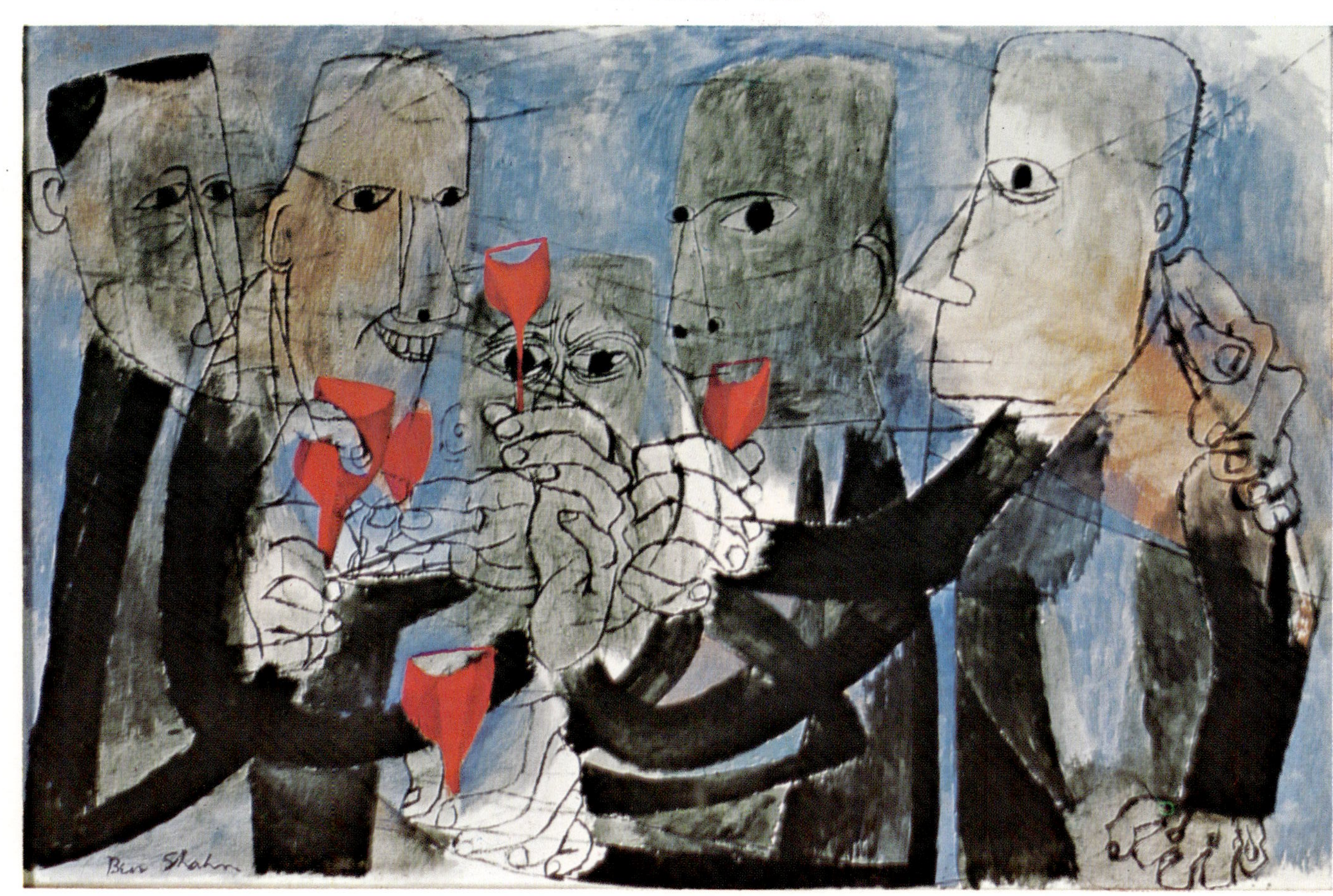

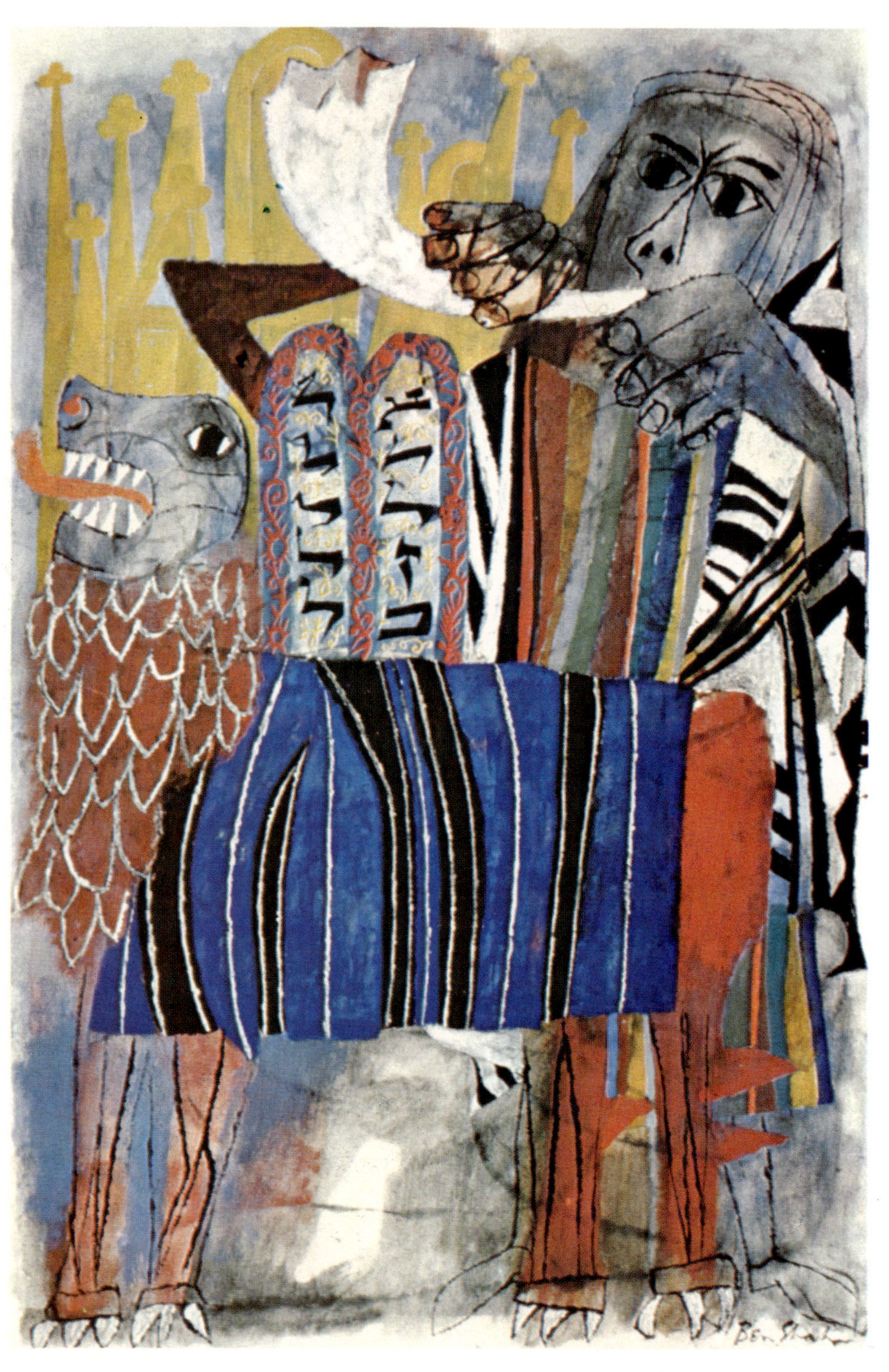

122 BEN SHAHN
The Third Allegory

awaits you at your coming, at your departure. But, beware! You cannot kill a child, a little child! For, surely then the very foundations of the entire universe with cosmos and chaos in it will be shaken, destroyed, and then changed. There will have to be another world-foundation, after a strange, terribly red, revengeful fire has killed you and your children's children, huddled together under the flaming ire and innocent" (but is not innocence the carrier of evil in the world? [*Plate 119*]).

And yet a little child had been killed one day, somewhere: the day of Sacco-Vanzetti coffins. The world's foundations were shaken, destroyed, and changed. But the *Torah* remained—unchanged. And Ben Shahn's second day of art's substitution was the day of the *Torah*'s—not the sword's—vindication of justice, the day not only of a little child's injurious death, but a child's resurrection: the co-sufferer's.

In the world of evil, capsized self-righteousness, all ruins now, Ben Shahn's resurrected, redeemed children—pale comrades of learning, of suspension, of terror also capsized, of vice, co-suffering, and games—are constructors of a new, transparent, "mobile-rigid" free and eventful world, all theirs. Broken, minute bricks of ruined homes, wounded walls and walls healed by the touch of the ghetto's passion-flower, multiplied over there, in the broken, yawning hole:

Child's toy, *aeternitas*-"ornament"!

Ben Shahn's playful calculated art of the ornamental: sheer "silliness," sheer "frivolity" for *Sophia*'s old pride! Ben Shahn's unending, interlaced "ornament"-landscape, "ornament"-infinity: his theodicy, his substitutions!

His subjects narrated: illustrations to a political angry choice, to a "commercialized" love meeting, a love convention, unequal, ugly, sharp-toothed? What does it matter now? And Ben Shahn's conception of pictorial space, the sharply reached goal of his "ornamental" linear perspective, flattened but so rapid and so rapidly convincing; its, this perspective's, own torment capsized also, thrusting all the converging lines rapidly forward; Ben Shahn's very personal discovery of *scientia signata*'s closeness—"ornament" too!—his typical structuring of an I-am-coming-upon-you volume, simply by placing an active and sharpened line over its obedient and splashed shadow, a masterly trick used also by Sesshu—what does all this matter? The yearning for *Torah*'s presence, the *techne* touch of *Torah,* here too, the touch of the ghetto's flesh, mud, wound, learning, despair, pride, and irony—this is what matters really: death, resurrection, child and co-sufferer, all in one image seen and touched through the transparency of Ben Shahn's substitution!

Facing us, a condemned, unhealthy little boy, grown up in the earth with the roots and the grain, a little corpse prematurely aged, holding his playball—not any fruit!—in his hand; is that only what he is? And the little girl facing him, her fiery, living hair as seen not by us, but by him, the little pale-faced one, seen only as a flashing air-and-fire, heaven-and-fire reflection, through the transparent stillness of the tombstones and the toy-like, capsized, Jacob's ladder *(Plate 120)*—who are they? Just a boy, dead, and a girl, alive, who have met once not to meet again?

No. Not altogether so. But Lazarus too, the friend of Christ, the buried and the resurrected one; that is, the resurrected story of Adam and Eve —the new Eve, the new apple in the hand of Adam, the new serpent, the new knowledge and new birth.

Third Day of American Theodicy

Third day of Ben Shahn's substitution: the wire

And the foundations of the old universe with chaos and cosmos and the heart in it were shaken, destroyed, then changed and rebuilt again.

And everybody knows—but nobody remembers it—that there was—there is—a *Witness* to this great shaking.

The Witness:

A little, insignificant, but testifying thing—a *res* ever present—the painter's third hallucination, chosen by him to substitute now the totality, unseizable otherwise, of the shaking evil-*persona:* the broken and forgotten *wire* of a *concentration camp's fence.* Very precisely, and so funny and decorative: Ben Shahn's new "trick" of outline drawing, his new pictorial *invenzione!* A substitution. So that the evil-*persona*—the blemish of our planet—could never be forgotten from this, visitation's, day on: *Quella cosa e più nobile che ha più eternità.*[17]

From Sacco and Vanzetti's changed and rebuilt icon; from the self-righteousness of a pact-scene *(Plate 121),* staged as evil's *equivoque* (a "*Disparate,*" added to all those of Goya)—festive wine, toast to old alliances? the Holy Grail's blood? blood of murdered children past and future?—to Ben Shahn's humanist *Credo,* surely that of a friend of the *Torah,* Luther's credo now (hammered too low and too late on the wall); and thence to man's, Ben Shahn's own, image of his "innermost body" revealed suddenly —as soul's first baby cry, as mind's first light flash!—in the clumsy, intricate, trailing fall of, say, this football player—all of it, all the imaginable subjects of Ben Shahn's curse, indignation political, social, moral, intellectual, of his exaltation, meditation and child-memory, all are transubstantiations now—yes! *theologically*—into the eucharistic bread and wine of his ultimate, the third, substitution: this pricky, lacerating and "uncomfortable" to behold wire of *that* Concentration Camp. (The precise yet hidden *that* is the Mysterious Companion himself again.)

Ben Shahn's *invenzione* of a barbed wire-line—why not, simply, a new prowess of a crafty decorator's hand, an ornamental, artisan, vocabulary enriched—an ornament after all, pure and simple? Why not indeed? This third day of *Dies irae,* the fanfare of the *shefer* blown, the brass and the flutes of his—America's—theodicy, cathedrals and towers of sounds not fingered any more but blown, as the wind bloweth where it wills *(Plate 122)*—they are spring's lovely sounds too, pretty pink and blue flower-and-women tunes of heart's desire, lighted dance tunes—King David now dancing in shiny-black and white robes before the vigilant and sacred ark-letters, all ancient voices of solitude-solidarity unheard or silenced, now finally exalted *in excelsis coeli,* by the brush of a Jew!

Ben Shahn's ornament, his own image-body of man-and-beyond-man's un-finity *is* flesh! Ben Shahn's flesh-image of man-and-his-innermost-body's "beyond" *is* ornament!

The art of Ben Shahn is the art at once of the ornament and of the flesh: the art of America.

And the great bird of Copley—America total—his two wings outstretched and both visible, is soaring high through light and clouds.

And whatever changes in the arts of how to paint minerals, plants, beasts, birds, humans, angels, and their letters and their names, might come—and should come!—from this time on, the two wings will continue to climb up the sky of America with the same rhythmic unison: no matter how uncompromising and absolute will be the loyalty to the ornament = continuity in, say, a Pollock, in a De Kooning, the neo-American, or to the ornament = *scientia signata* in a Wyeth, the "nails in the flesh," the wound of the "Man of Sorrows" will be there also forever—forever America's discovery.

"That is why," so concluded my witness's testimony and defense, "that is why America is the discovery of America.

As spring is of spring,

As *Torah* is of *Torah*,

As *amor intellectualis Dei* is, in art, the discovery of ornament and the discovery of flesh, the golden chain of Derbforgaill's love-and-death song between them all now."

The sound must seem an echo to the sense.[18]

Let the word journey be another name for spring, and a journey be the discovery of a journey: a journey that begins:

At the age of seventy-five, only fourteen years left to end his life's journey—but, truly, at what mysterious and unified time of a mysterious and unified life?—Hokusai wrote:

> From the age of six I had a mania for drawing the forms of things. By the time I was fifty I had published an infinity of designs; but all I have produced before the age of seventy is not worth taking into account. At seventy-three I have learned a little about the real structure of nature, of animals, plants, trees, birds, fishes and insects. In consequence, when I am eighty, I shall have made still more progress. At ninety I shall penetrate the mystery of things; at a hundred I shall certainly have reached a marvellous stage; and when I am a hundred and ten everything I do, be it but a dot or a line, will be alive. I beg those who live as long as I to see if I do not keep my word. Written at the age of seventy-five by me, once Hokusai, to-day Gwakio Rojin, the old man mad about drawing.[19]

A true journey's discovery of journey, this: Hokusai knew, his unfailing eye knew it for our sake, here and now, that a journey is the time of exchange of names—serpent's shedding off the slough, all in one and at once—the exact, "heraldic" time-knot where the rational-and-irrational (Hokusai's vision of his own life's chain of achievements and facts) is being renamed by my lady Iwai as honesty-and-generosity (Hokusai's *visitation* of his art's global attitude, his never repeated, ever beginning, ageless one-life).

Just that also which had been meant by another traveller, whose saying has been singled out for us: " . . . There is no man who is not incessantly being taught by his soul." One of his disciples asked: "If this is so, why don't men obey their souls?" "The soul teaches incessantly," Rabbi Pinhas explained, "but it never repeats."[20]

❖❖❖❖❖❖❖❖❖❖❖❖❖❖❖❖❖❖❖❖❖❖❖❖❖❖❖❖❖❖❖

At this very instant of Hokusai's essential time, Hokusai's compressed life-time—grapes chosen on rare and elected, sunny slopes, to be pressed into everybody's wine—freed from presumption, I say to the reader: "How I wish I too might start anew my own journey and say anew (looking back at our distant autumnal day, oh *peine d'amour!* yet touching today's spring day, not any more rainy, but in full glow of seeds, warmth, and questioning): Let the story of Japanese painting be a truly mysterious story today, that is, not only the story of an art mysterious but the story of a word, the word *mysterious,* mysterious and left alone, to remain so. For the mysterious is the discovery of the mysterious: at once unavoidable explanation and a failure of explanation. How I wish I might say anew: failure is not the opposite of success; let this, Japanese painting and its history, be a last exchange of gifts, mine and my lovely old lady's, dead: the ornament seen anew. A discovery of ornament-a-discovery . . .

❖❖❖❖❖❖❖❖❖❖❖❖❖❖❖❖❖❖❖❖❖❖❖❖❖❖❖❖❖❖❖

Journey Interrupted

THE READER (not politely any more, but in anger): Why the term *ornament* here again? A term, a name so abused, so vague, so sense-vague. Why not instead, in all directness of intention, the term *com-position,* this basic, and I would concede, "truly mysterious" structure of art? Why not give it the name *nonrepresentational art,* or *abstract expressionist,* or any other ready-made name that would justify, explain, and expand your obvious and obstinate pledge for today's thinking and feeling in art? Why the word *ornament* again, and again the word *discovery?* Sheer play of words?

I: And why not? A word's purity or loyalty to origins is seldom revealed in an explanation of a word by another word or aggregate of words, but does remain as part of the play, interplay, of words. Each word's meaning and sound (both sound out-sounded and still in-sounded) meet there, as if for the first time, *there* in the closest vicinity of mind's pre-split oneness itself; the tightly coiled oneness of image-idea-gesture uncoiling there (within each word's universe, a free play of energies!) the serpent-mind's sense-flow; a truly erotic shudder along the spine from eye and fang to tail's tip, from *idea* to smell, taste, and touch, from top to the bottom—all distinctions, verbal? visual? then becoming futile. Each word's universe, the whole of the serpent's sense-flow, as in music each harmonic chord's tonal universe, co-vibrates at will with another, vicinal word-universe—a flexible, both dissonant and consonant adhesion and bunching or play of tones and their over- and undertones, of words and their over- and under-words. A playing with words in the "heraldic" situ-ating, the dance, of meanings and sounds, joining the innermost body's dance.

Words, or aggregates of words, when explained by other words or aggregates of words, are *posited each upon each other,* the overlapping residual contours remaining then alone free and pure, fragments unexplained.

Words are in play when, attracted by the serpent's appeal—perdition? safety?—they *journey* back, and all at once, to their common origins: words are not posited then one upon another, but each stands playfully close by each other—in closest and rapidly uncoiled vicinity to each other.

Words in play are birds in seasonal migration, whose flight forms one common unbirdlike "abstract" pattern—a moving "ornament"—across the sky.

The word *ornament* when explained by the word *nonrepresentational* or *abstract-expressionist* either overlaps the resulting explanation or is shrunk underneath it. When in play (the "sheer play of words," cause of our journey's interruption), they are in close, "hypnotic" vicinity of each other: ornament, in close vicinity of, say, "nonrepresentational" art, but *not* this art. For the word *vicinity* itself is part of the same "heraldic" play. We play with the word *vicinity* in closest vicinity both to the word *association* and to the word *configuration* or *Gestalt.* Association: that is, psychological succession—"ornament" in *association* with "nonrepresentational." Configuration: that is, psychological adhesion-bunching—"ornament" in *adhesion* to "nonrepresentational."

Here, and in play, with no attempt to explain mind's primary operation of knowing or of judgment at all, we find ourselves in closest vicinity to the word *judgment,* the latter in its turn situ-ating itself in immediate vicinity to the two apparently opposite words *creativity,* or creative function, and *criticism,* or critical function, in man. A truly rare occasion of play, where the co-vibration of overtones, common to the harmonic triad or chord of both dissenting and consenting tone-words, can be registered.

Indeed: judgment is both evaluation and justification of its object-value—without their co-presence judgment is without existence: evaluation, that is to say readiness to reject; justification, readiness to accept. To reject what? To accept what? Precisely and at first: the vicinity of the word *readiness* itself. But readiness can only mean here readiness to reject or to accept that which is still new, totally new, unpredicted because unpredictable, a form new, not yet known, thus *monstrous* (here the "comic") in regard to the already known—truly a creation.

Readiness to accept is readiness to meet the coming of a monster, which, unpredictable yet expected, cannot but be the very readiness to create the new—the creative function itself.

And at the vicinity of the word *judgment,* readiness to reject cannot mean readiness to reject the not known, not judged yet: it simply means to be watchful over this very readiness to accept the monster, the new, the creation; it means the critical function in itself. Here, in the vicinity of the word *bottom*—judgment's bottom, or ocean's or history's or pre-split's—the "spontaneous" creative operation and the "structured" operation of criticism are in immediate vicinity to each other—almost reversible this time. We are nearing here, indeed, the vicinity of the word *discovery.* And when we find it—in the vicinity of spring's questioning all that preceded this word—we also reach the closest vicinity of our journey's goal: *amor intellectualis Dei* = ornament.

Ornament pure, loyal to origins; motion in itself; Paul Klee's "stroll for strolling's sake." Motion-litany:

Motion as *res-persona;*

Motion as vehicle of emotion, with neither profit-motive in it (emotion provoked), nor profit-goal for it (emotion explained, expressed, eliminated thus);

Motion-toy, the mysterious and playful toy of correspondence-substitution, of solitude-solidarity;

Motion as Aristotle's Prime Mover. And it is in the vicinity of this word-compound *Prime Mover* that we find suddenly the word *play* playing with the word *explanation* itself.

For when I say: Let the ornament be in the vicinity of what is truly mysterious, both as art and as a word, I am very close to adding this:

Let it be mysterious not only because any of the so-called "ornamental," say, linear elements in an "ornamental" ensemble could be traced back to some prehistoric, "mysterious" signalizations, a zigzag of the sky-god's destructive and creative thunderbolts, the horns of multi-phased moon-fertility; the multi-cross of stars' guiding orderliness, within and without man's will; the multi-petalled rosette of the scorching yet healing sun energy (all this, possibly, in the vicinity also of archaeological gossip, after all, with little play in it, little spring's planting in it, little discovery in it)—but because, precisely, of the word compound *Prime Mover*'s being in the vicinity of it. Prime Mover: Aristotle's cosmic "machine-tool," both body-detached and body-continued. At first—a continuous, "harmonious," rotary and concentric universe-cosmos; a tool-universe made of perfect circles—the revolving zones of heavenly bodies, each included in the others, according to the degree of the desire of "perfection" that each of these circles or mobile astral zones embodies. But dominating entirely this simplified rotary scheme of continued circles—either circles-within-circles or separate circles—there stands, both watching and acting, the discontinued, because independent, and separate, because immediate, principle-machine of motion and life: the famous Prime or First Mover of Aristotle's *Physics.* The entire complex of turning wheels is revealed, thus, as the result of a graduated transmission of an original mobility, and this transmission finishes or culminates logically in what is called *a thing moved by itself,* Aristotle's First Heaven from where all movement starts and within which we must discern a principle of movement in itself physically immobile, thus discontinued. It is true, this

Prime Mover, as the First Heaven is also called by Aristotle, creates the motion of all other heavenly circles *inasmuch* as his own intelligence or will invites him to do so. Thus, ultimately, in Aristotle's *Metaphysics* the "thing moved by itself" is still moved by something else, but by something that is not a body any more, not a physical but an absolute "spiritual" entity: Aristotle's God, the Supreme Discontinuity and the Supreme Continuity at once.[21]

But—and here is where play and explanation are in final, if accidental, vicinity to each other—Aristotle himself being in the vicinity of Greece's incessant urge to transfer the meaning of the word *universe-cosmos* to the word *universe-man,* the cosmic Prime Mover becomes a human Prime Mover, seen and felt by the human eye: ornament, vehicle of human emotion, the "mnemonic" circular continuity of movement-grace in art, and the immediacy of a "mobile" discontinuity, "mobile" rigidity.

This entire gearing of words in play, a play *ad infinitum,* unseizable, can now be seized—within the confines of our eye's self-search or journey—in the precise vicinity of the word *substitution:* transferred *in toto* to the truly mysterious word *journey.* Thus, I say: Let the word *journey* be another name for spring, and a journey be the discovery of a journey: a journey that begins.

THE READER: Let's go.

❖❖❖❖❖❖❖❖❖❖❖❖❖❖❖❖❖❖❖❖❖❖❖❖❖❖❖❖❖❖

And the journey into the eye begins.

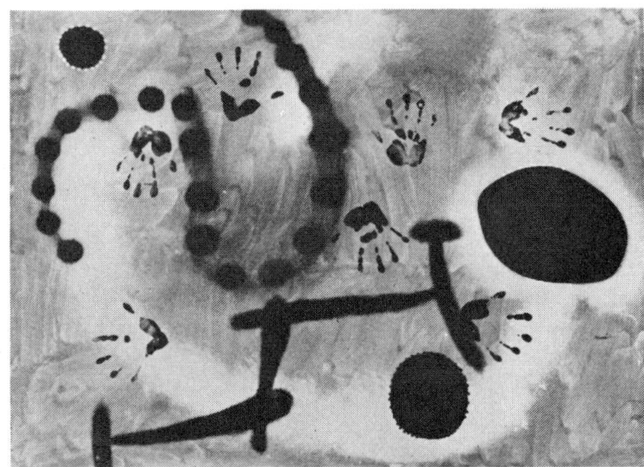

123 JOAN MIRO *Hope Returning* . . . . (1954)

Cosas veredes o Cid!

We have made a very long and a very strange voyage into the eye. I say we, because I was not alone in this adventure: my reader—the watcher—was with me. And he it was who asked me to start with the visit to all the places he had only read about: the places of the ghost's conversation, places of innermost body and thought *in autumn:* places of my lady Iwai's home, the home of innermost body and thought *in winter.* So we did; and only then continued our innermost road of spring. It was a long and strange voyage. But we came back in safety—as the poet said: "The Light of the Lord lies upon the Souls of the humble."[22]

And now we shall tell you—rapidly and in simplified mode—what we saw, or rather what was given to us to be seen there.

First Adventure:

> *Painting is an activity, and the artist will therefore tend to see what he paints rather than to paint what he sees. . . . The innocent eye is a myth. . . . For seeing is not just registering. It is the reaction of the whole organism to patterns of light that stimulate the back of our eyes.*[23]

When we reached the depth where the eye is almost sincere we saw this:

The immediate act or operation by which the eye seizes the outer world is made of two moments or stages, the mutual relation of which cannot be described either as a succession or as a simultaneity, but—similar in this respect to any construction of life—as an uninterrupted jet of one from the other, as a mutual completion. Two moments, two fundamental stages of the eye's labor: the *stage of synthesis* and the *stage of analysis.*

The stage of synthesis: the world of sight is given there as an *immediately expressive* totality, a block, a mass, a synthesis. Within this mass—a still amorphous but expressive mass—within this whole-block, all the particular form-elements are not yet expressed statically or plastically; they are not yet organized there, but *are organizing* themselves, following the general outline, or the synthetic direction of lines, colors, surfaces. It is an *irregular,* a *free* outline where all the ulterior plastic possibilities of the whole = synthesis are forming precisely that psychological frame which is called the visual apperception. (You are walking in the street. A passing face arrests your attention for a second. An unknown face of a stranger; an unknown look on that face. And, suddenly, you *see*—not only look at—this *look,* you apprehend it, you grasp—behind this look—unfailingly, and for yourself exclusively, intimately, the truth of a character, still void of precise acts or gesture; you capture the block, the totality of a personal expression where all the ulterior possibilities of a particular expressive act are given or offered to you, without being yet determined. Or, you are suddenly placed in front of an unknown building or a landscape, never seen before; you are suddenly introduced to a never-seen-before home: at first, the expressive whole of the given, its novelty, its *singularity,* is apprehended by you, before any detail might fix or parcel out your attention.)

It is a frame or a framing, a defining, all the same. This synthetic outline thus *hooks on to* another psychological universe, where the visual forms are already fully organized according to definite spatial rules, laws of matter, laws of geometry. That is how—continuation or completion?—the synthetic world gives way to, or is transformed into, an opposite universe: the analytic stage of the eye. Here, it is the particular, the detailed, that emerges, establishes and expresses itself at once and clearly: the seriated stability of a detailed, definite, clearly delimited—geometrized—form. (An object is perceived, any object: a stone, a hand, this flower or that leaf. How—in all sincerity!—how can we, by this visual act, comprehend *visually* the complex yet precise organization in space of this object, the external aspect of precisely this stone, or this leaf or that hand, were we not at the same instant already prepared, so to speak, or, rather, forced to this comprehension by the *labor rules* or the function of an innate geometry of the eye: the organizing labor or function of lines and curves, a certain harmony—a selected togetherness—of circles, various angles, ellipses, etc.?)[24]

Thus, the stage of synthesis is unity and multiplication all at once: all at once potential multiplicity and actual, global unity.

The stage of analysis is unity also, because it is connection between form-parts, a connection realized by geometrical rules which introduce there the narration of the visual world, its *legibility,* its *clarity;* it is also multiplicity because it reveals the individual integrity of each of those form-parts. We may define as follows:

Synthesis: not connection but adhesion; not stability, but *continuity, mobility,* absolute fullness of our visual contents, and thus inevitable "deformation" of the latter.

Analysis: connection, distinction, framing, series, static presence; and thus, fidelity to the "objective" appearance of space-contents.

We might say: one is sympathy-fusion, pure eye-feeling, participation; the other attentiveness, pure eye-comprehension, judgment.

That is how—in a simultaneity of these two stages—the world of sight is given to us.

❖❖❖❖❖❖❖❖❖❖❖❖❖❖❖❖❖❖❖❖❖❖❖❖❖❖❖❖❖

My description of the eye's elemental act may or may not be accepted as a correct description. It does not matter here. For there is a universal and elemental principle of style which dominates the entire and accessible panorama of the history of representative arts, whose double nature and activity appear to us—*without any possible glossing interference on our part* —as corresponding to what I described to be the double nature and activity of the eye: synthesis and analysis, mobility-continuity and stability-discontinuity.

As far as our historical perception can reach the past within the depth of time, we can infallibly ascertain that there have always existed, embodied in a given historical "style" or cycle, an art-mobility and an art-stability. There has always existed an art based on the dynamic and *deformative* togetherness of form-parts: an object-block, an object-"monster," the "bestiary" complex, for instance, of the "barbarians"—or ex-"barbarians"—Scythians, Sarmatians, Germans, etc. *(Plate 124),* or the frame-attraction, the frame-"hypnosis" of a Romanesque architectural ensemble *(Plate 125);*[25] or the animal-and-plant "mobile" inter-formation in an Iranian-Islamic "Gabri" ceramic piece *(Plate 126).* And there has always existed also an art based on the clear, seriated, plastically analyzed narrative quality of the visually observable space: the art of classical Greece, the art of classical China.

Stage of eye's analysis: art-narration; motion-stability; unity = connection between form-parts.

Stage of eye's synthesis: art-mimicry; motion-mobility; unity = adhesion of form-parts.

It is here, precisely, in the close vicinity of our own enjoyment (rather than of our communication), that the technical ability of art criticism on

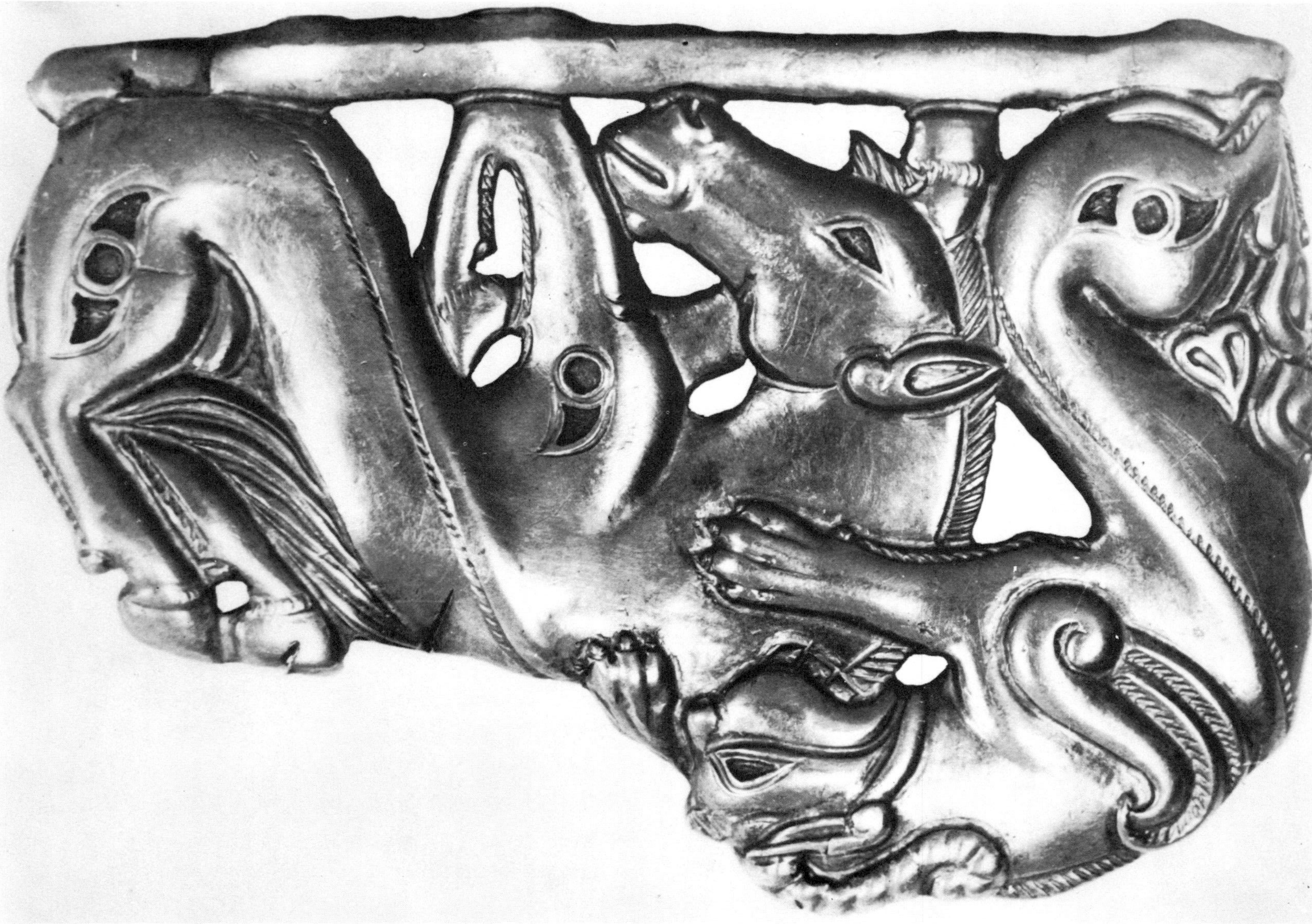

124. Scytho-Sarmatian Plaque (2nd century B.C.)

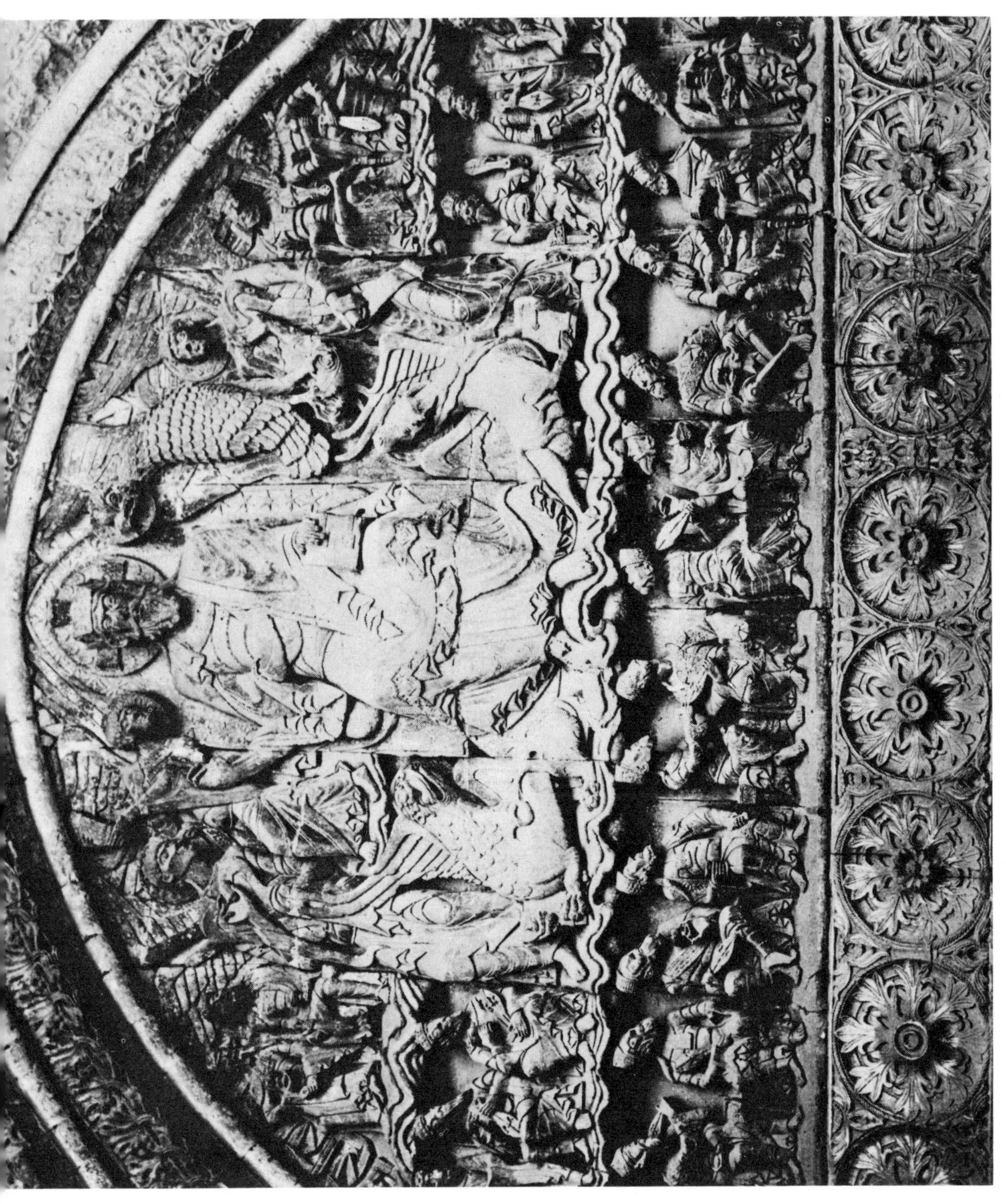

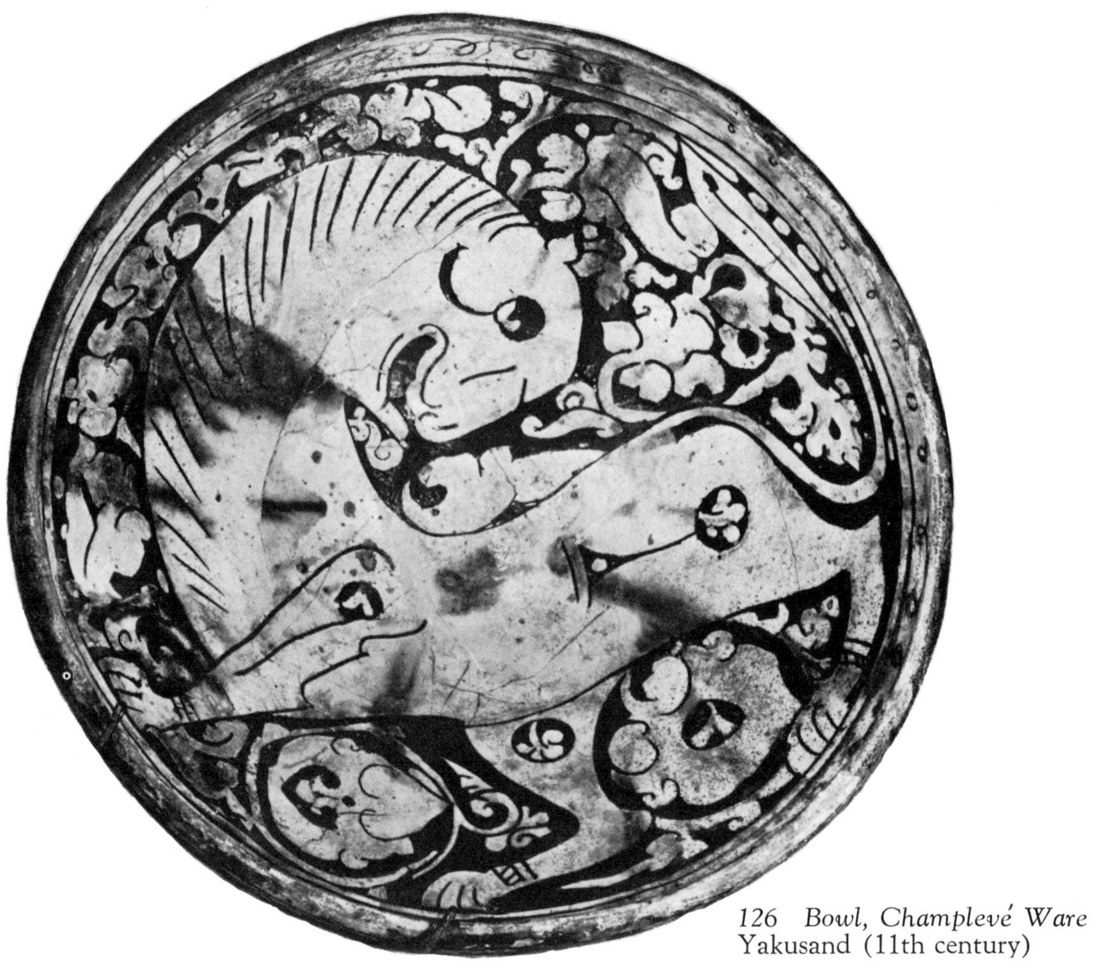

126 Bowl, Champlevé Ware
Yakusand (11th century)

the *what of the how* level situ-ates its own checking device. Namely: that within this frame of motion's two general divisions, movement-stability, movement-mobility, each of the two contains a second pair of subtler subdivisions: art's "mnemonic," structured, movement = grace, impression's idiom; art's movement = immediacy, the given, sudden, thus "mobilized" rigidity of a just-opened dike,[26] sensation's idiom.

That is to say, the behaviour of forms in space—their e-motion—can still reveal itself as "stability" in spite of the apparent, optical-discursive intercontinuity of their rhythms and themes, or, even when an apparent rigidity-obliquity is singled out there by us, as possibly "mobile" (a much more sophisticated distinction to be watchful over, already resulting from our eye's awakening to the possibility of a dikelike mobilization of the immobile itself or the arrested-stable). Both rhythmic systems would belong here to the art-stability, art-narration, when the essential elements of an image-compound (the representational or nonrepresentational subject-theme and its background, its beyond-theme, its "landscape") are represented as seriated, clearly delineated, *connected*—mnemonically—with each other, rather than *adhered to* within each other.

Similarly, yet in opposite direction, rhythms and themes either continuous-circular or discontinuous-oblique will belong to the world of art-mobility, when their interconnections, rather inter-adhesions, form one block-continuum, a new "monster"-block, the deforming immediacy of adhesion's preserve.

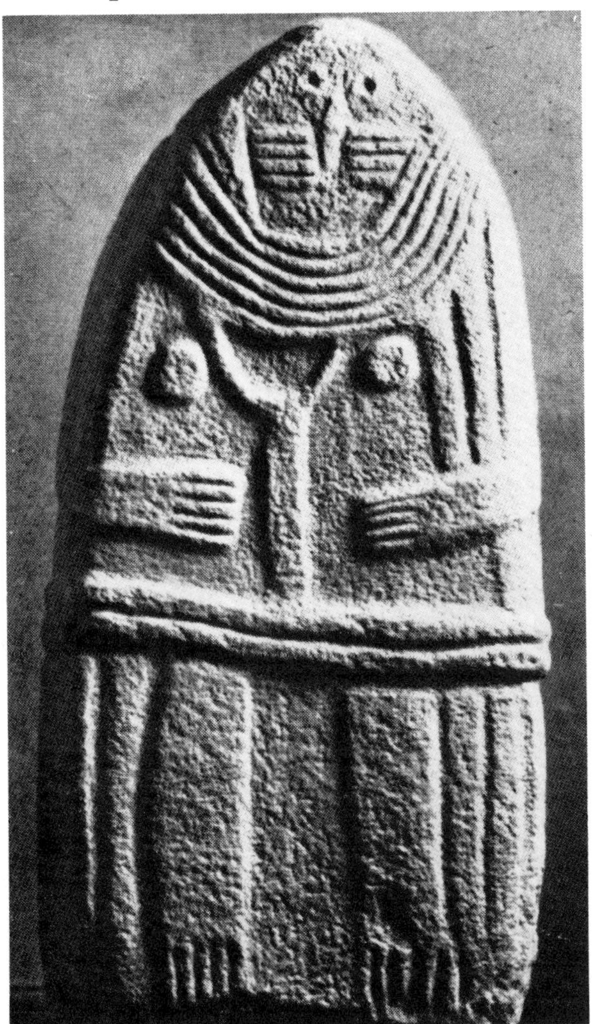

127 *Menhir* from Les Vidals, Tarn, France

Of course—and this is life's command everywhere—there cannot be a pure "mobile" style or "mentality" and a pure "stable" style or "mentality": style is always a certain equilibrium between both, equilibrium achieved under the hegemony of one of these two elemental stages of visual reality. There is a marked, and not an exclusive or absolute, tendency toward stability, toward narrative clarity and precision in the hallucinating close-to-things "naturalism" of the late Paleolithic. There is a marked tendency toward "mobility," toward "irregular" wholeness, toward block-conception in the so-called Neolithic art continuum. Here already is introduced that richly consequential techtonic o r g a n i z a t i o n—unknown to the Paleolithic—which, probably running parallel to analogous developments in social organization (and particularly in speech), consisted in a calculated adhesion of all the parts or elements of the whole of an object to the general frame or silhouette of this whole It is this "mobile" and "deforming" adhesion that precisely visualizes the magic-astral-sexual meaning of a Neolithic idol *(Plate 127)*, exactly as it will much later vivify a Romanesque sculpture or an Islamic-Iranian ornament. And why—generally speaking—is the Bronze Age so "stable"; why "mobile," the Iron Age? Did the Paleolithic and its art experience disappear entirely, submerged by the Neolithic "invasion," or could this culture persist historically, yet humbly, as a kind of fragmented, broken-up continuum, and then later re-appear in separated, yet "stylistically" interconnected zones of the "Bronze" culture: the Aegean ensemble, early Egypt, Sumer-Akkad, "Dravidian" India, etc.? How and how far into the "Iron" Age, along which of the two great directions, north or south, of the Euro-Asian historical cultural complex could the influence—if influence or diffusion there was—of the Neolithic revolutionary device penetrate? Essential historical questions—still mysterious for us. Be that as it may, the artistic destiny of both Europe and Asia is made of the interaction of the two basal and formative currents: "mobile" art-mimic and "stable" art-narration.

It is the art of stability, of spatial clarity, a rich and complicated yet legible imagery of logical poise, accessibility, and inventiveness; a powerful aesthetic tendency which ruled (in different or differently localized degrees of intensity, thus not totally excluding the opposite tendency) the art of Egypt throughout its entire history, the art of Greece, even the Hellenistic art, the art of Sumer, of Akkad, of Assyria. Facing it, the other current, northern, the current of "mobile" law, which from about the eighth-seventh centuries B.C., embraced a vast geographical area stretching from Mongolia and North China, through Siberia to the Caucasus and South Russia.[27]

❖❖❖❖❖❖❖❖❖❖❖❖❖❖❖❖❖❖❖❖❖❖❖❖❖❖❖❖❖❖

Thus we have two currents, two general, universal currents of human art. Among several more or less achieved and equally valuable "cyclic" solutions of the necessary synthesis-equilibrium of the two currents, among several great historical "styles," we have seen those few which seem to have expressed or realized this synthesis-equilibrium in the most typified and factually convincing way: the medieval art of the West, France, *par excellence;* the art of Japan; and in-between, the art of Islam, of Iran, *par excellence.* Hence the deep and real affinities between them. Indeed, emerging from this elemental duality of eye, and rooted historically in the mechanism of inner diffusion—often invisible or forgotten, yet organically active —of an identical "stable" or "mobile" ancestral culture, strange and unexpected stylistic similarities have been revealed to us. Art objects removed from each other both in time (distant periods) and space (distant geographical areas) sometimes become "stylistically" close to each other, deeply "mobile" or deeply "stable," reflecting, in this very similarity, correlative similarity of collective attitudes toward life, religion, morals, politics, etc.[28]

❖❖❖❖❖❖❖❖❖❖❖❖❖❖❖❖❖❖❖❖❖❖❖❖❖❖❖
❖❖❖❖❖❖❖❖❖❖❖❖❖❖❖❖❖❖❖❖❖❖❖❖❖❖❖❖❖❖

Here, at the crossing of several roads, we stopped for a while, in great amazement at the revelation of sudden, unexpected similarities, unrecognizable at the level of the *what* and the level of the *how.* Greatly intrigued also by what we already guessed the new *persona dramatis* of our journey, the pictorial art of Islam, would have to offer us, we boldly decided—was it mine, was it the reader's decision?—to leave our old and chosen road and to follow the one that opened right there, later to join again the other.

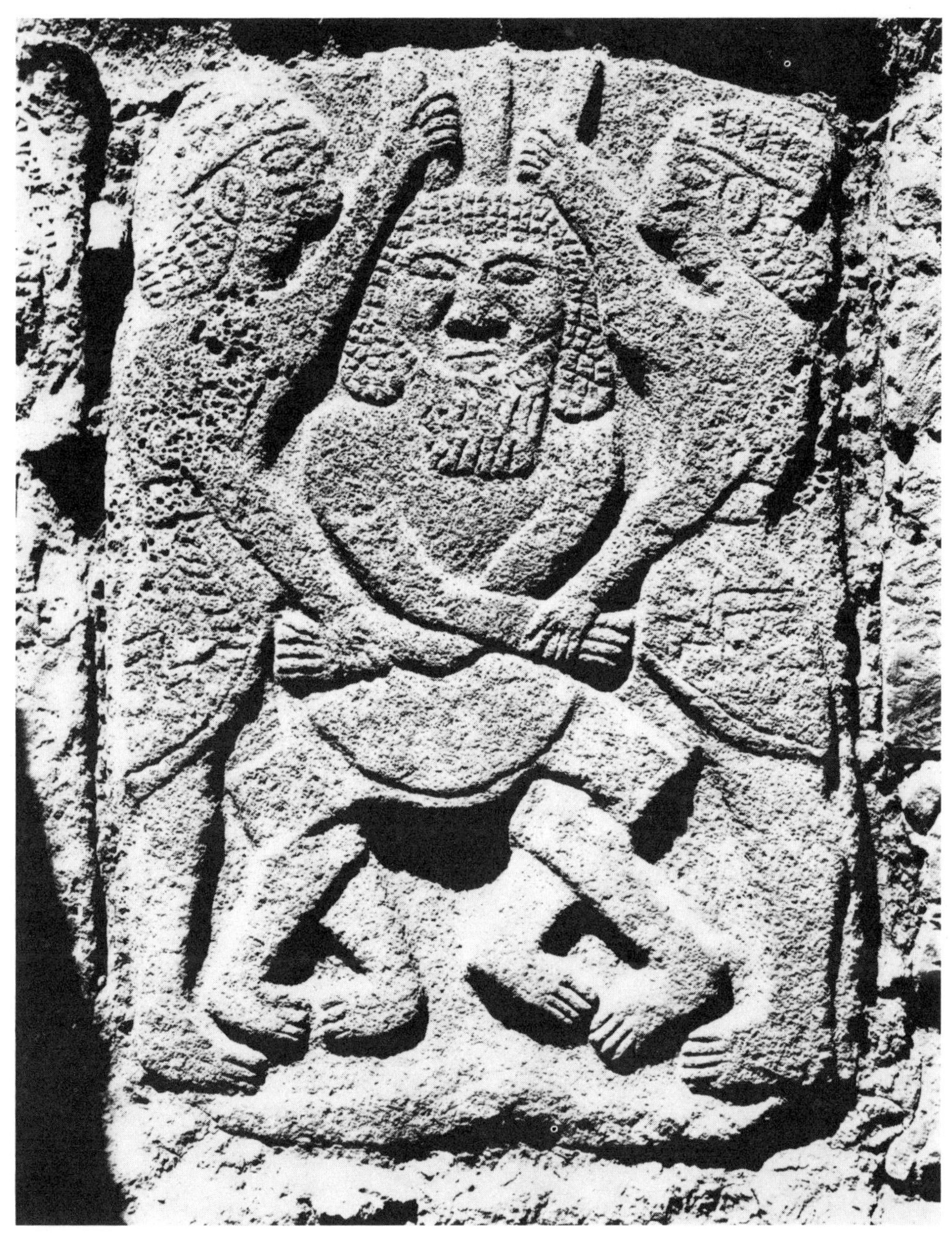

128 *Khuvava Slain by Gilgamesh and Engidu* (9th century B.C.)

Islam: the heir to the entire ancient Near East and to the West as well, with all their tremendous, inherent tensions and struggles, now for the supremacy of one of the two planetary principles of visual thought, now for their synthesis-equilibrium. And we saw, as in a dream of condensed and abstract splendor, alien to life's closer anxieties, an immense unrolling of history's events = attitudes. Here was Mesopotamia, its southern, Sumer-

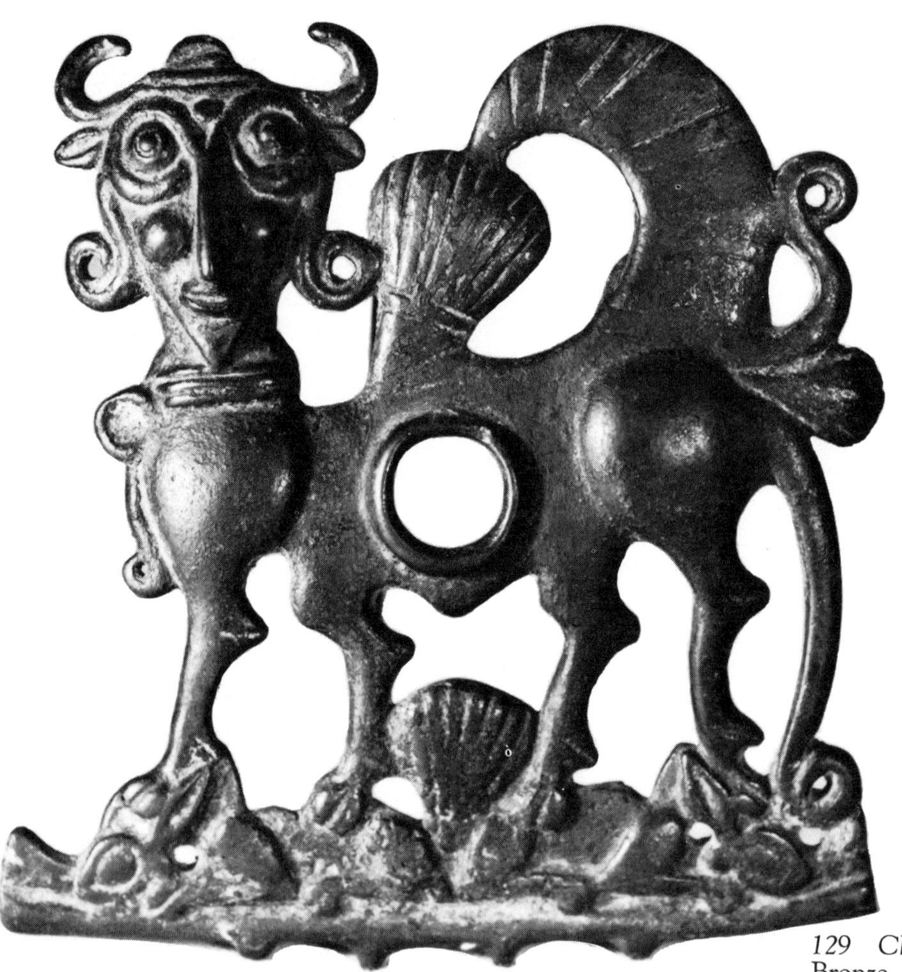

129 Cheek plaque of Bit
Bronze, Luristān
2nd-1st millenium B.C.

Akkadian "stability" facing the "mobility" of the northern—the Syro-Anatolian, "Hittite," zone *(Plate 128)*: Assyria partaking greedily, yet imaginatively, of both. Then: the first, properly Iranian international civilization, the Achaemenian (c. 550 B.C.—c. A.D. 330) in whose shaping—added to what the predominant "stability" of the Two Rivers' Bronze world, of Elam, of Egypt, even of Greece, had contributed—the "mobile" art of cultures more marginal, although not less powerful in historical impact, had played an ineffaceable role: the mountain region of Zagros, separating Mesopotamia from the Iranian Plateau, the zone of the so-called Luristān art *(Plate 129)*;[29] the near-Caspian and the outer or East Iran of pre-Islamic Central Asia.

Clear, legible, seriated, appeared to us the majestic processional imagery of the Persepolitan stone reliefs: poise, energy, rhythm-connection, consistency, smoothly presented plastic truth. Yet, underneath this narration, a secret and restless eloquence of "mobile" presence sometimes penetrated the voices of poise and serenity with a sudden—hence the more convincing "barbarian" beauty *(Plates 130, 131)*.

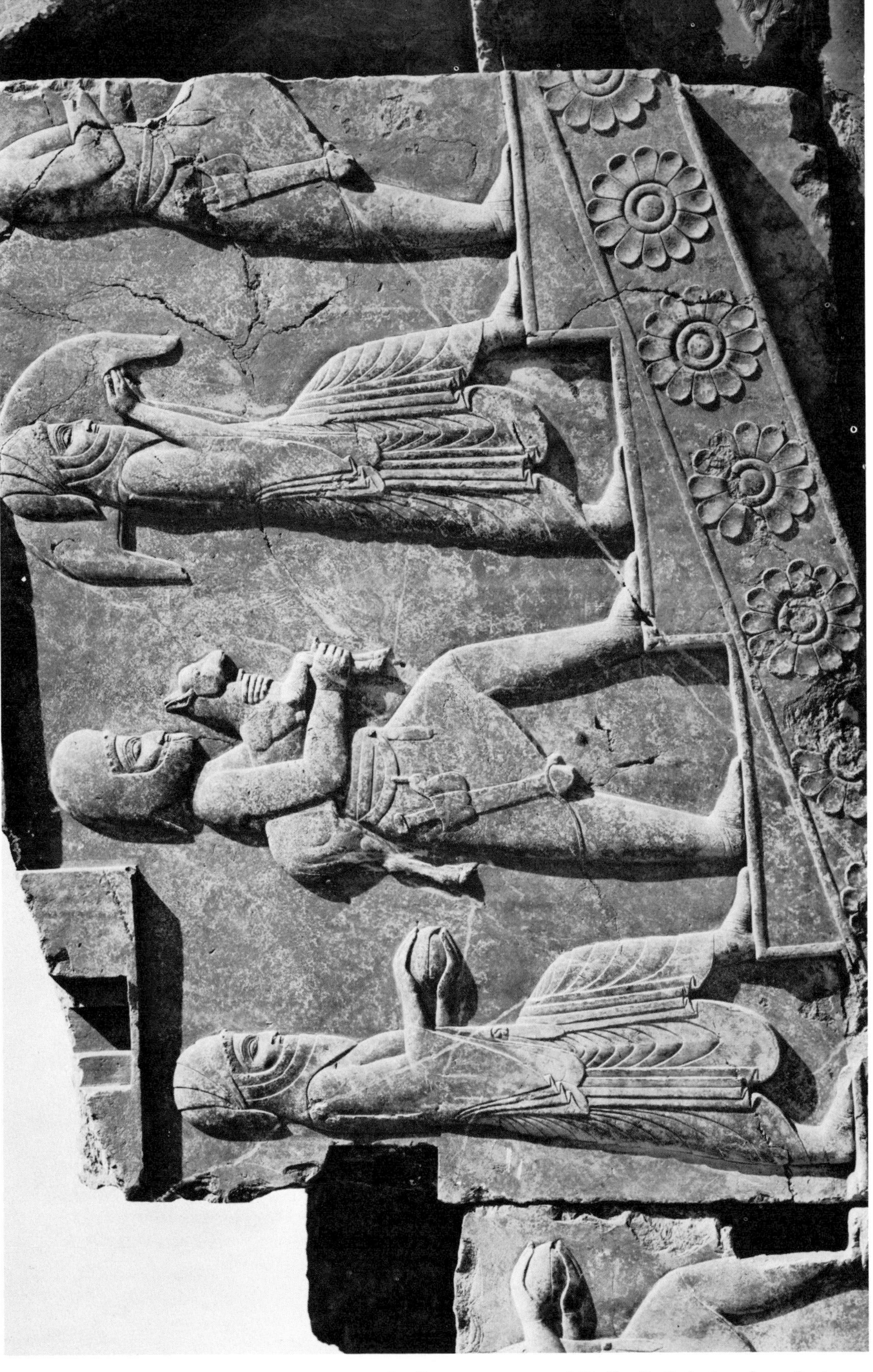

130 *Procession of Gift Bearers* Persepolis: Palace of Darius (late 6th-early 5th century B.C.)

(overleaf) 131 *Lion and Bull* Relief, Apadana Stairway Persepolis Terrace, Iran (late 6th-early 5th century B.C.)▶

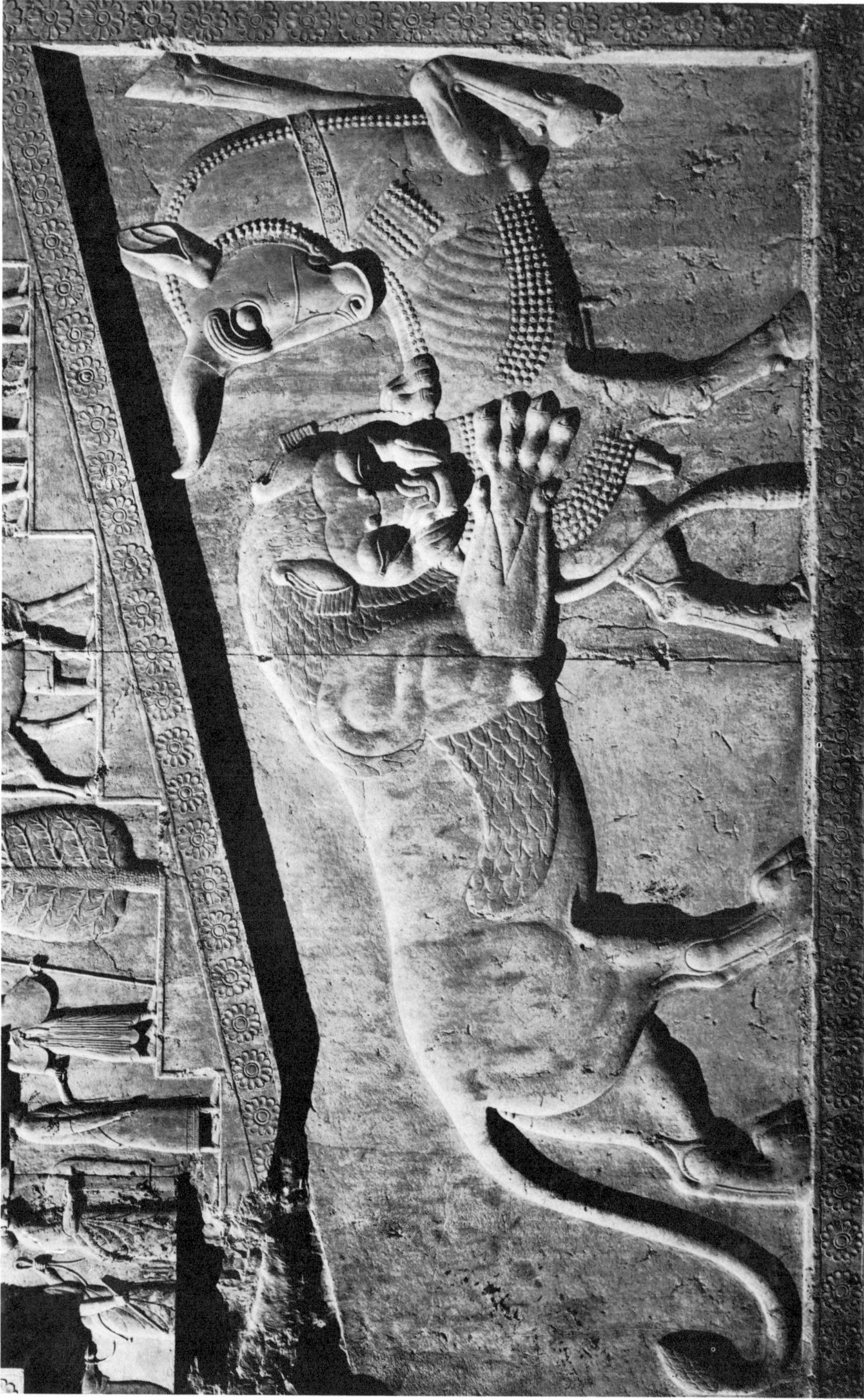

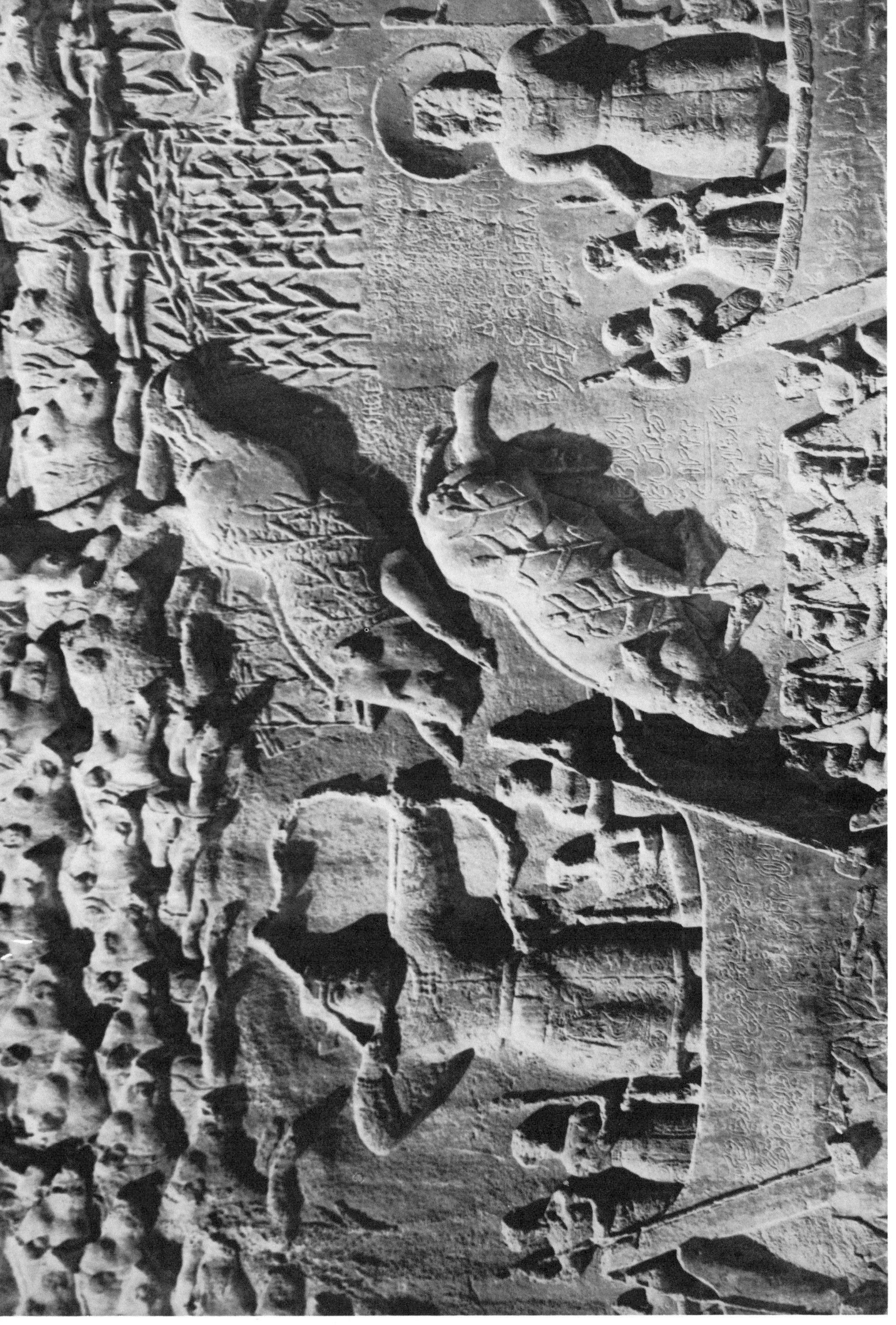

The inner drama of the Parthian art (c. 249 B.C.—c. A.D. 226) is still a mystery for us. Torn between the new loyalty to Hellenistic canon and the old loyalty to its ancestral steppe art-"mobility," long forgotten, submerged at first, then growing intenser and intenser in its impact and presence, this art, still so little known, is more than any other in closest vicinity to the drama of Islam itself.

The Sassanian art (c. 226—c. 642) appears at first "stable," majestic, both simplified and impetuous: so is the movement and the plastic consistency of the hunted animal masses on the reliefs of Taq-i-Bustān *(Plate 132)*; of the royal glories sculpted on the rocks of Naqsh-i-Rustam or Shapur, of the royal hunting prowess on the sumptuous silver vessels. But the most decisive moment or episode of the Iranian drama of synthesis is toward the end of this era, when, among the tumult, the last glamour of the aristocratic pride and the growing inner misery, political and social, the "northern" aesthetic formula began more and more to impose its "mobile" law, became more and more predominant. A new (provincial?) style arose: the late or immediately post-Sassanian silver plates with strange, "monstrous" images of interlaced animals and parts of animals, animals and plants fused in restless, "romanesque" ensembles *(Plates 133, 134)*. What happened?[30]

We can notice in history this very curious phenomenon: the decadence of an imperial civilization usually coincides with the renaissance of its deeply rooted popular ideology, an ideology submerged under the upper levels of the huge sociological structure. This historical phenomenon of decadence-renaissance—often realized with violence—must also have been the physiognomy of the late Sassanian Dynasty.[31] However, the Sassanian renaissance of the "popular," folklore ideology—still perforce unfinished—partially reflected in art, was but the eve of a real renewal. The great day was brought by a new and yet expected power: Islam.[32]

❖❖❖❖❖❖❖❖❖❖❖❖❖❖❖❖❖❖❖❖❖❖❖❖❖❖❖❖❖❖❖

And it was shown to us how great and central was the role of Iran—this vast being, so elastic in its political-geographical boundaries, and embracing in its cultural radiations, at many crucial moments of Asia's history, the entire Near as well as Central East—in the enactment of Islam's drama of growth and maturation.

The early history of Islam in Iranian countries is still an illegible page. Why, in the first place, was the Muhammadan conquest so sudden and rapid there; and in the second place, what is the meaning and the effect of the tenacious resistance in the Caspian zone of Iran: Dailam, the Greater Dailam of the medieval Islamic writers?[33]

The following explanation, synthetic, yet historically verifiable, might be suggested: The essentially democratic Islam must have appeared at first as a redeemer to the horribly oppressed Sassanian masses;[34] while it was the greatest enemy of the Sassanian feudal aristocracy. The truth of the former supposition is attested by the explosions of popular anti-feudal revolts, having both agrarian and urban-artisan bases, with which the first centuries of Islam are filled;[35] the truth of the latter, by the revival, likewise

◀(overleaf)

132 Tāq-I-Bustān Detail, rock reliefs, *Boar Hunt of Khusraw II* (6th-7th centuries)

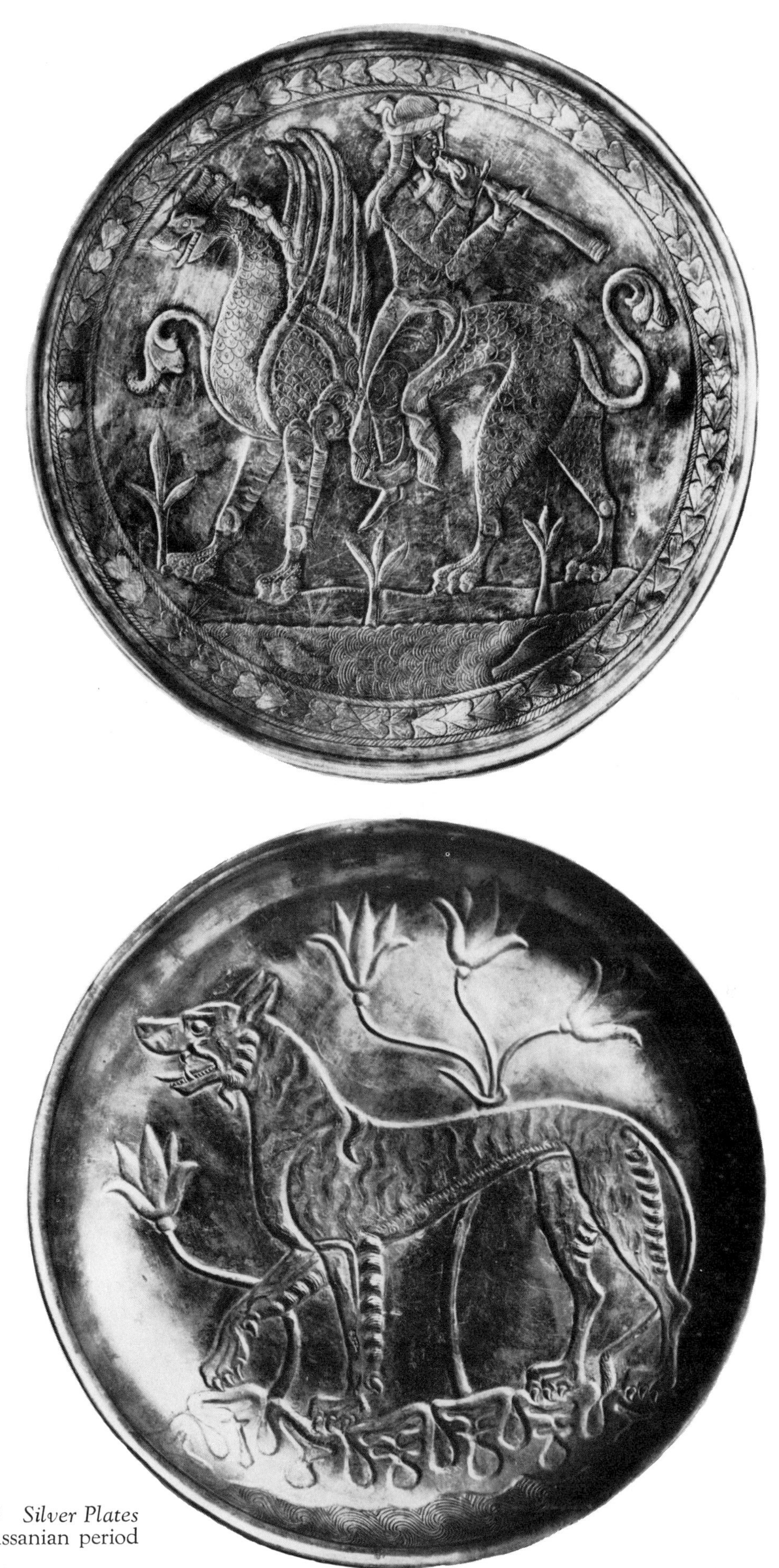

133, 134 Silver Plates
Late or post-Sassanian period

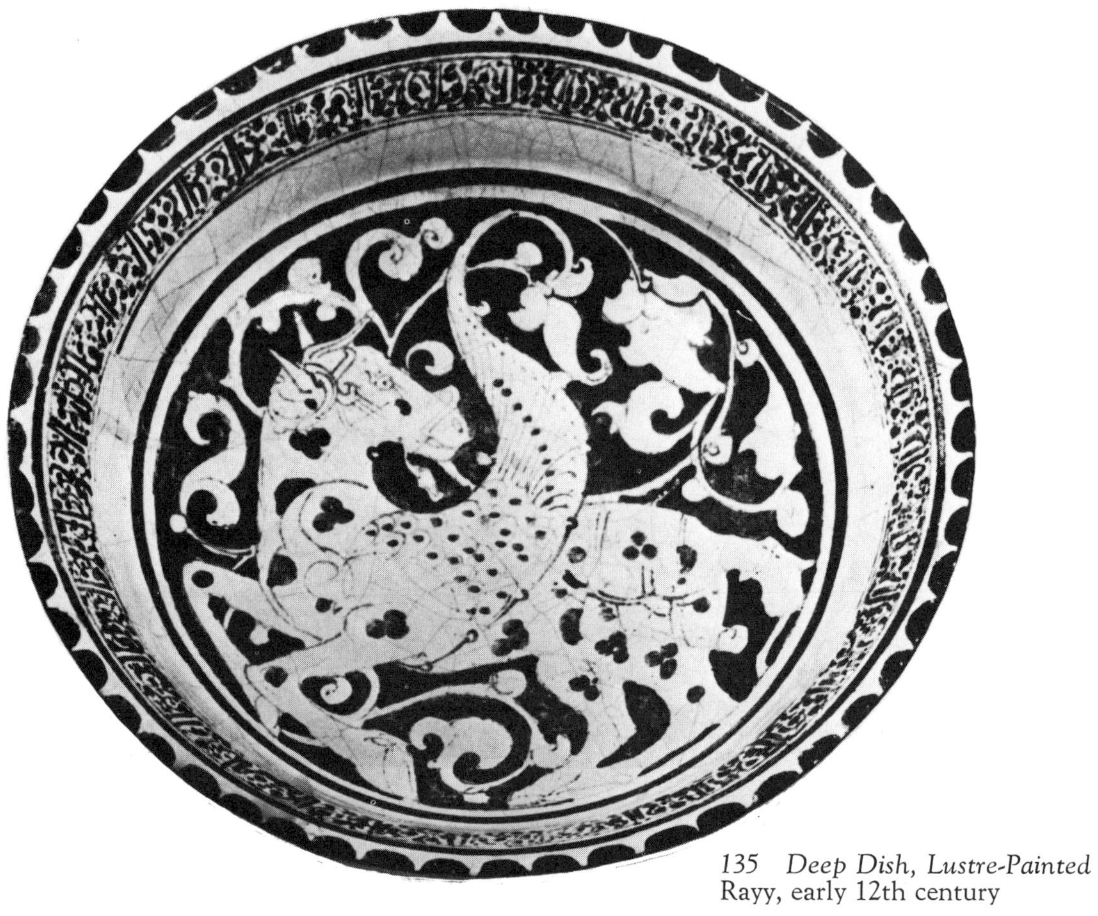

135 *Deep Dish, Lustre-Painted*
Rayy, early 12th century

revolutionary, of Sassanian religious-imperialistic ideals among the refugee aristocrats.

And it is in the near-Caspian provinces, the very crucible of Iranian destiny, that this double aspect of the deep Iranian traditions was most intensively fulfilled—at first in its feudal-aristocratic form (under local rulers), and then in its popular form with the infiltration of Islam under the latter's altogether revolutionary (dissenting) aspect: Shiʿism.[36]

We know how deeply Iranian was Shiʿism, if not in its "external" origin (Arabic ethnically and politically), certainly in its immediate diffusion, acceptance, and development; and we can already guess how profoundly connected in its "inner" origin it must have been with the lowest levels of the Iranian social, economic, and ideological structure.[37] Can we possibly—against the teaching of history—imagine that this Iranian Islamic renaissance (spread all over the Islamic world) did not affect the corresponding artistic ideology of the period?

Indeed it was in those northern or close-to-northern Iranian regions (which included all the culturally fertile zones of southern Caucasus and northeastern Iran), and at the very heart of this renaissance, both cultural and political (the formation of great Iranian feudal monarchies between the ninth and eleventh centuries: the Samanids, the Buyids, etc.),

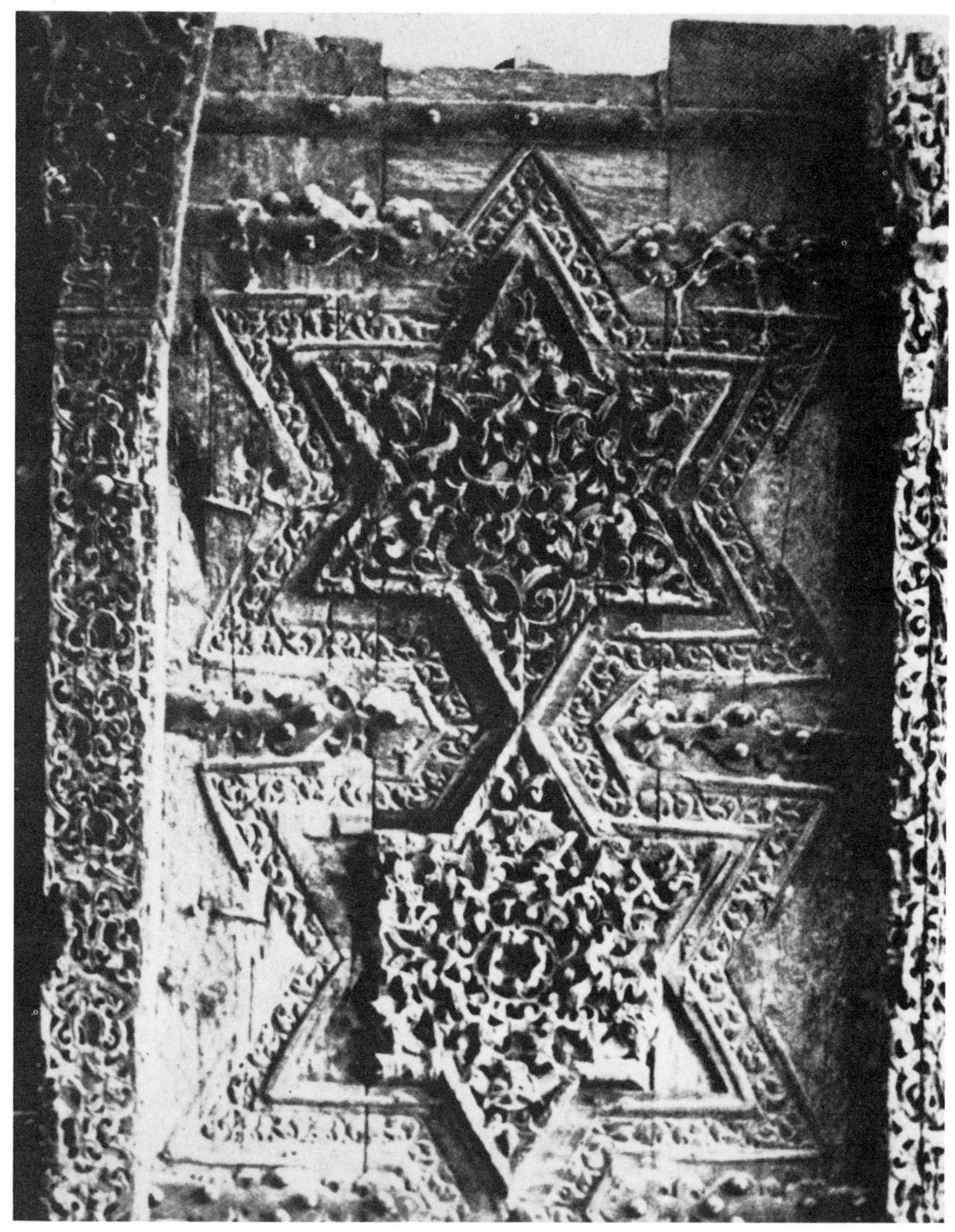

136 Wooden Door from Tomb of Mahmūd of Ghazni. Detail (ca. A.D. 1030)

that the "synthesis," the peculiar Iranian "equilibrium" was reached under the hegemony of the "mobile" law.

The Iranian Islamic "style" was born: the interlacing and systematically "deforming" animal-human, animal-and-plant style of the so-called "Gabri" pottery,[38] and related to it formally, all the ceramic art of other Iranian schools *(Plate 135)*, the ornamental architectural style of the "mobile" relief in stucco, wood *(Plate 136)*, brick, etc. The "personality" of Iran

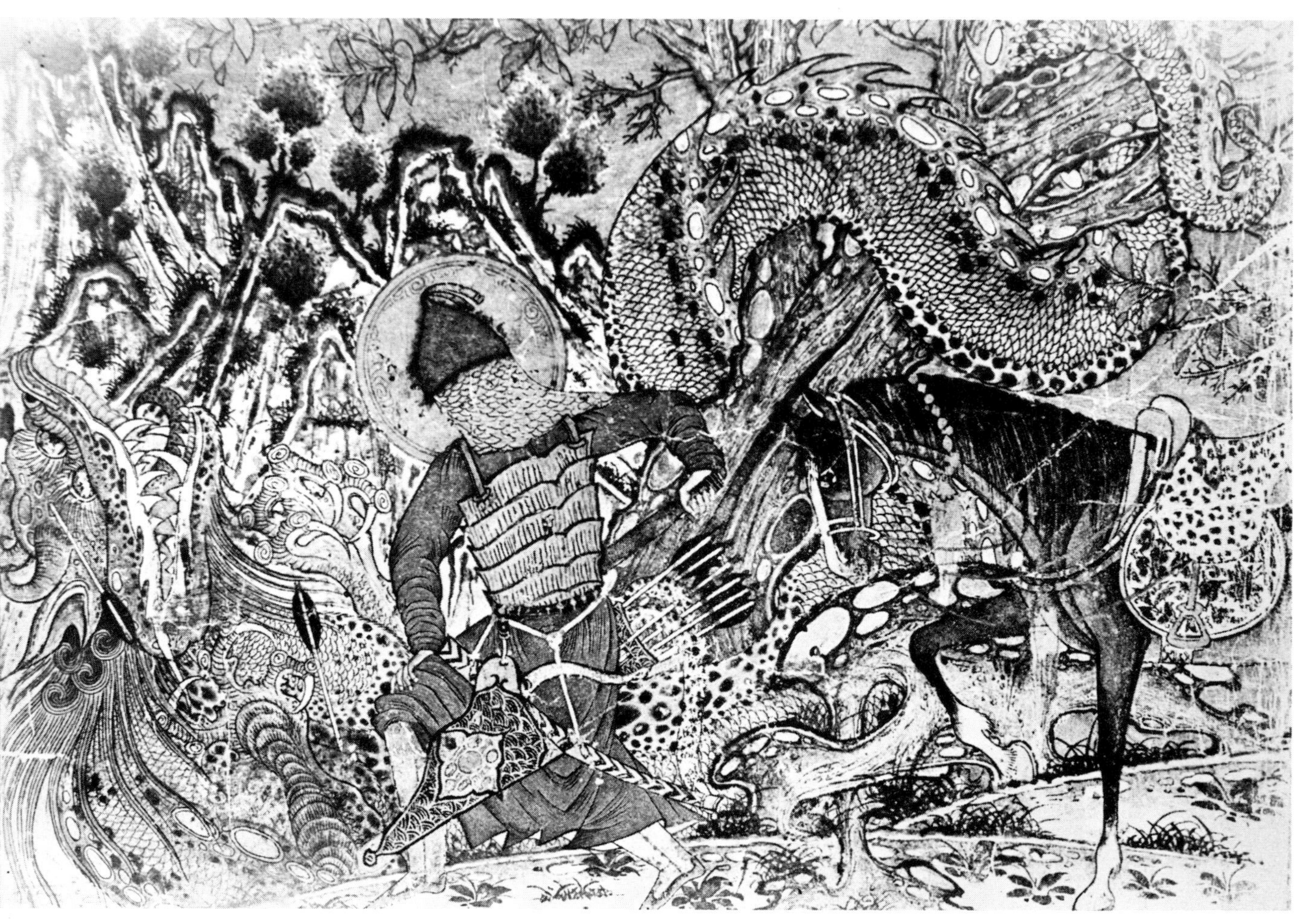

137 *Bahram Kills A Dragon* Page from Firdawsī, *Shah-Nameh* (Tabriz School, ca. 1340)

was formed, and all the subsequent periods of Iranian artistic destiny were the epic deeds of this same personality—this and no other. (It is of interest to note here the well-known fact that from the first Abbasid period—eighth-ninth centuries—through the two great successive waves of invasion—the Seljuq eleventh century and the Mongol thirteenth century—it was Central Asia, this still mysterious region with which the Scytho-Siberian culture must have had direct contact, that was a great source of artistic life for Iran, paralleling the European, Hindu, Egyptian, Chinese, and other influences.) But we must not forget the essential synthetic character of this personality: in all the artistic achievements or inventions of Islamic Iran there was an effort to attain a perfect fusion of the two antithetical psycho-historical tendencies. This effort at fusion is, basically, the whole imagery of Persia and her science of ornamentation.

It is in Iranian Islamic painting (book-painting, for that is principally what was left, undisturbed in its revelation, by the political cataclysms of Iranian history—the Mongol invasion in particular—and by the carelessness of men) that this is perhaps best revealed.

Two things stand out clearly at the very first approach to this art, especially of the most opulent (but not the "purest") period, the fifteenth and sixteenth centuries (the Timurid and particularly the beginning of the Safavid schools). One is the precision with which the shapes are silhouetted, and above all, the luminous tonal "stability" of their pure coloring; the second, and dominant, is the strange conception of space and perspective. This latter cannot be the result of technical ignorance. Intellectual curiosity and the advancement of mathematical science in Iran, the constant contact with the arts of other countries, especially of China and—more intensively and regularly since the Mongols—of western Europe, countries whose pictorial canons were directly opposed to those of Iran, make such a supposition inacceptable. The construction of perspective in Iranian painting is *determined:* it was the most dramatic visualization of the Iranian "mobile" equilibrium. Continuity, mutual "hypnotic" attraction, "romanesque" without-beginning-without-end wholeness of forms, all the bizarre language of pure eye-feeling is there. There already, in the thirteenth and fourteenth centuries Seljuq-Mongol (= Il-khanid) pictorial universe, an extremely complicated Syro-Mesopotamian-Iranian universe, where the resurrected voice of Asia's deepest past could make itself heard clearly and undoubtedly, in spite of other and younger voices, that of China, that of eastern Christianity.

Most glorious, unforgettable monuments of men's creativity: such, the "Morgan" Manāfi'al-Hayavān *(See Plate 98)*, such, the unrivalled, daring "Demotte" Shah Nameh![39] *(Plate 137)*.

In spite of its external, linear "stability," the Timurid-Safavid (fifteenth-seventeenth centuries) space remains inwardly the same "mobile" space. We know what this is in principle: at first, a "stable," static slipping of one perfectly flat surface into another, one behind or above the other, creating thereby a rich and highly decorative imagery, a fanciful depiction of the feudal life of those times. The floors of the royal halls, the palace gardens or the fields, are represented vertically on the first plane, and then, immedi-

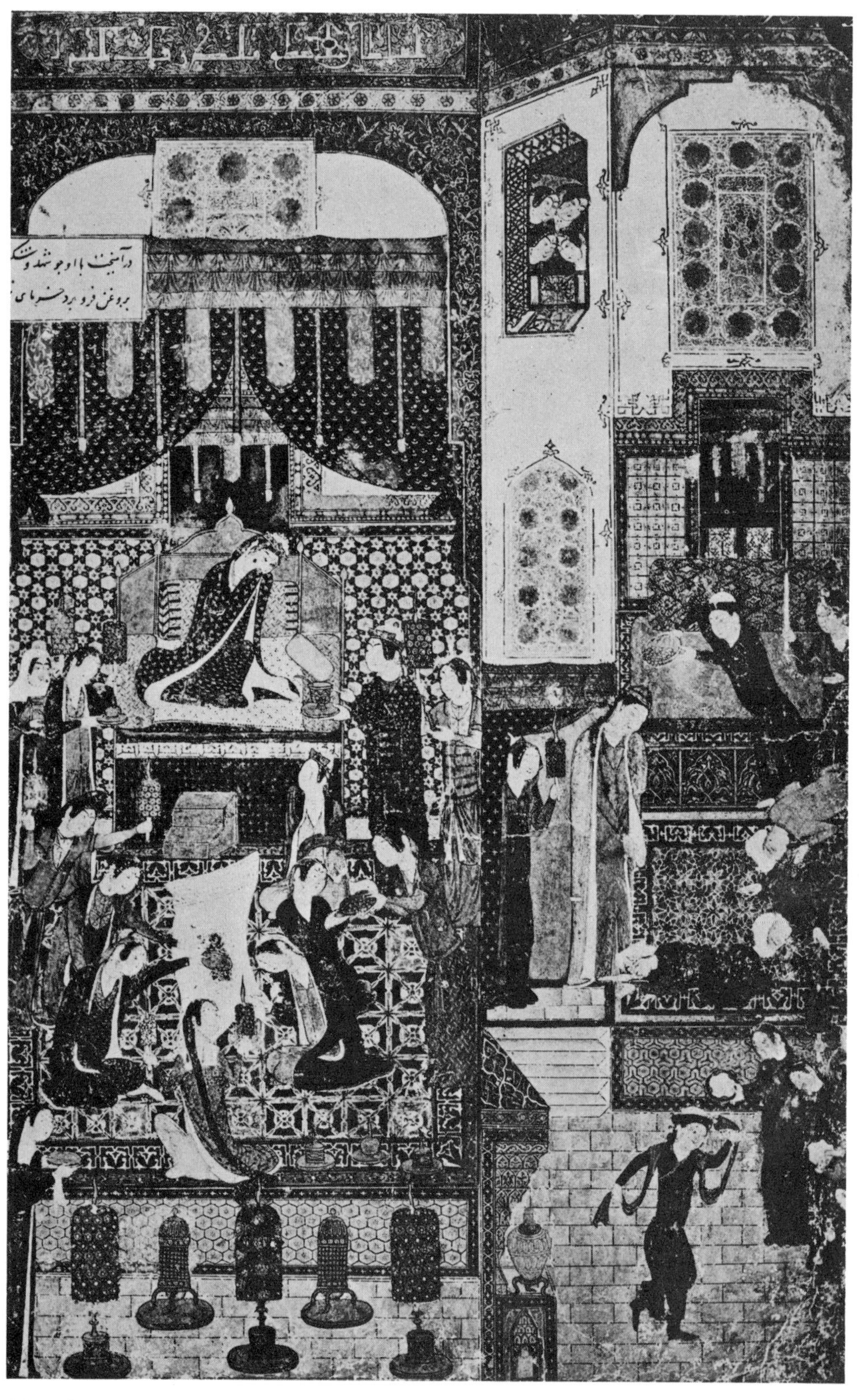

260

138 Junayd Naqqash Sultani *Wedding Celebrations of Prince Humay and Princess Humayun* (Baghdad, 1396)

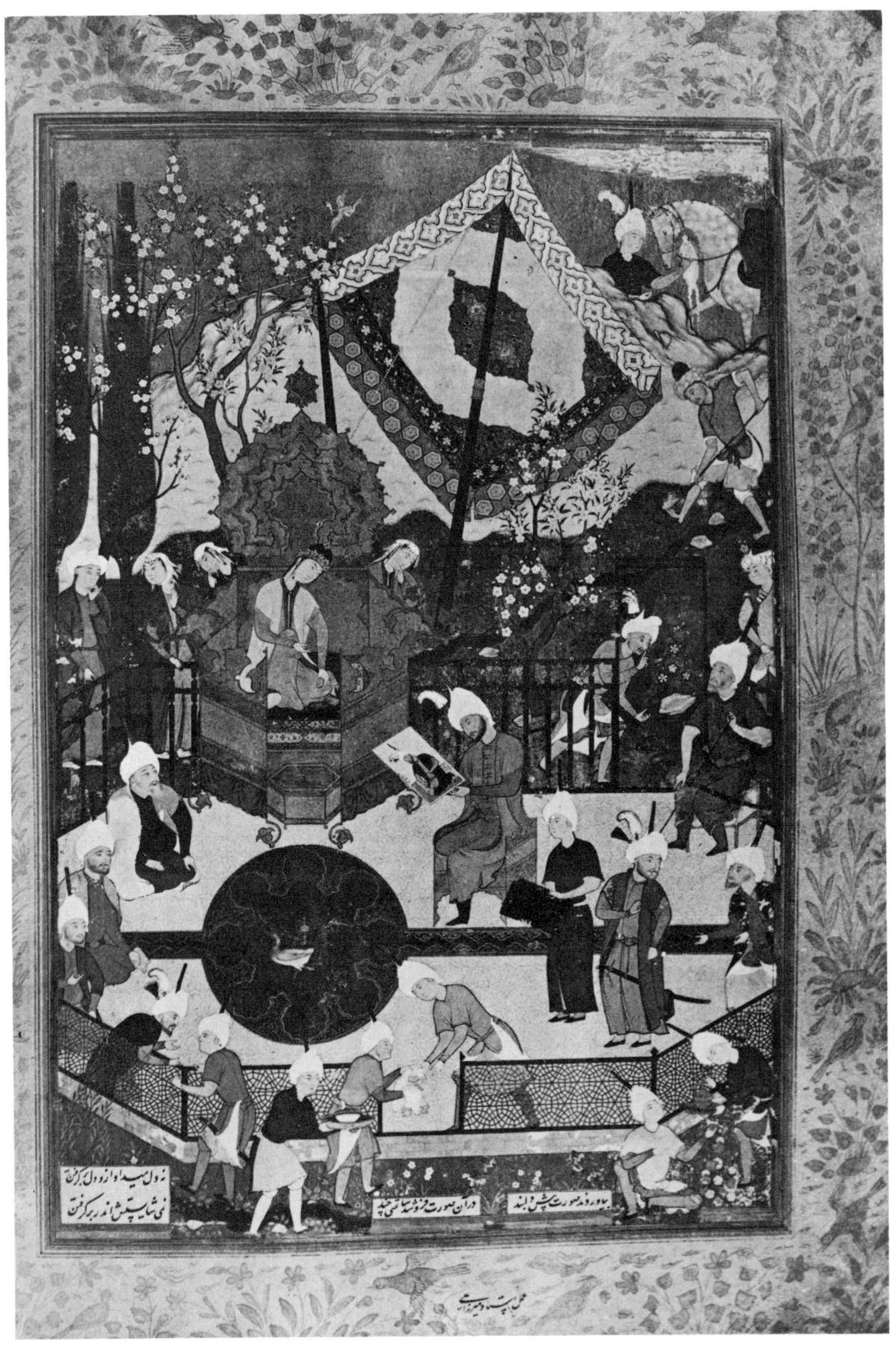

139 Mirza Ali *The Painter Shapur Bringing the Portrait of Khusraw to Shirin* (1539-43)

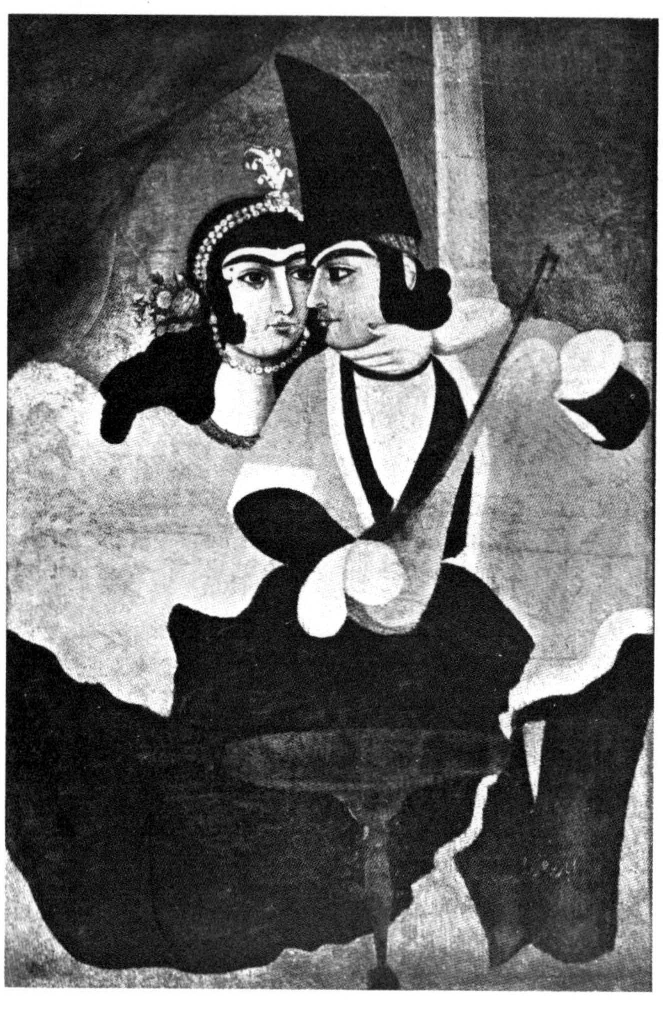

140 Artist unknown
The Lovers
18th century

ately, the eye passes on to succeeding planes, which follow each other vertically, or at opposite angles, with their princely banquets, hunting, battle, or love scenes. Yet the "mobile" equilibrium is there, convincing and communicative, perhaps more convincing and more communicative—because more "bizarre" and less easily fulfilled—than in other artistic media and in other periods of Iran.

Two methods, sometimes very simple and sometimes more complex in their construction, seem to dominate. According to the first method, usually a rectilinear scheme, a scene or rather part of a scene is continued in parts of other scenes, which mutually complete each other by an apparent juxtaposition (stability); actually, because they follow a conscious rhythm of intertwined surfaces, lines and colors, an *active* "mobile" perspective is thus created, a perspective which is not at once given to us statically-"objectively" (as in the three-dimensional "scientific" perspective created by the

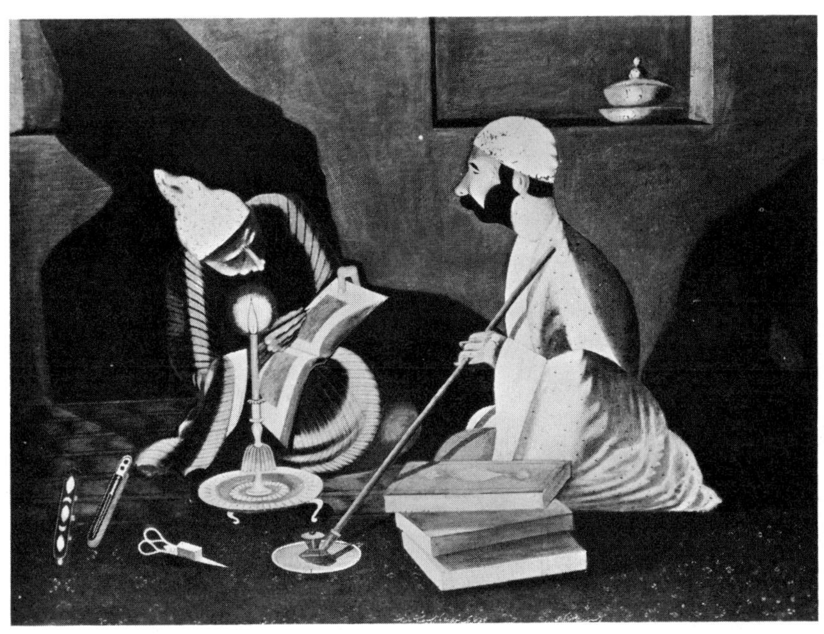

141 Artist unknown
A Reading Scene
19th century

Italian Renaissance), but which *we, the spectators, must reconstruct for ourselves by our own visual participation (Plate 138).*

The second method, cyclic or swirling, is no less intense. Two or more centers are given: for example, a circular or square basin is posed at the foot of the panel, and a richly ornamented canopy is set obliquely, in the upper part of the scene; while all around there is a circling dance of objects and personages, so arranged that the two spheres of action are fused, and by their persuasive and inviting poetry induce the eye to create a "mobile" perspective *(Plate 139).*

The art of Iran in subsequent centuries underwent a gradual, and what seems today to be a final decadence; it is often said that it no longer created, but merely repeated, unintelligently. This is not true, not quite true. We can sometimes see the "decadent" eighteenth-nineteenth century art imposing creatively—so powerful is the great tradition, the instinctive awareness of and the instinctive fidelity to it!—its never forgotten formula of "mobile" synthesis on the most energetic and by this time most welcomed formula of European "stable" three-dimensionality. What more convincing and revealing than this eighteenth-century painting, "Two Lovers" *(Plate 140),* so gracefully static and clear in its outlining, and so "mobile" in the "deformative" wholeness of its wavelike rhythm (two lovers—one being); and this extraordinary nineteenth-century oil painting, "A Reading Scene" *(Plate 141),* where the obvious, "cubistic" consistency of relief, perspective, chiaroscuro, is simultaneously both imposed (hallucinating Zurbaranian proximity of space) and dissolved into a "mobile" geometry of interconnected curves, sharp angles, dark and light surfaces, etc. (continuity of beings with things and of things with beings: great daring-do of intimacy).

But works like this are, probably, rare. Besides, their merit is more in the new—still confused—ways they suggest and encourage, than in their intrinsic achievement. The real greatness of the past is gone. Still, having once been so universal and so new, hence inexhaustible by virtue of its synthetic essence, is it possible that this grand art will not be reborn? Iran gave birth, without realizing it, to a unique aesthetic form; it remains for Iran to find it again, but in full consciousness of its worth.

Second Adventure

Thus, cultures distinct from each other open into each other because of the community of their inner struggles—however distinct will be their resulting final decisions. For the opening of a being is the closing—the hiding away—of all distinctions still present there. It is this promise of hope that gives life—life of creation—to Bistāmī's despair[40]—all Islam's creative despair: "The supreme degree of the doctrine of the Divine Unity is the denial of the Divine Unity."[41]

Transparency total.

Transparent to each other, distinctions wane away, still present; each opens into each other: our "verbal" consciousness into our "visual," and so forth—all these distinctions still so helpful not long ago—now waning away, definitely. Indiscriminatingly, in front of our road's new extension, we could say now:

The idiom—so mature—of our "verbal" interior provides us with a model. We must admire, indeed, the great patience and application with which, since its origins, thinking humanity has tried—and often succeeded—to learn all about the deep life of its "verbal" consciousness. (There is, in this fact, a "disturbing" proof of the natural, vitally selected, superiority or priority of this form of awareness over all other fraternal forms.) This consciousness or—what is the same thing—this culture is rich and subtle today. But its will or its ambition was always and is today unchanged. It always was and is this: to find a constant psychological law or some constant psychological laws around which, as if around an axis, the entire life-complex of this consciousness would or could be properly disposed. And suddenly a long-forgotten text came back to my memory: Descartes' solitary meditations on this subject, probably, in their utmost simplicity, the most earnest and the closest-to-satisfactory that we can find.

And what he said was given then to us both—travellers today, here, into the realm of the eye—as a guide:

> Of my thoughts some are, as it were, images of things, and to these alone properly belongs the name *idea;* as when I think (represent to my mind) a man, a chimera, the sky, an angel, or God. Others, again, have certain other forms; as when I will, fear, affirm, or deny. I always, indeed, apprehend something as the object of my thought but I also embrace in thought something more than the representation of the object; and of this class of thoughts some are called volitions or affections, and others judgments.
>
> Now with respect to ideas if these are considered only in themselves, and are not referred to any object beyond them, they cannot, properly

> speaking, be false; for, whether I imagine a goat or a chimera, it is not less true that I imagine the one than the other. Nor need we fear that falsity may exist in the will or affection, for, although I may desire objects that are wrong, and even that never existed, it is still true that I desire them. There thus only remain our judgments, in which we must take diligent heed that we be not deceived.[42]

Indeed, the whole psychical matter of man is, as it were, organized around this triple-faced axis:

1) The ideas-images ("representations") that we shall call *Descartes I*:—a perpetual source of mental and other images given directly, "naive" in their reflection and behaviour, juxtaposed and exclusive in their seriated appearance, and "true."

2) Judgments, or *Descartes II*:—the intellectual or logical disposition of those ideas-images, in accordance with their degree of proximity to or remoteness from the common point of usefulness, that is, in accordance with the degree of their affirmation or negation. Thus judgment—Descartes II—is the construction of a moral perspective ("in which we must take diligent heed that we be not deceived"). It is the creation of a moral space where all the "images" are projected and distributed now in the converging psycho-logical *linear* sense of depth and distance, in accordance with the directives of our mental categories (quantity, quality, relation, place, etc.). This rationally organized ensemble appears thus as a new and *autonomous* image-system, a closed system of graduated and interconnected images: an articulated mind-automaton *which moves or walks by itself*.

3) "Volitions or affections"—*Descartes III:*—this is fusion or interlacing of psycho-logical entities ("images" or "ideas"), a fusion effected by the force of their mutual attraction, which is the very principle of emotion. It is, therefore, creation of a new image-block, image-"monster" (a compound and "mobile" being), image-"ornament," a *new* "image-idea," as categorical, naive, whole, exclusive, limited in itself and "true" as the simple image, Descartes I.

❖❖❖❖❖❖❖❖❖❖❖❖❖❖❖❖❖❖❖❖❖❖❖❖❖❖❖❖❖❖

At this moment I could distinctly hear the reader's objection: The inner man being himself a fusion or a combination-result of all his psychological and other elements, how can one justify this threefold graduation, so rigid apparently, so arbitrary, and according to which the judgment-complex is "placed" between the image-complex and the volition-complex and not after the latter or before the first?

Yes, indeed, this inner fusion-combination exists: there is no "judgment" about anything without an image-idea or an emotion-volition in it, just as there could not be any "emotion" or any "idea-representation" where the two other psychic forces are not present somehow. But to say fusion or combination of elements is to imply delineation, at least mental, of the nature of each of these elements. Intellectual convenience demands it as a mental reservation, so to speak; as a thing understood and presupposed. And this demand is an ineluctable reality too. The "judgment" has its own mental nature; so has the "idea-representation"; so has the "emotion." Now what is the nature of a judgment? Judgment is an operation which situates images-ideas *already* given; thus, *past* images-ideas. And the nature of emotion? Emotion is the "labor" which gives birth to and situ-ates a new image-idea; new, therefore projected, as it were, toward a future action, a new image-idea yet to be. That is why, conformably to the time logic of these operations, and without forgetting their relative reality (that they are intercombined and cannot be "real" otherwise) we "place" judgment—Descartes II—between its past and its future, between the "idea" and the "emotion."

❖❖❖❖❖❖❖❖❖❖❖❖❖❖❖❖❖❖❖❖❖❖❖❖❖❖❖❖❖❖❖

There it is, then, the "moral" flame of the mind which penetrates and informs all conscious life, the life expressed in verbal "images-judgments-emotions" as well as in the images-judgments-emotions of the eye, of the touch, or of the ear (for human conscience is one, one compresence)! Awareness of the eye, awareness of the ear, etc.—their matter so rich and so differentiated takes its real shape only there, in the interior of this triple mold! And their language—through this form's creations—becomes clear, indeed. The eye says: I gather up the images, the naive, unmalicious representations given spontaneously to me (Descartes I): they are the whole of my dwelling. I possess them. Then I "judge" them (Descartes II), that is, I affirm their possession by disposing their presence in accordance with the degree of intensity of my "touching" them, or of my tactile attention to them. That is how distance is born: the spatial distribution of images according to their tactile-visual importance (the degree of their affirmation or negation). Distance or perspective is born—and also relief, the plastically graduated consistency of the images (the perspective of their inner contour). Here also, therefore, a *closed* system, well defined by the logic of my visual categories, visual quantity, visual quality, visual relation, etc., is constructed—a new, articulated image-system, *a space-automaton which can move or go by itself.*

But I cannot organize or judge my images without loving them (to hate them would mean to make them *visually* disappear or be nonexistent). I love, that is, I exercise "volition-affection" toward my images; which is to say that visually, the images-among-themselves-and-I are mutually attracted. I "deform" them, accordingly, so that their emotion-volition (Descartes III), liberated from the anatomic external limitation of these images, might take possession of them more freely also, and so fulfil their desire for union and fusion. Their (images-and-I) narrow embrace becomes then the very shape or the contour of a "new" image-idea (Descartes III = "new" Descartes I), an image-whole, an image-"monster": an idea-ornament. *The ornament is then born. For ornament is "affection-volition" of perspective: the "stability" of judgment in it becomes the "mobility" of desire.*

❖❖❖❖❖❖❖❖❖❖❖❖❖❖❖❖❖❖❖❖❖❖❖❖❖❖❖❖❖❖❖

Then we were shown great historical "cycles" or cultures and their epic struggles for self-affirmation; and within those cycles, great individuals struggling alone. And we saw that each "success"—each "physiognomy"—of a culture or of an individual was almost always the direct result of such a combination of the three inner degrees, Descartes I, II, III, and that one of them (and sometimes two) assumed the leading role.[43]

The epic struggle for self-affirmation in a given culture is a very long and sometimes obscure one: influences, impositions, diffusions, retreats toward dead traditions, or too rapid advances, etc. Too long and sometimes too obscure to be retold here. Yet the final "success," the "physiognomy" of each cycle appeared clear to us. Here was the ancient culture of the Nile. On Egypt's great stones, on its sculptured or painted woods, etc., we admired the human effort to affirm—with consummate knowledge—the truthfulness of the naive eye (an effort at transfer which is precisely the "moral" in the eye and in history). Long-storied bands arranged one above the other offered us, in spite of the absence of a formal or expressed perspective, the entire and detailed image-content of the latter. Triumph of Descartes I—pure, "true," seriated and hierarchic imagery—over Descartes II (judgment-perspective) and over Descartes III (emotion-"ornament"), that was ancient Egypt, before it was disturbed by extraneous influences. But how much more majestic and humanly touching appeared to us the "success" of Hellas! For it was there—as we have long known—that *judgment* was historically born and could freely mature into perspective and its laws of three-dimensionality. Since the early days of Attic grandeur—the experiments of Agatharchos of Samos (of the fifth century B.C.) who invented, they say,[44] the linear perspective for the stage paintings of his friend Aeschylos's plays; of Polygnotos the illustrious (fifth century); of Apollodōros, Zeuxis's teacher, who already knew, according to Plutarch, how to use in painting the gradation of light and shade, the gradation of tones—and continuing with the delicate and decisive achievements of Parrhasios and Zeuxis (beginning fourth century), from those "classical" acquisitions to the "Hellenistic" audacities of the Alexandrians and the Romans—we could follow the path of judgment's (Descartes II) ascendency. Thus it was in the Hellenic world that art could create the logically articulated space-automaton, *the thing which walks by itself*. Not in China, as one would legitimately be tempted to think. For since the time of T'ang's glory, China the faithful desired but one thing: harmony, or the reconciliation of Descartes I, II, and III. An overwhelming and total evidence of "image" plus perspective-"judgment," plus fusion-"volition" or "emotion," makes China's "physiognomy" all at once so convincing, beautiful, true, and also—in its message or trace of epic "struggle"—so "mediocre." Because—as a result of this reconciliation—the visual inner drama whose tension or strain is expressed in what we call "artifice" or "deformation" (the perspective-judgment, the articulated space automaton, and the "new" image-"ornament" are such "deformations") was, in China, "banalized" or lessened by the much more intense and creative new drama of the *verbal* struggle (the *narrated* poetry of Chinese painting). That is why many prefer China's more *verbally* accessible artistic visual message—prefer it to the "frivolity"—on the verbal level—of Japan's "ornament."

Thence, we were led to another art-culture whose confession amazed

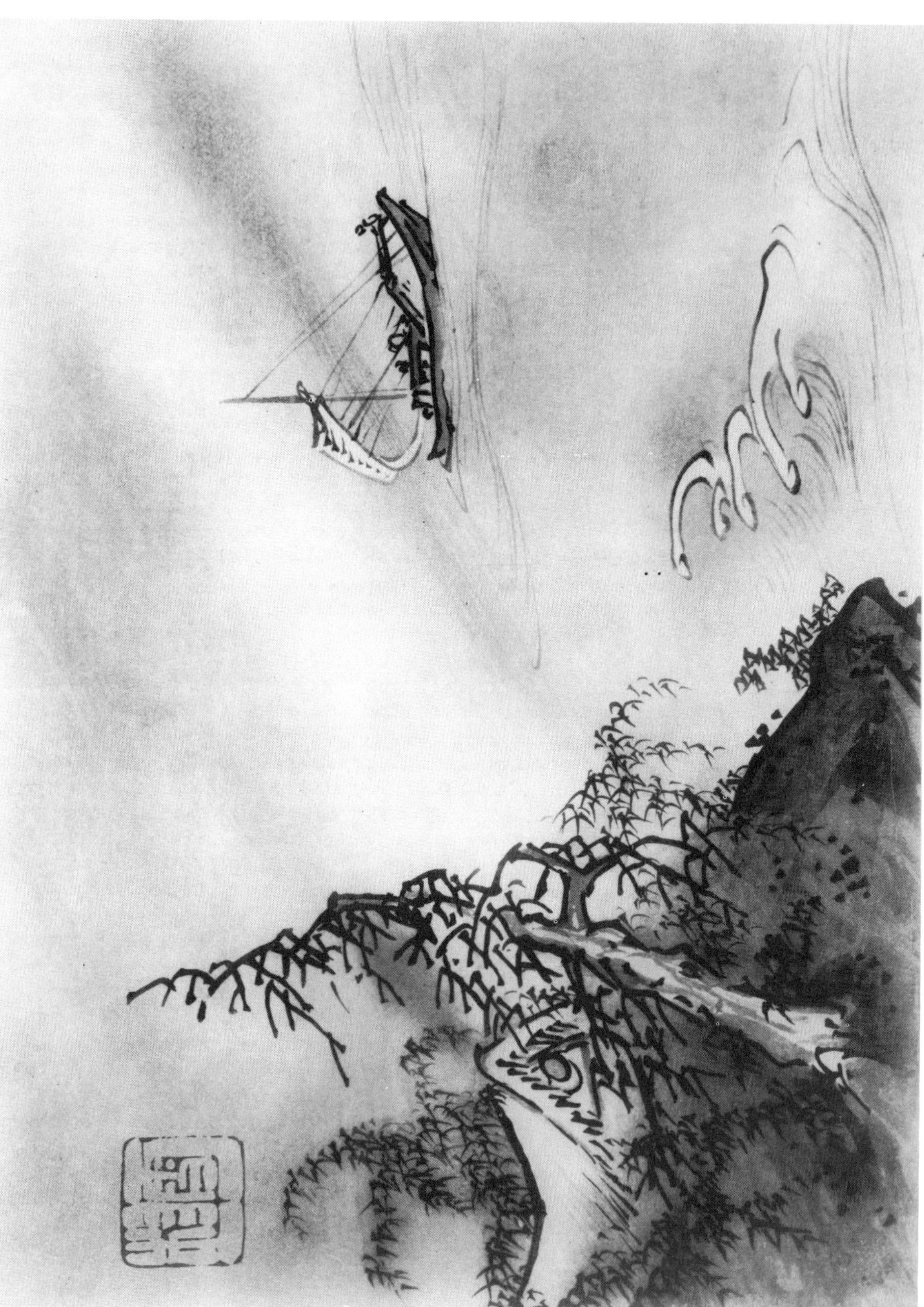

us greatly again. This was the strange and fascinating cycle of our medieval Occident, the so-called Romanesque art and its zone of influences to our own days. A strong yet "mobile" universe it was; thick and deep, full of forms continuing into each other, haunting each other, and finally, becoming fused together, transfigured into a new being, a being-and-its-hereafter, the being-"ornament": profound Romanesque victory of responsive volitive eye over the demon of isolation, victory of "volition"-emotion (Descartes III) over the naive image-idea and judgment-perspective (both, nevertheless, intensely present there)! *(See Plates 15 and 119).*

It was close—vicinal—to this style or cycle, and almost identical in its struggle and message (although so different in verbal imagery, the subject matter, the "expressive form"), that we found again the art of Islamic Iran, and even closer to the latter, the art of "our" Japan.

But yielding to my co-traveller's awakened curiosity—or fatigue: for it was late in the day already, and the journey had been long and fatiguing—I took with him a more wooded and smoother by-road, and we descended from the epic universe to the universe of the individual. We did not choose our visits—we just stopped at the homes of those who lived along the hem of the shorter road. There we saw the "deep" life of Uccello: the innate naiveté (Descartes I) of his eye, tormented yet victorious in the very midst of its judgment's prowess. And the life of a Sesson, the "romanesque mobility" of his so Japanese "ornament-*persona*": profound victory of responsive volitive eye over the demon of isolation, victory of "volition-emotion" (Descartes III) over the naive image-idea and over the judgment-perspective (both, nevertheless, intensively present there)! *(Plate 142).*

Thence we went to visit El Greco the Mobile—with him we descended to the very roots of the painter's eye.

El Greco's roots—his "innermost" struggles: the object *front face,* that is to say, the object's halt in space, its plastic jut-relief and its corresponding *schema,* the sphere: and opposite it, the object *profile,* the sliding flight of a line nearly straight and with no rest, upon the moving surface of extension! The wars of this Byzantine! Circle, sphere, the *face* (as such belonging technically to the imperative and the habits of El Greco's time, the Renaissance), twisted, thus drawn nearer to line's flight *ad infinitum,* sphere oblique, "rigid," El Greco's ellipsoid space. Descartes III—the "ornament"—triumphing: silhouette-"monster," perspective multi-axial, centrifugal, "mobile," space-profile, even when on the *what* level El Greco paints figures presented, or narrated, in front of us.

The towering home of Pablo Picasso—the most integral of all—we did not dare to re-visit. But then also, I wanted to show to my co-traveller the "innermost" home, unfamiliar to him, I knew, of another living artist whose creations became, long before our journey started, my second and personal "proof": Juan Miró, the "ornament's" poet, the "ornament's" philosopher, the "ornament's" painter, the *purest* of all, perhaps. The deep "ornament" of Juan Miró: poet's proof; child's proof, proof-event freed entirely from proving—serpent's shudder down, from pure idea to visitation, sound, smell, touch, taste: Miró's sex-and-constellations. A new monster, with no respectability about it (hence the *comic!*), only painter's subject = object of respect

◀142 Sesson *Wind and Waves* (Muromachi period, late 15th century)

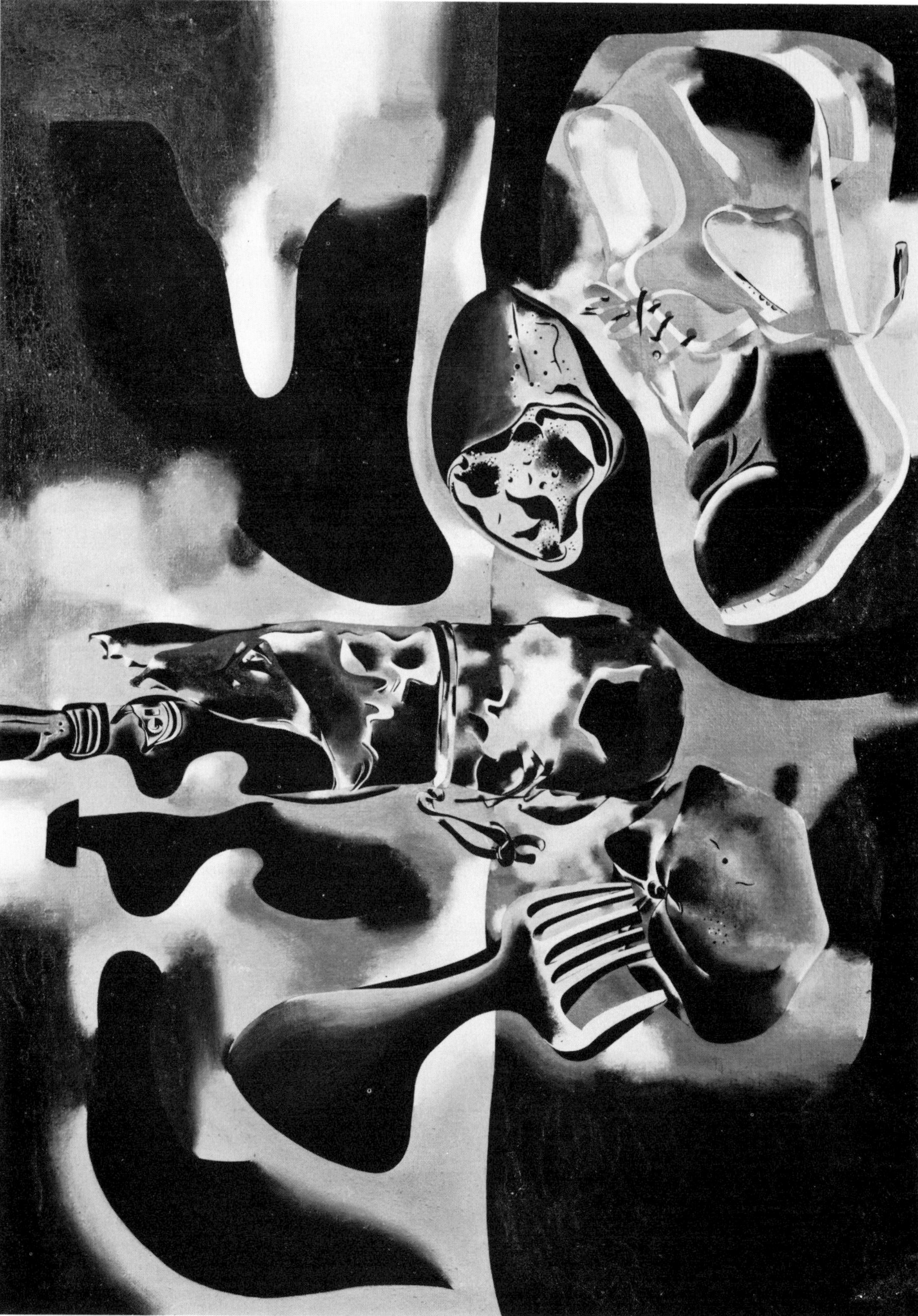

—bless the child's heart, the playful child-events, in the vicinity of a rose! For, indeed, if one could—and one can sometimes, now, for instance—see—understand—mimic in a single separable yet unseparably instantaneous time-knot, all of a rose's journey of opening from bud to flower expansion, one could then also re-make in one leap—serpent's knot-time of creation = critique—the whole of psyche-history's (of both the individual, Miró's or another's, any other's, and the planetary, Japan's or any other entity's) journey back home. That is to say, Miró's instantaneous return to the source of magician-artist-chieftain-or-dancer's universe of discourse.

And we saw the rose opened, its petals not superposed, opaque, one upon another, but each in the immediate vicinity of another, transparent, each present in each other, mutually, till the corolla is reached. At first: Miró's transparent fulfilment of a nostalgic promise—but this is the very promise of twentieth century *qua* twentieth century—the return to the *soma*-horizon. And we have seen already when autumn was here, and then winter, that this return is not a simple re-embodiment or re-collection of the past planetary cycle's primordial consubstantiality.

No; twentieth century is the discovery and the beginning of a new planetary cycle (we are ready for a new myth-monster!) a neo-*soma* horizon, a neo-consubstantiality, neo-Egypt-Dahomey-Shinto with a new "monstrous" dual being, present obscurely there, the neo-*pneuma* horizon, future as yet, and the new *nous* horizon, neo-India, neo-Greece-India-Yamato (are we ready to meet the monster?) about to flow and fulfil its new Kalpa destiny or cycle.

A new awareness too—the twentieth century's typical awareness of the discovery that something was lost during the last cycle's evolvement, and once found, must be re-installed today, in all its rights—re-stated as a directing and representative word neighbouring the word *discovery* itself: Descartes I, the idea-representation or the word image *per se*. Twentieth century is the discovery or re-discovery of the naive image-idea, this table, this star, this face—and of its inevitable vicinity—serpent's tail-in-head—to the image-new-image: the "deep ornament," Descartes III. Till the rim of Miró's corolla and throughout the transparency of his multi-petalled rose, this epoch-marking sovereignty of the re-installed idea-representation remains intact and omnipresent in his art.

But what makes Miró's art so unique is precisely this transparency—the playful ease with which he could see, comprehend, mimic, guide the inner events of his translucid journey. Thus, we saw that his was a "natural" urge—very "Mediterranean"?—to "stabilize" motion, to establish a movement-narration (vicinal to "judgment" rather than to "ornament" [*Plate 143*]) in the very midst of what his century had chosen to be the pictorial substance or medium, *par excellence:* space as a continuum-block.

Ever since, and remaining "stable," clear, seriated, all his effort, his nostalgia of a poet-painter, has been directed toward the missing contrary: the movement-mobility vicinal to "ornament."

And if he could create an art-mobility, all his own, without ever forgetting or betraying—quite the contrary!—his twentieth-century man's loyalty to the "image" as Descartes' idea-representation, it was because he

143 JOAN MIRO
Still Life with Old Shoe

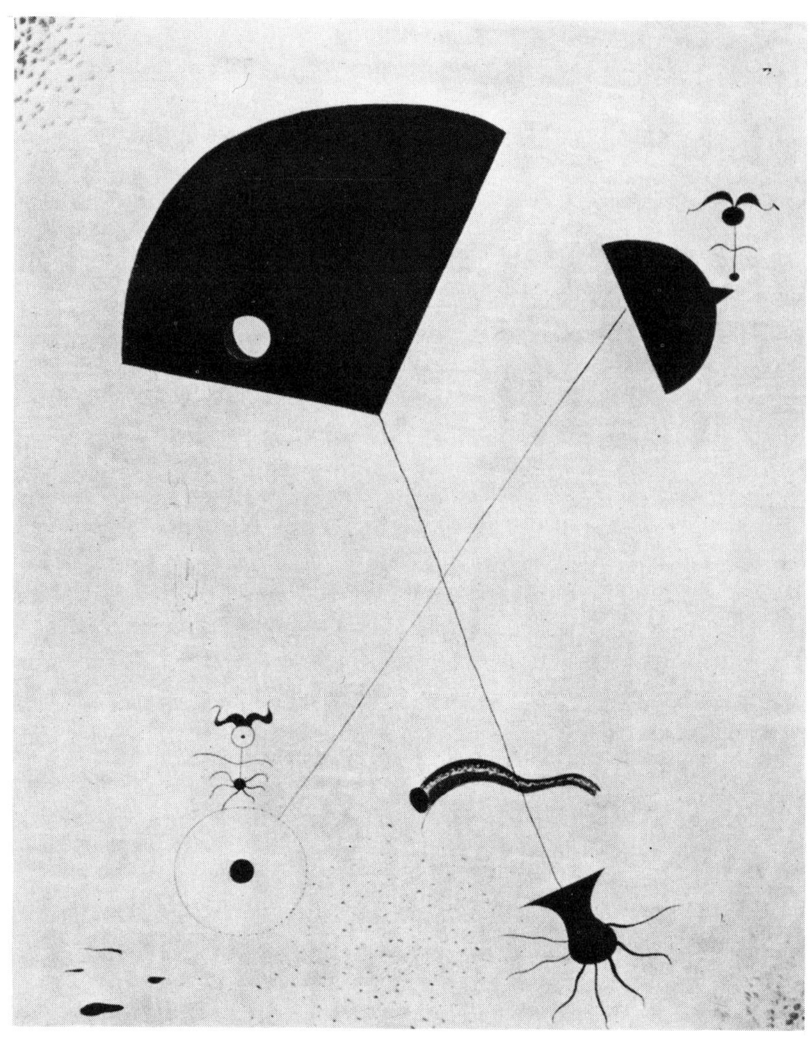

144 JOAN MIRO
Maternity

discovered also—he saw through the transparency of all the rose-petals—that something very close to the immediacy of motion itself was missing as yet, was absent in his experience, which he wanted integral, total, and immediate also. Miró knew what it was, and found where and how to make it his. And he saw that till then his world was the world of correspondence, the correspondence between mind's eye and the empirical eye, as well as between the total and the part: the world of impression. The universe of substitution, of the total seized totally by the part-witness—the world of sensation—was not there as yet.

And the poet-philosopher's uncompromising passion to seize the unseizable total—infinity—by finity, became his only, transparent, and transmitted as such to other eyes, central passion.

Now, only now, Miró's instantaneous journey could be followed with no interruption. From transparency to transparency, from substitution-identity to substitution-identity, his infinity, the total vagueness of its irrepressible urge and the vagueness intolerable of the word *infinity* itself was transferred *in toto*, into the finite precision—Miró's, no one else's—of an image-meaning gesture, Miró's *Image la Folle*, Miró's sex = constellations; transposed as such into the pictorial dryness and finite precision of his line-hair—decidedly "Maternity!" *(Plate 144)*—the female sex-hair, both creator and creature of the embryo in the future; of a perfect sky-breast, the uncompromising fullness of a thin, straight, dry sky-hair, floating in its own dry sky-emptiness. If one could see, understand, mimic in a single, instantaneous, time-knot all the petals of a rose open—in succession, yet not—from bud to full flower, one then could see, in one translucent time-knot this unseizable creative dryness of Miró's—the dryness of mathematics, of Plato, of father-sky—seized and completed (oh, fullness of a painter's new plunge into the oneness of correspondence-substitution, impression-sensation, feeling-idea!) by primeval wetness, drops of sky-blood, sky-sperm, mother-earth's sky.

And then—the processional dance-pose of back home coming: "Hope returning through the flight of constellations." The returning indeed: Miró's return to child's innermost eye, the serpent, all, the shudder along the spine from idea pure to smell, touch-taste and back: Fujiwara toy!

Third Adventure

When we left Miró and El Greco and all the others, and ascended back to our journey's chosen road, it was Islam's epic visitation that again met our eyes.

At this moment I could sense—but less distinctly than before—my cotraveller's objection.

We stopped for a short while and I said to him:

Yes, I know, you are in process now of reading the end of my fourth —Spring's—variation on the theme of Japanese painting (the fifth—Summer's—I warn you, to come in your absence). Yes, we are at the end of our journey, and yet, a confusing perplexity is still lingering in your mind: why, in the first place, Islamic painting again, when Yamato's is our goal or theme? Secondly, and in close connection with the first, do we still mean in using the word *ornament*, the same ornament total, West-East's final and total exchange of gifts, we have used before we met Descartes I-II-III?

I should try to answer you thus:

As a "heraldic" word-compound, the word *ornament*, vicinal to the pre-split word-compound *motion-per-se*, such as we have used, and meant it, undisturbed, before we met Descartes I-II-III, is neither an explanation of nor confusion with the singled-out word *volition* (= ornament-Descartes III) but is a word situ-ated heraldically in closest vicinity (= adhesion) to Descartes III as well as to Descartes I and Descartes II—three-limbed as it is. Our ornament total, West-East's final and total "exchange of gifts," is the co-presence of idea (= representation), of judgment (= perspective), of emotion (= ornament). Where one of these three is temporarily absent or hidden away, missing, precisely there will be situ-ated, in *substitution*, the creative élan of our consciousness—art's genesis as creative nostalgia for the missing. The intenser the drama of this substitution, the more revealing become both the nostalgic presence of what is missed or hidden, and the very technique of the substitution itself.

Now it so happens that in its innermost content and revelation the hidden drama of the Islamic world—(for us, the Islamic-Iranian painting)—is perhaps the most intense, thus revealing, of all the others. That is why the Islamic world is so intensely included in our story of Japanese painting: *it is Japanese painting, in transparent substitution.*

For the space of Iranian painting is neither a two-dimensional space, nor a three-dimensional. It is not a three-dimensional space in the sense that Greece and Rome, through Europe's later and novel teaching (since the Renaissance), have accustomed us to "judge" and to enjoy space-imagery: the articulated automaton-system, closed and "logical," of space "which walks by itself," the technique of "correct" perspective, of "natural" relief, of chiaroscuro, etc. The Iranian space is much more intense than that: it is neither two nor three-dimensional; *it is about to become three-dimensional.* Iran's charm and power, its "limitations" also—the "deformative," "illogical" absurdities of Iran's space construction—come from this *aboutness.* Hence its affinities with our own modern space-conception, which is *about* to overcome the impositions of an articulated and closed three-dimensionality. Hence also its neighbourliness to the Romanesque experience. For Iranian space is also dominated by Descartes III: volition-emotion. But its particularity, its uniqueness, consists in the ultimate alliance between this "volition"-image and the pure, naive first "image"-idea: alliance of Descartes I with Descartes III. The simple, "stable," seriated images of the Egyptian juxtaposition-scheme are kept integrally, in Iranian space-imagery, in the midst and for the sake of a most "mobile" will to transform those images in a fused and new "image-ornament," a collected-image. We have already seen how this radiant "stability" (clear silhouetting, purity of coloring) and this scytho-romanesque "mobility" became by their fusion the inner "success" of Iranian pictorial space. We have also seen how this "mobile" synthesis-formula there became a kind of space tool —the "spade" of the eye—which makes us, the "mobilized" spectators, participate in this act of "digging in."

And that, we saw, is how a psycho-plastic depth or perspective was created in Iran. Within this magic world you are not—you cannot be—placed *in front* of the organized space images, as if in front of a "system which walks by itself," but you are *within* it, *among* the images. You are not, therefore, aware of it. You are *about* to be so. Iranian "mentality" is not a struggle against "judgment"—Descartes II—but it is the will to "judge" (not for reconciliation's sake as in China, but for the plenitude of the eye's awareness); it is the effort to "judge" and, at the same time, the impossibility of so doing. Descartes II is missing there, and at the same time is aspired toward. This is the "secret" of Iranian pictorial space. Within or "among" this romantic, and in appearance, so cheerful imagery (pure radiant pigments, secure outlinings, etc.), very strange things happen; strange and "illogical" things, because new and at the same time future things (Descartes III = future "images"), things *about* to be totally "real." We can watch the sudden and tense "rigidity" of an evolving or moving image ("rigidity": the plastic reflex of what we saw is about to be the true, the immediate and not the mediated or "mnemonic" movement). Elsewhere, there will be here and there a sudden fusion of space and time, which means, sometimes, simultaneity of differentiated or remote actions and places: the "rigid" flattening of volumes, the what-is-an-earlier action becoming a later action, the what-is-farther-removed-from us becoming the nearer to us. And this simultaneity is revealed to us as an intended simultaneity, intended for the *moral* purpose of our total participation, of our image-judgment-volition participation in the represented, pictorially narrated, drama. Such, for instance,[45] is this unforgettable example of the purely Iranian style: a page from a Timurid Shah-Nameh, the slaying of Arjāsp the Turanian by the Iranian paladin Isfandiyār in the Brazen Castle and the rescuing of the two royal sisters, Humai and Bih Afrid *(Plate 145)*.[46] The captured princesses are already freed; they sit and talk peacefully with each other, while the violent action necessary for their rescue—Arjasp's tragic end—is being accomplished *behind* them: justice-intention and justice-fulfilment, justice-concept and justice-act being here, as they are ontologically, as they are also in the poem's intention, one and the same thing, one and the same moment. And so is everything else in the pictorial space here. The farther-removed-from-us objects—the emptied tower window of the prisoner sisters in the background—are plastically more consistent, thus in reality nearer to us, the spectators, than the flattened city walls of the foreground: one "rigidly mobile" block of active and space-building simultaneity achieved by means of geometrically complex interrelation (obliqueness of lines and surfaces) of architectural images. Neither a two-dimensional nor three-dimensional universe, but a *mobile* in-between universe, an *about* to be, more plenary than the simply plastic, universe of the eye: "ornament."

Such also is this other fifteenth-century episode of the Shah-Nameh *(Plate 146)*:[47] the profound and dangerously alive forest, and within, in the midst of it, the sleep of Rustam—Firdawsī's greatest hero—with the unequal struggle of Rustam's horse, Rakhsh, against the attacking lion. Here again is the same "mobile-rigid" block: we-within-the-trees-within-Rustam's-sleep-and-danger. The same new, whole, collected or collective image-ornament. A restless image, oblique and full, convincing and so gravely poetic. A tense and "difficult" world where "judgment" is both *missing* and *desired,* for we are really and in earnest *about to adhere* to the space-depth there.

It was in the middle of a legendary night when secretly, against all decorum of her sex and social position, the young Turanian Princess Tahmīna entered the palace chamber where a stranger was resting on his bed —the world-famous Iranian hero, Rustam, unexpected guest of her father, the king of Samangān. She came—bashful but decided—to tell him her love. And the secret of a beautiful night became here the secret of this daring girl's drama: that is how a Timurid artist painted the romantic episode of Tahmīna and Rustam, rich in future events chanted by Firdawsī. He painted a nocturne. Yet the fullness of a nocturne-image is not narrated

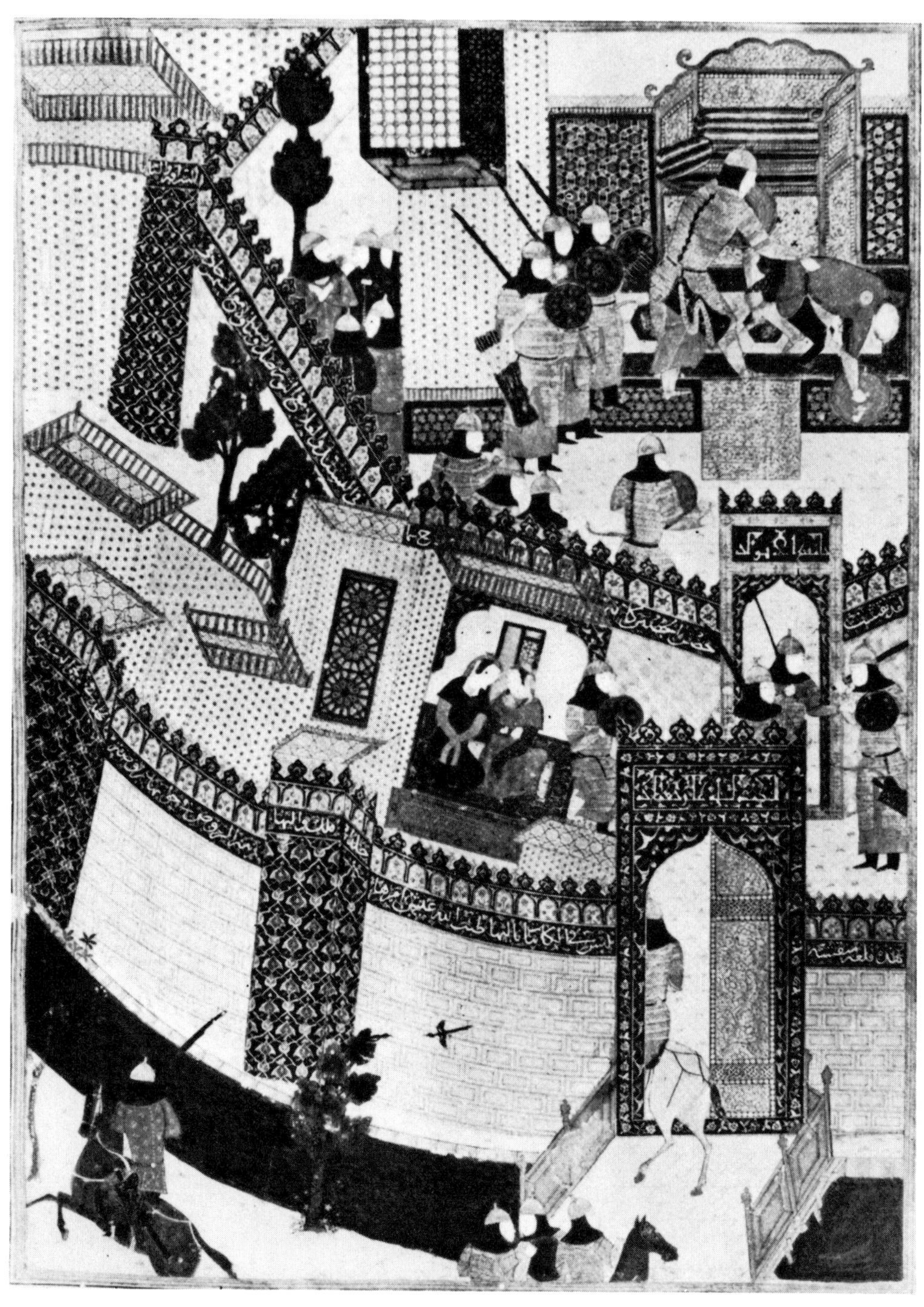

145 *Isfandiyār Slays Arjāsp in the Brazen Castle and Rescues His Sisters* Page from Firdawsī, *Shah-Nameh* (Herāt School, ca. 1429)

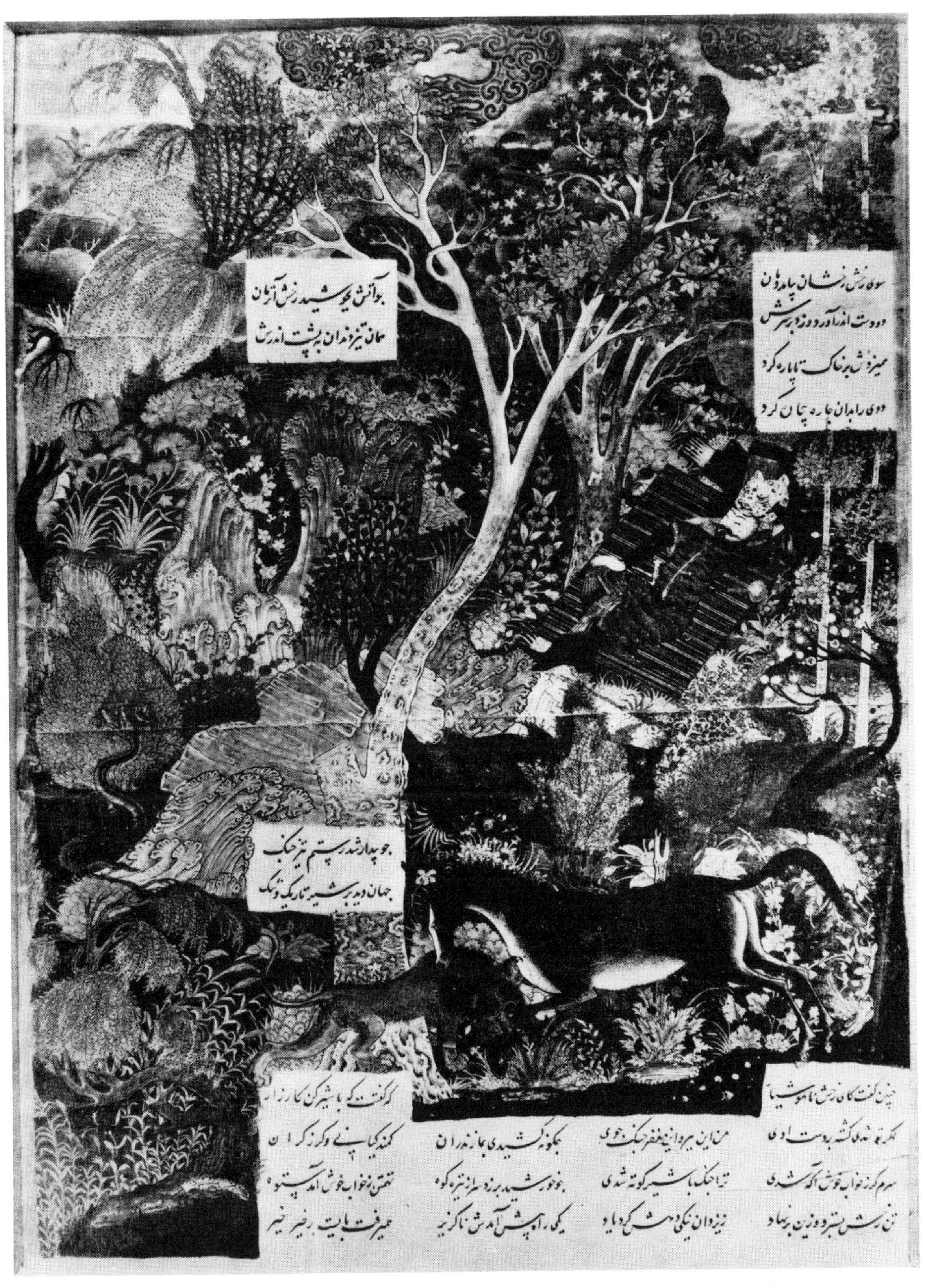

146 *Rustam's Sleep* Page from Firdawsī, *Shah-Nameh* (Herāt School, ca. 1450)

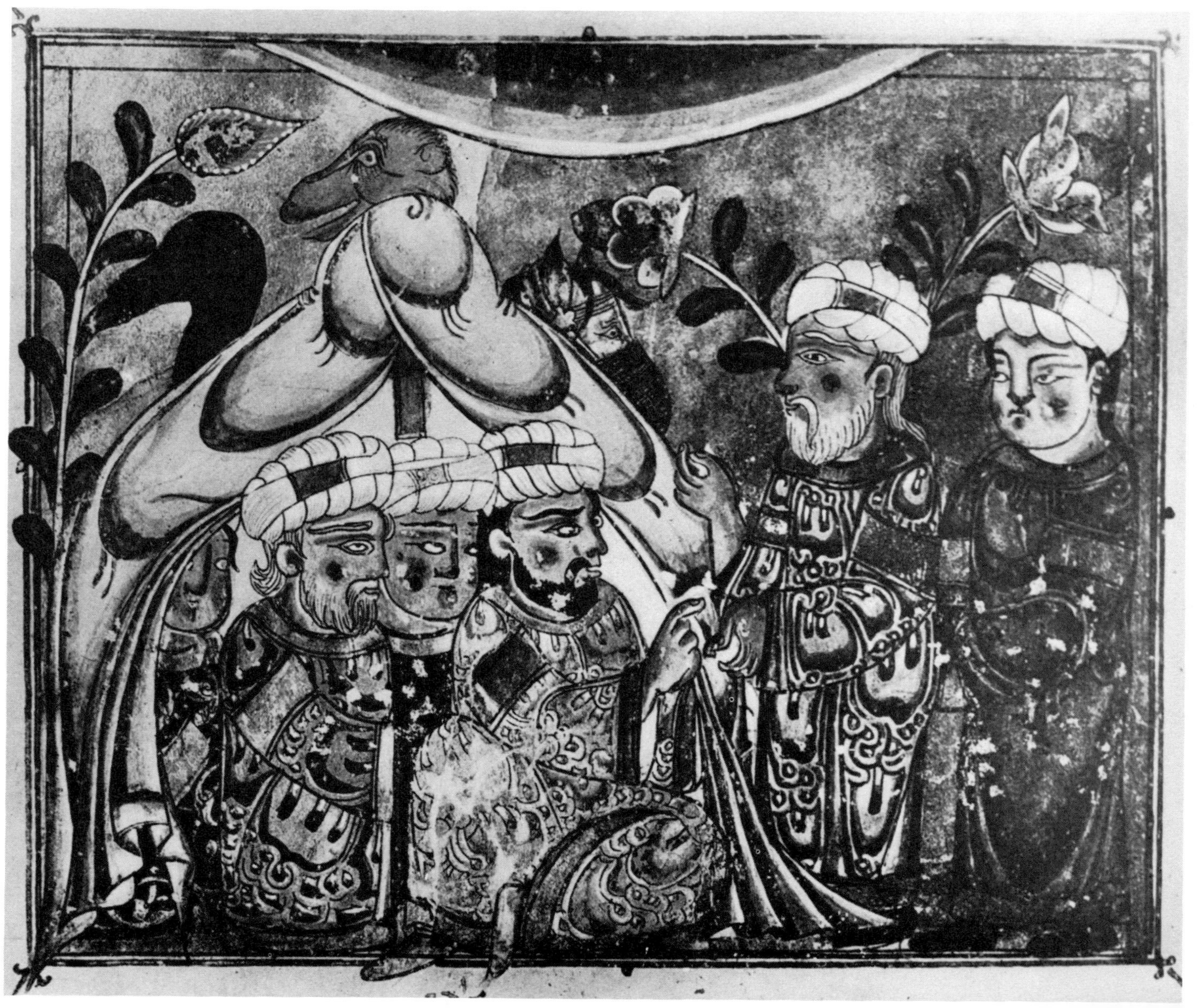

147 ARTIST UNKNOWN
The Twenty-sixth Assembly
14th century

here verbally-visually; it is *substituted totally*—prodigious compensation of the "about" uneasiness!—by an apparently or "naturalistically" arbitrary signalization: arbitrary, flat and "rigid" *mimic* of surfaces, colors, outlines, all of them converging—thus making meaningful the *mimic*—toward the large central panel, where, in contrast with the overhanging whiteness the golden-blue nocturnal sky is triumphant. A great night landscape—nocturnal sky full of stars—is there; but it is a "mobile," an "about"-to-be landscape. The temporarily acquired certainty of spatial depth, of nocturnal silence, of night's luminosity, is the result here of our—spectators'—"about" participation and "digging": subtle, delicate, prophetic deformation—"ornament"!

So also—but much more complex, because more urban-feudal (Mesopotamian) in its narrow-streets-tumult density, than the Iranian feudal-castle-like controlled poise—this other example: Al-Harīrī's Maqāmāt ("The Assemblies") in the National Library of Vienna, illuminated in 734 A.H. (1334 A.D.). Two episodes, particularly: the Fourteenth Assembly, called "of Mecca," in which it is related that while the narrator, Al-Harīth, is on the pilgrimage to Mecca, Abū Zayd, the old and shrewd hero-improviser of the Assemblies, and his son beg for food and a camel to enable them to continue their journey;[48] and the Twenty-Sixth Assembly, called "the Spotted," where Al-Harīth "having fallen into great poverty seeks assistance at the tent of a rich traveler whom he discovers to be Abū Zayd, who had been richly rewarded for composing a eulogy on the governor of Tūs."[49]

What a strange "new" monster-object, a totally "new" monster-space indeed, was manu-factured here by this fourteenth-century daring artist! Dense, tormented signal world of metal-like object-sensations, object-substitutions: obstinate memories of feudal cruelties, of sex, of implacable, unhuman things in nature—the folded watches of Salvador Dali!—and inside of this hardness a sudden center of tenderness, of poetry—water drops or pearl-tears?—all this said *exactly, concretely* there, in the ornamented aquatic folds of the robes, in the rigid metallic coolness of the tents, in the repeated anxiety of the camel head's silhouette; all this revived, reconstructed simultaneously by our antenna-like activity. *(Plate 147).*

Such, also, in spite of its "classical" poise, the about-volume of Bihzād (c. 1440—c. 1533), his "easy" and "pleasant" architecture-geometry of flattened one-within-the-other image-surfaces *(Plate 148).* What a sophisticated result—a taken-for-granted virtuosity—is already to be observed in this example of the late Timurid drama of space! It is the same Iranian drama, nevertheless. The same *about*-to-become fullness of volume, fullness of "image-judgment-emotion" through the participation technic, the "mobility" of the interconnected "far" and "near," "later" and "earlier." See how intensely near, closely present, is the tree-image in the distant center of the background and how *indifferent* toward, and thus distant from, the spatial "normality" of a closely observable image, is the "abnormal" verticality of the floor in the foreground! And see: the "far" and the "near," the "earlier" and the "later," are moving toward each other, they cross each other; thus

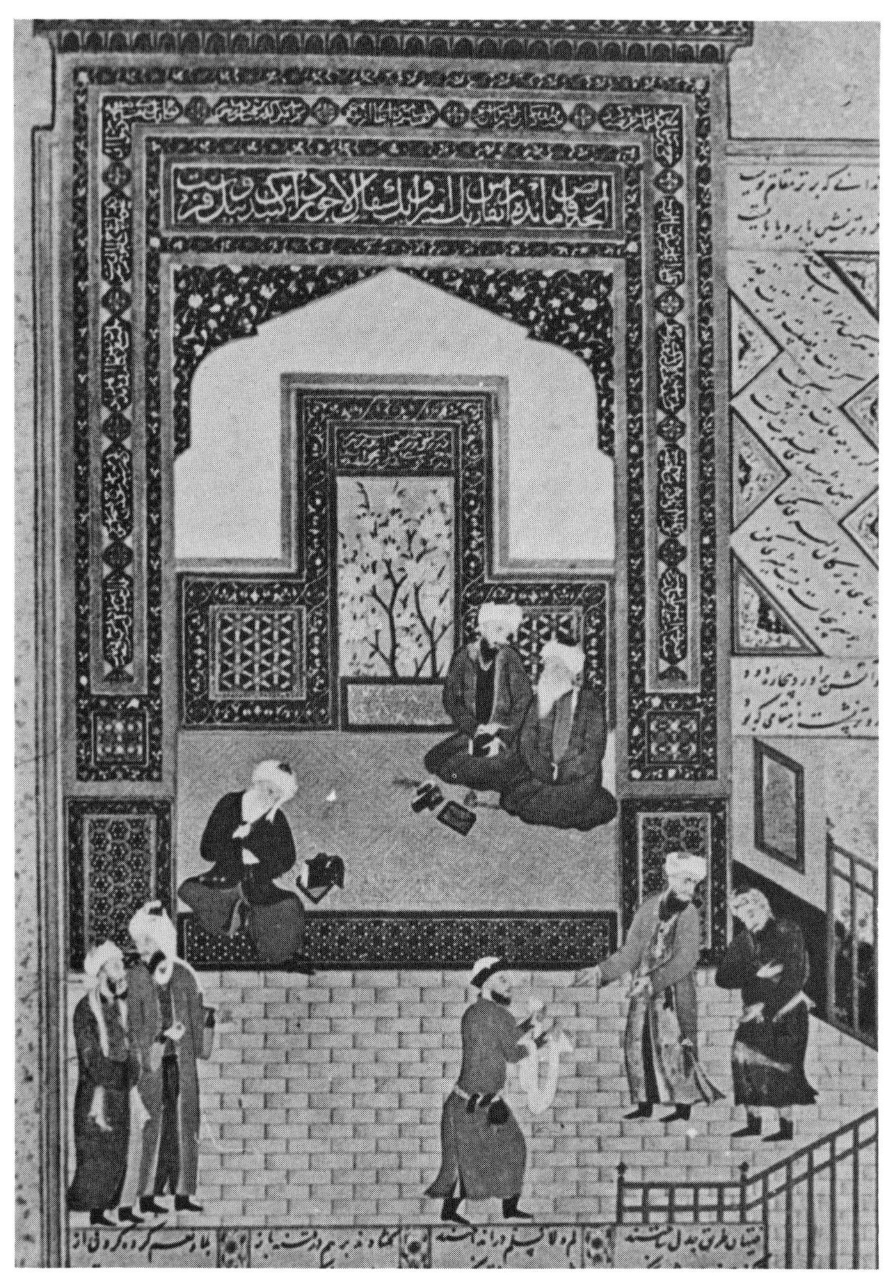

148 Bihzad *Scene in a Mosque* (Herāt School, ca. 1480)

the two-dimensional flatness of the whole is here but the temporarily "immobilized" result of this crossing, of this encounter of the two distances or dimensions: a temporary immobility and a temporary flatness, *about* to be changed into some new—unpredictable for us—"mobile" distance-dimension.

❖❖❖❖❖❖❖❖❖❖❖❖❖❖❖❖❖❖❖❖❖❖❖❖❖❖❖❖❖❖❖❖

But why did not Iran overcome this uneasy limitation of "about?" Why did not Iran include the fullness of the judgment-perspective (Descartes II) in the fullness of its visual equilibrium, and thereby create its own *final* space formula? This new formula, if invented, could have been as complete as that of Europe's Renaissance three-dimensionality (Brunelleschi, Alberti, Masaccio, etc.), more complete and richer, perhaps, because more dramatically matured through its stage of "about": not only the formula in-front-of-a-thing-which-walks-by-itself, but also the formula "within-the-thing."

Iranian "mentality," as was shown to us, is not a struggle against "judgment." It is the will, the effort, to "judge," the nostalgia-memory of "judgment"; and at the same time it is the impossibility of exercising "judgment," the some-thing-against-it preventing.

This obstruction, what is it?

❖❖❖❖❖❖❖❖❖❖❖❖❖❖❖❖❖❖❖❖❖❖❖❖❖❖❖❖❖❖❖❖

There is a zone of human actuality or human "material" achievement that is based on the inventiveness (thus, subjectivity) of human nature, and at the same time—within that inventiveness—is detached from the immediate condition of human control (objectivity understood in the sense of the same "independence" that physical-cosmic laws seem to enjoy). It is in this zone that we can reach a kind of direct reflection or reverberation of both logical rules and emotional actualities (in the form of "utility," for instance), a kind of automatic response of the inner man: the zone of *homo faber*. The official science of the beautiful neglects this zone, and therefore misses the "integral man." As Lynn White Jr. in his study: *Technology and Invention in the Middle Ages* rightly says:

> The history of technology and invention, especially that of the earlier periods, has been left strangely uncultivated. Our vast technical institutes continue at an ever-accelerating pace to revolutionize the world we live in; yet small effort is being made to place our present technology in the time-sequence, or to give to our technicians that sense of their social responsibility which can only come from an exact understanding of their historical function—one might almost say, of their apostolic succession. . . .
>
> Broadly speaking, technology is the way people do things. (In a certain sense there is even a technology of prayer.) Yet it is startling to reflect that we have, as a rule, only the vaguest notion of how the men . . . actually did things, and how, from time to time, they learned to do them better . . . .[50]

❖❖❖❖❖❖❖❖❖❖❖❖❖❖❖❖❖❖❖❖❖❖❖❖❖❖❖❖❖❖❖❖

To our question, why, granted that Europe and Iran, West and East, belong to the same historical current of visual realization, why did Europe create its formula of three-dimensionality (judgment-Descartes II), whereas the Near East, the East in general, did not, this time we, the travellers, propose a hypothesis:

Because the West discovered the "machine" and the East did not. Iran knew the tool, but not the machine. Iran belonged to the cyclic mentality of tool-facture (the *feudal* collective mentality) and not of machine-facture (the "capitalistic" collective mentality). A tool being, as it is usually formulated, "the continued hand," the tool-facture mentality is a *hand-* or *manu-*facture mentality. Its constructed or fabricated "object"—mental or plastic—is limited to the immediate, organic physical, one might say, bodily dependence on possession of space—mental or plastic: a between-the-eye-and-the-hand possession and certainty. The solemn laying on of the hand—token of the feudal principle of *personal* confidence—during the "hommage" and fief-granting ceremonies; the personal physical relation—of combined violence and protection—between the lord and the serf or between the personified Divinity and the praying soul of the sinner; the personal physical attachment to the soil; the directness of the individual participation in wars, and the individual physical, the hand-skill in feudal crafts and arts—all this goes deeply into the dense roots of human body, or hand, awareness, the roots of what we called the manufacture, the hand-facture "mentality." The resulting "object"—mental or plastic—does not "walk by itself" but "walks with us," because of us. The same is true (when compared with our post-Baconian and post-Cartesian "walking-by-itself object"—European science and philosophy) of the scholastic European theology, of the Islamic Science of Tradition (Hadīth), of the Jewish wisdom of the Talmud and their walking-because-of-us "object"-faith; and so also of the form (the *what of the how* form) of say, a Persian carpet—the whole of a paradise-garden possessed between-our-eye-and-hand; or the "compresence" of shape-"ornament"-and-us in Iranian pottery, metalwork, painting, or building.

The machine, on the other hand, is essentially *homo faber's* "success" in achieving the independence of the mind's function from the body's or the hand's function. It is the "technological" objectivation of judgment-Descartes II. It is—even if only temporarily or not indefinitely—"the thing which walks by itself." The *idea* of this independence was born (and this is part of my hypothesis), in classical Greece, although the machine as an *object,* as a precise technical device, was not created or applied in Greece.

The application of this principle of independence from the body, from the limitations of between-the-eye-and-the-hand, gave Europe the machine and the three-dimensionality of space—mental and plastic.

Now—and this was precisely my hypothesis—Islam, the Islamic Iran of our eye's journey, was *about* to create this three-dimensionality, because Iran was also *about* to create the machine.[51]

✣✣✣✣✣✣✣✣✣✣✣✣✣✣✣✣✣✣✣✣✣✣✣✣✣✣✣✣✣✣

Two things characterize at the outset all modern approach to the science of technics and to the history or the philosophy of mechanical inventions. First, an indecision in the definition of the notion of machine, when related to or compared with—either as contrast or as resemblance—the notion of tool. Second, a unanimous affirmation of uninterrupted, perhaps unilinear, evolution of all technical inventions, tools, and machines: no rupture or discontinuity seems to be discerned at any point of that evolution.

The tool is usually defined, broadly, as a "continued hand." The tool, says Francois Mentré, is undoubtedly a prolongation of the hand, this universal tool, so that the ensemble of tools exhausts the analysis of all the movements executed by the human hand or by both hands associated.[52]

Now this formula of a continued body (or hand, as an extreme result of our tactile consciousness) we saw emerging from our analysis of the visual possession of space. Only there, within the eye, this possession was automatic, self-given, while here, in the case of the tool, it is projected-*fabricated*, exactly as we saw fabricated a "new" art object. Yet the tool-possession is without the inner conflict-élan which is the very condition of creativeness or inventiveness in art. Thus, the tool stands exactly between the automatism of space, the automatic prolongation of the hand, and the "new," invented object of space, the art object.

And now, how is the machine to be defined? According to Stuart Chase:

> The learned professors have been at considerable pains in their attempts to make a distinction between tools and implements on the one hand, and machinery on the other. Nor have they arrived much of anywhere. The one is continually shading into the other. . . . . Where does the tool stop and the machine begin? A grindstone is widely held to be a primitive tool; a turret lathe is widely held to be a machine. Both spin around. What is the essential difference? The employment of non-human power, steam, oil, gas, has been defined as the difference. Well and good. Then everything worked by human hands and legs is a tool only, and bicycles, typewriters, adding machines, sewing machines, foot lathes, clocks, hand-pumps—are not machines. Which is absurd. . . . . [53]
>
> Its [the machine's] commonest function is to transform random energy into disciplined energy. It thus includes tools of all kinds, and mechanisms for more careful recording and measurement—the transit, for instance, or the telephone receiver.[54]

Lewis Mumford's definition is more decisive although none the less discouraging in its application:

> In back of the development of tools and machines lies the attempt to modify the environment in such a way as to fortify and sustain the human organism: the effort is either to extend the powers of the otherwise unarmed organism, or to manufacture outside of the body a set of conditions more favorable toward maintaining its equilibrium and ensuring its survival . . . .
>
> The essential distinction between a machine and a tool lies in the degree of independence in the operation from the skill and motive power of the operator: the tool lends itself to manipulation, the machine to automatic action. . . . The difference between tools and machines lies primarily in the degree of automatism they have reached. . . . [55]

The definition of a machine as a "thing-which-walks-by-itself" is thus here intimated or implied.[56] Yet confusing values with the use of values (machine-notion, tool-notion with machine-device and tool-device), Mumford concludes immediately:

> Moreover, between the tool and the machine there stands another class of objects, the machine-tool: here, in the lathe or the drill, one has the accuracy of the finest machine coupled with the skilled attendance of the workman. When one adds to this mechanical complex an external source of power, the line of division becomes even more difficult to establish.[57]

The vision of a unilinear continuity of evolution shared and accepted by all historians of human technics is but a natural consequence of their opinion about the continuity between the *notion* or *idea* of a machine and that of a tool. A luminous panorama of this evolution is projected—entirely or in sections—by all the investigators.[58] Light is thereby thrown, directly or indirectly, on many obscure or misinterpreted social and economic problems of humanity, so that many prejudices, barriers, and other miseries of history and historical criticism seem to be already rectified or even eliminated. "Technology knows neither chronological nor geographical frontiers": one must abolish "the conventional barriers between Greek and barbarian, Roman and German, oriental and occidental."[59]

Under this secure light of universal historical interrelations—Hellenistic, Byzantine, Muslim, Far Eastern converging contributions—the so-called Dark Ages of Europe are seen as the very laboratory of all future progress: we can watch, for example, the development of the fore-and-aft rig, this revolutionary nautical device which "would mark an epoch in the history of labor by eliminating the galley . . . . would cheapen sea transport by increasing the average speed of ships, and, by reducing the size of crews . . . would vastly extend the range of ocean voyaging";[60] we can see the diffusion and development of another invention, far-reaching in its economic and cultural repercussions, the northern wheeled heavy plow whose close connection with the introduction, at the end of the eighth century in northern Europe, of the three-field agricultural system and the additional spring sowing thus made possible, so greatly increased agricultural productiveness and stimulated the growth of wealth, order, and civilization in northern Europe from Charlemagne's period onward, etc.[61]

Particular, or "local" aspects of technology become, under this light, incorporated organically in the universal panorama: the broad historical role played by animal power, the horse, for example, and in special connection with the latter, the origin of the modern harness and the nailed shoe. It was Lefebvre des Noëttes's elucidation of this problem which contributed so greatly to our general historical awareness. Three inventions appeared in Europe, according to him,[62] toward the end of the ninth century and the beginning of the tenth, the modern horse collar,[63] the tandem harness, and the horse-shoe. "Taken together," explains, perhaps too enthusiastically, Lynn White, "these three inventions suddenly gave Europe a new supply of non-human power, at no increase of expense or labor. They did for the eleventh and twelfth centuries what the steam-engine did for the nineteenth. Lefebvre des Noëttes has therefore offered an unexpected and

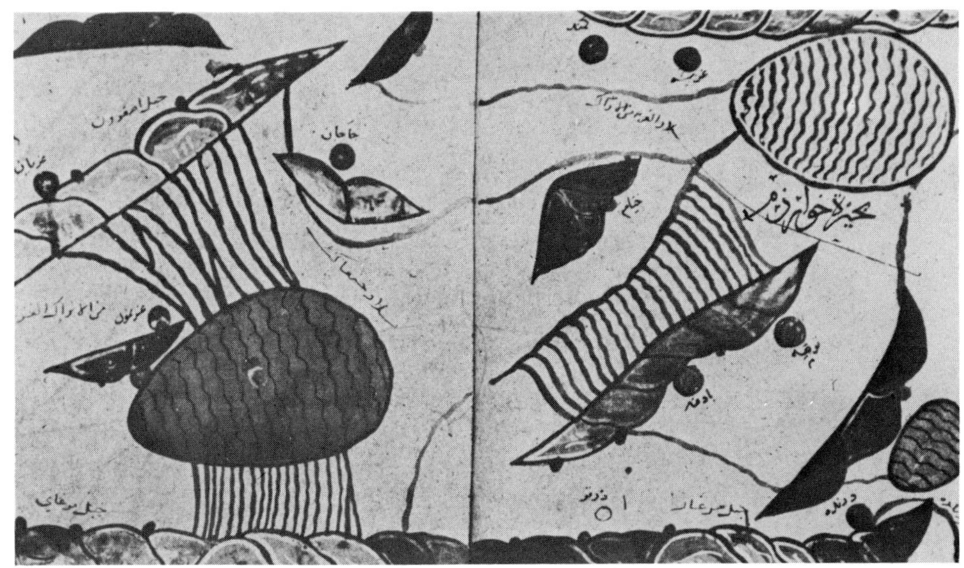

149 Al-Idrisi *Map* (12th century)

plausible solution for the most puzzling problem of the Middle Ages: the sudden upswing of European vitality after the year 1000."[64]

This progressive aspect (as well as many other analogous aspects) of the "dark" feudalism contrasts with the technological backwardness of the "luminous" antiquity. Because of the basic slavery system there, the use of animal (nonhuman) power in classic antiquity was incredibly inefficient. The yoke-system of horse harness (adequate to oxen) was a disastrous, strangulating device.[65] Neither did antiquity know how to protect the horse's foot. The foot protection was the sandal of leather or iron (sometimes even of silver or gold, in the imperial stables of Nero and his wife Poppaea),[66] bound to the horse's hoof mostly by cords, and used to cure rather than to protect.

Then, among many other examples of the universal historical value of the particular, "local" aspects of technology, let us not ignore the role played by the earth's raw materials in the shaping of our historical cycles or collective "mentalities": the evolution of metallurgy, for example, and the emergence of the great metal cycles or cultures, the Copper Age, the Bronze Age, the Iron Age. Or the importance of wood, nature's organic material of which, until our modern Western era (seventeenth-eighteenth centuries), tools and machines were made; its still insufficiently known "collective" repercussion in all the essential technics of those times, in fine arts, literature, every-day living, wars, etc. . . . Or the emergence of modern European cartography, which, running parallel (end fourteenth-fifteenth centuries) to the advance of exact scientific "three-dimensional" thinking (mathematics, physics, etc.) and the deepening of progressive social demands (beginning of feudal disintegration; growth of individual—"capitalistic"—awareness of freedom, of municipal necessities and liberties; geographical widening of trade's ambitions, etc.), gave to Europe the notion of "judgment," or perspective on a cosmic scale, the perspective of heavenly bodies and earth's facial traits. Invented contemporaneously with the rediscovery by European art of the Hellenic three-dimensionality—the "thing which walks by itself," in front of us—the modern map is likewise a three-dimensionally organized cosmic "thing which walks by itself" in front of us: the in-front-of-us position of planets, stars, nebulae, forests, rivers, cities, mountains, coasts, seas. . . . [67] What a totally different "thing," indeed, is the cosmographic space of the earlier Middle Ages, especially of the evolved Islamic cycle (the tenth and eleventh centuries)! The informative principle of this earlier cartography belongs to a totally different mentality too: not the in-front-of-us mentality but the my-body-among-seas-forests-coasts-skies mentality. We have the typical medieval synthetic-intuitive mentality with whose "permission" the earth's and the sky's anatomic silhouettes—the map's contents—could sometimes reproduce and deform such strange figures as animals or trees *(Plate 149)*: a very obscure, yet very creative collective-reflex-groping—still tribal, totemic, still physical visceral, sexual-magic-astral—of man's inner participation in the outer aspect of the world: Descartes I plus Descartes III.

Very important, almost central, was the role of Islam in the progress of our Western technology:

> It is probable that the Power Age [our Machine Age] would never have come to us, even as it never came to Egypt or to Greece, had we not adopted, some hundreds of years ago, Arabic [Hindu] numerals and particularly the Arabic cipher. The decimal system with its zero enormously simplified calculations. . . . The science of measurement must have remained in its infancy without the zero. . . . [68]

Yet the decisive—if not central—episode in technology's drama of continued evolution was the cultural "success" of the Hellenistic cycle—a legacy directly and creatively taken over by Islam. Now, this immensely important historical period which followed Alexander's feudal patriarchal and imperialistic adventure can be considered as a creative synthesis of the city-state (or world city-state, or world-state) and the feudal mentalities. It was a unique experiment in man's history, where the city-state's rational democratism—founded so contradictorily, therefore so fatally for its destiny, on slavery—and on the other hand, the theocratic—both despotic and communal (city-temple's "communism")—polity of the ancient East could combine for a while. What is more, this combination itself was formed so to speak with a view toward a new collective and additional complex: the dramatic fusion of city-state-city-temple with the new Macedonian ideal (or rather the old ideal peculiar to all late "patriarchal" stages) of feudal, constitutional and secular monarchy based, traditionally, on pan-tribal military equality, and economically, on serfdom.

From this tumultuous complex arose the Hellenistic culture which nourished both Europe and Asia of all the subsequent centuries; a culture in which the central idea of monarchic unity or unification could be totally reflected or expressed on all other levels of life—political, social, economic, as well as cultural: the "Hellenistic" emergence of world empires, Parthia, Rome; the growth of monotheism through the channels of Judaism and Stoicism; the gnostic universalism of the "Iranian" Mithraic creed, Christianity's greatest rival; and, finally, rising from this provocative background, as a result of the Hellenistic union of practical and abstract thinking, perhaps the most daring technological inventiveness human history has ever witnessed.[69]

In the center of this glorious technological period stands the figure of Heron of Alexandria.[70] We know him chiefly from his *Pneumatica.* Translated into English about the year 1600, this work, hitherto unknown to Europe, became the starting point of a technological revolution which gave us the modern Machine Age. Soon after, Edward Somerset (later the second Marquis of Worcester) and Dr. Papin studied with enthusiasm Heron's principles and by their experiments laid the foundation for the engine which opens our industrial era, the steam engine of Watt. Heron's book shows clearly that the Hellenistic engineers and scientists knew and understood the general principles of steam (including the use of the piston, the cylinder, and the valves), the principle of geared wheels which gave, in its later medieval European adaptation, the mechanical clock, and the modern principle of vacuum (practically translated into the principle of atmospheric pressure in the water pump, which was rejected by Aristotle and the mediaeval orthodox Western scholars[71] on the theological philosophical ground that vacuum or the discontinuity of eternal space is impossible because it contradicts the unicity and the plenitude of God's manifestation).

That is how Heron of Alexandria anticipated in the first century A.D. (or earlier) some of our modern notions of mechanics and physics. However, the full realization, in theory and in practice, of the value of these notions, he could not reach. What he could fully reach is the *about* of this realization. All his inventions remained ingenious scientific toys: the heat (hot air) engine which he built and named aeolipile led him only to the invention of a device for mysteriously opening and closing the temple's doors, and all his steam and atmospheric discoveries were used to build complex water-clocks with automata, the glory and luxury of Islamic ages.

Heron's about-to-be-machine "modernity" had to await centuries of social, economic, and scientific maturation in order to be systematically understood and applied. Meanwhile, between these two cycles, the Hellenistic and our own, technics continued their revolution through the constant refinements introduced there into the two main—feudally universal—sources of power and motion: water and wind. We know how great and beneficial during the mature feudal era was the role of water and windmills in their application to all kinds of industrial activities, the textile industry, mining, etc.[72]

While the feudal Near East of the subsequent Islamic periods remained stationary in its technological functioning, that is, *immobilized at the point of the "about" result reached by Heron,* medieval Europe, on the other hand, could, in its rapid social and economic transformation, advance with equal rapidity toward the acquisition of a fully evolved Descartes II point of view: rationalization of the entire life conception, rationalization of space and time, etc; in short, the moral, social, and scientific triumph of judgment's three-dimensionality. For at the end of antiquity, Europe, through the initial fusion of the decadent, already semi-feudalized Roman system with the German nomadic feudalism (a fusion which was much less the result of an "invasion of the Barbarians" than the consequence of a great social revolution by which the slave labor economy could be liquidated and thus serfdom or feudalism established), Europe could develop normally, unilaterally, so to speak, its feudal cycle and prepare, by inner differentiation and slow self-disintegration, the next cycle, called "capitalistic."

Iran could never reach this unilinear normality of fusion and development, first because Iran—*the entire East, rather*—could never entirely liquidate the slave labor system, this system having never been *totally* dominant there; second, and perhaps chiefly, because the Iranian historical evolution was repeatedly and one might say rhythmically interrupted by always the same traumatic event: the epoch-making invasion of feudal nomads or semi-nomads (Arabs, Turks, Mongols, etc.) which always meant a retrograde, regressive—yet in some respects also fresh, strong, and young—primitive tribal re-feudalization.

At the end of each of the great periods of Near and Central Eastern history, when the revolutionary self-disintegration of matured feudalism was *about* to be achieved, this drastic re-feudalization came invariably to reconstruct from within and with a richer content, the old building.[73]

It is this rhythmically repeated and intense *about*-achievement of its emancipation from feudal chains which makes so nonconservative the apparent "conservatism" of Iranian—the East's as a whole—evolution—social, economic as well as cultural—so rich internally in all sorts of refinements and nuances, so daring in its future-building creative intuitions.

Yes, there is undoubtedly a continued, uninterrupted history of the tool-and-machine evolution as affirmed or implied by modern historians of technical inventions. But somewhere in that history, there is discernible also the creative momentum by which was affected the break between or mutation from the tool to the machine. What is more, we must expect to find that this jump, or rupture of continuity, had its own causal genesis. And indeed, it is not within the material technical achievement itself—the machine as a mechanical object or device—that the revolutionary momentum of discontinuity from tool to machine was incorporated, but within something else, different in its aspect, yet connected by inner necessity to the technical achievement, namely, the concept of motion, or movement, the concept on which the exact definition of all mechanical devices is based. In other words, the technological revolution which would bring about a new and higher stage in the mechanical notion of movement, with all the resulting scientific and cultural repercussions, could be realized without practical implications: that is, without provoking the immediate invention or construction of the actual machine. The idea-machine would be given to the world nevertheless. This revolutionary idea-machine was born in classical Greece, while the "object"-machine, the machine as a mechanical power apparatus, remained totally unknown there.

Pre-Socratic Greece (except Heraclitos, the Mobile) knew the circle only. The uniform rotary continuity of the same effort—the perfect circle—gave them in its sense-mechanical hypostasis-substitution, the metaphysical (Parmenidian) certainty of my-body being within the body of cosmos, of my-body forming one circular body with the cosmos: the "continued," non-emancipated "hand." How physical was the metaphysical certitude of the pre-Socratics! And the mechanics of classical Greece was based on the development of this perfect "hand" or "tool" circularity: the five "simple machines" of antiquity, the wheel and axle, the lever, the pulley, the wedge, and the endless screw, all of them reducible to the basic and "circular" principle of the lever and all functionally related to the same and common purpose of moving weights.[74]

Then the break, the rupture of continuity came—the great "moral historical" revolution of post-Socratic Greece. Greece discovered the principle of detachment of "my-body" from itself; the awareness of "my-body" as a separate being, separated from me.

Instead of one circle-being, two intersecting circle-beings; reciprocity and coincidence of "me" and "my body"; "my" body, my awareness of a body-mind—the new and residual xx_1 figure—becoming then a "thing which walks by itself."[75] It is this detachment of the body, of "my" body through the consciousness of itself, the *return* to it, that is at the bottom of the Socratic technic of moral analytical self-watching: the watching of the watching of "my" body's behaviour. And the science of morals was born: Socrates's "know thyself."

But why *my* body? And in what relation to technology or technological awareness? It is only in reference to our body that motion can be apprehended elementally. The first conscious notion of movement comes from the verified relation between our body, which, as the center of our existence is always in movement (even when in repose), and other bodies (human or not human). And though these separate outer objects or bodies might move toward each other rather than toward me, even then the central *reference* remains in my body. It is only when I can finally detach myself from my body by means of a constructed and exact system of calculation or measurement (creation of a kind of a "logical" body parallel to mine), a system which is the direct result of the watching of my watching (genesis of abstract mathematics), only then can I also *judge* independently (free from my body) all the various movements effected in space and in time outside of me and including me ("my" body studied "objectively").

That is how the science of judgment—Descartes II—is born, the science of perspective or three-dimensionality: in art, in the syllogistic, categorical organization of thinking—the thinking of thinking; in mechanical or technological evolution.

The "thing which walks by itself," the idea-machine, was born.

This revolutionary mutation initiated by Socrates, incorporated in Plato's vision, still of the circle-tool, was fully realized only by Aristotle. Aristotle (whose probably great indebtedness to the scientific experience and generosity of the East must not be forgotten) is, thus, the real father of the idea-machine, the first to apply the Socratic principle of body-detachment to the general principle of motion. It is with him that the cosmos—its shape and its total, outer and inner, content—became such a system of interrelated mechanical and metaphysical movements which, by virtue of its continued initial impulse, could "behave" as a "thing which walks by itself." The Prime Mover, supreme continuity and supreme discontinuity. The "thing which walks by itself" was created—the concept of a machine. And the machine "mentality"—the notion of the machine, the "desire" for the machine—came to us from that Aristotelian source.

Through many subsequent stages and mutations of human scientific thinking, the practical embodiment of this notion and this desire could be finally realized.

The immediately post-Aristotelian period, the Hellenistic, took over with creative understanding and enthusiasm the Aristotelian message. The *about*-to-be-machine stage was reached: Heron and his technological prowess.

Asian Islamic culture inherited this result, perfected it, but did not, could not—and we saw partly why—provoke the next and the decisive mutation. Only Europe in its fully transformative process of social-economic and ideological conquests could find the necessary inner strength to complete the Aristotelian-Hellenistic revolution: only Europe could invent the machine-object. How? By creating an *automatically* controllable synthesis of the rotary and reciprocal movements.

> . . . . . There are two basic forms of motion: reciprocal and rotary. The normal device for connecting these—a device without which our machine civilization is inconceivable—is the crank. The crank is an invention second in importance only to the wheel itself; yet the crank was unknown to the Greeks and Romans.[76] It appears, even in rudimentary form, only after the Invasions: first, perhaps, in hand-querns, then on rotary grindstones. The later Middle Ages developed its application to all sorts of machinery.[77]

The pure rotary motion was the only mechanical motion known by classical antiquity, as we saw. The Hellenistic Eastern civilization was able to acquire the necessary knowledge of simple reciprocal motion: the geared wheels were already widely and ingeniously used. But the principle of gears was not sufficient in itself to promote the embodiment of the Aristotelian idea-machine in an object-machine. The principle of "mobile" reciprocated, "rigid" discontinuity had to be introduced in the pure rotary motion itself: a cranklike "discontinuity" which would make the gears a thing detached from the initial hand-continued circle or circles, a thing which would stop and move, move and stop again and again, and "walk by itself," had to be created. And it was created, indeed. It was created in the mechanical clock. "The primary mechanical elements of the clock with geared wheels had long been known. The use of weights as a driving mechanism extends far back into the pre-Christian period. The use of gears begins in a small way in the pre-Christian period and their use was widely extended in the milling industry. The use of such elements for the measurement of time was long an impossibility. . . . "[78]

They could not be applied to the mechanism of water clocks. The measurement of time could never be exactly controlled by these marvellous and so beautifully perfected works of mechanical art, the glory, and until about 1250, the almost exclusive monopoly of Muslim craftsmanship. Why? Because, explains Usher: "there was no means of controlling the force of the falling weight. Without some form of escapement, the falling weight would not measure time because it would move at an accelerating rate."[79]

An escapement[80] had to be invented. And it was. This was the decisive step toward the mechanical automatism or the real machine-object. A very primitive device, probably the earliest known form of an escapement, is to be found in a drawing in Villard de Honnecourt's famous *Album* (thirteenth century): a primitive and crude apparatus where, nevertheless, the motion of the wheel could be arrested so that "the fall of the weight would be periodically checked and released" there.[81] The principle of an "intermittent impulse"—principle-genesis of the machine-object—once launched, further rectifying inventions followed it, laboriously and sometimes dramatically. The application of springs to the driving mechanism of clocks at the beginning of the sixteenth century marked a real, systematically and not merely empirically realized advance in the evolution of the escapement principle;[82] perhaps the most decisive triumph of automatic accuracy and control was that gained by the seventeenth-century discovery[83] and perfecting of the pendulum—a very remarkable and influential moment in the history of technological progress.

How, by what means this clock automatism or the Aristotelian "discontinuity" embodied in the metal device (the escapement) was or ever became combined with another "discontinuity" principle (apparently anti-Aristotelian, but in reality very consistent with his metaphysical "discontinuity" doctrine), namely, with the principle of vacuum or discontinuity of eternal space;[84] how, by what means, this combination of mechanical and atmospherical "walking" devices culminated in the invention of the steam engine and the great industrial social revolution at the end of our own feudal cycle—all this is too well known and too much studied to be retold. The prophetic element in this drama, however, must be invoked here. The invention and the application of the steam engine was the culmination of the principle of crank-reciprocal mechanical motion. It gave to the world the Machine or the Power Age, but at the same time it gave the possibility of a new historical *mutation,* the possibility of an ultra- or extra-machine revolutionary move. By its *extreme* application or utilization, the modern machine complex *provoked the return to the pure rotary motion,* therefore, to the tool principle: to the principle of a total continuity or re-integration of our body-complex with the cosmic, the more-than-we body-complex.

It is generally appreciated that through the action of electricity, radio-electricity especially, the three components of the modern machine, the prime mover or the power engine, the transmission devices (the devices which transmit the motion and the power to the end-tools, belts, gears, levers, etc.), and the end-tools themselves, are more and more fused together in the sense of a uniform, continued (thus "circular") transformation of power into work or motion. The transmission devices especially become, more and more, integrated parts of the entire machine, more and more *identified* with the nervous system of our body. The *electrified mechanism* in its extreme delicacy, a delicacy which affects even the material used in it—new alloys, rare metallic earths and the lightest metals[85]—becomes a sensible being, almost a physiological means of yoking our own physico-psychic being to the sensibility of the surrounding universe: such is, for instance, De Forest's three-element oscillator or amplifier developed out of the Fleming valve, a complex and extremely delicate—"sensitive"—apparatus in which the only moving parts are electric changes.[86]

A great "moral" historical promise, perhaps the promise of a future light out of present darkness, invites our fatigued hope to take rest, if only for a while: our return, this time historically conscious, to a more back-to-the-tool, back-to-the-hand vision of ourselves and of what is more than ourselves.

❖❖❖❖❖❖❖❖❖❖❖❖❖❖❖❖❖❖❖❖❖❖❖❖❖❖❖❖❖

How different, and yet—because of its tenacious attachment to the tool or circular motion "mentality"—how near to ours, is the world of the East: a world both so incomplete in its Hellenistic "about" result or crystallization, and so more-than-complete, so prophetically ultra-modern in its proximity to that total technological result to which we, "modern" (without losing our past experience), seem to be "about" to return.

Water—water mills, water clocks, manuscripts and manuscripts, and more manuscripts buried in libraries of the Orient, full of illustrated descriptions of hydrostatic automatons, of water wheels, of balances, of elevations of water—that is what dominates absolutely the entire Eastern perspective of technology.

For water, as an *integrated* part of nature's body, inwardly intuited by us (and more directly than wind, for instance) as nature's "hand," is in itself neither a power which can create a "crank-discontinued" automatism, a mechanism *detached* from my body (provided we keep here in mind the elemental intuition of our moving body continued in the body of the outer world or nature), nor, naturally, a total and direct "continuation" of "my" body. Water is in-between: neither prolongation (nature's-hand-thus-my-"hand") nor rupture ("hand" detachment). Water is in-between. The *material* condition of the "about" mutation (Hellenistic East) is in it.

Now science, or scientific thinking-philosophy *tout court,* and technical invention are parallel in their historical growth; sometimes it is science which prefigures invention, sometimes it is invention which awakens science.

And so there is no better, or rather no more direct "proof" of this historical "about"-hypothesis than what the history of the Eastern-Islamic science, both speculative and experimental, can tell us.

It is an astonishing history, indeed: a daring and ingenious cycle which was "about" to reach the greatest heights of our modern Western cycle. Too complex and too long a history also to be revealed in a sketchy, and thus deforming, outline.

A few examples—patterns of the thinking of that cycle—must suffice here.

So, for instance, it was the mathematical and logical revision—one of Hellenistic "worries" already—of the famous Euclidian parallel postulate based on perceptual evidence, which led the mathematicians of Iran, Omar Khayyam in the eleventh century[87], Nāṣir al-dīn al-Ṭūsī in the thirteenth century[88] to the "about" establishment of a non-perceptual, non-Euclidian geometry, thus furnishing a basis for the European seventeenth- to eighteenth-century's problems of purely mathematical space, thence to the daring postulates of Gauss and Riemann, and finally, to Einstein's theory of relativity.

It was in the "international" and so restless thirteenth-century still Seljuq Iran that the doctrine of the plurality of space and time—this most daring modern "discovery"—was affirmed and defended by scholars like al-Ṭūsī and perhaps the Iranian Sufi, Fakhr-ud-Dīn 'Irāqī,[89] among others. Indeed this doctrine must be traced yet further back, to the main tenets of the famous atomistic or Ash'arite school of Islam. For it was in this school, especially in the writings of Ash'arī's—the founder's—great follower, al-Bāqilānī (d. 1013) that the modern atomistic doctrine of matter without mass—matter and life being conceived there as composed ultimately and exclusively of atoms of space and atoms of time—was "about" to be clearly formulated.[90]

On the other hand, contrasting with this matter-without-mass doctrine, it was in the thirteenth century also that the law of gravitation was enunciated (still empirically) by the great Iranian scholar and poet, Mawlānā Rūmī, in his chief work *Mathnawī*:

> Every particle in the Universe is coupled with every other particle and attracts it. Its attraction is quite like that of amber towards a straw. The sky and the earth are both like iron and magnet to each other . . . . The Earth remains hanging in space because the Heaven (heavenly bodies) attracts it on all sides. It is like an iron ball which if placed at the center of a dome built with magnetic stone, will remain fixed. The revolution of the sky (heavenly bodies) is due to attraction. Had this attraction not existed, the world would have faded out.[91]

About five centuries before Copernicus, al-Bīrūnī, one of the grandest figures of Islamic learning, testifies to the fact that a famous astronomer of his time (beginning of the eleventh century) believed in the earth's motion around the sun, and that the orbits of the planets are elliptical: the heliocentric doctrine was "about" to be established scientifically.[92]

It was Mawlānā Rūmī again who, in another astonishing and revealing passage of his *Mathnawī*, echoing, probably, a common scientific thought of his time, offers us the modern theory of biological universal evolution (still mystically veiled or conceived, it is true). He says:

> At first man was in the shape of the minerals and from that he changed to vegetables. For many years he lived in this vegetable form, oblivious of the struggles that he had made as a mineral. Then he changed from the vegetable to the animal, and forgot all about his past, i.e., the vegetable life, except the love that he had for the trees and the flowers at the time of the

spring. In this manner he was transformed from one stage to another, till the present state of consciousness and wisdom was reached.[93]

But, perhaps, the most striking "proof" of the "modernity" of all Islamic learning is to be found in the presence there and the propagation of what can be considered as one of the essential features of our Western modern science, one of the most far-reaching of all forms of mathematical freedom: namely, the scientific and philosophical idea of function.

Now, the idea of function or the "mobile" idea of number conceived as "pure relation" opposed to the "stable," static idea of number as "pure magnitude" was known already to al-Bīrūnī (973–1048 A.D.), in whose writings we can find—as a result of the deepest philosophical scientific reflection—this modern notion expressed by him quite specifically: al-Bīrūnī already knew that subtle, functional, and mathematical formula which is called now by us the Newtonian interpolation formula of the trigonometric functions.[94] It is the formulation of this idea of function as early as the beginning of the eleventh century by an Islamic Iranian thinker that completely nullifies the violent and inauspicious doctrine of "closed cultures" propagated by Oswald Spengler in twentieth-century Germany, according to which the idea of function would be the exclusive prerogative, the "symbol," as Spengler calls it, of the West, forever inaccessible or closed to the inferior mentality of the "closed" East.[95]

But cultures are not "closed." And it was, among other factors, the Islamic-Hellenistic culture, its "about" emancipation from the feudal mentality, that, through the channel of slow and hidden diffusion, could help all the struggling forces of the medieval West to overcome the latter's feudal limitations and to prepare, from within, Europe's external, political change or emancipation.

❖❖❖❖❖❖❖❖❖❖❖❖❖❖❖❖❖❖❖❖❖❖❖❖❖❖❖❖❖❖❖

The leaves, the flowers, the fruits of the tree of art are the *material* testimony of life's "invariant"; its roots are the very roots of life's material conditions. The entire tree—the richly leaved branches, the great trunk and the nude roots—is the "integral man": the synthesis of *homo loquens* and *homo faber.*

That is how—and not in any narrower sense!—our hypothesis was offered: Iran—Near East—was "about" to create its own formula of three-dimensional judgment—Descartes II—in art, because Iran was "about" to invent its formula of three-dimensional "machine" in life. So that this hypothesis becomes also—at the same time—this conclusion: Let the East —the entire East—possess the fullness of the "machine" mentality on all the levels of existence, and then, only then, Iran will overcome the "machine" by a conscious *return* to the "tool." Let the East—the entire East—become liberated through its own inner effort, and if required, with our nonmalicious help, from all the feudal chains of its life; and we shall see then how great, and beneficial even for us, will be again the "new" object created there; we shall see how, etc. etc.

But—"Allah knows best" . . . .

Our Last Adventure

The light of the day was rapidly abandoning our eye's landscape. It was the end of our journey. The silhouettes of things became more and more fused, and we could not distinguish any more what belonged to the eye's revelation properly and what was introduced there from elsewhere. Yet our inquiry was not finished. We were perplexed. In saying: "mobility-stability equilibrium"; in saying: "the art of the Persians was *about* to acquire it spatial fullness"—were we not indeed revealing the intimate mechanism of our own result-participation rather than theirs? Are we not therefore, and first of all, destroying that lovely and accessible to all, by all accepted, truth which is the simple poetical joy and ease of all Persian—or Japanese—art? Aren't we, with our difficult, complex and heavy "digging," destroying all this joy and ease: the simple and tangible poetry of Islamic Persia's figural, architectural, and *abstract* splendor; Persia's poise and playful grace; the triumph of rhythm in its imagery—crowded royal hunts, courtly mass symmetries, sky-and-flowers, trees-and-adolescence, tranquil sages and water, geometric fugues—and above all, that intimate sense of family, as life's center everywhere present there, from the cozy house-home of God to the cozy house-home of the lord, from a glistening, delicate and cozy lustrepiece to a cleverly-thought, delicate, dense and also cozy textile, a passionate sense of mother-and-father's peace, the truly *intellectual* ideal of nomads, infused so constantly into Iran's life sensitiveness?

So, perplexed, we advanced rapidly into the dying day: when the knotty roots are closer to our sight than the by-night-submerged branches.

❖❖❖❖❖❖❖❖❖❖❖❖❖❖❖❖❖❖❖❖❖❖❖❖❖❖❖❖❖❖

Why is it that no other historical cycle, so it appeared to us in final vision, had possessed and applied the principle of substitution in art more fully and more subtly (yet, at the same time in a most hidden way) than the Iranian-Islamic cycle? Why?

Because, as we saw before, the feudal mentality could acquire there, in its slow maturation and in its acute, several-times repeated "about" crises, a greater complexity and perhaps a greater skill in self-expressiveness than anywhere else. Interconnected with its material background—social and economic—this skilful "mentality" could generate a specific ideology, or a specific method in approaching reality, which became precisely the main support—the "permission"—of the image-deforming substitution technic in art: the ideology of Islam itself.

Now, in spite of all its labyrinthian external complexity, the historical formation of this ideology presents a luminous and simple inner view. We can discern there its origins, we can follow the path of its evolution.

Indeed, dominating in height and diversity of accidents the great summits of Islamic intellectual life of the first centuries—the pro-Aristotelian and neo-Platonist lofty speculations of the *falāsifa,* the arduous tenacity of the all-out-for-Qur'ān-and-Revelation Traditionalists—and emerging from the extreme and violent rational absolutism or rational spiritualism of the ninth- and tenth-century Muʿtazilite, stands all of the famous intellectual revolution of Al-Ashʿarī (d. 935).

Both reactionary in its reinforced traditionalism and progressive, new, in its liberation from the rationalistic absolutism, Ashʿarism is a typical Islamic creation of a method and philosophy of rational criticism and critical rationalism. Fully evolved under the discipline of al-Bāqīlanī (d. 1013), and perhaps best expounded in its purest speculative shape by the great Jewish non-Ashʿarite philosopher of Spain, Moses Maimonides (d. 1204) in twelve fundamental propositions of his *Guide of the Perplexed,*[96] this doctrine appears to us as the most original if not the extreme attempt of human thinking both to affirm and to limit the empire of pure reason. Ashʿarism prefigured if not surpassed in boldness the Kantian criticism itself. Duncan B. MacDonald comments:

> The object of the Ashʿarites was that of Kant, to fix the relation of knowledge to the thing in itself. Thus, al-Bāqīlanī defined knowledge (*ilm*) as cognition (*maʿrifa*) of a thing as it is in itself. But in reaching that "thing in itself" they were much more thorough than Kant. Only two of the Aristotelian categories survived their attack, substance and quality. The others, quantity, place, time and the rest, were only relationships (*iʿtibars*) existing subjectively in the mind of the knower, and not things. . . . [97]
>
> There exist only material atoms and their accidents, and so-called natural forms are also accidents . . . . Whatever is imaginable *(mutakhayyil)* is also rationally possible *(jâʿiz áqlî),* with the exception, naturally, of logical contradictions. . . . The existing has no necessity in itself but is dependent on the will of Allah. . . . [98] *The senses do not give certainty and their decision cannot be made the basis for any absolute proof* (burhān) . . . . The evidence of the senses, then, can never be accepted against a rational demonstration. Motion seems to our senses to be continuous, but we know by reason that it consists of a series of leaps and rests[99] . . . .

"Whatever is imaginable is also rationally possible. . . . The senses do not give certainty and their decision cannot be made the basis for any absolute proof." Here is the Ashʿarite "permission" to reconstruct, to place or to affirm as real a "substituted" natural image. For images are not "real" things: we might be forced by Allah's will (we call it "inspiration"; artistic, creative inspiration) to present or represent them *differently* than we sense-perceive them.[100]

Because of the element of intellectual violence which this categorical skepticism (form of metaphysical despair or pessimism which seems to be fatally attached to all Islamic speculation) concealed, pure Ashʿarism would have to face, in the long run, the usual danger of stratification and death were it not for the new life which was infused in its veins. And this new life, which became the very life of Islam itself, was the decisive cultural revolution made by the religious genius of an Iranian, al-Ghazzālī (d. 1111). It was a nonviolent revolution this time, a *via-media* reconciliatory revolution. For al-Ghazzālī reconciled two violences of Islam: the critical rational and the mystical. Indeed, parallel to the current of extreme Islamic rationalism there flowed another current of deeply human, lyrical aspiration toward truth, a current which came to be known to the world as Sufism. This method of individual search for truth or reality, with its prefiguration of the Beatitude of Identity, passed also, almost from the birth of Islam, through all the shades or degrees of self-affirmation; from the extreme suavity of the poetess Rābi'a al-'Adawiyya (d. 752) who said: "My sorrow is not for the things which make me grieve, but my sorrow is for the things for which I do not grieve,"[101] and who, it is reported, when asked: "Dost thou hate the Devil?" answered: "No." And when asked again: "Why not?" said: "Because my love for God leaves me no time to hate him";[102] and the extreme and rigid logistic of Hasan Basri's (d. 728) "science of hearts" (*'iln al qolub*);[103] to the extreme emotional-moral severity of al-Bistāmī (d. 875) who cried to God: "Thou obeyest me more than I obey Thee!"[104] and confessed to men: "I thought I had arrived at the very throne of God, and I said to it: 'O Throne, they tell us that God rests upon thee.' 'O Bāyazīd,' replied the Throne, 'we are told here that He dwells in a humble heart' ";[105] and finally reaching the supreme mystical violence of Islam, the *Ana'l Hakk* (I am the Truth!) of al-Hallāj the Martyr (executed in Bagdad in 922).

It was al-Ghazzālī's synthesis of these two opposite currents—Ash'arism, Sufism—that finally gave the world in its mature form what we call Islamic culture. Al-Ghazzālī "led men back from scholastic labors upon theological dogmas to living contact with, the study and exegesis of, the Word and the traditions,"[106] and to the emotional source of religious behaviour. From his time, Sufism, accepted by the Orthodoxy, became one of the firmest pillars of Islam, and Ash'arism, in the East chiefly, after a short period of struggle, the dominant philosophy and philosophical method.

The repercussion both in the field of speculative and practical thinking of this nonviolent revolution was immense. And it was from this joint action, the Sufi exigence of individual freedom for its truth-searching method and the Ash'arī affirmation of the nonvalidity of the criterion of our sense-data, that all the most daring formulations of Islamic scientific thinking—nonperceptual, purely abstract-mathematical and critical-experimental—came.

But there is something more in the Ash'arite doctrine, something more revealing than even the ontological skepticism of this philosophy—its "Critique of Pure Reason"—and that makes it really, in our opinion, the ideological basis of the "substitution," hypostasis, technic. This more is Ash'arī's "all-out" return to the traditionalist orthodox creed. Ash'arī, who before his conversion to strict orthodoxy (Sunnism), was a brilliant Mu'tazilite, thus a defender of the sovereignty of reason (*al-'akl*) and of free will, of God's pure spirituality or abstractness, of Qur'ān's human and not "eternal" creation, etc., suddenly, after a strange dream that, according to tradition, brought to an end his acute and sudden religious crisis, became the most ardent, convinced, and militant champion of a most "primitive," most "naive" form of faith. He textually and *uncritically* accepted the Revelation, such as it is, and all its objective, materialized contents: the reality, the tangible, concrete and not "allegorical" reality of Paradise and Hell; the Throne; the Balance; the Bridge stretched over the back of Hell; the Tank of Muhammad from which the believer, after his death, shall drink before entering the Garden of the Hereafter and after passing the Bridge; the Book, etc.

How could such an "obscurantist" move be performed by a critically emancipated Muʻtazilite? Only by a *total* change in the man's inner attitude toward reality, in the kind of interest in it and in its purpose. There is an illustrious document which shows us clearly what this change was. This document is Ashʻarī's creed. In reading it there is revealed to us immediately (especially when compared with other "creeds," that of al-Ghazzālī, for example) that the reality or truth which concerns the reformer exclusively *is not the reality of life,* but *the reality of death.* Here is the real key to the "psychological mystery" of his conversion. While for a philosopher—Muʻtazilite or any other of any time and any region—everything, including the speculation about death and the hereafter is, so to speak, visualized or proposed mentally—metaphysically or otherwise—in terms of life or life's interest and purpose, in Ashʻarī, as in all really religious thinking, it is life itself, life's object, life's being, that is posed and accepted in exclusive and concrete terms of death (the grave). Death is the life, death is the only figuration of life in Ashʻarī's creed;[107] while death is the transfiguration of life in al-Ghazzālī's creed.[108]

And it is here, in Ashʻarī's return to the Revelation and to its material contents, more efficaciously than elsewhere, that the presence and the role of the "hypostasis" technic becomes so obvious also. For the naive, textual —and not allegorical—acceptance of the Revelation is the delicate and "difficult" result of a substitution process. It is the hypostasis of faith by certitude; the substitution of the humanly accessible rationality of certitude for the unavoidable extra-rationality of faith: substitution and not reconciliation of faith and certitude (reason) as the Muʻtazilites and the Thomists wished to have it. In the uttermost depth of faith's genesis this substitution starts at first as an allegorical, a "meaningful" certitude (objects of Revelation considered or felt as rational poetical symbols or symbolical objects of faith and life after death). Then, from degree to degree of growing *rational* disdain toward any *extra-rational* exegesis, this still temporarily constructed certitude reaches finally the top of an absolute, *total* certitude by means of a total substitution of faith.

Now, death or life after death being the true reality and the true purpose of any religious faith, *qua* faith, this total substitution, death for life, means the substitution of the objects themselves for the symbolical value of the objects of faith. These objects are the familiar objects—the Book, the Bridge, the Tank, the Hand, the Pen—of our earthly life, death's contrary. And it is just because life is immediately given—in our imagination—as the contrary of death that all the familiar objects of life fit so exactly and immediately into such a substitution and that, therefore, all these objects continue to be in this total substitution the real, concrete—and not allegorical—objects of death or faith.

Through the channel of cultural interchange—scientific, philosophical, artistic—the subtle power of the Ashʻarite "hypostasis" must have been very influential in Islam as well as where Islam could culturally penetrate. We find it, this "total substitution" result, in the mysteriously three-levelled reality of al-Ghazzālī, his three simultaneous modes of all existence, the changing world of our senses, the eternal world of God's decrees, and the intermediary world of messengers, *alam-al-mulk, alam-al-malakūt* and *alam-al-jabarūt*[109] where great objects of worship are living not allegorically but really, actually, as illustrious personalities: Islam, Friday, Qur'ān. We find it in the convincing, closely present plasticity of Nizam's fancy. And so we found it ourselves in the hypostasis-formula of Iranian space.

❖❖❖❖❖❖❖❖❖❖❖❖❖❖❖❖❖❖❖❖❖❖❖❖❖❖❖❖❖❖

In Islamic Iranian art, more intensely than in any other art, more even than in Yamato's—and this was the chief result of our journey—ornament, the *deep* ornament or the *future* new image-emotion, new idea-representation, the "new object," Descartes I, is the hypostasis of visual space; the quality of decoration—its *what of the how*—is the concretized "symbol" of visual depth or perspective judgment.

Now, the "new" object, the "substitution" result, is, we saw, the result also of a precise, creative, and total historical moment. Thus a "new" object—in our case, the *Fourth Variation on the theme of Japanese painting,* the Iranian ornament-perspective, the Iranian "mobile" "about" formula—is the hypostasis of a precise and total momentum of the past, remote from or close to us. Art is the hypostasis—the substitution—of the past, remote or close, very remote or very close. But art is the integral man also, essentially. By saying "we participate," we say, *we of today complete a missing part in the integral man of that time—the man and his innermost body.* We are this part. For we are part of the integral man: participation means *our* participation added to *theirs,* the men and the events of the past, whose "object" becomes then ours.

And so we were led, without desiring it at all, to ask this last question: "Who are we, the until-now-missing fragment of the past?"

❖❖❖❖❖❖❖❖❖❖❖❖❖❖❖❖❖❖❖❖❖❖❖❖❖❖❖❖❖❖

At this very instant the last light of the day bestowed—as usually it does before things in light go away—its farewell on all the vastness of the eye's land, reaching, behind us, to the very entrance of our journey. And we saw ourselves there outlined in a "hypostatic"—substitution—pattern of human general behaviour.

Three circle-zones, intersecting and not tangential, formed this pattern of all human being and all human conduct. We contain in us all three of them, we all pass through each of them, but we choose or are given as our inner dwelling—and this is what we call our individuality!—one or the other of the three inner circle-zones of action.

And I saw that the first circle has to be named the circle of aesthetics, because *comfort* is its psycho-moral center; comfort in the sense of sufficient, satisfactory and satisfying achievement of "inner peace": exactly the feeling that beautiful things give us before we question them.

I saw then, that the second circle—the zone of the middle—was named moral, because its center is the *idea of perfection;* perfection in the sense of stability of the moral laws which everything categorically must be reduced or referred to, even—perhaps chiefly—the feeling of beauty and comfort.

But when we looked at the last circle of the inner man's behaviour and being, I saw that its name was not certain: some would call it the circle of metaphysics, some the circle of poetry, and others still, the circle of solitude. We liked best the name of poetry, but accepted as more convenient the name of metaphysics: its center is the *idea of perfectibility,* perfectibility in the sense of perfection's growth or activity, in the sense of Eros (Eros within beauty, within goodness, within truth, or within any other—if there be such other—purpose).

All our activity seemed to us colored with the color of that or those of the three circle-zones which dominates or dominate us; and it is this inner chemistry which defines a human being and his behaviour. So, for example, one can be a moralist or a metaphysician—professionally—and yet act in this field of morals or metaphysics as an *aesthetician,* as a man whose moral or metaphysical attitude toward life's conduct or life's enigma would be centered—by an organic choice—on the exigence of comfort, of moral or metaphysical comfort, of moral or metaphysical satisfaction received from that activity. And one can speak or write aesthetics, but if the inner—chosen or given—center is moral, the entire vision of beauty and art will be moral also, will be submitted to the categorical concept of what is perfect and necessary forever: Tolstoy, for instance. And it was the organic "choice" of the aesthetic-and-metaphysical hegemony that had limited or weakened, in the last instance, Dostoyevsky's moral vision; as on the other hand, aesthetic and moral tonalities gave the main color scheme to Emerson's philosophical panorama; but the metaphysical depth could not be reached thereby: the circle-perfectibility was half-eclipsed by the joint action of comfort-perfection.

And we could see then how the harmony of all the three circle-zones made the greatness of Goethe, for example, or of Spinoza, or of Rembrandt.

In art—our chosen concern here—this inner circle-chemistry defines the degree of our participation in—our behaviour toward—the integral past.

First circle: we enjoy art, we enjoy its comfort. We enjoy art as belonging to the past. For art and the study of art, even if it is today's art, belongs to the past.

And the past is comfortable: it is as such outside of our control, thus of our responsibility. We enjoy art, we enjoy the past, we enjoy history. *The past is in the time center of the circle-aesthetics.*

Second circle: ideas, rules, categories of reality. Permanence. Presence. The time center of this circle is the *present.* Art-comfort is rejected and with it past-comfort, history-comfort. Plato's *Republic.* A beautiful action is nearer perfection than a beautiful painting, or statue. People who struggle for the minimum of material aims, necessary and permanent comfort in life, hate the *aesthetical* comfort of the first circle-zone. They are attached to, they choose, the severe circle-perfection. The privileged—materially and mentally—are attached to the first.

Third circle: union of the other two. (Strange, yet to be expected, reapparition of Descartes I, II, III.) The circle-past becomes here the circle-idea, the permanence *and* the presence. A past is now an idea-permanence and an idea, any idea, any general concept is now forever a past, a certain, concrete past: terrifying thing—for our comfort—and so difficult to say!

Circle-perfectibility, Eros, where history (historicity) is the unique idea-truth and where art, which is almost-history and nothing else, becomes thus—almost—the unique witness of the unique Truth: the Mysterious Companion of any journey. And it was shown to us there, accordingly, that the time-center of this circle is the *future.* For the past, the history, the art of the circle-aesthetics means change—in the sense of transformation, of correspondence understood as comprehension or memory of change and motion; on the other hand, the idea, the present, the permanent in the circle-perfection means immobility, unspeakable immobility there, a timeless categorical arrest—total transfer, substitution (our sensation-blue = idea-blue). The union of both in the circle-Eros, past = present, past = idea, idea = past, becomes the only possible pattern of the future.

When we, lovers or students of art, are dominated by the rule of the aesthetic circle we contemplate and *enjoy* the artistic (the *what*) creation; when we enter the moral circle, we "judge" it (the *how*); when we are in the third circle, we participate in, we adhere to the integral man's total time—past, present, future.

There is a beautifully illuminated Iranian book of poetry decorated in the middle of the sixteenth century.[110] One of the twenty-eight miniatures *(Plate 150)* is, if not the most revealing at least the most eloquent of all: a brightly colored scene crowded with tents and people. It is profoundly "Iranian": "rigid mobility" of interconnected oblique lines and tonalities; flatness of silhouetting—flatness which is "about" to awake spatial depth—and all the poetry of a semi-nomadic, vanished close-family existence, familiar virtues and vices of fragile promiscuous peace; colors, faces, broken lines, and tents, tents, tents all over.

But you asked me—do you remember?—you asked me: "Did they, the Persians of that Shah Tahmāsp's time, know what we see in it?"

"No, of course not. Because they lived in it."

They, the Persians of Shah Tahmāsp's time, knew, just as their fathers and grandfathers did, the life lived in tents, the life within tents, within or with textiles, entirely, overwhelmingly. This new and unknown to us—banal for them—experience, could be realized naturally, automatically by them, *without* the awareness of this living. The living within tents-textiles; the particular textile smell; the among-textiles penumbra; the particular sweetness and warmth of textile shelter, childish, festive, erotic; the particular, subdued under-tent's-textiles acoustics—all this was closely and overwhelmingly known by them.

There is extant a descriptive text which helps us to understand better this extraordinary nomadic-like experience. It is the narrative of Tīmūr Lang's (Tamerlane) royal camp outside Samarqand, his imperial capital, made by the Spanish ambassador of King Henry III, Ruy González de Clavijo, in 1404: a naive and exact reconstruction of a completely new world, a world of textile-sensations and textile-perceptions.

 With the old chamberlain-ambassador we walked all through the in-

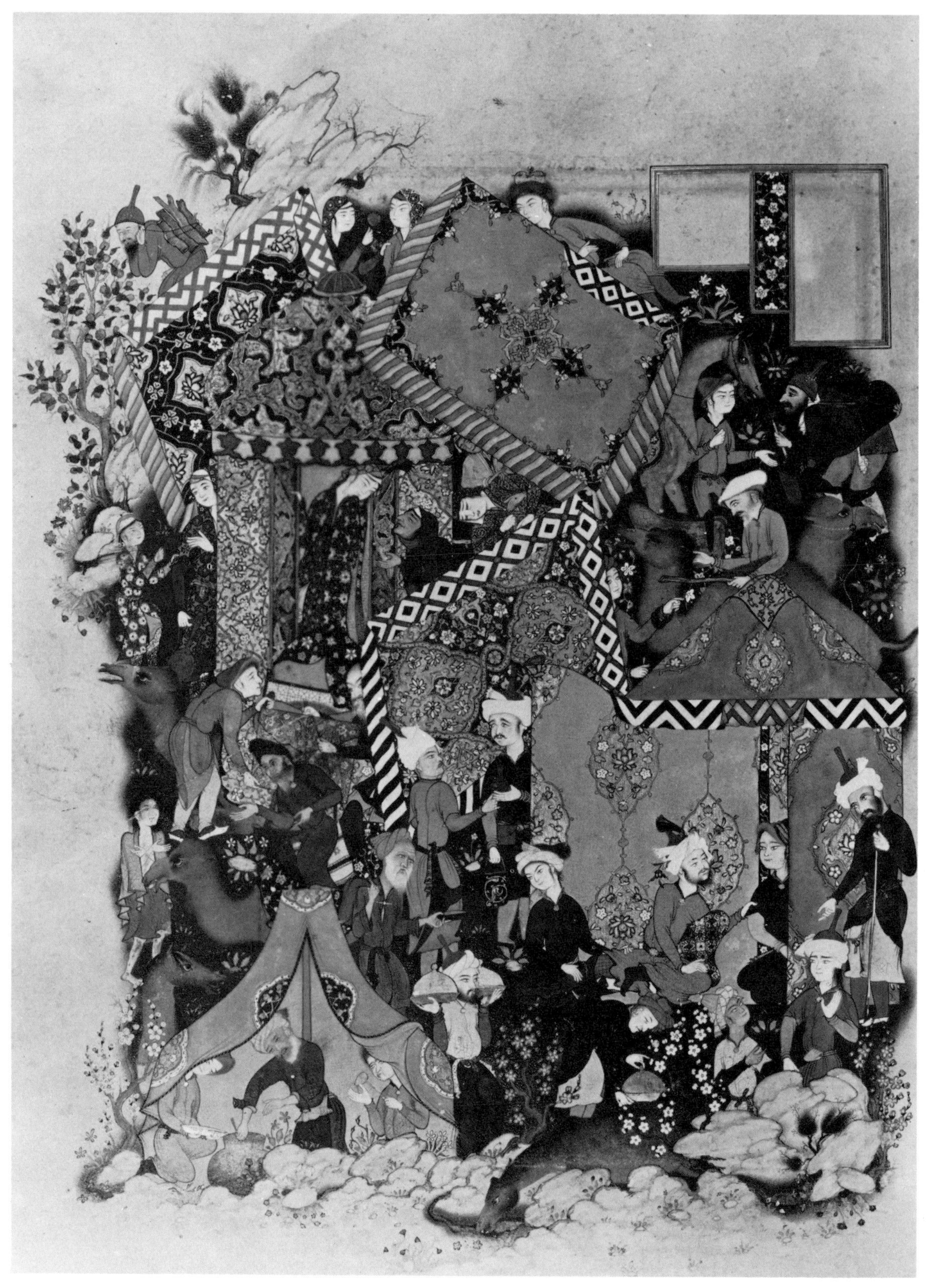

150 *Mejnun Comes to the Camp of Laila* Persian miniature (16th centry)

tricate labyrinth of textile corridors, covered passages between tents; among textile walls; along textile streets and bazaars; we penetrated into the splendor of royal palace chambers, the imperial tents, we lived within, with velvets, silks, embroideries. . . .

As regards us ambassadors we were that day taken over to the Horde, and in the great camp we found they had erected an innumerable number of extra tents all very beautiful to see, and for the most part these were erected on the bank beside the river. . . . These tents were marvelously fine, all one beside the other, very closely pitched, and thither they conducted us through a roadway where were all sorts of goods exposed on sale. . . . As soon as we had come near to where Tīmūr was in residence in the royal tents, they left us for a season to rest in the shade under a spacious awning. This we found to be made of a white linen stuff overset and let in with coloured embroidery, and the awning had wooden poles at the back which supported it by means of cords holding it taut. The like awnings were to be seen in many other parts of the camp and they are fashioned long and high in order to be open to the sun to catch the breeze. . . Nearby this awning where we were seated stood a very large high pavilion, in fact a very huge tent, and it was four square in shape. The ceiling of the pavilion was made circular to form a dome, and the poles supporting it were twelve in number each as thick round as is the chest of a man breast high. These poles were painted in colours blue and gold and otherwise. . . From each of these poles at its summit in the dome shaped ceiling there hangs one end of a great curtain in silk cloth that is thereto attached, and these curtains are looped up running from pole to pole, so as to make four archways. Round outside the four walls of the main tent of the pavilion there are *low galleries, like porticos*. . . The inner walls of the pavilion are lined with crimson tapestry very beautifully woven in patterns of diverse designs, further it is hung with silk stuffs of many colours in places worked over with embroidery of gold thread. The ceiling of the pavilion is its mark of greatest beauty for at the four corners are figured four eagles sitting with their wings closed. The exterior walls of the pavilion are made of silk cloth woven in bands of white and black and yellow that to us appeared made of silk sarsenet. . . From a distance . . . this great tent would appear to be a castle, it is so immensely broad and high. It is a wonder to behold, and magnificent beyond description. . . Round and about the pavilion on the ground outside is erected a wall of cloth, as might be otherwise the wall of a town or castle, and the cloth is of many coloured silks in diverse patterns. Along the wall-top are battlements. . . . This encircling canvas wall goes round a space of ground measuring across, may be, some 300 paces, and the wall itself is as high as a man on horse-back may reach up to. There is an arched gateway to it, with double doors without and within, all made of canvas as above described. . . Above the gateway rises a square tower of canvas with battlements, and as forsooth the encircling wall makes grand display of patterns and ornamentation in the stuff of which it is made. . . This forms the great Enclosure surrounding and shutting in the pavilion . . . and within its circuit stand many other tents and awnings. . .

Nearby again stood another tent. . . It was very richly made, the stuff being a red tapestry like shag-velvet. Then in a row there were four tents that were connected together by a passage way going from one way to the other, by which one could pass as might be through a corridor. . . Within

> the same great Enclosure we noticed quite a number of other tents, and nearby was another, a second Enclosure like the first, and as large in extent, shut in by an encircling wall of silk stuff, woven to look as though it were the pattern on a tile. In this wall there were opened at intervals window frames with shutters, but these window openings could not be passed through from without by any one, for each was guarded by a netting of thin silk tape. . . Alongside these first two Enclosures there is a third with canvas walls of a different make, with many tents and awnings. . . Further we noticed many other such Enclosures beyond and about. . . Each was of its own colour and design. . . These eleven Enclosures were indeed standing so near one to the other that between their outer walls, from the one to the next, the space was only sufficient for the width of a roadway. All these Enclosures aforesaid were occupied either by the wives of Tīmūr, or by the wives of his grandsons, and these princes and princesses have their abode therein, as does also his Highness likewise, both summer and winter .[111]
>
> Now on that Thursday the 9th of October Tīmūr commanded a feast to be made in honor of one of his grandsons whose marriage was about to be celebrated. We ambassadors again were invited. . . Further to celebrate this day of the royal wedding his Highness had given command by proclamation throughout the city of Samarqand that all the trading folk of the town, namely those who sold stuffs and those who sold jewels, with the hucksters and merchants for sale of goods of all and every sort, together with the cooks, butchers, bakers, tailors and shoemakers, in short all the craftsmen who were inhabitants of the capital, should betake themselves out for that day to the meadows where the great Horde was encamped. They were at the same time under obligation to bring out their tents to the camping place, and to sell there the goods and produce each of his trade, and thus the city was to remain empty of them all. The order further was given that each trade and craft should next arrange a gala show, where each man should display his skill making an exhibition throughout the Horde for the pleasure of all spectators.[112]

It was a great gala, indeed! And we saw the spectacle and greatly marvelled at it. With the old Castillian and the others, again we walked and walked all through the intricate penumbra-labyrinth of corridors of textiles, of walled street-textiles, entered palace-textiles, royal tents, artisans' tents, shops. . . . Bright colors, broken lines, oblique inclination of erected surfaces—tents and people and sky, sky, people and tents, a sea of textiles, silks, velvets, embroideries. . . . Overflowing, elemental, new ambience!

But not new for them, the Persians of 1404 or the Persians of 1535! For them it was a normal, natural, age-old ambience. And it could therefore provoke there that necessary and normal complex of inner responses that "hypostatically" led them toward certain "Iranian" artistic actions or experiences which we, now, cannot do or reproduce any more, only "enjoy" and "judge." Yet by penetrating artificially—with our contemplation-enjoyment tools—into this textile-life, we *challenge* the reality of a forever vanished past. In this process of participation-hypostasis, we distort at first the facts, because never did these people think as we must about their art: as of the "mobile," the "about," etc. But in distorting their reality we *force* the entrance to the past; thus we can penetrate—personally—into this past (event-past) and become these Iranians of 1535 A.D. for an intense and short moment of identity: a total, hypostatized moment of comfort, of perfection-"stability" and of "mobile" perfectibility-desire. We reach, through our sympathy-nostalgia within our innermost body, that degree of *moral-historical* perfection which life itself was reaching there, in Iran of those days. Sudden, total participation!

❖❖❖❖❖❖❖❖❖❖❖❖❖❖❖❖❖❖❖❖❖❖❖❖❖❖❖❖❖❖❖

We can, through art, participate in a past event. Can we equally influence it, correct it, change it?

We could not see any more. The night of our spring came rapidly and things became alike. And we had to go back. But just before we reached again the entrance to the other world, a gentle and friendly voice came through the nocturnal air. A friendly message:

Lucid shadows, Memory, good night!
What is lost is what is won
By day's dream. To be gone
Is to come for brighter light.
All is one; good night, good night!

VARIATION V
SUMMER

Summer:

A l'estiu tota cuca viu.

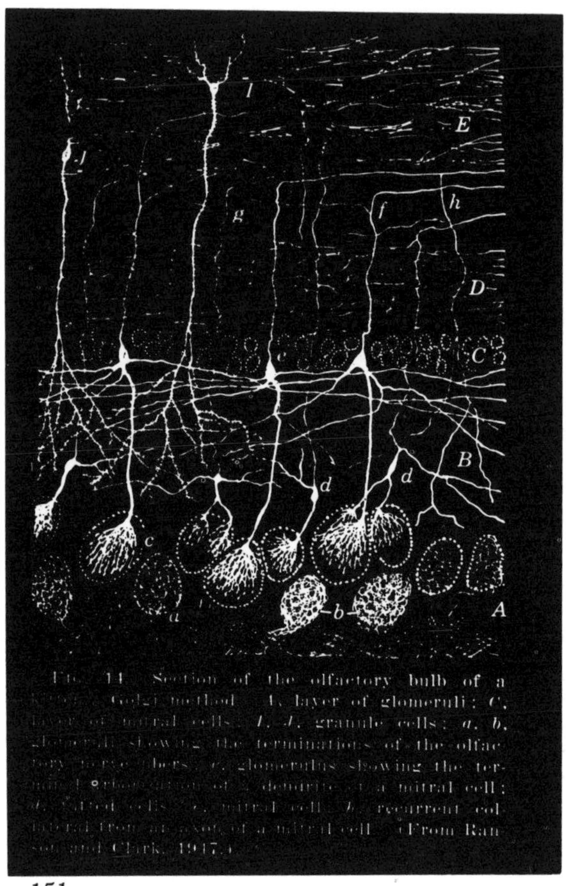

[illegible] 14. Section of the olfactory bulb of a [illegible]. Golgi method. A, layer of glomeruli; C, layer of mitral cells; *l*, *j*, granule cells; *a*, *b*, glomeruli showing the terminations of the olfactory nerve fibers; *c*, glomerulus showing the terminal arborization of [illegible] dendrite of a mitral cell; *d*, [illegible] cells; *e*, mitral cell; *h*, recurrent collateral from an axon of a mitral cell. (From Ranson and Clark, 1917.)

The Sense of Smell

Prelude to a Difficulty

Summer! It is good to be back.

The shortest possible distance between man's innermost and outermost body: his summer.

Just as smell is. Just as Child is. Just also—and this is what remains to be added now—as this painting, painted in Japan during its Momoyama period, was to me one day: just as bliss is.

Indeed, it all started—and we still can perceive the three interwoven circles, the aesthetic, the moral, and the metaphysical, of the inner man—everything started there with this Momoyama masterpiece of "ornament" and its "sublime" summer experience of smell as bliss and Child, lived among the painted flowers and flowery branches:

> *En una nocha escura, con ansias en amores inflamada,*
> . . . .
> . . . .
> *Quedéme y olvidéme*
> . . . .
> *dejando mi cuidado*
> *entre las azucenas olvidado.*[1]

The sense of smell: the least "sublime," the most material of all; a "low" or "inferior" and primeval, very ancient animal, chemical sense, yoked to taste, whose universe of stimulus-discourse starts at the arrival, upon the localized deep-nasal mucous, of the odorophore or osmophore particles: an obscure, tortuous moist = lipoid, dry = gaseous story of a nerve travelling from the olfactive cleft to the olfactive bulb of the brain.

And yet what is meant here, in my summer experience, is not the travelling experience of a particular flower scent evoked or awakened in a back-to-child echo-memory by the *scientia signata* of, say, those almost "real" blossoms, painted-bunched together by a dexterous Japanese *(See Plate 152)*, but truly, as well as suddenly, the sheer surprise and excitement, or exultation, in meeting—*entre las azucenas olvidado*—a visionary form-smell, an image-smell—*La Folle;* very similar to the form-taste, image-taste, so truly also, as well as suddenly, seen or discovered by Sartre's body-spade:

> The *sugary,* for example *expresses* the slimy when we eat a spoonful of honey or molasses, just as an analytical function expresses a geometric curve. This means that all qualities which are not strictly speaking flavor, represent the *matter* of flavor . . . . These qualities . . . on another level . . . express the visual aspect of the food. If I eat a pink cake, the taste of it is pink—thus I eat the pink as I see the sugary.[2]

The scent of the painted cherry blossom and the red fruit, painted: seen and heard, touched and mimicked, intellected and smelled, all at once! It is good to come back.

FIRST EPISODE, OR MOVEMENT

Adagio ma non troppo

In the Vicinity of the First Difficulty

Victis honor

Good to be back. The labor being finished and the four-arched bridge erected—over what? What else if not the new body's consubstantiality, its solitude-solidarity and the empty-full word *infinity* floating there, interstellar, inter-neuronic: the arch of the man-and-his-innermost body, arch one; the arch of the autumn-vision, arch two; the arch of the winter-sound, arch three; the arch of the spring-touch, arch four.

But the seasons are four. Where is the arch of our summer? The arch of summer *must* be there—given or built already. Indeed, it is there, it has been there from the start. It is the very arch of man's innermost and most ancient body.[3] To cross the new bridge is both to come out of it, to leave its last stone-support, and to come in to its start, back to its first stone: a back-forwarded bridge—not a straight Euclidian space-measuring one-pointed direction, but a multi-directional in-curved span, a strange, a very strange new "convention"-monster. And—why should this neo-consubstantial space structure be measured as being stranger than, say, the one signalled and tested already by Kepler's "convention" of the illimited and in-curved line, or by today's notion of the cosmos's body as light = electricity's curved, in-out, volume? (Twentieth century's concern about measure-conventions expresses itself thus: " . . . . . the comparison of size of distant rods cannot in any way be tested by an objective criterion, but rests on a convention only. We *name* certain widely separated rods equal in size, and that must be enough; for there is here not *cognition*, but a *convention*. We name such an agreement a co-ordinating definition since it achieves a co-ordination between real rods and the conception of spatial equality. Only on the basis of the convention does this conception have a real interpretation, correspond to anything in reality, and it is only when it thus acquires content that physical measurement becomes possible at all.")[4]

And furthermore, once the bridge is erected, what's so strange about the "project" of fusion—or con-fusion—between the physical-geometrical and the epistemological? Has not man's quest for the *what-of-the-how* of knowledge—the science of epistemology—been always the inescapable corollary (in spite of this being so jealously denied by "pure" philosophers) to the historical changes in the philosophy of nature? Greece: its cosmos-"convention," a still "two-dimensional" limited sphere, and its corollary, the Hellenic man's "coming out" as a limited, individuated-collective being, either—two-dimensionally—all mind-*res* or all mind-*persona,* a soul, a species, an abstracted certainty, an abstracted self-expression. And twentieth century: its own cosmic continuum-"convention," one only among any infinity

152 KANO SADANOBU *Cherry Blossoms and Pheasants*
Momoyama period ▶

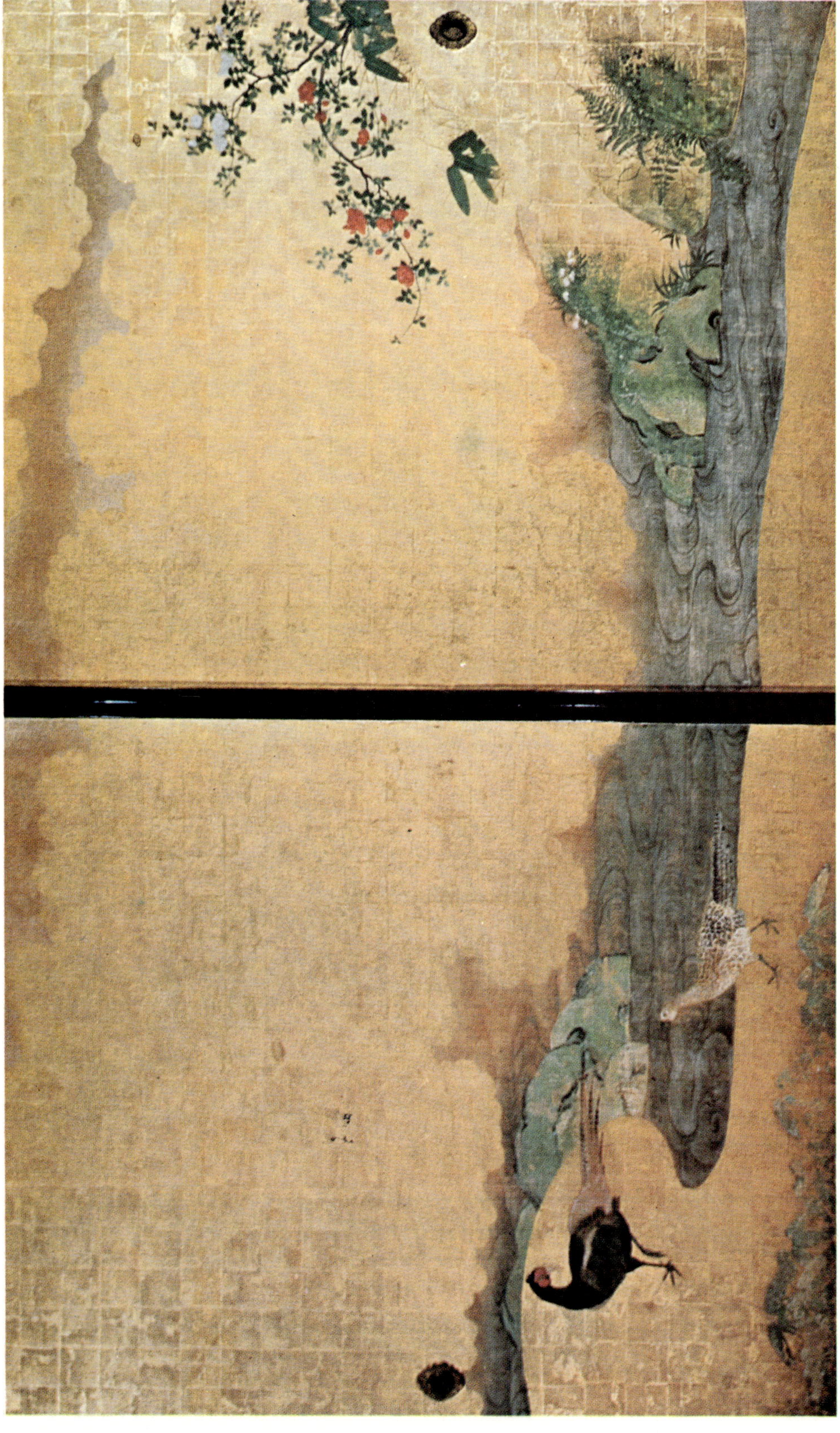

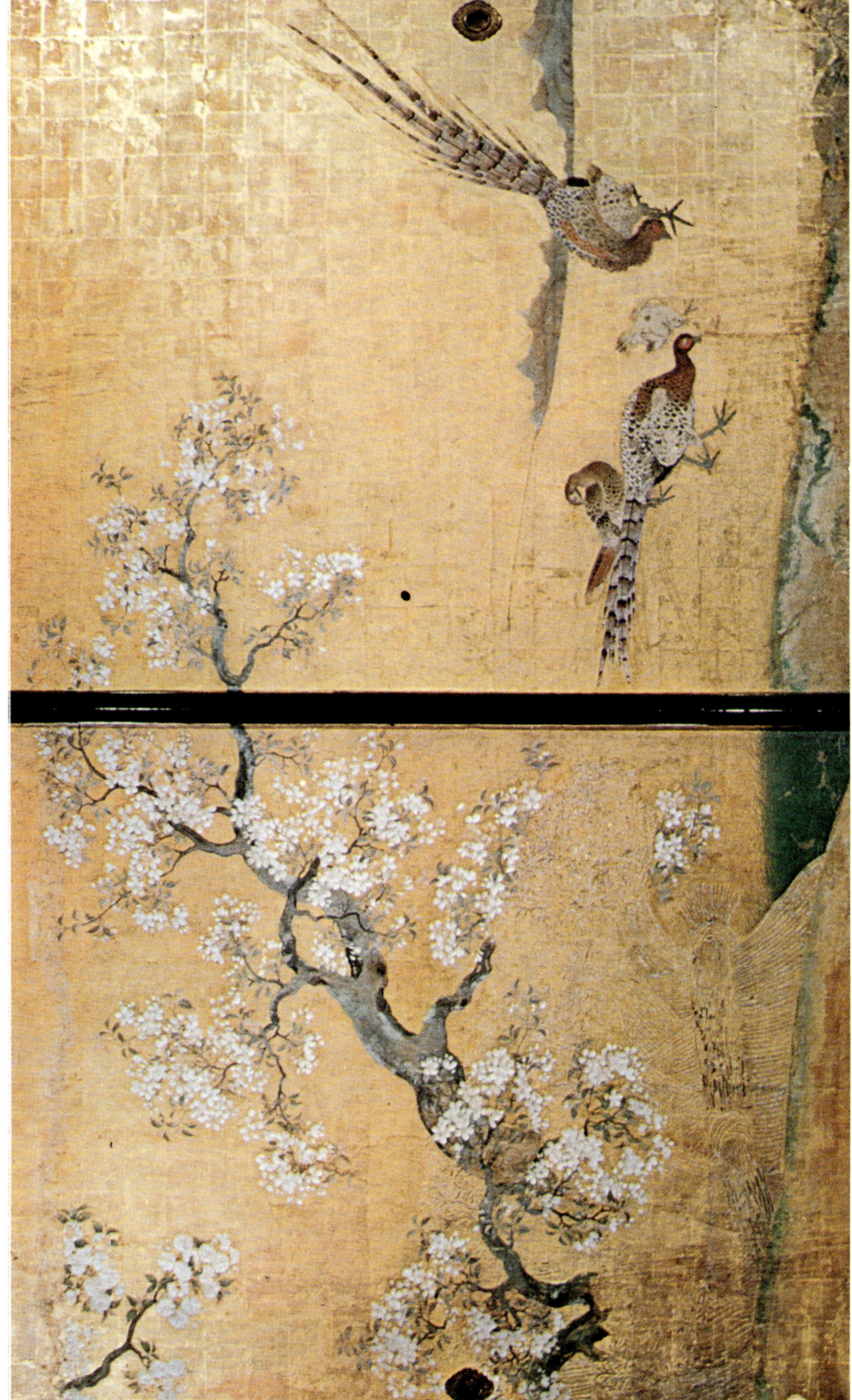

of probable other ones, and its epistemological, cognitive corollary, contemporary man's "coming out" as a collected individual, as an in-out continuum, as a curve of growth, as socialism-and-electricity, as probability and existence total, as *res = persona,* an abstracting and abstracted mind-stuff, an all-body expression.

✣✣✣✣✣✣✣✣✣✣✣✣✣✣✣✣✣✣✣✣✣✣✣✣✣✣✣✣✣✣✣✣

Summer: finished the labor. And the four-arched bridge rests upon its five stone foundations, the five stone-words planted upright in the flux under the bridge: *ready, peine, witness, discovery, vicinity.* And the word *ready,* which supports the innermost body's arch, grows into a garland of self-succeeding and radiating words that forms the curve of the arch itself: ready, myth, intensity, quantum, passion, logic, arbitrary, *peine.*

And *body's* last stone-word, *peine,* which functions already as autumn's great foundation stone, arches itself into autumn's *peine d'amour,* ghost, substitution, dance, witness. And autumn's last word, *witness,* builds up winter's curve: of witness, of history, of heraldic mind, of discovery. And *discovery,* spring's foundation stone and word affirms itself, along the spine of spring's arch, first, as the difficult equation-word *ornament*—bow's stretched curve joining *mud* and *amor intellectualis Dei*—then, as the stone-word *vicinity,* the vicinity of all that had preceded it. That is how the stone of the word *vicinity* became the foundation stone of both summer's last arch and innermost body's returning first arch: *ready = vicinity.*

Summer thus is in vicinity so close—the closest!—to the innermost body (the thinness of the skin being there the only separation from the outermost, interstellar, body), so indistinguishable from it, that it cannot be perceived or "proven" either as sight, or hearing, or even touch, but—in temporary and as yet uncorrected definition—only as smell (and taste).

Summer: the briefest intensity of a presence, a total presence of adherence with no category of relation in it as yet, only relation = vicinity, the two before the one, sex in vicinity of invention or of God, a total quantity witnessed as a total quality, wet-dry.

Summer: sensation-blue = idea-blue again: the true, the good and beautiful blue. Now and finally, the four-arched bridge, an infinity spanning the out-in blue bridge:

Blue-sensation-idea = body blue
Blue-sensation-idea = image blue
Blue-sensation-idea = sound blue
Blue-sensation-idea = touch blue
Blue-sensation-idea = smell blue

From farthest to nearest, from "highest" to lowest, from smell to the abstract, to the idea: the good and true and beautiful blue smell. In-out-coiled serpent, Kundalini,[5] genesis and goal of all energies and all tranquillities—India's great hallucination and art, the ascending shiver of Kundalini's evolvement = involvement from the root support, *Mūlādhāra*[6] to the liberating abode, *Satyaloka,* Yogi seed's supreme height, "which within the human body exists in the pericarp of the thousand-petalled lotus (*Sahasrāra*) in the highest cerebral center";[7] his-hers, Śiva-Śakti's self-ejecting power that "does not and need not stir from its place."[8]

✡

It is good to be back. Back to the Child, the *lieu* where poets are not to be chained as yet to the law of succession, the succession of their interpreted influences, but are released—the chain of reactions from smell to abstraction released—and bunched together, heraldic event-charges painted upon the shield of the individual, of the unique. Exactly that which is in the immediate vicinity of the outer-innermost body; an intense brevity of a rapid and sudden contact, sudden thus surprising, surprising thus exciting, and exciting because the contact here is *almost* simultaneity, but not really.

Exaltation, brief and lucid—the proving without proof: difficulty overcome. For I remember, while now at rest, I remember our "convention," which, at the bottom of judgment's act—the readiness in us both to accept and to reject, to justify and to evaluate[9]—made vicinal, almost reversible, the function of critique and the creative function. So that, by extension, critical "coolness" and creative "exaltation" themselves are in closest vicinity to each other. Creation (the coming of a new form: "I am ready to meet the new monster, watchfully") is cool. Critique, derivatively, explanation (the coming of a new form: "I am watchful over my readiness to meet the new monster") is exalted, is "hot."

SECOND EPISODE OR MOVEMENT
Andante molto espressivo
In the Vicinity of Another Difficulty

> But woe to you that are rich: for
> you have your consolation. St. Luke

The heat of summer's brief and lucid exaltation, summer's coolness: it is good to be back. Back to the Child, back to Japan who is the Child, back to the art of painting and of Japanese painting.

Back: I, Japan and history-without-proof.

I, the Mysterious Companion with no traveller or author there in need of companion any more. I, autumn's promise to come back—I am back. To say simply: that the Mysterious Companion is not any more but in Child's bliss to draw, the bliss to discover how to draw a totally real yet totally invented nose seen in front:—Child's delight, *trouble délicieux,* in another = self Child's involvement *(Plate 153)* within a continuous universe of pastel crayons; the delight of discreet color pallor; universe truly invented, universe of bliss, of shelter and invention, not of discourse: space almost complete—the hovering mother's. Exactly, the Momoyama four sliding doors from the Nagoya Castle *(See Plates 154, 155),* and my own, non-Japanese, of course, involvement *there* in a childhood's exalted and cool event—there? or here?—precisely here, at any child's summer moment and not at any other place in this book:

Far away, a little boy's escape from the danger and poison of school into the green delight of an end-of-his-little-town's meadow.

Trouble délicieux, a perverse delight, full of bliss, of course, known *a priori*: a meadow! Here it is, the high fence of the meadow, to be jumped or leaped over. Here—in a finite = substituted memory? In Kundalini's ever actual, *unarrested* and self-liberating *Prana* = Vitality shiver throughout all the six knot-centers, Cakras,[10] the six spinal arrests-and-departures of the one-pointed *samadhi,* or ecstasy-concentration! Here, at the foot of the rustic, compact, and battered fence, a massive and timely shock-surprise expects the boy: the nonchalant yet piercing and so familiar smell and sight of goat's dung. Can you sense the familiar, so promising smell and sight, suddenly new and unique? Exalted and brief summer familiarity with an image-smell at the foot of a fence—hot, very hot summer day, and perversity, and delight *a priori;* all the prophecy about sex and the secrets of loyalty, of intimacy, of sweat, fall and redemption—all, in closest vicinity to the comical and friendly word and image in the little town's dominant parlance: *tzygene bebkes!*

צִיגענע בּעפּקעס

Goat's little, round, shiny, innocent dungbeans: oh, but no!—red roses! Indeed, at the opposite foot of the same meadow fence now jumped or leaped over—red roses expect the boy, a bush full of them and their fragrance, the overflowing yet final, simply divine, smell of roses that has so often captivated speculative philosophers and poets alike.

One, only one, all-hugging shelter of child's surprise: red roses = *tzygene bebkes. Le Sacre de l'Eté.* The same fence having them both—roses, *bebkes*—the same fence separating them both, oh *peine d'amour* autumnal.

And the child: the child is hugging their presence and their separation in one big hug: he repeats in his own serpent's idiom *tzygene bebkes,* roses red!

Oh, but no: my own eye is hugging—Zen!—the *scientia signata* of the Momoyama gilded and painted doors. The prophetic body of *bebkes* = roses is in closest vicinity (so close as temporarily to make me, the center of creative sensibility and its resources—the isolated, inevitable "genius!"—indistinguishable from any other-than-mine body-and-center, anybody's *uomo cualunque's* body-and-genius; so close as temporarily to make the pre-split world be reborn) to the Japanese visionary conviction that bodies-kami, the nearer they are to our eye and touch *(See Plates 154, 155),* the less divided or fragmented (thus real and entire, exceptional, and sacred) they are, and the closer to becoming a painting-kami. The body-smell of *bebkes* =

roses and the body-vision of the Momoyama closeness and beauty are one body.

It was not a sudden awakening by the echo of childhood's experience in full correspondence with the eye's exalted touch of a painting, but it was the suddenness of the inner description of a bliss, the moving, "mobile-rigid" fulgurance of a "visionary circumstance of mind"—so brief, so exalted and rapid as to be seized only at the moment of its closest vicinity to another, no longer visionary-visual "circumstance," the moment when a body's sense-center—*Cakra?—is about to slide into another sense-center,* to be, then, substituted for it. And the substitution of this new and temporary infinity, the unseizable total of "my" Momoyama painting seized by the finite image-smell of it (and not, as it might well have been too, by, say, the image-sound)—this substitution of image-smell for the visual image is unavoidable. For substitution being an act of identity's self-transference, a free, "arbitrary" act not conditioned by a static, arrested choice of a form, but by a dynamic, moving, from-substitution-to-substitution choice—this journeying creativitiy *ex nihilo* cannot, within the confines of our innermost body, go farther or "lower" than the "lowest" sense-center of smell (and taste).

✡

But the initial and propelling Momoyama mirror-experience, the mirror-image of *bebkes*-roses, the image-smell of *bebkes*-roses, is mine, the author's, finite experience, my mirror, of course. And yet, why go into an extended description of a personal difficulty, which, because personal or self-ejected, is already overcome—useless? What does it matter to the world of art and art history or to the reader of this writing, that the author might be a poet, good or bad, with a flair for metaphysics and art history?

Oh, but a poet is none else but one who knows that the personal, *to be personal,* must be conveyed to an immanent companion, shared by "another," be "another's," that a passing summer impression—so convincingly personal—of a blue umbrella sliding gracefully along the icy pink of Sansovino's tower in Venice, and giving this tower its own blue, is not only personal any more: the bliss to give is in there—the presence of "another" someone, *res=persona,* is there to receive it—there, in closest vicinity to Asia's substitution of honesty-generosity for rational-irrational.

That is how *bliss is not happiness*: for bliss is what cannot be repeated —repeated by communication or communion. Exactly that which, in closest vicinity to the *conceptual*—dry—value given by theologians and by mystics (this time alike) to the chosen and avowedly *emotional*—wet—term or word *bliss,* could be provoked and repeated by them at will: when, for instance, in the presence of an intentionally called-in word-hallucination, God, or existence, or being-essence, or the active and the passive intellect, or man's soul (*forma corporeitas*? or isolation?) the unseizable body-totality of each of these theological or mystical terms could be seized, as a finite and total substitution in, say, Ibn Gabirol's or after him, in Grosseteste's (1175–1253) word-body *Light,* Light which "of its very nature diffuses itself in every direction in such a way that a point of light will produce instantane-

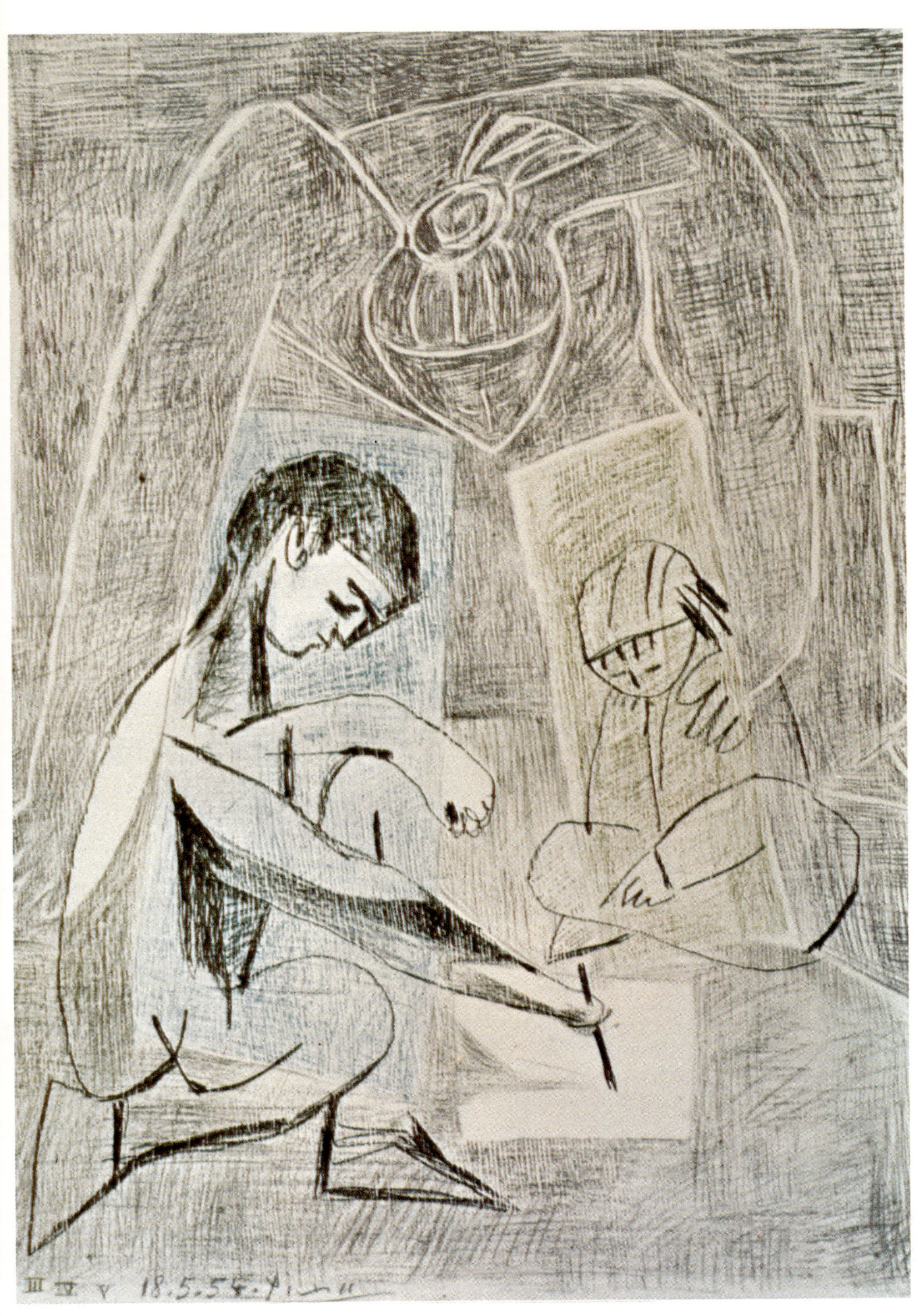

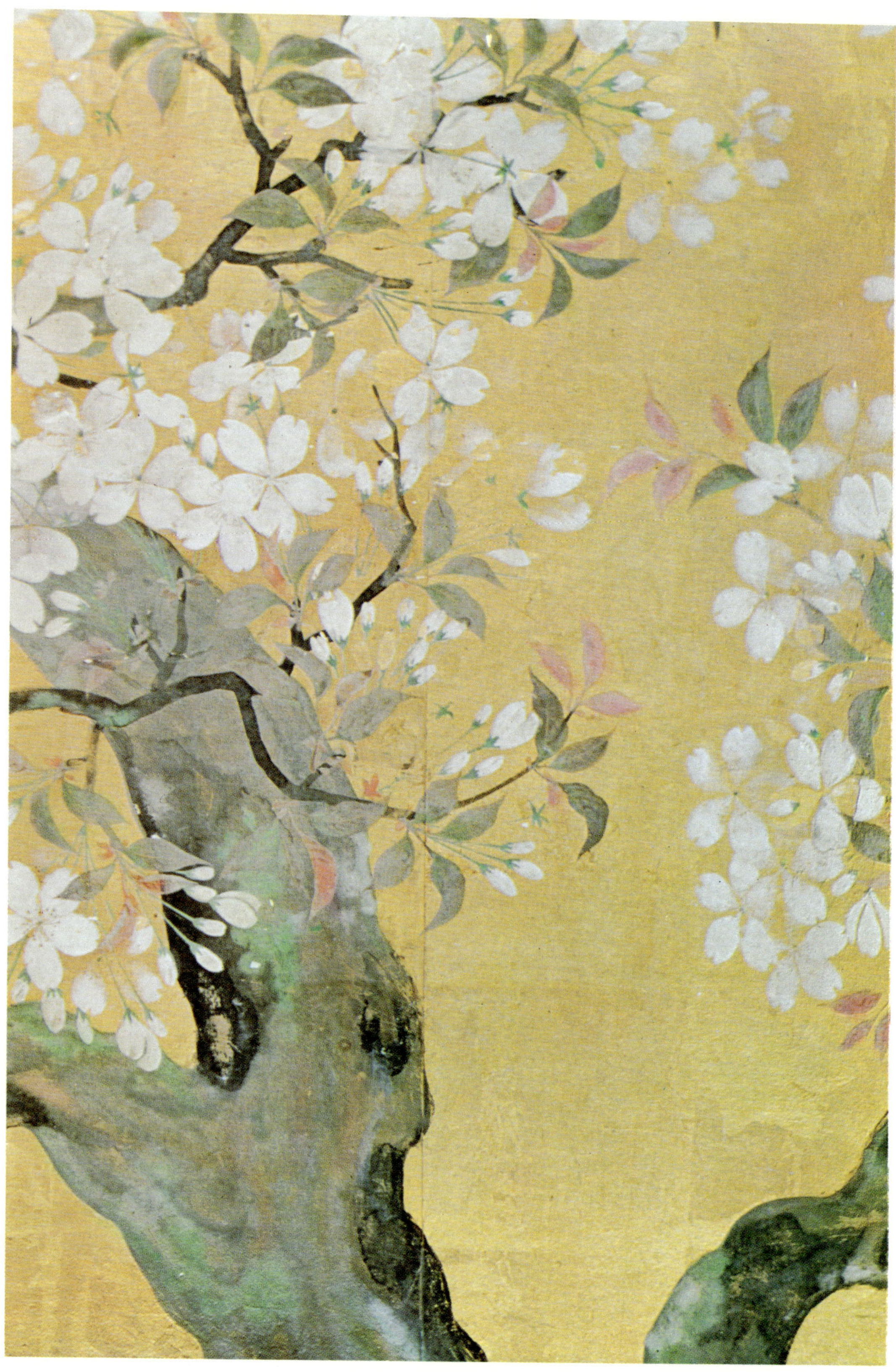

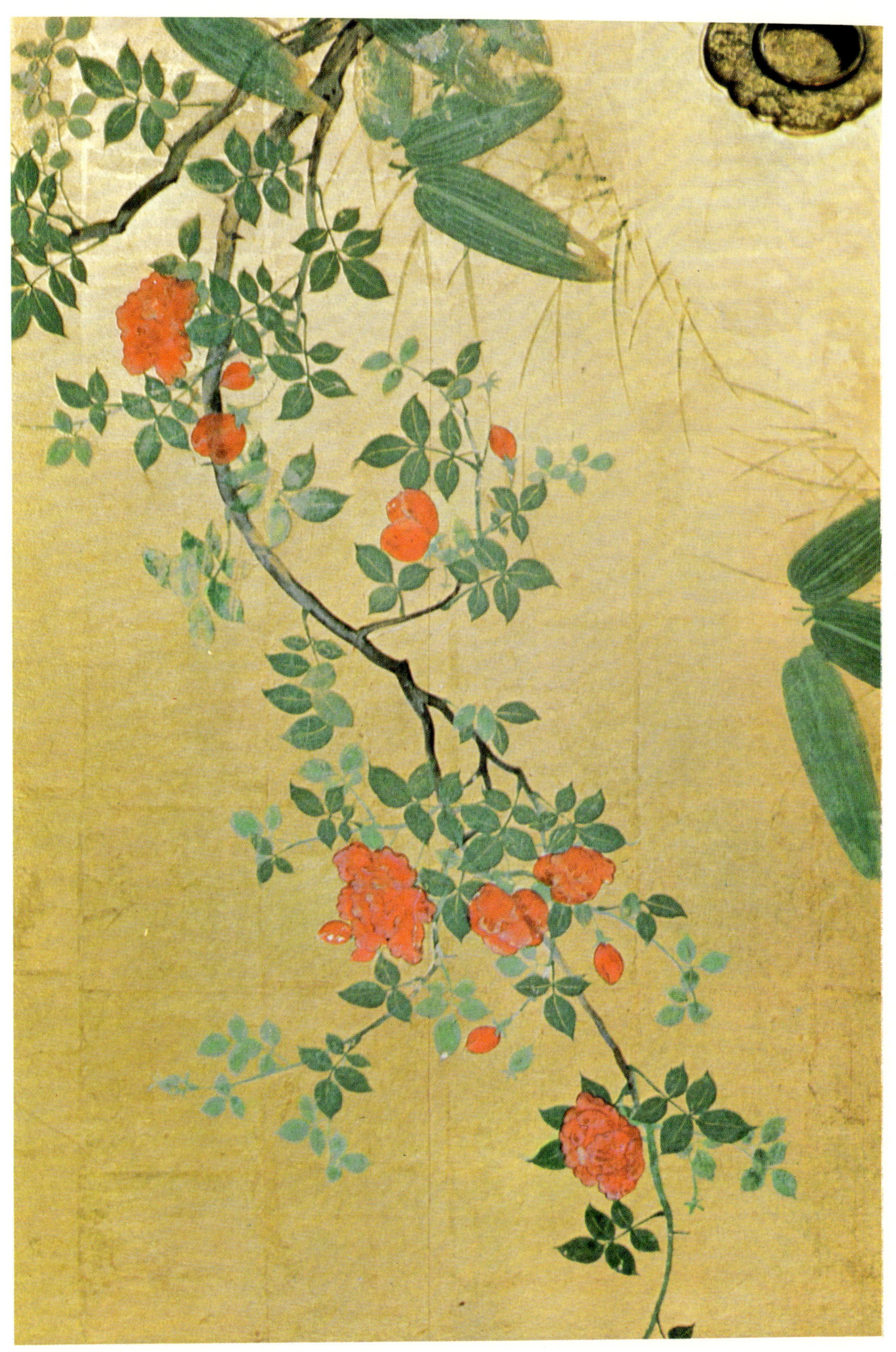

ously a sphere of light of any size whatsoever, unless some opaque object stands in its way."[11]

And Grosseteste's light-witness, journeying freely from substitution to substitution as it must, arrives at the bottom of my "Momoyama experience," arrives as summer-child-bliss-smell. More: as smell-image, as Japan-smell.

But why smell? And why the description of what is not to be described as yet—or any more?[12]

✡

E pur si muove

Is not the four-arched bridge standing there—over the word *infinity,* of course—its arch of summer in-curving itself into the arch of the innermost body; the sight, the hearing, the touch, and now the smell, all there? My book is almost finished: summer is smell is child is bliss is Yamato-e. All is said. Nothing else to say. Period.

But no: the description must go on. Because description is that which contains the urge of interpretation in itself. The urge and not the interpretation, of course. The urge of interpretation, which *qua* urge is description's self-sufficiency, to be satisfied to the very end: the only still possible *proof* left; an idea, stable, *fixe,* nailed there. Very similar to the Anselmian famous "ontological proof" and urge: that the idea of God—the urge in us to nail the imageless description of a God discovery-hallucination—God!—is the very idea of a proof that God is, thus is. The logical inevitability of such a proof and urge is precisely this—ours—here: summer is the child and the bliss and the smell-image-idea of Japanese painting.

But for God's sake (this very proof's sake), all this is not this, at all! Of course. And yet . . . . For if, as a contemporary West's mode of thought would have it,[13] any given "this" is never this, and this "this-not-this" in its turn is not this, and so forth, till the argument reaches the skin of our innermost body, even there the total concrete *thisness* of the very this-not-this self-multiplied model would still be standing, probably, solid, because of the mutual and multi-relationed leaning on each other of all the this-not-this elements of the model. And—temporarily—it is the stability of the "thisness" of such a model that is often referred to in psychology, and even in beyond-psychology, as the inescapable fact of symbolization in us, our very production of symbols.

My *bebkes*-roses image-smell is arrested in me, when this is feasible, as a symbol-compound, whose reduced-to-a-"schema"-(or "form") memory-content re-forms itself anew into the happy appreciation of my "Momoyama" experience.

A symbol is a "convention"-meaning or an organized set of such conventions, to be used pragmatically (thus historically, for a symbol is delimited by its historical necessity, by its appurtenances, and adhesive to the creativity of a given historical climate, religious, social, etc.; and it is becoming useless, therefore dangerous and obscurantist, when used or re-used beyond these "climatic"—however elastic—limits of necessity).

For a symbol is a choosy (thus again, historically chosen) "convention"—the nailing of a description's urge to interpret—which in itself is the result of another, more "elemental" choice: the self-organization as "sig-

◀154, 155 KANO SADANOBU
Cherry Blossoms and Pheasants Details (overleaf)

nals," or by elastic extension, as acts of "signalization," of all the underlying and freely floating this-is-not-this elements of the stabilized "thisness." A signal in us is the signalization-to-symbolization process itself, the heraldic act of situ-ating the elements of a symbol-model: not yet a condensed, self-enclosing point-sphere (= symbol) but a carefree point-line, sheer direction of change, free *signalling-curve*; not the expression or symbolic "projection" of the effect of influences on us, but still the expression of events in us. Elemental, watchful readiness: signal innermost; relation, not yet category of relation; sheer intensity, adhesion, presence—closest vicinity to the domain of the image-touch, the *index* of the touch, of the witness, but not the witness, not as yet the touch: lower, still "lower," higher, still "higher," serpent's point-curve from foot to head!

Signal's domain: domain of the head: of the foot.

The revered Śamkarācārya sings: "Kuharinī,[14] thou sprinklest all things with the stream of nectar which flows from the tips of Thy two feet; and as thou returnest to Thine own place, Thou vivifiest and makest visible all things that were aforetime invisible; and on reaching Thy abode Thou resumest thy snake-like coil and sleepest."[15]

The sense of smell—the earth, the feet—and its instantaneous shiver throughout the entire gamut of ascending-descending sense forms is, now and here, the Witness-Touch, at once witnessing and filling Kundalini's unimpeded, *whole* becoming. (How strangely mirrored in this, Asia's, essential testimony of a cognitive, total being-becoming is, among so many similar images of twentieth-century thought, this theory—perhaps the strangest and most daring of all—Fermi's theory of gas! "According to this new theory," says the French scholar Louis de Broglie, "no two of the individual entities forming the gas can be in the same state of motion and have the same energy—a view which at first must certainly appear paradoxical. How, indeed, can it be possible for an atom at one end of a vessel containing gas to prevent another atom at the other end being in the same state of motion as itself? It seems inexplicable, except on the assumption that in a certain sense each individual entity composing the gas fills the whole of the receptacle.")[16]

Now, the sense of smell—this quantic unit of intensity in our body's entire signal-universe—smell as a particularized form-content of knowing, what would it be? How would the "heraldic" convention of the two signal-words "schema" (or form) and "image" be *situ*-ated there?

In autumn I would have tried to answer thus: "My Mysterious Companion would say this or this . . . . "

In winter: "My lady would say this or this . . . . "

In spring: the discovery of spring would suggest or show this or this . . . .

But now, in summer—the shortest possible season and distance between the innermost and outermost bodies—the answer could only be tried in the vicinity of a rapid answering itself:

That the "heraldic" foundation of smell is not the "normal schema-givenness" *plus* the image-need structured and added there. Nor is it the visionary givenness—the visitation of the *Image-la-Folle* with the schema-need, the form-lucidity "added" heraldically to it.

Nor is it, as organized sound's—music's—root-knowledge would perhaps be, the schema *and* structured image given together, thus, not situated, but situ-ating our innermost body's other roots of knowing in accordance with the will, or choice, of what is "signalled" or given there: either the will of words in music, or of visions, or of sounds, of touch, or of smell.

Nor is smell, as touch is, the pure, unimpeded givenness of the schema-and-image: Hallucination = reality permanent and undifferentiated. But smell, the closest to touch, is schema and image fused together, intermingled.

Smell is schema imaged, an image schematized—the very root of speculation. Smell is speculation, itself in closest vicinity to the speculation about smell. Not a symbolic fixation of an *else* yet-to-be-known, but smell-signal's direction—a smell-curve in our body—aimed at this else:

This is not this is this. (How great a help is Gertrude Stein's help here, her red rose-watering, and not war-watering help!)

Smell is the Child is the bliss is a painting is a rose-*bebke* is a smell-image is not this is always something else.

Smell is always something else lain upon the awakened and lucid horizon where the two bodies meet: it is the nostalgia in man, and nostalgia is the smell of smell of bliss of Child. And Child does not know the bliss, Child does not know the smell: bliss, child, smell, Japanese painting are *outside* bliss, or smell or child. They are the undistinguishable fullness and part—a summer's sheltered corner—of our entire and very ancient innermost body.

Do I mean by "outside" the *lieu* of our nostalgic and poignant—the most poignant of all particular memory-traces in us—memory of childhood? No, certainly.

But, very precisely, I mean at once the outside of such a memory-trace, of *our* memory, and the *inside* of the all-filling *matter* of memory itself, the very stuff our innermost body is made of.

Child is what is very ancient in us—the ancient age in us and its melancholy: not what memory is but what memory is not already. For that which we don't remember is the very matter of memory, its stuff (and if, as it is sometimes believed, a young child, as well as a young animal, is less olfactive,[17] it is simply that childhood is the very stuff of the olfactive, with no traces yet of loss or of "memory" there, and that it is this innermost stuff as it grows and expands which, together with the "traces" it overwhelmingly accumulates, becomes the "remembering," nostalgic adult or "grownup").

And the bliss too is that which we don't remember as yet or already: the nostalgia—*la peine d'amour!*—of what *in* the memory is not *our* memory. This is the bliss to be communicated.

That is why smell is always something else—a *deus absconditus* to be discovered as spring is, to be given as summer is (given in summer's vicinity to what the word-signal *grace* meant once, when it was history's living and necessary *res-persona*): the briefest intensity of presence—uncoilment, instantaneity, but not entirely so—bliss, and the nostalgia in it.

If smell is the child and is the bliss, it is only because it is part and fullness of that which is fully our body's memory—the fulgurant descent into the *else*: look, please, into the nocturnal, starry mystery of a dog's eye and the story told there of the ancient brain, the "nose-brain"[18] of the proto-humans, the prosimian's living in the trees, then after millions of years the snuffing in the earth and the moist dense dark, the crafty, creative smell world of insects, and the urge to descend, the descent with the myth of *Okeanos,* the earnestness of descent and of return such as only Japanese Noh knew how to tell.

And the smell of a rose.

The smell of a rose is not in the rose nor in an obstinate memory of a rose, but in "another" rose cut out directly from the stuff of body's memory, a nostalgic else-rose—a *painted rose,* for instance, the bliss to paint the bliss of a rose. It is this, rightly or wrongly worded, that the defenders of "abstraction" in the arts have earnestly in mind today: the uncoilment of the serpent's foot = head, smell = idea, the "another" rose in Boucher's painting of a painted rose, in Raphael's painting of "another" Madonna, in Korin's "another" cranes, in Mondrian's "another" painting of Mondrian-angle's schema = Mondrian-angle's-image.

There, smell-else and nostalgia-else are wedded to each other: bliss and melancholy, inseparable.

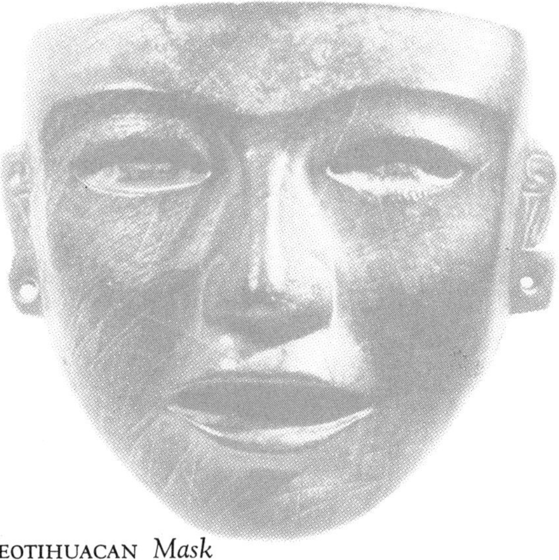

156 TEOTIHUACAN *Mask*
Pre-Aztec

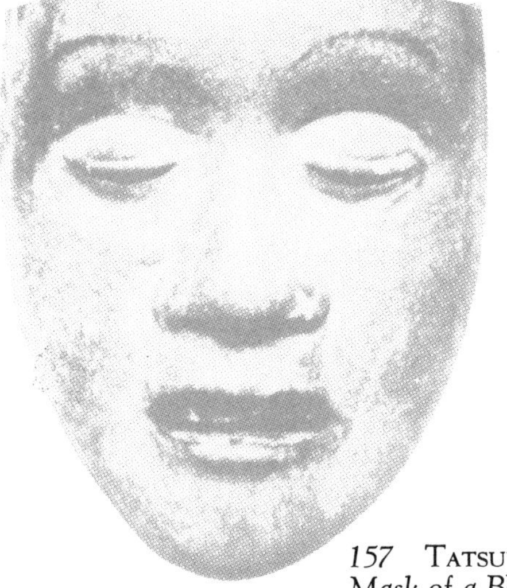

157 TATSUYEMON
Mask of a Blind Woman
14th century

Look: floating over the moody mirror of the word *infinity,* and bypassing the four-arched bridge, look: the two faces *(Plates 156, 157).*

Surely this one is not just the mask of a dead youth, that one, not just the mask of a returning young woman dead—but they are a twin mask surely of early love—how inseparable, the bliss and melancholy of their pallor!—surely of death—how they resemble each other!

And yet, they have never met, never could meet: how could the mask of an Aztec dead youth and the Noh mask of a young woman's ghost ever meet?

Floating, inseparable, the twins of death. Not because of one-death (for how would one know about this or that of death's structure beyond what its image-schema's self-combining has to uncoil for us—and thanks be given for that little!) but because death, the very "else" lain upon the horizon of the body and upon the two lonely faces, is so ancient—as ancient as our innermost body is, as memory's matter which fills it is: not lovely Juliet, not lovely Romeo, but the story that happened long, very long ago, uncoiled now by Shakespeare's brief and lucid and ancient intensity about them, the smell, the touch, the sound, the logos of their ancient story.

How wonderfully full of death is the world! How silly to give or to bring there still "another" death—oh, lovely masks mirrored now—look!—so close to each other, in the waters of another and surely beautiful painting of Yamato *(Plate 158).*

Volez, bienheureux oiseaux,
Messagers de la victoire
Sur les éternelles eaux
Des filles de la Mémoire
Je voy venir la gent noire.[19]

The two masks float—now over the word *infinity* itself and its bridge, now beyond it, mirrored in the restless *painted* wind—oh, but so discreet! A lonely exchange of gifts—Japan! My unforgettable winter lady, Iwai!—the immense and so fully closing on us moon, the loud blue of feudal flowers there and the humble field flowers, yellow; the trouble of high grasses and the same rhythm of all the living and dead there, under the same wind . . .

And no echo of the *painted* lullaby:

Sleep, sleep, child, of death dead,
lifelike—all alike!—death.
Sleep, don't move
don't move with the little child-wind

(no: it is not this—but an aroma, seen in the mirror of the two masks), the pestilent little zephyr that makes the moon's foot-grasses and flowers move with the same regular and continuous rhythm—not "oblique" any more, not only Japan's—it's not necessary any more!—but Greece's and China's too, a continuous, quiet, circular and full rhythm. For the two faces are floating free. And their time is dead as their death itself is: a time very precise—*aeternitas?*—slowly, very slowly, quietly, very quietly, the two faces lean together over the mirror of grasses, flowers, and the moon—no space, no time, no categories, only what is, what the Diamond Sutra teaches, the Japanese mask and the Aztec mask inseparable, the same.

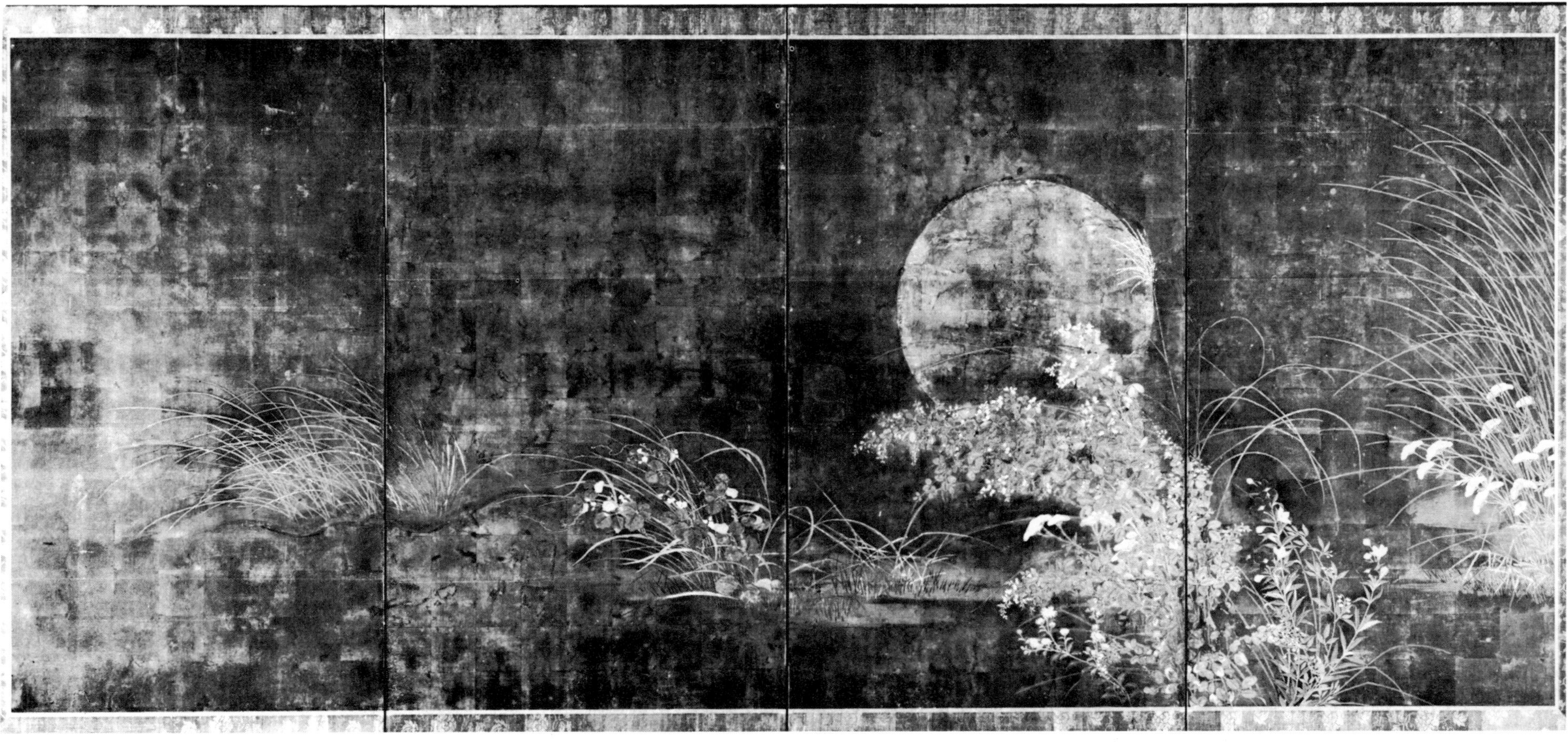

158 *Grasses, Flowers and Full Moon* Kano screen (Momoyama period, late 16th century)

From below the mirror's song:

Sleep my lunar beautiful pale child
bayūshkī-bayū
oh death dead sweet
quiet forgotten ancient with no resurrection
living life live death,
sleep oh peace dead too
bayūshkī-bayū lunar
live no-peace!—

from below the flowers and grasses painted in traditional earnest of Japan comes by way of surprise, by way of rapidity—how *rapid,* the uncoilment! how *surprising* the brevity and the persistence all at once, of summer's passion, *bebkes-roses!*—by way of excitement—surprising, its signal-curve in our body!—comes the smell.

Sleep, lonely twin face: smell is awakened and watchful. Smell is your first awakening, the awakening that replaces your sleep, everywhere in every *thing,* in every body.

Bliss and melancholy in everybody's "another" rose: smell is the *uomo cualunque*'s awakened "else," his "substituted" awakening—oh, innermost body's matter-and-memory, all, of all, of every life, of all possible and real lives ever lived, unseizable!

Lonely and so *average,* the chance meeting, the seizure of the unseizable whole, of the captive masks, this one surely not just a mask of an Aztec youth dead, that one surely not just a Noh mask of a young woman dead and returning, but a twin mask, surely, of love and death and chance, average, "mediocre," passed by.

✡

THIRD EPISODE, OR MOVEMENT
Andante molto cantabile ed espressivo
In the Vicinity of the Third Difficulty

Genius is the memory of mediocre lives.[20]

. . . the last difficulty.

That the description must go on. And yet description must stop somewhere, where description and its urge of interpretation and the interpretation itself culminate in summer's lucid and brief exaltation.

It is a start-to-be, winter's *middle,* that returns and testifies upright and anew. For winter is—as now summer is—a part of the same bridge. At winter's birth and at winter's death nothing starts with the start but starts somewhere in the middle.

And so it was built into the entire bridge and throughout its four arches that what is the middle is always the beginning of a new difficulty; a new start or difficulty is always in the middle of a season's thought. Such, the thought's hunting adventure right here and now—autumn's reawakening?—: "What forest being, animal or monster, am I hunting when I say: *smell is speculation"?*

How can smell, so immediately one with body's matter = memory, be (and I don't say how can it become, but how can it *be,* for then it would not be the hunting thought's difficulty) a "cool," disembodied *speculation?*

But is not speculative thought such an adventure of mind and man's will whose goal and method, whose "project," of self-confirmation (both the desire to possess the *object* of thought *qua object* and its possession already as a *subject* of thought) advances "normally" along reason's—or judgment's—road, the road of the intuitive man who, guided by the syllogistic and dialectic stability of facts and influences duly interpreted, is led to the summit of what is called logical conviction or proof, but whose final arrival there must be confirmed or "signalled"—how "abnormal" and contradictory this!—by the non-intuitive "logic of the arbitrary": the "heraldic" man, his touch, his moral index, his reality, the proving without proof of the Witness—the Witness himself?

Irreconcilable contradiction; scandal of human mind and will! And yet, here it is precisely, in mid-summer, spring's returning discovery of spring—mind's discovery of the *third way:* the way of *techne-touch.*

So close to the body, so one with the body as to be at once the "in" and the "out" in it—here it is, the attraction, the irresistible *charm* of speculative thought in history and man!

Its neoconsubstantial pre-split "normalcy" is thus re-established.

Somewhere, in its "else," the birth of a precise difficulty-speculation.

Bliss and melancholy are wedded: my image = smell, smell = idea, *bebkes*-roses, speculation!

From below the mirror's song:

Sleep, my lunar child
bayūshkī-bayū
oh death dead
ancient with no resurrection
living life live death
oh peace dead
bayūshkī bayū
live no-peace!

from below the flowers, the grasses, the moon, and the little child-wind *painted,* comes by way of surprise, by way of rapidity, by way of exaltation, smell!

. . . . . The only possible companionship with Japanese painting, mysterious, romantic, honest companionship indeed, creation and critique equated.

The sense of smell is speculative thought in man, because smell is a smell-image made precise somewhere in the middle of the sense; and the image here is not "justified" or given only by memory's correspondences, an image-impression evoked by a given "that" smell, but simultaneously, an image-substitution, a substitution of a *constructed* "another" rose—a painted visited hallucination, indeed!—for such a *given* smell—this rose!

Indeed, this is how—in repeated speculation again—schema or form and *Image-la-Folle* are fused together in smell: smell is indifferently image schematized and schema imaged.

And this is why, also, poignantly, smell's *res-persona* or self (*who* is the bliss to paint, *who* is the child, *who* is the companionship of Japan) is both inside and outside the body—just as speculation itself must be.

And speculation it is, in full.

When smell is *inside* body—an observable, physical sense, a "pure" simple sense, loyal to its "physical" origins of matter and memory consubstantial, it is body's very sameness, undistinguishable from body's own matter-and-memory physicality.

And being thus, both the oscillating *in* of the body and its oscillating *out*, it becomes, when observable, "studied," a true speculation about this *in* and this sameness. Smell becomes the hypothesis, a truly scientific, experimental, hypothesis of matter's, matter-and-memory's, "ultimate secret."

Ever deeper and deeper, beyond the physical-chemical, the biochemical, the electronic-neural, beyond the matter of light itself and its speed's limit, the unimaginable image of wave-and-particle's "atom of energy"; and beyond what is lying still deeper in wait there, matter's equation with movement "pure" and its heraldic middle start, its very being, *emotion*, smell, in a *dry* return-shock, might become the very checking of science's own "speculative" possibilities or "proofs" and their objectivity.

Here is what, in a succinct theoretical resumé, a scientist, expert in the "chemical senses," has to say and suggest to us:[21]

> In the olfactive bulb the arrangement of cells and axons[22] provides a convergence of pathways and a return route back to the glomerulus itself by way of collaterals, so that a kind of closed reverberating circuit is formed. [*Speculatively* and within smell's own stimuli-universe-of-discourse, wouldn't this be a "hooking" of the schema's and image's fusion = circuit?] . . . . It is this "feedback" that accounts in part for the great sensitivity of the sense of smell.
>
> . . . Of the chemical senses smell is the most acute. In terms of concentrations of molecules it has been estimated that olfaction is 10,000 times as sensitive as taste.
>
> Organic compounds make up the greatest class of odorous substances.[23] Both total molecular structure and the presence of osmophoric groups and arrangements within the molecule appear to influence odor.[24]
>
> Theories that point to such molecular effects as infrared absorption, ultraviolet absorption, Raman effect, etc.,[25] to account for the essential step in stimulation have been presented ever since Faraday first noted that many odorous materials strongly absorb radiation in the infrared region of the spectrum . . . . When monochromatic light shines through pure substances, spectroscopic analysis reveals scattering into the longer and shorter wavelength regions. The difference between the wavelengths of incident and reflected light is the Raman shift. *It is independent of the light used and is a unique characteristic of any one substance.* Raman shifts between 140 and 350 millimicrons, according to the theory, are odorous. . . . Such substances frequently have different odors. Many suggestive correlations of this sort have been made; but disturbing exceptions have been found. Glycerin, which has a Raman shift in the critical region, is odorless [very unconvincing: even glycerin might be odorous for a sensitive nose] . . . . .

Infrared spectroscopy is a powerful technique for the analysis of molecular structure. Infrared absorption and the Raman effect both depend on the oscillation of the atoms in the molecule around their mean positions. Because the masses and distances involved in molecular structure are so small, frequencies of oscillation are of the order of 10^{13} to 10^{14} cycles per second. It is this frequency range that determines the infrared absorption. Every organic substance has a unique infrared absorption spectrum which cannot be matched by any other substance.[26]

One wonders: the ligamen Raman effect—smell, a still humble and prudent seed and voice—what flowers and fruits would it bear?

The Raman effect itself, although essentially physical in nature, is another parameter by which the behavior of atoms within the molecules and of the molecules themselves may be determined independently of their state of aggregation.[27]

. . . In Raman spectra a molecule is bombarded with radiation of wavelength much greater than the size of the molecule. . . . It may be a long wave, or red light or short wave, or ultra violet . . . using X-rays one deals essentially with a static arrangement [of atoms in a molecule], with the Raman effect, one deals not with a static, but with a dynamic situation. Here it is primarily a question of the *motion of the atoms in a molecule* and only indirectly of their position in a space.[28]

✡

In a dry, speculative return-shock, when smell is temporarily our "out" 's *cool* speculation about the *exalted* "in" of the total body, smell is perhaps a prophecy about the "ultimate proof" of matter and memory as one volume-motion.

But smell is the fusion of schema and image—the circuit of these two basal components of knowledge. In smell they are indistinguishable from each other: impression-correspondence, sensation-identity, one and the same experiencing of smell; the *mnemonic* and the *immediate* movement, the finite stability of the circular-continuous and the infinite mobility of the rigid, discontinuous "oblique," one and the same direction there of change, of growth in us.

And it is thus when smell (arrested temporarily as if for the sake of this instant of argument here) becomes our oscillating "out," that its very being, the oscillating "in," can be "imagined"—in a *wet,* still speculative, return-shock, a *wet* yet brief and lucid exaltation—as a "coming out" again, a new and exclusive *Image-la-Folle,* a hallucination, painter's hallucination: smell-image, the total substitution = "else" for a given particular physical smell.

Here is where smell is still another prophecy about the coming of a new image, image-monster, the "another," the "else" at the end of smell-planting nerves: a story, an invented imagery of bliss and nostalgia.

Is it the smell of such a story? Is it the story of such a smell? Which? Tell me, child, my Mysterious Companion; tell me, "Bliss-to-paint," my Mysterious Companion; and you, the "else" of all return, the "else" of Noh's ghost and of my questioning itself, my Mysterious Companion "else," tell me which! Death mask of an Aztec youth, young woman's Noh mask, both of them floating apart from each other, reflected together, close to each other now, in the mirror of a mysterious painting of Japan—my Mysterious Companion, tell me which!

I speak—and thus evoke for the last time the true intent of this book—of a closed-in, framed painting painted in the Far Eastern style and manner.

✡

I speak of an experience lived in front of a certain forest, a simple, average pine tree wood that could be seen or, in all fairness to the evocation here, contemplated, from an old wooden porch each of whose large openings were framing the view exactly as if of a separated picture—somewhere in a wood-and-lake corner of one of Japan's islands, or right here, where this is being written, in a wood-and-lake inland corner of North America's Maine.

This framed view was not a natural view, it was a painting—its inner volume-movement, both continuous and oblique, defining it thus.

A painting indeed: but of a Face—of this forest's "another" Face—a forgotten and returning glance upon it, a story at the end of nerves' curve, an image-smell, I must say—not a painting of fragrant living trees standing there in front of me and of the porch, day after day in midsummer, rows behind rows of slender worshippers, such exactly as are formed in the mosque's sanctuary at the hour of common prayer against the *qibla* wall.

But—whose "another" Face and whose glance on the Face? Tell me . . . I only see the trees.

July 14 in the morning

Again and again I see the forest's living and fragrant pine trees against the luminous and transparent-green curtain of the wood's farthest-from-my-eye-end—the *qibla* wall with the *mihrab*-glance upon it—and suddenly I see, for I see better now, all the worshippers surrounding, at a powerful old-roots distance from it, the grand and studied gesture of their oldest tree that stands there, isolated and powerfully branched: a grand gesture suddenly so familiar, a suddenly frozen arrest of a shiver, Amida's embrace and enlightenment of everybody and everything.

Here, the main performer—by my choice!—of the dance of the Face, the witness of the Face, not the *Shite* himself but his "else" and his same, the *Shite-Zure,* my Mysterious Companion, my old isolated Central Tree!

But tell me, whose *Face* it is?

July 14 in the late afternoon

When I sit on the porch facing not one of its windows' frames, where the grand overpowering gesture appears in the middle—a true picture then—but the porch's door which hides the *grand personnage* from my eye, the picture disappears, the Face is lost. Nothing would have happened with my pine wood if I had not seen it in myself, framed by one of the porch's partitions, as a picture of a Face, a hallucination visited and organized, a lucid and exalted exactitude, very brief—still summer's.

Later, the day soon finishing

How transparent all! The old isolated tree in the middle of the day's latest luminosity, transparent from its age and its ancient roots, is much more transparent than the other, slender, trees surrounding his dance-pose. And the green curtain of the forest's visible end—the *qibla* wall—its luminosity is bunched together, petals upon petals of transparency, with the old tree's transparency—one transparent new form born in a forest. Out of what substance born?

Dried twigs and branches of pine trees in regular rows, their Franciscan aspect and color give a sharp brownish crystallinity to the free air around the twigs and branches where the sky, seen through them, blazes and where, within this airy substance, the crystalline late day's flight of birds makes with it one soft and crystalline silence and volume of bliss. There, this crystal lends its new brownish tints to old copper of twigs and branches themselves, ascending even to the pines' summits and thence descending again, and swiftly, to their suspended needle-clouds, green and grey. Between the branches and twigs and the air itself is born there a new substance common to them all: this brown crystallinity.

Yet, branches and twigs and the air are segregated from each other: in *solitude-solidarity*—the substance of the new form. And it is this, probably, that creates, as art creates (making thus a painting of it and not a "natural" view) the threshold of a Look, of a Glance, like a new light that comes forth from eyes in love. And indeed, from under the crystal and the sky's blaze flares up the game of another light in the forest, the twilight's light of pure gold, not of copper only: always the game of "another" light, of the "else."

July 16 in the morning

The porch is all fragrance (my coming story is guided by its spell, of course), the pine aroma, red and white, India's shelter and sonority—more! —this aroma's adhesion: you can touch here the memory of the Mediterranean warm heart of the pine, the spreading sweetness and strength of the good man's hand. Red (Taira) and white (Minamoto) fragrance—in substitution, a finite smell-story.

July 16 in the afternoon

The Look of the Forest.

There he is, always the same, the *Grand Personnage,* his body isolated, immobile, rooted—not the *Shite*'s multi-branched supreme Dance, but the *Shite*'s same-else, the *Shite-Zure,* the witness by my choice.

The whole forest moves around him, away from him (this being precisely the *Shite-Zure*'s identity dance), with him, up to the confines of the green curtain—a green rival luminosity, "another" luminosity, the abode of somebody forgotten—the "else" appearing from beyond the green limit, somebody witnessed by the dance.

There: the Look in a forgotten Face.

I sit on the porch angry and tired and resigned. Simply, pine trees in front of me.

Simply too, the irresistible contemplation of their beyond-of-them, my one-pointed *Dhyana* till I squeeze out from it the Face. Of a Goddess? Why not? But the Face is still someone else: nostalgia and smell are inseparable; try to separate them: impossible!

✡

. . . Once upon a time there was a young man in love with a young girl, who loved him too. They married. The young woman died soon after. This was long ago in the man's life. The man married another, begot children, was happy, contented, and prosperous. Very quietly and normally his first love was forgotten. The Face of the once loved first wife was forgotten.

And now, while I was sitting there in front of the deepened transparency, unintentionally and unprepared at first, but then more and more awakened to a presence, because of the forest's watchful silence and its crystal and the dance of the forest's old tree, the attendance of all other trees, and the new light from behind the curtain—transparency upon transparency, lotuses upon lotuses—the true Face slowly, sweetly emerged, the first wife's Face came back. It brought ruins with it and it brought bliss, communicated bliss: the Face of the forgotten one came back, the ghost of a forgotten life. It is a face in a forest—of someone lost returning, a return never to be forgotten, and yet it is, it was forgotten: a faint smell vanishing ("The Face of *Ecce Homo* on Veronica's kerchief: the Witness real, the co-sufferer," tinkles the curtain at the far end of the forest).

And because of a forest somewhere in a corner of Japan's island or in a corner of Maine's inland, all is in ruins now: the man, his second wife, their children, their well-being—ruined.

But the green luminous curtain tinkles sweetly: "The Face of the *Ecce Homo* on Veronica's kerchief. The witness of what is forgotten: the Lost Presence. And a ghost of the first wife is not regret nor a wound any more. It is a presence of bliss and nostalgia wedded. So that the sacred Face could not be forgotten."

But I who write this cannot see—how could I, who never knew the fact of that man's first wife, dead?—the Face I wished to see in the forest. The story is all and very suddenly imagined, imposed irresistibly and experienced as identity with the pine trees' aroma: as the image of a curvature, or a direction of growth and change in me given quietly by the forest's very aspect. From behind my green curtain's "else" the redeeming Noh melancholy and bliss of the Lost is returning.

Somewhere in the middle of the forest's Face appears—starting at the middle of the green luminous mihrab-glance—the story of the first wife. The curve continues (for a curve is the very *aspect* of change's direction, is what returns and at the same time what delays the return, that is, what is the very duration of change; perhaps, as duration, not a change at all, but a *situ*ated point in space where "another" point-*situ*ation is, or has been, or is going to be; a curve is my innermost body's appurtenance to the "else"). The first wife's face, unique and first, just as unique and as first was the forest for my eye, is now the Face on Veronica's kerchief, the Face forgotten, present, a *Veronica* in everything—the bridge four-arched over infinity itself—the sacred Face. And the Face is the grand *Shite-Zure* gesture, the Face of the tree's dance = aroma, a unique and first curve (substitution is always of the unique and first for the unique and first) returning to its origins. It is a return after all, even as the summer's arch is the curved return to the innermost body's. The curve of the story returns to what was lost and found in the forest: A "feedback" circuit, return to the Veronica-smell, to the first wife's ghost, to the speculation about it, to the sudden uselessness of a painted hallucination-smell, the profitless *amor intellectualis Dei,* the ornament, the ornament-smell.

All the lucid and brief exaltation of summer's fable: the image-smell and the smell-image of Momoyama sliding doors = *tzygene-bebkes = roses,* Yamato-e.

✡

Everything and everybody are their own "else": the writing of this book is its else, the one who is loved is his or her else and so is a red rose and bliss wedded to nostalgia. So is a revolution and industry and light, or *la peine d'amour,* or smell; the same and the else of Veronica, an imprint of the Face on a cloth or on a forest.

Everything is the curve of growth that incurves itself in me. And I am—we are—at once formed by it and a form of it: *Natura naturata* and *natura naturans.*

July 16, early afternoon

Sitting on the porch. The *Shite-Zure* is there, splendid, the old grand pine tree, unique and total: certainly a substitution *per se,* immobilized for the sake of such a moment. Certainly he cannot but be at once the Witness and the Face.

And the crystal again. All is repeated: bliss is what cannot be but a repeated communication and communion.

This is how the story of a lost and found Face in a forest was born.

Same day, late afternoon, evening approaches

Sitting on the porch: dried copper-gold branches and twigs, indeed, very dry in me.

Nothing—only a slight nascent shame creeping in somewhere: how forgetful all this.

Why is the story of Veronica's face a story-curve? Why a curve? And why smell-image and not sound-image at the nerves' end?

✡

Smell is speculative thought, speculatively a smell = idea: a speculation. The trap in a forest.

A hunted forest beast or monster is trapped, and the description, its urge of interpretation and the interpretation itself stopped abruptly; stopped in the vicinity of the word *curve.* For any sense-abstracting, inner act in us—any creative = critical expression of sources of inspiration in life—has a content—a subject matter—extensible, on its *what* level, *ad infinitum,* yet limited also by our body's innermost horizon, and in depth, by our innermost body's ocean bottom.

In order to be such an expression at all of such a content, the latter must be—and is indeed (precisely as the primeval act of creation = critique in us)—reduced to a maximum obtainable degree of self-contraction or intensity. The content of our experiencing must be changed into a new, "another" content. We call it Form (this is how—in art—form as content's passion and formalism as content's gossip about this passion have nothing to do with each other).

Form, at its maximum content-reduced degree of intensity, is, in our body's space, the *tracery* of such a transference from total content to a total form—exactly where the *what-of-the-how* is situ-ated and where sensation-infinity is seized as an isolated part or fragment of it. It is thus the very tracery of the direction—the very process—of change or growth in us: a *curvature,* rounded or "rigid"-mobile, as the case might be.

All creation of a form in art is directly inspired by the inner, in-visual, aspect of a particular curvature in us: a musical theme or thought is a *curve;* a linear limit, or a color, or a volume in space is a *curve.* And smell is a *curve.* The smell of a rose, of a violet, is the curve of "another" rose, another "violet"; so is equally the "offensive" smell. (Stink is the disintegration of a curvature-smell to be re-integrated anew.)

And if, in summer's halt, I single out the smell-and-image curve and not, say, sound-and-image or sound-and-smell, as I could or should perhaps do, it is because smell is the most vicinal, the closest, to the innermost body's limit. While a musical sound-thought and a visual image can easily join each other in a metaphor or an intuited and expressed poem (the "pure" element of the "verbal" being here placed, as it were, directly above the auditive, which is directly above the visual upon the scale or the spine of our sense-abstracting process, serpent's shiver), the conjunction of the image and the smell (both being, in downward direction on the same scale, closer to each other than to the summit-abiding "verbal") does not lend itself easily to, say, a metaphor, a verbal-visual formulation, but to body's immediacy of a touch-form, that is, to what precisely is between them and what thus unites them: touch with no category of relation in it as yet, pure pleasure-gratuity, profitless play or growth: a *curve,* a curvature with all its possible variables included. Touch-image = touch-smell. Ornament: *bebkes*-roses. Smell. Smell-image. Speculative thought = smell-idea.

For when I say *curve* I can think and visualize it as such. But previously—simultaneously?—I must draw or trace it manually-mentally, so to speak. I must be helped here by my "manual" memory of having already sketched many curves. It is thus that I "draw" the in-skin curve of a melody or an odor. But couldn't I as well say or think a curve as a self-traced, self-drawing manifestation of the curving function itself, that is, as an instantaneous—or very rapid—ligament between the content-free symbolizing "abstract," vicinal to the visual, and the signalizing kinæsthetic, vicinal to smell-touch?

Would not the *sensuousness* of the curve in mathematics be such a self-drawn being—the mathematical obsession with the *creativity* of the curve, and still floating there in spite of all, the old angelological world intuited or touched by the precision of zodiacal curved astrology?

It is in the vicinity of the word *curve* that the Wittgenstein-Russell notion of transferability from one sense-structure's idiom into another, the intertranslatability of sense-data or sense-contents[29] is surely *situ*-ated.

And if Plato's Triad itself, the True, the Beautiful, the Good, was conceived and kept by Plato as one, only one, being (ultimately the True), it was because the trajectory of this being's self-manifestation or self-tracing was also a one, only one, curvature in Plato, "invented" there in the vicinity of the word-signal *curve,* in the immediate vicinity of its intermeaning's exaltation and surprise.

Indeed, what arouses a curve's being in us is the initial and double impact of an opposition: at once *excitement or exaltation* that comes from our meeting with the same, the expected, and *surprise* that comes from our meeting with the new, the unexpected, the "else."

Now, this is exactly what we find, not only at the threshold, or at the arousing moment, of any sense-presence in us, but as the very content-form, and the dwelling itself, of the most subtle sense, smell, from the beginning to the culmination of its curve.

And so, "speculatively," what is meant here by this vicinity to the word *curve* and its meaning-complex is not to be met in any possible sense datum experience, not even in the reversibility of our sense-structures, but, again, to be met as the intertranslatability of their idioms, with a primordial *curve*-idiom, *curve*-pattern, underlying and sustaining all of them: smell.

How? Neither exaltation nor surprise (surprise: this lever that moves exaltation to its ending or consummation) are distractions from a particular and given-in-us sense-presence—a visual or auditive, or a "verbal" experience. On the contrary, they become the intensification of such a sense-experience, the tenacity of this presence. So that, and because of this intensification and its energy-propelling tenacity (the irreversible uniqueness of a sight's curve or a tune's curve), our attention thus energized is led suddenly to the *opening into* another sense experience (which could also be an opening into the very notion or hypothesis of the "intertranslatability"). And this opening is usually not the opening of or into a "superior," but of or into an "inferior" sense: as if there were no energy left—exaltation and surprise having consumed all—to climb up the scale of sense-hierarchy and reach the inner heaven's "superiority," say, the "verbal"—the "spiritual"—but energy enough to descend down and down, lower and lower in the scale—to reach and to rest, *entre azucenas olvidado,* among the oozes of innermost body's ocean-bottom.

All the energy of my available attention is thus canalized into the narrowest passage made in me by a *new* object of concentration or contemplation, the corner of a street, a wall's ivy creeping up, the smell of grass, the *bebkes*-roses, the co-vibration of overtones—so that in clinging to such an object (a *fac-simile* of an unseizable sensation-infinity seized by the finite) as entirely as I can or will, I detach myself at the same time from all the rest in and around me—all the rest which is almost all that immensely fills existence at large (for my corner of a street, or wall's ivy, is so very humble, so insignificant, occupies so little space; my *bebkes*-roses are so "silly" when compared, say, with the importance of sober business in life, real war, real revolution, real decisions of mind)!

And then, only then, the great secret Night—*la noche escura*—everybody's *peine d'amour,* creates the return to the sources, the neo-Platonic curving back, or my own going down down into the eye of a dog, the pre-man's nights on trees, smell, smell-and-image, the "else," the image-else, the smell-else, Child, Bliss and Japan's Painting, and the sacred Face lost, found: Veronica.

Exaltation-and-surprise: is not this what the Mysterious Companion meant, when he said: "I am the bliss and the appreciation of art, simply"?

Exaltation, surprise—the threshold of each and any sense-construction, the threshold of smell, of course; but also smell's whole dwelling; our discovery or finding of ourselves *among* the excitement-and-surprise, among, within, the very content-form of the smell-curve:

Cezanne's exaltation, Cezanne's excitement-surprise co-vibrating with our sudden discovery of being among, within it, among, within the weight of smell, at the chosen and secret corner of any of his creations. And the growth of excitement, exaltation and surprise—oh, how astonishing and astonished is here our attentive appreciation of Cezanne's "else"—at the touch, the sound, the idea, the incurving *weight* pulling us down, down, resting only where smell itself rests, and where human art starts and ends: in Yamato, in China, or in Islam.

✵

All is quiet for a short instant now. In front of these chosen, and probably final, masterpieces of Eastern art let us rest.

They are masterpieces of Korean painting, indeed. At this art's closest to its self-reliance and its self-expression in the heraldic history of painting, somewhere in the middle between China's correspondence-solidarity and Japan's identity-substitution, Korean painting reached its full maturity at the precise time of the Far East's late *Renovatio:* when China's revendication of the long-neglected—betrayed even—"artisan" sacredness had created a new, "another," transferred pictorial expression, the Ch'ing porcelain; when Japan's Ukiyo-e made anew of the art of painting a living kami-presence, a living kami of a painted autumnal leaf, a kami of Bodhisattva-"ornament," a kami of Yamato-e space, of its oblique "rigid"-mobility, a kami painted image-smell.

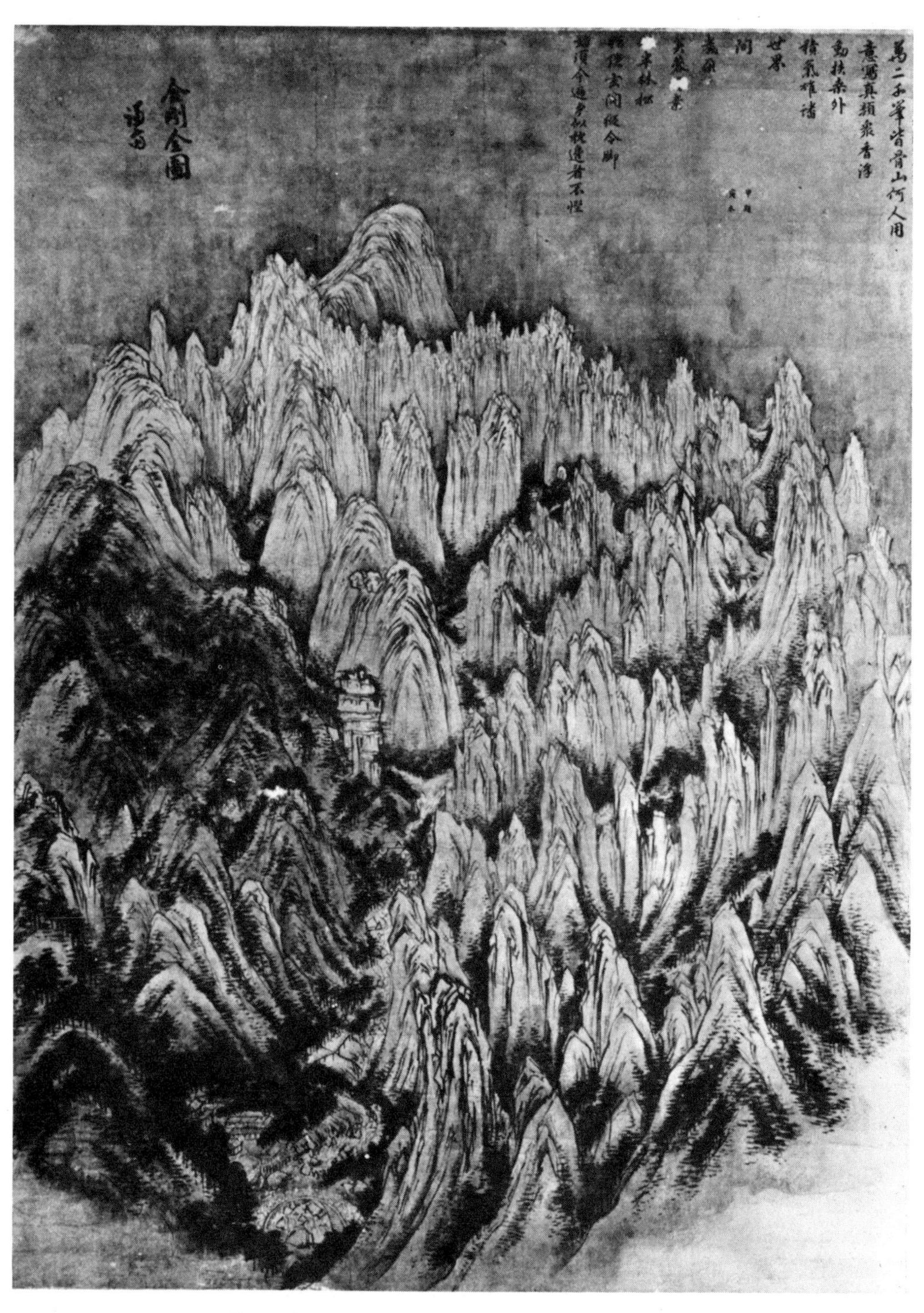

159 CHŌNG SŌN *The Diamond Mountain* (18th century)

The "Diamond Mountain" *(Plate 159)*, by Chōng Sōn (1676-1759) is all this. A loyal portrait of a vertiginous mountain made of ascending and sky-piercing crystal blocks? Oh, yes! But it is this mountain's painting, its "else": the very word *diamond*, sparkling, compound, is signalized here naively, surprisingly, by its image-replica. A diamond mountain indeed—in verbal substitution. And suddenly discovering itself among the excitement-and-surprise of a discovery, our eye, in sensuous down-fall, reaches the oozes: a diamond smell at the end of the *curve*.

And the lovely "Spring" *(Plate 160)* by Yi In-Mun (1746-1825), the loveliest young blushing face ever painted! Delicate *trouble délicieux*, color washes, shiny, slippery, changing, neither pink—yet all is pink!—nor blue—yet all is blue!—nor yellow—all yellow!—Dufy-like technique of shining afar, of color's and line's *glissade* one under the other, fragile, moving curve of change, the immediate vicinity of excited surprise—what will happen now in the painting?—delicate shiver of the "else" here too—"another" shiver: transparent image-smell, truly spring.

. . . . One wonders . . . one muses . . . at the end of this brief and lucid exaltation of a summer moment . . . .

For it is at this intensely quiet moment when a painting or any other object = *persona*—any other result of contemplation—is about to reveal itself as "incomprehensible," as not *willing* to be comprehended (or to be comprehended not as, say, Yi In-Mun's spring story—a subtle and truthfully told story to be sure, of mount-water-sky-trees—but, more modestly, as a way of painting itself)—it is then that the surprise-and-joy of meeting someone or something comes so close to me, to us, becomes so "my body" as not to be ever able to make me, us, know "what" it is!

It is at this very moment of quieter intensity that through the opened narrow interstices of a nascent judgment in us (the "monster" of nascent creation = critique), the closest-to-the-bottom sense in man insinuates itself; the animal sense *par excellence*, smell.

But—one wonders, one muses again—the brain-soil is fertile, the soil of the "else" is fertile: the grain of a sense when sown grows very rapidly into a one-pointed *curve* of matured self-change, irresistibly into its grown "else," the "another" of its self.

The sense of smell, Yi In-Mun's hallucination of a painted spring, insinuates itself through the interstices of a nascent judgment, *not as smell only*, not even as an image-smell exclusively, but as a guiding idea leading all other senses: an idea-smell. (With no other proof for this than the fusion of schema and *Image-la-Folle;* in front of me.) . . . . Wondering—musing—further: A smell is—*speculatively*—a smell-idea, the *what-of-the-how* of an idea, as idea, as its self-sustaining value or profitless meaning, thus its *moral* essence, the *amor intellectualis Dei* of it. In a visionary image, smell is bliss, because it contains and keeps awakened the impetus toward the moral eventfulness—moral conduct—in the best of man and his planetary history. Such as, in an illustrious example, the immense fertility-centered cycle of the ancient "magic," still pre-moral man, a cycle whose fully symbolized gossip-content of sympathetic profit-and-power magic would not stop there in its evolvement, but taking suddenly another route, that is, continuing its

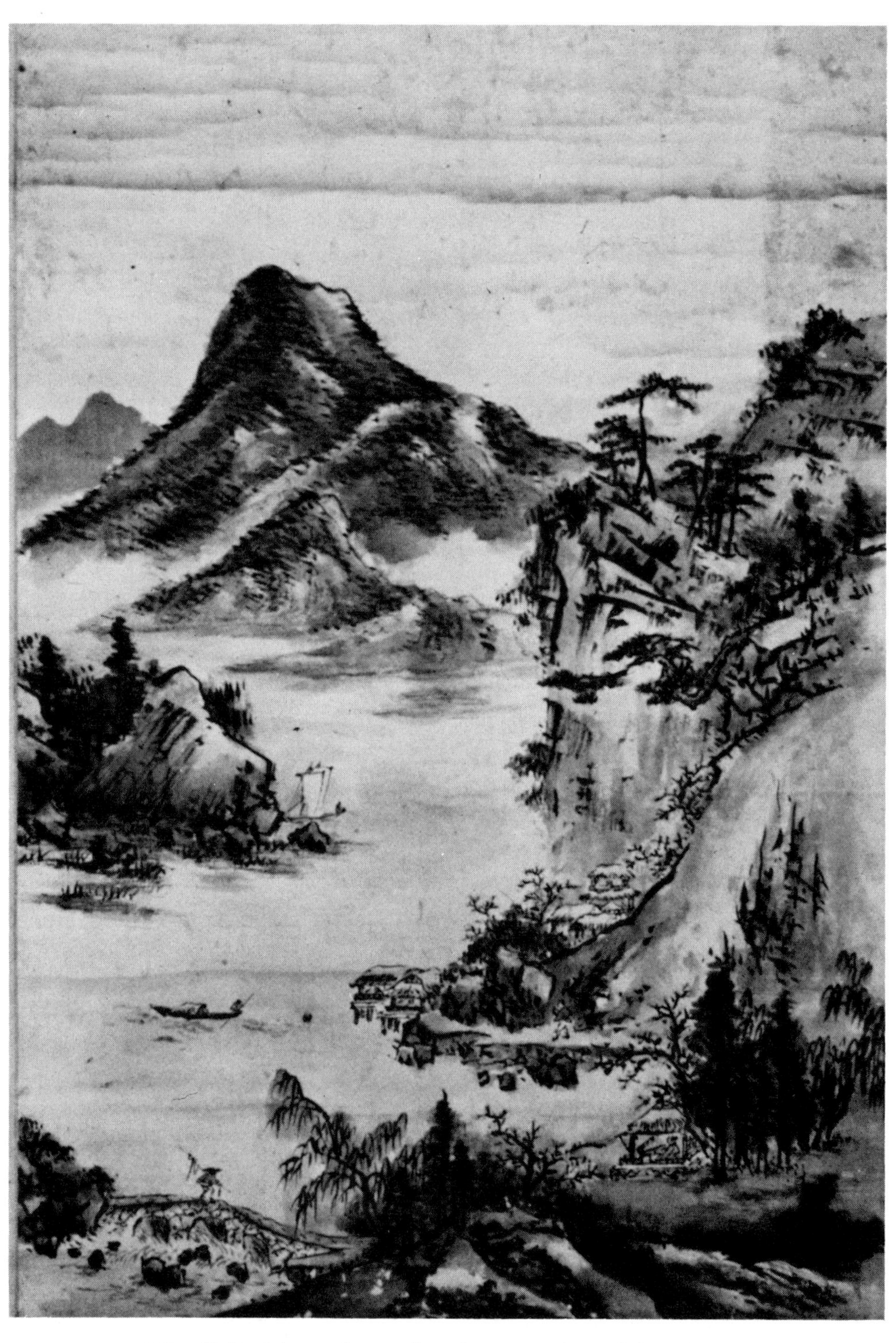

160 Yi In-Mun *Spring Landscape* (late 18th century)

other, "signalizing," trajectory born still in the pre-split universe of consubstantiality, and passing beyond the vicinity of all the fertility cultures' acquired wealth, touched at the end the poverty or purity of a new content, the ultimately reduced, form-content-to-form, content of man's *moral* exaltation and suprise, ancient man's first conscious exaltation and surprise; the image-idea-smell of the Ten Commandments' Law.

Prophetically: here and now.

Here and now: just as the Child was in this book, just as a smell is in this book, just as bliss is here and now. And just as Japan and Japanese Painting are not here any more . . . .

Sudden Epilogue

Right. The author of this book is not here any more. And I, his Mysterious Companion, am here to make, in my companion's stead, the last bow:

The book *is* on Japan and Japanese painting—the only culture that is child-and-art culture, smell-and-art culture, bliss-and-art culture. The only one that remains to give testimony today to man's innermost body's consubstantiality with man's beyond-man. Japan and Japanese painting—part of the past cycle-Kalpa, where, at the beginning, *soma* gave birth both to *pneuma* and *nous,* are present: in the book's loyalty to this.

But touching the end of that cycle's curvature, both continuing and separating from it, a new planetary cycle slowly arose—we, of today, are the bewildered observers and participants in it—already arousing in its own curvature a similar or homologous direction of growth.

Today's new Monster, the new cycle of a new consubstantiality, is just beginning to emerge: a great trouble, a great convulsion—the new Body! —and a great change. Shall we live in a new "another" "pre-split" world? Shall we witness a tragic, yet creative, new event of another split?

That is why Japan and Japanese painting are not there, in the book, any more. And yet the *curve* of their witnessing for the entire past remains the same: Japan and Japanese painting remain there: as the curve of the witnessing itself.

The same direction of change and growth is starting to frame the future of the new cycle: the new *soma* is ready to sprout as future *new pneuma,* or future *new nous.*

And the meaning of the curve is the intended meaning of this book: *Yoga* as *history and as art of painting.*

Through and through, the book and the curve are evolved in the vicinity of Serpent's coil that encircles both the old cycle and the new nascent one—Kundalini-Yoga, the liberation, the union with Paramātma-Cit, the self supreme; her = his, Śiva = Śakti's, I = Kundali-Śakti's body, at once continued in the great Body, or in *correspondence* with it, as *pneuma,* as my individual breath, *pinda* or *vyasti prāna,* one with the universal breath or *Prāna,*[30] and identified with the great Body and breath, substituting it, as *nous:* I = Kundalini's instantaneous uncoilment—both *pneuma* and *nous*— from smell to idea: a difficult *un-* and *in*coiling within "another" time measure of bliss, ascending-descending the six *cakras* or six degrees of subtle structures:

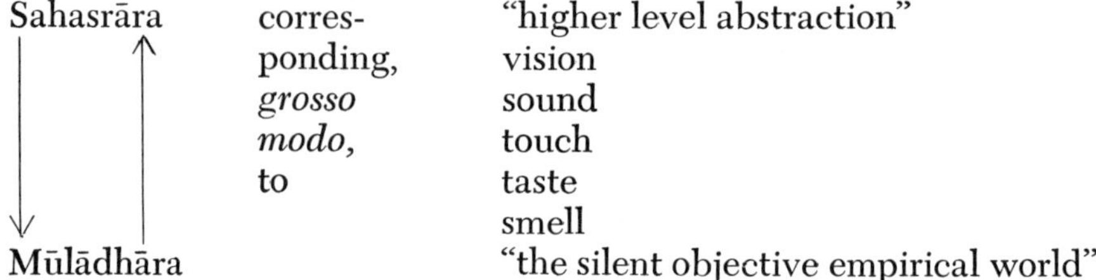

But today we are—insolently, nonchalantly, "vulgarly," possessively—we are the small children of neo-*soma. Everything, everybody is Yogi:* "Everybody is *dada.* Everybody is the director of dada."[31]

We, of the neo-Body's nascent cycle—its neo-*nous* and its neo-*pneuma* still close to the moisture of the earth there, inherent but not self-evidenced, present, moving, revolving, kicking the innermost's belly, close to the feet ("Kuharini, Thou sprinklest all things with the stream of nectar which flows from the tips of Thy two feet; and as Thou returneth to Thine own place, Thou vivifiest and makest visible all things that were aforetime invisible, and on reaching Thy abode Thou resumest thy snake-like coil and sleepest"),[32] *we of the neo-consubstantiality,* we don't want Yoga, we don't need Yoga, either Dhyana-Yoga, the intellective power of liberation (Buddhist Zen?) or Kundalini-Yoga, *soma*'s "else" liberation (Amidist Buddhism?).

We reject the Yoga of the elite of the old cycle, still working in us, still tempting us—the wounded sick Yoga. Its almost invisible, yet surely persisting wound of post-split's treason is still there, in spite of all. Still there, the subtle hidden old scar of poisonous treason in history. For the elite the center of radiation toward the Embrace is still not the lowest = highest immediacy, *Ghanda,* Smell = Foot,[33] as Vedanta and all Asia would admit or accept in the apparent earnest of their sayings and writings—the lowest for the highest!—but *Sábdā* or in-sound = *Logos,* the very Brahman manifested as sacred letter, that which is still in-between, the middle's only exalted Truth, the tantric elite's truth, but not plenitude-void.

And single-handed, I, who replace the absent, the one whom I don't accompany any more, in single-handed decision, I change the entire tantric wisdom—I transfer the entire tantric weight and depth into the brief and lucid and finite exaltation of everybody's, anybody's cognition and experiencing, into the Child, the bliss, the nostalgia and the smell of an image-touch: the wisdom of art by divine substitution.

I say: for the new consubstantial cycle—the new-fish-kami, the new *nous*-kami, the new *pneuma*-kami—give me, oh loyalty to the origins, purity!—give me at first, the neo-paganism (the new Yoga, I concede) of a new and rapid visitation, the integral monster; the *neo-substitution of art for logos*—from Ukiyo-e to Miró, from Raphael to Mondrian and Le Corbusier.

And only after, afterward, bestow on me the gift of the new Ten Commandments.

But first: everybody's, anybody's "another" rose: *Satori* amongst the *vulgar-kami.*

This is what I, this book's substitution, meant, when, substituted for the Face of Veronica's return, I performed the last *mie* of Return, I, the *Shite-Zure,* at the end of his Noh:

ACT I

I am Kumagai no Jirō Naozane, the rude warrior from the Land of Musashi in the East. At the battle of Ichi-no-Tani by the Suma beach I murdered the young and beautiful Taira no Atsumori and became the repentant monk Rensei . . . I carry throughout the universes of innumerable Kalpas the desire of Atsumori's last smile . . . . and now I must go to the Suma beach . . .

CHORUS

The scene is of great mountainous beauty. Proper for the enacting of so melancholy a Noh.

WAKI

How true. Indeed, I came here not with the times but through the events. My journey hither—eight hundred years!

(Enter SHITE *as an old woman clad in hanging rags.)*

SHITE

I am the old weary woman—alas! alas!—of younger day. No being else here. . . . I bring myself before the gods in the hope to see once again, once only! my last bliss. I am in search—oh, fraternal Kami of Help, help me!—of a lost form. . . .

. . . .

WAKI

The old woman in rags speaks very strangely. Her voice is the voice of another.—Who are you? Tell me.

SHITE

I lost a single fragrance, a scent around my coming death, around my flute close to my armour.

WAKI

Is she Atsumori?—Oh, moment of fullness and deception—remain.

CHORUS

So futile a desire? How could it be a torment of truth? I wonder.

SHITE

A fragrance seen—and I lost its form—

WAKI

I start to believe. Are you Atsumori?

SHITE-ZURE

(appearing in grand grey kimono, cross-and-lengthwise tormented by a light purple garland of davallias) I am the Today within our Kalpa's frame—I am also the eight hundredth year of this Noh. Today I am what we all become. I heard, I saw—before dying at the Suma beach, the scent just mentioned—and more fragrance still—

WAKI

Thus Atsumori's life has come to an end.

SHITE

It was the evening before the great battle. Do you remember?

WAKI

Yes, oh yes—the feast at the fort.

CHORUS

Feast of abundance—feast of torch lights—

WAKI

And the music of Atsumori: his flute singing a song of bliss—

SHITE

I am tired, too. Look at the old woman in rags. How old I am. Oh, tell them how beautiful was my boyish face and the splendor of my courtly attire.

. . . .

SHITE

I faced my giver of death at the wild Suma beach with a smile.

WAKI

I can't help you.

CHORUS

I shall not help you.

SHITE

I can't see the smile.

WAKI

I shall not see your scent.

WAKI and SHITE

Let's pray. Separate.

ACT II

SHITE

(reappearing as the real Atsumori, wearing the mask of a young man—juroku) Look! Look! It is over. The beautiful head, still radiant, is there, severed, soiled with blood and sand and dirt. Close to the young warrior's limbs is the sheathed flute, and still closer——oh, Heian sentiment!—is a fragrant branch of plum-tree. Naozane has wept. I hear him say: "I shall bring you back the Form of your bliss—the Fragrance you saw."

WAKI

I see, I smell the growth of the Child in my hand's warmth. I shall never find your smile. So helpless a love!

CHORUS

(muted) So helpless.

SHITE

Useless.

CHORUS

Useless? Oh, useless clarity of adults' laws—begone.

WAKI

Farewell.

(He sinks to the floor and hides his head in his sleeve. His fan is unfolded. SHITE *bends over him, his open fan covering the* WAKI*'s.)*

CHORUS

Pity's smile—Form Supreme nowhere lost.
Like the palpitating cluster of hungry birds over
the deep sea's plenty—fish! big fish! big fishes!
—its splashing jumps out and in the blue
and luminous offing; like the cluster of fishermen's boats swiftly
reaching the long looked for
spot—guided by the excitement
of wings over fins;
like these three dark clusters

of death, profit, and desire,
each separate, each
different from each other,
yet yoked each to each other by
the drive of inner event
one and the same—
so also are to each other
the two separate desires of our Noh—
the passing smile of a dying Child; the scent's passing
bliss received by the eye.
One sameness of two flames. . . .

SHITE-ZURE

(standing behind the SHITE-WAKI*'s closed group. His sumptuous costume of Act 2, grey on grey, frames them as with some great bird's wings.)* Desires interchanged—birds in flight. . . . It is a thing real. The faint vanity of desire, of pleasure, of nostalgia and search—the Form visible of a forgotten—present—fragrance—is Amitabha. Bliss in Immediacy.

WAKI and SHITE

How?

SHITE-ZURE

The Release from the Wheel, itself so inexorable and terrifying a law of yore is transferred, ever more fraternal, now, today—why not? why not? from the still *external* Ocean of Becoming to the innermost flow of human *ontos:*

Buddhist psyche-*ascent* became—I am here to recognize it!—my twentieth-century's psyche-*descent* into brain's intimacy where the lowest and elemental joins the highest decisions of abstracting.

Not any more our deliverance from the chain of senses, but the innermost deliverance of the senses themselves—freedom for each and solidarity with each: the Touch is seen, the Fragrance is seen. The Sight is a Scent and the Sound is the Touch. Unto the deepest, Socialism and Fragrance—Cosmos's *satori*—in Vision's Form.

CHORUS

The Chain is released, oh, beautiful, compassionate Face, oh beautiful, compassionate Form-Scent!

We see the roots: It is not dark.

WAKI and SHITE

Show me.

SHITE-ZURE

I am the today. How incongruous here! Thus: I raise the banner—the Form, the Scent, the One—how incongruous!—of *uomo cualunque*'s Liberation: Socialism *de profundis*—Form so humble, fragrant hut *(Plate 161)* of Ise, shelter to all, from the sacredness of a primeval small-number family living

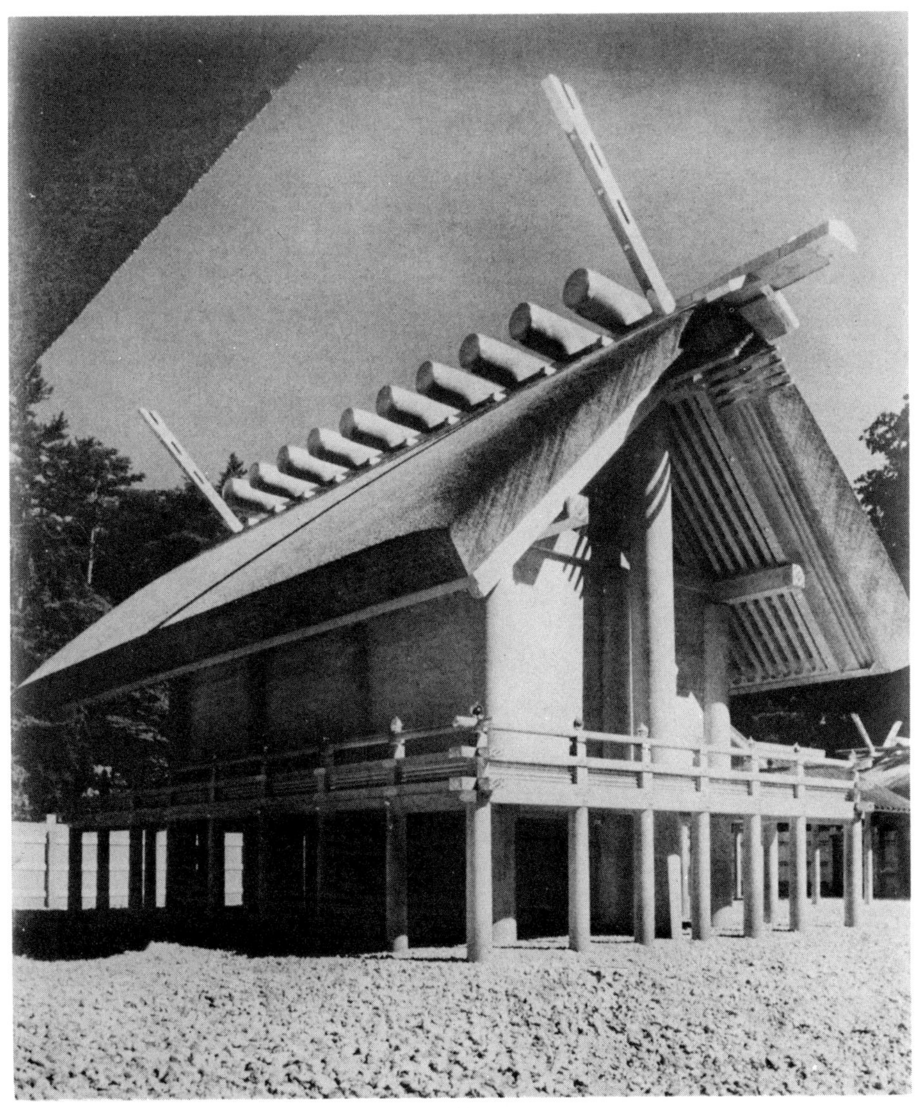

161 Ise, most venerated Shinto Temple in Japan

there together, to the sacredness of the greatest-number family living there together—*égalité, fraternité, liberté* told anew—final secret of Yamato. I pray the prayer of thanks—in purest white—all-kamis! Kami-scent, kami-smile, kami-desire!

SHITE and WAKI

"If I attain the Buddhahood
In the whole world and its ten spheres
Of all that dwell here none shall call on my name
And be rejected or cast aside."

FINIS

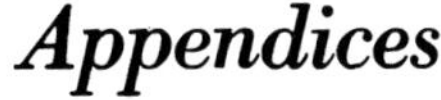
Appendices

NOTES

VARIATION I

1. At the entrance to the Itsukushima-jinja, temple built in 811, restored in the 15th century, and in the 16th by Hideyoshi.

2. "This is the spirit that Beauty must ever induce, wonderment and a delicious trouble, longing and love and a trembling that is all delight." Plotinus, *The Enneads,* tr. by Stephen MacKenna (London, 1956), p. 59.

3. Louis Sullivan, quoted by Siegfried Giedion, *Space, Time and Architecture* (3rd ed., Cambridge, 1954), p. 413.

4. The Tibetan icon of Eternity-Power as the embrace: Shiva-Shakti, Male-Female, One.

5. *Paul Klee on Modern Art,* Introduction by Herbert Read (New York, 1945), p. 51.

6. From John Carter Covell, *Under the Seal of Sesshu* (New York, 1941).

7. See Ernest Fenollosa, *Epochs of Chinese and Japanese Art* (New York, 1912), II, 42, 43, 82, *et passim. Nōtan:* almost untranslatable term; literally, *Nō* = thick, deep, strong + *Tan* = of delicate flavour; tasteless, flat, thin. Applied to painting, it would mean that subtle and interiorized sense of darkness-light which characterizes the pictorial line, mass, and even color.

8. Paul Henry Láng, *Music in Western Civilization* (New York, 1941), p. 443.

9. William Cohn, *Chinese Painting* (London, 1948), p. 72.

10. Cassius J. Keyser, quoted by Alfred Korzybski, in *Science and Sanity* (2nd ed.; Lancaster, Pa., 1941), p. 188.

11. In Northrop's formulation. *See* F. S. C. Northrop, *The Meeting of East and West* (New York, 1946), *passim.*

12. Paul Klee, *The Inward Vision* (New York, 1958), p. 25.

13. Bertrand Russell, Introduction to Ludwig Wittgenstein, *Tractatus Logico-Philosophicus* (London, New York, 1922), p. 23.

14. Jean Robinet, *L'Evolution des espèces,* p. 187.

15. *Statements by the Artist* (New York, 1941), pp. 12, 13. (Italics mine.)

16. Gordon Childe, *What Happened in History* (Penguin Books, 1946), *passim.*

17. " . . . to hope till Hope creates/ From its own wreck the thing it contemplates." Percy Bysshe Shelley, *Prometheus Unbound,* lines 573-74.

VARIATION II

1. In the sense of Giedion's *Mechanization Takes Command* (New York, 1948).

2. An excellent, concise and exhaustive resumé of this epistemological problem and of Kant-Cassirer's illumination of it is to be found in Charles W. Hendel's Introduction to Ernst Cassirer, *The Philosophy of Symbolic Forms* (New Haven, Conn., 1953), Volume I.

3. In J. W. T. Mason's definition of Shinto, the "creative impetus buried in the subconscious knowledge life has of itself." *The Meaning of Shinto* (New York, 1935), p. 15.

4. Langdon Warner, *The Enduring Art of Japan* (Cambridge, Mass., 1952), p. 47. The ordinary way of handling the makemono, a narrow scroll which cannot be hung. It is "unrolled horizontally on the mat from the left and gathered in by the right hand."

5. Translated, together with several other Noh plays, by Ernest Fenollosa and Ezra Pound, in *"Noh" or Accomplishment, A Study of the Classical Stage of Japan* (New York, 1917), pp. 151-64.

6. *Locus cit.*

7. *Ibid.,* p. 164.

8. P. Mus, *Le Bouddha Paré* (1928); quoted by A. K. Coomaraswamy in his introductory essay, "On the Nature of Buddhist Art," in Benjamin Rowland, Jr., *The Wall-Paintings of India, Central Asia and Ceylon* (Boston, 1938), p. 24.

9. Erwin Panofsky, *Early Netherlandish Painting* (Cambridge, Mass., 1953), pp. 9-10.

10. From the Noh play *Nishikigi,* translated by Fenollosa and Pound, *opus cit.,* pp. 131-49.

11. Mrs. C. A. F. Rhys Davids, *A Manual of Buddhism* (New York, 1932), p. 142—where she continues thus: "But he [the man-*Nāmā*] was not then considered as being *mind* in any way. [Italics mine.] Mind was a collective way of wording man's inner activities, such as knowing, purpose, speech, feeling, becoming and the like. He could thus be appraised in many ways. He was he, but his *karṃan,* or action was manifold, both inward and outward."

12. Melville J. Herskovits, *Dahomey. An Ancient West African Kingdom* (New York, 1938), *passim.*

13. H. and H. A. Frankfort and others: *The Intellectual Adventure of Ancient Man. An Essay on Speculative Thought in the Ancient Near East* (Chicago, 1946), pp. 62-70, *et passim.*

14. Persian mystic Junayd (9-10th century), quoted in E. G. Browne, *A Literary History of Persia* (New York, 1922), I, 427.

15. J. W. T. Mason, *opus cit.,* p. 115.

16. *Ibid.,* pp. 63, 114, 117, *et passim.*

17. "Shinto cannot be understood unless the fact that everything is Kami be accepted as reality"—not symbolically. *See* J. W. T. Mason, *The Spirit of Shinto Mythology* (Tokyo, 1939), p. 88.

18. *Ibid.,* p. 80.

19. Not in the apparently similar Indian sense of the humblest corresponding to the loftiest, but in the precise Japanese sense of definite body = presence.

20. *Records of Ancient Matters,* published in A.D. 712, translated by Basil Hall Chamberlain in *Transactions of the Asiatic Society of Japan* (Supplement, Vol. 10, Yokohama, 1882). These are closer, in their Shinto narrative, to the original,

unwritten, sources than the more detailed but more "Chinese" Nihongi Chronicles of Japan, first published in A.D. 720.

21. Mason, *The Spirit of Shinto Mythology, op. cit.*, p. 62.

22. Yoni Noguchi, *Through the Torii* (Boston, 1922), pp. 1-7. (Italics in this passage are mine.)

23. "He [the pilgrim] may easily spend an entire day in this fashion. However, for his rest and delectation, at each of these places, there are tea houses, commanding excellent views of the plain below, where may be purchased food for the worshipper's physical nourishment and wine to make glad his heart. By the time all the holy places have been visited . . . some of the faithful are so well fortified with saké, which is the essence of rice and therefore a most appropriate drink for Inari believers [Inari: food divinity's pantheon], that their staggering gait and red faces cannot be attributed wholly to the exertion of climbing the mountain." Reverend D. C. Buchanan, *Inari: Its Origin, Development, and Nature* (Asiatic Society of Japan, 1935), p. 104.

24. *Mikoto* (*Mi* = divine, *Koto* = thing) is in Shinto mythology an alternative word for Kami. A man is *Mikoto,* a Kami is *Mikoto,* the Emperor is *Mikoto, Sumera* (whole?) *Mikoto. See* Mason: *The Meaning of Shinto, op. cit.*, pp. 157-59.

25. *Ibid.*, pp. 93-97. (Italics mine.)

26. Thus now—of the two official post-Meiji divisions of Shinto in today's Japan, the Jinja or Shrine Shinto, a cult for development of national unity only, whose shrines, under the control of the Department of Home Affairs are declared *not to be religious institutions,* and the sectarian Shinto, Kyōha Shinto, recognized by the Department of Education, which controls it, as a religion equal in rights and value to any other religion of the country—of these two, the first, the Jinja, would be the real, elemental Shinto . . . of course.

27. This cosmic happening, its consequences and its solution, is given in the 1932 ed. of Chamberlain, *Kōjīki*, pp. 63-70 (Cf. footnote 20).

28. Buchanan, *op. cit.*, p. 93.

29. Chamberlain translation, *op. cit.*, p. 58.

30. Early Nara period, 646-710; Nara was Japan's capital from *ca.* 710 to *ca.* 784.

31. Buchanan, *op. cit.*, p. 126.

32. *Ibid.*, p. 121.

33. Ruth Benedict, *The Chrysanthemum and the Sword, Patterns of Japanese Culture* (Boston, 1946), p. 288.

34. "A ritual or magic [power-full] circle . . . . a diagram used in invocations, meditation and temple services," *A Buddhist Students' Manual,* Christmas Humphreys, ed. (London, 1956), p. 156.

In its dual modality, either as a typically Lamaist, anthropomorphic multi-figural yantra-picture, embracing in its circular pattern the whole Dhyana Buddha Universe-image, with all its radiations, or as a yantra-diagram, the *mandala* could approximately be defined thus: " . . . In Hindu devotional tradition yantra is the general term for instruments of worship, namely, idols, pictures, or geometrical diagrams. A yantra may serve as (1) a representation of some personification or aspect of the divine, (2) a model for the worship of a divinity by inner meditation, face to face in one's heart, when the outer elements of worship have been discarded by the initiate, (3) a kind of chart or program for the gradual evolution of a vision and identification of the Self with its contents, namely, with the divinity in its gradual manifestation and transformations. In this case the yantra contains dynamic elements. It is, thus, a pattern to guide the production of inner visualizations, meditations, and experiences. On the one hand, these reflect the reality of the divine essence, and the process of its production of the universe. But, on the other hand, the cosmic process and the stratifications and gradations of evolution are reflected or copied in the structure of the human organism, body and psyche, so that these blueprints for the yoga-work of the devotee-initiate have a psychological as well as a cosmic meaning.

"Thus, yantra is an instrument for curbing the psychic forces by concentrating them on the pattern offered, and in such a way that one's power of visualization will reproduce this very pattern. The pattern may indicate a static vision of a divinity to be worshipped, a superhuman power to be contacted, or it may develop a series of visualizations which grow and unfold from each other, forming the links or steps of a process. The latter is the richer . . . . " From Henry R. Zimmer's notes for his lecture on "Śrī-Yantra and Śiva-Trimūrti," posthumously printed in *The Review of Religion* VIII, 1 (New York: Columbia University Press, November, 1943).

35. Buchanan, *op. cit.*, p. 124.

36. *Ibid.*, p. 125.

37. Arnold Hauser, *The Social History of Art* (New York, 1951), I, 372, 373, 452; II, 919.

38. Lady Murasaki's *Genji Monogatari* (11th century).

39. A Buddhist saying quoted by Junjirō Takakusu, *The Essentials of Buddhist Philosophy,* ed. by W. Chan and Charles A. Moore (2ND ed.; Hawaii, Honolulu, T. H. 1949), p. 90.

40. "The ideas peculiar to Zen," says Takakusu (*op. cit.*, pp. 163, 164), "may be summarized as follows: 'From mind to mind it was transmitted, not expressed in words or written in letters'; 'it was a special transmission apart from the sacred teaching.' 'Directly point to the human mind, see one's real nature and become an enlightened Buddha.' Or, 'the very body or the very mind is the Buddha.' . . . .

"The basic idea of Zen is the identity of *ens* and non-*ens*. 'The true state is no (special) state'; 'the gate of *Dharma* is no gate'; 'holy knowledge is no knowledge.' The mutual identification of two opposed ideas, such as black and white, good and evil, pure and impure, or the like, results from deep meditation. 'The ideal body has no form, yet any form may come out of it.' 'The golden mouth has no word, yet any word may come out of it.' . . . . "

41. In the dense forest-thought of India, the whole Indic universe, dark, immense and moist, the piercing and dry clarity of the Two = One doctrine shines through the darkness, enlightening all there, from the obscurity of the tree-roots to the wind-shaken tree-summits. Such is the Mahayana Buddhist doctrine (most nourished and nourishing fruit of India's soil) of "totalist" psycho-cosmic causation, the theory of the Presence, of Thus-ness or Such-ness, *tathā-tā*, "the state (-tā) of being 'so' (tathā)" [a] and not of Thisness or Thatness *(Tattva)*, these or those phenomena's vital energy,[b] the supreme theory of the "unimpeded interdiffusion of all particulars"—or *jijimuge* in Japanese,[c] in its last wind-shaken summit's light, the law of self or ego-lessness, the one-pointedness of mind. This is also, both in Hindu-Upanishadic and "esoteric" Buddhist thought, the oneness of the static = dynamic two in all-existence-as-becoming, the "wayfarer's" existence.[d]

Very concretely Two = Oneness is the image-abstraction (both icon and idea) of Shiva-Shakti in Embrace (Shiva, the static Creator-destroyer of self-creativity and self-creatureness, one with his Māyā-Energy Consort, his multi-imaged, multi-named Shakti), the Yab-Yum, Embrace of Adi-Buddha,[e] origin-goal of the never-ceasing flow of all His Emanations, all the Dhyana or meditation Buddhas and Bodhisattvas of the "esoteric" tantric micro-macrocosmoses, one with his Consort Shakti, the "Wisdom of the Yonder Shore," *Prajnā-Pāramitā*. The Two = One, the Embrace, produces thus, contains and illuminates the obscurest terms of Buddhist thought, the thought about the Sameness = Else, the thought-chain of unending yet end-pointed equations:

1) *prajnā* = *karuna* (in gross translation, wisdom = compassion, and compassion not in the sense of a co-sufferer's sentiment, but in the matter-of-factness of knowing that everybody and everything co-exists in both destruction, thus self-and-else's destruction, and salvation, thus self-and-else's salvation), actively linked with the essential Buddhist equation:

2) mind = matter; mind-only = mind-stuff.[f] "The Mind and Body are effects of Prakṛti [or mind-evolving-first energy-Shakti]. Both having the same origin, each as such, whether as Mind or Matter, are 'material' things—that is, they are of the nature of forces."[g] "In other words, Consciousness (Cit) as the ultimate experiencing principle, pervades and is at base all being. Every cell of the body has a consciousness of its own. The various organic parts of the body which the cells build have not only particular cell-consciousness, but the consciousness of the particular organic part which is other than the mere collectivity of the consciousness of its units. Thus there may be an abdominal consciousness. And the consciousness of such bodily region is its Devatā—that is, that aspect of Cit which is associated with and informs that region. . . . Then there is the subtle form or body of these Devatās, in the shape of Mind—supersensible 'matter' . . . and sensible 'matter'—namely, ether, air, fire, water, earth. . . . . "[h]

As Zimmer interprets it: . . . "Whatever seems to exist is the result of *parikalpa*, 'creation from within,' i.e., 'imagination.' But such magically creative thought is possible only because there exists a kind of eternal repository (*ālaya*, 'abode') from which can be drawn the substance of every possible image and idea. This is the so-called *ālaya-vijñāna*, 'repository consciousness,' which is thought in and by itself; thought without the thing that is thought; thought therefore that is 'void' *(śūnya)*. This is termed *tathātā* 'the suchness,' and is the *positive* aspect of the Void."[i] Hence, actively linked to this:

3) *plenum* = *void* (*śūnyāta* = voidness), "*Śūnyāśūnya* (void yet non-void)."[j] For: "Perfect emptiness or Void comprehends all things. . . . The doctrine of Void. . . . is in reality Non-Void, i.e., not one-sided, abstracted Void, because it can comprehend anything whatever."[k] And " '*śūnya*' negatively means 'Void' but positively 'relative,' i.e., 'devoid of independent reality' or 'devoid of specific character.' Thus *Śūnyāta* is non-entity and at the same time 'relativity,' i.e., the entity only as in causal relation. . . . "[l] For: "The state of Samādhi [or concentration-ecstacy] 'is. . . . the Void Itself.' "[m]

4) Which thus, finally—towering Two-One achievement!—equates the Impermanent, that which is "it is the else," with that which is "it is"

[a] *See* Heinrich Zimmer, *Myths and Symbols of Indian Art and Civilization*, Joseph Campbell, ed. (New York, 1946), p. 145.

[b] *See* Takakusu, *op. cit.*, p. 137; and Arthur Avalon, *The Serpent Power* (16th ed., Madras, 1958), *passim*.

[c] *See* Christmas Humphreys, *Buddhism* (Penguin Books, 1958) p. 151 *et passim*.

[d] The Pāli root-word *bhu* and its derivatives, *bhāva*, *bhāvati*, etc., all are related to *becoming*, *"make become"; see* Mrs. Rhys Davids, *op. cit.*, pp. 88, 92, 116, 120, *et passim*.

[e] Mahavairocana Buddha, the great Sun Buddha of the beginnings.

[f] *Cit, citta, sukṣma.*

[g] Avalon, *op. cit.*, pp. 50, 51.

[h] *Ibid.*, pp. 162, 163.

[i] Zimmer, *Philosophies of India*, Joseph Campbell, ed. (New York, 1951), p. 526.

[j] Avalon, *op. cit.*, p. 184.

[k] Takakusu, *op. cit.*, p. 107.

[l] *Ibid.*, p. 106.

[m] Avalon, *op. cit.*, p. 183.

—Samsāra = Nirvana. (The effort on the part of Western as well as Indian and Far Eastern scholarship to make comprehensible and admissible [never of course "finally" and "successfully"] in the West all these dense, dark, immense, yet out-and-in illuminated precise terms, is truly admirable. In particular when one considers the competent and infallible loyalty of a man like Arthur Avalon [Sir John Woodroffe].)

The basic two-oneness of India's teaching, the "one-pointedness of 'contemplation on reality'" *(sambōdhi)* is thus defined and summarized by Arthur Avalon: "All that is manifest is Power (Śakti) as Mind, Life and Matter. Power implies a Power-Holder. . . . The Power-Holder is Śiva. . . . The two as they are in themselves are one. They are each Being, Consciousness and Bliss. These three terms are chosen to denote ultimate Reality, because Being or 'Is-ness,' as distinguished from particular forms of Being, cannot be thought away. . . . These three terms stand for the ultimate creative Reality as it is in itself. By the imposition upon these terms of Name (Nāma) and Form (Rūpa) or Mind and Matter, we have the limited Being-Consciousness and Bliss which is the Universe.

"Rest implies Activity, and Activity implies Rest. Behind all activity there is a static background. Śiva represents the static aspect of Reality and Śakti the moving aspect. The two, as they are in themselves, are one. All is *Real,* both *Changeless* and *Changeful.* [Italics mine.] Māyā is not in this system 'illusion,' but is . . . . 'the Form of the Formless' . . . . The world is *its* form and these forms are therefore Real.

"Man is then as to his essence the static Power-Holder, or Śiva who is pure Consciousness; and, as Mind and Body, he is the manifestation of Śiva's Power, or Śakti or Mother. He is thus Śiva-Śakti."[n]

42. *See* August Karl Reischauer, *Studies in Japanese Buddhism* (New York, 1917), pp. 158-68.

43. Avalon, *op. cit.*, pp. 291-92.

44. *Ibid.*, p. 50.

45. Rhys Davids, *op. cit., passim.*

46. *See* footnote 41.

47. "Amida Butsu, . . . before he became a Buddha and while he was still the Bosatsu Hōzō (Bodhisattva Dharmakara), many aeons ago, made a great vow in which he vowed that he would not enter the full bliss of Buddhahood until he had worked out a way of salvation for all men, including even the lowest sinners. He remained true to his vow and after many incarnations of self-sacrificing lives he finally succeeded in heaping up so much merit that he became the great Amida Butsu, the Buddha of Eternal Life and Light who offers every man entrance, or rather birth, into his Pure Land of Bliss. . . . . The believer is told to call upon the name of Amida in the prayer Namu Amida Butsu which probably means, 'I adore Thee,' or 'Have mercy upon me, Thou Buddha of Eternal Life and Light.' He who does this shall be saved." Reischauer, *op. cit.*, p. 111.

Amidism as a creed already widely practiced in the Far East as early as the 6th century emerged as a typically Japanese formulation during the late Heian era. As a doctrine it is distinguished from other types of Buddhism mainly by its insistence upon *tariki* or "reliance upon the strength of another," and not upon *jiriki,* one's own strength. The main tenet of the Pure Land or Jōdo belief was expressed in words that the founder of Jōdo, the celebrated Hōnen Shōnin, also called Genku (1133-1212), wrote on his deathbed: "The method of final salvation that I have taught is neither a sort of meditation such as that practiced by many scholars in China and Japan in the past, nor is it a repetition of the Buddha's name by those who have studied and understood the deep meaning of it. It is nothing but the mere repetition of the name of the Buddha Amida without a doubt of his mercy. . . . ." G. B. Sansom, *Japan, a Short Cultural History* (London, New York, 1931), p. 321.

The Jōdo school was founded in 1175, but it was Shinran Shōnin who in 1225 established the Jōdo Shinsu or Shin, the True Pure Land Sect, who gave Amidism its final Japanese Substitution content: the formula *Nembutsu* (Namu Amida Butsu) pronounced = salvation given.

48. A.D. 1395

49. William M. Ivins, Jr., "On the Rationalization of Sight, etc." (New York: Metropolitan Museum of Art Papers, No. 8, 1938), pp. 16-26, esp. 16, 17.

50. Korzybski, *op. cit.*, pp. 34-35, 416-17, 421, 477, *et passim.*

51. Referred to by Ivins, *op. cit.*, p. 12.

52. Benda's *Trahison des Clercs.*

53. *See* supra I, 32.

54. "Shōgun. The word means 'General' or 'Commander,' but it is generally used as an abbreviation of *Sei-i-tai-shōgun* (q. v.), a title conferred by the Court upon Military Dictators." Sansom, *op. cit.*, p. 533: Index.

The power of the shōgun being the very power of the Emperor, yet without the Emperor ceasing to be Emperor, the institution of the shogunate, though relatively late (early 13th century), is the most concrete manifestation of rule by substitution.

55. Such was the substitution-rule of the famous Fujiwara regents—the kwambaku, or kampaku—an office established toward the close of the 9th century (888). A substitution-rule. And the typically Japanese substitution-power of woman-and-child. "The true basis of Fujiwara power," says George Sansom, "was not the rank or the ability of Fujiwara men, but the matrimonial success of Fujiwara women . . . . . it is a Fujiwara

[n] *Ibid.*, pp. 23, 24.

dowager empress and not the ruling emperor whose wishes determine the succession to the high post of Regent and Dictator. . . . . " *A History of Japan to 1335* (Palo Alto, Calif., 1958), I, 155.

"The choice of a consort for the sovereign," comments Captain Frank Brinkley, R.N., "should be legally limited to a daughter of their [the Fujiwara] family, five branches of which were specially designated to that honour through all ages. When a son was born to an emperor, the Fujiwara took the child into one of their palaces, and on his accession to the throne, the particular Fujiwara noble that happened to be his *maternal grandfather* [italics mine] became regent of the empire; . . . . for the Fujiwara did not allow the purple to be worn by a sovereign after he had attained his majority, or, if they suffered him to wield the sceptre during a few years of manhood, they compelled him to abdicate . . . . From 1073, for more than half a century, there sat on the throne titular emperors, with titular regents, chancellors and ministers, while during each reign, not far away, in a palace of his own, keeping imperial state, and assisted by his own officers, was an abdicated emperor in holy orders who, in name a monk, was in fact a ruler. . . . The government . . . . appeared to consist of an emperor, delegating [?] his authority to a regent who controlled a council of state and the ministerial boards; and of an ex-emperor whose commands overrode those of the occupant of the throne." *Encyclopaedia Britannica,* "Japan" (13th ed., 1926) XV, 258, 259.

The political origins and structure of the shogunate proper are summarized by Brinkley: " . . . by the middle of the 12th century the . . . influence of the Fujiwara had paled before that of the Taira and the Minamoto; and a question of succession to the throne marshalled the latter two families in opposite camps, thus inaugurating an era of civil war which held the country in the throes of almost continuous battle for 450 years. . . . At first the Minamoto were vanquished . . . [Taira's] supremacy had lasted 22 years." The Taira were defeated at the famous sea battle at Dan-no-ura in 1155. At Kamakura. . . . Yoritomo, the victorious Minamoto, "obtained for himself the title of *sei-i-tai-shōgun* (Barbarian-subduing-Generalissimo), and just as the office of regent (kwambaku) had long been hereditary in the Fujiwara family, so the office of shōgun became thenceforth hereditary in that of the Minamoto. . . . Kamakura then (after the death of Yoritomo [1198]) became the scene of a drama analogous to that acted in Kiōto from the 10th century.

"The Hōjō family, to which belonged Masa [Masa-ko], Yoritomo's consort, assumed towards the Kamakura shōgun an attitude similar to that previously assumed by the Fujiwara family towards the emperor in Kiōto. A child, who on state occasions was carried to the council chamber in Masa's arms, *served as the nominal repository of the shōgun's power* [italics mine], the functions of administration being discharged in reality by the Hōjō family, whose successive heads took the name of *shikken* (constable) . . . . Children occupied the position of shōgun in Kamakura under authority emanating from children on the throne in Kiōto; and members of the Hōjō family as shikken administered affairs at the mandate of the child shōguns. Through all three stages [in reality one substitution-stage!] in the dignities of mikado, shōgun and shikken, the strictly regulated principle of heredity was maintained, *according to which no Hōjō shikken could ever become shōgun; no Minamoto or Fujiwara could occupy the throne."* (Italics mine.) *Ibid.,* pp. 259-60.

And this structure never ceased, throughout all subsequent political upheavals and changes, never ceased to be the very pattern of Japan's polity. At the beginning of the 14th century the supremacy of the Hōjō shikken was shaken, and from the ensuing bloody tangle came (ca. 1335) a new substitution-rule: the Ashikaga Shogunate. "What the regents had been to the emperors and the constables to the Minamoto shōguns, that the wardens (kwanryō) were to the Ashikaga shōguns." *Ibid.,* p. 260.

After the bloodiest era of continuous civil wars (beginning with the outbreak of the so-called Ōnin Wars, ca. 1467) and the 16th-century reconstruction era, the era of the three great warrior-organizers, Oda Nobunaga (1534-1582), Toyotomi Hideyoshi (1537-1598) and Tokugawa Iyeyasu (1542-1616), followed by the last historical embodiment of the shogunate, the Tokugawa era (ca. 1603 or 1615 to 1867)—throughout all these changes, the same, essentially the same substitution-principle had been at work, and still is working today underneath Japan's global transformation.

56. H. Jeffrey, "Theory of Probability," (1939) quoted in William S. Beck, *Modern Science and the Nature of Life* (New York, 1957), p. 170.

57. W. S. Beck, *op. cit.,* p. 155.

58. The famous *Kabuki,* but especially *jōruri* or puppet-drama playwright (ca. 1653-1724), considered the "Shakespeare of the Japanese stage," the greatest Japanese dramatist.

59. Quoted in *Kabuki,* by Yomazo Hamamura, Takashi Sugawara, Junji Kinoshita, Hiroshi Minami, tr. by Fumi Takano (Tokyo, 1956), p. 68.

60. *See* Variation II, pp. 55, 56.

61. Fenollosa and Pound, *op. cit., p.* 108.

Indeed, no matter how different chronologically may have been the origin and evolvement as well as the social and religious-philosophical, primarily Buddhist, content and conditions of each of the three main forms of Japanese theater, the solemn Noh drama (the Sarugaku-no Noh, commonly known as Nōgaku or Nō, glory of the Zen—aristocratic Ashikaga period), with all its classically ordered six-modal complexity of subject matter[a]

[a] Fenellosa-Pound, *op. cit.,* pp. 14-15.

and the two much younger—Tokugawa, *par excellence*—Kabuki and Bunraku (puppet)—shows, they all originally and ultimately owe their existence to the dance. "Né de la danse, le *nô* ne pouvait pas ne pas donner une importance particulière à la mimique, *mono-mane* . . . . 'imitation des choses' . . . . 'C'est à la sculpture et à la peinture qu'empruntent le plus volontiers leurs comparaisons ceux qui ont traité de cette 'beauté de la forme'."[b]

Much has been written about the history of Japan's theater, of the Noh form particularly, and much remains still very vague and confused: "The early stage of development of both the *Noh* dance and the *Noh Kyôgen* [a realistic short comedy played without music, a necessary interlude between the Noh performances]," says Shigetoshi Kawatake, "is by no means clear, but there is one distinct source which is traceable to *Gigaku*. This *Gigaku* was introduced by Koreans in the early part of the 7th century, but it is considered to be typical of a mask dance which originated in Central Asia and prevailed in India and China.

"The traditional way of performing this *Gigaku* was later combined with *Sangaku* (sometimes called *Sarugaku*) also imported from China, and later, in the days of the Kamakura period (13th century), after a dormant interval of several centuries, a new art, the *Noh*, was evolved from *Ennen-no-mai*, a kind of variety dance performed in temples. In those days the *Noh* attempted to express a story through the medium of dance and music. This *Noh* dance of *Ennen* was taken into *Dengaku*, which had been developed from a folk-dance, and later came to be known as *Dengaku Noh*. The *Sangaku* players who adhered to this tradition have also contributed to the further development of the dance, but it was not until the end of the 14th century, when the third Ashikaga Shôgun, Yoshimitsu, had especially encouraged its practice, that it reached its present stage of perfection.

"A father and son, Kannami and Seami, have contributed. . . .

"In its early days, the *Noh* dance was regarded socially as of low grade, but once it had been taken to the Court of the Shôgun as a ritual dance, it soon developed into a classic form of art. . . . .

"As it has been mentioned already, the *Noh* dance and the *Noh Kyôgen* contributed much to the development of *Kabuki*, but it must be remembered also that they influenced the puppet plays as well. . . .

"The *Noh* play is a sort of ballet performed by masked players, and we must trace it back to the period of *Bugaku* [Quite confusing, the sudden introduction of this new form!] . . . .

"Even at present, *Bugaku* is preserved as Court music (music for Court rituals). When first introduced at the end of the 7th century from China, India, Pohai and Korea, it was a grand mask dance, but early in the 9th century, the crude music and dances imported hitherto being in a disorderly state, were set in order and properly Japanized by the great musicians and dancers of the Heian period.

"*Bugaku* is performed on a stage especially erected for the purpose, with the accompaniment of an orchestra. . . .

" . . . *Bugaku* is a composition of music and dance brought to its perfection about 1,000 years ago, and may safely be claimed as the source of all forms of music and dance in Japan."[c]

62. *Op. cit.*, p. 63.

63. *Ibid*, p. 193.

64. " . . . . *mie* . . . singularly typifies the art of the Kabuki actor [as well as Noh's] . . . . It has been immortalized in the prints and drawings of the artist Sharaku, that strange genius. Time and time again, his prints depict the moment when the actor has reached the climax in his acting and poses rigidly for a moment to impress his emotion and fiery ardour on the audience. . . .

"There are different kinds of *mie*, but they all have a common aim, the actor must impose himself upon the audience . . . . what is called *nirami*, literally glare . . . . The actor draws himself up into a pose and gestures, often with the palms outwards and fingers outstretched, at the same time he performs what is called *senkai*. In this he moves his head several times with a circular motion, the body and shoulders remaining rigid, and finally ceases the action either full face or full profile to the audience. By this time his eyes are dilated as though about to leap from their sockets and the pupils slowly turn inwards. This is *nirami*. . . . .

"The *mie* has a motionless quality about it; it is the climax to all preceding movement. . . . . " A. C. Scott, *The Kabuki Theatre of Japan* (London, 1955) p. 105, 106.

And in *Kabuki* one reads the following description of the climatic moment in the famous play *Ichinotani Futaba Gunki*—the battle scene between the rude Kumagai and the youth Atsumori: "You see now in the middle of the stage Kumagai and Atsumori rising slowly from beneath by means of a special elevator. The two warriors do not move at all. They are frozen in their position with the former holding the latter to the ground. This kind of appearance is technically called *seridashi* (push-up). The actors are raised from the cellar below in certain fixed poses. This, of course, is done by the elevator which exposes first the face, then the body, and finally the legs. The actors, in a fixed pose, make their appearance without batting an eyelash, like a group of dolls, accompanied by music coming from the window in the left corner of the stage. Here Kumagai and Atsumori appear from below frozen at the climax of their mortal fight. It is all far beyond logic or reality. . . . .

[b] Noel Peri, *Le Nô* (Tokyo, 1944), p. 51.

[c] *Development of the Japanese Theatric Art* (Tokyo, 1935), pp. 12-14.

"It is here that the essential impact of the puppet theater of Japan, both as stage technique and philosophy of the theater is manifested most convincingly."[a]

Albert Maybon has emphasized this aspect very eloquently (if sometimes erroneously. But who, not even, say, a Peri, could be "accurate" to the end when speaking of these matters?): "Ce théâtre [Kabuki] porte si bien la marque de celui des marionnettes que, en dépit des quelques réformes scéniques de ces dernières années, inspirées par un souci de vraisemblance, on a laissé dans le sillage de l'interprète un assistant qui a quelque chose des animateurs de fantoches. Comme eux il est vêtu et voilé de noir, comme eux, collé, non pas toujours, mais dans maints épisodes, au *corps* du personnage qu'il sert; il l'aide au cours de la représentation à changer de costume, à revêtir des armures, à prendre une attitude, il lui met en main un objet, lui glisse un siège, lui ouvre un chemin . . . L'acteur . . . est . . . comme un être artificiel dont il faut qu'on s'occupe. L'aide est donc toujours présent et attentif. On lui donne le nom . . . d' 'ombre'."[b] [Italics mine.]

And this revealing, although indirect, example of Japanese transfer of the puppet-mind's attitude toward art (Chikamatsu's "Art is the layer that lies between the skins of truth and falsity") into Kabuki's daring realism: "Dans *Koïtsukami* il [the *hanamichi,* the famous "flower path" or actor's passage—that came to Kabuki directly from the Noh stage—"projecting at right angles from the left hand side of the stage and running clear through the pit" and connected with a small green-room partitioned from the audience by a curtain. The old Kabuki used to have "a second *hanamichi* which was about half the width of the other"[c]] est transformé en ruisseau qui se déverse dans un étang, sur le plateau circulaire: ce n'est pas une simple figuration liquide, c'est bien de l'eau dans laquelle plonge et nage un acteur représentant une carpe; et afin de ne pas être incommodés par les éclaboussures, les spectateurs des premiers rangs endossent un vêtement caoutchouté."[d]

65. Quoted in Donald Keene, *The Battles of Coxinga* (London, 1955), pp. 93-95.

66. Peri, *op. cit.,* p. 26.

67. *Ibid.*

68. *Ibid.* pp. 27-28.

69. *Kabuki, op. cit.,* p. 93.

70. *Ibid.*

71. "Quand, en xii[e] siècle, la Chine enseigna au Japon la cabale, mimes et danseurs devinrent des sortes de magiciens. C'est alors que l'on vit les premières marionnettes aux mains des bateleurs. En des temps plus anciens, des figurines, à peu près semblables, avaient été offertes aux dieux les jours de sacrifices, et le peuple s'était accoutumé à leur prêter une âme. Il les considéra, à plus forte raison, comme des êtres doués de vie quand elles s'animèrent à leurs yeux; il regarda aussi comme d'extraordinaires enchanteurs ceux qui les faisaient mouvoir, leur donnant un nom qui signifiait 'apte à changer l'esprit de l'arbre,' ou 'apte à donner la vie au bois.'

"Les bords de la rivière Yodo, qui coule entre Kyôto et Osaka, étaient le lieu favori des montreurs de marionnettes. Attirés par le succès de ces représentations, tous les histrions aimés du peuple, les bouffons, les jongleurs et ces comédiennes qui faisaient rire avec leur face poudrée et cramoisie se donnaient rendezvous sur les tréteaux de Yodo." Maybon, *op. cit.,* p. 30.

72. One of the three surviving scrolls of the original, now preserved by the National Museum, Tokyo.

[a] *Op. cit.,* p. 13.

[b] *Le Théâtre Japonais* (1925), p. 86.

[c] *Kabuki, op. cit.,* pp. 1, 55.

[d] Maybon, *op cit.,* p. 83.

VARIATION III

1. "It was in the city of Aomori, on the northern tip of Japan's main island of Honshu, that Munakata received his limited formal education. He was born there in 1903, the third son of a blacksmith, an old-fashioned man who sired an old-fashioned brood, six boys and six girls.

"The family belonged to the Zen sect of Buddhism, but it was dominated by the spirit of Shinto. The elder Munakata was a craftsman in the old tradition, and he kindled his forge with a sense of ancient ritual. [In 1928 Shiko Munakata began the career of a woodcut artist; he has worked intensely in this medium as well as in oil painting. A strongly religious element which has never left him manifested itself in his work with the publication of his *Kegon-fu* in 1937. A special prize at the Imperial Academy's Art Exhibition was awarded in 1938 to his *Utō Hanga Saku* series of 31 prints, based on the Noh play *Utō* (*Birds of Sorrow,* translated into English in 1947). His works were first exhibited in the West in Locarno (1951), in Sao Paulo (1952), in New York at the Willard Gallery (1952).] 'I want to strip my work of "effects",' said Munakata. 'It must flow naturally from my materials, from the way of the chisel and the way of the block.' . . . To the title of each of his series Munakata adds the words *hanga saku.* 'In common usage *saku* means a picket fence,' he says, 'but it also connotes a custom practiced in the pilgrimages made around the island of Shikoku. At each station, after praying at the temple, the pilgrim pounds a stake in the ground. It is an act which signifies a continuing effort.

" 'I have the same feeling about my prints. No print is complete in itself. It is one more stake in the ground. It is one more step toward the goal of a lifetime. . . . ' " Quotes from *Shiko Munakata (1903—),* ed. by Yojuro Yasuda, tr. by Oliver Statler (Kadansha Library of Japanese Art No. 12 [Rutland, Vt.—Tokyo, 1958]) pp. 7-8, 82.

2. Masaoka: born 1866 (two years before the

Meiji Restoration), son of a samurai. Died in 1902, of tuberculosis. He took the name of Shiki, which means the cuckoo, on the first day he spit blood. A legend has it that the cuckoo is so careful about the way he practises singing that he spits blood.

3. *Haiku:* a three-line, seventeen-syllable poem, uniquely Japanese. Each *haiku* is an entire Buddhist universe in a single seasonal subject.

4. For instance, F. S. C. Northrop, *op. cit.*

5. The bloodiest and initial stage of the civil wars that devastated Japan during the later part of the 15th century and throughout the 16th.

6. Oda Nobunaga (1534-1582); Toyotomi Hideyoshi (1537-1598); Tokugawa Iyeyasu (1542-1616).

7. Like his celebrated Kitano Tea Party: "In October, 1587, he announced publicly in Kyōto, Ōsaka and other cities that he would hold a great tea ceremony in the next month. Everybody was invited to attend, from his richest vassals down to the humblest peasants, who were told that they need bring only a kettle and a cup and a mat to sit upon. The fête lasted ten days, there were plays and music and dancing. Hideyoshi exhibited his art treasures, as did other great collectors of the day." Sansom, *Japan, A Short Cultural History* (revised ed.; New York, 1943), p. 438.

8. The "Nightless City" on the outskirts of Edo, with its 2,000 courtesans—they say—its famous actors, theatres, and places of entertainment.

9. Ernest F. Fenollosa, *Epochs of Chinese and Japanese Art, op. cit.* (revised ed.), with note by Professor Petrucci, who proves the factual inadmissibility of Fenollosa's Pacific-Americas-Japanese thesis.

10. "The present print [representing two actors, Ichikawa Komazo as Chubei and Nakayama Tomisaburo as Umegawa] shows all the beauty that Kabuki has: its colours, types, music, and all the accomplishments necessary in the production of these Kabuki plays. The black of the background shows an effect similar to that of the black which may be said to constitute the colour and tone of the whole of Kabuki." Teruji Yoshida, *Sharaku. A Complete Collection* (Tokyo, 1952), I, 64. "Notes on Print 34."

11. A courtesan of high status.

12. Ink and water painting.

13. Sansom, *Japan . . . , op. cit.*, p. 507.

14. The synthesis toward the end of the 15th century of the Ashikaga "Kanga" or Chinese style and the Yamato-e or "Tosa" style.

15. A crest, family insignia.

16. Yuzuru Okada, *Japanese Family Crests* (Japan, 1941). Tourist Library #37.

17. Anne Marie Louise d'Orléans, Duchesse de Montpensier (1627-93), granddaughter of Henri IV, and first cousin of Louis XIV.

18. It is revealing to study here how all the varieties of collective expressions correspond to the variety of shades in the character of such splits as have taken place in the "barbarism" of, say, Oceania, or Black Africa, more persistently and expressively.

19. Gordon Childe, *op. cit.*, pp. 69-70, 78, 79, *et passim.*

20. Rhys Davids, *op. cit.*, p. 110 *et passim.*

21. Techne: See Horace M. Kallen, *Art and Freedom* (New York, 1942), p. 49.

22. Benjamin Farrington, *Science and Politics in the Ancient World* (London, 1939), pp. 21, 60, 129.

23. "The key lay in the Keplerian processes, in which Desargues [the great promoter of the projective idea in geometry (1639)] indulged very freely, of regarding opposite ends of a straight line as coincident, and straight lines as circles with centres at infinity," H. T. Pledge, *Science Since 1500* (London, 1939), p. 75.

24. "Escapement. — In watch and clock making, the mechanism which intervenes between the motive power and the regulator; causing an intermittent impulse to be given to the latter." Hawkins' *Mechanical Dictionary*, p. 218.

25. Charles Picard, *Les Origines du Polythéisme Hellénique. L'art Créto-Mycénien* (Paris, 1930), pp. 58, 59, 91.

26. Louis Massignon, *Salmān Pāk et les Prémices Spirituelles de L'Islam Iranien* (Publications de la Societé des Études Iraniennes et de l'Art Persan, No. 7 [Tours, France, 1934]), pp. 28-29.

27. See Kallen, *op. cit.*, pp. 94-96: on *collegia* and the repercussion of their influence upon guilds.

28. George Sarton, *Introduction to the History of Science* (Baltimore, 1931) II, Part I, pp. 154, 156.

29. "Not all the craftsmen seeking safety and freedom [during the early medieval period] sought them *via* the churchly vocation. Not only had many taken sides with the barbarian invaders when the latter broke the Empire; many others had fled to their protection. There is the tale of a company of such, master-craftsmen, who had found their way to Comacina, a little island on Lake Como, and there maintained a collegium under the protection of the Lombard chieftains. Sometimes known as Casari or Casarii, the record refers to them as constituting, toward the end of the sixth century, a 'University of Free Masons.' But they were not masons and carpenters merely; they counted also as architects, painters, statuaries. They practiced modifications of the ancient form of fellowship—of its membership fee, its common meals, its initiations and other rites and ceremonies, and of its co-operative business enterprise. They took contracts for building and all arts connected with building. They sent companies of craftsmen of every required sort to any place to do the work. These, while on the job, lived together in *Lodges,* or *Temples,* or *Bauhaüser*. . . . . Charlemagne is said to have considered such [their occupations] as 'conspirations dangerous to the state.'" Kallen, *op. cit.*, pp. 95-96.

30. The *shite* is the doer, the main actor; the *waki* ("side") is the supporting actor. The *tsure* is the "companion," hence *shite-zure* and *waki-zure*, or *tsure-waki*. See Peri, *op. cit.*, pp. 26-31.

31. "The basic cycle of Hindu cosmology, *Kalpa*, a 'day of Brahmā,' or 4,320 million earthly years. . . . The longest cycle . . . . after which the whole universe returns to the ineffable world-spirit, until another creator god is evolved." A. L. Basham, *The Wonder That Was India* (New York, 1959), p. 320.

32. Found close to the dead boy's armour. Peri, *op. cit.*, p. 156.

33. Ichi-no-tani, Ni-no-tani, San-no-tani, among which part of the Taira army was massed. See Peri, *op. cit.*, pp. 117-18, for the detailed topography of the famous battle.

34. The fearful and despotic Taira chief who died in 1181.

35. The battle was fought at the beginning of the year 1184.

36. This expression usually refers to young girls of the nobility, however, the *Gempei seisui ki* also uses it for young men. Peri, *op. cit.*, p. 121.

37. From Shunkai Nō (Monumenta Nippónica IV, No. 1, January 1941), p. 247.

38. The title of Tomomori, the commander of the Ikuta front. Peri, *op. cit.*, p. 120.

39. A title given to young men of great families. *Ibid.*

40. *Ibid.*, p. 123.

41. See Arthur Waley's translation of Seami's "Atsumori" in *The Nō Plays of Japan* (New York, 1922), p. 44.

42. Verse quoted from the *Ise monogatari* by Peri (*op. cit.*, p. 273, footnote 2), who explains that *davallies* are the *shinobu*, a fern signifying "to remember and to love."

43. Peri, *op. cit.*, p. 119.

44. Strips or bits of gold leaf often used for ornamental patterns in clothing, painting, etc. A technique particularly favored during the Fujiwara period.

45. For the most daring socio-political issues involved in present-day China's opening wide and wild to its "total" change had several times in China's Great Past already been subjected to political scrutiny and experiment.

46. The Kusha School (Realism: *Ens* School); The Jōjitsu School (Nihilism: Non-*ens* School); The Hossō School (Idealism: Both *Ens* and Non-*ens* School); The Sanron School (Negativism: *Neither* Ens *nor* *Non*-ens *School*); the Kegon School (Totalism). Takakusu, *op. cit.*, pp. 57-126.

47. See Footnote 9, Variation III.

48. Variation I, 26ff.

49. See Reischauer, *op. cit.*, pp. 158-68; and Zimmer, *Philosophies of India, op. cit.*, p. 530, footnote 80, by the editor.

50. Variation I, 30, *et seq.*

51. *"Impression fausse,"* Paul Verlaine, *Choix de Poésies* (Paris, 1900), p. 319.

52. Léo Bronstein, *Fragments of Life, Metaphysics and Art* (New York, 1952), *passim.*

53. Ananda K. Coomaraswamy, *Yaksas.* Parts I, II (Washington, D. C., 1928-31), II, 20, *et passim.*

54. See Footnote 41, Variation II.

55. J. Huizinga, *The Waning of the Middle Ages* (London, 1927), pp. 211-12.

56. Fox-Davies leading the phalanx with his classical *Complete Guide to Heraldry.*

57. "Taking as our starting-point the definition of a blazon considered by Fox-Davies to be one of the best, namely that a coat of arms 'requires the twofold qualification that the design must be hereditary and must be connected with armour,' Saracenic blazons are blazons in the full sense of the word." L. A. Mayer, *Saracenic Heraldry* (New York, 1933). Introduction.

Whereas in Japan the "use of family crests for decorative purposes certainly forms a singular characteristic of Japanese Heraldry as against the armorial bearings in the West. But this is by no means strange when it is remembered that the historical fact is that many Japanese crests take their origin from decorative patterns." Okada, *op. cit.*, p. 89.

58. *Japanese Family Crests, op. cit.*

59. And more about Japan's heraldry: "Bien que l'on ne connaisse pas la date exacte de l'invention des armoiries au Japon, leur usage remonte à une époque très reculée, sans doute contemporaine, . . . de l'apparition du blason en Europe. Déjà . . . . aux Xe et XIe siècles . . . . des guerriers en renom avaient adopté des couleurs et des emblèmes distinctifs qui les faisaient *reconnaître de loin* [italics mine] sur les champs de bataille; l'épopée héroïque . . . (XIIe siècle) à rendu . . . célèbres les *feulles de bambou* et l'étendard blanc des Minamoto, le *papillon* et la bannière rouge des Taira . . . . La fleur de *kiri* du blason impérial, ou *kiri-mon*, . . . son origine se perd dans la nuit des temps. Quant au *chrysanthème*, qui l'accompagne aujourd'hui, son adoption est attribuée à l'empereur Go-toba-ténnô (1184-1198) qui eut, dit-on, *la fantaisie* [italics mine] de graver sa fleur de prédilection sur la soie d'un sabre qu'il venait de forger de ses propres mains.

"Le blason japonais ne paraît pas avoir jamais été symbolique comme celui de la chevalerie européenne. Le goût, la fantaisie du fondateur de *chaque* famille, ou peut-être quelque *circonstance fortuite,* [italics mine] semblent avoir seuls présidé au choix de son emblème distinctif, autant du moins que nous pouvons en juger par ce que l'histoire rapporte de l'origine des *trois feuilles de mauve appointées* de l'illustre maison de Tokougawa. Après une grande victoire, . . . Il y eut cependant, à une époque tardive, des lois réglementant l'usage des armoiries, mais dans la noblesse militaire seulement. En 1642, le Shô-goun Iyé-mitsou décrète que tous les Daimïos, Hatamotos et Samouraïs devront avoir deux mons:

. . . . *Djô-mon*, 'armes réglementaires' qui est le blason originel de la famille, l'autre *Kahé-mon*, 'armes exceptionelles,' destiné à distinguer les diverses branches d'une même maison, ou les familles différentes possédant les mêmes armoiries." L. de Milloué et S. Kawamoura, *Coffre à trésor, Étude Héraldique* (Paris, 1896), p. viii-xi.

And how Western this sounds: " . . . les règlements très sévéres, auxquels était naguère encore asujettie la noblesse japonaise, imposent aux Daïmiôs, Hatamotos et Samouraïs de ne se servir que *d'objets, armes ou autres*, marqués exclusivement de leurs armoiries familiales, *sans tolérer la moindre fantaisie*." [Italics mine.] *Ibid.*, p. vi.

And how applicable, on the other hand, to Japan would be the following statement about the initial role of badges in Western heraldry! "Badges . . . . accidental bearings which do not affect the original arms . . . . whilst they may have been granted by the Sovereign, they were mostly assumptions and often *allusive to* some *particular circumstance* or event connected with the family or individual possessing them. . . . Badges were figures assumed as the *distinctive mark* of an individual or clan for display on standards, liveries, buttons and so forth. They were *often charges* taken from the *arms* and have sometimes been of the same device as the crest. But they all differ from the crest in that they have no connection whatever with the helmet . . . ; they were for the use of servants, dependants, retainers and partisans [Red, White Rose!] as well as for the *individual or family* of which they were the emblem; they were worn by women and there were often more than one.

" . . . Badges were an important part of early heraldry and, indeed, of the *lives* of the English people in those times therefore. . . . " [Italics mine.] Sir Christopher Lynch-Robinson, *Intelligible Heraldry* (London, 1949), p. 99.

And more: "We may regard the latter half of the twelfth century as the earliest period to which we can trace the use of arms in the proper sense.

"Early in the thirteenth century the practice began of embroidering the family ensigns on the surcoat worn over the hauberk or coat of mail, whence originated the expression 'coat of arms.' Arms were similarly embroidered on the jupon, cyclas, and tabard, which succeeded the surcoat; and displayed on the banners and pennons of knights, or floating from the shafts of their lances; they were also enamelled or otherwise represented on furniture, personal ornaments, and weapons.

"In the infancy of arms great latitude was allowed in representing the *charge* [italics mine] fixed on or inherited. It was used singly, or repeated, or in any attitude which the bearer chose, or which the form of his shield suggested. But as coats of arms multiplied, confusion could only be obviated by restraining the bearers' fancy, and regulating the number, position, and colour of the charges, and the attitudes of such animals as were represented on the shields; and in the course of time Sovereigns found it necessary to interfere with the unrestricted assumption of arms within their respective realms, and to regulate the bearing of them. . . .

" . . . . Even in the beginning of the fifteenth century there was probably a good deal of assumption of arms *proprio motu*, and the *Boke of St. Alban's* contains the rather startling dictum that any one might assume arms *at his own hand*, provided they *had been borne by no one else*." [Italics mine.] George Burnett, in John Woodward and George Burnett, *A Treatise on Heraldry, British and Foreign* (Edinburgh-London, 1892), pp. 32-33, 35.

60. J. H. Probst-Biraben and A. Maitrot de la Motte-Capron, "*Dc l'Influence Mediterranéene sur les Signes Lapidaires en Europe Centrale,* and *La Croix Gammée Mediterranéene*," in *Bulletin de la Société de Géographie d'Alger et de l'Afrique du Nord* (Année 44), 1939.

61. See Footnote 10, Variation III.

62. [Attributed to] Dame Juliana Berners, *The Boke of Saint Albans containing treatises on Hawking, Hunting and Cote Armour. Printed at Saint Albans by the school master-Printer in 1486.* Reproduced in Facsimile with Introduction by William Blades (London, 1881).

63. Variation II, 41-42, 85.

64. Form or schema, similar to Gestalt, or Configuration, psychology's basal "field"-structural position, according to which our "neutral functions and processes with which the perceptual facts are associated in each case are located in a continuous medium; and . . . . the events in one part of this medium influence the events in other regions in a way that depends directly on the properties of both in their relation to each other. . . . " Wolfgang Köhler, *Dynamics of Psychology* (New York, 1940), p. 55.

So that we do not first perceive all the separate elements of an experience, and then, subsequently, combine them into an organized group. The whole mass of data is experienced as a unit, more or less satisfactory and complete.

65. See Footnote 55, Variation II.

66. "*Sophrosyne:* the ideal of self-restraint, discipline and moderation . . . . *kalokagathia,* the ideal of a right balance between bodily and spiritual, physical and moral qualities. . . . " Hauser, *op. cit.*, I, 84.

67. *Ibid.*, I, 81-83.

68. Variation I, 17.

69. The Sassanian era, c. 225 A.D. c. 650 A.D.

70. Ruben Dario on New York.

71. Bronstein, *op. cit.*, pp. 35-37.

72. Variation I, 24.

73. Lynn White, Jr., in *Speculum, A Journal of Medieval Studies,* XV, No. 2 (Cambridge, Mass., April, 1940), p. 153.

74. H. F. Hallett, *Aeternitas, A Spinozistic Study* (Oxford, England, 1930), p. 158. "Ab-

stract extension is merely the place of instantaneous *puncta*. . . . "

75. Variation I, 24-25.

76. *Ibid.*, 7-8.

77. Ludwig Bachhofer, *A Short History of Chinese Art* (New York, 1946), p. 105. *See also*, pp. 94-97, 107.

78. Yùan: c. 1279-1368; Ming: c. 1368-1644; Ch'ing: c. 1644-1912.

VARIATION IV

1. C. T. Ramuz — I. Stravinsky, *Story of the Soldier*.

2. Meisetsu (2nd half 19th century), Harold J. Isaacson, tr.

3. Giordano Bruno, *Eroici Furori*.

4. *The World of Sholem Aleichem*, drawings by Ben Shahn. A brochure (1953) for the production of the play of that title given at the Barbizon Plaza in New York City.

5. S. Giedion, *op. cit.*, pp. 29, 111.

6. Paul Valery, *L'Idée Fixe*.

7. From "Death of Lugail and Derbforgaill" an old Celtic Irish tale, quoted in *Speculum* (January, 1959), p. 48. (The Ms. H. Trinity Coll. 318, fo. 728 reads: "Between her two wings," instead of "between her ribs." Note 28.)

8. Mazdakite: a pre-Islamic (6th century) socio-religious movement, "communistic," whose influence on Islamic culture was immense.

9. "In the broader sense, the name Ḳarmaṭian means the great movement for social reform and justice based on equality, which swept through the Muslim world from the ninth to the twelfth centuries. . . .

" . . . The movement was based on reason, tolerance and equality, with a system of graduated initiation and the ritual of a gild, which—encouraging the rise of the trade gild movement and universities—seems to have reached the West and to have influenced the formation of European gilds and freemasonry." Louis Massignon, "Karmatians," in *Encyclopedia of Islam*, No. 29 (London, 1923), p. 767.

10. Oskar Hagen, *The Birth of the American Tradition in Art* (New York, London, 1940) p. 2.

11. " . . . *scientia signata*, the doctrine [known and much meditated upon by Renaissance as well as late Mediaeval 'artisan'-philosophers and 'artisan'-scientists] of signatures, which was held to contain a key to the occult power of all natural substances and spiritual essences. In order to achieve, in accordance with this doctrine, the desired effect of the radiation of energy from all the minerals, plants, animals and other forms of life in the picture, it was necessary that their 'signatures,' i.e. their form-creating essential forces [the so-called *vis vitalis or* 'organic functional force of life'], should be profoundly understood and given permanent form [a bird had to be recognized as that bird's essence]." Wilhelm Fränger *The Millenium of Hieronymus Bosch*, tr. by Eithne Wilkins and Ernst Kaiser (Chicago, 1951), page 151.

12. "Drapery painting had, unfortunately, always meant as much to him [Copley] as face-painting and now [after 1774, when he left America and went to England, never to return] it began to mean everything." Gordon Washburn, Rhode Island School of Design Museum *Bulletin* (1945), p. 51.

13. "He [Copley] matched always the colors on his palette with the tints of each sitter's face, before starting work on the canvas." Virgil Barker, *Ibid.*, p. 139.

14. Describing so eloquently the funerals in old New England, James Thomas Flexner writes: "Only in imagination can we return to these unpaved streets, mingle under jutting second stories with the awestruck Puritans who, so Judge Sewall tells us, not only leaned out of every window but perched 'on fences and trees like pigeons.' The procession comes at a death's pace, slow, so slow. The horses have become creatures from a fabulous world: their hooves are muffled, they wear long black stockings, each equine face . . . transmuted by a picture on its forehead into a skull. Hangings thrown over the horses' flanks, placards in the mourners' hands, speak both of vanity and its defeat. The deceased, now locked in that coffin, and perhaps depicted as he looked in the first still moments of death; hour-glasses and other symbols of passing time are rendered in somber colors. In imagination standing beside our ancestors, we marvel at the majesty of an early American art *dedicated to death and resurrection.*" [Italics mine.] *Flowers of Our Wilderness* (Boston, 1947), p. 29.

15. The massacres during the Cossacks' uprising under Chmielnicki and the turbulent times in Poland and the Ukraine (c. 1648-1660); the subsequent emergence of Hasidism, founded by Baal-Shem Tov (1700-1760), the *Possessor of the Good Name*, a term signifying "a man who lives with and for his fellow-men on the foundation of his relation to the Divine." Martin Buber's Introduction to the *Tales of the Chasidim. The Early Masters* (New York, 1947), p. 13.

16. *Saint Catherine of Siena. As Seen in Her Letters*, tr. & ed. with an Introduction by Vida D. Scudder (London; New York, 1905), pp. 113-14.

17. Leonardo da Vinci.

18. Pope, *Essay on Criticism*.

19. In the Preface to his "Hundred Views of Fuji." Quoted by Stewart Dick, *Arts and Crafts of Old Japan* (Chicago, 1905), p. 57.

20. Martin Buber, *op. cit.*, p. 121.

21. For the explanation and resolution of the apparent contradiction between the ultimate views on the doctrine of the genesis of motion offered by Aristotle in his *Physics* and those given by him in his *Metaphysics*, see the excellent study by Jean Paulus: *"La théorie du Premier Moteur chez Aristotle," Revue de Philosophie. Nouvelle Serie*, (1933), pp. 259-94, 394-425.

22. Yehuda Halevi (c. 1085-c. 1140).

23. E. H. Gombrich, *Art and Illusion,* Bollingen Series XXXV (New York, 1960) p. 298.

24. The Gestalt theory would locate this inner and elemental geometry at the moment-synthesis and not, as here, at the moment-analysis.

25. Léo Bronstein, *Altichiero. L'artiste et son oeuvre* (Paris, 1932), pp. 74-75.

26. Variation 1, 24.

27. All these and other combined vital motivations contradict flatly the racist-northern "scythian" thesis of Strzygowski, who has also, of course, noticed what we call the "mobile" character of this art. Moreover, the Celtic-Scandinavian art—"northern" also!—often appears rather "stable" than "mobile." The seriated, although rhythmically interconnected images—strange objects and strange beings seen in "diving" perspective—on the Gunderstup golden vase (4th century B.C.) offer the best proof of this.

28. What more revealing and convincing than the "stylistic" identity of interests which led medieval architects, both western and eastern, to adopt (if not to create) as their most genuine necessity and expression the "mobile" structural formula: the squinch in Iran, a vertical "mobile" device for the passage of a square (groundplan) into a circle (the dome): and the "gothic" rib in France, a horizontal-"mobile" device for the vault's *elastic solidity.*

29. An extensive mountain region which separates Mesopotamia from the Iranian Plateau. Luristân, which belongs to this region, is situated near the West-Persian border. An extraordinary artistic culture (the famous Luristân bronzes) flourished there II-I Mill. B.C.

30. J. Orbelli and C. Trever *Sassanian Silver and Gold Objects* ([in Russian], Moscow-Leningrad: 1935, pp. xxiii-xxiv), have suggested that at least some of the plates showing the interlaced style have been influenced by the techniques of other crafts—textiles, wood carvings, etc. But textile designs influenced craftsmen in other media, in Coptic Egypt, for instance, yet there is no trace of the "monsters" typical of this style.

31. On the Sassanian decadence and on its causes generally, see: Christensen, *L'Iran sous les Sassanides* (Paris, 1936), pp. 93-95; on aspects of social protest, as, for instance, the movement for the emancipation of women: *ibid.,* p. 325; on the great revolutionary religious-communistic movement of Mazdak (6th century), and above all, the traditional Iranian elements in his innovations: *ibid.,* pp. 339-40.

32. A parallel phenomenon of deep folk-cultural revival (sometimes reaching the Neolithic cultural level) provoked by an analogous social-historical cause—the introduction of Christianity—is offered by the "Coptic" culture of Egypt. Since the 3rd century the indigenous Christian "art of the people" became there the expression of a revolutionary-traditional religious movement (Monophysitism) as opposed to the feudal aristocratic (the Imperial Byzantine church) camouflage of apostolic democratism.

33. See V. Minorsky, *La domination des Dailamites* (*Publication de la société des Études Iraniennes,* No. 3., Paris, 1932), p. 2.

34. The lower agricultural classes, reduced economically to a state of slavery by the class of *dihkans* or smaller Sassanian landowners and oppressive tax collectors. See Christensen, *op. cit.,* pp. 107, 135, 139, 254, 316, 352, 508; and W. Bartold (in Russian), *The Place of the Caspian Region in the History of the Muslim World* (Baku, 1925), pp. 20-21.

35. On the history and causes of these violent movements, *provoked also by the disillusionment of the Islamized masses, when official Islam in its turn became oppressive,* see Bartold, *ibid.,* pp. 20, 21, 32, 35; *Turkestan,* E. J. W. Gibb Memorial Series V (London, 1928), pp. 183, 190; T. H. Kramer, "Persia. Historical and Ethnologic Survey," *The Encyclopedia of Islam,* III, 1042. See also Footnote 9, IV, on the great Karmatian movement.

36. The Alids—also refugees—by their popularity among the Caspian masses, and by their influence as powerful "democratic" Imams, prepared the way for the great Dailamite Iranian dynasty, the Buyids (Minorsky, *op. cit.,* pp. 5-9). The Shi'ite dynasties, the Ziyarids, the Buyids, represented a synthesis of the popular Iranian and imperialistic Sassanian aspirations (Bartold, *op. cit.,* p. 32). The double character of Shi'ism, the revolutionary-aristocratic and the revolutionary-popular, is a known fact: for instance, the role of opposition played by the Iranian aristocratic Shi'ite Imamite party in the Abbasid State, at the 10th-century Caliphal court in Bagdad (Massignon, *La Passion d'al-Husayn ibn Mansour al-Hallaj, martyr mystique de l'Islam* [Paris, 1922], I, 11, 142, 143). For the revolutionary-popular aspect of Shi'ism, considered as such by the orthodox or Sunnite dynasts, Samanids, Seljuqs, etc., *see* Bartold, *Musulman Culture,* tr. by Shahid Suhrawardy (Calcutta, 1934), pp. 73-78, 80-81.

37. On Kūfa of the first century of the Hijra—the capital of the Shi'as—and its Iranism, *see* Massignon, *Salman Pak . . . . , op. cit.,* pp. 11-12. On the connection between Shi'a and the working classes: *ibid.,* p. 29.

38. This systematic deformation—could it not be simply the result of a well-known Islamic theological restriction in the representation—sinful repetition of Allah's most creative act—of living beings, especially human beings? But we know that the restriction was a recommended one; it was not a total or absolute prohibition. See Massignon, "*Les Méthodes de réalisation artistique des peuples de l'Islam,*" *Syria* II (1921), pp. 47-49. Massignon quotes also an old *hadîth* [p. 52], in which Ibn 'Abbâs recommends to a Persian artist that he obviate his orthodox scruples by cutting off the heads of the animals, and by

endeavoring to make them resemble flowers. But the value of that testimony is weakened by the fact that the advice is directed to a *Persian* artist, and the expedient might simply have been a utilization of a possibly existing Persian artistic practice. Moreover, the character of fusion or interlacing-deforming is not at all an Islamic invention—to cite, at random, the ornament of the Irish-Northumbrian illuminated Gospels.

39. Illuminated at Bagdad, according to some in the first half, according to others in the second half, of the 14th century.

40. Bāyazīd of Bistam (in northern Persia), a famous Sufi, who died in 261 (875) or 264 (877-78). According to the *Encylclopedia of Islam,* his doctrine is known to us only from occasional utterances handed down by Attar amongst others. From these it is clear that he was a convinced pantheist and very probably the first to introduce the doctrine of Fanā (Nirvana).

41. Browne. See footnote 14, Variation II.

42. René Descartes, *The Meditations and Selections from the Principles,* tr. by John Veitch (Chicago, 1908): Meditation III, "Of God: that he exists," pp. 45-46.

43. *See* Frantz Brentano's commentary on Descartes' Meditation III: *Vom Ursprung Sittlicher Erkenntnis* (Leipzig, 1921), pp. 15-17.

44. E. Bertrand, *Etudes sur la peinture et la critique d'art dans l'antiquité* (Paris, 1893), pp. 171, 207.

45. For not all Iranian miniatures—far from it! —have achieved or intended this tense Iranian drama of "about."

46. School of Herāt; dated 1429; Library of the Gulistan Palace, Tehran. *A Survey of Persian Art,* Arthur Upham Pope and Phyllis Ackerman, eds. (London, 1937) V. pl. 874.

47. c. 1450. Probably from Herāt (formerly in possession of Kirkor Menassian, New York). *Ibid.,* 881.

48. Sir Thomas W. Arnold and Prof. Adolf Grohmann, *The Islamic Book, A Contribution to its Art and History from the 7th-17th Centuries* (New York, 1929), II, pl. 46A; and *The Assemblies of Al-Harīri,* tr. by T. Chenery (1867), I, 181-85.

49. Sir T. W. Arnold, *op. cit.,* pl. 47B; The *Assemblies,* pp. 258-64.

50. In *Speculum:* A Journal of Medieval Studies, XV (Cambridge, Mass., April, 1940), n. 2, p. 141.

51. Machine and tool always understood in the inner philosophical-historical sense of collective machine and tool "mentalities," historical machine and tool "styles."

52. "Une thèse de Karl Marx sur le developpement du machinisme," *Revue d'Économie Politique* (Année 51, n. 4, 1937), p. 1225.

53. *Men and Machines* (New York, 1929), pp. 22-23.

54. *Ibid.,* p. 24.

55. *Technics and Civilization* (New York, 1934), p. 10.

56. Is a trap—this most primitive "automatic" device—a machine then? No, because a trap is a "thing which walks by itself" once only and cannot repeat or continue the initial automatic move. It does not "walk by itself" properly; for to "walk," that is, to show a sort of independence from the initial act, is to repeat or to be able to repeat this act (the initial act itself, any initial act, being always a dependent act somehow and anyhow, ultimately).

57. Mumford, *op. cit.,* p. 10.

58. In this respect it is A. P. Usher's panorama, offered in his classic *A History of Mechanical Inventions* (New York, London, 1929, revised 1954) which is until now by far the most convincing and suggestive one. But see also the huge bibliography at the end of his work and of Mumford, *op. cit.*

59. Lynn White, Jr., *op. cit.,* p. 143.

60. *Ibid.,* p. 145.

61. *Ibid.,* pp. 151-53.

62. Commandant Lefebvre des Noëttes, *La Force motrice animale à travers les ages* (Paris, 1924), pp. 94-100, 109.

63. Perhaps—and this of utmost importance for the historian of Near Eastern cultures—a central-Asiatic, nomadic-feudal invention of the steppes. *See* A. G. Handricourt, *"De l'origine de l'attelage moderne," Annales d'histoire économique et sociale,* VIII (1936), pp. 515-522, cited by White, *op. cit.,* p. 155.

64. White, *op. cit.,* p. 154.

65. "It is noteworthy that relatively efficient harness for horses appeared in China under the Han dynasty." Usher, *op. cit.,* p. 133 (1929 ed.). Now, China of this dynastic period (c. 200 B.C.-c. 300 A.D.) was already living under a fully evolved feudalism.

66. F. M. Feldhaus, *Technik der Vorzeit, der geschichtlichen Zeit und der Naturvölker* (Berlin, 1914), V, 535.

67. "The Hereford Map of 1314 might have been done by a child: it was practically worthless for navigation. That of Uccello's contemporary, Andrea Banco, 1436, was conceived on rational lines. . . . By laying down the invisible lines of latitude and longitude, the cartographers paved the way for later explorers, like Columbus. . . . " Mumford, *op. cit.,* p. 2.

68. Pope Silvestre II, born in 940, was one of the first Europeans to understand the grandeur of Islam's contribution. Educated in Islamized Spain, he became as head of the illustrious school of Rheims one of the earliest builders of Europe's future.

69. We consider erroneous Rostovtzeff's socio-economic interpretation of this Hellenistic technologic progressiveness: "Some modern scholars have found the cause of the weakness of the ancient industry in the existence of slave labour. They explain that the cheapness of slave

labour, the docile character of the slaves, and the unlimited supply, which permitted a constant increase of the numbers of workmen, prevented the invention of labour-saving machinery and thus made it impossible to build up factories. Against this theory I would point out that ancient industry reached its highest level in the Hellenistic period when it was based wholly on slave labour. It began to decay under the Roman Empire when slaves were gradually replaced, even in the field of industry, by ever-increasing numbers of free workmen. . . . " *The Social and Economic History of the Roman Empire* (Oxford, 1926), p. 303.

But Rostovtzeff should have remembered that 1) the Hellenistic period was an era where slavery and growing serfdom (feudalism) were normally intermixed, creating there, precisely, a complex and youthful culture, revolutionary in all fields, with creative and constructive oppositions and contrasts within it, and not only corrosive contradictions; 2) the Roman Empire was a petrified city-state (or world-state) system of social and political existence, violently re-enforced by dictatorship after the civil wars, and that this desperately mended system soon started to crack all over, giving way to all kinds of corrosive forces and activities, both from within and from without. It is the strange, contradictory, monstrous aspect of the old and familiar forces—in our case those of the slave-labor system—that, when they become decaying, thus unrecognizable forces, they can give us the impression of novelty, of the contrary of themselves, of *new* forces, in this case, the impression of a non slave-labor, of rather a feudal or even a "capitalistic" system. In appearance we see in late Rome masses and masses of freed-men active everywhere; in reality, we see these masses of ex-slaves, when still unprivileged, joining the masses of city paupers and colons, forming with them one restless, rebellious bloc of semi-slaves, semi-serfs. One can say, therefore, that if there was already feudalization in late Rome (Roman *possessio precaria,* the embryo or prototype of the future fief), it was there rather the result of a self-destructive decay-process in a dying slavery system; while in Alexandria or Seleucia this feudalization was a normal fruition of a millennia-long social and economic life-process.

70. Pupil of the illustrious Philo of Byzantium who is said to be the pupil of Ctesibus (3rd or 2nd cent. B.C.). "References in the texts of Hero make it difficult to assign any date prior to [the] second half of the first century B.C. Some writers now identify Hero with the later part of the second century A.D. but such a view is not easily supported. . . . " Usher, *op. cit.,* p. 46.

71. But known by Muslim and also Jewish scholars, for instance: the learned physicist-philosopher Abū Bakr Muhammad b. Zakāriyya al-Rāzī (b. 864, d. c. 925), who affirmed that void exists. Solomon Pines, "Some Problems of Islamic Philosophy," *Islamic Culture* XI (1937), n-1, p. 75.

72. In connection with the Hellenistic "modernity" it is important to remember also how dependent on Hellenistic learning—through the channel of Syriac-Christian—chiefly Nestorian—Sabaean teaching and diffusion—was the culture of Iran from Sassanian times (3rd-7th century, A.D.) and perhaps even earlier, during the Parthian period (3rd century B.C. to 3rd century A.D.).

73. So it is that at the end of the Sassanian era we can already see this pre-"capitalistic" self-disintegration of feudalism almost triumphant on all levels of the highly sophisticated Iranian social and cultural life: in the growth of cities, the ever-increasing role of the market, the increasing class differentiation among the artisan serfs themselves, the consequent appearance (or further development) of guilds, and finally, as an organic repercussion of all this, the exasperation of the monarchic absolutism, the rigidity and weakening of the aristocratic-bureaucratic scale, the social-religious restlessness among the horribly exploited artisan and agrarian masses (the ascetic-communistic movement of Mazdakism), etc., etc. ("I have observed," writes Burzōe, illustrious 6th-century court physician and philosopher, in his autobiography [Christensen, *op. cit.,* p. 425, translation mine] "that there exist many religions and many faiths, and that even their own followers are divided among themselves. Some of them received their faith from their fathers, some others have been forced by fear and violence to accept it. . . . Yet each pretends to be the exclusive possessor of truth and justice and considers all the others as being full of aberrations and mistakes . . . . each one despises, attacks and condemns the faith of others . . . . so finally I decided to address myself to the learned and the heads of each religion. . . . I have studied and observed a great deal. But I saw that all these men could only give me their traditional chimeras; they all praised their own religion and insulted the religion of others. I, therefore, recognized clearly that all their conclusions were based on illusions and that they did not speak at all in the name of equity.") Sassanian society was *about* to realize what Europe of the 17th and 18th centuries realized so completely.

But we know what happened. A fresh semi-nomadic feudal force, violently dynamic and as restless (socio-economically) as the Sassanian imperial complex was itself, came to reorganize everything: the Arabic-Islamic wave of re-feudalization. The progress reached by the Sassanians was not destroyed, but the feudal basis was reinforced, and a new "cycle" arose, both progressive (or more complex in its contents) and regressive (more firmly feudal), the Abbasid "farming-bureaucratic" feudalism, which at the end of the 10th century, in the politically emancipated East Iran—the Samanid kingdom—could in its turn reach the maturity of the same *about:* a "bourgeois" revolution—in the country, in the rich and already semi-emancipated cities, among the sophisticated, daring and "rationalist" (Mu'tazile) intelligentsia of Islam—was in the air. But from the steppes of Central Asia came the feudalized Turkish semi-nomads: the Kara-Khānids (who, helped by the Samanid "Fifth-Columnists," took Bukhara, the capital of the Samanid Empire, in 999 A.D.), and a little later came the democratic-minded Seljuqs, the builders of another Iranian world empire. A new, re-feudalized "cycle" emerged again. The so-called Seljuq era was the era of a refreshed, reorganized, reinforced military feudalism (with the dominant military role of the iqtā, roughly, the Islamic fief). Yet, in its social-intellectual expression, the Seljuq era was more refined, deeper, more mature than the preceding. Thus, with all the inherited richness and "modernity" (the having "about" overcome the decomposed feudalism) of the preceding experience, Iran had to go back again, and rebuild, on the same socio-economic foundation, the same old building. A strange, tragic and fascinating destiny! And it was the same thing at the end of this richly evolved, really "international," Seljuq "cycle" (under the East Iranian Khwarīm Shahs, Seljuzids' political and cultural heirs), when, in 1220, the heathen Mongols came—a less progressive wave than was the Turkish-nomadic one, almost a still tribal-matriarchal steppe formation. And the same thing happened at the end of the Timurid period, so brilliant, so "modern" in its non-religious, very secular (by Mongol inheritance) splendor, when the progress of the mature anti-feudal or self-destructively feudal forces was stopped (at the beginning of the 16th century) by a new and retrograde wave of refreshed feudalism. This time, and fatally for Iran, it was not, as in all previous and analogous traumas of Iranian history, a wave of re-feudalization politically exterior to Iran (invasion of peoples from without) but a tribal-religious wave coming from within Iran proper—a curious reactionary revival of some of the ancestral, pre-Islamic Iranian formulae: the socio-economically prejudicial rule of the Shi'ite Safawis (16th-18th century).

74. Usher, *op. cit.*, p. 69.

75. See Variation III, 190-91.

76. Known to Heron, but not utilized systematically.

77. White, *op. cit.*, p. 154.

78. Usher, *op. cit.*, p. 153 (1929 ed.)

79. *Ibid.*

80. See Footnote 24, Variation III.

81. The records of St. Paul's Cathedral in London—particularly a reference to a clock keeper in the account rolls for the year 1286—mark probably the first stage of this revolutionary career.

82. This would include the improvement of the verge escapment and of the foliot balance, as well as the much needed greater regularity given (by the Swiss master Jacob Zech, between 1525 and 1540) to the unequal power of the mainspring, so that this inequality could be "compensated by applying it [the spring] to a driving barrel of varying diameter known as a fusee," Usher, *op. cit.*, p. 272 (1929 ed.).

83. Perhaps an Arabic Spanish, early XIth-century discovery. *Ibid.*, p. 276.

84. This discontinuity which was—as mentioned before—known to the Hellenistic scientists and was rejected later by the scholastic medieval learning, was "discovered" and applied only in the 17th- and 18th-century European experiments on vacuum pumps.

85. Mumford, *op. cit.*, p. 231.

86. *Ibid.*, p. 234.

87. D. E. Smith, "Euclid, Omar Khayyām and Saccher," *Scripta Mathematica* III (1935), pp. 5-10.

88. Tūsī's work on Euclid was printed in Rome, 1594; John Wallis introduced it to the University of Oxford about the middle of the 17th Century. The effect of it was immense.

89. Mohammad Iqbal, "A plea for deeper study of the Muslim scientists," *Islamic Culture* III (1929), n. 2, pp. 204-08.

90. Time atomism: a prefiguration of the monadology of Leibnitz. See Duncan B. MacDonald, *Development of Muslim Theology, Jurisprudence and Constitutional Theory* (New York, 1903), p. 200. This far-reaching and very modern theory of time atoms combined with the atoms of space might be of Indian origin: the philosophical scheme of the sautrântikas, a Buddhist sect which originated in the 2nd or the 1st century B.C. See MacDonald, "Continuous recreation and atomic time in Muslim scholastic theology," *Isis* No. 30 (Vol. IX, 2) (Cambridge, Mass., 1927-28), pp. 342-44.

91. The English translation of this extraordinary text is given by M. Razī-ud-din Siddiqui in his study "The Contribution of Muslims to Scientific Thought," *Islamic Culture* XIV (1940), n. 1, p. 34.

92. The translation of the curious and convincing al-Bīrūnī's testimony is also given by Siddiqui, *op. cit.*, p. 41.

93. *Ibid.*, p. 35.

94. " . . . I had a vague recollection," writes the author of this study, "of the idea of function in Al-Bêrûnî, and, not being a mathematician, I sought the help of Dr. Zîa' -ud-Dīn of Aligarh who very kindly gave me an English translation of Al-Bêrûnî's passage, and wrote to me an interesting letter from which I quote the following:—'Al-Bêrûnî in his book *Qanûn-i-Mas 'ûdî*, used Newton's formula of Interpolation for valuing the various intermediary angles of Trigonometry functions from his tables which were calculated for every increase of fifteen minutes. He gave Geometrical proof of [the] Interpolation formula. In the end he wrote a paragraph saying that this proof can be applied to any function whatsoever, whether it may be increasing or diminishing with the increase of arguments. He did not use the

word function, but he expressed the idea of function in generalising the formula of Interpolation from Trigonometrical function to any function whatsoever. I may add here that I drew the attention of Prof. Schwartzschild—Professor of Astronomy in the Göttingen University—to this passage, and he was so much surprised that he took Prof. Andrews with him to the library, and got the whole passage translated three times before he began to believe it.' " Iqbal, *op. cit.*, pp. 203-04.

95. *Ibid.*, p. 205.

96. MacDonald, "Continuous . . . , " *op. cit.*, pp. 328-29.

97. MacDonald, *Development . . . , op. cit.*, p. 201.

"Nature" is not necessary at all. Matter—in the sense of Aristotelian "potentiality" does not exist. Nor "spirit" in its concrete, autonomous, traditional-philosophical sense.

There is no matter-mass: only atoms of space and atoms of time, and the void or milieu of *energy* between them.[a] Allah's absolute will, Allah's uninterrupted miracle of creation— the only reality. " . . . There is no such thing [for the Ash'arites] as a nature in things," we read in MacDonald's account of the twelve Propositions of Maimonides, "at best there is a certain simulacrum of continuity through Allah's generally acting according to a certain habit or custom (*'âda*)."[b]

"There are 'accidents' (*a'râd*), in the exact logical sense of non-permanent qualities, which are qualities, or ideas (*ma'āni*) added to the idea (*ma'nâ*) of the atom. In consequence, there is no body which has not one or more of them. These accidents are in opposed couples, as life and death, motion and rest, knowledge and ignorance, combination and separation, and an atom must have one or other of a couple. . . . [This doctrine of negative accidents is, historically, one of the great novelties introduced in philosophy by Ash'arism.] But that certain accidents go with one another does not mean that an accident can exist in another accident. That would lead at once to a doctrine that there is a 'nature' in things, distinguishing, e. g., iron from butter. The Atomists are absolutely opposed to the idea of 'nature' . . . Only Allah has qualities (sifât)."[c]

"The accident does not last two atoms of time. This means that when Allah creates a material atom he creates in it whatever accidents he wills, along with it, at the same moment. . . . . "[d]

Thus, " . . . We must eliminate the conception of causality from the universe except as to the immediate, moment by moment, working of Allah. . . [e]

" . . . So the natures of animals and the natures of men, and sense and reason are all accidents, like whiteness and blackness, and the difference between one species and another species is like the difference between individuals in the same species. Thus there are only momentarily existing individuals, as the will of Allah, from moment to moment, decrees; and our logical apparatus of genus and species is only a convention in that will."[f]

98. MacDonald, "Continuous . . . " *op. cit.*, Propositions IX and X, pp. 334-35. (Italics mine.)

99. *Ibid.*, Proposition XII, pp. 336-37. (Italics mine.)

100. But in the midst of all this, what about free will, man's free choice (affirmed on the other hand so categorically by the Mu 'tazila, the bitter enemies of the Atomists)? What about our consciousness and man's original responsibility? The Ash'arite answer to that is a "substitution" answer; it is also the most astonishing and violent torsion ever given to reason's rectitude by reason itself: the so-called doctrine of "acquiring for one's self" (*iktisâb*). Allah "creates in the mind of the supposed actor an 'accepting as his own' of his supposed act. Man is thus a cinematographic automaton with the belief added that he is doing it all himself." *Ibid.*, p. 333. Supreme prowess or trick of myth-making substitution!

101. Quoted by Margaret Smith, *Rabi 'a the Mystic and her Fellow-Saints in Islam* (Cambridge, Mass., 1928), p. 56.

102. E. G. Browne, *The Literary History of Persia* (London, 1902), I, 229.

103. L. Massignon, *Essai sur les origines du lexique technique de la Mystique Musulmane* (Paris, 1922), p. 169.

104. *Ibid.*, p. 247.

105. Margaret Smith, *Studies in Early Mysticism in the Near and Middle East* (London, 1931), p. 238.

106. MacDonald, *Development. . . , op. cit.*, p. 238.

107. See W. C. Klein's translation of the entire text in his Abu'l-Hasan 'Ali ibn Ismā'īl al-Aš'arī's Al-ibānah 'an uṣūl ad-diyānah (The Elucidation of Islām's Foundation), American Oriental Series XIX (New Haven, 1940), pp. 31-57.

108. MacDonald, *Development . . . , op. cit.*, pp. 300-03.

109. *Ibid.*, pp. 234-35.

110. The "Haft Aurang" of Jāmī (28 miniatures, 1533-34 A.D.) Phyllis Ackerman, *Guide to the Exhibition of Persian Art* (New York, 1940) p. 260, Case 16B.

111. *Clavijo, Embassy to Tamerlane, 1403-1406,* tr. from the Spanish by Guy Le Strange (London, 1928), pp. 237-243.

112. *Ibid.*, p. 248.

---

[a] E. Belayev, in *Bolshaya Sovietskaya Encyclopedia* XXIX (1935), p. 382.

[b] MacDonald, "Continuous. . . , " *op. cit.*, Proposition VI, p. 332.

[c] *Ibid.*, IV, p. 330.

[d] *Ibid.*, VI, p. 331.

[e] *Ibid.*, VII, p. 334.

[f] *Ibid.*, VIII, p. 334.

VARIATION V

1. San Juan de la Cruz (1549-91). Number 101 in *Oxford Book of Spanish Verse.*

2. Jean Paul Sartre, *Existentialism and Human Emotions* (New York, 1957), pp. 88, 89.

3. Variation I, *passim.*

4. Hans Reichenbach, *Atom and Cosmos. The World of Modern Physics,* tr. by E. S. Allen (New York, 1957), p. 43.

5. "Kundalini (the coiled one), who is known by various names, such as the Śakti, Isvarī (sovereign lady). . . . . . This Śakti is the Supreme Śakti (Parā-śakti) in the human body, embodying all powers and assuming all forms. . . . .

"She the 'Serpent Power' sleeps coiled up in the Mūlādhāra . . . " Avalon, *op. cit.,* p. 224.

Mūlādhāra (from Mulā, root), the lowest center or *cakra* in our body, from which Kundalini's ascension toward the supreme union with Shiva starts. "A description of the Cakras involves, in the first place, an account of the Western anatomy and physiology of the central and sympathetic nervous systems . . .

"The Tāntrik theory regarding the Cakras . . . is concerned on the *Physiological* side . . . with the central spinal system, comprising the brain or encephalon, contained within the skull, and the spinal cord, contained within the vertebral column . . . " *Ibid.,* p. 103.

But: "It is a mistake . . . to identify the Cakras with the physical plexuses. . . These latter are things of the gross body, whereas the Cakras are extremely subtle vital centres of various Tāttvik operations. In a sense we can connect with these subtle centres the gross bodily parts visible to the eyes as plexuses and ganglia. But to connect or correlate and to identify are different things" (*Ibid.,* p. 161). In the Mūlādhāra, the lowest earth-feet-smell root-cakra in our body-Body, Kundalini-Śakti sleeps (rests) coiled (Yoni) around the Śiva-in-sleep (lingam) to be aroused —our wish for union laboring for and with this—for her upward rush through the more and more "subtle" Cakras-Lotuses till she reaches the supreme, the seventh Lotus-center, the Sahasrāra, where at the crown of the head the two-oneness of Śiva-Śakti's embrace, self-liberation, is realized.

6. Avalon, *op. cit.,* p. 296.

7. *Ibid.,* p. 43.

8. *Ibid.,* p. 303.

9. Variation IV, p. 239.

10. Avalon, *op. cit.,* p. 103.

11. "De Luce" quoted in Gordon Leff, *Medieval Thought from Saint Augustine to Ockham* (New York, 1958), p. 188.

12. "Comparer ou égaliser l'intensité des deux odeurs différentes est . . . difficile, et sans valeur en l'absence d'un critère de comparaison. C'est pour cette raison qu'il n'a pas été possible jusqu'à présent de préciser et d'établir une unité permettant d'exprimer objectivement l'intensité des odeurs, comme on exprime les intensités sonores de différentes fréquences, ou les intensités lumineuses de diverses couleurs. On ne trouve pas comme dans la vision un équivalent de la lumière blanche, servant de répère et permettant par égalisation d'exprimer l'intensité des lumières colorées. L'intensité d'une odeur est toujours l'intensité d'une odeur specifique. Jacques Le Magnen, *Odeurs et Parfums* (Paris, 1949), p. 36.

" . . . on ne peut, comme on définit une couleur complexe comme le pourpre par des longueurs d'ondes, définir l'odeur dite de camphre par la stimulation à l'aide du camphre. Car toute une série d'autres corps entre lesquels l'on n'aperçoit pas jusqu'à présent de relations, provoquent également cette odeur dite de camphre. . . . L'unité chimique que représente la nature de la molecule stimulante ne correspond pas . . . à une unité qualitative sensorielle définissable." *Ibid.,* p. 45.

("L'odeur de boeuf grillé, agréable . . . quand venant d'une cuisine . . . devient repoussante [venant de] *l'Iris foetidissima.*") *Ibid.,* p. 42.

And " . . . Cette fonction individualisatrice des perceptions olfactives est cependant exceptionnelle au niveau de la connaissance consciente. . . . L'individuation des espèces chimiques s'exerce en relation étroite avec les grandes fonctions organiques: conservation de l'individu, nutrition, respiration, vie sexuelle, et c'est dans leur aptitude à la satisfaction ou à la non-satisfaction de ces besoins organiques, que les odeurs sont profondement marquées, beaucoup plus que les autres sensations, des tonalités affectives de l'agréable ou du désagréable. C'est là le caractère psychologyque essentiel des odeurs. Un bruit, une couleur, une sensation tactile, peuvent être indifférente. Presque toutes les odeurs peuvent être immédiatement classées et percues comme agréable ou désagréable." *Ibid.,* p. 79.

13. Korzybski, *Science and Sanity,* op cit., *passim.*

14. "Kuhara is a cavity; Kuharinī would then be She [the Śakti] whose abode is a cavity—the cavity of the Mūlādhāra" (Avalon, *op. cit.,* p. 475, ftnote 1). Kuharinī is thus Kundalī-in-the-cavity, the Mūlādhāra cavity, the subtle abode of earth, feet, the sense of smell.

The following is a gross and only partial scheme of the Cakras, the five "lower" Tāttvik Cakras (the gross-subtle perception centers); the sixth, the Ajnā center, the threshold of Buddha; and the seventh, the supreme Sahasrāra, not being called Cakra at all. This scheme combines the schemas of Avalon (*ibid.,* pp. 125,141):

Main or Essential Cakras

1) Mūlādhāra: its gross-body situation: spinal center of region below genitals . . . its regnant Tattva [thisness, "reality"] and its quality: Pṛthivī [earth]; cohesion, stimulation . . . Mūl ādhāra . . . Gandha (smell) . . . (earth); the Jñānendriya [the sense of knowledge] of *smell;* the Karmendriya [the sense of action] of *feet.* Yellow.

2) Svādhiṣṭhāna: spinal center of region above the genitals . . . ; contraction, stimulating sense of taste. Svādhiṣṭhāna: Rasa (*taste*) . . . . (water) . . . . the Karmendriya of *hands*. White.
3) Manipūra: Spinal center of region of the navel . . . . producing heat and stimulating sight-sense of color and form. . . . Rūpa (sight) . . . . fire . . . . the Karmendriya of *anus*. Red.
4) Anāhata: Spinal center of region of the heart . . . . general movement, stimulating sense of *touch*. Sparśa (touch) . . . . (air) . . . . the Karmendriya of *penis*. Smoky.
5) Viśuddha: Spinal center of region of the throat . . . . space-giving, stimulating sense of hearing . . . Śabda (*sound*) . . . . (ether) . . . . the Karmendriya of *mouth*. White.
6) Ājñā Center of region between the eyebrows . . . . Manas (mental faculties) . . . . "the Lotus of Command."
7) Sahasrāra: "Above the Ajñā is the causal region and the Lotus of a thousand petals, with all the letters, wherein is the abode of the supreme Bindu Paraśiva" (Avalon, *op. cit.* p. 141). [Bindu "literally means a point and the dot . . . which denotes in Sanskrit the nasal breathing. . . . in its technical Mantra sense it denotes that state of active Consciousness or Śakti in which the 'I' or illuminating aspect of Consciousness identifies itself with the total 'This.' It subjectifies the 'This,' thereby becoming a point (*Bindu*) of consciousness with it. When Consciousness apprehends an object as different from Itself, it sees that object as extended in space. But when that object is completely subjectified, it is experienced as an unextended point. This is the universe-experience of the Lord-experiencer as Bindu" (*Ibid.*, p. 34).]

15. Quoted by Avalon, *op. cit.*, p. 283.
16. *Philosophical Studies in Quantum Physics* (Paris, 1939), p. 231.
17. Le Magnen, *op. cit.*, p. 17.
18. "In fact, the first prosimians had what amounted to a nose-brain. The cortex came into being largely as an overgrowth of ancient smell centers." John Pfeiffer, *The Human Brain* (New York, 1955), p. 19.
19. Joachim du Bellay (1524-1560): "Contre les Poètes envieux."
20. Bronstein, *Fragments* . . . . . . op. cit., p. 64.
21. Carl Pfaffman, "Taste and Smell," in *Handbook of Experimental Psychology*, ed. by S. S. Stevens (New York, 1951), p. 1160.
22. "The appendage of the neuron which transmits impulses away from the cell." *American College Dictionary.*
23. It is curious to read in another author: "Odorophores . . . are substances which either do not possess life, are released by the onset of death, or are produced by metabolic processes and then thrown off." Ralph Bienfang, *The Subtle Sense* (Norman, Oklahoma, 1946), p. 21.
24. Pfaffman, op. cit., p. 1162.
25. Raman effect or, as it is also called, a new radiation theory, a theory of light and molecule interconnection, was announced in 1928 by the Indian scholar Sir C. V. Raman and his associates (earlier and independently foreseen by others, in particular clarity, by Smekel).
26. *Op. cit.*, pp. 1167-68. (Italics mine.)
27. James H. Hibben, "The Raman Effect and Its Chemical Applications, with theoretical discussions by the author and Edward Teller." (American Chemical Society Monograph #80, New York, 1939), Preface.
28. *Ibid.*, p. 17. (Italics mine.)
29. See Variation I, p. 22.
30. Prāna or Prānik = vital energy of which the *Nādis* or "nerves" are the conduits, "subtle channels." It is through them that Prāna's "solar and lunar currents run. Could we see them, the body would present the appearance of those maps which delineate the various ocean currents." Avalon, *op. cit.*, p. 110.
31. Tzara and others.
32. Avalon, *op. cit.*, p. 283.
33. *Ibid.*, p. 142.

Notes for Introduction

1. Sherman E. Lee, *Japanese Decorative Style* (Cleveland, 1961), p. 2.

2. Hōnen Shōnin (1133-1212). Quoted from George B. Sansom, *Japan, a Short Cultural History* (New York, 1943), p. 328.

Illustrations

1. Seashore, Kanagawa Ken. *See* F. M. Trautz, *Japan, Korea and Formosa* (Berlin: Atlantis-Verlag, 1930).
2. Haruna Shrine. Trautz, *op. cit.*
3. Pagoda in the Ishiyamadera, in the so-called Tahōtō style of architecture. Trautz, *op. cit.*
4. Eaves and brackets, Phoenix Hall. Heian period (11th century). Uji, near Kyoto, Japan. *See* Katsukichi Hattori, editor, *Collected Illustrations of Old Architecture* (Kyoto: Kyoto University Architectural Association, 1927-36).
5. Elevation, Phoenix Hall. *See* illustration number 4, *op. cit.*
6. Artist unknown. Wooden image of Ashikaga Yoshimasa, 8th shogun of the Ashikaga family, in priestly costume. Muromachi period (late 15th century). Ginkakuji Temple, Kyoto, Japan. New York Public Library print, reproduction of plate in: Shiichi Tajima, *Masterpieces Selected from the Fine Arts of the Far East.* Vol. 15: Kanroku Kubota, editor (Tokyo: The Shimbi Shoin Ltd., 1920).
7. Mu-ch'i: Bull-headed shrike on old pine tree. Ink on paper. Southern Sung (13th century). Privately owned. New York Public Library print reproduced from Tajima, *op. cit.,* Vol. 4.
8. Niten: Shrike on dead tree. The artist was famous in Japan as Miyamoto Musashi, a samurai (1584-1645). Kakemono, painted in sumi on paper. Early Edo period (17th century). Nagao Museum, Kanagawa Ken. Barney Burstein transparency.
9. Sesshu (1420-1506): Winter landscape. From a pair of kakemono painted in sumi on paper. Muromachi or Ashikaga period. National Museum, Tokyo.
10. Chao Po-Chü: The entry of the first Emperor of the Han Dynasty into Kuan-chung (detail). Handscroll; color on silk. Sung Dynasty (12th century). Museum of Fine Arts, Boston.
11. Attributed to Fujiwara-no-Nobuzane (1176-1265?): Kitano Tenjin Engi (detail: Michizane's burial place). Emakimono, painted in colors on paper. Kamakura period. Section two of the fifth in a set of nine scrolls about the life of Sugawara-no-Michizane (845-903). Michizane has died in exile, and on the way to the burial place, the ox having refused to go farther, Michizane is buried at the spot. There are several versions of these scrolls. The section reproduced here is from the one at the Kitano Temmangū Monastery in Kyoto, and is considered the *Kompon* engi, or original version. It was produced during the Jōkyū era (1219-1221).
12. Kaigetsudo Ando: Yoshiwara courtesan, "Beauty." Kakemono, painted in colors on paper. Edo period (early 18th century). Tokyo National Museum. Barney Burstein transparency.

13. Head of Apollo. Western pediment, Temple of Zeus, Olympia (ca. 470 B.C.). *See* Walter Hege and Gerhart Rodenweldt, *Olympia* (Berlin: Deutscher Kunstverlag, 1936).
14. Prophet (probably Isaiah). Detail, south portal, St. Pierre, Moissac (12th century). Photo Marburg.
15. Agnolo Bronzino (1503-1572): A young woman and her little boy. Panel. Photo, National Gallery of Art, Washington, D. C. Widener Collection, 1942.
16. Tintoretto (1518-1594): Moses striking water from the rock. Scuola di San Rocco, Venice. Photo Alinari.
17. Pablo Picasso: Les Demoiselles d'Avignon. (Spring 1907). Oil on canvas. Collection the Museum of Modern Art, New York. Acquired through the Lillie P. Bliss Bequest. Photo Soichi Sunami.
18. Giorgio de Chirico: The Sacred Fish (1919). Oil on canvas. Collection, the Museum of Modern Art, New York. Acquired through the Lillie P. Bliss Bequest. Photo Soichi Sunami.
19. Pablo Picasso: Guernica (mural, 1937). Detail. Oil on canvas. On extended loan to the Museum of Modern Art, New York, from the artist. Photo Soichi Sunami.
20. Ogata Korin (1658-1716): Matsushima (screen). Edo period. (Detail of same screen overleaf). Courtesy Museum of Fine Arts, Boston. Barney Burstein transparency.
21. Korin: Azaleas Edo period (early 18th century). Private collection, Tokyo.
22. Korin: Walking Cranes (screen, detail). Edo period (early 18th century). Courtesy of the Smithsonian Institution, Freer Gallery of Art, Washington, D. C. Transparency Raymond Schwartz.
23. Korin: Irises (screen). One of a pair of sixfold screens. Colors on gold paper. Middle Edo period. Nezu Art Museum, Tokyo. Reproduction of plate from *Selected Masterpieces by the Three Artists of the Koetsu School* (Tokyo: The Shimbi Shoin Ltd.).
24. Nike. From the parapet of the Temple of Athena Nike (c. 410-407 B.C.), Acropolis Museum, Athens.
25. Ch'ên Jung: Dragon (detail). A section, part IV, from a long scroll, dated 1244, of nine dragons appearing through clouds and waves. Courtesy Museum of Fine Arts, Boston.
26. Giotto: The Kiss of Judas. Fourteenth century. Scrovegni Chapel, Padua. Photo Alinari.
27. Artist unknown: Portrait of Ariwara Yukihira. Kamakura period (c. 1185-c. 1333). Colors on silk. Private collection, Tokyo, Japan. *See* Tajima, *op. cit.*, Volume II (1913). Barney Burstein transparency.
28. Sesshu (1420-1506): Ama-no-hashidate (detail). Kakemono, painted in sumi with slight coloring, on paper. Kyoto National Museum.

29-35. Koetsu-Sotatsu: Seven sections of a Poem Scroll. Painting ascribed to Tawaraya Sotatsu (early 17th century), calligraphy by Hon-ami Koetsu (1558-1637). Early Edo period. Emakimono, painted in sumi and gold and silver ink on paper. The poems are from *Kokin Wakashū,* an ancient anthology. Hatakeyama Collection, Tokyo.

36. Katsukawa Shunshō (1726-93): Tragic ghost. Woodblock print of Danjūrō V as the ghost of elderly woman named Higaki in the play *Sugata no Hana Yuki no Kuronushi* (1776). Signed Katsu Shunshō.

See Louis Ledoux, *Japanese Prints of the Ledoux Collection, Harunobu & Shunsho* (New York: E. Weyhe, 1944).

37. Attributed to Mu-ch'i: Wild Goose. Painted on silk. Sung dynasty (13th century). Berlin Ethnographical Museum. Courtesy Metropolitan Museum of Art, New York. Photo Taurgo.

38. Kogyo: Illustration of Nō Dance (ca. 1910). Woodblock print. Scene from play *Hagoromo.* Dance of Tennin on seashore of Miho. The Metropolitan Museum of Art, New York. Gift of T. Ito, 1919.

39. Torii Kiyonobu I (Kiyonobu the First) ca. 1664-1729: Heikuro and Heikichi. Tanye print. Hosoban. About 1710. Kanda collection. New York Public Library print reproduced from plate in Yone Noguchi, *The Ukiyoye Primitives* (Tokyo: privately published, 1933).

40. Okumura Masanobu (ca. 1686-1764): An actor as a girl dancing (about 1715). British Museum, London. New York Public Library print reproduced from plate in J. Hillier, *Japanese Masters of the Colour Print* (London: Phaidon Press, 1954).

41. Katsukawa Shunshō (1726-93): Danjūrō V as Tomomori in the play *Yoshitsune Senbon Zakura* (1784). Signed Shunshō ga. Courtesy Museum of Fine Arts, Boston. Barney Burstein transparency.

42. Shunshō (1726-93): Danjūrō IV as the Thundergod in the Noh play *Sugawara,* in which the ghost of Michizane returns as Raijin, the thundergod, to torment his betrayer (1776). Signed Shunshō ga. Courtesy, Museum of Fine Arts, Boston. Barney Burstein transparency.

43. Kiyomasu I: Danjūrō II in the play *Shibaraku.* Tanye print (1714). Kanda Collection. *See* Noguchi, *op. cit.*

44. Katsukawa Shunshō (1726-93): The Black Danjūrō. The fifth Danjūrō in the role of Sakata no Kintoki in the play *Shitenno Tonoi no Kisewata* (1781). Signed Shunshō gwa. *See* Ledoux, *op. cit.*

45. Attributed to Fujiwara-no-Nobuzane (1176-1265?): Portrait of Kodai-no-kimi or Ko-ōgimi, a poetess (a fragment from the scroll-painting of the 36 major poets). Kakemono, painted in colors on paper. Kamakura period (13th century). Courtesy, The Museum Yamato Bunkakan, Nara, Japan.

46. Artist unknown: Nawa Noren (rope curtain). Early Edo period (ca. 1650). Twofold screen, painted in colors on gilded paper. Courtesy Mrs. Taki Hara, Tokyo, Japan. Barney Burstein transparency.

47. Artists unknown: Fan-shaped Hoke-kyō. Consecrated at the Shitennōji Monastery in the year 1188 (late Heian period). Kakemono, ink and colors on paper. Number 47 is a leaf from one of 10 decorated fan-shaped albums in which the Lotus Sutra (Hoke-kyō) was copied by a group of court nobles and Buddhist priests. The design was printed on decorative fan papers from a woodblock, and colors added by the artist. The scriptures were superimposed upon the design, which had no relation to the text of the sutra. Tennōji-ku, Osaka, Japan.

48. Paul Klee: Twittering machine (1922). Water color, pen and ink. Collection, The Museum of Modern Art, New York. Photo Soichi Sunami.

49. Artist unknown: Spring and summer landscape. Momoyama period (16th century. One of a pair of sixfold screens "Landscapes with Sun

and Moon" painted in colors on gilded paper. Kongōji Monastery, Osaka, Japan.

50. Artist unknown: Heiji monogatari emaki (detail). Kamakura period (13th century). A detail of section one of the scroll owned by the National Museum, Tokyo, Japan. Barney Burstein transparency.

51. Shiko Munakata: The barking of a dog (1953). From a series of woodblock prints called *Ryuri Hanga Saku* and based on songs by Isamu Yoshii, published in the Kodansha Library of Japanese Art (No. 12) and in an American edition (Brattleboro, Vermont: Charles Tuttle). Reproduced here courtesy of Mr. Munakata.

52. Munakata: The Mother. From a catalogue of an exhibition of woodblock prints, sponsored by the Museum of Folk Crafts, Tokyo. One of a series of 30 prints called *Uto Hanga Saku,* based on the Noh drama *Uto.* Courtesy of the artist.

53. Munakata: Vultures (1953). See note for Number 51.

54. Munakata: Dragonflies. From *Seitensho Hanga Kan* (Tokyo: Hobunkan Ltd.) Reproduction here courtesy of the artist.

55. Kaigetsudo Dohan: Courtesan (ca. 1715). Handpainting on paper. Kuki Collection. *See* Noguchi, *op. cit.*

56. Artist unknown: Westerners in Japan (Namban byōbu). Early Edo period. Section four of one of a pair of sixfold screens painted in color on gold paper. Imperial Household collection. One of the earliest pairs of this type of screen "depicting Southern Barbarians," of which some forty are still in existence — all painted ca. 1590 - ca. 1630. *See* Yashiro Yukio, editor, *Art Treasures of Japan* (Tokyo: Kokusai Bunka Shinkokai, 1960). Barney Burstein transparency.

57. Shêng Mou (Tzū-chao): The deep white clouds (1348). Yüan dynasty. Private collection, New York. *See* Osvald Sirén, *Chinese Paintings in American Collections* (Paris-Brussels: Librairie Nationale d'Art et d'Histoire. G. Vanvert, Publisher, 1927).

58. Artist unknown: Cretan Priest-King (?). Reconstructed. Original true fresco (2nd mill. B.C.?), found in Palace of Knossos. Museum, Kandia. Photo Fogg Art Museum, Harvard University, Cambridge, Mass.

59. Ise. Most venerated Shinto shrine in Japan. *See* Kenzo Tange and Noboru Kawazoe, *Ise Prototype of Japanese Architecture* (Boston: Massachusetts Institute of Technology, 1965). Photo Yoshio Watanabe.

60. Max Beckmann: The Actors (triptych). Oil on canvas. Busch-Reisinger Museum, Harvard University, Cambridge, Mass. Barney Burstein transparency.

61. Artist unknown: The Wise and the Foolish Virgins. From the so-called Rossano Gospels (or Codex Purpureus), 6th century, Syro-Byzantine. Cathedral Treasury, Rossano, Italy. Photo Hirmer Verlag, Munich.

62. Mathias Grünewald: Crucifixion (detail, polyptych). Altarpiece painted for the monastery at Isenheim, and completed in 1515. Museum, Colmar, Alsace. *See* Nikolas Pevsner and Michael Meier, *Grünewald* (London: Thames and Hudson, 1958).

63. Artist unknown: The Angel at the Sepulchre. A recto folio from the Book of Pericopes of Henry II. (The facing verso folio is an illustration of the Three Marys confronting the Angel.) Ottonian manu-

script (early 11th century). State Library, Munich. Photo Hirmer Verlag, Munich.

64. Beckmann: The Actors (detail). *See* note for illustration 60. Barney Burstein transparency.

65. Juan Gris (1887-1927): Le Canigou. Oil on canvas. Albright-Knox Art Gallery, Buffalo, New York. Barney Burstein transparency.

66. Attributed to Fujiwara-no-Nobuzane: Kitano Tenjin Engi (detail). From Section 3 of the Fifth Scroll. *See* note for illustration 11. Here, Michizane's ghost begs the abbot to justify him to the ruler, and the abbot refusing, Michizane spits pomegranate seeds which start the palace fire.

67. Pablo Picasso: The Three Dancers (1925). Oil on canvas, owned by the artist. © SPADEM 1963 by French Reproductions Rights, Inc. Photo Soichi Sunami. The Museum of Modern Art, New York.

68. Attributed to workshop of Pasquier Grenier: Hector and Adromache. A section of the Trojan War series. Silk and wool. Flemish tapestry, late 15th century; made in Tournai. The Metropolitan Museum of Art, New York. Fletcher Fund, 1939.

69. Ascribed to Fujiwara-no-Nobuzane (1176-1265): Murasaki Shikibu Nikki E-maki (detail). Four scroll-paintings in color on paper, illustrating the diary of the court lady Murasaki Shikibu, who wrote the *Tale of Genji*. Kamakura period (late 12th-early 13th century). Fujita Art Museum, Osaka. *See* Tajima, *op. cit.*, Vol. II.

70. Illasamsos: Dura-Europos wall painting (last quarter, 1st century A.D.). Second figure of three ministrants (photo taken before fresco was damaged by Arabs in 1922) on the Wall of Bithnanaïa in Hall II. The paintings are in the Zeus-Baal Temple in the Dura-Ṣâliḫîyah Fortress, at Dura-Europos, a Greek city buried in the heart of the Syrian desert on the west bank of the Euphrates. *See* James H. Breasted, *Oriental Forerunners of Byzantine Painting*. Oriental Institute Publications, Vol. I (Chicago: University of Chicago Press, 1924).

71. Sculptor unknown: Yakshi. Stone torso from south gate at Sāñchī, Bhopal, India. Early Andhra period (72-25 B.C.). Courtesy Museum of Fine Arts, Boston.

72. Sculptor unknown: Seated Sakyamuni. Stone sculpture from T'ien Lung Shan, Cave XXI, north wall. Chinese, T'ang dynasty (ca. 684-ca. 755). Courtesy Fogg Art Museum, Harvard University, Cambridge, Mass. Grenville L. Winthrop Bequest.

73. Sesshu (1420-1506): Daruma and Eka ("Priest Eka cutting off his arm" given as the title by the artist, who added the statement, "Sesshu at the age of seventy-seven"). Kakemono, painted in ink with light coloring on paper. Collection Sainen-ji, Aichi. Photo Richard Edwards.

74. Sesshu: Detail of illustration number 73.

75. Artist unknown: The Great Bodhisattva (Padmapani). Detail, wall-painting in Cave I at Ajantā, Gupta period (late 6th century).

76. Artist unknown. Bodhisattva Kannon. Detail of wall-painting in color on white clay priming. Nara period (late 7th or early 8th century). Formerly in the Golden Hall, Hōryū-ji, Nara, and almost totally destroyed by fire in 1949. The painting of which this is a detail represents the Land of Amida, who is pictured in the center, with the

Bodhisattvas Kannon and Seishi on either side. Twenty-five small figures surround the trinity. *See* Yukio, *op. cit.*

77. Artist unknown: A Buddhist image, probably the head of one of the Malla princes from Kuśinagara (ca. A.D. 700). Detail of a wall-painting found at Kyzil (Central Asia). Museum für Völkerkunde, Berlin. *See* A. von Lecoq, *Die Buddhistische Spätantike in Mittelasien.* Vol. 3: *Die Wandmalereien* (Berlin: Verlag Dietrich Reimer, 1924).

78. Sculptor unknown: Funerary statue (2nd mill. B.C.) called the "Great Throned Goddess" by Max von Oppenheim. From the Palace of Kaparu at Tell Halaf, Mesopotamia (9th century B.C.). Formerly in the Oppenheim Collection, Berlin, it was destroyed during World War II. Photo reproduced from plate in Oppenheim, *Tell Halaf. A New Culture in Oldest Mesopotamia* (New York: G. P. Putnam's Sons, 1933). *See* Henri Frankfort, *The Art and Architecture of the Ancient Orient,* a volume in the Pelican History of Art series edited by Nikolas Pevsner (Baltimore, Maryland: Penguin Books, 1954).

79. Ben Shahn: Man with Cow. Drawing. Illustration from program brochure for "The World of Sholem Aleichem." © 1953, by Ben Shahn and R. L. Leslie. Reproduced here courtesy of Ben Shahn.

80. Sculptor unknown: Crucifix (detail), bronze, 11th century. At Stephanskapella, Werden am Ruhr, Germany. Photo Dr. William Kästner. *See* Max Hauttmann: *Die Kunst des Frühen Mittelalters* (Berlin: Propyläen-Verlag, 1929).

81. Velázquez (1599-1660): Venus and the Mirror. Oil on canvas. Reproduced by courtesy of the Trustees, The National Gallery, London.

82. Edouard Manet (1832-1883): Olympia. Musée du Louvre, Paris. Photo Draeger.

83. Sculptor unknown: Lapith woman. From western pediment of the Temple of Zeus, Olympia. First half 5th century B.C. (ca. 470). *See* Hege, *op. cit.*

84. The Mihrab from the Great Mosque of Cordoba (10th century). *See* Henri Terrasse, *L'Art Hispano-Mauresque des origines au XIIIe Siècle* (Paris: Editions G. van Oest, 1932).

85. Brunelleschi (1377?-1446): Interior of the Pazzi Chapel, Church of San Croce, Florence, Italy. Photo Alinari.

86. Ben Nicolson: Relief (1939). Synthetic material, painted. Collection, The Museum of Modern Art, New York. Gift of H. E. Ede and the artist. Photo Soichi Sunami.

87. Detail of a lekythos (ca. 440 B.C.) by the Achilles painter, representing a woman and a girl. *See* L.D. Casky, with the cooperation of J. D. Beazley, *Attic Vase Paintings in the Museum of Fine Arts, Boston* (New York: Published for the Museum by the Oxford University Press, 1931). Photo Barney Burstein.

88. Ascribed to Ku K'ai-chih (ca. 344-405): The admonitions. Detail of the 7th picture in a scroll that "illustrates the Admonitions of the Instructress to the Palace Ladies, *i.e.* a moralizing text by the poet Chang Hua (232-300)." The text of this section is: " No one can endlessly please: affection cannot be for one alone." British Museum, London. It is believed that the original was done in the early part of the T'ang dynasty (618-906). " . . . an example of a stylistic tradition that probably goes back to Ku K'ai chih, . . . " but to what extent

this is his is a problem. *See* O. Sirén, *Chinese Painting,* Vol. I (New York: The Ronald Press Co., 1956).

89. Liang K'ai (active c. 1200): Ideal portrait of the Poet Li T'ai-po. Southern Sung period (late 12th - early 13th century). National Museum, Tokyo. K'ai was a painter at a Ch'an monastery. *See* O. Sirén, *op. cit.,* Vol. III plate 331.

90. Attributed to School of Arras: Annunciation. Wool, some metal thread. Flemish tapestry, early 15th century. The Metropolitan Museum of Art, New York. Gift of Harriet Barnes Pratt, 1949, in memory of her husband, Harold Irving Pratt.

91. A pilgrim on his travels. Detail from painting on south wall, cave 217, at Ch'ien-fo tung (Caves of the Thousand Buddhas). Early T'ang period (ca. 660). The caves are situated close to the Tun-huang oasis on the westernmost border of China proper. The painting is from a Sūtra depicting Avalokiteśvara as Protector against calamities. *See* Basil Gray, *Buddhist Cave Paintings at Tun-Huang* (London: Faber & Faber). Photo Tun-huang Institute.

92. North Wei Caves. Detail from upper part of the north wall, Cave XXI, Lung-men (Northern Wei dynasty, ca. 386-557), Lo-yang, China. *See* Daijo Tokiwa in collaboration with Professor T. Sekino, *Buddhist Monuments in China,* Part II, (Tokyo: The Society for the Study of Buddhist Monuments, 1925-30).

93. Yen Hui: The Taoist Immortal, Li T'ieh-kuai. Yüan dynasty (14th century). Chion-ji Temple, Kyoto. *See* Tajima, *op. cit.,* Vol. 9.

94. Velázquez: Las Hilanderas (detail). Oil on canvas. Museo del Prado, Madrid.

95. Ben Shahn: Drawing. See note for illustration 79.

96. Frank B. Gilbreth: Girl folding handkerchief. Cyclograph record of a movement. Courtesy Lillian M. Gilbreth. *See also* Siegfried Giedion, *Mechanization Takes Command* (New York: Oxford University Press, 1948).

97. Fragonard (1732-1806): Seated Pasha. Sepia drawing. Musée du Louvre, Paris.

98. Il Khānid School (Mesopotamia): Pair of elephants, from Manāfi 'Al-Hayavān, an illuminated manuscript (dated Marāgha 1296) of a bestiary compiled in the 11th century by Ibn Bakhtishū, a physician to the Caliph of Baghdad. Pierpont Morgan Library, New York. Photo Iranian Institute.

99. Torii Kiyonobu I (ca. 1664-1729): Two actors in the play called *Saya-ate.* Ink-print (ca. 1700). British Museum, London. New York Public Library reproduction of plate from J. Hillier, *op. cit.*

100. Attributed to the Koetsu School: Coxcombs, maize and morning glories. Detail. Edo period (17th century). Courtesy of the Smithsonian Institution, Freer Gallery of Art, Washington, D. C.

101. Unknown American artist: Running before the Storm. Oil on canvas. Courtesy, the Museum of Fine Arts, Boston, Mass. Barney Burstein transparency.

102. Unknown American artist: Meditation by the Sea. Oil on canvas. Courtesy, Museum of Fine Arts, Boston, Mass. Barney Burstein transparency.

103. Rafael Peale (1774-1825): After the Bath. Detail (1823). Courtesy, Nelson-Atkins Art Gallery, Kansas City, Missouri.

104. Benjamin West (1738-1820): Mrs. Peter Beckford. Oil on canvas. The Metropolitan Museum of Art, New York. Bequest of John R. Morron, 1950.
105. Thomas Cole (1801-1848): The Oxbow. Oil on canvas. The Metropolitan Museum of Art, New York. Gift of Mrs. Russell Sage, 1908.
106. Joshua Shaw: The Deluge (1804). Formerly attributed to Washington Allston (1779-1843). Metropolitan Museum of Art, New York.
107. John Singleton Copley (1738-1815): Mrs. Thomas Boylston. Oil on canvas. Fogg Art Museum, Harvard University, Cambridge, Mass. Barney Burstein transparency.
108. Copley: Eleazer Tyng. Oil on canvas. National Gallery of Art, Washington, D. C. Gift of the Avalon Foundation. National Gallery of Art transparency.
109. Copley: Eleazer Tyng (detail). See note for 108 above.
110. Gilbert Stuart (1755-1828): Mrs. Perez Morton. Oil on canvas. Courtesy, Worcester Art Museum. Gift of the grandchildren of Joseph Tuckerman.
111. George Caleb Bingham (1811-1879): Fur traders descending the Missouri (ca. 1845). Oil on canvas. The Metropolitan Museum of Art, New York. Morris K. Jesup Fund, 1933.
112. George W. Bellows (1882-1925): Dempsey and Firpo (1924). Based on a drawing made at the time of the fight on November 14, 1923. Oil on canvas. Whitney Museum of American Art, New York.
113. Albert Pinkham Ryder (1847-1917): Moonlight Marine. Oil on wood. The Metropolitan Museum of Art, New York. Samuel D. Lee Fund, 1934.
114. Thomas Hart Benton: July Hay. Oil on canvas. Courtesy Mr. Benton and the Metropolitan Museum of Art, New York.
115. John Marin: Lower Manhattan (1920). Watercolor. Collection, the Museum of Modern Art, New York, Philip L. Goodwin Collection. Photo Soichi Sunami.
116. Jacques Levine: The White Horse. Oil on canvas. Collection of Museum of Art, University of Oklahoma, Norman.
117. Hyman Bloom: Corpse of an elderly male (1945). Oil on canvas. Courtesy of Mr. Bloom and Brandeis University, Waltham, Massachusetts. Gift of Henry Crapo. Barney Burstein transparency.
118. Ben Shahn: The Passion of Sacco and Vanzetti (1931-32). Tempera. Collection of the Whitney Museum of American Art, New York, gift of Edith and Milton Lowenthal in memory of Juliana Force. Whitney Museum transparency.
119. Ben Shahn: Allegory (1948). Tempera. Courtesy the artist. Privately owned. Barney Burstein transparency.
120. Ben Shahn: Sound in the mulberry trees (1948). Smith College Museum of Art, Northampton, Massachusetts. Barney Burstein transparency.
121. Ben Shahn: "Pact." Tempera. From the Joseph H. Hirshhorn Foundation. Barney Burstein transparency.
122. Ben Shahn: The Third Allegory (1955). Watercolor. Courtesy Mr. & Mrs. Irving Levick, Buffalo, New York. Barney Burstein transparency.
123. Joan Miró: Hope returning . . . . (L'espoir nous revient par la fuite des constellations), 1954. Oil on canvas. Galerie Maeght, Paris.

124. Scytho-Sarmatian plaque (2nd century B.C.). Found in Maikop, Russia. Hermitage Museum, Leningrad. Photo Taurgo, made from New York University negative.

125. Tympanum, St. Pierre de Moissac (detail). Early 12th cent. Archives Photographiques, Paris. Metropolitan Museum of Art photostat. Reproduced from John Evans, *Art in Medieval France, 987-1488* (New York: Oxford University Press, 1948).

126. Bowl, Champlevé ware, Yākusand (11th century). Plate reproduced from *A Survey of Persian Art from Prehistoric Times to the Present.* (London: Oxford University Press, 1938), by permission of the editor, Arthur Upham Pope.

127. Neolithic idol. Menhir from Les Vidals, Tarn, France. Metropolitan Museum of Art photostat of plate from José Pijoán, *Summa Artis, Historia General del Arte,* Vol. VI, *El Arte Prehistorico Europeo* (Madrid: Espasa-Calpe, S.A., 1934).

128. "One of over 200 small reliefs that formed a dado round the south side of the Palace [of Kaparu at Tell Halaf, Mesopotamia]." Ninth century B.C. Courtesy, Walters Art Gallery, Baltimore, Maryland. *See* Frankfort, *op. cit.* Photostat Metropolitan Museum of Art, New York, of plate in Oppenheim, *op. cit.* Note: Baron von Oppenheim referred to the orthostat by the title used with the illustration on page 240 of this volume, but there is some doubt that this is the actual subject. Frankfort calls it simply "two figures dispatching a third."

129. Cheek plaque of bit, bronze, Luristān (2nd-1st mill. B.C.). Collection Ackerman-Pope. Photo Iranian Institute, *see above.*

130. Procession of Gift Bearers, Palace of Darius (late 6th - early 5th century B.C.). Persepolis, Iran. Section of the procession on the left end of the stairway on the south side of the palace. Photo The Oriental Institute, University of Chicago, Illinois.

131. Lion and Bull. Relief, Apadana stairway, Persepolis Terrace, Iran (late 6th - early 5th century, B.C.). A relief repeated over and over again on the stairway. Photo Oriental Institute, *loc. cit.*

132. Tāq-I-Bustān, details of rock reliefs. Boar hunt of Khusraw II. Sassanian (6th-7th century A.D.). Pope, *op. cit.* Photo Iranian Institute.

133. Plate, silver, partially gilt, carved and engraved with flute-player on fantastic animal. Late Sassanian. Hermitage Museum. Pope, *op cit.* Photo Iranian Institute.

134. Plate, silver, partially gilt, carved and engraved with fantastic animal and lotuses. Late Sassanian. Bibliothèque Nationale, Paris. Pope, *op. cit.* Photo Iranian Institute.

135. Deep dish. Lustre-painted ware. Rayy, early 12th century. Metropolitan Museum of Art, New York. Pope, *op. cit.* Photo Iranian Institute.

136. Wooden doors (detail) from the so-called tomb-tower of Mahmūd of Ghazni, now known to have been built for a later Ghaznevid prince, *circa* first half of the 12th century. Museum of Delhi, India. Metropolitan Museum of Art photostat of plate from Emanuel La Roche, *Indische Baukunst,* Vol. I (Munich, 1921).

137. Bahrām kills a dragon. Page from Firdawsī, the "Demotte" Shah Nameh. Tabrīz School (ca. 1340). Private collection. Pope, *op. cit.* Photo Iranian Institute.

138. Junayd Naqqash Sultani: Wedding celebrations of Prince Humay

and Princess Humayun. Page from a manuscript of the Diwan of Khwaju Kirmani, copied at Baghdad in 1396 by Mir 'Ali Tabrizi. British Museum, London. Metropolitan Museum of Art photostat of plate from Basil Gray. *Persian Painting. Miniatures of the XIII-XIV Centuries* (New York: Iris Books, Oxford University Press, 1940). *See* text note 39, Variation IV.

139. Mīrzā 'Alī: The painter Shāpūr bringing the portrait of Khusrau to Shīrīn. From a manuscript of Nizāmi executed for Shāh Tahmāsp. Tabriz. (A.D. 1539-43).

140. Artist unknown: Two Lovers. Oil painting, 18th century. Courtesy, Arthur Upham Pope. Photo Iranian Institute.

141. Artist unknown: A Reading Scene (19th century). Oil painting. Courtesy Arthur Upham Pope. Photo Asia Institute Archive.

142. Sesson (1504 - ca. 1589): Wind and waves. Painted in sumi with slight coloring on paper. Muromachi period (16th century). Courtesy Fumihide Nomura, Kyoto, Japan. Photo New York Public Library Prints Division.

143. Joan Miró: Still life with old shoe. Oil on canvas, painted in 1937. Collection, James Thrall Soby, New Canaan, Conn. Photo Soichi Sunami, Museum of Modern Art, New York.

144. Joan Miró: Maternity. Oil on canvas, painted in 1924. Collection Roland Penrose, London, England. Photo Soichi Sunami, Museum of Modern Art, New York.

145. School of Herāt: Isfandiyār taking the brazen hold. Page from Firdawsī, Shah Nameh, dated A.D. 1429. Library of the Gulistan Palace, Tehrán. Pope, *op. cit.* Photo Iranian Institute.

146. School of Herāt: Page from Firdawsī manuscript, Shah Nameh. Rustam's Sleep. The sleeping Rustam with Rakhsh killing the lion. British Museum, London. Pope, *op. cit.* Photo Iranian Institute.

147. Al-Hariri: "The Spotted," Twenty-sixth episode in Maqāmāt (The Assemblies), illuminated manuscript (1334). National Library of Vienna. Photo Iranian Institute. *See* text notes 48, 49, Variation IV.

148. Bihzād: Scene in a Mosque. Herāt School (c. 1480). Pope, *op. cit.* Photo Iranian Institute.

149. Mahammad Al-Idrīsī: Map (12th century). From Konrad Müller, *Mappae Arabicae,* Vol. 6: *Idrīsī-Atlas.* (Stuttgart: Müller, 1927).

150. Majnūn comes to the camp of Lailā. Miniature from the *Haft Aurang* ("Seven Thrones"), the seven Mathnavi poems of Jāmī. Persian manuscript (1556-65). Kevorkian Collection. Courtesy of the Smithsonian Institution, Freer Gallery of Art, Washington, D.C. *See* text note 110, Variation IV.

151. Section of olfactory bulb of a kitten. Plate, Ranson & Clark, 1947, taken from Carl Pfaffman, *op. cit.,* Variation V, Note 21.

152. Kano Sadanobu (1597-1623) and others: Cherry Blossoms and Pheasants (1614). Four sliding doors painted in color on gilded paper. Momoyama period. Nagoya Municipality.

153. Pablo Picasso: Le petit peintre. A lithograph. Reproduced by kind permission from a copy owned by Professor Frederick B. Deknatel. © SPADEM 1966 by French Reproduction Rights, Inc.

154-155. Details of illustration number 152. Outer left and outer right wings of the doors.

156. Tatsuyemon: Yorobishi. Noh mask (14th century) of a blind

woman. *See* Friedrich Perzyński, *Japanische Masken, Nō und Kyōgen* (Berlin: 1925).

157. Pre-Aztec mask. Brownish stone sculpture from the ancient city of Teotihuacán in central Mexico. Private collection, Mexico. *See* Franz Feuchtwanger, *The Art of Ancient Mexico* (London: Thames & Hudson, 1954). Photo Irmgard Groth-Kimball.

158. Kano screen: Grasses, Flowers and Full Moon. Momoyama period (late 16th century). Courtesy of the Smithsonian Institution, Freer Gallery of Art, Washington, D.C.

159. Chōng Sōn (1676-1759): The Diamond Mountain. Collection of Mr. Sohn Jaihyong, Seoul, Korea.

160. Yi Inmun (1745-1821): Spring Landscape. Collection Mr. Chun Hyong-pil, Seoul, Korea.

161. Ise Temple. *See* note for illustration no. 59, above.